THE

The Modern Cy-près Doctrine

RACHAEL P. MULHERON
BCom, LLB (Hons) (UQ), LLM (Adv) (UQ), DPhil (Oxon)
Solicitor of the Supreme Court of Queensland and of the
High Court of Australia

Routledge
Taylor & Francis Group

LONDON AND NEW YORK

First published 2006 by UCL Press

The name of University College London (UCL) is a registered trade mark
used by UCL Press with the consent of the owner

2 Park Square, Milton Park, Abingdon, Oxon OX14 4RN
711 Third Avenue, New York, NY 10017, USA

Routledge is an imprint of the Taylor & Francis Group, an informa business

First issued in paperback 2016

British Library Cataloguing in Publication Data
A catalogue record for this book has been requested

Library of Congress Cataloging in Publication Data
Data available

ISBN 978-1-138-97628-3 (pbk)
ISBN 978-1-84472-086-6 (hbk)

Typeset in Sabon by
RefineCatch Limited, Bungay, Suffolk

To William Orville Dalton

Summary of Contents

Preface		xv
Table of Cases		xvii
Table of Legislation		xliii
List of Abbreviations		lvii
Notes on Mode of Citation		lxi
Chapter 1	Introduction	1
Part I The *Cy-près* Doctrine in the Context of Trusts		19
Chapter 2	Charitable Trusts: *Cy-près* Delineation	21
Chapter 3	Charitable Trusts: General *Cy-près*	53
Chapter 4	Charitable Trusts: Statutory *Cy-près*	91
Chapter 5	Charitable Public Appeal Funds	143
Chapter 6	Non-Charitable Trusts	169
Part II The *Cy-près* Doctrine in the Context of Litigious Remedies		213
Chapter 7	Class Actions *Cy-près*: An Introduction	215
Chapter 8	Class Actions *Cy-près*: Principles	253
Chapter 9	*Cy-près* Specific Performance	279
Chapter 10	*Cy-près*—More than a Doctrine?	303
Bibliography		315
Index		331

Contents

Preface   xv
Table of Cases   xvii
Table of Legislation   xliii
List of Abbreviations   lvii
Notes on Mode of Citation   lxi

CHAPTER 1   *INTRODUCTION*
  A INTRODUCTION   1
     1. The *Cy-près* Doctrine: Traditional Definition   1
     2. Redefining the *Cy-près* Doctrine   2
  B ORIGINS OF THE CY-PRÈS DOCTRINE   5
  C WHAT THIS BOOK COVERS   18
     1. Division of Chapters   18
     2. Further Miscellaneous Applications   13

PART I
THE CY-PRÈS DOCTRINE IN THE CONTEXT OF TRUSTS

CHAPTER 2   *CHARITABLE TRUSTS:* CY-PRÈS *DELINEATION*
  A INTRODUCTION   21
  B JUDICIAL AND PREROGATIVE CY-PRÈS   21
     1. The Width of Judicial *Cy-près*   21
     2. The Uncertainties of Prerogative *Cy-près*   23
  C ADMINISTRATIVE SCHEMES   26
  D CONSTRUING DISPOSITIONS TO AVOID 'FAILURE' OF CHARITABLE
     GIFTS   30
     1. Augmentation: Where a Defunct Charitable Donee Continues
       in Modified Fashion   33
       (a) The relevant rule of construction described   33
       (b) Pre-requisites for the rule of construction to apply   35
     2. A Gift on Trust for the *Purposes* of a Defunct Unincorporated
       Charity   39
       (a) The presumption described   40
       (b) Pre-requisites for a 'purpose gift' to an unincorporated
         charity   41
     3. A Gift on Trust to a Defunct Charitable Corporation   44
  E OUSTER OF CY-PRÈS BY THE DONOR   46
     1. Where a *Cy-près* Power is Already Given to theTrustees   46

2. Gift-over Provisions   48
3. Other Scenarios   51

CHAPTER 3   *CHARITABLE TRUSTS: GENERAL* CY-PRÈS

A   INTRODUCTION   53
B   EXCLUSIVELY CHARITABLE PURPOSES   54
   1. Defining the Purposes as Charitable   54
   2. Providing a Gift-over   57
C   IMPOSSIBILITY OR IMPRACTICABILITY   58
D   GENERAL CHARITABLE INTENTION   63
   1. Some Preliminary Conundrums about a 'General Charitable
      Intent'   65
     (a) *Should* a general charitable intent be required for initial
        failure?   65
     (b) Is actual proof of a general charitable intent required for
        subsequent failure?   66
     (c) Can a general charitable intent be displaced entirely by the
        out-and-out gift rationale?   67
     (d) Is a general charitable intent required for left-over
        surpluses?   70
   2. What is the Date for Determining Whether Failure was 'Initial'
      or 'Subsequent'?   72
     (a) Charitable trusts under will   72
     (b) Charitable trusts *inter vivos*   73
   3. How is a 'General Charitable Intent' Fathomed?   75
E   APPLYING THE PROPERTY CY-PRÈS   86

CHAPTER 4   *CHARITABLE TRUSTS: STATUTORY* CY-PRÈS

A   INTRODUCTION   91
B   RELATIONSHIP BETWEEN STATUTORY CY-PRÈS AND OTHER LAW   93
   1. *Cy-près* Doctrine under General Law   93
   2. Administrative Scheme-making Doctrine   95
   3. Impact of the European Convention on Human Rights   96
   4. Where No Scheme Required Prior to Statute   97
C   THE 'ENGLISH VERSION' STATUTORY CY-PRÈS   98
   1. Triggers for the Statutory *Cy-près* Jurisdiction   99
   2. The 'Spirit of the Gift' Requirement   112
D   VARIATIONS UPON THE ENGLISH STATUTORY THEME   118
   1. The Requirement of a General Charitable Intent   118
     (a) Abolishing the requirement   119
     (b) Presuming the requirement   121
   2. Other Triggers for the *Cy-près* Jurisdiction   122
E   APPLYING THE PROPERTY CY-PRÈS   125
   1. What is the Original Reference Point for the Donor's
      Intention?   125

2. Can Extrinsic Evidence be Relied Upon? 126
3. How Close Must the *Cy-près* Application Be? 128
F SOME PROCEDURAL ASPECTS OF THE *CY-PRÈS* JURISDICTION 139

CHAPTER 5 *CHARITABLE PUBLIC APPEAL FUNDS*
A INTRODUCTION 143
B OVER-SUBSCRIBED PUBLIC CHARITABLE APPEALS 145
1. Initial Failure or Subsequent Failure? 145
2. Application of *Cy-près* at General Law 146
3. Effect of Charities Act 1993, s 14 148
C UNDER-SUBSCRIBED PUBLIC CHARITABLE APPEALS 149
1. Initial Failure or Subsequent Failure? 149
2. At General Law: The Identifiable and Traceable 'Named
Donors' 150
(a) Presumption of a resulting trust/conditional gift 151
(b) Rebutting the presumption of a resulting trust 152
(c) The backstop position: *bona vacantia* 157
(d) Conclusion: Identifiable donors under general law 158
3. At General Law: The Anonymous Donors 158
(a) No resulting trust 158
(b) Anonymous donations 'cross-infecting' identifiable
donations 160
(c) Are anonymous donors always fixed with a general
charitable intent? 161
(d) Are identifiable donors 'infected' with a general charitable
intent by anonymous donors? 161
(e) Conclusion: Anonymous donors 162
4. Effect of Charities Act 1993, s 14 163
(a) Seeking simplification 163
(b) Criticisms of the provisions 164

CHAPTER 6 *NON-CHARITABLE TRUSTS*
A INTRODUCTION 169
B NON-CHARITABLE TRUSTS 169
1. Anomalous Cases 176
2. Mixed Persons/Purposes Trusts 178
(a) A question of construction 179
(b) What if the purpose is impossible or impracticable to
fulfil? 182
(c) The application of *cy-près* 185
3. Non-charitable Purpose Trusts 186
(a) Why should non-charitable purpose trusts be
recognised? 186
(b) If they *are* recognised, should the *cy-près* doctrine apply
to them? 190

    (c) Legislative enactments permitting pure purpose trusts   194

    (d) Canadian proposals for reform   199

C   NON-CHARITABLE PUBLIC APPEALS   202

  1. Resulting Trust Back to the Donor   202

  2. *Cy-près* Applications of Donated Monies   206

    (a) The available options   206

    (b) Some statutory examples   207

  3. Public Appeals for Private Persons   210

PART II
THE CY-PRÈS DOCTRINE IN THE CONTEXT OF LITIGIOUS REMEDIES

CHAPTER 7   CLASS ACTIONS CY-PRÈS: AN INTRODUCTION

A   INTRODUCTION   215

B   THE WIDE AND NARROW MEANINGS OF 'CY-PRÈS'   216

  1. The *Cy-près* Doctrine in its 'Narrow Sense'   217

    (a) Price-rollback *cy-près*   218

    (b) Organisational-distribution *cy-près*   222

  2. The *Cy-près* Doctrine in its 'Wider Sense'   224

    (a) A wider connotation of damages *distribution*   224

    (b) A wider connotation of damages *computation*   224

    (c) Coupon recovery   227

C   A SNAPSHOT OF LEADING CLASS ACTION JURISDICTIONS   229

  1. Australia   230

  2. Canada   232

    (a) Statutory invocations   232

    (b) Divided views   234

  3. United States   236

    (a) Creative judicial decision-making   236

    (b) The practicalities   242

D   THE ALTERNATIVES TO A *CY-PRÈS* DISTRIBUTION   244

  1. Plaintiff Fund-sharing   245

  2. Escheat to the Government   247

  3. Reversion to the Defendant   250

CHAPTER 8   CLASS ACTIONS CY-PRÈS: PRINCIPLES

A   INTRODUCTION   253

B   RELATIONSHIP BETWEEN CLASS ACTIONS CY-PRÈS AND CHARITABLE TRUSTS CY-PRÈS   253

  1. The Analogies   253

  2. Defining the Purpose of the Class Actions *Cy-près* Doctrine   254

    (a) Focusing upon the 'donor' of the monies   255

    (b) Focusing upon the intended recipient of the monies   258

C   TRIGGERS FOR *CY-PRÈS* IN CLASS LITIGATION   259

D   A SUFFICIENT DEGREE OF OVERLAP — 263
  1. To What Extent will the *Cy-près* Distribution Benefit Original
     Class Members? — 264
  2. Geographical Scope of the Original Class — 266
  3. Will Non-class Members Receive a Windfall from the *Cy-près*
     Distribution? — 268
  4. Will the *Cy-près* Distribution Promote the Purposes of the
     Underlying Cause/s of Action? — 269
E   CHOOSING THE CY-PRÈS RECIPIENTS IN CLASS ACTION LITIGATION — 270
  1. How Close must the Relationship between *Cy-près* and
     Original Purpose Be? — 270
  2. Focusing upon the *Cy-près* Recipient — 274
F   CY-PRÈS IN UNITARY LITIGATION — 276

CHAPTER 9   CY-PRÈS *SPECIFIC PERFORMANCE*
A   INTRODUCTION — 279
B   SETTING THE CONTEXT — 281
  1. Finding a 'Middle Ground' in Contractual Remedies — 281
  2. The Triggers for *Cy-près* Property Transfer — 284
C   WHO MAY APPLY FOR A CY-PRÈS SPECIFIC PERFORMANCE ORDER? — 286
  1. Applications for *Cy-près* Specific Performance by the Innocent
     Party — 286
  2. Applications for *Cy-près* Specific Performance by the Contract-
     breaker — 291
D   FURTHER CONDITIONS FOR CY-PRÈS SPECIFIC PERFORMANCE — 294
  1. The *Cy-près* Order must fit the 'Spirit of the Contract' — 295
     (a) Degree of difference between Contractually Described
         Property and available property — 295
     (b) No contradiction with the terms of the contract — 297
  2. Other Specific Indicators of *Cy-près* Specific Performance
     Suitability — 299
E   SOME CONCLUDING COMMENTS — 301

CHAPTER 10   CY-PRÈS—*MORE THAN A DOCTRINE?*
A   REVISITING THE DEFINITION — 304
B   SOME FURTHER COMMON THEMES — 309
C   CONCLUDING OBSERVATIONS — 313

Bibliography — 315
Index — 331

Preface

THE CY-PRÈS DOCTRINE has been a hitherto rarely considered subject in the legal literature. Apart from the wonderfully lucid and thoughtful works by LA Sheridan and VTH Delany, *The Cy-près Doctrine*, published in 1959, and by EL Fisch, *The Cy-près Doctrine in the United States*, published in 1950, this area of law has since attracted limited individual attention. Rather, it is usually considered as a somewhat difficult member of the large family of charitable trusts jurisprudence. In order to remedy that scenario in part, this book places the spotlight upon the *cy-près* doctrine in its current important manifestations, seeking to show how the 'difficult member' has garnered significant attention—both judicial and statutory—outside of its traditional environs.

This book arose out of a confluence of my teaching, research and legal practice across quite disparate areas. I found it intriguing that the *cy-près* doctrine, so-called, should manifest the philosophy of 'as near as possible' in various strands of the law. Throughout my teaching of the Trusts syllabus in Australia and England, the '*cy-près* doctrine', of course, featured prominently in the field of charitable trusts. Through my research and writing in the field of comparative class actions,[1] the doctrine emerged as a 'hot topic' of monetary relief in class action regimes, accompanied by the frequent judicial admission that class actions *cy-près* was drawing upon charitable trusts *cy-près* by analogy. Still further, whilst in legal practice in Australia, I witnessed specific performance being sought on behalf of clients, with a measure of compensation, when what was contracted for could not be literally conveyed, giving rise to the commonly attributed label of '*cy-près* specific performance'.

These various exposures to some form of the doctrine generated my considerable curiosity about the 'near enough is good enough' mantra in respect of property and monetary transfers. Case law research across several jurisdictions uncovered and confirmed other areas of modern application of the doctrine that have opened up those areas to both flexibility and pragmatism. Naturally, all of this invites the questions of whether there is some new and overarching definition which should now be attributed to the *cy-près* doctrine, whether there is a doctrinal symmetry of analysis that truly renders it a body of '*cy-près* law' in the modern context, and whether we can expect this legal concept to play an even greater role in the future.

As always, the production of this book has been a concerted team effort. The support, encouragement, wise counsel and good humour provided by my

---

[1] *The Class Action in Common Law Legal Systems: A Comparative Perspective* (Hart Publishing, Oxford, 2004).

parents, my friends, and my colleagues at Queen Mary University of London throughout the undertaking of this work, are gratefully appreciated. Hearty thanks are also due to editor Briar Towers, for her constant support and assistance, and to all the team at UCL Press, for providing essential editorial, typesetting and other assistance, in order to bring the book to fruition. The work has also benefited from useful discussions with Ross Cranston, Alastair Hudson, Geraint Thomas, and Keith Uff, from all of whom I derived both benefit and insights. My thanks also to Louise Sylvan for providing helpful materials. Lastly, the book has benefited tremendously from the proofreading undertaken by my parents; but, as ever, all remaining errors are solely my responsibility.

For the sake of clarity and readability, the work has been prepared according to the style notes and modes of citation outlined at page lxi. The law is stated, from the materials that were available to me, as at 31 July 2005, although it has been possible to make selective reference to later developments where appropriate.

Rachael Mulheron
London
September 2005

Table of Cases

AUSTRALIA

Annandale, Re [1986] 1 Qd R 353 79
ANZ Executors and Trustee Co Ltd v Trustee for the Presbyterian
    Church of Australia (NSW SC, 12 Jun 1990) 84
Armenian General Benevolent Union v Union Trustee Co of
    Australia Ltd (1952) 87 CLR 597 (HCA) 27
Association of Heads of Independent Girls Schools of Victoria v
    Attorney-General (Victoria) (Vic SC, 27 Oct 1989) 46
Aston v Mt Gambier Presbyterian Charge [2002] SASC 332,
    84 SASR 109 .... 58, 81, 93–95, 101, 119
Attorney-General (New South Wales) v Fulham [2002]
    NSWSC 629 (19 Jul 2002) 73, 93, 109–110, 114–115,
                                           121, 129, 170
Attorney-General (New South Wales) v Perpetual Trustee Co Ltd (1940)
    63 CLR 209 (HCA) 60, 66, 76, 77, 79, 121, 125, 127
Attorney-General (New South Wales) v Public Trustee (1987)
    8 NSWLR 550 (CA) 83
Australian Elizabethan Theatre Trust, Re; Lord v Commonwealth
    Bank of Australia (1991) 30 FCR 491 .... 153, 181

Bacon v Pianta (1966) 114 CLR 634 (HCA) 182
Banyo Seminary Trust, Re [2000] QSC 215 112
Barry, Re [1971] VR 395 (Master) 78
Beggs v Kirkpatrick [1961] VR 764 .... 144, 148, 149, 151, 153, 154,
                                  157, 158, 161, 162, 163
Bianco (decd), In re; Cox v Attorney-General (Victoria)
    (Vic SC, 23 Sep 1997) 34, 127
Burnside City Council v Attorney-General (South Australia) (1993)
    61 SASR 107 (Full Ct) 51

Cauvin v Phillip Morris Ltd [2002] NSWSC 736 277
City of Burnside v Attorney-General (South Australia) (No 2)
    (SA SC, 1 May 1998) 95, 123
Commissioner for Fair Trading v Thomas (NSW SC, 3 Jun 2004) 277
Commissioner for Railways and Trustees of St Barnabas' Church,
    Bathurst, Re (1887) 8 LR(NSW) Eq 22 60
Constable (decd), Re [1971] VR 742 83

Corporation of the Synod of the Diocese of Brisbane,
Re [1995] QSC 334 104
Crowther v Brophy [1992] 2 VR 97 103

Daniels (decd), Re [1970] VR 72 83
Darwin Cyclone Tracy Relief Trust Fund, Re Trust Deed Relating to;
Adermann v Corporation of the City of Darwin (1979) 39 FLR 260
(NT SC) 144, 146–8
De Little, In re; Union Trustee Co of Australia Ltd v Attorney-General
[1943] St R Qd 31 16

Edwards v Attorney-General (NSW) [2004] NSWCA 272 181
Ethel Pedley Memorial Travelling Scholarship Trust (1949) 49
SR (NSW) 329 (Eq), Re 150
Executor Trustee and Agency Co of South Australia Ltd v Warbey
(No 2) (1973) 6 SASR 336 .... 77, 79

Fellows v Sarina (NSW SC, 9 May 1996) 78
Findlay's Estate, In re; Tasmanian Trustees Ltd v Launceston Girls'
Home (1995) 5 Tas R 333 77
Foran (decd), Estate of; Mair v Attorney-General (New South Wales)
(NSW SC, 20 Nov 1987) 43, 83
Forge v Dorsman (NSW SC, 10 Jul 1990) 86
Forrest v Attorney-General (Victoria) [1986] VR 187 .... 93, 102, 112,
113, 116, 126, 141
Fowler v Geelong College and Kardinia International College
(Geelong) (Vic SC, 13 Dec 1996) 93, 100, 110–12, 126–8

General Assembly (Clare Trust) Inc v Attorney-General
(South Australia) [1991] SASC 2832 123
Godfree (decd), Re [1952] VLR 353 83
Goodson (decd), Re [1971] VR 801 31
Gray v Australian Cancer Foundation for Medical Research [1999]
NSWSC 492 126
Gray v Australian Cancer Foundation for Medical Research (No 2)
[1999] NSWSC 725 113
Green v Trustees of the Property of the Church of England in Tasmania
(Tas SC, 31 Aug 1992) 73

Heydon v NRMA Ltd (2000) 36 ACSR 462 (NSW CA) 15
Hunter Region SLSA Helicopter Rescue Service Ltd v Attorney-General
(New South Wales) [2000] NSWSC 456 .... 26–7, 95

Ipswich City Council v Attorney-General (Queensland) [2004]
QSC 252 .... 81, 112

Kean Memorial Trust Fund, Trustees of the v Attorney-General
  (South Australia) (2003) 86 SASR 449 .... 93–4, 102, 110
King v Poggioli (1923) 32 CLR 222 (HCA) 287

Leahy v Attorney-General (New South Wales) [1959]
  AC 457 (PC) 171, 182
Lovett v Permanent Trustee Co Ltd (NSWCA, 24 Mar 1987) 132

McCormack v Stevens [1978] NSWLR 517 79
McLean v Attorney-General (New South Wales) [2002]
  NSWSC 377 .... 79, 84, 121, 122
McLean v Attorney-General (New South Wales) [2003]
  NSWSC 853 132
Mills, Re [1934] VLR 158 83
Misra v Hindu Heritage Research Foundation Ltd (NSW SC,
  21 Jun 1996) 152–3, 160
Modbury Primary School, In re the former (1997) 69 SASR 497 57
Moore (decd), Re; Austrust Ltd v United Aborigines Mission and
  Attorney-General (New South Wales) (1991) 55 SASR 439 72
Morton v Attorney-General (Victoria) (Vic SC, 23 Dec 1996) 102
Mother Theresa Celine v Union Fidelity Trustee Co of Australia Ltd
  (VSC, 14 Apr 1987) 125
Murdoch v Attorney-General (Tasmania) (Tas SC, 4 Aug 1992) 83

National Trust of Australia (NSW) v Amour (NSW CA, 3 Dec 1997) ... 51

Pace (decd), Re (1985) 38 SASR 336 .... 83, 127
Parker (decd), In re; The Ballarat Trustees, Executors and Agency
  Co Ltd v Parker [1949] VLR 133 28
Peacock's Charity, Re [1956] Tas SR 142 66
Peacock, In re (Tas SC, 16 Dec 1992) 51
Pedulla v Nasti (1990) 20 NSWLR 720 177
Peirson Memorial Trust, In the matter of [1995] QSC 308
  (7 Dec 1995) 93, 100, 103, 110, 114–15
Penny v Cancer & Pathological Research Institute of
  Western Australia (1994) 13 WAR 314 .... 115, 136–7
Permanent Trustee Co Ltd v Attorney-General (New South Wales)
  [1999] NSW SC 288 (9 Apr 1999) 122
Permanent Trustee Co Ltd v Attorney General (re Byrne's Estate)
  (No 2) (NSW SC, 1 Mar 1995) 142
Permanent Trustee Co Ltd v Attorney General (re Byrne's Estate)
  (NSW SC, 12 Dec 1994) 142
Perpetual Trustee Co Ltd v Braithwaite (NSW SC, 29 May 1992) 128

Perpetual Trustee Co Ltd v John Fairfax & Sons Pty Ltd (1959)
  76 WN(NSW) 226 177
Perpetual Trustee Co Ltd v Minister for Health of the State of
  New South Wales (NSW SC, 13 Dec 1990) 83
Perpetual Trustees Co Ltd v State of Tasmania [2000] Tas SC
  (6 Jun 2000) 175
Perpetual Trustee Co Ltd v University of Newcastle (NSW SC,
  12 Nov 1991) 103
Perpetual Trustees Tasmania Ltd v Attorney-General (Tasmania)
  (Tas SC, 18 Nov 1993) 48, 58, 148
Perpetual Trustees Tasmania Ltd v Attorney-General (Tasmania)
  (Tas SC, 12 Apr 2002) 125
Phillips v Roberts [1975] 2 NSWLR 207 (CA) 28, 127, 129
Public Trustee v Attorney-General (New South Wales)
  (NSW SC, 10 Feb 1994) 36, 83–4, 86
Public Trustee v Attorney-General (New South Wales),
  Jarrett, Muller and Davies (1997) 42 NSWLR 600 ...... 54, 56, 99, 121
Public Trustee of Queensland v State of Queensland [2004]
  QSC 360 80–1
Public Trustee of Queensland as Trustee of the Anzac Cottages Trusts v
  Attorney-General (Queensland) [2000] QSC 175 .... 93, 100, 112, 115,
                                                        116, 139
Public Trustee (Estate of Hodge (decd)) v Cerebral Palsy Association of
  Western Australia Ltd [2004] WASC 36 31,
                                                         39, 46

Queensland Rugby Football League Ltd v Worrell (2000) 35 ACSR 555
  (Qld SC) 16

Radmanovich v Nedeljkovic [2001] NSWSC 492
  (15 Jun 2001) 183, 204
Roman Catholic Trusts Corporation for the Diocese of Melbourne v
  Attorney-General (Victoria) (Vic SC, 19 Nov 1993) 102
Roman Catholic Trusts Corporation for the Diocese of Melbourne v
  Attorney-General (Victoria)[2000] VSC 360 .... 81, 102
Royal Agricultural and Industrial Association v Chester (1974)
  48 ALJR 304 (HCA) 179
Royal North Shore Hospital of Sydney v Attorney-General
  (New South Wales) (1938) 60 CLR 396 (HCA) 1, 58, 76

Scott v Anti-Cancer Council of Victoria (Vic SC, 5 Sep 1996) 102
Sir Moses Montefiore Jewish Home v Howell & Co (No 7)
  Pty Ltd [1984] 2 NSWLR 406 46
Smith, Re [1954] SASR 151 83

South Eastern Sydney Area Health Service v Wallace (NSW SC,
      24 Nov 2003) 35
Stevedoring Employees Retirement Fund Pty Ltd v Association of
      Employers of Waterside Labour (NSW SC, 1 Mar 1995) 5
Strathalbyn Show Jumping Club Inc v Mayes [2001] SASC 73 181
Sumner v Sumner (1884) 10 VLR (E) 261 28
Sydney Homoeopathic Hospital v Turner (1959) 102 CLR 188
      (HCA) 45–6

Taylor v Attorney-General (New South Wales)
      (NSW SC, 24 Apr 1987) 41
Tidex v Trustees Executors and Agency Co Ltd [1971]
      2 NSWLR 453 181
Tyrie (decd), Re [1970] VR 264 79
Tyrie (decd) (No 1), Re [1972] VR 168 83

Williams v Attorney-General (New South Wales) (1948)
      48 SR (NSW) 505 72
Wilmott (decd), Re; Uniting Church in Australia Property Trust (Vic) v
      Royal Victorian Institute for the Blind (SC Vic, 2 Dec 1999) 50, 73

Yeomans v Yeomans [2005] QSC 85 (19 Apr 2005) 181

CANADA

Abercrombie Estate v Etobicoke (City) Board of Education (Ont SCJ,
      9 Feb 2004) 34
Adamson Estate v McIntyre (1997), 70 ACWS (3d)
      200 (Ont Gen Div) 84
Alfresh Beverages Canada Corp v Hoechst AG (2002), 16 CPC (5th)
      301 (SCJ) 223, 234, 260–1, 274
Aquila v Hamilton General Homes (1971) Ltd (SCJ, 24 Jun 2004) 294
Avalon Consolidated School Board v United Church of Canada (1983),
      42 Nfld & PEIR 8 (Newfoundland SC) 73

Bilz v Community Care Access Centre (1998), 84 ACWS (3d) 1231
      (Ont Gen Div) 29
Boudreau v Reneault (1911), 123 Alta LR 333 (SC) 295
Boy Scouts of Canada, Provincial Council of Newfoundland v
      Doyle (Newfoundland CA, 26 Jun 1997) 66, 68, 70
British Columbia (Official Administrator) v Ridge Meadows Association
      for Community Living (1999), 86 ACWS (3d) 464 (BC SC) 83
Brooks Estate, Re (1969), 4 DLR (3d) 694 28
Bruce Estate, Re (PEI SC, 5 Aug 2004) 77, 127

Bryson v Egerton (1999), 25 RPR (3d) 113 (BC SC) 294
Buchanan Estate, Re (1996), 61 ACWS (3d) 841 (BC SC) 84

Canada Trust Co v Cantol Ltd, Re (1980), 103 DLR (3d) 109
  (BC SC) 204
Canada Trust Co v Ontario Human Rights Commission, Re (1990),
  69 DLR (4th) 321 (Ont CA) 58, 66, 67
Charlesworth Estate, Re (1996), 62 ACWS (3d) 632 (Man QB) 78, 80,
  85, 127
Christian Brothers of Ireland in Canada, Re (2000), 47 OR (3d) 674,
  184 DLR (4th) 445 (Ont CA) 2, 41, 46
Conforti v Conforti (1990), 39 ETR 32 (Ont Gen Div) 41
Conroy Estate, Re (1973), 35 DLR (3d) 752 (BC SC [Probate]) 24–5
Cox, Reference Re Herbert Coplin [1953] 1 SCR 94 78

Fidelity Trust Co v St Joseph's Vocational School of Winnipeg (1984),
  27 Man R (2d) 284 (QB) 73
Fitzgibbon, Re (1922), 69 DLR 524 (SC) 66
Fitzpatrick, Re; Fidelity Trust Co v St Joseph's Vocational School of
  Winnipeg (1984), 6 DLR (4th) 644 (Man QB) 10
Ford v F Hoffmann-La Roche Ltd (SCJ, 23 Mar 2005) 223, 234, 260,
  267, 274, 276
Ford v F Hoffmann-La Roche Ltd (SCJ, 23 Mar 2005)
  (separate decision) 216
Fraser Estate, Re (2000), 99 ACWS (3d) 525 (PEI SC) 77, 83, 128

Gilbert v Canadian Imperial Bank of Commerce (2004),
  3 CPC (6th) 35 (SCJ) 260–1, 264
Granfield Estate v Jackson (1999), 87 ACWS (3d) 205 (BC SC) 29

Halifax School for the Blind v Attorney-General [1935],
  2 DLR 347 156
Hunter, Re; Genn v Attorney-General (British Columbia) (1973),
  34 DLR (3d) 602 (BC SC) 66, 72, 83

Johnston Estate v Cavalry Baptist Church for Ganaraska Woods
  Retreat Centre (2002), ACWS (3d) 752 (SCJ) 83, 125, 128

Keewatin Tribal Council Inc v Thompson (1989), 61 Man R (2d) 241
  (QB) 181
Kunze Estate, Re (Sask QB, 9 May 2005) 41

Landucon-Yonge Ltd v Safeguard Real Estate Ltd (1992), 30 RPR (2d)
  87 (Ont Gen Div) 294
Leer Estate, Re (Sask QB, 13 Jun 2005) 83

LeMesurier v Andrus (1986), 54 OR (2d) 1, 25 DLR (4th) 424
(Ont CA) 293

Machin, Re (1979), 9 Alta LR (2d) 296, 101 DLR (3d) 438
(Alta SC) 31
Montreal Trust Co v Richards (1982), 40 BCLR 114, [1983]
1 WWR 437 (BC SC) 24, 25, 83

Nakonechny Estate, Re (2003), ACWS (3d) 620 (Alta QB) 83
Nicola Valley Lumber Co v Meeker [1917] 31 DLR 607 (BC CA) 295
Northern Ontario Fire Relief Fund Trusts, Re (1913), 4 OWN 1118,
11 DLR 15 (SC) 148
Nova Scotia (Attorney-General) v Axford (1885), 13 SCR 294 1

Ontario Asphalt Block Co v Montreuil (1913), 15 DLR 703
(Ont Sup Ct App Div) 287

Power v AGNS (1903), 35 SCR 182 49
Public Trustee and Toronto Humane Society, Re (1987),
60 OR (2d) 236, 40 DLR (4th) 111 22
Punch v Chisholm (1874), 9 NSR 469 (CA) 295

Raaber v Coll-in-Wood Farms Ltd (1971), 14 DLR (3d) 234
(Alta SC App Div) 281, 285, 295
Ramsden Estate, Re (1996), 139 DLR (4th) 746 (PEI SC) 29
Roberts, Re (1958), 26 WWR 196 (Alta CA) 29
Rowland v Vancouver College Ltd (2001), 94 BCLR (3d) 249,
205 DLR (4th) 193 (BC CA) 31, 41

Sheppard v Bradshaw (1921), 50 OLR 626, 64 DLR 624 (SC) 29, 202
Skariah v Praxl (1990), 73 OR (2d) 1, 70 DLR (4th) 27 (HC) 295
Smith v Canadian Tire Acceptance Ltd (1995), 22 OR (3d)
433 (Gen Div) 233
Stefanovska v Kok (1990), 73 OR (2d) 368 (HC) 294

Tesluk v Boots Pharmaceutical plc (2002), 21 CPC (5th) 196 (SCJ) ... 223,
234–6, 258, 260, 261, 263, 265
Toronto Aged Men's and Women's Homes v Loyal True Blue and
Orange Home (2003), 68 OR (3d) 777 (SCJ) 29
Tufford, Re (1984), 45 OR (2d) 351, 6 DLR (4th) 534 (Ont CA) ... 31, 71

Wallace v Nichol [1951], 1 DLR 449 (Ont CA) 285, 287
Waller v Roach (BC SC, 14 Jul 1982) 285
Walt Estate v Williams (1997), 73 ACWS (3d) 558 (BC SC) 77

Weatherhead Estate v Canada (1995), 57 ACWS (3d) 682
(New Brunswick CA) 83
Webb and Reeves v Dipenta [1925] SCR 565, [1925]
1 DLR 216 .... 281, 295
Weninger Estate v Canadian Diabetes Association (1993),
2 ETR (2d) 24 (Ont HC) 84, 128
Wilson v Patterson (1918), 39 DLR 642 (Alta SC) 281, 287, 295
Wilson Estate v Loyal Protestant Association (BCSC, 31 Jan 1986) 73
Wright, Re (1923), 56 NSR 364 (CA) 29

ENGLAND

Abbott Fund, In re Trusts of the; Smith v Abbott [1900] 2 Ch 326 143,
146, 151, 152, 154, 181, 210
Aberconway's Settlement Trusts, In re; McLaren v Aberconway [1953]
Ch 647 (CA) 181
Adderley v Dixon (1824) 1 Sims & St 607; 57 ER 239 281
Air Jamaica Ltd v Charlton [1999] 1 WLR 1399 (PC) 204–5
Andrew's Trust, In re; Carter v Andrew [1905] 2 Ch 48 210
Anonymous (1678) 2 Freeman 40; 22 ER 1045 (Curia Cancellarie) 9
Armitage (decd), In re; Ellam v Norwich Corporation [1972]
1 Ch 438 61
Arms (Multiple Sclerosis Research) Ltd, In re [1997]
1 WLR 877 (Ch) 45
Ashton Charity, In re (1856) 22 Beav 288 97
Aspinalls v Powell and Scholefield (1889) 60 LT 595 285
Astor's Settlement Trusts, In re; Astor v Scholfield [1952]
Ch 534 .... 170–3, 190, 201
Atkinson's Will Trusts, In re; Atkinson v Hall [1978]
1 WLR 586 (Ch) 203
Attorney-General v Andrew (1798) 3 Ves 633; 300 ER 1194 .... 9, 61
Attorney-General v Baxter (1684) 1 Vern 248; 23 ER 446
(Lord Keeper) 9
Attorney General v Bishop of Worcester (1851) 9 Hare 328;
68 ER 530 142
Attorney-General v Boultbee (1794) 2 Ves 380; 30 ER 683 58
Attorney General v Coopers' Co (1812) 19 Ves 187; 34 ER 488 28
Attorney-General v Day [1900] 1 Ch 31 106
Attorney-General v Earl of Craven (1856) 21 Beav 392 60
Attorney-General v Gibson (1835) 2 Beav 317n 61
Attorney-General v Guise (1692) 2 Vern 266; 23 ER 772 (HC Ch) 8
Attorney-General v Ironmonger's Co (1841) Cr & Ph 208;
41 ER 469 .... 87, 101, 134

Attorney-General v Ironmongers' Co (1844) 10 Cl & F 908;
    8 ER 983 .... 5, 86, 126
Attorney-General v Lady Downing (1767) Wilm 1 (C) 13 7
Attorney-General v London Corporation (1790) 3 Bro CC 171 61
Attorney-General v Peacock (1675) Finch 245 8
Attorney-General v Platt (1675) Finch 222. 7–8
Attorney-General v Price [1912] 1 Ch 667 48
Attorney-General v Vint (1850) 3 De G & Sm 704; 64 ER 669 61
Attorney-General v Whitchurch (1896) 3 Ves 114 86

Bagshaw (decd), In re; Westminster Bank Ld v Taylor [1954]
    1 WLR 238 (Ch) 34, 36
Bankers Trust Co v Namdar [1995] NPC 139 (Ch) 280, 295, 299
Barclays Bank Ltd v Quistclose Investments Ltd [1970]
    AC 567 (HL) 181
Barlow v Grant (1684) 1 Vern 255 210
Barlow Clowes International Ltd v Vaughan [1992]
    4 All ER 22 (CA) 159
Barnes v Derby Diocesan Board of Finance [2003] Ch 239 98
Barnes v Wood (1869) LR 8 Eq 424 300
Beaufort Western Ltd v Fellows (CA, 26 May 2000) 281
Bennett (decd), In re; Sucker v Attorney-General [1960] Ch 18 24–6
Besterman's Will Trusts, Re (Ch, 21 Jan 1980) 55
Beswick v Beswick [1968] AC 58 (HL) 282–3
Biscoe v Jackson (1887) LR 35 Ch D 460 (CA) 60, 76, 79
Bowes, In re; Earl Strathmore v Vane [1896] 1 Ch 507 183–4
Bowman v Secular Society [1916–17] All ER Rep 1 (HL) 77
Bradwell Will Trusts, In re; Goode v Board of Trustees for the
    Methodist Church Purposes [1952] Ch 575 61
Braithwaite v Attorney-General [1909] 1 Ch 510 .... 145, 154, 205
British Red Cross Balkan Fund, In re; British Red Cross Society v
    Johnson [1914] 2 Ch 419 .... 145, 159
British School of Egyptian Archaeology, In re; Murray v Public Trustee
    [1954] 1 WLR 546 (Ch) 69, 73, 146, 148, 150, 156–7
Broadbent (decd), Re; Imperial Cancer Research Fund v Bradley [2001]
    EWCA Civ 714 .... 40, 43, 69
Brown v Burdett (1882) 21 Ch D 667 175
Buck, In re; Bruty v Mackay [1896] 2 Ch 727 61
Bucks Constabulary Widows' and Orphans' Fund Friendly Society
    (No 2), In re [1979] 1 WLR 936 (Ch) 205

Campden Charities, In re (1881) 18 Ch D 310 (CA) 59
Catherall (decd), In re; Lloyds Bank Ltd v Griffiths
    (Ch, 3 Jun 1959) 176, 190

Cato v Thompson (1882) 9 QBD 616; 47 LT 491 (CA) 283, 290,
293, 300
Cedar Holdings Ltd v Green [1981] 1 Ch 129 (CA) 285, 289–90, 299
Chichester Diocesan Fund and Board of Finance v Simpson [1944]
AC 341 (HL) 55
Church Patronage Trust, In re; Laurie v Attorney-General [1904]
2 Ch 643 (CA) 174, 189
Clifford, In re; Mallam v McFie [1912] 1 Ch 29 179
Colonial Bishoprics Fund 1841, In re; Goode v Board of Trustees for
Methodist Church Purposes [1935] Ch 148 61
Commissioners for Special Purposes of the Income Tax v
Pemsel [1891] AC 531 (HL) 54, 56, 109, 134,
135, 136, 143, 169
Conservative and Unionist Central Office v Burrell (Inspector of Taxes)
[1980] 3 All ER 42 (Ch) 153
Construction Industry Training Board v Attorney-General
[1971] 1 WLR 1303 (Ch) 10
Construction Industry Training Board v Attorney-General [1973]
Ch 173 (CA) 25
Co-operative Insurance Society Ltd v Argyll Stores (Holdings) Ltd
[1998] AC 1 (HL) 281–3
Cooper's Conveyance Trusts, In re; Crewdson v Bagot [1956]
1 WLR 1096 (Ch) 48–9, 58, 147
Corporation of the Master Wardens and Court of Assistants of the
Mystery or Art of Brewers of the City of London v Attorney-General
(Ch, 23 Jul 1999) 105
Couchman's Will Trusts, In re; Couchman v Eccles [1952] Ch 391 29
Cox (decd), In re; Baker v National Trust Co [1955] AC 627 (PC) 78
Cunnack v Edwards [1895] 1 Ch 489 154
Cunnack v Edwards [1896] 2 Ch 679 (CA) 153, 203, 205

Da Costa v De Pas (1754) Amb 228; 27 ER 150 86–7
Davis, In re; Hannen v Hillyer [1902] 1 Ch 876 .... 28, 82
Davis v Richards & Wallington Industries Ltd [1990]
1 WLR 1511 (Ch) 204–5
Dawson's Will Trusts, In re; National Provincial Bank Ltd v
National Council of the YMCA Inc [1957] 1 WLR 391 (Ch) 33–4
Dean, In re; Cooper-Dean v Stevens (1889) 41 Ch D 552 .... 174, 176
Denley's Trust Deed, In re; Holman v HH Martyn & Co Ltd [1969]
1 Ch 373 .... 179–86, 201
Dingle v Turner [1972] AC 601 (HL) 56
Re Diplock; Wintle v Diplock [1941] 1 All ER 193 (CA) 55
Dominion Students' Hall Trust, In re; Dominion Students'
Hall Trust v Attorney-General [1947] Ch 183 .... 62, 87, 96, 102

Durham v Legard (1865) 34 Beav 611; 55 ER 771 . . . . 290, 300
Dyke v Walford (1848) 5 Moo PCC 434; 13 ER 557 23

Edis's Declaration of Trust, In re; Campbell-Smith v Davies [1972]
   1 WLR 1135 (Ch) 40, 45
Endacott (decd), In re; Corpe v Endacott [1960] Ch 232 (CA) . . . 170, 173,
                                                                         176, 177, 201
Evans Marshall & Co Ltd v Bertola SA [1973] 1 WLR 349 (CA) 282

Falcke v Gray (1859) 4 Drew 651; 62 ER 250 282
Faraker, In re; Faraker v Durell [1911–1913] All ER Rep 488
   (CA) 33–9, 42, 104
Fawcett and Holmes, In re Contract between (1889) LR 42 Ch D 150
   (CA) 296
Finger's Will Trusts, In re; Turner v Ministry of Health [1972]
   1 Ch 286 . . . . 22, 40, 44–5, 80, 82, 84
Fisher v Hill (1612) Duke 82 8
Flight v Booth (1834) 1 Bing NC 370; [1824–34] All ER Rep 43
   (Ct of Com Pleas) 286, 295, 297
Foveaux, In re [1895] 2 Ch 501 108
Fraser, In re; Yeates v Fraser (1883) LR 22 Ch D 827 28
Funds Raised for and Donated to NHS Hospitals (1995)
   3 Decisions of the Charity Commissioners 35 75
Frere, In re; Kidd v Farnham Group Hospital Management Committee
   [1951] Ch 27 34

Gardner's Will Trusts, Re; Boucher v Horn [1936] 3 All ER 938
   (Ch) 28–9
Gates v Jones (1690) 2 Vern 266 8
Gaudiya Mission v Kamalaksha Das Braham (Ch, 14 Mar 1997) 28
Gibson v South American Stores (Gath & Chaves) Ltd [1950]
   Ch 177 (CA) 49, 70
Gilchester Properties Ltd v Gomm [1948] 1 All ER 493 (Ch) 285, 301
Gillingham Bus Disaster Fund, In re; Bowman v Official Solicitor
   [1958] Ch 300 . . . . 143–4, 153–4, 159, 163, 202–5, 210
GKN Bolts and Nuts Ltd (Automotive Division) Birmingham Works,
   Sports and Social Club, In re [1982] 1 WLR 774 (Ch) 205
Glass' Will Trusts, In re [1950] Ch 643 37
Goldney, In re; Goldney v Queen Elizabeth Hospital for Children
   [1946] WN 158 (Ch) 43
Goldschmidt (decd), In re; Commercial Union Assurance Co Ltd v
   Central British Fund for Jewish Relief and Rehabilitation [1957]
   1 WLR 524 (Ch) 77, 82, 85
Good's Will Trusts, Re; Oliver v Batten [1950] 2 All ER 653 (Ch) 79

Gosling v Gosling (1859) Johns 265; 70 ER 423 183
Gott, In re; Glazebrook v University of Leeds [1944] 1 Ch 193 27
Grant v Dawkins [1973] 1 WLR 1406 (Ch) 286
Grant's Will Trusts, In re; Harris v Anderson [1980] 1 WLR 360
   (Ch) 180
Guild v Inland Revenue Commissioners [1991] STC 281 79
Guild v Inland Revenue Commissioners [1992] 2 AC 310 (HL) 10

Halsey v Grant (1806) 13 Ves Jun 73; 33 ER 222 295
Hambermehl v Attorney-General (Ch, 31 Jul 1996) 48
Hanbey's Will Trusts, In re; Cutler's Co v President and Governors of
   Christ's Hospital, London [1956] Ch 264 49
Harris v Sharp (CA, 21 Mar 1989) 73–5
Harwood, In re; Colman v Innes [1936] Ch 285 . . . . 59, 80–2, 85
Hawkins (decd), In re; Hawkins v Hawkins [1972] 1 Ch 714 4
Heilbut Symons & Co v Buckleton [1913] AC 30 (HL) 301
Henry Wood National Memorial Trust, In re; Armstrong v
   Moiseiwitsch [1966] 1 WLR 1601 (Ch) 149, 151, 159, 166
Hetherington (decd), In re [1990] Ch 1 (CA) 24
Hillier's Trusts, In re; Hillier v Attorney-General [1954]
   1 WLR 9 (Ch) 150, 158, 204
Hillier's Trusts, In re; Hillier v Attorney-General [1954]
   1 WLR 700 (CA) 70, 150, 152, 154–6, 159–62, 204
Hobourn Aero Components Ltd's Air Raid Distress Fund,
   In re [1946] Ch 86 203
Hobourn Aero Components Ltd's Air Raid Distress Fund,
   In re [1946] Ch 194 (CA) 143
Hooper, In re; Parker v Ward [1932] 1 Ch 3 176
Humberston v Humberston (1716) 1 P Wms 332 14
Hunter (decd), Re; lloyds Bank Ltd v Girton College, Cambridge [1951]
   Ch 190 41
Hutchinson's Will Trusts, In re; Gibbons v Nottingham Area No 1
   Hospital Management Committee [1953] 1 Ch 387 . . . . 34, 37

Ingleton Charity, Re; Croft v Attorney-General [1956] Ch 585 51
Inland Revenue Commissioners v Broadway Cottages Trust [1955]
   Ch 20 (CA) 201
Internet Trading Clubs Ltd v Freeserve (Investments) Ltd plc
   (QB, 19 Jun 2001) 282–3

Jackson and Haden's Contract, In re [1906] 1 Ch 412 (CA) 298
Jacobs v Revell [1900] 2 Ch 858 . . . . 288, 297–8
Jenkins's Will Trusts, In re; Public Trustee v British Union for the
   Abolition of Vivisection [1966] Ch 249 . . . . 55, 80

Jones v Attorney-General; R v Wain (1994) 2 Decisions of the
 Charity Commissioners 33 143
Jones v Edney (1812) 3 Camp 285 297
Jones v Williams (Ch, 15 Mar 1988) 205

King Bros (Finance) Ltd v North Western British Road Services Ltd
 [1986] 2 EGLR 253 (Ch) 288
King, In re; Kerr v Bradley [1923] 1 Ch 243 .... 59, 71, 103
Knox, In re; Fleming v Carmichael [1937] Ch 109 .... 79, 80, 82
Koeppler Will Trusts, In re; Barclays Bank Trust Co Ltd v Slack
 [1986] Ch 423 (CA) 41

Laing Trust, In re JW; Stewards' Co Ltd v Attorney-General [1984]
 Ch 143 .... 95, 99, 112
Lambeth Charities, Re (1853) 22 LJ Ch 959 142
Latimer v Commissioner of Inland Revenue [2004] UKPC 13 49
Lawton (decd), In re; Lloyds Bank Ltd v Longfleet St Mary's Parochial
 Church Council [1940] Ch 984 77
Lepton's Charity, In re; Ambler v Thomas [1972] 1 Ch 276 ...... 93, 100,
              102, 111–12, 117, 128
Lipinski's Will Trusts, In re; Gosschalk v Levy [1976] 1 Ch 235 180
Lipmans Wallpaper Ltd v Mason & Hodghton Ltd [1968]
 2 WLR 881 (Ch) 287
Little (decd), In re; Barclays Bank Ltd v Bournemouth and East Dorset
 Hospital Management Committee [1953] 1 WLR 1132 (Ch) 41
Liverpool and District Hospital for Diseases of the Heart v
 Attorney-General [1981] Ch 193 .... 15, 22–3
Liverpool City Council v Attorney-General (Ch, 15 Apr 1992) 23
Lord Nuffield (as Trustee for the Nuffield Foundation) v
 Inland Revenue Commissioners (1946) 28 Fam Cas 479 (KB) 28
Lucas, In re; Sheard v Mellor [1948] Ch 424 (CA) 34, 38, 43
Lysaght (decd), In re; Hill v Royal College of Surgeons [1966]
 1 Ch 191 .... 56, 60, 62, 76, 96, 102

McPhail v Doulton [1971] AC 424 (HL) 193
Mayor of Lyons v Advocate-General of Bengal (1876) LR 1
 App Cas 91 (PC) 49, 85
Meyers (decd), In re; London Life Association v St George's Hospital
 [1951] Ch 534 .... 41, 45
Mills v Farmer [1814–23] All ER Rep 53 (Ch) 28, 76
Mitchell's Will Trusts, In re (1966) 110 Sol Jo 291 (Ch) 79
Moggridge v Thackwell (1802) 7 Ves 6; [1803–1813] All ER
 Rep 754 (Ch) 7, 23–5
Monk, In re; Giffen v Wedd [1927] 2 Ch 197 (CA) 70, 84, 146–7

Monypenny v Dering [1843–60] All ER Rep 1098 (CA) 4
Moon's Will Trusts, Re; Foale v Gillians [1948] 1 All ER
    300 (Ch) 60, 72
Morgan (decd), Re; Cecil-Williams v Attorney-General [1955]
    1 WLR 738 (Ch) 62
Morgan's Will Trusts, In re; Lewarne v Minister of Health [1950]
    1 Ch 637 .... 31, 34–6
Morice v Bishop of Durham (1805) 10 Ves 522; [1803–13] All ER
    Rep 451 (Ch) 171, 180
Mortlock v Buller (1804) 10 Ves 292 (HL) 286
Mountgarret, In re; Mountgarret v Ingilby [1919] 2 Ch 294 14
Murray v Thomas [1937] 4 All ER 545 (Ch) 24
Mussett v Bingle [1876] WN 170 176

National Anti-Vivisection Society v Inland Revenue Commissioners
    [1948] AC 31 (HL) 108, 139–40
Niyazi's Will Trusts, In re [1978] 1 WLR 910 (Ch) 76
North Devon and West Somerset Relief Fund Trusts, In re;
    Hylton v Wright [1953] 1 WLR 1260 (Ch) 58, 66, 70, 71, 143, 144,
                                          147, 148, 152, 155, 204
North Shields Old Meeting House, In re (1859) 7 WR 541 97
Nottage, In re; Jones v Palmer [1895] 2 Ch 649 (CA) 179

Oldham Borough Council v Attorney-General [1993] Ch D 210
    (CA) 1, 93, 95, 97–8
Osoba (decd), In re; Osoba v Osoba [1979] 1 WLR 247 (CA) 181,
                                                       184, 210
Ovey, In re; Broadbent v Barrow (1885) 29 Ch D 560 42
Owen v Williams (CA, 21 Nov 1985) 298

P & O Overseas Holdings Ltd v Rhys Braintree Ltd
    (Ch, 5 Jul 2001) 285
Packe, In re; Sanders v Attorney-General [1918] 1 Ch 437 79
Paice v Archbishop of Canterbury (1807) 14 Ves 364 24
Palmer v Abney Park Cemetery Co Ltd (Ch, 4 Jul 1985) 205
Parke's Charity, In re (1842) 12 Sim 329 97
Patten, In re; Westminster Bank Ltd v Carylon Sussex [1929]
    2 Ch 276 170
Payling's Will Trusts, Re; Armstrong v Payling [1969]
    1 WLR 1595 (Ch) 73
Peel's Release, In re [1921] 2 Ch 218 .... 50, 70
Peggs v Lamb [1994] Ch 172 .... 105–9, 112
Perrin v Morgan [1943] AC 399 (HL) 127

Pettingall v Pettingall (1842) 11 LJ Ch 176 176
Philipps v Attorney-General [1932] WN 100 61
Pirbright v Salwey [1896] WN 86 176
Potts v Hickman [1940] 4 All ER 491 (HL) 4
Price v Strange [1978] Ch 337 (CA) 283, 286, 288
Progress Aviation SA v Americom Leasing Group Inc
    (CA, 15 Mar 1988) 302
Puckett and Smith's Contract, In re [1902] 2 Ch 258 (CA) 296–7
Purday v Johnson [1886–90] All ER Rep 1111 (Ch) 82
Pyne, In re; Lilley v Attorney-General [1903] 1 Ch 83 24

R v District Auditor No 3, Audit District of West Yorkshire
    Metropolitan CC; ex p West Yorkshire Metropolitan CC [1986]
    RVR 24 (QB) 182, 185
R v York Health Authority; ex p Nicholas (QB, 1 May 1992) 112
Rainbow Estates Estates Ltd v Tokenhold Ltd [1999] Ch 64 282–3
Raine (decd), In re; Walton v Attorney-General [1956] Ch 417 ..... 71, 84
Raineri v Miles [1981] AC 1050 292
Randell, In re; Randell v Dixon (1887) 38 Ch D 213 49
Recher's Will Trusts, In re; National Westminster Bank Ltd v
    National Anti-Vivisection Society Ltd [1972] Ch 526 170
Resch's Will Trusts, In re; Le Cras v Perpetual Trustee
    Co Ltd, Far West Children's Health Scheme v Perpetual Trustee
    Co Ltd [1967] 3 All ER 915 (PC) 28
Richmond Parish Charity Lands Richmond Corporation v
    Morell, Re [1965] RVR 590 (CA) 26
Riverpath Properties Ltd v Brammall (Ch, 31 Jan 2000) 288
Roberts (decd), In re; Stenton v Hardy [1963] 1 WLR 406
    (Ch) 31, 34–5, 37, 40, 42, 45
Robertson, In re; Colin v Chamberlin [1930] 2 Ch 71 .... 58, 71
Robinson, In re; Besant v The German Reich [1931] 2 Ch 122 28
Robinson, In re; Wright v Tugwell [1923] 2 Ch 332 60
Royal Holloway and Bedford New College (1993) 1 Decisions of the
    Charity Commissioners 21 .... 102, 132–3
Royce, In re; Turner v Wormald [1940] Ch 514 .... 71, 84
Rudd v Lascelles [1900] 1 Ch 815 .... 284–7, 290, 293, 295,
                                                    297, 299–300
Rutherford v Acton-Adams [1915] AC 866 (PC) 287, 290–5, 301
Ryan v Mutual Tontine Westminster Chambers Association [1893]
    1 Ch 116 (CA) 283
Rymer, In re; Rymer v Stanfield [1895] 1 Ch 19 (CA) 42–3, 59, 76, 82

Sanders' Will Trusts, In re; Public Trustee v McLaren [1954] Ch 265 ... 56
Sanford v Gibbons (1829) 2 Hare 195n 25

Satterthwaite's Will Trusts, In re; Midland Bank Executor and
  Trustee Co Ltd v Royal Veterinary College [1966] 1 WLR 277
  (CA) 55, 59, 79–80, 82
Saunders v Vautier (1841) 4 Beav 115 183
Schwabacher, Re (1907) 98 LT 127 282
Selinger's Will Trusts, Re; Midland Bank Executor and Trustee Co Ltd v
  Levy [1959] 1 WLR 217 (Ch) 15
Servers of the Blind League, In re [1960] 1 WLR 564 (Ch) 38
Seven Seas Properties Ltd v Al-Essa [1988] 1 WLR 1272 (Ch) 286
Shaw (decd), In re; Public Trustee v Day [1957] 1 WLR 729
  (Ch) 170, 190
Shelton's Settled Estate, In re; Shelton v Shelton [1945] Ch 158 47
Shepherd v Croft [1911] 1 Ch 521 .... 285, 296–7
Sick and Funeral Society of St John's Sunday School, Golcar,
  In re [1973] 1 Ch 51 205
Simon v Barber (1829) 3 Hare 195n 25
Simpson (HM Inspector of Taxes) v Grange Trust Ltd [1935] AC 422 ... 4
Sky Petroleum Ltd v VIP Petroleum Ltd [1974] 1 WLR 576 (Ch) 282
Slatter's Will Trusts, In re; Turner v Turner [1964] Ch 512 ...... 34, 36–8,
                                                           41, 82, 86
Slevin, In re; Slevin v Hepburn [1891] 2 Ch 236 (CA) 48–9,
                                                           72–3, 147
Smith, In re; Public Trustee v Smith [1932] 1 Ch 153 (CA) 24
Societe des Industries Metallurgiques SA v The Bronx Engineering
  Co Ltd [1975] 1 Lloyd's Rep 465 (CA) 282
Songest, In re; Mayger v Forces' Help Society [1956] 1 WLR 897
  (CA) 25
Spence (decd), In re; Ogden v Shackleton [1979] Ch 483 .... 42–3, 63,
                                                           79–80, 82–3
Spence's Estate, Re; Barclays Bank Ltd v Stockton-on-Tees Corporation
  [1937] 3 All ER 684 (Ch) 29
SSSL Realisations (2002) Ltd (t/a Save Service Stations Ltd) (in liq),
  Re [2004] EWHC 1760 (Ch) 283
Stanford, In re; University of Cambridge v Attorney-General [1924]
  1 Ch 73 .... 58, 70–1
Stemson's Will Trusts, In re; Carpenter v Treasury Solicitor [1970]
  Ch 16 .... 35–8, 45
Stephens, Re; Giles v Stephens (1892) 8 TLR 792 108
Sudbrook Trading Estate Ltd v Eggleton [1983] 1 AC 444 (HL) 281

Tacon, In re; Public Trustee v Tacon [1958] Ch 447 (CA) 72, 74
Talbot, In re; Jubb v Sheard [1933] Ch 895 77
Thames Guaranty Ltd v Campbell [1985] 1 QB 210 (CA) 280,
                                                           287, 299

Tharp, Re; Longrigg v The People's Dispensary for Sick Animals of
the Poor Inc [1942] 2 All ER 358 (Ch) 10, 82
Thomas v Attorney-General [1936] 2 All ER 1325 (Ch) 170
Thomas v Dering (1837) 1 Keen 729; [1835–42] All ER
Rep 711 . . . . 281, 295, 299–300
Thompson, In re; Public Trustee v Lloyd [1934] Ch 342 . . . . 172, 176
Thorley v Byrne (1830) 3 Hare 195n 25
Tito v Waddell (No 2) [1977] Ch 106 283
Topfell Ltd v Galley Properties Ltd [1979] 1 WLR 446 (Ch) 288–91,
295, 300
Town Investments Ltd v Department of the Environment [1978]
AC 359 (HL) 171
Trimmer v Danby (1856) 25 LJ Ch 424 176
Twinsectra Ltd v Yardley [2002] UKHL 12, 2 AC 164 . . . . 182, 201

Ulrich v Treasury Solicitor [2005] 1 All ER 1059 (Ch) 174, 203
Ulverston and District New Hospital Building Trusts, In re; Birkett v
Barrow and Furness Hospital Management Committee [1956]
1 Ch 622 (CA) 69–70, 146–51, 154–64, 206
United Bank of Kuwait plc v Sahib [1997] Ch 107 (CA) 280
University of London Medical Sciences Institute Fund, In re; Fowler v
Attorney-General [1909] 2 Ch 1 (CA) 149, 151–2, 156, 159

Vandervell v Inland Revenue Commissioners [1967] 2 AC 291
(HL) 191
Varsani v Jesani [1999] Ch 219 (CA) 28, 58, 92–3, 100, 111–14, 128
Varsani v Jesani (Ch, 31 Jul 2001) 96
Vernon's Will Trusts, In re; Lloyd's Bank Ltd v Group 20 Hospital
Management Committee (Coventry) [1972] Ch 300 . . . . 25, 34, 37,
39–40, 44–5
Von Ernst & Cie SA v Inland Revenue Commissioners [1980]
1 WLR 468 (CA) 40

Wallis v Solicitor-General of New Zealand [1903] AC 173 (PC) 60
Waring, In re; Hayward v Attorney-General [1907] 1 Ch 166 37
Watson v Burton [1957] 1 WLR 19 (Ch) 285, 288, 292–3, 296–8
Watt, In re; Hicks v Hill [1932] 2 Ch 243 . . . . 41, 65
Watts v Spence [1976] Ch 165 289
Wedgwood, In re; Sweet v Cotton [1914] 2 Ch 245 . . . . 37, 40
Weir Hospital, In re [1910] 2 Ch 124 (CA) 58, 87, 111
Wells, Re; Swinburne-Hanham v Howard [1932] All ER Rep 277
(CA) 23
Welsh Hospital (Netley) Fund, In re; Thomas v Attorney-General
[1921] 1 Ch 655 . . . . 66, 71, 145–8, 152–3, 155, 158–61, 204

West Cheshire Water Board v Crowe [1940] 2 All ER 351 (KB) 4
West Sussex Constabulary's Widows, Children and Benevolent (1930)
  Fund Trusts, In re; Barnett v Ketteringham [1971] Ch 1 145–7,
                                                150–3, 157–9, 163, 203–5
Westdeutsche Landesbank Girozentrale v Islington London Borough
  Council [1996] AC 669 (HL) 157
Westminster, City of v Duke of Westminster [1991] 4 All ER 136
  (Ch) 4, 59, 86, 93
Whitby v Mitchell (1889) LR 42 Ch D 494 13
Whitby v Mitchell (1890) 44 Ch D 85 (CA) 13–14, 193
White v White (1778) 1 Bro CC 12; 28 ER 955 7
White's Trusts, Re (1886) 33 Ch D 449 73
White's Will Trusts, In re; Barrow v Gillard [1955] 1 Ch 188 73
Whitworth Art Gallery Trusts, Re; Manchester Whitworth Institute v
  Victoria University of Manchester [1958] Ch 461 60
Wicks v Firth (Inspector of Taxes) [1983] 2 AC 214 (HL) 180
William Denby & Sons Ltd Sick and Benevolent Fund,
  In re; Rowling v Wilks [1971] 1 WLR 973 (Ch) 153
Williams and Glyn's Bank Ltd v Boland [1981] AC 487 (HL) 285, 290
Willis, In re; Shaw v Willis [1921] 1 Ch 44 (CA) 27, 76
Wilson, In re; Twentyman v Simpson [1913] 1 Ch 314 .... 61, 76, 79
Withall, In re; Withall v Cobb [1932] 2 Ch 236 .... 34, 36, 38
Wokingham Fire Brigade Trusts, In re; Martin v Hawkins [1951]
  Ch 373 .... 71, 146–7, 157
Wood, In re; Barton v Chilcott [1949] Ch 498 173
Woodhams (decd), In re; Lloyds Bank Ltd v London College of Music
  [1981] 1 WLR 493 (Ch) 77, 79, 84, 96, 102
Wright, In re; Blizard v Lockhart [1954] Ch 347 (CA) 49, 72–3, 147
Wykes' (decd), In re; Riddington v Spencer [1961] Ch 229 203

HONG KONG

Attorney-General (Hong Kong) v Pon Yup Chong How Benevolent
  Association [1992] 24 HKCU 1 (SC) 2

INDIA

Merchant v Shaifuddin [2000] 1 LRI 1028 (SC App) 1

NS Rajabathar Mudaliar v MS Vadivelu Mudaliar (1970) 1
  SCC 12 128

State of Uttar Pradesh v Bansi Dhar [1974] AIR 1084 (SC) 1, 51

IRELAND

Magee v Attorney-General (Irish HC, 25 Jul 2002) 132

Olivia Fund Committee, In re; Doyle v Attorney-General (Irish HC,
    Ch, 22 Feb 1995) 164

Prescott (decd), In the matter of; Purcell v Pobjoy [1990] 2 IR 342 82

Representative Church Body, The v Attorney-General [1988]
    IR 19 .... 1, 112
Royal Kilmainham Hospital, In re; Attorney-General v
    British Legion [1966] IR 451 (HC) 77, 112

Worth Library, In re The [1994] 1 ILRM 161 .... 56–7, 86

MALAYSIA

Tai Kien Luing v Tye Poh Sun [1961] 1 MLJ 78 (OCJ Penang) 2

NEW ZEALAND

Alacoque v Roache [1998] 2 NZLR 250 (CA) 77, 84, 94, 120
Amelia Bullock-Webster (decd), Re [1936] NZLR 814 137
Attorney-General, ex rel Rathbone and McKay v Waipawa Hospital
    Board [1970] NZLR 1148 (SC) 120, 140

Baptist Union of New Zealand v Attorney-General [1973]
    1 NZLR 42 (SC) 30

Centrepoint Community Growth Trust, Re [2000] 2 NZLR 325 137
Collier (decd), Re [1998] 1 NZLR 81 .... 2, 29, 57, 65, 99, 120–1

Door of Hope, Re the (1905) 26 NZLR 96 137

Gift for Life Trust, Re (NZ HC, 9 Nov 2000) 94
Goldwater (decd), Re [1967] NZLR 754 137

Harding (decd), Re [1960] NZLR 379 137

Lushington (decd), Re; Manukau County v Wynyard [1964]
    NZLR 161 (CA) 1, 79

McElroy Trust, Re [2002] 3 NZLR 99 94
McElroy Trust, Re [2003] 2 NZLR 289 (CA) 94, 123–4
McIntosh (decd), Re [1976] 1 NZLR 308 57
Martin (decd), Re [1968] NZLR 289 137

Palmer (decd), Re; White v Feltham Children's Home Trust Inc
   [1939] NZLR 189 137
Palmerston North Halls Trust Board, Re [1976] 2 NZLR 161 ..... 94, 120
Pettit, Re [1988] 2 NZLR 513 .... 55, 77, 83, 94
Public Trustee v Attorney-General [1923] NZLR 433 137

Tennant, Re [1996] 2 NZLR 633 .... 55, 109, 137
Twigger, Re [1989] 3 NZLR 329 .... 94, 125, 128, 136–7

Waite (decd), Re; Cox v New Zealand Insurance Co Ltd [1964]
   NZLR 1034 (CA) 84
Westphal (decd), Re [1972] NZLR 792 14
Wilson Home Trust, Re [2000] 2 NZLR 222 137

NORTHERN IRELAND

Currie, In re; McClelland v Gamble [1985] NI 299 (Ch) 76–7, 80, 127

Dunlop (decd), Re (1984) 19 Northern Ireland Judgments Bulletin 72
Dunwoodie, In re [1977] NI 141 66

Londonderry Presbyterian Church House, Trustees of the v
   Inland Revenue Commissioners [1946] NI 178 (CA) 174

Millar (decd), In re; Millar v Ben Hardwick Memorial Fund
   (NI Ch, 5 Sep 1997) 2

Nesbitt v Attorney-General for Northern Ireland
   (Ch, 17 Apr 1991) 55, 80

SCOTLAND

Ballingall's Judicial Factor v Hamilton, 1973 SLT 236 29
Borland, Re 1908 SC 852 60

Davidson's Trustees v Arnott, 1951 SC 42 (IH 2 Div) 73

Guild v Russell [1987] SCLR 221 (Court of Session) 1

McCaig's Trustees v Kirk-session of United Free Church of Lismore,
1915 SC 426 175

Smart (Trustee of the Mining Institute of Scotland Benevolent Fund
and of the Mining Institute of Scotland Educational Trusts) 1994
SLT 785 (Court of Session, Outer House) 111

SINGAPORE

Hwa Soo Chin v Personal Representatives of the Estate of
Lim Soo Ban (decd) 1994 2 SLR 657 (HC) 2

SOUTH AFRICA

Wit Deep and Knights Central Joint Medical Society, Ex p, 1918
WLD 13 1

UNITED STATES

'Agent Orange' Products Liability Litigation, In re, 597 F Supp 740
(EDNY 1984) 217, 219, 236, 238
'Agent Orange' Products Liability Litigation, In re, 611 F Supp 1396
(EDNY 1985) 215, 223
'Agent Orange' Product Liability Litigation, In re, 818 F 2d 179
(2d Cir 1987) 243, 274–5
Airline Ticket Commission Antitrust Litigation, In re, 268 F 3d 619
(8th Cir 2001) 216, 260, 265
Airline Ticket Commission Antitrust Litigation Travel Network Ltd v
United Air Lines Inc, 307 F 3d 679 (8th Cir 2002) 216, 238,
267–8, 270, 276
Al Barnett & Son Inc v Outboard Marine Corp, 64 FRD 43
(D Del 1974) 254
Allapattah Services Inc v Exxon Corp, 157 F Supp 2d 1291
(SD Fla 2001) 238, 243, 246, 273

Bebchick v Public Utilities Commission, 318 F 2d 187
(DC Cir 1963) 218–19
Board of Trustees of the Museum of the American Indian v Board of
Trustees of the Huntington Free Library and Reading Room, 610
NYS 2d 488 (NY App Div 1994) 138
Boeing Co v Van Gemert, 444 US 472, 100 S Ct 745 (1980) 238, 245,
250–1

Boyle v Giral, 820 A 2d 561 (Ct App 2003) 237
Brewer v Southern Union Co, 1987 US Dist LEXIS 15940
    (D Colo 1987) 215, 219, 220–2, 224, 246,
                                                      252, 266, 268
Brewer v Southern Union Co, 83 F 1173 (D Colo 1987) 252
Buchholz Mortuaries Inc v Director of Revenue, 113 SW 3d 192
    (S Ct Mo 2003) 237

Cavalier v Mobil Oil Corp and Chelmette Refining LLC,
    898 So 2d 584 (La App 4 Cir 2005) 237
City of Philadelphia v American Oil Co, 53 FRD 45 (DNJ 1971) 217,
                                                      221, 268, 271
Colson v Hilton Hotels Corp, 59 FRD 324 (ND Ill 1972) ... 218, 220, 238
Compact Disc Minimum Advertised Price Antitrust Litigation,
    In re, 2005 US Dist LEXIS 11332 (D Maine 2005) 215, 252,
                                                      264–5, 267–8, 275
Compact Disc Minimum Advertised Price Antitrust Litigation,
    In re, 2005 US Dist LEXIS 16468 (D Maine 2005) 265, 275
Compact Disc Minimum Advertised Price Antitrust Litigation,
    In re, 2005 US Dist LEXIS 22273 (D Maine 2005) 275

Daar v Yellow Cab Co, 67 Cal 2d 695, 63 Cal Rptr 724 (1967) 220
Democratic Central Committee of District of Columbia v
    Washington Metro Area Transit Commission, 84 F 3d 451
    (DC Cir 1996) 216, 218–20, 237, 260, 263
Department of Energy Stripper Well Exemption Litigation,
    In re, 578 F Supp 586 (D Kans 1983) 215, 249, 258–9
Drennan v Van Ru Credit Corp, 1997 US Dist Lexis 7776
    (ND Ill 1997) 237, 244

Eisen v Carlisle & Jacquelin, 52 FRD 253 (SDNY 1971) 217, 219, 226
Eisen v Carlisle & Jacquelin, 479 F 2d 1005 (2d Cir 1973) 219, 222,
                                                      225, 226, 238
Eisen v Carlisle & Jacquelin, 417 US 156, 94 S Ct 2140 (1974) 219,
                                                      226, 238
Evans v Abney, 396 US 435 (1970) 1

Fears v Wilhelmina Model Agency Inc, 2005 US Dist LEXIS 7961
    (SDNY 2005) 270
Fears v Wilhelmina Model Agency Inc, 2005 US Dist LEXIS 10764
    (SDNY 2005) 274
Fogie v Thorn Americas Inc, 190 F 3d 889 (8th Cir 1999) 238
Folding Carton Antitrust Litigation, In re, 557 F Supp 1091
    (ND Ill 1983) 215, 217, 236, 237, 240, 241, 246, 253

Folding Carton Antitrust Litigation, In re, 744 F 2d 1252
(7th Cir 1984) 224, 238, 246, 249, 251, 261
Folding Carton Antitrust Litigation, In re, 934 F 2d 323
(7th Cir 1991) 273
Friedman v Lansdale Parking Authority, Fed Sec L Rep (CCH) P98,
676 (ED Pa 1995) 217, 238, 251, 269

General Motors Corp Pick-up Truck Fuel Tank Products Liability
Litigation, In re 55 F 3d 768 (3d Cir 1995) 227

Harvard College v Society for Promoting Theological Education,
3 Gray 280 (Mass 1855) 87
Hayes v Arthur Young & Co, 1994 US App LEXIS 23608
(9th Cir 1994) 245–6, 262
Hodgson v YB Quezada, 498 F 2d 5 (9th Cir 1974) 249
Hodgson v Wheaton Glass Co, 446 F 2d 527 (3d Cir 1971) 249
Holocaust Victim Assets Litigation, In re, 2000 US Dist LEXIS 20817
(EDNY 22 Nov 2000) 240, 243
Holocaust Victim Assets Litigation, In re, 302 F Supp 2d 89
(EDNY 2004) 237
Holocaust Victim Assets Litigation, In re, 311 F Supp 2d 407
(EDNY 2004) 215, 264, 266, 271
Hotel Telephone Charges, In re, 500 F 2d 86 (9th Cir 1974) 225,
238, 254
Houck v Folding Carton Administration Commission, 881 F 2d 494
(7th Cir 1989) 267–8

Jones v National Distillers, 56 F Supp 2d 355 (SDNY 1999) 218, 222,
237, 242, 258–9, 272–3

Keele v Wexler, 149 F 3d 589 (7th Cir 1998) 244
Kestenbaum v Emerson, 1981 US Dist LEXIS 14794 (SDNY 1981) ... 252

Late Corporation of the Church of Jesus Christ of the Latter-Day
Saints v US, 136 US 1, 10 S Ct 792 (1889) 6
Lindy Bros Builders v American Radiator & Standard Sanitary Corp
(ED Pa, 28 Feb 1978) 237
Local 28 of the Sheet Metal Workers v EEOC, 478 US 421,
106 S Ct 3019 (1986) 276
Local Number 93, International Association of Firefighters v
City of Cleveland, 478 US 501, 106 S Ct 3063 (1986) 243

Mace v Van Ru Credit Corp, 109 F 3d 338 (7th Cir 1997) 218, 238,
259, 261
Market Street Railway Co v Railroad Commission of California,
28 Cal 2d 363, 171 P 2d 875 (1946) 237, 262

Matzo Food Products Litigation, In re, 156 FRD 600 (DNJ 1994) 215,
                    238–9, 242–5, 255–6, 259–60, 271
Memorex Securities Cases, In re, 61 FRD 88 (ND Cal 1973) 217
Mexico Money Transfer Litigation, In re, 164 F Supp 2d 1002
    (ND Ill 2000) 221, 244, 261, 268, 274
Mexico Money Transfer Litigation, In re, 267 F 3d 743
    (7th Cir 2001) 237, 262
Microsoft Corp Antitrust Litigation, In re, 185 F Supp 2d 519
    (DM 2002) 244, 259–60, 262–4
Milne, In re Succession of, 89 So 2d 281 4
Mirfasihi v Fleet Mortgage Corporation, 356 F 3d 781
    (7th Cir 2004) 254–5, 258
Molski v Gleich, 318 F 3d 937 (9th Cir 2003) 254, 256
Motorsports Merchandise Antitrust Litigation, In re, 160 F Supp
    2d 1392 (ND Ga 2001) 218, 242, 245, 262, 272–3
Mui v GPU Inc, 851 A 2d 799 (Sup Ct 2004) 237

Nabal v BJ's Wholesale Club Inc, 2002 US Dist LEXIS 15106
    (ED Pa 2002) 245, 252
Nelson v Greater Gadsden Housing Authority, 802 F 2d 405
    (11th Cir 1986) 267

People v Thomas Shelton Powers MD Inc, 3 Cal Rptr 2d 34
    (Ct App 1992) 237
Phenylpropanolamine (PPA) Products Liability Litigation, In re,
    214 FRD 614 (WD Wash 2003) 217, 226–7
Powell v Georgia-Pacific Corp, 843 F Supp 491 (WD Ark 1994) 245,
                    251, 271
Powell v Georgia-Pacific Corp, 119 F 3d 703 (8th Cir 1997) 215,
                    237–8, 242–3, 245, 260–3, 266, 268
Pray v Lockheed Aircraft Corp, 644 F Supp 1289
    (DDC 1986) 215–16, 252
Pruitt Cloud Land Trust v Powell Mountain Coal Co Inc,
    1996 US Dist LEXIS 5499 (WD Va 1996) 245

Reich v Dominick's Finer Foods Inc, No 78CH5667
    (Ill Cir Ct Cook Co, 11 Jul 1980) 220
Rodriguez v Berrybrook Farms Inc, 1990 US Dist LEXIS 14646
    (MD 1990) 262

Schwartz v Dallas Cowboys Football Club Ltd, 362 F Supp 2d 574
    (ED Pa 2005) 215, 223, 246, 264, 267, 269–70
Shults v Champion International Corp, 821 F Supp 520
    (ED Tenn 1993) 271

Simer v Rios, 661 F 2d 655 (7th Cir 1981) 217–18, 237, 252,
                                                             255, 257, 261
Six (6) Mexican Workers v Arizona Citrus Growers, 641 F Supp 259
    (D Ariz 1986) 216, 224, 252, 262, 276
Six (6) Mexican Workers v Arizona Citrus Growers, 904 F 2d 1301
    (9th Cir 1990) 217, 221, 224–6, 237, 243, 245, 249,
                                 251–2, 254, 256, 260, 264–5, 269, 271, 274–5
St Louis v McAllister, 218 SW 312 (1920) 110
State of California v Levi Strauss & Co, 41 Cal 3d 460, 715 P 2d 564,
    224 Cal Rptr 605 (1986) 218, 220–3, 244, 247, 249, 260–1
State of Illinois v JW Petersen Coal & Oil Co (ND Ill 1976) 237
State of New York v Keds Corporation, 1994 US Dist LEXIS 3362
    (SDNY 1994) 260–2
State of New York v Reebok International Ltd, 903 F Supp 532
    (SDNY 1995), aff'd, 96 F 3d 44 (2d Cir 1996) 242, 261
State of New York v Salton Inc, 265 F Supp 2d 310
    (SDNY 2003) 260–1
Superior Beverage Co v Owens-Illinois Inc, 827 F Supp 477
    (ND Ill 1993) 237, 241, 271, 273

Thatcher v Lewis, 76 SW (2d) 677 (1934) 110
Three Mile Island Litigation, In re, 557 F Supp 96
    (MD Pa 1982) 223, 244
Toys 'R' Us Antitrust Litigation, In re, 191 FRD 347 (EDNY 2000) ... 242

United States v Exxon Corp, 561 F Supp 816 (DDC 1983) 249

Valquez v Avco Financial Services, No NCC 11933,
    B (LA Superior Court 1984) 275
Van Gemert v Boeing Co, 553 F 2d 812 (2d Cir 1977) 238, 242, 246
Van Gemert v Boeing Co, 573 F 2d 733 (2d Cir 1978) 215, 255
Van Gemert v Boeing Co, 739 F 2d 730 (2d Cir 1984) 248, 250
Vitamin Cases, In re, 107 Cal App 4th 820 (Ct App 2003) 237

Weber v Goodman, 1998 US Dist LEXIS 22832
    (EDNY 1998) 216–18, 242, 258–9
Wells Fargo Securities Litigation, In re, 991 F Supp 1193
    (ND Cal 1998) 216, 237, 245, 270–1
West Virginia (State of) v Chas Pfizer & Co, 314 F Supp 710
    (SDNY 1970) 223, 236–7, 241, 243, 249
Wilson v Southwest Airlines Inc, 880 F 2d 807 (5th Cir 1989) ... 238, 251
Windham v American Brands Inc, 565 F 2d 59 (4th Cir 1977) ... 225, 238

Yeager's Fuel Inc v Pennsylvania Power & Light Co, 162 FRD 482
    (ED Pa 1995) 225

Table of Legislation

ANGUILLA

Trusts Ordinance 1994
 s 15(1) 198
 s 49 198

AUSTRALIA

Federal

Federal Court of Australia Act 1976
 Pt IVA 230, 232
 s 33Z(1)(f) 230
 s 33ZA(1) 230
 s 33ZA(5) 230

Federal Court of Australia Amendment Act 1991, s 3 230

Income Tax Assessment Act 1936, s 78(1)(a) 144

New South Wales

Charitable Trusts Act 1993
 ss 9–11 91
 s 9(1) 124
 s 10(1) 121
 s 10(2) 121
 s 23 55

Dormant Funds Act 1942
 s 2... 209
 s 2(1) 166
 s 5A 209
 s 11 209
 s 11(2) 209
 ss 12, 13 209
 s 18 209

Unclaimed Money Act 1995
s 6 247
s 10 247

Northern Territory

Associations Incorporation Act 1990, s 22 16

Queensland

Charitable Funds Act 1958
s 2 208
s 5 .... 166, 208
s 20(1) 208

Collections Act 1966
s 35A(1) 208
s 35B(1) 207–8
s 35B(2) 208
s 35B(10) 208
s 35C(4) 208
ss 35B–35D 166

Trusts Act 1973
s 104 55
s 105 .... 91, 93
s 105(1)(a)(i) 100
s 105(1)(a)(ii) 101
s 105(1)(b) 103
s 105(1)(c) 103
s 105(1)(d) 104
s 105(1)(e)(i) 106
s 105(1)(e)(ii) 107
s 105(1)(e)(iii) 109

South Australia

Collections for Charitable Purposes Act 1939
s 16 167

Trustee Act 1936
s 69A 55

s 69B 52, 91, 94
s 69B(1)(a)(i) 100
s 69B(1)(a)(ii) 101
s 69B(1)(b) 103
s 69B(1)(c) 103
s 69B(1)(d) 122
s 69B(1)(e)(i) 106
s 69B(1)(e)(ii) 107
s 69B(1)(e)(iii) 109, 110
s 69B(3) 119, 140
s 69B(6) 100

Tasmania

Variation of Trusts Act 1994

s 4 55
s 5 91
s 5(2) 123
s 5(3)(a)(i) 100
s 5(3)(a)(ii) 101
s 5(3)(b) 103
s 5(3)(c) 103
s 5(3)(d) 122
s 5(3)(e)(i) 106
s 5(3)(e)(ii) 107
s 5(3)(e)(iii) 109
s 11 .... 163, 167

Victoria

Charities Act 1978

s 2 91
s 2(1)(a)(i) 100
s 2(1)(a)(ii) 101
s 2(1)(b) 103
s 2(1)(c) 103
s 2(1)(d) 104
s 2(1)(e)(i) 106
s 2(1)(e)(ii) 107
s 2(1)(e)(iii) 109
s 3 .... 163, 167

Property Law Act 1958
  s 131 55
  s 131(2) 54

Ripon Peace Memorial Trust Act 1961 144

Western Australia

Charitable Collections Act 1946
  s 16 167
  s 16(1) 209–10

Charitable Trusts Act 1962
  s 7 91
  s 7(1) 119, 123, 136
  s 7(3) 119

Trustee Act 1962, s 102 55

BAHAMAS

Purpose Trusts Act 2004
  s 3 195
  ss 8(2), (3) 196

BARBADOS

International Trusts Act 1995, c 245
  s 10 197
  s 14(1) 197
  s 14(2) 197

BELIZE

Trusts Act (revised edn 2000), c 202
  s 15 199
  s 45(1) 199

BERMUDA

Trusts (Special Provisions) Act 1989
  ss 12A–12D 198
  s 12B(2) 198

Trusts (Special Provisions) Amendment Act 1998 198

BRITISH VIRGIN ISLANDS

Trustee (Amendment) Act 2003, ss 11, 12 197

Trustee Ordinance 1961, c 303
  s 84 197
  s 84(15) 197
  s 84(16)(a) 198
  s 84(17) 198

BRUNEI

International Trusts Order 2000, Constitution of Brunei Darrusalam
  s 75 196
  s 77(3) 196
  s 84 196

CANADA
Alberta

Class Proceedings Act 2003, SA 2003, c C–16.5
  s 34 233
  s 34(1) 265
  s 34(5) 245

British Columbia

Class Proceedings Act 1996, RSBC 1996, c 50
  s 34 233
  s 34(1) 234, 265
  s 34(5)(b) 248
  s 34(5)(c) 250

Law and Equity Act, RSBC 1979, c 224 200

Manitoba

Class Proceedings Act 2002, CCSM c C 130
  s 34 233
  s 34(5)(b) 248
  s 34(5)(c) 250

Escheats Act, CCSM, c E140, s 1 247

Newfoundland and Labrador

Class Actions Act 2001, SNL 2001, c C–18.1
  s 34 233
  s 34(5)(b) 248
  s 34(5)(c) 250

Nova Scotia

Trustee Act, RSNS 1989, c 479, s 52(3) 207

Ontario

Class Proceedings Act, SO 1992, c 6
  s 24 233
  s 25 233
  s 26(1) 233–5
  s 26(4) 233, 235, 258, 265, 268
  s 26(5) 233
  s 26(6) 233, 269
  s 26(10) 248, 250

Escheats Act, RSO 1980, c 142 247

Escheats Act, RSO 1990, c E20 247

Perpetuities Act, RSO 1990, c P9, s 16 201

Quebec

Civil Code of Quebec, CCQ
  arts 1268, 1270 195

Code of Civil Procedure, RSQ c C–25
  arts 1034, 1036 233

Saskatchewan

Class Actions Act 2001, SS 2001, c C–12.01
  s 37 233
  s 37(5)(b) 248
  s 37(5)(c) 250

CAYMAN ISLANDS

Special Trusts (Alternative Regime) Law 1997
  s 6(3) 195
  s 11 195

Cayman Islands Trust Law 2001
  s 104(1) 195
  s 391 195

COOK ISLANDS

International Trusts Act 1984, s 12(2) 199

CYPRUS

International Trusts Law 1992, ss 2, 7(3) 199

ENGLAND AND WALES

Chancery Amendment Act 1858, c 27, s 2 286

Charitable Trusts Act 1853, c 137 91

Charitable Trusts Act 1914, c 56 10

Charitable Trusts (Validation) Act 1954, c 58 203

Charitable Uses Act 1601 (Eng), 43 Eliz 1, c 4 174

Charities Act 1960, c 58
  s 13 .... 10–11, 91, 97
  s 14 163

Charities Act 1992, c 41
  s 15 163

Charities Act 1993, c 10
  s 3(4) 108
  s 4(1) 108
  s 13 ...... 11, 35, 91–3, 96–100, 102, 107, 113, 130, 134, 140–1, 196
  s 13(1) 99, 129
  s 13(1)(a)(i) 100
  s 13(1)(a)(ii) 100–2, 112
  s 13(1)(b) 103
  s 13(1)(c) 35, 103–4, 112
  s 13(1)(d) 104, 107, 112
  s 13(1)(e)(i) 106
  s 13(1)(e)(ii) 107, 140
  s 13(1)(e)(iii) 100, 109, 112
  s 13(2) 99–100
  s 13(3) 142
  s 13(4) 106
  s 13(5) 48, 139
  s 14 .... 148–9, 159, 163–7
  s 14(1)–(7)) 163
  s 14(3) 164
  s 14(7) 149, 165
  s 15 91
  s 16(1) 33, 92
  s 16(1)(a) 27–8, 104
  s 16(3) 92
  s 16(10) 28, 92
  s 17 91
  s 18 140
  s 18(1) 92
  s 28 140
  s 29 97
  s 64(2) 47
  s 74 113
  ss 74(2), (3) 104
  s 74(4) 33
  s 74(5) 104
  s 75 113

Charities Act 1993, c 10 – *continued*
   Sch 3 106

Charities (*Cy-près* Advertisements, Inquiries and Disclaimer)
   Regulations 1993 163

City of London Parochial Charities Act 1883, 46 and
   47 Vict, c 36 .... 10, 91

Civil Procedure Rules 1998, Pt 19.III 229

Courts of Justice Building Act 1865, c 48 144

Endowed Schools Act 1869, c 56 .... 10, 91

Friendly Societies Act 1793 (33 Geo 3, c 54), s 14 154

Human Rights Act 1998, c 42, s 6(1) 96

Law of Property Act 1925, c 20, s 161(1) 13

Local Government Act 1933, c 51, s 268(3) 61

Misrepresentation Act 1967, c 7, s 2(1) 301

National Health Service Act 1946, c 81 .... 34, 150

Pension Schemes Act 1993, c 48, s 163 174

Reverter of Sites Act 1987, c 15 17

Trustee Act 1925, c 19, s 63 .... 160, 203

GRENADA

International Trusts Act 1996, s 18 197

IRELAND

Charities Act 1961
   s 47 .... 91, 132
   s 47(1)(a)(i) 100

Charities Act 1961 – *continued*
s 47(1)(a)(ii) 101
s 47(1)(b) 103
s 47(1)(c) 103
s 47(1)(d) 104
s 47(1)(e)(i) 106
s 47(1)(e)(ii) 107
s 47(1)(e)(iii) 109
s 48 163–4

ISLE OF MAN

Purpose Trusts Act 1996 199

JERSEY

Trusts (Jersey) Law 1984, art 38(2) 196

Trusts (Jersey) Law 1984 (revised edn 2004), art 42(2) 197

Trusts Amendment (No 3) (Jersey) Law 1996, art 7 196

LABUAN (MALAYSIA)

Offshore Trusts Act 1996, Act 554
s 4(3) 199
s 18(2) 199

LIECHTENSTEIN

Law of Trust Enterprises 1928 195

MAURITIUS

Trusts Act 2001
s 19 199
s 59 199

MONTSERRAT

Trust Act 1998, s 25 197

NAURU

Foreign Trusts, Estate and Wills Act 1972, ss 6, 6(2) 199

NIUE

Trusts Act 1994, s 16 199

NEVIS

International Exempt Trust Ordinance 1994
  s 8 199
  s 11 199

NEW ZEALAND

Charitable Trusts Act 1957
  Pt III 94, 136
  Pt IV 167
  s 32 . . . . 55, 91, 121
  s 32(1) 94, 119–20, 123, 136
  s 32(3) 119–20
  s 34) 141
  s 61B 55

Perpetuity Act 1964, s 10 14

Religious, Charitable and Educational Trusts Act 1908
  s 15 137

NORTHERN IRELAND

Charities Act 1964
  s 22 91
  s 22(6) 140
  s 23 163

ST KITTS

Trusts Act 1996
  s 13 196
  s 58(2) 197

ST LUCIA

International Trust Act 2002
  s 21 198
  s 22 198

ST VINCENT AND THE GRENADINES

International Trusts Act 1996
  s 12 197
  s 15 197

SCOTLAND

Charities and Trustee Investment (Scotland) Act 2005 91

Education (Scotland) Act 1946, 9 and 10 Geo 6, c 72, s 116(2) 112

Law Reform (Miscellaneous Provisions) (Scotland) Act 1990
  s 9 .... 91, 111
  s 9(1)(a)(i) 100
  s 9(1)(a)(ii) 101
  s 9(1)(b) 103
  s 9(1)(c)(i), (ii) 104
  s 9(1)(d)(i) 106
  s 9(1)(d)(ii) 107
  s 9(1)(d)(iii) 109

SEYCHELLES

International Trusts Act 1994
  s 13 196
  s 14(1) 196
  s 64 196
  s 65 196

SINGAPORE

Charities Act 1984, s 22 163

UNITED STATES

Federal

Class Action Fairness Act of 2005, 28 USC § 1712(a) 239

Federal Rules of Civil Procedure
  r 23 .... 225, 236, 240–1, 248, 252, 268–9
  r 23(b)(3) 225

Private Securities Litigation Reform Act of 1995, s 78u-4(a)(6) 239

Rules Enabling Act 225, 241
  28 USC § 2072(b) (1982) 241

Securities Exchange Act 1934, r 10(b) 269

28 USC §§ 2041, 2042 248

California

Code of Civil Procedure, s 384(b) 237

Probate Code, ss 15203, 15204 195

INTERNATIONAL CONVENTIONS

European Convention on Human Rights 1950, arts 9, 14 96–7

List of Abbreviations

[147]	paragraph 147
11	page 11
§ or s 67	section 67
A-G	Attorney-General
ALI	American Law Institute
ALRC	Australian Law Reform Commission
Am	American
Ann	Annual
Ass	Assurance
Assn	Association
Aust or Aus	Australian
BC	British Columbia
BC	Borough Council
c	chapter
CC	City Council
Ch Comm	Charity Commission *or* Charity Commissioners
Comm	Commission *or* Commissioner
Corp	Corporation
CP	Consultation Paper
CUP	Cambridge University Press
decd	deceased
DP	Discussion Paper
ex p	*ex parte*
fn	footnote
Govt	Government
Ins	Insurance
Intl	International
L	Law
Litig	Litigation
LJ	Law Journal
LRC	Law Reform Commission
L Rev	Law Review
NSW	New South Wales
NZ	New Zealand
OLRC	Ontario Law Reform Commission

OUP	Oxford University Press
PD	Practice direction
pp	pinpoint or pages
Prod/s	Product/products
Q	Quarterly
Qld	Queensland
Rep	Report
Rev	Review
Soc	Society
ST	Settlement Trust or Settlement Trusts
Uni	University
ULP	University of London Press
US	United States
Vic	Victoria
WT	Will Trust or Will Trusts
Ybk	Yearbook

LEGISLATION

CPA (Ont)	Class Proceedings Act 1992, SO 1992, c 6
CPA (BC)	Class Proceedings Act, RSBC 1996, c 50
FCA (Aus)	Federal Court of Australia Act 1976 (Aus)
FRCP	Federal Rules of Civil Procedure (US)

LAW REPORTS

AC	Appeal Cases (1891–)
All ER	All England Law Reports
App Cas	Appeal Cases (1875–90)
Ch	Chancery Division (1891–)
Ch D	Chancery Division (1875–90)
CLR	Commonwealth Law Reports
DLR	Dominion Law Reports
FLR	Federal Law Reports (Aus)
ILRM	Irish Law Reports Monthly
IR	Irish Reports
Lloyd's Rep	Lloyd's List Law Reports
LMELR	Land Management and Environment Law Reports
NSWLR	New South Wales Law Reports
NZLR	New Zealand Law Reports
QB	Queen's Bench (1891–)
QBD	Queen's Bench Division (1876–90)

Qd R	Queensland Reports
SALR	South Australian Law Reports
SASR	South Australian State Reports
SC	Session Cases (Scotland)
SLT	Scottish Law Times
Sol Jo	Solicitor's Journal
TLR	Times Law Reports
VLR	Victorian Law Reports
VR	Victorian Reports
WAR	Western Australian Reports
WLR	Weekly Law Reports (UK)

COURTS

CA	Court of Appeal (of the jurisdiction referred to by the reporter series)
Ch	Chancery Division
Div Ct	Superior Court of Justice (Divisional Court of Ontario)
FCA	Federal Court of Australia
Fam CA	Family Court of Australia
Full FCA	Full Bench of the Federal Court of Australia
Gen Div	Ontario Court of Justice (General Division)
HCA	High Court of Australia
HL	House of Lords
PC	Privy Council
QB	Queen's Bench Division
SC	Supreme Court (of the relevant jurisdiction)
SCC	Supreme Court of Canada
SCJ	Superior Court of Justice (Ontario)
SDNY	United States District Court Southern District New York (sample jurisdiction only)
2d Cir	United States Court of Appeals Second Circuit

JOURNALS

ALJ	Australian Law Journal
All ER Ann Rev	All England Law Reports Annual Review
ASCL	Annual Survey of Commonwealth Law
CJQ	Civil Justice Quarterly
CLJ	Cambridge Law Journal
Can BR	Canadian Bar Review

Conv	Conveyancer and Property Lawyer
JBL	Journal of Business Law
LQR	Law Quarterly Review
LS Gaz	Law Society Gazette
LSJ	Law Society Journal
NILQ	Northern Ireland Legal Quarterly
NLJ	New Law Journal
NZLJ	New Zealand Law Journal
PCB	Private Client Business

Notes on Mode of Citation

1. When available in a primary or secondary source, paragraph numbers will be used as pinpoints in preference to page numbers.

2. In each jurisdiction, the court is referred to in parentheses in all instances where it is not obvious from the report series or mode of citation which court made the decision.

3. The expression 'English law' should be understood to include the law of Wales, and not to include the laws of Scotland or Ireland (unless indicated otherwise).

4. Throughout this book, the masculine personal pronoun is used, for the sake of convenience, and as and where appropriate, should be taken to denote the feminine pronoun. Moreover, in accordance with the style advocated by BA Garner, *A Dictionary of Modern Legal Usage* (OUP, New York, 1987) 502, the term 'testator' will be treated throughout as denoting both the masculine and feminine gender.

5. For the sake of consistency and uniformity, the expressions, '*cy-près*' and '*Cy-près*', will be used wherever occurring throughout the book.

6. The scholarship and opinion of many entities and persons are referenced throughout this book, and have been cited, referenced and pinpointed in accordance with British citation conventions. All reasonable efforts have been made to pinpoint as accurately and fulsomely as possible. It should be noted that wherever quotations appear, and in the interests of brevity, footnotes within those quotations have not been reproduced, and the conventional usage of 'footnotes omitted' should be assumed throughout.

1

Introduction

1. The *Cy-près* Doctrine: Traditional Definition

TRADITIONALLY, AND STATED in its simplest of terms, the *cy-près* doctrine is the vehicle by which the intentions of a donor (settlor or testator) may be given effect 'as nearly as possible' in circumstances where literal compliance with the donor's stated intentions cannot be effectuated. Accordingly, in the law of charitable trusts, the *cy-près* doctrine states that where a donor has directed a gift of money or property to a charitable object (purpose), but has expressed a general charitable intention that is impossible or impractical to effect, the courts will allow the intention to be carried out in an approximate fashion.

In this, its most traditionalist context, the doctrine has received widespread judicial recognition and adoption. Indeed, from the materials explored in developing this book, it could be said that the doctrine has virtual universal acceptance, at least in common law jurisdictions. This generalisation is evidenced by the referenced materials from a number of widespread and culturally-diverse jurisdictions. By way of introduction and illustration, examples are taken of the following: England,[1] the United States,[2] Australia,[3] Canada,[4] New Zealand,[5] Ireland,[6] Scotland,[7] South Africa,[8] India,[9]

---

[1] Eg: *Oldham BC v A-G* [1993] Ch D 210 (CA) 221.

[2] Eg: *Evans v Abney*, 396 US 435, 437 (1970).

[3] Eg: *Royal North Shore Hospital of Sydney v A-G (NSW)* (1938) 60 CLR 396 (HCA) 415 (Latham CJ) 428 (Dixon J).

[4] Eg: *Nova Scotia (A-G) v Axford* (1885), 13 SCR 294.

[5] Eg: *Re Lushington (decd), Manukau County v Wynyard* [1964] NZLR 161 (CA) 172 (North J), 181 (McCarthy J).

[6] Eg: *The Representative Church Body v A-G* [1988] IR 19, 22.

[7] Eg: *Guild v Russell* 1987 SCLR 221 (Court of Session, Outer House) 222.

[8] Eg: *Ex p Wit Deep and Knights Central Joint Medical Society* 1918 WLD 13.

[9] Eg: *Merchant v Shaifuddin* [2000] 1 LRI 1028 (SC App), and no longer *only* applicable to testamentary gifts, since: *State of Uttar Pradesh v Bansi Dhar* [1974] AIR 1084 (SC). Cf the position when LA Sheridan and VTH Delany, *The Cy-près Doctrine* (Sweet & Maxwell, London, 1959) 24, and fn 44, was written.

Singapore,[10] Malaysia,[11] Hong Kong,[12] Northern Ireland,[13] and elsewhere.[14] One of the most succinct, yet fulsome, definitions of the traditional *cy-près* doctrine is provided by the *American Restatement of the Law (Second), Trusts*:

> If property is given in trust to be applied to a charitable purpose, and it is or becomes impossible or impracticable or illegal to carry out the particular purpose, and if the settlor manifested a more general charitable intention to devote the property to charitable purposes, the trust will not fail but the court will direct the application of the property to some charitable purpose which falls within the general charitable intention of the settlor.[15]

Such is the clarity of enunciation in this definition that it has been cited with approval by courts from New Zealand[16] to Canada,[17] and by leading academic charity texts.[18] (The definition has since been redrafted by the American Law Institute,[19] although not, in this author's opinion, for the better.[20]) Notably, current law dictionaries from several jurisdictions also define the doctrine singularly by reference to its charitable trusts genesis.[21]

2. Redefining the *Cy-près* Doctrine

Whilst historically (and 'historical' may be traced to 'Roman law') the doctrine has its roots, by and large, in the context of the law of charitable trusts, notably

---

[10] Eg: *Hwa Soo Chin v Personal Representatives of the Estate of Lim Soo Ban (decd)* 1994 2 SLR 657 (HC).

[11] Eg: *Tai Kien Luing v Tye Poh Sun* [1961] 1 MLJ 78 (OCJ Penang).

[12] Eg: *A G (Hong Kong) v Pon Yup Chong How Benevolent Assn* [1992] 24 HKCU 1 (SC).

[13] Eg: *In re Millar (decd); Millar v Ben Hardwick Memorial Fund* (NI Ch, 5 Sep 1997).

[14] Eg, in Jersey Islands: *Re the Greville Bathe Fund* [1973] IJJ 2513. Further, all jurisdictions which have implemented non-charitable purpose trust statutory regimes (considered in Chapter 6) have either expressly or impliedly acknowledged within those regimes that the charitable trusts *cy-près* doctrine comprises part of their body of law.

[15] American Law Institute, *Restatement of the Law (Second), Trusts* (ALI Publishers, St Paul Minn, 1959) Vol II, § 399, p 297.

[16] *Re Collier (decd)* [1998] 1 NZLR 81, 93.

[17] *Re Christian Brothers of Ireland in Canada* (2000), 47 OR (3d) 674 (CA) [71].

[18] H Picarda, *The Law and Practice Relating to Charities* (3rd edn, Butterworths, London, 1999) 295; LA Sheridan and VTH Delany, *The Cy-près Doctrine* (Sweet & Maxwell, London, 1959) 4. Also preferred as the definition of choice by: EL Fisch, *The Cy-près Doctrine in the United States* (Matthew Bender & Co, Albany NY, 1950) 2, citing the version in the *First Restatement* (1935) which was in similar terms.

[19] See: ALI, *Restatement of the Law (Third), Trusts (Tentative Draft No 3)* (ALI Publishers, St Paul Minn, 5 Mar 2001) § 67, p 189–90.

[20] The revised definition permits *cy-près* where 'it is or becomes wasteful to apply all of the property to the designated purpose'—too wide a trigger power, in this author's opinion. The triggers for the *cy-près* jurisdiction, in the Commonwealth context, are explored in ch 4, sections C and D.

[21] In Australia, eg: PE Nygh and P Butt (eds), *Australian Legal Dictionary* (Butterworths, Sydney, 1997) 316. In England, eg: JB Saunders (ed), *Words and Phrases Legally Defined* (Butterworths, London, 1988) vol 1, 394; D Greenberg and A Millbrook (eds), *Stroud's Judicial Dictionary of Words and Phrases* (6th edn, Sweet & Maxwell, London, 2000) 594. In the United States, eg; *Words and Phrases* (Permanent edn, West Publishing Co, St Paul Minn, 1968) vol 10A, 558–78; BA Garner (ed), *Black's Law Dictionary* (8th edn, West Group, St Paul Minn, 2004) 415.

in the last three decades, the '*cy-près* doctrine' has marched (both judicially and legislatively) into other legal territory where 'as near as possible' is considered appropriate for a wide range of circumstances. For example, the doctrine has been applied where court-awarded damages cannot be distributed to the particular victims who succeeded in litigation against the defendant. This has particularly (although not exclusively) occurred in the multi-party context in which the victims are not identifiable nor readily able to participate in the damages award. It has also been applied where fines have been awarded against corporate defendants in the quasi-criminal context of consumer protection, and where orders for specific performance cannot be carried out. The doctrine has lately traversed into even more uncharted territory; for example, it has been statutorily embraced in the context of non-charitable purpose trusts, vehicles that are commonly used to minimise tax liability.

Thus, with quiet benevolence, the 'as near as possible' decree has gained a legal foothold in circumstances pertaining to the transfer of property or money that extend far beyond its origins in charitable law. In this light, an overarching definition of the *cy-près* doctrine which both embraces its modern manifestations and encompasses its traditional application in charitable trusts law, could be framed as follows:

Where:

- property is (or is to be) given by A to B for a designated purpose, under a legally enforceable obligation (the 'original transfer'); AND
- it is or becomes impossible, impracticable, illegal or infeasible for the designated purpose to be effected; AND
- in accordance with relevant objective factors, it is legally appropriate that the original transfer be carried out by approximation; THEN
- by court or other superior order, the original transfer can legally be altered in a material respect—namely, the designated purpose for which the property is given, or the nature of the property transferred for the designated purpose, or the recipients of the property, are altered—to approximate 'as near as possible' the original transfer.

This definition ties together the many applications of the 'as near as possible' legal mantra that will be discussed in following chapters. It approximates the sentiment used by the American Law Institute whereby the term can be used to refer to 'reformations or judicial modifications . . . in which some modified effect is given to dispositions that would otherwise exceed what the law allows'.[22] Notably, the definition is wider than the traditional charitable trusts definitions

---

[22] ALI, *Restatement of the Law (Third), Trusts (Tentative Draft No 3)* (ALI Publishers, St Paul Minn, 5 Mar 2001) 191.

cited at the commencement of this chapter, yet it is narrower than the extremely wide 'doctrine of approximation' which some courts in the United States have coined as synonymous with the *cy-près* doctrine.[23] It is also narrower than a mere substitution of one mode of achieving a general intent by another mode of achieving that same intent, a further definition to be found in American legal sources[24] and in early English case law.[25] Specifically, the boxed definition adopted above pertains to *property transfers*, where some alternative purpose or recipients, or even the property itself, is amended 'as near as possible' to the originally contemplated transfer.

This definition does not, nor is it intended to, encompass scenarios where some courts (although English courts have indicated otherwise[26]) have made reference to '*cy-près*' in circumstances where statutes are 'dynamically' interpreted 'as near as possible' to their original wording (taking into account changed societal, economic, political or technological circumstances);[27] or where legal rules are applied, not directly, but as nearly as the nature of the circumstances permit;[28] or where covenants in leases have arguably become obsolescent and warrant redrafting.[29] In these instances, clearly '*cy-près*' is being used synonymously with 'as near as possible', but in a context com-

---

[23] Eg: *In re succession of Milne*, 89 So 2d 281, 287 ('The "*cy-près* doctrine" as applied in the United States is the "doctrine of approximation" '), and also cited in: *Words and Phrases* (Permanent edn, West Publishing Co, St Paul Minn, 1968) vol 10A, 570.

[24] Eg: S Rapalje and RL Lawrence, *A Dictionary of American and English Law* (Lawbook Exchange Ltd, Union NJ, 1997) 334 ('Where a person has expressed a general intention and also a particular mode in which he wishes it carried out, but the intention cannot be carried out in that particular mode, the court before whom the matter comes will in certain cases direct the intention to be carried out *cy-près*, ie, as nearly as possible in the mode desired').

[25] Eg: *Monypenny v Dering* [1843–60] All ER Rep 1098 (CA) ('The doctrine of *cy-près*, as I understand it, is nothing more than the giving effect to a general at the expense of a particular intent. It is this. Where there is a valid particular intent and a valid general intent and the former, in the opinion of the court, not effectuating all the intention of the testator, the court looks to his general intent and will effect that general intent at the sacrifice of the particular intent').

[26] See, eg: *Potts v Hickman* [1940] 4 All ER 491 (HL) 507 (in relation to the interpretation of s 1 of the Landlord and Tenant Act 1709, '[t]here is obviously no room for an equitable or *cy-près* construction'). Also: *West Cheshire Water Board v Crowe* [1940] 2 All ER 351 (KB) 352 ('[t]his being a statutory body, its powers are, therefore, determined by the express words of the statute creating it. That statute did not give it the power which it now claims. . . . There is . . . no *cy-près* doctrine dealing with cases of this sort, and it has to be kept strictly within its powers'); *Simpson (HM Inspector of Taxes) v Grange Trust Ltd* [1935] AC 422 ('[i]t is a recognised rule in the construction of the Income Tax Acts that taxation cannot be imposed by analogy or by implication or by any sort of *cy-près* doctrine': Lord Wright).

[27] As discussed, eg, in: JC Coffee, 'The Mandatory/Enabling Balance in Corporate Law: An Essay on the Judicial Role' (1989) 89 *Columbia L Rev* 1618, 1686–87 ('a court is entitled to re-interpret and update a statute's intent in light of new and changed circumstances', citing argument); WN Eskridge, *Dynamic Statutory Interpretation* (Harvard Uni Press, Camb Mass, 1994), especially ch 2 (the *cy-près* perspective reviewed in and commented upon in: P Mitchell, 'Just Do It! Eskridge's Critical Pragmatic Theory of Statutory Interpretation (Book Review)' (1996) 41 *McGill LJ* 713, 728).

[28] Eg: *In re Hawkins (decd); Hawkins v Hawkins* [1972] 1 Ch 714, 723 ('I cannot apply the rule directly, and can do no more than apply it *cy-près*, as nearly as the nature of the administration of estates permits').

[29] Argued unsuccessfully in: *City of Westminster v Duke of Westminster* [1991] 4 All ER 136 (Ch).

pletely unrelated to property transfers. The use of the term in these respects is coincidental, bearing no relationship to the *cy-près* doctrine as redefined above, and will not comprise any further discussion in this book.

In that regard, the purpose of this book is threefold: first, to identify, in common law jurisdictions, the modern scenarios in which the *cy-près* doctrine has been applied or contended for, whether judicially, legislatively or by law reform; secondly, to critique the marked differentiation that exists between common law countries' reception to *cy-près* in its various guises, and to explore the ways in which encroachment of the doctrine has generated different controversies and conundrums; and thirdly, to highlight that, whilst the doctrine is traditionally discussed in the context of trusts, succession and charity law, it occupies greater omnipresence in modern legal jurisprudence. This three-fold purpose provides the grounds for vigorous and lively debate about the requirements of legal accuracy, and whether 'as near as possible' might not mutate to 'next best' as the utility and wider opportunities from the doctrine become more refined in the future. It is intended that this book will inform that debate by identifying the theoretical and pragmatic underpinnings and policy of the *cy-près* doctrine in its modern applications.

B ORIGINS OF THE *CY-PRÈS* DOCTRINE

The derivation of the expression '*cy-près*',[30] the doctrine's historical development, and even the term's pronunciation,[31] are matters upon which there is some disagreement. Although this book concentrates upon the modern applications of the doctrine, both charitable and otherwise, a few words about its very beginnings may be instructive for an understanding of the doctrine's continuing evolution.

Although most strongly associated with charitable trusts, it was not always so, as Justice Young described:

> The earliest extant recorded use of the term [in English literature] was by *Littleton on Tenures* (1481) with reference to conditions precedent concerning legal estates. Then, in Fitzherbert's *La Grande Abridgment* (1516) tit *Subpoena* there is reference to a decision where a settlor settled property on his daughters, but later had a son, where the court held that the son was the beneficiary on the basis that had the settlor known he was to sire a son, he would not have disinherited him, and the chancellor should carry out the settlor's intentions.[32]

---

[30] Seemingly, an Anglo-French term, derived from the expressions, 'aussi-près que possible' ('as near as possible') or 'ici-près' ('near here'), as noted in *A-G v Ironmongers' Co* (1844) 10 Cl & F 908, 922, 8 ER 983, although note the opinion of LA Sheridan and VTH Delany that the precise derivation of the term is doubtful: *The Cy-près Doctrine* (Sweet & Maxwell, London, 1959) 5.

[31] Pronunciation varies across jurisdictions, typically 'see pray' in England and the Commonwealth jurisdictions, but 'sigh pray' in the United States.

[32] *Stevedoring Employees Retirement Fund Pty Ltd v Assn of Employers of Waterside Labour* (NSWSC, 1 Mar 1995) 5.

Within the context of charitable trusts, the doctrine had religious origins, and was exercised by the ecclesiastical courts, as Sheridan and Delany describe:

> there is little doubt that [the *cy-près* doctrine] came into the common law by way of the Court of Chancery, which in turn borrowed it from the ecclesiastical courts. The defective jurisdiction of the latter tribunals in the case of creditors led to an early intervention by the Chancellor in this field, armed with his power to direct account. Later, there came a parallel intervention on behalf of legatees, as more and more of the jurisdiction passed to the Chancellor, he adopted from the ecclesiastics the civil law rules by which, in their courts, the construction of legacies had been governed.[33]

As the above passage highlights, two key features were associated with the *cy-près* doctrine in its embryonic stages of development.

First, it is commonly observed that it was a device of Roman, not Christian, law. Several Roman law and charity scholars endorse this view. Jolowicz notes that, where ecclesiastical corporations were dissolved, the church was under a duty to apply its property 'to objects analogous to those for which the corporation had existed ... closely connected with the preferential treatment given charitable legacies which is also at the root of the English *cy-près* doctrine'.[34] Grigsby explains that under Roman law, any donations that were given for illegal public purposes were applied *cy-près* 'at least one hundred years before Christianity became the religion of the empire'.[35] Fisch suggests that the English chancellors simply carried over their training in Roman law to resurrect the doctrine.[36] Ford and Hardingham point to the writings of Modestinus, an official in the administration of Rome about AD 240, who explained how, when a public show for which the testator had left an annual income in the testator's memory was illegal to conduct, 'after calling together the heirs and the leading men of the state, there must be consideration as to the purpose for which the trust ought instead to be employed, to the end that the testator's memory might be honoured in some other fashion which is lawful.'[37] Likewise, Buckland observes that Roman law applied 'something like the *cy-près* doctrine' in permit-

---

[33] LA Sheridan and VTH Delany, *The Cy-près Doctrine* (Sweet & Maxwell, London, 1959) 7, referencing: G Spence, *Equitable Jurisdiction of the Court of Chancery* (London, 1846) Vol I, 578–80.

[34] HF Jolowicz, *Roman Foundations of Modern Law* (Clarendon Press, Oxford, 1957) 138.

[35] WE Grigsby, *Commentaries on Equity Jurisprudence* (first English edn, Stevens and Haynes, London, 1884)§ 1169, citing, at fn 2: 'per Ld Ch Justice Wilmot, Wilmot's Notes, pp 53–54, citing Dig Lib 33, tit 2, ss 16, 17, De Usu et Usufruct Legatorum'.

[36] EL Fisch, *The Cy-près Doctrine in the United States* (Matthew Bender & Co, Albany NY, 1950) 4.

[37] HAJ Ford and IJ Hardingham, *Trusts Commentary and Materials* (6th edn, Law Book Co, Sydney, 1990) 711, citing: H Modestinus, *Responsa* (9th book) (trans). Also: HA Picarda, *The Law and Practice Relating to Charities* (3rd edn, Butterworths, London, 1999) 297, citing his own earlier work on the topic: 'Charity in Roman Law: Roots and Parallels' (1992/93) *Charity Law and Practice Rev* 9, 13–14. Similar words, purportedly by Modestinus, are noted in: EL Fisch, *The Cy-près Doctrine in the United States* (Matthew Bender & Co, Albany NY, 1950) 3–4, noting their citation by the US Supreme Court in: *Late Corp of the Church of Jesus Christ of the Latter-Day Saints v US*, 136 US 1, 52, 10 S Ct 792 (1889); and in: LA Sheridan and VTH Delany, *The Cy-près Doctrine* (Sweet & Maxwell, London, 1959) 7 and fn 33.

ting money left to a town to be applied to other public uses that benefitted the community as a whole, or allowed property given for the purpose of public games upon which the Roman Senate had forbidden the community from spending any money, to be applied for other public purposes.[38] However, Jones, whilst prepared to admit that *cy-près* was known to the Romans, contends that its origins are obscure and conjectural.[39] It is certainly true that very early English judicial pronouncements about the doctrine also speculate about a possible linkage with Roman law.[40]

The second notable early feature of the doctrine was that the ecclesiastical courts apparently embraced the *cy-près* doctrine in the belief that its application would bestow upon a testator heavenly rewards. Whilst the doctrine may have had 'secular justification' as well (maintaining property for the public benefit, generation after generation),[41] the desire to save a testator's soul was crucial, as Wilmot J described:

> Charity was an expiation of sin, to be rewarded in another state; and therefore, if political reasons negatived the particular charity given, this court thought the merits of charity ought not to be lost to the testator, nor to the public, and that they were carrying on his general pious intention . . . The court thought that one kind of charity would embalm his memory as well as another, and being equally meritorious, would entitle him to the same reward. . . . It is plain that they looked at the motive of the gift, the immortalizing the memory of the donor, which was the only future reward a Pagan could enjoy. For this law was made 100 years before Christianity was the religion of the Empire. . . . The reason, which animates the law, applies as forcibly to a legacy given to a charitable use under the Christian dispensation.[42]

Thus, it was considered that charitable dispositions should not, for the sake of the testator's soul, be permitted to fail. As Gray explains,[43] there was, in mediaeval times, a close connection between the last will and the last confession, with the testator's 'first thought' (or, perhaps more accurately, his last thought), not on how his property would be distributed, but upon the future welfare of his immortal soul; that the notional division of a testator's property into three parts—for his wife, for his children, and for himself—favoured gifts to charity, for the third part could be disposed of outside his immediate kin, and was

---

[38] WW Buckland, *Equity in Roman Law* (ULP, London, 1911) 116.

[39] G Jones, *History of the Law of Charity 1532–1827* (CUP, Cambridge, 1969) 73–74.

[40] *White v White* (1778) 1 Bro CC 12; 28 ER 955, cited by Lord Eldon in: *Moggridge v Thackwell* (1802) 7 Ves 36; [1803–1813] All ER Rep 754 (Ch) 758 ('In what the doctrine originated, whether, as supposed [in *White*], in the principles of the civil law as applied to charities, or in the religious notions entertained formerly in this country, I know not'); and also: *A-G v Platt* (1675) Finch 222.

[41] Noted in: HA Picarda, *The Law and Practice Relating to Charities* (3rd edn, Butterworths, London, 1999) 296, citing: *Report of the Committee on the Law and Practice relating to Charitable Trusts* (Cmd 8710) (HMSO, London, 1952) (*Nathan Committee Report*) [71].

[42] *A-G v Lady Downing* (1767) Wilm 1 (C) 13.

[43] H Gray, 'The History and Development in England of the *Cy-près* Principle in Charities' (1953) 33 *Boston Uni L Rev* 30, 32–34. Also described in: LA Sheridan and VTH Delany, *The Cy-près Doctrine* (Sweet & Maxwell, London, 1959) 8–9.

usually applied to charity because of the testator's wish to enter the kingdom of heaven; and for any residue not disposed of and for one third of intestates' estates, these were appropriated to charity. Gray concludes that 'it is not too much to see in these [mediaeval rules of inheritance] the . . . beginnings of a wide and liberal construction of charitable gifts which ultimately developed into the *cy-près* doctrine.'[44]

Not all, however, were convinced of this justification; Winder famously noted that it was not for the courts to consider 'the testator's welfare in the hereafter . . . why should not the Court discourage the Attorney-General's attempt to obtain for him further supernatural rewards?'[45] As Nathan further points out,[46] the motivation was not altogether altruistic either. The 'privilege' of the *cy-près* doctrine which charitable gifts attracted was, in a sense, self-motivated: the Church stood to gain directly through gifts for the advancement of religion, and indirectly in that almost all educational services were within its remit at the time. Thus (argues Nathan), charity was crucial to the scope and depth of services which the Church provided, and it was in the interests of the ecclesiastical courts to single out charitable bequests for special treatment. The *cy-près* doctrine was but one manifestation of that. It is also interesting to note the thesis propounded by Willard,[47] that charitable gifts of the most public-spirited type were sought to be encouraged by any and all means, including by invocation of the *cy-près* doctrine by which one type of charity could be matched by another, given the extent of selfish 'superstitious worship of relics and idle pilgrimages, with their gross excesses and inevitable liability to perversion and abuse', which had prevailed during the middle ages and which the Chancery courts were subsequently keen to discourage.

The first 'modern' case applying the *cy-près* doctrine has been said to have been decided in 1612,[48] with some further examples from 1675 frequently noted.[49] From this author's own examination of the series of early reported Chancery decisions, a couple of interesting 17th century cases conveniently illustrate the application of the doctrine:

> *Attorney-General v Guise*[50]—the testator gave an annual sum for the education of Scotchmen at the University of Oxford so as to enter holy orders and of the Church of England, and then go forth to Scotland 'to propagate the doctrine and discipline of

---

[44] Gray, *ibid*, 33.

[45] WHD Winder, 'Cy-près Application of Surplus Funds' (1941) 5 *Conv* 198, 211.

[46] HL Nathan *et al*, *The Charities Act 1960* (Butterworths, London, 1962) 2–3.

[47] J Willard, 'Illustrations of the Origin of Cy-près' (1894) 8 *Harvard L Rev* 69, 87 (quote), 91–92.

[48] *Fisher v Hill* (1612) Duke 82, cited by H Gray, 'The History and Development in England of the Cy-près Principle in Charities' (1953) 33 *Boston Uni L Rev* 30, 31.

[49] *A-G v Peacock* (1675) Finch 245; *A-G v Platt* (1675) Finch 222. Also cited in Gray, *ibid*, 31, and see further discussion of cases decided during this same century in: G Jones, *History of the Law of Charity 1532–1827* (CUP, Cambridge, 1969) 74–93.

[50] (1692) 2 Vern 266; 23 ER 772 (High Court of Chancery). This case also refers to *Gates v Jones* (1690) 2 Vern 266, in which the testator bequeathed a gift 'to maintain popish priests'; purpose declared to be superstitious and void; property applied *cy-près*.

the Church of England there'; by an Act of Parliament, Presbyterians had settled in Scotland, and the terms of the will could not be carried out; 'yet it ought to be performed *cy-près*; and the substance of it may be pursued; that is to propagate the doctrine and discipline of the Church of England, though not in the form and method intended by the testator'

Attorney-General v Baxter[51]—testator gave a devise to 'poor ejected ministers', many ejected for 'want of titles, and . . . fit objects of charity'; concern that to benefit such ministers would 'encourage and keep up a perpetual schism in the church, which the law would not endure'; the Lord Keeper decreed the devise for the maintenance of another clergyman, the chaplain at Chelsea College (this decree was ultimately reversed by the Lord Commissioners, and the sum was ordered to be paid according to the will)

Although Lord Loughborough declared toward the very end of the 18th century that the doctrine 'ought never to be mentioned again in this court',[52] it was a mere four years later, in 1802, that the seminal decision of *Moggridge v Thackwell*[53] was delivered by Lord Eldon, of which more will be said later. Formal early collections of equity cases from the 17th and 18th centuries,[54] the regularity with which this case is cited in 20th century case law, and historical commentary,[55] all confirm that this is the leading modern authority for the *cy-près* doctrine.

It is evident too that the application of *cy-près* in the 17th century was not without controversy, as Lord Freeman's note, accompanying an anonymous case of 1678, demonstrates: 'The doctrine of *cy-près*, though frequently disapproved, and its extension, farther than adjudged cases have already gone, declared improper, is, within those limits, firmly established.'[56] Echoes of this dilemma about the appropriate width to be afforded to the doctrine have resonated to the present time. As later chapters will demonstrate,[57] both legislatures and judiciaries have struggled to define what the triggers for the *cy-près* jurisdiction ought to be, how to adjudicate whether a general charitable intent has been manifested by the donor, and how 'near' the *cy-près* recipients should be to the original purpose or beneficiary. Not so very much has changed over 350 years!

Thereafter, throughout the 18th and 19th centuries, the *cy-près* doctrine continued to be applied, both at general law and by wide-ranging, situation-specific,

---

[51] (1684) 1 Vern 248; 23 ER 446 (Lord Keeper), and discussed in further detail in: G Jones, *History of the Law of Charity 1532–1827* (CUP, Cambridge, 1969) 81.
[52] *A-G v Andrew* (1798) 3 Ves 633, 650, cited in: LA Sheridan and VTH Delany, *The Cy-près Doctrine* (Sweet & Maxwell, London, 1959) 6.
[53] (1802) 7 Ves 36; [1803–1813] All ER Rep 754 (Ch).
[54] See, eg: AE Randall, *Leading Cases in Equity* (Stevens and Sons, London, 1912) 10–12.
[55] As noted by: H Gray, 'The History and Development in England of the *Cy-près* Principle in Charities' (1953) 33 *Boston Uni L Rev* 30, 31, 41 ('monumental judgment') 42 (*Moggridge* 'reviewed all cases of indefinite gifts from earliest times down to his day . . . for all practical purposes, the law on indefinite gifts was established then once and for all').
[56] See: *Anonymous* (1678) 2 Freeman 40; 22 ER 1045 (Curia Cancellarie) and see note (2) therein (precise authorship unknown, but generally attributed to the Hon Richard Freeman).
[57] See, generally, chh 3–5.

statutes,[58] and moves to reform the doctrine persisted in England, which push culminated eventually with the passage of s 13 of the Charities Act 1960.[59] Insofar as it has been applied to charitable trusts, the *cy-près* doctrine has continued to receive a mixed judicial reception in England over the last four decades. At one end of the spectrum, it has been described as 'peculiar',[60] and at the other end, has been primarily viewed through a prism of benevolence—comprising one extremely significant manifestation of the 'benignant approach',[61] the 'bias', some would say,[62] frequently adopted with respect to any trust evincing a general charitable intention.[63]

C WHAT THIS BOOK COVERS

Extending the three purposes nominated in section A above, this book is principally devoted to a discussion of the modern extended range of the presently possible applications of the *cy-près* doctrine, so as to explore 'its march' away from its traditional auspices, the charitable trusts context.

1. Division of Chapters

The book is divided into two Parts. Part I deals with the doctrine within the context of trusts. The jurisdictional coverage within this Part will concentrate upon English judicial and statutory developments, with extensive references

---

[58] City of London Parochial Charities Act 1883, 46 and 47 Vict, c 36; Endowed Schools Act 1869, c 56; Charitable Trusts Act 1914, c 56.

[59] See the excellent historical discussion of this period in, eg: HL Nathan, *The Charities Act 1960* (Butterworths, London, 1962) 1–7; S Petrow, 'The History of Charity Law' in G Dal Pont, *Charity Law in Australia and New Zealand* (OUP, Oxford, 2000) 47–57.

[60] *Construction Industry Training Board v A-G* [1971] 1WLR 1303 (Ch) 1308 (Pennycuick VC). It has even been questioned whether the term, 'the *cy-près* doctrine', is 'quite accurate' and the 'right expression' to describe the court's scheme-making powers: *Re Tharp; Longrigg v The People's Dispensary for Sick Animals of the Poor Inc* [1942] 2 All ER 358 (Ch) 362, but such doubts have not been borne out over the decades since.

[61] The phrase used by Lord Keith in *Guild v Inland Revenue Commissioners* [1992] 2 AC 310 (HL) 322 to describe the general approach, as manifested in that case by different rules of construction (when the language in a charitable disposition is susceptible of two constructions, choose the one that would make it effectual rather than void).

[62] *Re Fitzpatrick; Fidelity Trust Co v St Joseph's Vocational School of Winnipeg* (1984), 6 DLR (4th) 644 (Man QB) 648.

[63] Early equity texts consistently noted how Chancery courts were disposed to treat charitable trusts with more favour, and with a more liberal construction, than they would in the case of a gift to an individual, eg: HA Smith, *The Principles of Equity* (Stevens and Sons, London, 1882) 28; LS Bristowe and WI Cook, *The Law of Charities and Mortmain* (Reeves and Turner, London, 1889) 139; TA Roberts, *The Principles of the High Court of Chancery* (Wildy and Sons, London, 1852) 12–13; EHT Snell, *The Principles of Equity* (Stevens and Haynes, London, 1868) 90. Note also, the extra-curial comments in GFK Santow (the Hon), 'Charity in its Political Voice—A Tinkling Cymbal or a Sounding Brass?' (1999) 18 *Australian Bar Rev* 225, 228; and by: ALI, *Restatement of the Law (Third), Trusts (Tentative Draft No 3)* (ALI Publishers, St Paul Minn, 5 Mar 2001) 191.

to case law and enactments emanating from other jurisdictions with a strong affinity with English legal frameworks, such as Australia, Canada, Ireland, Northern Ireland, Scotland and New Zealand, to illustrate divergences of view, or to better illustrate particular conundrums with the doctrine, as and where appropriate. United States charitable trusts law will not be compared within this Part.[64]

To commence this Part, Chapter 2 delineates the boundaries of the *cy-près* doctrine by examining those scenarios that fall outside its strict ambit—where application of the doctrine would be wrongful, misdirected or unnecessary. For example, the chapter explores the contexts where the charitable disposition does not 'fail', where the doctrine is ousted by the donor, and where prerogative *cy-près* should apply instead.

Chapter 3 descends into the particularities of the general charitable *cy-près* doctrine. The chapter considers the triggers for the doctrine at general law, the significance of finding a general (as opposed to a specific) charitable intention in the case of *initial* failure of the charitable object, and the degree of 'closeness' required by the general law with which the substituted '*cy-près*' scheme must comply.

Chapter 4 considers the scope of the *cy-près* scheme-making power as it has been developed by statute. An overarching statutory *cy-près* regime was introduced into English law in 1960,[65] re-enacted in 1993,[66] and introduced via similar legislative regimes elsewhere in parts of the Commonwealth. This chapter examines and critiques the statutory *cy-près* doctrine from various perspectives, for example: does the statutory *cy-près* regime represent a code; what triggers serve for invoking statutory *cy-près*; and how have other jurisdictions *departed* from England's statutory *cy-près* regime? It could be said that the legislative march has its modern beginnings around this time across a range of jurisdictions—illustrative of the cross-fertilisation which occurs in response to common (and universal) societal needs.

Chapter 5 considers the problematic scenario of charitable public donations which are not, for various reasons, used for the purpose for which they were donated. Where trustees who are responsible for the monies discover that they cannot spend any or all of them, and where the rules of the public appeal do not provide for what is to happen in this scenario, then the role of *cy-près*, and the ultimate destination of the unused donations, presents considerable legal difficulties. The general law and statutory solutions to these problems are explored in detail in this chapter.

---

[64] Excellent treatments of the *cy-près* charitable trusts doctrine in the United States are to be found in, eg: American Law Institute, *American Restatement of the Law (Second), Trusts* (ALI Publishers, St Paul Minn, 1959), vol II, 297–307; by the same Institute: *Restatement of the Law (Third), Trusts (Tentative Draft No 3)* (ALI Publishers, St Paul Minn, 5 Mar 2001) 189–210; and in: AW Scott and WF Fratcher, *The Law of Trusts* (4th edn, Little, Brown and Co, Boston, 1989), vol IVA, 476–557.

[65] Charities Act 1960, s 13.

[66] Charities Act 1993, s 13.

Chapter 6 diverts from the traditional charitable context to examine the extent to which the *cy-près* doctrine has been recognised and applied in the context of non-charitable trusts. The ability to alter the application of property 'as near as possible' to the original purpose, within the context of the non-charitable purpose trust, and the mixed persons/purposes trust, for example, is scrutinised in this chapter—in addition to the problem of unused monies that were donated to non-charitable public appeals.

Part II of the book departs from the trusts context, to consider the application of the doctrine to litigious remedies of damages and specific performance. The jurisdictional coverage within this Part will change somewhat from that adopted for Part I, in that the there will be a concentrated focus upon developments in Canada and the United States, where the doctrine within this context is at its most sophisticated and innovative, as well as from other jurisdictions such as Australia and England.

Chapter 7 commences this Part with a discussion of the doctrine as applied to class actions litigation—where damages are applied 'as near as possible' to the original purpose for which they were awarded (or paid via settlement). The chapter considers matters such as the precise definition of *cy-près* in this context (in the midst of great terminological confusion), and the alternatives to a *cy-près* distribution that may provide legally better solutions in this context.

Chapter 8 explores the particularity of *cy-près* in class actions—the triggers for the doctrine, the degree of closeness required between the recipient of the *cy-près* benevolence and the original purpose of the lawsuit, and the relationship between the charitable trusts and class actions applications of the doctrine.

Chapter 9 concludes this Part with an examination of 'specific performance *cy-près*', whereby the court may exercise its discretion to award substituted specific performance where a party cannot transfer the property originally intended for transfer under contractual obligation. The chapter also draws parallels between substituted specific performance and the more traditional charitable *cy-près* doctrine.

To close, Chapter 10 draws together the various strands of the *cy-près* doctrine in its modern manifestations as presented in earlier chapters. The commonly-arising difficulties with any alternative application of property—for a different purpose, to a different recipient, even different property—are highly correlative between applications. This chapter will critically analyse how the overarching definition adopted for this book encompasses the doctrine in all of its manifestations, and will draw out various common themes that have been apparent to date.

It will be evident from this summary that the *cy-près* doctrine has expanded and marched into territories uncharted, and perhaps uncontemplated, when the charitable trusts *cy-près* was burgeoning and developing. Some of the complex circumstances in which the doctrine has manifested are legal innovations of the past ten to thirty years. In that respect, the doctrine warrants a close and considered study, because it is an examplar of legal enunciation that 'near enough is good enough'. It is put that if we are prepared to countenance such pragmatism (with respect to distribution of money or property or compensation, or in respect of contractual performance), the theoretical framework governing the doctrine's march into other areas needs to be 'cleverly crafted'. The conundrum of a 'near enough is good enough' mantra is only legally supportable if its ambit is clearly delineated and defined.

2. Further Miscellaneous Applications

Certain *cy-près* applications of property, in narrow situation-specific contexts, are briefly mentioned here for the sake of completeness, but will not be discussed further.

The rule in Whitby v Mitchell. As Pascoe notes, '[t]he doctrine of *cy-près* saved limitations from the destructive effects of two rules: the rule in *Whitby v Mitchell*[67] and the rule against perpetuities.'[68] According to the first-mentioned rule, and in the words of Kay J, 'the law as to land has always been that you cannot limit an estate to an unborn person for life, with remainder to the issue of that unborn person', for the reason that landowners should not be permitted to tie land up for as long as possible, so as to 'make successive limitations of life interests to unborn persons and to the children of those unborn persons. That has always been treated as being an invalid limitation of real estate.'[69] An application of the *cy-près* doctrine sought to soften the effects of this rule in *Whitby v Mitchell* by providing that, where the testator had manifested a general intention that a particular unborn devisee and his issue should take certain property, the court would uphold that general intention to provide for the issue of the devisee by vesting an estate tail[70] in the issue. This meant that '[t]he testator's general intention would be more closely effectuated if the eldest son was given an entail than if he took a mere life estate.'[71] The rule in *Whitby v Mitchell* was abolished by s 161(1) of the Law of Property Act 1925,[72] and the

---

[67] (1890) 44 Ch D 85.

[68] S Pascoe, 'Solicitors: Be Bold—Create Entailed Interests' [2001] *Conv* 396, and see text accompanying fnn 69, 70 thereof.

[69] *Whitby v Mitchell* (1889) LR 42 Ch D 494 (first instance decision) 500.

[70] A 'tail' means the limitation of an estate so that it can be inherited only by the donor's issue or class of issue. An interest in tail may be created by a trust in any property, real or personal. The limitation finds expression in a number of different but related terms, eg, a 'tail female' was a limitation to female heirs; a 'tail special' was a tail limited to specified heirs of the donee's body; and a 'tail general' was a tail limited to the issue of a particular person, but not to that of a particular couple. See generally: BA Garner (ed), *Black's Law Dictionary* (8th edn, West Group, St Paul Minn, 2004) 1492; DM Walker, *The Oxford Companion to Law* (Clarendon Press, Oxford, 1980) 1205; J Burke, *Jowitt's Dictionary of English Law*, vol 2 (2nd edn, Sweet & Maxwell, London, 1977) 1738.

[71] S Pascoe, 'Solicitors: Be Bold—Create Entailed Interests' [2001] *Conv* 396, citing (at fn 75): RE Megarry, 'Perpetuities and the *Cy-près* Doctrine' (1939) 54 *LQR* 422, 423.

[72] The section provided: 'The rule of law prohibiting the limitation, after a life interest to an unborn person, of an interest in land to the unborn child or other issue of an unborn person is hereby abolished, but without prejudice to any other rule relating to perpetuities.'

cy-près doctrine appears to have no further role to play in this regard. In any event, it has been said that this manifestation of the doctrine had 'no direct connection' with charitable trusts *cy-près*.[73]

Dispositions that offend the rule against perpetuities. Where a testator devised a perpetual series of life estates to a person and his issue in succession, that creation of a series of successive life estates to unborn persons in perpetuity was void. However, as Pascoe explains, 'if there was gift over on failure of issue sufficient to show an intention to give an estate tail, in such a case, the first generation that was unborn at the testator's death took an estate tail by *cy-près*.'[74] Sheridan and Delany note that, in respect of both this and the preceding application of the doctrine, they 'probably developed out of the doctrine of equity that the general intent must overrule the particular intent.'[75] The doctrine appears to have no role to play in English law, given the comments by Pascoe that 'Maudsley . . . proposes as one solution to the problem of the rule against perpetuities giving the court a power to adjust a void limitation to render it valid, altering as little as possible and observing the settlor's or testator's intention as far as possible. . . . It has not, however, received much support in England. As Maudsley states, there would be no chance that English courts would adopt *cy-près* to reform the perpetuity rule. The English courts show a great reluctance to exercise any power to "rewrite the instrument" for any of the parties.'[76] In contrast, for example, New Zealand's Perpetuity Act 1964 (NZ), s 10 provides, *inter alia*:

> where it has become apparent that, apart from the provisions of this section, any disposition . . . would be invalid solely on the ground that it infringes the rule against perpetuities, and where the general intentions originally governing the disposition can be ascertained . . . the disposition shall be reformed so as to give effect, if possible and as far as possible, to those general intentions within the limits permitted under the rule against perpetuities.[77]

Application to conditions precedent that were attached to testamentary gifts. At common law, where such a gift depended upon a condition that could not be strictly performed, the legacy would lapse. However, it developed that if the

---

[73] RA Pearce and J Stevens, *The Law of Trusts and Equitable Obligations* (Butterworths, London, 1995) 214. For further discussion, see: *Halsbury's Laws of England*, vol 35 (4th edn reissue, Butterworths, London, 1996) [1004]; LA Sheridan and VTH Delany, *The Cy-près Doctrine* (Sweet & Maxwell, London, 1959) 11–15.

[74] S Pascoe, 'Solicitors: Be Bold—Create Entailed Interests' [2001] *Conv* 396, citing (at fn 80): *Humberston v Humberston* (1716) 1 P Wms 332. Note, eg, *In re Mountgarret; Mountgarret v Ingilby* [1919] 2 Ch 294, where it was held that the *cy-près* doctrine did not apply in the scenario at hand. On this application of the doctrine, but for a differing viewpoint, see: EB Histed, 'Finally Barring the Entail' (2000) 116 *LQR* 445.

[75] LA Sheridan and VTH Delany, *The Cy-près Doctrine* (Sweet & Maxwell, London, 1959) 13.

[76] S Pascoe, 'Solicitors: Be Bold—Create Entailed Interests' [2001] *Conv* 396, and text accompanying fn 94ff.

[77] The section was considered and applied, but without reformation, in: *Re Westphal (decd)* [1972] NZLR 792, 795.

condition precedent could be performed substantially, the gift should be carried into effect.[78] The application of the *cy-près* doctrine in these circumstances depends (as with the charitable trusts application, which we will see later[79]) upon the existence or otherwise of a gift-over provision:

> When there is no disposition upon non-compliance with the terms of the condition [precedent], either in time or collateral circumstances, a liberal construction is to be put upon the performance, under authority of the testator's intention, inferred from the absence of any disposition over, that he meant the legatee to receive the legacy, upon the condition being performed *cy-près*, or in substance . . . But when there is a limitation over of the legacy on noncompliance with its specific terms, the construction is less liberal, a strict and literal performance being required; as it is presumed, from the disposition over of the legacy to another person, that the testator meant, if the terms which he imposed were not literally fulfilled, the second object of his bounty should succeed to the bequest.[80]

Application to the dissolution of corporations. The memorandum of association of a company limited by guarantee may typically provide:

> If, upon the winding up or dissolution of the Company, there remains after satisfaction of all its debts and liabilities any property whatsoever, the same shall not be paid to or distributed among the members of the Company, but shall be given or transferred to some other institution having objects similar to the objects of the Company, such institution to be determined by the members of the Company at or before the time of dissolution, and in default thereof, by the Chief Judge, and if and so far as effect cannot be given to the aforesaid provision, then to some charitable object.

This particular clause, at issue in *Heydon v NRMA Ltd*,[81] was termed in that case to be 'analogous' to *cy-près* in charitable trusts.

In the case of a charitable corporation, its dissolution clause may look like this:

> If the Charity is dissolved, the assets (if any) remaining after provision has been made for all its liabilities must be applied in one or more of the following ways: (a) by transfer to one or more other bodies established for exclusively charitable purposes within, the same as or similar to the Objects; (b) directly for the Objects or charitable purposes within or similar to the Objects, or (c) in such other manner consistent with charitable status as Charity Commission approves in advance.[82]

---

[78] LA Sheridan and VTH Delany, *The Cy-près Doctrine* (Sweet & Maxwell, London, 1959) 10–11, and see the early cases cited at fnn 41, 42.

[79] See pp 48–50, 57–8.

[80] *Re Selinger's WT; Midland Bank Executor and Trustee Co Ltd v Levy* [1959] 1 WLR 217 (Ch) 222–23, citing: Roper's *Law of Legacies* (4th edn, 1847) 769.

[81] [2000] NSWCA 374; 36 ACSR 462. For a similar clause, and discussion thereof, in the context of an incorporated association, see: *Liverpool and District Hospital for Diseases of the Heart v A-G* [1981] Ch 193, and cl 9 of the Memorandum reproduced therein.

[82] See: F Quint, *Charity Law Association Model Documents—Memorandum and Articles of Association for a Charitable Company Limited by Guarantee* (NGO Finance, London, 1997) cl 8.

It has been suggested that the corporate *cy-près* doctrine can afford to be more expansive than the charitable trusts *cy-près* doctrine, because 'there is less reason in the case of corporations to pay special attention to the wishes of donors'.[83]

Application to dissolution of incorporated associations. At common law, the unincorporated non-profit association was not recognised as a separate legal entity. In order to provide a framework in which such entities could operate, legislatures in several jurisdictions such as Australia, Canada and the United States, introduced statutory recognition and incorporation, although not always with desirable uniformity.[84] One aspect of the regulatory regimes governing incorporated associations must entail what is to occur with the surplus where the association is wound up, and there remains considerable assets after the payment of the association's debts. A *cy-près* distribution of assets to an organisation with similar objects may be countenanced by a provision in the association's constitution,[85] or in the relevant statute under which the association derives legal recognition.[86]

Again, the doctrine is probably not as strict as the charitable *cy-près* doctrine. In *Queensland Rugby Football League Ltd v Worrell*, the court noted that all that is required in such cases is some choice of similarity of objects, for which 'a good deal of latitude [is] necessarily permitted', compared to the stricter charitable trusts *cy-près* doctrine where the donor's intent must be considered.[87]

Application to powers of appointment. For testamentary powers of appointment of realty, where there is no substantial conformity in the appointment, the court may find a general intention and execute the particular intention *cy-près*. According to *Halsbury's*, this application will not be extended further, but appears to still exist:[88]

> Under the doctrine, the court has construed an appointment to an object for life with remainder in tail to his first and other sons who are not objects, as an estate tail in the appointee, provided that to do so will neither omit any object intended to be included nor include any object intended to be omitted.[89]

---

[83] OLRC, *Report on the Law of Charities* (1996) 504, referring there to religious and charitable corporations.

[84] See, for informative discussion: S Sievers, 'Incorporation and Regulation of Non-Profit Associations in Australia and Other Common Law Jurisdictions' (2001) 13 *Australian J of Corporate Law* 120, 126.

[85] See, eg, the clause in: *Queensland Rugby Football League Ltd v Worrell* [2000] QSC 381; 35 ACSR 555 (SC Qld).

[86] See, eg: Associations Incorporation Act 1990 (NT), s 22, applied in: *Alice Springs Town Council v Mpweteyerre Aboriginal Corp* (1997) 115 NTR 25 (CA) (reiterating that the judge was bound 'under s 22 to ensure that any surplus assets were disposed of *cy-près*').

[87] [2000] QSC 381; 35 ACSR 555 (SC Qld).

[88] *Halsbury's Laws of England* (4th edn reissue, Butterworths, London, 1996) vol 36(2), [275], and see further: *In re De Little; Union Trustee Co of Australia Ltd v A-G* [1943] St R Qd 31 (SC).

[89] *Halsbury's, ibid*, vol 5(2), [275].

Situation-specific statutory manifestations of the doctrine.   The Reverter of Sites Act 1987 came into force in England to allow, in certain circumstances, for the sale and *cy-près* distribution of the charitable sites. For sites that were originally used for religious or educational purposes in certain cases, the statute permits the creation of a *cy-près* scheme 'in favour of the local community generally, or in favour of the young people of that community, rather than necessarily for the purposes of education, worship, etc'.[90] Some other statutory provisions allowing for a change of trust objects are noted elsewhere.[91]

---

[90] As discussed in: D Evans, 'Reverter of Sites Act 1987' [1987] *Conv* 408, 413.

[91] LA Sheridan, *The Barry Rose Charity Statutes* (Barry Rose Law Publishers, Chichester, 1998) 108–9. For some further miscellaneous applications of the doctrine in the US context, see: EL Fisch, *The Cy-près Doctrine in the United States* (Matthew Bender & Co, Albany NY, 1950) 203–4.

Part I

The *Cy-près* Doctrine in the Context of Trusts

Part I considers the *cy-près* scheme-making power, as it pertains to charitable and non-charitable dispositions of property on trust. First, however, the boundaries of the judicial *cy-près* power are delineated for the sake of clarity.

2

Charitable Trusts: Cy-près *Delineation*

A INTRODUCTION

WHEN COMMENCING CONSIDERATION of the charitable *cy-près* doctrine, it is important to delineate the boundaries of the doctrine by identifying those areas where reliance upon the doctrine is unnecessary and, indeed, misdirected. It is not for every scenario where a donor has directed a disposition to a charitable object, and which is impossible or impracticable to effect, that recourse must be had to the *cy-près* doctrine. Figure 2.1 illustrates where the traditional *cy-près* doctrine fits within the wider context of problematical charitable dispositions, and points to how the doctrine is examined within this, and subsequent chapters of this Part. As the figure shows, a variety of techniques may be employed to save the charitable disposition, and prevent the ultimate of last resorts, the lapse[1] or failure of the gift.

B JUDICIAL AND PREROGATIVE CY-PRÈS

1. The Width of Judicial Cy-près

At the outset, it is important to distinguish between judicial and prerogative *cy-près* powers. The judicial *cy-près* doctrine 'enables the court (or the Charity Commissioners) to make a scheme for the application of the property for other charitable purposes as near as possible to those intended by the donor.'[2] This manifests where property is given by the donor on trust for charitable purposes, and the purposes cannot be carried out in the precise manner intended by the donor.

The judicial *cy-près* power is, however, somewhat wider than that, for provided that there exists *some* person or body which is under a legally binding obligation to distribute assets for charitable purposes, then the court can intervene to exercise the spectrum of its inherent supervisory equitable jurisdiction, including its *cy-près* powers. That person or body is commonly a traditional

---

[1] Lapse means the return (or resulting back) of the beneficial interest in the property to the settlor or to his personal representatives (ie, the trust lapses) or, if the settlor is deceased, to his residuary estate or distributed on an intestacy, whichever is appropriate.

[2] JE Martin, *Hanbury and Martin Modern Equity* (17th edn, Sweet & Maxwell, London, 2005) 451.

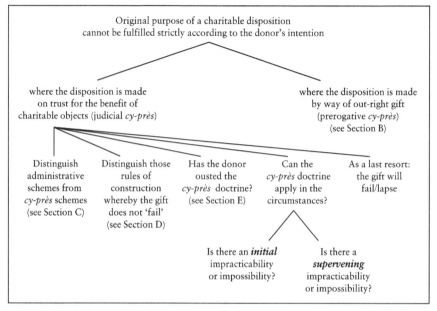

Figure 2.1 *The framework for* cy-près *analysis*

trustee. However, a charitable corporation, for example, may be sufficiently bound by various obligations to dispose of its property for exclusively charitable purposes *as though it were a trustee*—that will be sufficient to allow the judicial *cy-près* power to be invoked, if necessary.[3]

This question arose for direct consideration in *Liverpool and District Hospital for Diseases of the Heart v A-G*,[4] in which a liquidator sought directions as to whether the surplus assets of a charitable corporation upon winding up should be distributed amongst the members or should be applied *cy-près*. (Any assets that had been given to this corporation were given to it *beneficially*, for the company to own outright, and *not* given for the purposes of the company, which purposes may continue in another form[5]—a distinction that is discussed later in the Part[6]). A preliminary question was whether, in those circumstances, the court had jurisdiction to order a *cy-près* scheme, given that the company did not hold its assets on trust in the strict sense, but it was bound to use its assets for charitable purposes. Slade J held that it did, and based the court's capacity for intervention upon the following reasoning:

---

[3] As explained in: *Re Public Trustee and Toronto Humane Society* (1987), 60 OR (2d) 236, 40 DLR (4th) 111, although the court was not dealing there with a *cy-près* power, but rather whether certain expenditures were appropriate for a charitable corporation.

[4] [1981] Ch 193.

[5] *In re Finger's WT; Turner v Ministry of Health* [1972] 1 Ch 286.

[6] See pp 44–6.

the so-called rule that the court's jurisdiction to intervene in the affairs of a charity depends on the existence of a trust means no more than this. The court has no jurisdiction to intervene unless there has been placed on the holder of the assets in question a legally binding restriction arising either by way of trust in the strict traditional sense or, in the case of a corporate body, under the terms of its constitution which obliges him or it to apply the assets in question for exclusively charitable purposes. For the jurisdiction of the court necessarily depends on the existence of a person or body who is subject to such obligation and against whom the court can act *in personam* so far as necessary for the purposes of enforcement.[7]

Whilst the judicial *cy-près* power could be invoked in this scenario, the situation will differ where there is no effective and imperative dedication of the property to charity, but merely a gift to a corporation that it is obliged to use and apply according to its statutory powers, some of the motives of which are to employ the property for charitable purposes (ie, the provision of a public park or recreation ground). In that case, there is no possibility of the Attorney-General's being able to enforce the 'trust' in favour of the public (because there is no charitable trust in place), and there is no place for operation of the *cy-près* doctrine.[8]

2. The Uncertainties of Prerogative *Cy-près*

Prerogative *cy-près* powers, on the other hand, are invoked where a gift is made simply to a charity, which gift cannot be carried into effect, and where the gift is given 'without the vestiges of trusteeship' (ie, at the very least, no trustees are stipulated).[9] Strictly speaking, the property the subject matter of that gift which was made to charity in general terms is then *bona vacantia*,[10] and hence belongs to the Crown, with the sovereign as 'constitutional trustee'.[11] It is then up to the Crown to deal with the property *cy-près*. Thus, as one court succinctly put it: '[a] gift to charity not upon a trust is disposed of by the Crown ... This is the prerogative *cy-près*. Where a trust is involved the court has its own jurisdiction.

---

[7] [1981] Ch 193, 214. See also: JE Martin, *Hanbury and Martin Modern Equity* (17th edn, Sweet & Maxwell, London, 2005) 454, fn 72.

[8] *Liverpool CC v A-G* (Ch, 15 Apr 1992), comprising an unsuccessful attempt to widen the application of the principle in *Liverpool and District Hospital, ibid*.

[9] G Dal Pont, *Charity Law in Australia and New Zealand* (OUP, Oxford, 2000) 249 (quote); JE Martin, *Hanbury and Martin Modern Equity* (17th edn, Sweet & Maxwell, London, 2005) 451; and the leading example of which is: *Moggridge v Thackwell* [1803–1813] All ER Rep 754 (Ch). On prerogative powers generally, see, eg: R Brazier, *Ministers of the Crown* (Clarendon Press, Oxford, 1997) ch 12; LL Blake, *The Royal Law* (Shepheard Walwyn, London, 2000) 53–56.

[10] Property that has no owner, in which case it belongs to the Crown: *Re Wells; Swinburne-Hanham v Howard* [1932] All ER Rep 277 (CA), citing both *Dyke v Walford* (1848) 5 Moo PCC 434; 13 ER 557, and *Blackstone's Commentaries* (8th edn) vol 1, 298. The Crown or the Duchy of Lancaster or Cornwall take *bona vacantia* property, according to: J Mowbray *et al, Lewin on Trusts* (17th edn, Sweet & Maxwell, London, 2000) 20–159.

[11] *Moggridge v Thackwell* [1803–1813] All ER Rep 754 (Ch) 765.

This is referred to as a judicial *cy-près*'.[12] Thus, the distinction solely depends upon whether the charitable disposition (which cannot be carried into effect) was created by direct gift or by trust.

Where the charitable disposition was created by direct gift, the question has arisen as to whether or not a court has jurisdiction to exercise its judicial *cy-près* power in any event, effectively replacing the prerogative *cy-près* power and directing of its own accord the *cy-près* disposition of the property. Two views have been expressed on 'this rather obscure subject'.[13] In *In re Bennett (decd); Sucker v A-G*,[14] Vaisey J opined that 'under a very long series of authorities (not altogether consistent and not altogether easy to interpret), it falls to be dealt with by the royal prerogative.' In this case, the testatrix gave a 25% share of her residuary estate to 'The Hospital for Incurable Women of Brompton Road London'. No hospital of that name existed. Further, notwithstanding the nomination of executors and trustees, the will contained no trusts. The executors requested that the court direct a *cy-près* scheme for the disposition of the gift, but Vaisey J refused: 'in a simple case such as this, as between the jurisdiction arising from the royal prerogative and the ordinary equitable jurisdiction of the court ... this is a case in which the royal prerogative must be appealed to, to enable justice to be done.'[15] Certain other judicial[16] and academic[17] opinion supports the view that the court lacks jurisdiction to order what should be done with the property in the absence of a trust, and that its distribution must be directly effected by the Crown under Sign Manual[18] by virtue of its prerogative *cy-près* power.

---

[12] *Montreal Trust Co v Richards* (1982), 40 BCLR 114, [1983] 1 WWR 437 (BC SC) [45] (references omitted).

[13] *In re Bennett (decd); Sucker v A-G* [1960] Ch 18, 25 (Vaisey J).

[14] *Ibid*, 24.

[15] *Ibid*, 25.

[16] *In re Pyne; Lilley v A-G* [1903] 1 Ch 83, citing with approval on this point: *Moggridge v Thackwell* [1803–1813] All ER Rep 754 (Ch); and *Paice v Archbishop of Canterbury* (1807) 14 Ves 364. See also, in cases where a scheme under the Sign Manual was accepted as proper: *In re Hetherington (decd)* [1990] Ch 1 (CA); *Murray v Thomas* [1937] 4 All ER 545 (Ch) 547 ('If there is an existing trust which the court can administer, the court has jurisdiction to direct a scheme. If there is no trust which the court can administer, it is a sign manual case'); *In re Smith; Public Trustee v Smith* [1932] 1 Ch 153 (CA) 169 (testator bequeathed his entire estate to 'my country England to and for own use and benefit absolutely'; a charitable bequest; money ordered to be handed over to the person designated under the Sign Manual to be applied for the advantage of the country's people).

[17] J Warburton, *Tudor on Charities* (8th edn, Sweet & Maxwell, London, 1995) 305 ('The jurisdiction of the court is founded on the existence of a trust, and where there is no trust the application of the fund is beyond the jurisdiction of the court, and rests with the Crown alone'); also cited in: *Re Conroy Estate* (1973), 35 DLR (3d) 752 (BCSC [Probate]) [12]; DG Cracknell (ed), *Charities: The Law and Practice* (Thomson Sweet & Maxwell, London, 1994–) [looseleaf] para 1.56 ('Where there is a gift to charity which does not take the form of an express or implied trust, the court and the Charity Commissioners lack jurisdiction to make a scheme'); also: LA Sheridan and VTH Delany, *The Cy-près Doctrine* (Sweet & Maxwell, London, 1959) 66; JG Riddall, *The Law of Trusts* (6th edn, Butterworths, London, 2002) 17.

[18] The Sign Manual encompasses those formal documents (warrants, commissions or orders) by which the monarch's wishes or commands in executive matters are conveyed, and which documents are used to put into operation the powers conferred by the common law or by statute (eg, appointments of judges occurs under the royal Sign Manual: *Halsbury's Laws of England*

Other authorities in England[19] and elsewhere,[20] and significant academic opinion,[21] however, have preferred the more expedient view that where property is given for charitable purposes in circumstances in which no trust is created, the court has the jurisdiction to supplant the Crown and make the *cy-près* scheme itself. Under this approach (presumably pursued with the Crown's approval), the court would preserve the royal prerogative in form, and distribute the fund *bona vacantia* precisely as it would for any property disposed of for failed charitable purposes. Effectively, under this approach, whether a court declares that a direct gift was given with a general charitable intention and must be upheld and disposed of in accordance with the wishes of the Crown, or the court gives directions itself for what is to happen to the property with the informed concurrence of the Attorney-General, the principle is the same.[22]

The separation between judicial and prerogative *cy-près* powers has, in the past, been labelled a vexed and ambiguous one.[23] The situation is not assisted by the fact that some judicial opinions on the matter have been expressed on the basis that there was a trust when there was not, or *vice versa*.[24] For example,

---

(4th edn reissue, Butterworths, London, 1996) vol 8(2), [906], [908]. It literally means the signature or 'royal hand' of the Queen: S Bone (ed), *Osborn's Concise Law Dictionary* (9th edn, Sweet & Maxwell, London, 2001) 352.

[19] *Construction Industry Training Board v A-G* [1973] Ch 173 (CA) 186 ('Where the Crown invokes the assistance of the courts for such purposes, the jurisdiction which is invoked is, I think, a branch of the court's jurisdiction in relation to trusts'); *In re Vernon's WT; Lloyd's Bank Ltd v Group 20 Hospital Management Committee (Coventry)* [1972] Ch 300, 303 ('a charitable purpose will not fail for lack of a trustee but will be carried into effect either under the Sign Manual or by means of a scheme').

[20] Eg: *Re Conroy Estate* (1973), 35 DLR (3d) 752 (BCSC [Probate]); approved on this point in: *Montreal Trust Co v Richards* (1982), 40 BCLR 114, [1983] 1 WWR 437 (BCSC).

[21] In Canada: OLRC, *Report on the Law of Charities* (1996) 398 fn 19, 402. In England: J Hackney, 'Trusts' [1974] *ASCL* 514 (allowing court to make the scheme 'the sensible answer. The distinction between judicial and prerogative *cy-près* has little to recommend it today'). In Australia: G Dal Pont, *Charity Law in Australia and New Zealand* (OUP, Oxford, 2000) 250.

[22] *Re Conroy Estate* (1973), 35 DLR (3d) 752 (BCSC [Probate]) [18].

[23] *Moggridge v Thackwell* (1802) 7 Ves 36; [1803–1813] All ER Rep 754 (Ch) 765 ('I have great difficulty in my own mind' on the topic, noting that 'authority meets authority and precedent clashes with precedent': Lord Eldon LC). Later, a leading treatise seemed less than impressed with Lord Eldon's attempts in this case, noting that "[i]t is nevertheless difficult to find from the reported cases an exhaustive statement or explicit rule as to the respective rights of the Crown to direct the disposition of a charitable gift under the sign manual . . . Lord Eldon's statement was . . . by no means clear': CE Shebbeare and CP Sanger, *The Law of Charitable Bequests* (2nd edn, Sweet & Maxwell, London, 1921) 209.

[24] Eg: some authorities have been cited in support of the court's power to assist the Crown, eg: *Sanford v Gibbons* (1829) 2 Hare 195n; *Simon v Barber* (1829) 3 Hare 195n; *Thorley v Byrne* (1830) 3 Hare 195n, all cited in *In re Bennett (decd); Sucker v A-G* [1960] Ch 18, 20–21, but with the suggestion that they involved dispositions on trust. Also: *In re Songest (decd); Mayger v Forces' Help Society* [1956] 1 WLR 897 (CA) was cited in *Re Conroy Estate* (1973), 35 DLR (3d) 752 (BCSC [Probate]) [8], but in *Songest*, the testatrix's residuary was plainly given on trust for 'the Disabled Soldiers Sailors and Airmen's Association'—the approval of the Attorney General was sought there presumably because the gift was directed toward caring for disabled men who had been in the service of the Crown, *not* because it was a direct gift that would require an exercise of prerogative power. For a useful exposition of the English law on this subject, see: *Re Conroy Estate* (1973), 35 DLR (3d) 752 (BCSC [Probate]) [11]–[18].

Picarda points out that, in his view, the decision in *Bennett* ought to have turned upon judicial, not prerogative, *cy-près*, because:

> if the presence of a trust removes the case from the jurisdiction of the Crown and brings it into the jurisdiction of the court, it is difficult to see how any testamentary gift is applicable under the Royal Prerogative, since all the property of the deceased devolves upon his personal representative upon trust. The point was not argued in *Re Bennett* and perhaps if the attention of Vaisey J had been directed to it, he might not have held the gift to be applicable under the Royal Prerogative.[25]

However, the issue may not be especially significant now, given that: no case law that turns upon the distinction has been generated in England since *Bennett*[26] was decided over 40 years ago; whether a gift is given on trust or not is probably only a matter of drafting coincidence;[27] some legislative *cy-près* schemes clearly extend the court's jurisdiction to charitable gifts rather than charitable trusts;[28] and as Martin notes,[29] the distinction between the two types of *cy-près* has not always been observed in any event.

As an aside, in modern times, it is not the Sovereign who directs under Sign Manual to which specific charitable objects the property should be applied; in 1986, this power was delegated to the Attorney-General.[30]

Throughout the remainder of this Part, unless otherwise indicated, the expression, 'a gift to charity' and the like should be taken to mean 'a gift *on trust* to charity'. In other words, no further instances of direct gifts that invoke prerogative *cy-près* powers will be considered in this Part.

Finally, before leaving this section, it is perhaps pertinent to note a third alternative, quite apart from judicial and Crown-directed *cy-près* schemes. Where the charitable trusts are founded by statute, and the trusts are no longer practicable, they can only be altered by an Act of Parliament, such that any *cy-près* scheme must be settled in that fashion—an instance which arises occasionally in the case reports.[31]

C ADMINISTRATIVE SCHEMES

As noted in *Hunter Region SLSA Helicopter Rescue Service Ltd v A-G for NSW*,[32]

---

[25] HAP Picarda, *The Law and Practice Relating to Charities* (3rd edn, Butterworths, London, 1999) 331.

[26] [1960] Ch 18.

[27] J Hackney, 'Trusts' [1974] *ASCL* 514. Also cited in: Dal Pont, below.

[28] A point made by: G Dal Pont, *Charity Law in Australia and New Zealand* (OUP, Oxford, 2000) 250, referring to the Victorian, Western Australian and New Zealand schemes.

[29] JE Martin, *Hanbury and Martin Modern Equity* (17th edn, Sweet & Maxwell, London, 2005) 451. See also, the several instances of confusion noted in: LA Sheridan and VTH Delany, *The Cy-près Doctrine* (Sweet & Maxwell, London, 1959) 69–71.

[30] As noted in: *Report of the Ch Comm for England and Wales* (1989) [38].

[31] Eg: *Re Richmond Parish Charity Lands Richmond Corp v Morell* [1965] RVR 590 (CA).

[32] [2000] NSWSC 456 (22 May 2000) [3].

the *cy-près* scheme is only one subspecies of the genus scheme, and schemes other than *cy-près* schemes may be implemented where there is lack of clarity as to the particular objects, or where there are no trustees, or where there is not proper machinery for the management and control of the trust property, or regulating its distribution and application. In giving those instances, I am not intending to be exhaustive.

Whilst it is true that there must be a threshold certainty for charitable trusts,[33] certainty of object is loosely fashioned. There must be certainty as to the property that is subject to the trust, and it must also be certain that the donor intended to devote that property to a charitable purpose. If these conditions are fulfilled the gift cannot fail for uncertainty.[34] In *Re Gott; Glazebrook v University of Leeds*, it was remarked, '[n]o doubt, when a purpose is stated, no charitable trust is created unless the purpose is certainly charitable, but, given that certainty, uncertainty as to the particular charitable purpose intended is . . . immaterial',[35] and that one of the advantages of this category is that 'a trust for charitable purposes does not fail for uncertainty'.[36] It is perceived that the need for the purposes of a charitable trust to be articulated with certainty is not as pressing as in the case of private trusts because, in the former, the Attorney-General has authority to enforce charitable trusts and to request that the court exercise its jurisdiction to settle a scheme for their administration.[37] The mere existence of the court's inherent scheme-making power deems a charitable trust to have sufficient certainty of object, and it then becomes a question of which scheme-making power is exercised, and how.

In circumstances where the court must nominate a specific charitable purpose to be benefited in circumstances where the terms of the charitable trust are ambiguous, or where the machinery for carrying out the charitable purpose requires greater definition, or completely breaks down,[38] the court (or the Charity Commissioners[39]) will approve an administrative scheme to assist

---

[33] *Viz*, certainty of intent and certainty of subject-matter.

[34] *Armenian General Benevolent Union v Union Trustee Co of Australia Ltd* (1952) 87 CLR 597 (HCA) 614.

[35] [1944] 1 Ch 193, 197.

[36] *Ibid*.

[37] GE Dal Pont and DRC Chalmers, *Equity and Trusts in Australia and New Zealand* (LBC Information Services, Sydney, 1996) 377, citing: *Morice v Bishop of Durham* (1804) 9 Ves 399, 405. Called the 'doctrine of deviation' in US trusts law: EL Fisch, *The Cy-près Doctrine in the United States* (Matthew Bender & Co, Albany NY, 1950) 3.

[38] Eg: *In re Willis; Shaw v Willis* [1921] 1 Ch 44, 51–52 (bequests made to charities to be selected by named person X who predeceased testator; testator had intent to benefit charitable purposes generally, leaving only mode of application to selection of X; where selection by X impossible, court carried testator's intention into effect by way of administrative scheme).

[39] Pursuant to Charities Act 1993, s 16(1)(a) (the provision permits the Commissioners to exercise concurrent jurisdiction with the High Court in charity proceedings for the purposes of 'establishing a scheme for the administration of a charity', which includes a *cy-près* scheme). For an expansive discussion of the role of the Charity Commissioners in English charity law, see, eg: P Luxton, *The Law of Charities* (OUP, Oxford, 2001) 553–58; Ch Comm for England and Wales, *Ch Comm Origin and Functions* (CC1, 1992).

achievement of the donor's intention.[40] Note that this is not a *cy-près* scheme; in no circumstances are the purposes of the trust altered, and hence, this is not a *cy-près* application of the property. The purposes to be benefited are the very objects which were instructed by the testator, and the court merely 'fills up the details' of the donor's charitable intention.[41] Administrative schemes have been employed to provide certainty, for example, to gifts on trust for 'charitable purposes';[42] for 'the relief of poverty';[43] to 'charitable uses or purposes';[44] for 'promoting the gospel in foreign parts';[45] for 'the work of the Lord';[46] and for charitable uses 'as I have by writing under my hand . . . directed' (no directions were found).[47]

Both *cy-près* and administrative schemes fall within the inherent jurisdiction of the court to deal with the administration of charities.[48] Additionally, both types of schemes fall within the concurrent jurisdiction of the court and the Charity Commissioners;[49] and both mirror the same motivation—a benevolent attitude toward the upholding of charitable gifts wherever possible. The two main points of distinction between an administrative scheme and a *cy-près* scheme are: (a) the latter entails some alteration in the trust's purposes, whereas the former does not; and (b) the latter requires proof of a general charitable intention whereas the former does not.

The Ontario Law Reform Commission compared the two scheme-making powers in this manner:

---

[40] Administrative schemes can function more broadly than this, their other uses including: appointing trustees upon the death of the original trustees, refusing to act, or non-existent: *In re Fraser; Yeates v Fraser* (1883) LR 22 Ch D 827; managing how a charitable residuary gift is to be distributed amongst substitutes for named institutions which did not exist: *In re Davis; Hannen v Hillyer* [1902] 1 Ch 876; or managing the trust fund after it has been misapplied: *A G v Coopers' Co* (1812) 19 Ves 187; 34 ER 488, 490–91. For a more comprehensive list, see, eg: *Halsbury's Laws of England* (4th edn reissue, Butterworths, London, 1996) vol 5(2), [171]; G Dal Pont, *Charity Law in Australia and New Zealand* (OUP, Oxford, 2000) 256–58.

[41] *In re Robinson; Besant v The German Reich* [1931] 2 Ch 122, 128–29; *Varsani v Jesani* [1999] Ch 219 (CA) 234–35 (Morritt LJ); *Phillips v Roberts* [1975] 2 NSWLR 207 (CA) 222–25 (Mahoney JA); *In re Parker (decd); The Ballarat Trustees, Executors and Agency Co Ltd v Parker* [1949] VLR 133, 136.

[42] *Sumner v Sumner* (1884) 10 VLR (E) 261, 267, and example cited in: J Martin, *Hanbury and Martin Modern Equity* (16th edn, Sweet & Maxwell, London, 2001) 395.

[43] General example provided in: OLRC, *Report on the Law of Charities* (1996) 398.

[44] *In re Dobinson; Maddock v A-G* [1911] VLR 300, 309. See also the example in *Re Gardner's WT; Boucher v Horn* [1936] 3 All ER 938 (Ch) of EG giving all her residuary estate for the purpose of creating a fund, 'EG Charity', with no further instructions given.

[45] *Mills v Farmer* [1814–1823] All ER Rep 53 (Ch) 60.

[46] *Re Brooks Estate* (1969), 4 DLR (3d) 694.

[47] *A-G v Syderfen* 1 Vern 224.

[48] *In re Resch's WT; Le Cras v Perpetual Trustee Co Ltd, Far West Children's Health Scheme v Perpetual Trustee Co Ltd* [1967] 3 All ER 915 (PC), citing: *In re Robinson, Besant v The German Reich* [1931] 2 Ch 122, 128. Also: *Phillips v Roberts* [1975] 2 NSWLR 207 (CA) 222 (Mahoney JA). Both strands are part of the court's 'special jurisdiction' in relation to charitable trusts: *Gaudiya Mission v Kamalaksha Das Braham* (Ch, 14 Mar 1997). See also, the discussion in: *Lord Nuffield (as Trustee for the Nuffield Foundation) v IRC* (1946) 28 Fam Cas 479 (KB).

[49] Charities Act 1993, s 16(1)(a), subject to s 16(10), whereby the Court has sole jurisdiction where the matter is contentious or where a special question of law or fact is involved.

The *cy-près* doctrines . . . permit a court to alter the objects. The power of the court to devise a scheme, by contrast, applies only to ensure that a charitable trust does not fail at the outset for want of certainty or for want of specification of projects or modalities. The distinction—supplying specifics versus altering objects—although logically valid, is often difficult to draw. . . There is some confusion in the case law that arises out of this difficulty. It is contributed to by the law's use of the word 'scheme' for the outcome of both . . . However, the confusion causes no real harm since the doctrines are motivated by the same spirit and they seek to accomplish the same general objective.[50]

Examples of the confusion referred to in the above passage, whereby schemes that are truly administrative schemes have been termed *cy-près* schemes and *vice versa*, have occurred sporadically in various jurisdictions such as Canada,[51] New Zealand,[52] Scotland[53] and England,[54] and even recently, there has been judicial indecision as to whether the particular scheme permitted by the court properly pertained to the purposes of the trust or to the administrative machinery for performing the trust.[55]

Of course, ring-fencing the *cy-près* power for the scenario of *amending the trust's purposes*, and hiving off other scenarios to be dealt with by powers found elsewhere (whether in the court's inherent jurisdiction, in statute, or in the trust instrument itself) maintains a purity of doctrine: 'eliminating a source of much

---

[50] OLRC, *Report on the Law of Charities* (1996) 399. See also: *Halsbury's Laws of Australia* (Butterworths, Sydney, 1991–) [looseleaf] [75–695].

[51] Eg, Canada: *Re Roberts* (1958), 26 WWR 196 (Alta CA); *Sheppard v Bradshaw* (1921), 50 OLR 626, 64 DLR 624 (Sup Ct); *Re Wright* (1923), 56 NSR 364 (CA, Chisholm J), all of which are cited in: DWM Waters, *Law of Trusts in Canada* (2nd edn, Carswell, Toronto, 1984) 612, 620 as incorrect applications of a *cy-près* scheme where none was required, with the criticism that 'Canadian courts sometimes give the impression that they assume that all schemes have as their purpose the *cy-près* application of the trust funds': at 620. This view is borne out by more recent examples, where the *cy-près* doctrine has been referenced for other than a change of the trust's purposes, eg: *Granfield Estate v Jackson* (1999), 87 ACWS (3d) 205 (BCSC) [41]–[44]; *Bilz v Community Care Access Centre* (1998), 84 ACWS (3d) 1231 (Ont Gen Div) (uncertainty as to which institution was meant to take the bequest); *Re Ramsden Estate* (1996), 139 DLR (4th) 746 (PEI SC) (change of trust administrator).

[52] Eg, see C Rickett, 'Politics and Cy-près' [1998] *NZLJ* 55, 57, who explains how the *cy-près* doctrine ought to have played no part in the analysis in *Re Collier (decd)* [1998] 1 NZLR 81, and that, at best, an administrative scheme to sharpen the definition of a potential charitable purpose was the only scheme that ought to have been contemplated.

[53] Eg: *Ballingall's Judicial Factor v Hamilton* 1973 SLT 236 (residuary estate divided between 'heart diseases and cancer research'; *cy-près* scheme approved), and see J Hackney 'Trusts' [1974] *ASCL* 514, who notes how this case truly entailed an administrative scheme.

[54] Eg: *Re Spence's Estate; Barclays Bank Ltd v Stockton-on-Tees Corp* [1937] 3 All ER 684 (Ch) ('even if the corporation [trustee] should refuse the gift, the gift would not fail, and, in such case, a scheme would be necessary for its application *cy-près*'; however, in the event of a trustee refusing to act, an administrative scheme would be required); *In re Couchman's WT; Couchman v Eccles* [1952] Ch 391 ('Whether it is correct to call it a *cy-près* application, or simply a scheme for the carrying out of the original purpose, does not much matter in this case'; an administrative scheme appears the better view in this case); *Re Gardner's WT; Boucher v Horn* [1936] 3 All ER 938 (Ch) (EG gave all her residuary estate for the purpose of creating a fund, 'EG Charity', with no further instructions given; note the debate among counsel as to whether this was a *cy-près* or an administrative scheme).

[55] *Toronto Aged Men's and Women's Homes v Loyal True Blue and Orange Home* (2003), 68 OR (3d) 777 (SCJ) [31]–[43].

confusion, as well as giving the doctrine its avowed meaning'.[56] To illustrate, the court's discretion to enlarge the powers contained in a trust instrument in certain defined circumstances does not extend to alterations that would amend the basic purpose of the charity. In *Baptist Union of New Zealand v A-G*,[57] the New Zealand Supreme Court criticised the path which the applicant had chosen (for an order to enlarge powers under the trust) in order to change the method of operating a charity set up to provide a home for children, in circumstances where the contemplated changes would amount to a change of purpose. Woodhouse J chastised that '[t]he essential route in the present case is via the appropriate [*cy-près*] provisions of the Charitable Trusts Act 1957 and the issue is no mere question of procedure. It goes to jurisdiction.'[58] His Honour suggested[59] that the *cy-près* route had deliberate advantages that the incorrectly-chosen route did not, namely, publication and advertisement of the proposed scheme, and scrutiny by the Attorney-General.

D CONSTRUING DISPOSITIONS TO AVOID 'FAILURE' OF CHARITABLE GIFTS

The *cy-près* doctrine will only apply where the original purpose of a gift on trust has failed (in the legal sense of 'failure' in this context, namely, impossibility or impracticability). Therefore, if, by some means of construction, it can be found that the gift (although problematical) has not 'failed', then this has several advantages.

First, it is not necessary to incur the expenses and delays of applying for a *cy-près* scheme. It may ultimately be necessary for the court to give directions as to how the trust property will be applied, but that is not a *cy-près* scheme. Secondly, it will not be necessary to find a paramount general charitable intent, for that requirement only arises where there has been an initial failure of the charitable purpose. Indeed, it is incorrect to look for a general charitable intention where the gift has not failed.[60] Thirdly, where one of the rules of construction discussed in this section applies, there is no question of the gift failing, and thus lapsing and falling into residue, away from charity (a further manifestation of 'the leniency with which the court treats charitable gifts'[61]).

A variety of rules of construction which will preclude a 'failure' of the problematical gift are outlined in the table which follows, and are then con-

---

[56] A point also reiterated in: EL Fisch, *The Cy-près Doctrine in the United States* (Matthew Bender & Co, Albany NY, 1950) 177–78.

[57] [1973] 1 NZLR 42 (SC).

[58] *Ibid*, 43.

[59] *Ibid*, 44.

[60] This point is forcefully made in: J Martin, 'The Construction of Charitable Gifts' (1974) 38 *Conv* 187, 188, and also: JE Martin, *Martin and Hanbury Modern Equity* (17th edn, Sweet & Maxwell, London, 2005) 453–54; G Moffat, *Trusts Law Text and Materials* (4th edn, CUP, Cambridge, 2005) 908.

[61] *Halsbury's Laws of England* (4th edn reissue, Butterworths, London, 1996) vol 5(2), 120.

sidered further in turn.[62] Some of these rules are, by judicial admission, artificial. They are the product of 'an enlarged construction',[63] depend upon 'very refined arguments',[64] and introduce considerable 'further complications in the law'[65]—all of which are the consequence of courts' striving to uphold bequests in favour of intended charitable donees wherever possible. As a further point of controversy, whether the rules are mutually exclusive, or could be cumulative in an appropriate scenario, is not entirely clear either.[66] Despite their difficulties, the rules considered in this section have been judicially followed in Australia[67] and Canada,[68] although where marked differences in principle occur between England and these Commonwealth jurisdictions, these are noted.

It is important to reiterate that these rules of construction, and the *cy-près* doctrine, operate 'in tandem'. If the gift does indeed fail because it cannot be salvaged via one of these rules, then the *cy-près* doctrine may well step in to prevent the property from lapsing and falling into residue (if the gift was made with a general charitable intention, in cases of initial failure of the gift). The correct analysis is to consider whether the following rules can salvage the gift, in a pre-*cy-près* stage of the analysis. If the charity beneficiary does not enjoy any success there, then the last resort is to accept that the gift has 'failed', and to seek to apply the gift *cy-près*.[69]

---

[62] For further detailed English commentary, see, eg: HAP Picarda, *The Law and Practice Relating to Charities* (3rd edn, Butterworths, London, 1999) ch 26; JG Riddall, *The Law of Trusts* (6th edn, Butterworths, London, 2002) 13–15; J Martin, 'The Construction of Charitable Gifts' (1974) 38 *Conv* 187; RBM Cotterrell, 'Gifts to Charitable Institutions: A Note on Recent Developments' (1972) 36 *Conv* 198; G Moffat, *Trusts Law Text and Materials* (4th edn, CUP, Cambridge, 2005) 908–10.

[63] *In re Morgan's WT; Lewarne v Minister of Health* [1950] 1 Ch 637, 642.

[64] *In re Roberts (decd); Stenton v Hardy* [1963] 1 WLR 406 (Ch) 413.

[65] Noted in: RP Meagher and WMC Gummow (eds), *Jacobs' Law of Trusts in Australia* (6th edn, Butterworths, Sydney, 1997) [1084].

[66] As Cotterrell notes, they would appear to be mutually exclusive, in that the donor would surely have one aim uppermost in his mind, but that Goff J in *In re Finger's WT* seemed to adopt the cumulative approach: RBM Cotterrell, 'Gifts to Charitable Institutions: A Note on Recent Developments' (1972) 36 *Conv* 198, 199.

[67] See, for recent discussion/endorsement of relevant English law by the Western Australian Supreme Court: *The Public Trustee (Estate of Hodge (decd)) v Cerebral Palsy Assn of Western Australia Ltd* [2004] WASC 36, and earlier, by the Supreme Court of Victoria in: *Re Goodson (decd)* [1971] VR 801.

[68] See, eg, for discussion/endorsement of relevant English law in various provinces: *Rowland v Vancouver College Ltd* (2001), 94 BCLR (3d) 249, 205 DLR (4th) 193 (BCCA); *Re Tufford* (1984), 45 OR (2d) 351, 6 DLR (4th) 534 (Ont CA); *Re Machin* (1979), 9 Alta LR (2d) 296, 101 DLR (3d) 438 (Alta SC); and see also, for academic consideration of pertinent English/Canadian law: DWM Waters, *Law of Trusts in Canada* (2nd edn, Carswell, Toronto, 1984) 614–619; OLRC, *Report on the Law of Charities* (1996) 398–422.

[69] DWM Waters, *Law of Trusts in Canada* (2nd edn, Carswell, Toronto, 1984) 615; RBM Cotterrell, 'Gifts to Charitable Institutions: A Note on Recent Developments' (1972) 36 *Conv* 198, 199; P McLoughlin and C Rendell, *Law of Trusts* (MacMillan Publishers, London, 1992) 278–79; HAP Picarda, *The Law and Practice Relating to Charities* (3rd edn, Butterworths, London, 1999) 328; G Dal Pont, *Charity Law in Australia and New Zealand* (OUP, Oxford, 2000) 289.

	The disposition conveying the charitable gift on trust	The problem with the gift	Construing the disposition: the gift will not fail (and no *cy-près* scheme will be required) if . . .
A	T leaves £10,000 for the Multiple Sclerosis Relief Charity, Redgate [this is an unincorporated association]	prior to T's death, the Multiple Sclerosis Relief Charity ceased to exist; it has been amalgamated with other small charities in Redgate to form the Redgate Care Society (or otherwise taken over by another entity)	the Multiple Sclerosis Relief Charity is construed to have continued in modified form—the gift is construed to augment the funds which are held for the MS Relief Charity; the gift is thus transferred to the Redgate Care Society for its use
B	As above	prior to T's death, the Multiple Sclerosis Relief Charity changed its name to the Redgate Benevolent Charity for the Sick	as above, the gift is construed to augment the funds of the Multiple Sclerosis Relief Charity
C	As above	prior to T's death, the Multiple Sclerosis Relief Society had ceased to exist; there was no amalgamation, taking over, or change of name	the gift is construed as a gift for the purposes of the Multiple Sclerosis Relief Charity, which are for the relief of multiple sclerosis sufferers in Redgate— if that purpose can be carried out by other means, the gift will be applied to those purposes
D	T leaves £10,000 for the Multiple Sclerosis (Redgate) Ltd [a company limited by guarantee]	prior to T's death, Multiple Sclerosis (Redgate) Ltd is wound up	the gift is construed as a gift for the purposes of the company, which are for the relief of multiple sclerosis sufferers in Redgate—if that purpose can be carried out by other means, the gift will be applied to those purposes

1. Augmentation: Where a Defunct Charitable Donee Continues in Modified Fashion

(a) The relevant rule of construction described

A charity may 'disappear' via amalgamation. The constitution of the charitable trust may confer upon the trustees an express power to amalgamate with other charities with similar purposes; or the charity may comprise a 'small charity' which is statutorily permitted to amalgamate in specified circumstances;[70] or the trustees may make application to the Charity Commissioners for permission to do so;[71] or the amalgamation may occur informally.[72] Where, under scenario A, the Multiple Sclerosis Relief Charity amalgamates with another charity at some point prior to the testator's death, such that its functions are assumed by a successor institution, then the court may regard the original charity as still being in existence but merely continuing in another form—so that any gift on trust to the charity by its original name passes to augment the funds of the successor charity. On this basis, the gift in scenario A will be validly applied for the benefit of the Redgate Care Society, the charitable institution now administering the trust funds of the defunct charity.

The leading example of this rule of construction remains the early case of *In re Faraker; Faraker v Durell*,[73] in which a testatrix bequeathed a legacy of £200 to 'Hannah Bayly's Charity' for the benefit of widows living in Rotherhithe. In 1905, six years prior to the testatrix's death, the Charity Commissioners created a scheme under which this nominated charity (and its fund) was consolidated with the funds of 13 other charities under the name, 'Consolidated Charities'. The funds (amalgamated) from all 14 charities were thereafter held by this successor charity as one fund 'for the benefit . . . of the poor of the ancient parish of Rotherhithe'. No express provision was made in this 1905 scheme for widows in Rotherhithe. The question was whether the legacy of £200 had failed. It was held not.[74] Hannah Bayly's Charity had not ceased to exist, for its objects were subsumed within those of the consolidated charity; to omit to refer to widows in those objects was a mere 'slip'; and the Commissioners had no power to end the life of the Hannah Bayly's Charity, and certainly not by virtue of the administrative scheme which they undertook in

---

[70] See: Charities Act 1993, s 74(4).

[71] Charities Act 1993, s 16(1), under the exercise of the Charity Commissioners' concurrent jurisdiction with the High Court.

[72] As in: *In re Dawson's WT; National Provincial Bank Ltd v National Council of the YMCA Inc* [1957] 1 WLR 391 (Ch) 396 (the 'Church Association of 13–14 Buckingham St Strand London' amalgamated informally with the 'National Church League (Inc)' which had similar objects, to form the 'Church Society'). For other scenarios/cases illustrating informal amalgamations, see: *Halsbury's Laws of England* (4th edn reissue, Butterworths, London, 1996) vol 5(2), [148].

[73] [1911–1913] All ER Rep 488 (CA) 493.

[74] At first instance, Neville J held (reported at *ibid*, 491) that the legacy had lapsed, the charity intended to be benefited being extinct; the decision was reversed unanimously on appeal.

1905.[75] Thus, the legacy took effect in favour of the Consolidated Charities. The *Faraker* principle has been applied upon numerous occasions since.[76]

The rule of construction can also apply where, prior to the gift taking effect, some administrative aspect of the charity is legally altered by the trustees acting either pursuant to the trust instrument[77] or under an administrative scheme by the Charity Commissioners.[78] A charitable bequest to a named institution or object may become problematical where there has been a change of name, or a change of the trustees, or even a change of site of the charitable operations. In these circumstances, the property can be validly applied to the 'new' charity and the gift will not lapse.

Therefore, under scenario B, there is no scope for the gift of £10,000 to the Multiple Sclerosis Relief Charity to be applied *cy-près*. It has been judicially reiterated that this is not a *cy-près* application, but merely an exception to the circumstances in which a trust will fail.[79]

---

[75] *Ibid*, 493–94.

[76] Eg, in none of the following cases did the original charitable gift lapse, instead, it was dedicated to the purposes of the successor charitable institution or object, such that the testator in each case intended to contribute to the endowment of the charity in reconstituted form: *In re Morgan's WT; Lewarne v Minister of Health* [1950] 1 Ch 637, 638 (gift of residuary estate to Passmore Edwards Cottage Hospital; following nationalisation of health service in 1946, the hospital buildings etc vested in Minister of Health free from trusts, and existing management committee dissolved); *In re Withall; Withall v Cobb* [1932] 2 Ch 236, 242 (gift of residuary estate to Margate Cottage Hospital; at time of testatrix's death, all this hospital's work, staff, patients, had been transferred to new hospital, 'Margate and District General Hospital'); *In re Lucas; Sheard v Mellor* [1948] Ch 424, 430 (gifts of legacy and residuary estate to 'the Crippled Children's Home, Lindley Moor, Huddersfield'; 'the Huddersfield Home for Crippled Children' had been carried on at Lindley Moor since 1916, but was closed before the date of the will; under a scheme by the Charity Commissioners, a new charity, 'the Huddersfield Charity for Crippled Children' was established for sending crippled children to holiday or convalescent homes). Also see, for further endorsement and/or application of the *Faraker* principle: *In re Hutchinson's WT; Gibbons v Nottingham Area No 1 Hospital Management Committee* [1953] 1 Ch 387, 393–94; *In re Vernon's WT; Lloyds Bank Ltd v Group 20 Hospital Management Committee (Coventry)* [1972] Ch 300, 303; *In re Bagshaw (decd); Westminster Bank Ld v Taylor* [1954] 1 WLR 238 (Ch); *In re Dawson's WT; National Provincial Bank Ltd v National Council of the YMCA Inc* [1957] 1 WLR 391 (Ch); *In re Slatter's WT; Turner v Turner* [1964] Ch 512; *In re Roberts (decd); Stenton v Hardy* [1963] 1 WLR 406 (Ch); *In re Frere (decd); Kidd v Farnham Group Hospital Management Committee* [1951] Ch 27.

[77] See, eg: *In re Bagshaw (decd); Westminster Bank Ld v Taylor* [1954] 1 WLR 238 (Ch), wherein the objects and name of the original charity 'B & District War Memorial Cottage Hospital' was legally altered through machinery in the trust deed to 'B & District 1914–18 War Memorial Charity', the new objects being to provide (a) such additional hospital benefits of a charitable nature for the benefit of the inhabitants of the district as might not be provided under the National Health Service Act, 1946, and (b) charitable assistance for necessitous ex-service men or women of the district or their dependants. The charity continued to maintain the hospital.

[78] See, eg: *In re Faraker; Faraker v Durell* [1911–1913] All ER Rep 488 (CA); *In re Lucas (decd); Sheard v Mellor* [1948] Ch 424, wherein schemes established by the Charity Commissioners altered the names and objects of the charities concerned.

[79] Eg: *In re Bianco (decd); Cox v A-G (Vic) (Vic SC, 23 Sep 1997); Abercrombie Estate v Etobicoke (City) Board of Education* (Ont SCJ, 9 Feb 2004) [15].

(b) Pre-requisites for the rule of construction to apply

It is pertinent to note that, given the wide definition of *cy-près* triggers to be found under the statutory *cy-près* regime contained in s 13 of the Charities Act 1993,[80] the *Faraker* scenario would probably now fall within the *cy-près* regime proper. However, the rule of construction outlined above remains important (ie, bypassing the statutory *cy-près* scheme), given that where a donor makes a specific gift in favour of a specific charitable institution, which *did* exist but which has been shut down or is otherwise defunct, then there is rarely room to infer a general charitable intention; the intention was specific, and no *cy-près* order will be possible.[81] Hence, where a gift cannot be given to the precisely intended charitable donee, and where there is no general charitable intent to enable a *cy-près* application to occur, then the purported reliance upon the *Faraker* principle to salvage the gift is useful.

It requires the establishment of two pre-requisites:

Overlap of the purposes of the original and the successor charities.   Both judicial[82] and academic[83] opinion suggests that the *Faraker* construction will not apply where the objects of the successor charity are manifestly different from those of the original defunct charity. If they are substantially dissimilar, then the *cy-près* jurisdiction would need to be invoked (and if it could not, then the gift would lapse). In *Faraker*,[84] the defunct charity's purposes (relieving the poverty of widows) was held to be subsumed within the consolidated charity's purposes (relieving the poverty of poor persons in the parish, even though the scheme was silent about widows' poverty). As Farwell LJ commented, until the 'happy event' of no poor widows living in Rotherhithe, there would be no room for any *cy-près* scheme.

In contrast, where a testator bequeathed his residuary estate to a charitable organisation, the Rationalist Endowment Fund Ltd, but its assets were later passed (upon dissolution) to the Rationalist Press Association Ltd, whose objects did not include the relief of poverty, the gift failed.[85] The purposes were too dissimilar, and the principle in *Faraker* did not apply. Sometimes the first

---

[80]   In particular, s 13(1)(c), considered further: pp 103–4.

[81]   See pp 81–2.

[82]   Note that, in *In re Morgan's WT; Lewarne v Minister of Health* [1950] 1 Ch 637, 642, the court required proof that the work of the hospital stipulated in the will had always been and was still being carried out on the premises of the newly named hospital. For a more recent example of hospital oncology functions being transferred from one hospital to its statutory successor, which enabled a *cy-près* scheme in favour of the latter hospital to be carried into effect, see: *South Eastern Sydney Area Health Service v Wallace* (NSWSC, 24 Nov 2003) [19].

[83]   Eg: JE Martin, *Hanbury and Martin Modern Equity* (17th edn, Sweet & Maxwell, London, 2005) 455; *Halsbury's Laws of England* (4th edn reissue, Butterworths, London, 1996) vols 5(2) [140]–[141].

[84]   *In re Faraker; Faraker v Durell* [1911–1913] All ER Rep 488 (CA) 493.

[85]   *In re Stemson's WT; Carpenter v Treasury Solicitor* [1970] Ch 16, 26. See also: *In re Roberts (decd); Stenton v Hardy* [1963] 1 WLR 406 (Ch) 413, 416 for a similar conclusion.

instance and successor institutions share very little in common. For example, where a masonic hospital (the recipient of the bequest) ceased to exist in its original character, and was 'carried on' as a private hospital under a new name, character and ownership, the *Faraker* principle was also inapplicable—for one thing, the purposes of the private hospital, as a commercial enterprise run for the profit of its shareholders, were held to be non-charitable.[86]

Assume, for the moment, that the objects of the defunct and the successor charity do overlap. An associated question is whether the bequest of the testator must be applied as it would have been applied by the original charity, or whether *any* application falling within the objects of the amalgamated successor charity will suffice. Again, referring to our example, scenario A (in the previous table), must T's gift of £10,000 be applied for the benefit of the relief of multiple sclerosis sufferers, or can it be used for any one of the purposes for which the Redgate Care Society has been formed? There is some inconsistency on this particular point in English law. On the one hand is the view that the effect of the *Faraker* principle is to defeat the testator's intention to some extent, because a *similarity in purpose* between defunct and successor charities need not be accompanied by a similarity in *expenditure patterns*.[87] Certainly, in that case, Kennedy LJ suggested that there was no obligation upon those administering the bequest to give 'one penny to a widow'. On the other hand, it has been suggested elsewhere[88] that the property should be applied by the successor charity strictly in accordance with the testator's intention to benefit the original charity; and that if it were not, the Attorney-General could, by application, seek that order.[89]

Even though this first pre-requisite focuses upon the respective purposes of the defunct and replacement charities, it must be emphasised that, under this rule of construction, the gift is being construed as a gift to the *charity itself*, and *not* as a gift solely to its purposes. It is that particular point that distinguishes this *Faraker* rule of construction from the second rule of construction which will be considered in Section 2 below.

The continued existence of the original charitable trust.   The *Faraker* construction of a gift also depends upon the continued existence of the original charity in some tangible form, for the gift is taken to augment the endowed trust funds of that donee charity. It has been said that the *Faraker* principle can only apply 'to a charity founded as a perpetual charity';[90] that there must remain

---

[86] *Public Trustee v A-G (NSW)* (NSWSC, 10 Feb 1994) 12.

[87] JE Martin, *Hanbury and Martin Modern Equity* (17th edn, Sweet & Maxwell, London, 2005) 455. Cf: G Watt, *Trusts and Equity* (OUP, Oxford, 2003) 318, who regards the question as uncertain.

[88] *In re Morgan's WT; Lewarne v Minister of Health* [1950] 1 Ch 637 (ordered that legacy be paid to successor charity hospital management committee; to be available only for the work that had been carried on at the Passmore Edwards Cottage Hospital nominated by the testator, which had been taken over following nationalisation).

[89] *In re Withall; Withall v Cobb* [1932] 2 Ch 236, 241–42, cited with approval on this point in: *In re Slatter's WT; Turner v Turner* [1964] Ch 512, 523.

[90] *In re Bagshaw (decd); Westminster Bank Ld v Taylor* [1954] 1 WLR 238, cited with approval in: *In re Stemson's WT; Carpenter v Treasury Solicitor* [1970] Ch 16, 22.

in existence funds perpetually dedicated to the charity;[91] and that it does not apply to a case where the donee charity was liable to dissolution under its own constitution.[92] For this reason, Watt makes the practical point that '[e]ven after amalgamation it may be wise to leave the basic administration of the original charity intact to avoid problems of the sort that arose in *Re Faraker*.'[93]

Some cases indicate that the original charity may subsist in another form by the most tenuous means. For example, in *In re Wedgwood; Sweet v Cotton*,[94] a legacy to 'Saint Mary's Home for Women and Children of 15 Wellington Street Chelsea' was challenged as invalid when, prior to the testatrix's death, the name of the charity changed, its location changed to Trafalgar Square, and it operated under different management. Nevertheless, it was held that the gift was valid: there was no material alteration in substance, nor any break in the continuity of the institution.[95] In another case, a gift was upheld to a school that was only operating on one day a week at the time of the testatrix's death, but was 'still existing—in a poor way it may be, but it is still alive, not dead, even if it be moribund.'[96] The artificiality of the *Faraker* rule has been called into question by Waters, who notes that if the testator was a member of a group of persons who banded together for some charitable cause, and that institution amalgamates with others rather than wind up and disband, 'is it legitimate to find continuing identity in the [institution] . . . when what the testator foresaw as an institution has really gone?'[97] Despite such misgivings, the law remains that a charity will not be taken to have ceased to exist if there continues to be funds held in trust for the purposes of the charity,[98] and if the change is 'merely in its mechanical aspect'.[99]

The situation will be quite different where the charity has ceased to exist altogether, 'by exhaustion of all its assets and cessation of its activities'.[100] The *Faraker* principle will not apply to save a gift that was made to a charity that could dissolve itself by virtue of the powers contained in the trust instrument. In *In re Stemson's WT*, Plowman J stated the proposition thus:

---

[91] *In re Slatter's WT; Turner v Turner* [1964] Ch 512, 527; DJ Hayton and C Mitchell, *Hayton and Marshall Commentary and Cases on the Law of Trusts and Equitable Remedies* (12th edn, Sweet & Maxwell, London, 2005) 511; HAP Picarda, *The Law and Practice Relating to Charities* (3rd edn, Butterworths, London, 1999) 334.

[92] *In re Stemson's WT; Carpenter v Treasury Solicitor* [1970] Ch 16, 25; *In re Roberts (decd); Stenton v Hardy* [1963] 1 WLR 406 (Ch) 413–14; *In re Hutchinson's WT; Gibbons v Nottingham Area No 1 Hospital Management Committee* [1953] 1 Ch 387, 393 ('if it is a gift for the general work of that charity and is to be construed as a gift in augmentation of the funds of the charity, there cannot be a lapse because the charity cannot die').

[93] G Watt, *Trusts and Equity* (OUP, Oxford, 2003) 319.

[94] [1914] 2 Ch 245. See also; *In re Glass' WT* [1950] Ch 643.

[95] *Wedgwood, ibid*, 250.

[96] *In re Waring; Hayward v A-G* [1907] 1 Ch 166, 171.

[97] DWM Waters, *Law of Trusts in Canada* (2nd edn, Carswell, Toronto, 1984) 616.

[98] Noted in *In re Stemson's WT; Carpenter v Treasury Solicitor* [1970] Ch 16, 26.

[99] *In re Vernon's WT; Lloyds Bank Ltd v Group 20 Hospital Management Committee (Coventry)* [1972] Ch 300, 304.

[100] *Ibid*, 304.

a charitable trust which no one has power to terminate retains its existence despite such vicissitudes as schemes, amalgamations and change of name so long as it has any funds. It follows, in my judgment, that where funds come to the hands of a charitable organisation, such as REF, which is founded, not as a perpetual charity but as one liable to termination, and its constitution provides for the disposal of its funds in that event, then if the organisation ceases to exist and its funds are disposed of, the charity or charitable trust itself ceases to exist and there is nothing to prevent the operation of the doctrine of lapse.[101]

The outcome and reasoning in this case (and others like it[102]) have been criticised[103] on the basis that, by saying that the gift must lapse if there are no continuing funds, takes away from the main point that the funds were devoted to charitable purposes—and that, what ought to be asked instead is whether the *purposes* to which the funds were to be devoted still exist. However, the line of authority persists.

Significantly, in *Stemson*, Plowman J was dealing with a corporate charity, not an unincorporated association. Whether the *Faraker* principle applies at all to defunct charitable corporations, which are liable to dissolution by the inherent nature of their constitutions, is doubtful—although views are not entirely consistent on this point in English law either. Certainly, the decision in *Stemson*[104] supports the proposition that the *Faraker* principle has no application where the charity is a company, any more than it has where there is bequest to an unincorporated charity with a clause in its constitution enabling it to be wound up. In *Stemson*, the residuary gift was made to the company Rationalist Endowment Fund Ltd (REF), the memorandum of association of which contained a clause to the effect that on a winding-up, any surplus assets should be transferred to some other institution having similar objects. The REF was dissolved in 1965 and, pursuant to that clause, it transferred its assets to the Rationalist Press Association Ltd, a charitable company, although with no objects for the relief of poverty corresponding with those of REF. Plowman J held that the gift to the REF was a gift to the corporation outright; that this charitable trust ceased to exist when the REF ceased to exist, so that the residuary gift lapsed.[105] Thus, the case stands for the proposition that there can be no continuity of the charity, and the *Faraker* principle cannot apply, where the original charitable corporation is dissolved, and where another which has similar objects benefits from a clause applying those assets to like

---

[101] *In re Stemson's WT; Carpenter v Treasury Solicitor* [1970] Ch 16, 26. Also see: *In re Slatter's WT; Turner v Turner* [1964] Ch 512, 526 ('The hospital had no endowments which were dedicated to its general work, and through which . . . it could sustain its existence'; no general charitable intent either, so the gift lapsed).

[102] *In re Withall; Withall v Cobb* [1932] 2 Ch 236; *In re Lucas; Sheard v Mellor* [1948] Ch 424 (CA); *In re Slatter's WT; Turner v Turner* [1964] Ch 512.

[103] J Martin, 'The Construction of Charitable Gifts' (1973) 38 *Conv* 187, 191.

[104] *In re Stemson's WT; Carpenter v Treasury Solicitor* [1970] Ch 16, 22, and citing earlier authority, eg: *In re Servers of the Blind League* [1960] 1 WLR 564 (Ch).

[105] See: *In re Stemson's WT; Carpenter v Treasury Solicitor* [1970] Ch 16, 26.

charities upon termination: '[t]ermination is termination, however similar the purposes.'[106]

The decision in *In re Vernon's WT; Lloyd's Bank Ltd v Group 20 Hospital Management Committee (Coventry)*,[107] however, offers some contrast. A residuary gift was left to a charitable corporation, the 'Coventry and District Crippled Children's Guild' which owned an orthopaedic hospital. Following nationalisation of the health service, the company was dissolved and the hospital vested in the Minister of Health. The decision does not support the view that *Faraker* has no application to companies which have been wound up—for in that case, the legacy to the incorporated guild survived: 'the bequest took effect at the death of the testatrix in favour of the charity then being conducted by [the NHS hospital management committee] in unbroken continuance of the charity which at the date of the will was being conducted by the incorporated guild.'[108]

The decision in *Vernon* has caused some consternation. It has been suggested by courts elsewhere[109] that *Vernon* should be restricted to its facts, and that the decision would have been different if, instead of there being a *compulsory* transfer of its property following nationalisation, the guild had been wound up and had transferred its property elsewhere. In that event, it is unlikely that the gift would have survived. Cotterrell[110] advances the most likely view that *Vernon* is an instance of the judicial policy to save charitable gifts 'at all costs', but in doing so, the requirement that the assets must be subject to continuing trusts for charitable purposes has been all but removed, leaving the first pre-requisite (a cross-over of purposes) to alone provide some doctrinal consistency.

We now turn to the second of the possible rules of construction that can be used to save a charitable bequest, but avoid the employment of the *cy-près* doctrine.

2. A Gift on Trust for the *Purposes* of a Defunct Unincorporated Charity

If the charitable gift cannot be construed as a gift to an apparently defunct association that can be identified as a continuing institution, there is another possible course by which to save the gift, regardless of any *cy-près* analysis.

---

[106] JD Davies, 'Trusts' [1969] *ASCL* 393, 394.

[107] [1972] Ch 300.

[108] *Ibid*, 305.

[109] See: *The Public Trustee (Estate of Hodge (decd)) v Cerebral Palsy Assn of Western Australia* [2004] WASC 36, seeking to reconcile the two cases. This decision favoured the *Stemson* view.

[110] RBM Cotterrell, 'Gifts to Charitable Institutions: A Note on Recent Developments' (1972) 36 *Conv* 198, 201–2.

(a) The presumption described

Where a gift is made to a named unincorporated charitable institution, and that charity no longer exists under that name or indeed, at all, the following presumption ('the *Vernon* presumption') applies:

> Every bequest to an unincorporated charity by name without more must take effect as a gift for a charitable purpose. No individual or aggregate of individuals could claim to take such a bequest beneficially. If the gift is to be permitted to take effect at all, it must be as a bequest for a purpose, *viz.*, that charitable purpose which the named charity exists to serve. . . . A bequest to a named unincorporated charity, however, may on its true interpretation show that the testator's intention to make the gift at all was dependent upon the named charitable organisation being available at the time when the gift takes effect to serve as the instrument for applying the subject matter of the gift to the charitable purpose for which it is by inference given. If so and the named charity ceases to exist in the lifetime of the testator, the gift fails.[111]

Where the presumption applies, then gifts to unincorporated charities are perceived as 'purpose trusts',[112] whereby the institution is a 'mere conduit pipe'[113] for the matching of the property to the charity's purpose.

   This rule of construction means that where, under scenario C of the previous table, the purposes of the MS Relief Society of Redgate were to provide for the relief of suffering caused by the disease, then if the existence of the particular institution carrying out that purpose did not matter to the validity of the gift, it becomes a question of seeking to locate a trustee who *can* carry out the purposes of the trust. Provided that the purposes are still in demand, and can be carried out by other means by some entity which promotes those same purposes, the gift will not lapse. The problem is a reasonably common one—'bequests to a named college, school, hospital, or Home which, prior to the death of the testator, has closed down, moved, amalgamated, expanded or undergone some other potentially significant change, such as a scheme altering its objects'[114]—and the presumption of a purpose trust has rescued many gifts from lapse in England[115] and elsewhere.[116]

---

[111] *In re Vernon's WT; Lloyds Bank Ltd v Group 20 Hospital Management Committee (Coventry)* [1972] Ch 300, 303 (Buckley J).

[112] *In re Edis's Declaration of Trust; Campbell-Smith v Davies* [1972] 1 WLR 1135 (Ch) 1146.

[113] *Von Ernst & Cie SA v Inland Revenue Commissioners* [1980] 1 WLR 468 (CA) 480.

[114] *Re Broadbent (decd); Imperial Cancer Research Fund v Bradley* [2001] EWCA Civ 714, [36].

[115] Eg: *In re Wedgwood; Sweet v Cotton* [1914] 2 Ch 245 (legacy to 'Saint Mary's Home for Women and Children of 15 Wellington Street Chelsea'; change in name, location and management of the charity; no lapse; 'legacy in question is not given to any person or association, but really for a charitable purpose or object, namely, the carrying on of the work of St Mary's Home'); *Re Finger's WT; Turner v Ministry of Health* [1972] 1 Ch 286 (gift of residuary to the unincorporated association, the 'National Radium Commission'; Commission wound up, and its work and assets transferred to Minister of Health; gift was a purpose trust for the work of the Commission; no indication in the will to make that body the essence of the gift); *In re Roberts (decd); Stenton v Hardy* [1963] 1 WLR 406 (gift of residuary to 'Sheffield Boys' Working Home (Western Bank, Sheffield)'; home sold and proceeds of sale transferred to 'Sheffield Town Trust'; no lapse; gift 'not so correlated with the physical

Again, this is strictly not a *cy-près* application of the property; rather, the gift takes effect as if the testator had articulated the *purposes* of the association[117] (although isolated judicial statements adhere to the *cy-près* doctrine in such circumstances[118]). If those purposes continue in *some* form, then there is: no 'failure' of the gift; no need to consider whether the purposes are 'impossible or impracticable' so as to trigger the *cy-près* doctrine; and no need to hunt for any general charitable intent that would be required for initial failure of purpose under the *cy-près* doctrine. Instead, what is looked for under the *Vernon* presumption is that the gift should be construed as one to *purposes*, and not as a gift to the specific charitable association. The fact that this presumption avoids any *cy-près* analysis is vitally important, because if a bequest is made to a charitable institution which does not exist at the date that the gift takes effect, the *cy-près* analysis will only serve to save this bequest if the donor had a general charitable intention (given it is a case of initial failure)—and that general charitable intent can be very difficult to prove where a gift to a named institution is made.

The *Vernon* presumption has rightly been criticised as an example of the 'blurred thinking which confuses so much of this area of the law. For what else is the ascertainment that the testator meant purposes as opposed to a specific institution than a discovery of general charitable intent?'[119] To this criticism may be added that there abound pedantic distinctions as to whether the gift was for an institution or for a purpose, as the following discussion of the prerequisites will show.

(b) Pre-requisites for a 'purpose gift' to an unincorporated charity

Have the purposes of the charity ceased to exist?   If the purposes of the defunct unincorporated charity have ended, such that it is not possible for the work to be

premises where the institution was located that it failed when those premises ceased to exist'). Presumption also approved and/or applied in, eg: *In re Slatter's WT; Turner v Turner* [1964] Ch 512; *In re Watt; Hicks v Hill* [1932] 2 Ch 243; *In re Meyers (decd), London Life Assn v St George's Hospital* [1951] Ch 534; *In re Little (decd); Barclays Bank Ltd v Bournemouth and East Dorset Hospital Management Committee* [1953] 1 WLR 1132 (Ch); *In re Koeppler WT; Barclays Bank Trust Co Ltd v Slack* [1986] Ch 423 (CA); *Re Hunter (decd); Lloyds Bank Ltd v Girton College, Cambridge* [1951] Ch 190.

[116] Eg, in Australia: *Taylor v A-G (NSW)* (NSWSC, 24 Apr 1987) 10–13 (bequest of half of residuary estate to 'Lourdes TB Hospital at Killara' failed; hospital ceased to operate after testator's death; construed as a trust for the purposes of the institution, and that such purposes carried on because the religious order which had run the hospital were involved in the care of aged and infirm needy persons; gift applied *cy-près*). In Canada: *Rowland v Vancouver College Ltd* (2001), 94 BCLR (3d) 249, 205 DLR (4th) 193 (BCCA) [54]–[55]. Rule of construction also approved, but not applied, in: *Re Kunze Estate* (Sask QB, 9 May 2005) [26]–[29].

[117] *English Private Law* (OUP, Oxford, 2003), vol 1, [4.521].

[118] *Conforti v Conforti* (1990), 39 ETR 32 (Ont Gen Div) [8] ('a gift to an unincorporated charitable association is a gift for its purposes and, therefore, the gift will not lapse, notwithstanding the disappearance of the association and institution itself. If the purposes of the former institution are still being carried out by some other body, the gift is applicable by way of *cy-près*'). Also see: *Re Christian Brothers of Ireland in Canada* (2000), 47 OR (3d) 674, 184 DLR (4th) 445 (Ont CA) [75]; *Taylor v A-G (NSW)* (NSWSC, 24 Apr 1987) 10–13.

[119] DWM Waters, *The Law of Trusts in Canada* (2nd edn, Carswell, Toronto, 1984) 615.

carried on in any fashion, then the gift will lapse. As Farwell LJ wryly noted in *In re Faraker; Faraker v Durell*,[120] an institution set up for the relief of poverty of those living in a parish, once defunct, is likely to have its purposes met by other entities.

It may be, however, that the purpose truly has 'died', as occurred in *In re Slatter's WT*.[121] In 1955, a testatrix gave her residuary estate to her trustees on trust 'for the Malahide Red Cross Hospital, of . . . New South Wales, Australia', this hospital having been set up in 1926 for the treatment of patients suffering from tuberculosis. The campaign against tuberculosis in that state was so successful that the hospital became redundant and closed down prior to the testator's death. It was held that the gift could not be saved, and fell into residue. The *Faraker* principle (considered in the previous section) did not apply, because the hospital had no funds dedicated to its general work through which it could sustain its existence (failure of the second pre-requisite); and the *Vernon* presumption could not apply because, on closing down, the hospital's work was not transferred elsewhere, nor could it be construed as a bequest for the benefit of the work performed by the Red Cross generally.[122] This decision hardly supports the mantra that courts will lean in favour of charity, and against lapse, wherever possible. The decision has been criticised[123] on the basis that, whilst TB may have diminished in the locality, surely some scheme could have been devised to apply the gift to the *purposes of TB eradication* more generally. Thus, whether the purposes have 'ceased to exist' is a matter of subjective discernment.

Is the continued existence of the original charity essential to the gift?   If the continued existence of the *particular institution* in that particular place and no other is construed as being a vital part of the testator's intention, then the *Vernon* presumption will not be possible to invoke. In that event, the gift will fail where the specified institution no longer exists.[124]

It has been said that '[t]he cases which have been cited on the point, whether a gift is to a particular institution or a charitable purpose, are not easy to reconcile',[125] and indeed, some pedantic distinctions abound in this area. For example, a gift has been construed as one in favour of a particular (defunct) institution rather than in favour of the successor because of the fact that only one key word in the name of the original charity has been repeated in the successor charity's name;[126] the fact that a 'Home' in one name does not equate

---

[120] [1911–1913] All ER Rep 488 (CA) 494; also see 493 (Cozens-Hardy MR).
[121] [1964] Ch 512.
[122] *Ibid*, 526–27.
[123] J Martin, 'The Construction of Charitable Gifts' (1974) 39 *Conv* 187, 191.
[124] Eg: *Clark v Taylor* (1853) 1 Drew 642; *In re Rymer; Rymer v Stanfield* [1895] 1 Ch 19 (CA); *In re Ovey; Broadbent v Barrow* (1885) 29 Ch D 560, 565.
[125] *In re Roberts (decd); Stenton v Hardy* [1963] 1 WLR 406 (Ch) 415.
[126] *In re Spence (decd); Ogden v Shackleton* [1979] Ch 483.

to an 'Association' in the other name;[127] the fact that the testatrix referred in the bequest to 'the patients' of an 'Old Folks Home', thereby indicating a gift to *those patients* rather than any intention to make a gift to the old people of that district;[128] and that whenever a gift is made, say, to a home for sick children, the motive might be to help with the healing of sick children, but that is not enough to construe the gift as for the carrying on of that particular work.[129] Clearly, these are very narrow parameters by which to judge whether a gift is to a purpose or to a particular institution. Indeed, if one considers that every gift to a particular charitable institution must arguably comprise a gift for its purposes, then it is difficult to draw sensible and consistent distinctions.[130]

A further problem is that some courts have indicated that whether the gift is for a purpose or for an institution is a matter of 'impression'—which, of course, does little for the precedential development of this presumption. In *Estate of Foran (decd); Mair v A-G for NSW*,[131] the testator purported to gift property by will to 'Our Lady of the Sacred Heart Hospital'. No such institution existed, and the court refused to construe this as a 'purpose trust' of the type described above. The evidence of the document itself apparently did not support such a finding:

> The idea that the testator had some charitable object which he wished to achieve, in the achievement of which Our Lady of the Sacred Heart Hospital was employed as a means, but not in a way which made those means essential for the carrying out of his intention, simply has no expression in Mr Jones' will.... The use of the word 'Hospital' in the description might be enough, when taken with the activities of the hospital, to make the gift a charitable gift for the purposes for which the institution was conducted [but] . . . I do not see a clear answer in this particular case.[132]

The most recent leading English example is that of *Re Broadbent (decd); Imperial Cancer Research Fund v Bradley*,[133] in which the testatrix bequeathed a one-third share of her residuary estate to 'The Vicar and Church Wardens of St Matthews Church Stalybridge for the general purposes of such Church but with the request that the money be used primarily for the upkeep of the fabric

---

[127] *Ibid.* Cf: *In re Lucas; Sheard v Mellor* [1948] Ch 424 (CA), where gifts to 'the Crippled Children's Home Lindley Moor Huddersfield' successfully took effect as gifts to 'The Huddersfield Charity for Crippled Children'.

[128] *In re Spence (decd); Ogden v Shackleton* [1979] Ch 483, 493, 496.

[129] *In re Goldney; Goldney v Queen Elizabeth Hospital for Children* [1946] WN 158 (Ch) (gift to St Luke's Home for Sick Children, which had closed down, lapsed; not intended for the purpose of assisting sick children generally).

[130] Note the similar criticism by RP Meagher and WMC Gummow, *Jacobs' Law of Trusts in Australia* (6th edn, Butterworths, Sydney, 1997) [1084]; and *Halsbury's Laws of England* (4th edn reissue, Butterworths, London, 1996) vol 5(2), [141].

[131] (NSWSC, 20 Nov 1987).

[132] *Ibid*, [29]. See also the rather vague words of Lindley LJ in *In Re Rymer; Rymer v Stanfield* [1895] 1 Ch 19, 35 ('You must construe the will and see what the real object of the language which you have to interpret is.... It is a gift of £5,000 to a particular seminary ... and I do not think it is possible to get out of that. I think the context shews it').

[133] [2001] EWCA Civ 714.

of the Church'. The church, which was owned by trustees pursuant to a 1913 charitable trust deed, suffered from an ongoing state of disrepair and falling attendances. It was closed, sold and demolished, and the site used for residential development, prior to Mrs Broadbent's death. Having exercised their power of sale conferred by the 1913 trust deed, the trustees had a continuing duty to apply any proceeds of sale to other religious or charitable purposes that they considered proper.

In these circumstances, it was held that the testatrix's gift did not fail. Three factors were especially important. First, the bequest was not expressly or impliedly tied to the existence of the particular building called 'St Matthew's Church' and the wish to maintain the fabric of the building were precatory words only. Secondly, after the sale, new charitable trusts were created under the 1913 deed, and the 'general purposes of such Church' could encompass applying the proceeds of sale to those new endeavours. Thirdly, the trustees still held the bulk of the proceeds of sale on trust, which funds could be augmented by the testatrix's residuary gift.[134]

3. A Gift on Trust to a Defunct Charitable Corporation

In the obverse scenario to that of bequests to unincorporated associations (where there is a rebuttable presumption that a gift is for a charitable purpose), a bequest to an incorporated charity is presumed to be an absolute gift to be used as part of its general funds. If the corporate charity no longer exists, the gift will fail.

In that regard, gifts to corporations which no longer exist are treated under English law similarly to gifts to natural persons who die before the gift takes effect.[135] The gift occurs 'simply as a gift to [the company] beneficially, unless there are circumstances which show that the [company] is to take the gift as a trustee.'[136] Thus, under scenario D, a gift to Multiple Sclerosis (Redgate) Ltd, no longer existing at the time of T's death, is presumed to fail.[137] Then, it is only if the testator had a general charitable intention when making the bequest to the corporation that the *cy-près* doctrine will save the bequest from lapsing, as the facts of *In re Finger's WT; Turner v Ministry of Health*[138] demonstrated.

---

[134]   *Ibid*, [25]–[28].
[135]   Also noted in: P Todd and G Watt, *Cases and Materials on Equity and Trusts* (5th edn, OUP, Oxford, 2005) 402.
[136]   *In re Vernon's WT; Lloyds Bank Ltd v Group 20 Hospital Management Committee (Coventry)* [1972] Ch 300, 303.
[137]   As Moffat succinctly states, 'the purposes die with the company': G Moffat, *Trusts Law Text and Materials* (4th edn, CUP, Cambridge, 2005) 909.
[138]   [1972] 1 Ch 286 (residuary gift to no-longer-existing National Council for Maternity and Child Care (a body corporate); nothing in the will from which to imply a trust for the carrying on of the council's work; but general charitable intent existed, given the 'very special' circumstances: almost the whole estate was devoted to charity; the Council was itself merely a co-ordinating and supportive body for numerous constituent charitable bodies; and the testatrix regarded herself as having no relatives; applied *cy-près*).

Despite some academic[139] and judicial[140] misgivings about the somewhat anomalous results to which it can give rise, the presumption that gifts to charitable corporations are absolute gifts and not gifts for charitable purposes has been frequently approved[141] and applied[142] in England.

As noted above, the presumption is rebuttable, such that it is open to the beneficiary to seek to prove that the gift was for the *purposes* of the nominated corporation, and not to the corporation itself. It is only rarely that reported cases can be found in English law where a gift will be construed to have been given on trust for the purposes of the company's charitable objects, such that if the company is wound up prior to the testator's death, the gift will validly be applied to other purposes similar to those of the company.[143] The Charity Commissioners have, however, noted[144] that, by a combination of the words used by testators when making their gifts, or by the wording of public appeals instituted by charity corporations, or by virtue of the terms of their memoranda of association, it is a 'very common occurrence' for charity corporations to hold their property on trust for charitable purposes, rather than as part of their general property. Where this is so, and the charity corporation ceases to exist prior to the testator's death, a gift made to that corporation that takes effect after that date will not fail, but can be used by another entity for similar charitable purposes.

Notably, in Australia, the presumption in respect of bequests to corporations outlined above does not hold, and a deliberate departure from the English view has occurred. The Australian High Court noted in *Sydney Homoeopathic*

---

[139] RBM Cotterrell, 'Gifts to Charitable Institutions: A Note on Recent Developments' (1972) 36 *Conv* 198, 203 ('[t]he average donor probably neither knows nor cares whether the donee charity has corporate status or not, and, if he does know, there is, in general, no reason why this should influence his intention either to make his gift to the institution itself or to benefit particular purposes of which it is the instrument'); J Martin, 'The Construction of Charitable Gifts' (1973) 38 *Conv* 187, 195–96 (pointing to a conflict between *Re Meyers* and *Re Finger's*); P McLoughlin and C Rendell, *Law of Trusts* (MacMillan Publishers, London, 1992) 279; HAP Picarda, *The Law and Practice Relating to Charities* (3rd edn, Butterworths, London, 1999) 342.

[140] *In re Finger's WT; Turner v Ministry of Health* [1972] 1 Ch 286, 294 ('I would have thought that there would be much to be said for the view that the status of the donee, whether corporate or unincorporate, can make no difference to the question whether as a matter of constitution a gift is absolute or on trust for purposes': Goff J); *In re Roberts (decd); Stenton v Hardy* [1963] 1 WLR 406 (Ch) ('The mere fact that there is a gift to an unincorporated charity does not seem to me to be enough to enable me to come to the conclusion that it is a gift for charitable purposes').

[141] Eg: *In re Edis's Declaration of Trust; Campbell-Smith v Davies* [1972] 1 WLR 1135 (Ch) 1146 ('A gift to a corporation without more is . . . simply a gift to the body itself not requiring the implication of any trust').

[142] Eg: *In re Stemson's WT; Carpenter v Treasury Solicitor* [1970] Ch 16; *In re Vernon's WT; Lloyds Bank Ltd v Group 20 Hospital Management Committee (Coventry)* [1972] Ch 300; *Re Arms (Multiple Sclerosis Research) Ltd* [1997] 1 WLR 877 (Ch).

[143] *In re Meyers (decd); London Life Assn v St George's Hospital* [1951] Ch 534, 541 (legacies given to some hospitals formerly administered by incorporated bodies but renationalised in 1946 and no longer existing under original name or constitution; gifts did not lapse; given that their work was being continued, 'the gifts to them ought to be construed in the same way as the gifts to the hospitals which had never been incorporated').

[144] *Report of the Ch Comm for England and Wales* (1971) [22]–[25].

Hospital v Turner[145] that a company does not necessarily hold a charitable bequest outright, and that 'if the objects of a body are limited to altruistic purposes, it is as an instrument of altruism that it is likely to attract bene-factions'. Very often in that case (remarked Kitto J), the donor should be taken to have intended a purpose trust, to be held on trust for the purposes stated in the company's memorandum of association.[146] It has since been held by some Australian State courts that the rule articulated in the English cases of *Vernon's WT* and *Finger's WT* should not apply, and that, instead, 'a disposition to a charitable corporation is to be treated as having presumptively the necessary elements creating a trust, so that the disposition to such a charitable corporation takes effect as a trust for the purposes of the corporation rather than as a gift to it'.[147] This simplified position, also recently enunciated by the Ontario Court of Appeal,[148] has received academic approval in England.[149]

E OUSTER OF CY-PRÈS BY THE DONOR

The judicial *cy-près* power can be ousted by a number of further means, noted here for the sake of completeness:

1. Where a *Cy-près* Power is Already Given to the Trustees

First and foremost, if the governing instrument of the charity itself[150] reserves an appropriate power to the trustees of the charity to amend the governing instrument (ie, a 'private *cy-près* power'[151]), and so permitting the objects of the charity to be altered, then there is no need to rely upon the judicial *cy-près* power.

---

[145] (1959) 102 CLR 188 (HCA).

[146] *Ibid*, 221.

[147] *Sir Moses Montefiore Jewish Home v Howell and Co (No 7) Pty Ltd* [1984] 2 NSWLR 406, 416, cited with approval in: *The Assn of Heads of Independent Girls Schools of Vic v A-G (Vic)* (SC Vic, 27 Oct 1989); *Public Trustee (Estate of Hodge (decd)) v Cerebral Palsy Assn of Western Australia Ltd* [2004] WASC 36.

[148] Eg: *Re Christian Brothers of Ireland in Canada* (2000), 47 OR (3d) 674, 184 DLR (4th) 445 (Ont CA) [74] ('The public policy which the courts wish to implement is to save charitable gifts and to apply them as far as possible to the purposes intended by the donor . . . To do that, the court can determine that a gift was intended as a trust, even though left to a corporate charity, in order to save the gift where the particular corporate charity is no longer available to receive the gift').

[149] RA Pearce and J Stevens, *The Law of Trusts and Equitable Obligations* (3rd edn, Butterworths, London, 2002) 546–47.

[150] This could be: a trust deed, a will, a constitution, a conveyance document, a Royal Charter, a scheme drawn up by the Charity Commissioners, or other formal document: Charity Comm for England and Wales, *Small Charities* (2004) 2.

[151] EL Fisch, *The Cy-près Doctrine in the United States* (Matthew Bender & Co, Albany NY, 1950) 223.

Such a clause has been strongly recommended[152] on the basis that (a) the trustees will need to apply for a *cy-près* scheme where, due to impossibility or impracticability, it becomes necessary for the trustees to depart from the terms of the trust and alter the objects, or else the trustees will be in breach of trust; (b) without such a clause, the courts (or Charity Commissioners) can only act if there is a *cy-près* trigger; an express power to amend the charity's objects may, according to its terms, be exercisable in cases where the *cy-près* triggers do not actually exist. Where a private *cy-près* power exists in a will (by adopting wording such as, 'or as nearly corresponding thereto as the circumstances of the case will admit'[153]), then those words compel execution of the will's terms *cy-près*, if the specified mode of performance is not possible.

Recommended *cy-près* clauses have been helpfully drafted for various legal structures under which a charity may operate.[154] For example, for a charitable trust:

> This Deed may be amended by supplemental deed on a resolution of the Trustees but no amendment is valid if it would make a fundamental change to the Objects or to this clause or destroy the charitable status of the Trust.[155]

For an unincorporated charitable association:

> This constitution may be amended at a general meeting by a two-thirds majority of the votes cast, but the members must be given 21 clear days' notice of the proposed amendments. No amendment is valid if it would make a fundamental change to the Objects or to this clause or destroy the charitable status of the Association.[156]

A 'fundamental change' is one that would not have been within the reasonable contemplation of the donor when making the donation to the trust or to the association.

For a charitable corporation, a company may usually alter its objects clauses by special resolution, although where any alteration directs or restricts how the property may be applied, that amendment is ineffective unless consented to by the Charity Commissioners.[157]

---

[152] P Luxton, *The Law of Charities* (OUP, Oxford, 2001) 270, 575; LA Sheridan and VTH Delany, *The Cy-près Doctrine* (Sweet & Maxwell, London, 1959) 134 ('The bestowal of a discretion upon trustees is in the nature of a personal *cy-près* power created by the settlor, and provided it is properly exercised, it will often prevent the necessity of an application to the court'). Also see: Ch Comm for England and Wales, *Responsibilities of Charity Trustees* (1992) 17.

[153] Eg: as were at issue in: *In re Shelton's Settled Estate; Shelton v Shelton* [1945] Ch 158.

[154] For discussion of the various possible legal structures, see: D Simon, 'Shopping for the Best Charitable Structure—Some Thoughts for Would-be Settlors and Trustees' (2000 Aug) *Trusts and Trustees* 16.

[155] See: F Quint, *Charity Law Association Model Documents—Trust Deed for a Charitable Trust* (NGO Finance, London, 1997) cl 8.

[156] See: F Quint, *Charity Law Association Model Documents—Constitution for a Charitable Unincorporated Association* (NGO Finance, London, 1997) cl 12.

[157] Charities Act 1993, s 64(2).

Significantly, whether or not the governing documents of the charity contain a power to amend the purposes, the trustees must constantly review their effectiveness; they are statutorily obliged to do so.[158]

2. Gift-over Provisions

The *cy-près* doctrine only applies where, on a true construction of the trust deed or will, the property has been given to charity, absolutely and perpetually.[159] In some circumstances, however (called, in some quarters, 'gifts of limited duration'[160]), the donor may expressly provide what the trustees are to do if the objects of the charitable bequest are impossible or impracticable to fulfill—in which case there is no necessity to have recourse to the *cy-près* doctrine at all. Effectively, wherever the instructions in the trust instrument are precise and performable in the event of failure of the charitable bequest (eg, that the trust property is to be applied to another institution or purpose), a *cy-près* distribution cannot be carried out.[161]

In the alternative, there may be some indication that the donor has reserved an interest to *himself*, should the charitable bequest fail. Where it was the donor's intention that, once the particular way specified by him for giving effect to his charitable intentions had been carried out, the property should pass in a certain direction, the doctrine is ousted.[162] In the early case of *In re Slevin; Slevin v Hepburn*,[163] Kay LJ contemplated that such cases may exist: 'it is possible that a will might be so framed as that a subsequent failure of the object of the charitable gift might occasion a resulting trust for the benefit of the testator's estate.'

Where, on the other hand, the court is satisfied that the donor never contemplated the possibility that the manner in which he wished his purposes to be

---

[158] Charities Act 1993, s 13(5); and see too, Ch Comm for England and Wales, *Responsibilities of Charity Trustees* (1992) 17.

[159] *In re Cooper's Conveyance Trusts; Crewdson v Bagot* [1956] 1 WLR 1096 (Ch) 1102, citing: HG Carter and MF Crawshaw, *Tudor on Charities* (5th edn, Sweet & Maxwell, London, 1929) 141.

[160] See, eg: *Halsbury's Laws of England* (4th edn reissue, Butterworths, London, 1996) vol 5(2), [165].

[161] For discussion, see: JG Riddall, *The Law of Trusts* (6th edn, Butterworths, London, 2002) 1–2; LA Sheridan, *Keeton and Sheridan's The Modern Law of Charities* (4th edn, Barry Rose Law Publishers, Chichester, 1992) 255; *Halsbury's Laws of Australia* (Butterworths, Sydney, 1991–) [looseleaf] [75–700]; OLRC, *Report on the Law of Charities* (1996) 411; AJS Paines, 'Charity and the NHS—Use or Abuse' (1994) 5 *PCB* 338, 342–43.

[162] *Perpetual Trustees Tasmania Ltd v A-G (Tasmania)* (S Ct, 18 Nov 1993, Zeeman J) 9 (no contrary intention evident there; 'the deceased clearly intended that he part with the trust property once and for all and did not even contemplate the possibility that the manner in which he wished his objects to be carried out might cease to be capable of being given effect to'; property applied *cy-près*); *Hambermehl v A-G* (Ch, 31 Jul 1996) ('if the charitable trusts immediately came to an end on the operation of the reverter, there would be . . . a complete determination of the trust, so that there would be no power to direct any *cy-près* application', citing: *A-G v Price* [1912] 1 Ch 667).

[163] [1891] 2 Ch 236 (CA) 239.

carried out might cease to be capable of being given effect to, and what should happen to the property in the event of failure, the *cy-près* doctrine applies. It is a question of construction.

Key indicators of ouster have included the following:

Valid gift-over provision. There are two possible scenarios: where a donor creates a trust for charitable purposes with a valid gift-over provision to other objects (charitable or non-charitable) if the prior trust fails;[164] or expressly stipulates that, upon a failure of the object of the charitable bequest, the property should revert to the donor or to his estate.[165] These types of clauses have been sufficient to deny the doctrine's application (although successful examples of such a disposition have been judicially noted to be rare[166]).

The leading case in which the *cy-près* doctrine was ousted in this way occurred in *In re Randell; Randell v Dixon*.[167] The testator bequeathed a sum of money on trust to pay the income to the church vicar, so long as he permitted the pews to be occupied free, but in case pew rents were ever demanded, the trust monies were to be dealt with as part of her residuary estate. The gift-over was valid, and no *cy-près* distribution of the monies was permitted.

An invalid gift-over provision, which nevertheless precludes any cy-près. Suppose that the gift-over provision with which the donor sought to control the property, should the initial charitable bequest fail, was held to be invalid as offending the rule against perpetuities. Nevertheless, it may be held that the testator indicated that he intended to limit his gift to the amount necessary for the particular purpose named and for no more.[168] That particular construction will also oust the *cy-près* doctrine.

An illustration of this occurred in *In re Cooper's Conveyance Trusts; Crewdson v Bagot*.[169] By deed dated 1864, land and buildings thereon were

---

[164] RP Meagher and WMC Gummow, *Jacobs' Law of Trusts* (6th edn, Butterworths, Sydney, 1997) [1070]; DWM Waters, *Law of Trusts in Canada* (2nd edn, Carswell, Toronto, 1984) 627, citing: *Power v AGNS* (1903), 35 SCR 182. For an English example, see: *In re Hanbey's WT; Cutler's Co v President and Governors of Christ's Hospital, London* [1956] Ch 264 (bequest to a charity school, with a gift-over in favour of Christ's Hospital if first charitable gift impracticable to carry out; court declined to order any *cy-près* scheme, and ordered that the gift-over take effect).

[165] Noted, eg, in LS Bristowe and WI Cook, *The Law of Charities and Mortmain* (Reeves and Turner, London, 1889) 144, citing, in fn (e): *Mayor of Lyons v Adv-Gen of Bengal* (1876) LR 1 App Cas 91 (PC) 115.

[166] *In re Slevin; Slevin v Hepburn* [1891] 2 Ch 236, 239 (having acknowledged that a charitable gift could be of limited duration, '[w]e have not been referred to any such case, nor have we found any'; no resulting trust found here). See later: *In re Wright; Blizard v Lockhart* [1954] Ch 347 (CA) 362 ('Once money is effectually dedicated to charity, whether in pursuance of a general or a particular charitable intent, the testator's next of kin or residuary legatees are for ever excluded'; absolute gift held there).

[167] (1887) 38 Ch D 213. This, and other case of its type, are discussed more fulsomely in: *Gibson v South American Stores (Gath & Chaves) Ltd* [1950] Ch 177 (CA).

[168] Cf: *Latimer v Commissioner of Inland Revenue* [2004] UKPC 13, [39], where such a construction was not tenable, further discussed in D Morris, 'Casenote' (2004) 18 *Trust Law Intl* 155.

[169] [1956] 1 WLR 1096 (Ch).

conveyed by a donor to trustees for use as an orphanage for young girls. Due to changes of policy, the orphanage was forced to close in 1954. The grant contained a gift-over, on failure of the trust, to the persons entitled to the Levens Hall mansion house. That gift-over was void as contravening the rule against perpetuities. The question for the court was whether the land and buildings and any proceeds of sale were held on valid charitable trusts to be applied *cy-près*, or whether there was a resulting trust for the estate of the grantor, long since deceased. The latter view prevailed, and the property could not be applied *cy-près*. On a true construction of the 1864 deed, and particularly bearing in mind the inclusion of the gift-over provision, the donor had evinced an intention that the charity was only for a limited time and purpose, and that the charity was intended to continue only so long as it could be carried on as an orphan girls' home. When the charity could no longer be carried on, the undisposed-of interest resulted to the donor's estate.[170] In spite of academic criticism,[171] the decision has recently been followed elsewhere.[172]

The decision in *In re Peel's Release*[173] provides a neat contrast. P granted an acre of land to his trustees to permit it to be used 'for ever thereafter' as a school for the education of the poor children of the parish. The deed also provided that, if the purposes 'either not take effect, or, having taken effect, shall afterwards cease or determine or be defeated, or the precise objects . . . become prevented', then the land and school-house should revert to the donor's heirs. The school was built, but over the years, the trust income was insufficient to pay for a school mistress or to maintain the buildings, and the school closed. The gift-over was void under the rule against perpetuity, and there could be no reversion to the heirs under that clause. Nevertheless, the heirs argued that the mere inclusion of a gift-over provision in the *inter vivos* deed indicated that the donor had thereby excluded the *cy-près* doctrine from applying, so that the property should result to them. This was rejected. A *cy-près* scheme was ordered, on the basis that the gift-over provision could not oust the *cy-près* jurisdiction, when the bequest used the words, 'for ever thereafter', for those words, indicating that the settlor intended the gift to charity to be absolute and perpetual, took precedence.

---

[170] *Ibid*, 1103.

[171] P Luxton, *The Law of Charities* (OUP, Oxford, 2001) 561; HA Picarda, *The Law and Practice Relating to Charities* (3rd edn, Butterworths, London, 1999) 319 ('it is to be hoped that [*Cooper's*] will not be given further support'); LA Sheridan and VTH Delany, *The Cy-près Doctrine* (Sweet & Maxwell, London, 1959) 114 ('It is submitted, however, that this [abortive] gift over . . . negatived an intention to have a resulting trust, and that the *cy-près* doctrine should have been applied').

[172] *Re Wilmott (decd); Uniting Church in Australia Property Trust (Vic) v Royal Victorian Institute for the Blind* (SC Vic, 2 Dec 1999) (testator wanted house 'for indigent old ladies in the City of Melbourne' established; home closed, due to changing accommodation requirements and inability to attract a caretaker for the premises; charitable gift construed as a gift for a particular charitable use and for a limited time only; no *cy-près* scheme ordered).

[173] [1921] 2 Ch 218.

3. Other Scenarios

In other cases, the very terms of the trust instrument or will, the nature of the recipient, or surrounding circumstances, negative any indication that a perpetual gift to charity was meant, and the *cy-près* doctrine will not apply.

There must be a continuing trust.   Although it is an obvious point, it bears repeating that the court's power to make a *cy-près* scheme depends upon the subsistence of a trust. As one authority made clear, the doctrine relies upon 'the continuance of the trusts as binding on the trustees unless and until varied by law, because if the charitable trusts immediately came to an end on the operation of the reverter, there would be . . . a complete determination of the trust, so that there would be no power to direct any *cy-près* application'.[174]

Conditional gifts compared with trusts.   A trust of property conveyed for charitable purposes must be distinguished from a conditional gift for charitable purposes. If the conditions which must be satisfied before the recipient can take are not fulfilled, and if the disposition is construed as a conditional gift, then the gift will fail, and there will be no question of the *cy-près* doctrine being invoked. If, on the other hand, the disposition is construed as a charitable trust, which suffers from initial impossibility of performance, and if a general charitable intention is to be found, then the *cy-près* doctrine applies.

It has been said that this is 'a way out of the *cy-près* type problem which is not often utilised',[175] and certainly, its occurrence does appear to be rare. In a recent decision in New South Wales,[176] the Court of Appeal was not satisfied that sufficient consideration had been given to this distinction, and the matter was referred back to trial to determine whether the clause in the testator's will conveying the residuary estate to the National Trust was a trust for charitable purposes (rather than a conditional gift, which had been held at first instance), and if so, whether the property should be applied *cy-près*.

Statutory preclusion.   Occasionally, it has been argued that statutory fetters preclude the operation of the *cy-près* doctrine. This was argued, for example, in *Burnside CC v A-G (South Australia)*.[177] The Council purchased land for use as a public recreation ground at a reduced price, on the understanding that it would hold that land as trustee under declaration of charitable trust. The land was

---

[174] *Re Ingleton Charity; Croft v A-G* [1956] Ch 585, 592.

[175] J Hackney, 'Trusts' [1975] *ASCL* 455, discussing how this distinction was utilised in *State of Uttar Pradesh v Bansi Dhar* [1974] AIR 1084 (SC) (gift of money for a hospital conditional upon State government matching donor's contribution; State never paid money; conditional gift which failed; money resulted back to donor's estate).

[176] *National Trust of Australia (NSW) v Amour* (NSWCA, 3 Dec 1997). For a similar point of distinction, in favour of a trust rather than a conditional gift, see, eg: *In re Peacock* (Tas SC, 16 Dec 1992).

[177] (1993) 61 SASR 107 (Full Ct).

classified as parklands. The Council sought a declaration that it could sell the parklands (known as the Olympic Sports Field) and apply the proceeds *cy-près*.[178] At first instance, it was held that the Council could not sell the land because it was prohibited by statute from selling parkland; and hence, this prohibition overrode any *cy-près* powers that the court may have exercised in relation to the charitable trust. On appeal, that was overturned; it was held that the court did have the power to consider an application to sell the land and to apply the proceeds *cy-près*. The *cy-près* jurisdiction was not ousted, and as Kelledy notes, '[i]n the absence of clear and unequivocal provisions to the contrary, it should always be open to the court to consider an application of trust property *cy-près*'.[179] This is an observation true of all scenarios in which ouster of the *cy-près* jurisdiction is contended.

---

[178] The relevant *cy-près* power is contained in Trustee Act 1936, s 69B.

[179] M Kelledy, 'Trusts, Charities and "Parklands"—The Olympic Sports Field Case' (1995) 1 *Local Govt LJ* 65, 67.

3

Charitable Trusts: General Cy-près

A INTRODUCTION

SIMPLY STATED, THE general law doctrine of *cy-près* applies wherever a trust is used as a method for dedicating property to charity, and where that property cannot be applied in accordance with the intention of the donor. The doctrine enables the court (or, in England, most commonly the Charity Commissioners) to make a scheme for the application of the property for some other charitable purpose 'as near as possible' to the purpose designated by the donor. It will be recalled that, where the gift is made directly with no trust device employed, and the gift fails, the Crown must deal with the property under its prerogative *cy-près* jurisdiction. This chapter will proceed on the basis that the settlor or trustee has used a *trust* to dedicate the property to charity.

The general doctrine of *cy-près* requires that several issues be systematically examined (and in this order[1]). As a preliminary matter, the gift must be directed toward a charitable object (considered in Section B). Next, it must be manifest that the charitable object has become impossible or impracticable to carry out (the so-called *cy-près* triggers). The treatment of this issue under general law will be dealt with in Section C—somewhat briefly, for that aspect of the doctrine has been substantially reformed by statutory *cy-près*, the subject of study in the next chapter. As a further issue, in the case of *initial* failure of the charitable object which is impossible or impracticable to carry out, a general (as opposed to a specific) charitable intention must be proven (Section D). Lastly, some substituted scheme for application of the property which is 'as near as possible' to the donor's intention must be devised. The extent to which that standard, 'as near as possible', must be satisfied will be considered in Section E. Throughout this and the following chapter, emphasis will be placed upon English charitable trusts jurisprudence. However, to the extent that any significant developments in other Commonwealth jurisdictions such as Australia or in Canada differ or else provide a neat illustration of a legal point, these will be highlighted as and where appropriate.

---

[1] The order of treatment of the legal issues is very important to avoid doctrinal confusion, as international commentary has reiterated. Eg, in Australia: *Halsbury's Laws of Australia* (Butterworths, Sydney, 1991–) [looseleaf], 'Cy-près Schemes', [75–705]; in England: M Chesterman, *Charities, Trusts and Social Welfare* (Weidenfeld and Nicolson, London, 1979) 277; in Canada: OLRC, *Report on the Law of Charities* (1996) 403; and in the United States: EL Fisch, *The Cy-près Doctrine in the United States* (Matthew Bender & Co, Albany NY, 1950) 129 and ch 5.

B EXCLUSIVELY CHARITABLE PURPOSES

As a prerequisite to the invocation of any *cy-près* jurisdiction, the purpose for which the gift was originally made must be exclusively charitable. The court cannot apply the property *cy-près* under the traditional auspices of the doctrine if it is not dealing with an *absolute charitable trust*.

Two difficulties can arise when seeking to satisfy this prerequisite: it may be more likely that the bequest is non-charitable (or mixed charitable/ non-charitable which cannot be rendered exclusively charitable by 'blue pencil' statutes); or there may be a gift-over provision that precludes any absolute (also termed an 'out-and-out') gift to charity. Both conundrums have proven to be stumbling blocks when courts have been requested to exercise their jurisdiction to approve a *cy-près* scheme.

1. Defining the Purposes as Charitable

A role for *cy-près* only arises when the trust property was given for exclusively charitable purposes. That is, the trust must fall into at least one of the *Pemsel's* categories[2] of charity—for the relief of poverty, for the advancement of education, for the advancement of religion, or for other purposes beneficial to the community not falling within any of the first three categories—and it must contain some element of benefit to the public generally. Essentially, there are two limbs to proving that a bequest is charitable at law: 'firstly, an element of *benefit*, eg, the relief of poverty, and secondly, an element of *public* benefit.'[3]

As an alternative, where the trust contains a mixture of charitable and non-charitable purposes which are impossible or impracticable, statutory assistance may (where available via 'blue pencil statutes'[4]) be called upon to strike out the non-charitable purposes and to retain the remaining charitable purposes as the sole purposes of the gift, provided that what remains satisfies the testator's presumed intention. Then, a *cy-près* scheme can be drafted.

This two-step course was adopted, for example, in *Public Trustee v A-G (NSW), Jarrett, Muller and Davies*,[5] in which a gift of the testatrix's entire estate

---

[2] *Commissioners for Special Purposes of the Income Tax v Pemsel* [1891] AC 531 (HL) 583 (Lord Macnaghten).

[3] HA Delaney, 'Charitable Status and *Cy-près* Jurisdiction: An Examination of Some of the Issues Raised in *In Re The Worth Library*' (1994) 45 *NILQ* 364, 366 (original emphasis).

[4] These statutes have the effect of validating trusts that are for mixed charitable and non-charitable purposes by omitting the non-charitable portion and construing them as trusts for charitable purposes only. See, eg, Property Law Act 1958 (Vic), s 131(2): 'Any such trust shall be construed and given effect to in the same manner in all respects as if no application of the trust funds or any part thereof to or for any such non-charitable and invalid purpose had been or could be deemed to have been directed or allowed.'

[5] (1997) 42 NSWLR 600, 621 (political trust). For further discussion, see: PW Young (the Hon), 'Charity and Politics' (1997) 71 *ALJ* 839.

to the Federal Council for the Advancement of Aborigines and Torres Strait Islanders failed. The Council, which had ceased to exist some eight years prior to the testatrix's death, had a number of charitable and non-charitable (political) purposes among its main objects, but the latter were capable of severance[6] so that the bequest was 'exclusively charitable', and a *cy-près* scheme was approved. Similarly, in the New Zealand case of *Re Pettit*,[7] a bequest of the residue 'for the general purposes of the Doctors' Widows Fund' failed (there was no such fund), but the bequest was deemed to include some charitable purposes, in that the testatrix clearly intended to benefit a class of doctors' widows who may be needy or aged or impotent. Thus, this was an 'imperfect trust provision'[8] which could be construed as if the residue was applied to exclusively charitable purposes; the word 'general' was replaced by the word 'charitable'; and the court applied the residue to three institutions similar to what the testatrix had in mind, under its *cy-près* power.[9]

   In the absence of such statutory 'blue-pencil' provisions, however, there is no room for manoeuvre. It is not possible for the court to make a *cy-près* scheme for a failed non-charitable gift, even if that gift is one of a series of gifts which are charitable, and is closely related to the charitable gifts. This invokes the principle memorably described by Buckley J, '[i]f you meet seven men with black hair and one with red hair you are not entitled to say that here are eight men with black hair.'[10] In less evocative but equally forthright terms, Lord Wright earlier explained in *Chichester Diocesan Fund and Board of Finance v Simpson* that, where the disposition was made to 'charitable or benevolent objects' and was struck down as invalid, courts have refused to apply the *cy-près* doctrine to cases that mix both charitable and non-charitable (ie, benevolent) purposes: 'the court washes its hands of the administration [such as its *cy-près* scheme-making powers] and holds the entire bequest invalid.'[11] It is certainly

---

[6] Under Charitable Trusts Act 1993 (NSW), s 23. Similar provisions exist in all other Australian States: Property Law Act 1958 (Vic), s 131; Trustee Act 1962 (WA), s 102; Variation of Trusts Act 1994 (Tas), s 4; Trustee Act 1936 (SA), s 69A, Trusts Act 1973 (Qld), s 104.

[7] [1988] 2 NZLR 513. Also mooted as potentially applicable, had one of the four bequests not been charitable, in: *Re Tennant* [1996] 2 NZLR 633, 637. *Re Pettit* is critiqued on this point in: CEF Rickett, 'Charitable Attitudes to Charity' [1989] *NZLJ* 431.

[8] Within the definition of the Charitable Trusts Act 1957 (NZ), s 61B.

[9] Charitable Trusts Act 1957, s 32.

[10] *In re Jenkins's WT* [1966] Ch 249, 256. Cf: *In re Satterthwaite's WT; Midland Bank Executor and Trustee Co Ltd v Royal Veterinary College* [1966] 1 WLR 277 (CA) (testatrix left residuary estate to nine animal protection and animal treatment organisations; one of the nine bequests was to a defunct non-charitable anti-vivisection society; six were charities; one was the 'London Animal Hospital'; the last-mentioned could be applied *cy-près*; there was an overriding general charitable intention on the part of the testator, via the medium of kindness to animals, notwithstanding that one of the beneficiaries was not charitable at law). Later authorities have pointed out the difficulty in reconciling these two cases, eg, in Northern Ireland: *Nesbitt v A-G for Northern Ireland* (Ch, 17 Apr 1991).

[11] [1944] AC 341 (HL) 356 (and earlier, for discussion of 'charitable or benevolent' failing for uncertainty, see: *Re Diplock; Wintle v Diplock* [1941] 1 All ER 193 (CA)). The point is also discussed in *obiter* in: *Re Besterman's WT* (Ch, 21 Jan 1980) (exclusively charitable purposes; but no general charitable intention evident; hence no *cy-près* scheme would have been possible, had the Taylorian at Oxford ceased to exist).

not the function of the doctrine to expand the categories of legally charitable purposes.[12]

It follows that if the court holds that the trust is not a valid charitable one, because either the trust purposes satisfy none of the four *Pemsel* heads of charity exclusively, or they are not for the public benefit, the *cy-près* analysis has absolutely no room in which to operate. The gift will lapse, and result back to the donor or to his estate. Occasionally, this result appears to have been favoured as a matter of policy, and at the expense of the *cy-près* doctrine. As Lord Cross noted,[13] some early attempts to argue that funds held on trust for the relief of poverty were *not* charitable trusts were driven by a desire to ensure that the bequests were returned to the donors or to the estates of the testators, and not applied away from their families, *cy-près*.

It has also been judicially[14] and academically[15] reiterated that it is not permissible, once the gift fails to satisfy *Pemsel's* legal definition of charity, to then hinge the *cy-près* doctrine on a finding that the testator had a 'general intention to benefit charity' when making the bequest. That is not sufficient to permit *cy-près*, if the purposes themselves are not charitable at law.

In notable examples from other jurisdictions, the task of proving that the property was devoted to exclusively charitable purposes, before any *cy-près* scheme could even be countenanced, has not always been straightforward or free from confusion. To take some examples:

from Ireland:

> In *In re The Worth Library*,[16] a bequest was made, under will dated 11 November 1723, to Dr Stevens' Hospital in Dublin of a large and valuable collection of books. The hospital closed in 1988, and the collection was moved to Trinity College Dublin. Application was made for a *cy-près* scheme to permit the library to be permanently housed at the College rather than at the former hospital. However, before dealing with this point, the court struggled to find that the bequest was for the 'public benefit', given that the books were bequeathed to three named office-holders of the hospital. The court eventually held the bequest to be a valid charitable gift under the fourth *Pemsel* head of

---

[12] G Dal Pont, *Charity Law in Australia and New Zealand* (OUP, Oxford, 2000) 299; A Hudson, *Equity and Trusts* (4th edn, Cavendish Publishing, London, 2005) 895.

[13] *Dingle v Turner* [1972] AC 601 (HL) 617.

[14] *Public Trustee v A-G (NSW), Jarrett, Muller and Davies* (1997) 42 NSWLR 600, 609 (the common law *cy-près* doctrine requires that 'before a general charitable intention becomes relevant, the Court must find that the gift is for a charitable purpose'); *In re Sanders' WT; Public Trustee v McLaren* [1954] Ch 265, 273–74; *In re Lysaght (decd); Hill v Royal College of Surgeons* [1966] 1 Ch 191, 201–3.

[15] For further reiteration of this point, see: C Rickett, 'Politics and Cy-près' [1998] *NZLJ* 55, 55–56, and earlier, by the same author: 'Charitable Attitudes to Charity' [1989] *NZLJ* 431, 433; *Halsbury's Laws of Australia* (Butterworths, Sydney, 1991–) [looseleaf], 'Cy-près Schemes', [75–705]; JE Martin, *Hanbury and Martin Modern Equity* (17th edn, Sweet & Maxwell, London, 2005) 457; *Halsbury's Laws of England* (4th edn reissue, Butterworths, London, 1996) vols 5(2), [201]; LA Sheridan and VTH Delany, *The Cy-près Doctrine* (Sweet & Maxwell, London, 1959) 29–30.

[16] [1994] 1 ILRM 161.

charity, on the basis that the library offered a haven of 'intellectual relaxation' for the hospital's office-holders, and as such, was for the benefit of the charity represented by the hospital.[17] A *cy-près* scheme (unspecified in the report) was approved.

from New Zealand:

> In *Re Collier*,[18] the testatrix bequeathed her residuary estate on trust 'to form a charitable trust' for four specified objects: to promote ideas of 'world peace', that the terminally ill be able to die with dignity, voluntary euthanasia, and to promote a government enquiry into the death of the testatrix's friend. None of these objects was held to be charitable at law. The court, however, permitted a *cy-près* application of the residuary estate, finding a general charitable intent in relation to the second-named purpose, especially in the light of 'the general reluctance of Courts to render a construction leading to an intestacy'. The decision has been criticised by Rickett as being wrongly decided ('[i]t is quite illegitimate to use the *cy-près* doctrine to save as charitable— justified on a [general charitable] intention test—a gift which was not charitable').[19]

and from Australia:

> In *Re the former Modbury Primary School*,[20] the A-G (South Australia) sought to invoke a statutory *cy-près* scheme for an alleged trust for educational purposes. The donor had conveyed land to the Crown in 1881, upon the expectation that a primary school would be built there. After 80 years, the site became too small for the primary school, and the land was thereafter used for a community library and for a tertiary college. The A-G sought approval for a *cy-près* scheme for the use of the land. It was held to be unnecessary, as there was no trust for the advancement of education on these facts, merely a political trust of governmental obligation, falling short of a charitable trust. The Minister was thus free to dispose of the land without requiring any court approval or *cy-près* scheme.

Conceptually, therefore, it is important that the doctrine of *cy-près* is not misused or misapplied, so as to simply convert a non-charitable to a charitable trust by saying, 'there is a general charitable intent evident here', and thereafter apply the property to analogous purposes.

2. Providing a Gift-over

The *cy-près* jurisdiction at general law is predicated on the basis that the donor intended to make an absolute and perpetual gift to charity, and that it becomes

---

[17] For a critique of this and other aspects of this case, see: HA Delaney, 'Charitable Status and *Cy-près* Jurisdiction: An Examination of Some of the Issues Raised in *In Re The Worth Library*' (1994) 45 *NILQ* 364.

[18] [1998] 1 NZLR 81. Cf: *Re McIntosh (decd)* [1976] 1 NZLR 308 (SC) (bequest to provide for patients in various hospitals 'creature comforts, additional to what they may have now or at any time hereafter may enjoy, or actual necessities'; held to be for charitable so-called 'luxuries', namely, for care, recreation and recovery of patients, that is, for the relief of the 'aged, impotent and poor people'; *cy-près* scheme appropriate).

[19] C Rickett, 'Politics and *Cy-près*' [1998] *NZLJ* 55, 55–56.

[20] (1997) 69 SASR 497, 500–1.

apparent—either when the gift is to take effect (initial failure) or after the gift has taken effect and been successfully performed for some period of time (subsequent failure)—that carrying out this charitable purpose will be impossible or impracticable. The general position (albeit with limited exception[21]) is that property cannot be considered as dedicated to charity if the donor has expressly provided, at the time of the initial donation, how he wishes the property to be distributed if the charitable purpose should indeed fail or end.[22] As discussed previously, where the donor anticipates the trust's failure, and makes a gift-over in default (whether to another object, or by stipulating that the property should return to himself on a resulting trust), or if he only intends to dedicate the gift to charity for a limited period, then it is not a perpetual dedication to charitable purposes.[23] A *cy-près* scheme in those circumstances will be inappropriate.

C IMPOSSIBILITY OR IMPRACTICABILITY

Traditionally, according to oft-cited expressions of the general doctrine of *cy-près*, it has been invoked only when a reasonably high threshold of difficulty was encountered (all emphasis is the author's):

> there can be no question of *cy-près* until it is clearly established that the directions of the testator *cannot be carried into effect*[24]

> if the particular means is *impracticable*, it is open to the court to frame a scheme *cy-près* for the attainment of the general objects mentioned in the will[25]

> the circumstances in which it was considered appropriate to [invoke *cy-près*] were originally confined to those where it was demonstrated that the original purpose had become impossible or impractical to carry out. In the 19th century, at least, *impossibility or impracticality were narrowly defined*[26]

All of these judicial pronouncements state the triggers for *cy-près* in somewhat differing language. The semantics of the language used in this regard is

---

[21] *Aston v Mt Gambier Presbyterian Charge* (2002) 84 SASR 109 (16/39ths of a residuary estate was left to the 'Scot's Presbyterian Church Building Fund of Mount Gambier'; no such fund ever existed; cl 4 of will provided that, in event of failure of any residuary gift, it fell to be shared with other residuary beneficiaries; did not preclude this from being an exclusively charitable bequest).

[22] *In re Cooper's Conveyance Trusts; Crewdson v Bagot* [1956] 1 WLR 1096 (Ch) 1102 (Upjohn J); *In re North Devon and West Somerset Relief Fund Trusts; Hylton v Wright* [1953] 1 WLR 1260 (Ch); *In re Stanford; Uni of Cambridge v A-G* [1924] 1 Ch 73; *In re Robertson; Colin v Chamberlin* [1930] 2 Ch 71; *Perpetual Trustees Tasmania Ltd v A-G (Tasmania)* (Tas SC, 18 Nov 1993); *Re Canada Trust Co v Ontario Human Rights Comm* (1990), 69 DLR (4th) 321 (Ont CA).

[23] See pp 48–50.

[24] *In re Weir Hospital* [1910] 2 Ch 124 (CA) 132 (Cozens-Hardy MR). For an elegant enunciation, over 100 years earlier, see: *A-G v Boultbee* (1794) 2 Ves 380, 387; 30 ER 683, 687.

[25] *Royal North Shore Hospital of Sydney v A-G (NSW)* (1938) 60 CLR 396 (HCA) 415 (Latham CJ), and see earlier at 414. Also: *A-G (NSW) v Adams* (1908) 7 CLR (HCA) 124–25 (Isaacs J).

[26] *Varsani v Jesani* [1999] Ch 219 (CA) [14].

illustrated perfectly by the variations that occurred throughout early (pre-statute) editions of that seminal text, *Snell's Principles of Equity*. Snell himself noted that the *cy-près* doctrine could only be invoked where 'literal execution of the trusts of a charitable gift become inexpedient or impracticable',[27] but authors of subsequent editions altered this formula in favour of the following: 'inexpedient or impracticable (that is to say, impossible)';[28] and then 'impossible, or at least highly undesirable'.[29] These adjustments of wording were arguably no accident, but rather, a sign of the shifting sands of the appropriate *cy-près* threshold.

Notably, statutory intervention has lowered the threshold somewhat from the strict standard countenanced above, as discussed in the next chapter. The stricter triggers of impossibility or impracticability that justified a *cy-près* application under the general law (and the 'working tests' that were developed to lend some consistency to the law[30]) remain relevant, however, even under the statutory treatments. These general law scenarios can be usefully summarised in the following list:[31]

- the charitable gift is made to a charity that has ceased to exist,[32] or which never existed;[33]
- the charitable purpose was accomplished in full, either from the charitable bequest itself[34] or from external funding sources,[35] and there

---

[27] EHT Snell, *The Principles of Equity* (Stevens and Haynes, London, 1868) 90.

[28] A Brown, *Snell's Principles of Equity* (16th edn, Stevens and Haynes, London, 1912) 71.

[29] HG Rivington and AC Fountaine, *Snell's Principles of Equity* (17th edn, Stevens and Haynes, London, 1915) 95.

[30] As termed in: *Westminster CC v Duke of Westminster* [1991] 4 All ER 136 (Ch) 142 (Harman J).

[31] For alternative lists, with references to different illustrative authorities, see those collected in: JG Riddall, *The Law of Trusts* (6th edn, Butterworths, London, 2002) 180–81; *Halsbury's Laws of Australia* (Butterworths, Sydney, 1991–) [looseleaf], 'Cy-près Schemes', [75–730], [75–735]; HAJ Ford and WA Lee, *Principles of the Law of Trusts* (2nd edn, Law Book Co, Sydney, 1990) 892–907; G Dal Pont, *Charity Law in Australia and New Zealand* (OUP, Oxford, 2000) 294–99; DWM Waters, *Law of Trusts in Canada* (2nd edn, Carswell, Toronto, 1984) 620–22; *Halsbury's Laws of England* (4th edn reissue, Butterworths, London, 1996) vol 5(2), [149]–[156], [205].

[32] Eg: *In re Rymer; Rymer v Stanfield* [1895] 1 Ch 19 (CA) (gift to seminary; ceased to exist; but no *cy-près* scheme ordered in all the circumstances).

[33] Eg: *In re Harwood; Colman v Innes* [1936] Ch 285 (gift to the Peace Society of Belfast; no such society could be shown to have ever existed; *cy-près* scheme ordered). Sometimes, the sources from which the list of charities is compiled are not sufficiently accurate, eg, from the London telephone directory, as in *In re Satterthwaite's WT; Midland Bank Executor and Trustee Co Ltd v Royal Veterinary College* [1966] 1 WLR 277 (CA).

[34] Eg: *In re King; Kerr v Bradley* [1923] 1 Ch 243 (gift for installation and maintenance of stained-glass memorial window in church; substantial surplus after sum set aside for maintenance; *cy-près* scheme ordered).

[35] Eg: *In re Campden Charities* (1881) 18 Ch D 310 (CA) (gift on trust for the relief of poverty in Kensington; very large increase in the funds available for the relief of poverty arose; *cy-près* scheme ordered). For further schemes to widen the purposes of this same trust over 100 years later, see: *Report of the Ch Comm for England and Wales* (1990) [80]–[81].

is no need for any further monies to be devoted to it, leaving an unspent surplus;

- the charitable purpose cannot,[36] or can no longer,[37] be fulfilled because the need for it has entirely disappeared over time;
- whilst it cannot be said that the charitable purpose has been fulfilled, past experience indicates that any need for it in the future is extremely unlikely;[38]
- the trust property provided by the donor is insufficient in amount to carry out the charitable purpose;[39]
- the charitable purpose required the use of land which could not ever be found,[40] or the land comprising the trust property was impossible for the purpose,[41] or ceased to be available,[42] or ceased to be appropriate;[43]
- the donor specified conditions or restrictions upon those who could benefit from the charitable purpose, which the trustees refused to accept (ie, disclaimed) the gift, either at the outset[44] or with the passage of time,[45] because those conditions were viewed to be repugnant (and where the identity of the trustees selected by the donor was essential to the donor's intention[46]);

---

[36] Eg: *Re Moon's WT; Foale v Gillians* [1948] 1 All ER 300 (Ch) (X directed that, after X's wife's death, legacy by will to Methodist church for purposes of missionary work; at date of widow's death, church had been destroyed during WWII bombing; *cy-près* scheme ordered).

[37] Eg: *A-G v Earl of Craven* (1856) 21 Beav 392 (by will dated 1687, gift of money for burying persons who had died from plague; by 1856, plague had been eliminated for several years; *cy-près* scheme ordered).

[38] Eg: *Re Borland* 1908 SC 852 (income for support of young men from locality intending to enter ministry of Church of Scotland; for two decades after charity founded, no applications for support had been made; *cy-près* scheme ordered).

[39] Eg: *Re Whitworth Art Gallery Trusts; Manchester Whitworth Institute v Victoria Uni of Manchester* [1958] Ch 461 (income of charitable corporation founded by royal charter inadequate to conduct museum and art gallery; *cy-près* scheme ordered).

[40] Eg: *Biscoe v Jackson* (1887) LR 35 Ch D 460 (CA) (gift to establish soup kitchen and attached cottage hospital in parish; no suitable land could be found; *cy-près* scheme ordered).

[41] Eg: *A-G (NSW) v Perpetual Trustee Co Ltd* (1940) 63 CLR 209 (HCA) (testator left property, 'Milly Milly', to be used as a farm for training 'orphan lads' in agricultural methods; homestead too small for the purpose, plant antiquated; *cy-près* scheme ordered).

[42] Eg: *Re Comm for Railways and Trustees of St Barnabas' Church, Bathurst* (1887) 8 LR(NSW) Eq 22 (land given on trust for charitable purposes resumed; *cy-près* scheme ordered).

[43] Eg: *Wallis v Solicitor-General of NZ* [1903] AC 173 (PC).

[44] Eg: *In re Lysaght (decd); Hill v Royal College of Surgeons* [1966] 1 Ch 191 (gift to Royal College of Surgeons for studentships for those other than Jews and Roman Catholics; trustees refused to accept on those terms; *cy-près* ordered; conditions dispensed with).

[45] Eg: *In re Robinson; Wright v Tugwell* [1923] 2 Ch 332 (fund for endowment of evangelical church, with condition that black gown should be worn in the pulpit; trust came into effect 1889; by 1923, wearing a black gown in the pulpit detrimental to teaching and practice of evangelical doctrines; *cy-près* scheme ordered; condition dispensed with).

[46] Otherwise, the maxim ordinarily states, 'equity will not let a trust fail for want of a trustee'; this scenario is an exception to that maxim: S Wilson, *Todd and Wilson's Textbook on Trusts* (7th edn, OUP, Oxford, 2005) 305.

- the charitable institution to which the gift was made on trust disclaimed the gift;[47]
- the charitable purpose was an illegal mode of achieving a lawful purpose;[48]
- whilst legal when the donor framed it, the charitable trust became illegal,[49] or at least, a change in the law rendered the achievement of the purpose impracticable[50] or unnecessary;[51]
- the persons who were intended to benefit from the charitable purpose either ceased to exist altogether,[52] dwindled in number so as to make the trust unworkable,[53] or ceased to come forward to receive any benefits from the trust;[54]
- the trustee selected by the donor to administer the charitable trust could not do so because of statutory prohibition (and where the identity and personality of the chosen trustee was not essential to the donor's charitable intention);[55] or
- the donor left money for a charitable purpose that never came into effect.[56]

Hence, it is evident that there was an extensive list of scenarios that could fulfill the requirements of failure—'impossibility' or 'impracticability'—so as to trigger the *cy-près* jurisdiction.

---

[47] Eg: *A-G v Andrew* (1798) 3 Ves 633; 300 ER 1194 (bequest to found scholarship declined by college A; applied *cy-près* to establish a scholarship at a neighbouring college). Note the rules associated with disclaimer by beneficiaries of testamentary gifts: 'if the intended donee disclaims, the subject-matter of the gift either passes to the residuary legatee or, if the donee was the residuary legatee or sole beneficiary under the will, the deceased's estate passes to the next-of-kin under the intestacy rules. If the next-of-kin disclaim, the property becomes *bona vacantia*': J Hill, 'The Role of the Donee's Consent in the Law of Gift' (20010) 117 *LQR* 127, fn 100.

[48] Eg: *A-G v Vint* (1850) 3 De G & Sm 704; 64 ER 669 (bequest to provide poor inmates of workhouse with a 'point of porter each'; doubt whether bringing alcohol into workhouse was legal; gift applied *cy-près* to allow other beverages).

[49] Eg: *In re Bradwell Will Trusts; Goode v Board of Trustees for Methodist Church Purposes* [1952] Ch 575 (gift of income was settled for a period that exceeded the permissible accumulation period).

[50] Eg: *In re the Colonial Bishoprics Fund 1841; Goode v Board of Trustees for Methodist Church Purposes* [1935] Ch 148 (gift to endow cathedral at Cape Town for Church of England in 1841; self-government of colony granted in 1850, depriving Crown of prerogative power to establish bishopric that colony would recognise; *cy-près* scheme ordered).

[51] Eg: *A-G v Gibson* (1835) 2 Beav 317n (trust for the abolition of slavery in the colonies; legislation passed which achieved that object).

[52] Eg: *A-G v London Corp* (1790) 3 Bro CC 171 (trust for the propogation of the Christian religion amongst 'the infidels of Virginia'; no 'infidels' left in Virginia; *cy-près* scheme ordered).

[53] Eg: *In re Buck; Bruty v Mackay* [1896] 2 Ch 727.

[54] Eg: *Philipps v A-G* [1932] WN 100.

[55] *In re Armitage (decd); Ellam v Norwich Corp* [1972] 1 Ch 438 (gift of residuary estate for nursing homes for elderly women; trustee local authority prohibited under Local Government Act 1933, s 268(3) from acting as trustee of 'eleemosynary charities'; gift applied *cy-près*).

[56] Eg: *In re Wilson; Twentyman v Simpson* [1913] 1 Ch 314 (gift by will to pay salary of school master, to teach at specified school; school never built; no *cy-près* scheme ordered (no general charitable intention); but the A-G could enquire how far the intentions of the will could be carried out).

These strict requirements of failure were not always stringently adhered to, however. For example, in *In re Dominion Students' Hall Trust; Dominion Students' Hall Trust v A-G*, in which a trust was established for a students' hall of residence for American and Commonwealth students of 'European origin', Evershed J noted that the word 'impossible' should be construed widely, such that:

> it is not necessary to go the length of saying that the original scheme is absolutely impracticable. Were that so, it would not be possible to establish in the present case that the charity could not be carried on at all if it continued to be so limited as to exclude coloured members of the Empire. . . . But times have changed, particularly as a result of the war; and it is said that to retain the condition, so far from furthering the charity's main object, might defeat it and would be liable to antagonize those students, both white and coloured, whose support and goodwill it is the purpose of the charity to sustain. The case, therefore, can be said to fall within *the broad description of impossibility.*[57]

A simple and useful illustration of the wide approach toward the doctrine is manifest in *Re Morgan (decd); Cecil-Williams v A-G*.[58] A testator bequeathed £3,000 for the purchase of a piece of land as a public recreation ground for amateur activities for the health and welfare of the community. The trustees took the view that a recreation ground was not what the community required at all, when it already possessed a cricket pitch and football ground. Rather, the better idea (the Council considered) was to build an indoor gymnasium. There was no doubt that a recreation ground could have been purchased and equipped, as the testator envisaged (ie, it was both possible and practicable)—but the court agreed to a *cy-près* scheme for the provision of a hall for indoor recreation.

By the employment of wide-scope reasoning, these decisions tended to allow for purposes that better served contemporary society than those which the donor chose—a liberal approach to the *cy-près* doctrine, which was public policy-oriented,[59] but which also fell outside the scope of the strict threshold tests generally propounded by the courts. However, particularly in cases of subsequent failure, where there was no risk of the gift lapsing (or of next-of-kin arguing for return of the property to them, given its perpetual dedication to charity), there was little motivation or interest, at times, to overhaul charitable trusts of a rather useless kind—all of which served as the prelude to the re-definition of wider *cy-près* triggers, courtesy of statute.[60] This reform will be considered in detail in the following chapter.

---

[57] [1947] Ch 183, 186. See also: *In re Lysaght (decd); Hill v Royal College of Surgeons* [1966] Ch 191 (gift to Royal College of Surgeons for establishment of studentships, except for Jews and Roman Catholics; restriction removed *cy-près*).

[58] [1955] 1 WLR 738 (Ch).

[59] DWM Waters, *Law of Trusts in Canada* (2nd edn, Carswell, Toronto, 1984) 622.

[60] *Report of the Committee on the Law and Practice Relating to Charitable Trusts* (Cmd 8710) (HMSO, London, 1952) (*Nathan Committee Report*) [104]–[105].

Next, however, it is relevant to consider a further element of the general doctrine of *cy-près*, which is also equally as pertinent under the statutory *cy-près* schemes as it was under the general law.

The general law doctrine of *cy-près* turns upon whether there was an initial or subsequent failure of the charitable purpose. Essentially, proof that the donor had a general charitable intent when making the charitable gift is a pre-requisite for cases of initial failure, but not for cases of subsequent failure of the charitable purpose. There are numerous other contrasts between these two strands of the doctrine, as the following table illustrates:

	Initial failure	Subsequent failure
what it means	• at the point that the charitable gift is intended to take effect, it is unable to take effect in the precise terms specified	• where the charitable gift does take effect as intended, and is performed for a while, but then the charitable purpose cannot be performed any longer
example	• Charity X does not exist at the date that the gift is supposed to take effect, either because it has closed down, or never existed[61]	• monies are given to research for a cure for small pox; an effective vaccination is developed, rendering further research obsolete
what happens if the trust fails?	• the primary position is that if the trust fails, the gift lapses; if an *inter vivos* gift on trust, then a resulting trust in favour of the donor is presumed to arise; if the gift is *by will*, then the gift either lapses into residue, or if it is the residuary estate itself that fails or if no residuary gift is nominated under the will, the gift passes on intestacy to the donor's next of kin	• if the donor provides what is to happen to the property if the charitable purpose fails, then those wishes must be fulfilled; otherwise, the gift cannot lapse, or fall into residue—there is no possibility of a resulting trust—once dedicated to and used for charity (when the gift takes effect), it is always dedicated to charity and available for its use, and a *cy-près* scheme must occur

---

[61] A fairly common occurrence where a testator has failed to realise that the charity closed prior to his death, eg: *In re Spence (decd); Ogden v Shackleton* [1979] Ch 483, 496.

	Initial failure	Subsequent failure
is a 'general charitable intention' required? Why or why not?	• the property will be applied *cy-près* to other charitable purposes **only** when the donor is proven to have had a 'general charitable intention'—that is, the donor intended to benefit charity generally, and the gift to that specific purpose was merely one manifestation—allowing the court to choose another 'example' of a charitable purpose—but if there is no general charitable intention, the property will be 'lost to charity' (per box above)	• in order to invoke the *cy-près* jurisdiction, it is **not** necessary to find that the donor had a 'general charitable intention' when making the gift; such an intention is presumed—once the property has been dedicated to charity, the court presumes that the donor intended that the gift to charity was perpetual—if the gift fails, another charitable purpose will be selected under a *cy-près* scheme to carry on that charitable intention—there is no question of the property being 'lost to charity'

It will be appreciated that a donor's estate must be excluded from taking the failed gift by way of resulting trust where there has been *subsequent* failure (unless the *cy-près* doctrine is somehow ousted by a valid gift-over). Having been applied to charity after the gift took effect, the trust property is devoted to charity. There is no point in the donor or his estate claiming that property back, in cases of subsequent failure. It has been suggested that this particular rule 'reflects the quasi-corporate perception of charity in general by the Chancery judges'[62]—once applied, always applied. A perusal of the Charity Commissioners' *Annual Reports* over the last twenty years also suggests that both the significance of proving a 'general charitable intention', and the chances of the testator's estate ever receiving the property back on resulting trust, have greatly diminished, because most *cy-près* schemes drawn up in the modern age are to modernise trusts that have operated for years (ie, cases of subsequent failure), for which proof of a general charitable intent is not required. The occurrence of initial failure, and the consequent need to prove a general charitable intent, also have greatly dissipated.[63]

---

[62] J Hackney, *Understanding Equity and Trusts* (Fontana Press, London, 1987) 159.
[63] Also noted in: M Chesterman, *Charities, Trusts and Social Welfare* (Weidenfeld and Nicolson, London, 1979) 278.

1. Some Preliminary Conundrums about a 'General Charitable Intent'

(a) Should *a general charitable intent be required for initial failure?*

It has been suggested[64] that the need to prove a general charitable intention in the case of *initial* failure arose from 18th century cases, as a legal device to try to protect the expectations of heirs from claims by charities for failed charitable gifts *cy-près*. Where a general charitable intent on the part of the donor could not be proven, the property went by way of resulting trust back to the heirs, ensuring that the property was kept in the family. In these more modern times, when '[c]harity is always favoured by equity',[65] such rationale is considerably weaker.

New Zealand courts have gone so far as to state that, in the case of initial failure, there should be a *presumption* in favour of finding a general charitable intent, as a matter of 'public interest'.[66] Unless rebutted, such a presumption would prevent failed charitable gifts from falling into residue. A number of policy reasons have been advanced for the view that charities should prevail over next-of-kin—that charity plays a key socio-economic role; that the charity sector has evolved because the public and private sectors could not meet demand, and it should be supported for that reason; that modern charities often tackle social issues that governments will not; and that charities are innovative and politically useful, often comprising delivery vehicles for state funding programmes.[67] This view has also been academically supported on the additional bases that the gift should be upheld to preserve as many charitable trusts as possible;[68] if the trust failed, the property would pass to relatives of the testator that he probably wished to exclude or had already provided for;[69] and a presumption would save costly preparation and trial time in having to prove the existence of so esoteric a concept as a general charitable intention.[70]

The Australian High Court has certainly come close to favouring an outright presumption also, opining in 1940 that, in cases of initial failure, a general charitable intent is not difficult to divine, 'requir[ing] no more than a purpose

---

[64] G Jones, *History of the Law of Charity 1532–1827* (CUP, Cambridge, 1969) 139 (the courts 'were determined to "find" a general charitable intention, and were not concerned to nurture the selfish ambitions of the heir and next-of-kin'). Also: DJ Hayton, *The Law of Trusts* (4th edn, Sweet & Maxwell, London, 2003) 126 ('If the settlor did not have the requisite general or paramount charitable intention then a resulting trust arises, the courts originally being most reluctant to disinherit heirs in favour of charity'); G Moffat, *Trusts Law Text and Materials* (4th edn, CUP, Cambridge, 2005) 911.

[65] As expressed, eg, in: *In re Watt; Hicks v Hill* [1932] 2 Ch 243, 246 (Lord Hanworth MR).

[66] *Re Collier (decd)* [1998] 1 NZLR 81, 95 (that such an approach is 'more intellectually honest').

[67] *Ibid*, 95.

[68] RG Sisson, 'Relaxing the Dead Hand's Grip: Charitable Efficiency and the Doctrine of *Cy-près*' (1988) 74 *Virginia L Rev* 635, 643; G Dal Pont, *Charity Law in Australia and New Zealand* (OUP, Oxford, 2000) 309.

[69] CEF Rickett, 'The Dead Hand's Grip' [1988] *NZLJ* 335, 337, also citing Sisson, *ibid*.

[70] OLRC, *Report on the Law of Charities* (1996) 405; and see also, the comments in: OLRC, *The Law of Trusts* (1996), vol 2, 471.

wider than the execution of a specific plan involving the particular direction that has failed.'[71] However, as discussed shortly, modern Australian case law tends to indicate that State courts are utilising a series of factors by which to closely assess whether such a 'general charitable intention' exists, belying any suggestion of a presumption in favour of a *cy-près* distribution.

Interestingly, the contention that a general charitable intention should be *presumed* (in cases of both initial and subsequent failure) has been picked up and enacted in at least one statutory *cy-près* scheme, whilst other statutory regimes have sought to *abolish* the requirement altogether (considered next chapter[72]).

(b) Is actual proof of a general charitable intent required for subsequent failure?

The short answer to this is 'no'. Some courts state that a general charitable intent should be presumed in cases of subsequent failure,[73] some say that it is a fictitious exercise to hunt for one in these circumstances,[74] others say that it is simply irrelevant.[75] Whichever of these one adopts, the lack of any need to find such an intent—because of the ongoing dedication to charity—can accord with pragmatic realities. As Sheridan notes, the trust may fail a long time after it first operated, and any possible next-of-kin claiming under a resulting trust could be very remote from the donor.[76] Of course, the timeframe may be much shorter, and it is then that the *cy-près* doctrine can appear at its most incongruous. As Dal Pont points out, there is much to be said for treating initial and subsequent failure symmetrically, for 'it is somewhat odd that the testator's intention is critical if failure occurs immediately before his death, but not immediately subsequent to it. The simplest way of avoiding this artificiality is simply to apply the same principles to *both* initial and subsequent failure cases.'[77]

Unfortunately, some case law from across the jurisdictions[78] has clouded

---

[71] *A-G (NSW) v Perpetual Trustee Co Ltd* (1940) 63 CLR 209 (HCA) 225 (Dixon and Evatt JJ).

[72] See pp 118–22.

[73] See p 64, Table.

[74] *Boy Scouts of Canada, Provincial Council of Newfoundland v Doyle* (Newfoundland CA, 26 Jun 1997) [149]–[150].

[75] Eg: in Northern Ireland: *In re Dunwoodie* [1977] NI 141, 145.

[76] LA Sheridan, *Keeton and Sheridan's The Modern Law of Charities* (4th edn, Barry Rose Law Publishers, Chichester, 1992) 259.

[77] G Dal Pont, *Charity Law in Australia and New Zealand* (OUP, Oxford, 2000) 292, fn 61.

[78] Eg, in England: *In re Welsh Hospital (Netley) Fund* [1921] 1 Ch 655; *In re North Devon and West Somerset Relief Fund Trusts; Hylton v Wright* [1953] 1 WLR 1260 (Ch), referenced in DJ Hayton and C Mitchell, *Hayton and Marshall Commentary and Cases on the Law of Trusts and Equitable Remedies* (12th edn, Sweet & Maxwell, London, 2005) 514 as 'illogical cases'. In Canada: *Re Canada Trust Co v Ontario Human Rights Comm* (1990), 69 DLR (4th) 321 (Ont CA); *Re Hunter; Genn v A-G (BC)* (1973), 34 DLR (3d) 602 (BCSC); *Re Fitzgibbon* (1922), 69 DLR 524 (Sup Ct), and see the earlier authorities collected at: OLRC, *Law of Trusts* (1996) vol 2, 456, fn 133. In Australia: *In re Peacock's Charity* [1956] Tas SR 142; *Parker v Moseley* [1965] VR 580. See also the further cases collected in: LA Sheridan, *Keeton and Sheridan's The Modern Law of Charities* (4th edn, Barry Rose Law Publishers, Chichester, 1992) 260, fn 142; *Halsbury's Laws of England* (4th edn reissue, Butterworths, London, 1996) vol 5(2), [164] fn 3; and in HA Picarda, *The Law and Practice Relating to Charities* (3rd edn, Butterworths, London, 1999) 315, fnn 17–1.

the *cy-près* doctrine by seeking to find a general charitable intent in cases of subsequent failure—much to the chagrin of academic commentary.[79] But is it so entirely irrelevant? The editors of the Dominion Law Reports argue[80] that, whilst it may not be legally correct to hunt for a 'general charitable intent' in the case of subsequent failure, that very intent is probably relevant when asking how the property should actually be applied *cy-près*. The whole point of the exercise is to select charitable purposes which are similar or related to those that the donor originally stipulated. Thus, '[i]n order to discover another purpose that is as near as possible to the original intent of the donor, it may be necessary to inquire what, generally, the donor was attempting to accomplish. Can it really be said that this question is substantially different from the search for a general charitable intent?'.[81]

Additionally, Sheridan remarks[82] that, in most cases of subsequent failure where the courts have incorrectly hunted for a general charitable intent, the error has been insignificant because a general charitable intent has been found to exist in any event. Nevertheless, for the sake of doctrinal clarity in cases of subsequent failure, the courts should plainly be enquiring what the general intent of the testator was in order to determine what similar purposes the property could be applied to, not to determine whether a *cy-près* application should be permitted at all. There is much to be said for the correct result being reached via the correct route.

(c) Can a general charitable intent be displaced entirely by the out-and-out gift rationale?

One of the most controversial questions surrounding the role of the general charitable intent is whether it can be entirely displaced, in cases of initial failure, by the out-and-out gift rationale. According to this theory, once property is devoted to charity perpetually, out-and-out, then upon failure of the charitable object, the property must be applied to some other charitable purpose— regardless of any general or specific charitable intention being found. In this context, an 'out-and-out gift' means that the donor made his gift to charity, never intending to regain the property, so that, should that purpose not be possible, the trust property was to be applied towards *some* charitable purpose,

---

[79] See OLRC, *ibid*, and Sheridan, *ibid*, and Waters, below.

[80] See Annotations at commencement of case report for *Re Canada Trust Co v Ontario Human Rights Comm* (1990), 69 DLR (4th) 321 (Ont CA), citing also: SG Maurice and DB Parker (eds), *Tudor on Charities* (7th edn, Sweet & Maxwell, London, 1984) 268; DWM Waters, 'Comment on *Re Hunter*' (1974) 52 *Can BR* 598, and by the same author: *Law of Trusts in Canada* (2nd edn, Carswell, Toronto, 1984) 629. That commentary is also to be found at: LA Turnbull, 'Case Comment' (1991) 38 *Estates and Trusts Rep* 47.

[81] See Annotations at commencement of: *Canada Trust Co, ibid*.

[82] LA Sheridan, *Keeton and Sheridan's The Modern Law of Charities* (4th edn, Barry Rose Law Publishers, Chichester, 1992) 260.

no matter what events should unfold.[83] Essentially, such a view 'adopt[s] the pragmatic position that *cy-près* should be invoked where donors part with their entire interests in the trust properties, dedicating them to specific charitable objects, notwithstanding the absence of overriding general charitable intent beyond the chosen modes of their benevolence.'[84] The question is whether out-and-out gifts form a separate category that will give rise to the *cy-près* doctrine when the gift fails.

That the matter has been controversial for a long time is manifestly evident. In the very first edition of the leading charity work by Tyssen, the author seemed to propound the out-and-out theory as a separate category for permitting *cy-près*.[85] In the second edition of that work in 1921, a different author disagreed, contending that there was no such category, and that, in cases of initial failure, there *must* be found a general charitable intention before the gift would be applied *cy-près*.[86] Leading commentary of the *cy-près* doctrine in the 20th century is divided, with one maintaining the out-and-out theory as an alternative to finding a general charitable intention,[87] and with another finding the theory 'hard to sustain'.[88] On one occasion when the view was put forth in the *Canadian Bar Review*,[89] it was met by an spirited rebuttal (at least in the Canadian context) in the same journal issue.[90] The Australian version of *Halsbury's*[91] confounds the matter by referring to the fact that the *cy-près* doctrine applies where an out-and-out gift is made to a charitable object, but then devotes the rest of the discussion to the more orthodox analysis of initial versus subsequent

[83]   LA Sheridan and VTH Delany, *The Cy-près Doctrine* (Sweet & Maxwell, London, 1959) 37 ('By "out-and-out gift" we mean a disposition which clearly involves no expectation by the donor that he or his successors will ever get the property back').

[84]   *Boy Scouts of Canada, Provincial Council of Newfoundland v Doyle* (Newfoundland CA, 26 Jun 1997) [150].

[85]   AD Tyssen, *The Law of Charitable Bequests* (William Clowes & Sons, London, 1888) 440 (a first category of *cy-près* is where 'a testator has devoted property for ever to the performance of some charitable purpose . . . it is settled law that property once devoted to charity is so devoted for ever'). Initial versus subsequent failure of the charitable purpose, with one requiring a general charitable intent and the other not, is considered by this author to be a fourth category.

[86]   GE Shebbeare and CP Sanger, *The Law of Charitable Bequests* (2nd edn, Sweet and Maxwell, London, 1921) 184.

[87]   LA Sheridan and VTH Delany, *The Cy-près Doctrine* (Sweet & Maxwell, London, 1959) 37–38, and see the earlier definition at 5; and by: LA Sheridan, 'The *Cy-près* Doctrine' (1954) 32 *Can BR* 599.

[88]   HAP Picarda, *The Law and Practice Relating to Charities* (3rd edn, Butterworths, London, 1999) 325.

[89]   LA Sheridan, 'The *Cy-près* Doctrine' (1954) 32 *Can BR* 599.

[90]   ECE Todd, 'The *Cy-près* Doctrine: A Canadian Approach' (1954) 32 *Can BR* 1100.

[91]   *Halsbury's Laws of Australia* (Butterworths, Sydney, 1991–) [looseleaf] [75–700], which provides, in part, 'In order for the court to order a *cy-près* scheme, one of the following must occur: 1) there is a case of initial impossibility, and either (a) an out-and-out intention to benefit charity, or (b) a general charitable intention, plus a possible mode of effecting that intention . . .'. No detailed exploration of that first limb, as an exclusive and independent ground for *cy-près*, is provided in the following paragraphs.

failure, and the need to find a general charitable intention in the case of the former. The English version of *Halsbury's*[92] gives rise to some uncertainty too, with one reference appearing to support the out-and-out theory,[93] whilst another reference does not.[94] All of this highlights the uncertainty with this aspect of the *cy-près* doctrine.

For various reasons, it is submitted that the out-and-out theory is far from convincing:

- where the gift fails *ab initio*, modern case law insists that, where there is no general charitable intent, the gift will fail, no *cy-près* is possible, and the gift will revert to the donor (or to his estate)—regardless of whether the donor ever expected to see the property back, or not;[95]
- references to an out-and-out gift theory, as an alternative to finding a general charitable intent, could not be located by this author in either reported or unreported case law in England over the last twenty years;
- some judicial statements have sought to clarify that the out-and-out theory cannot sustain a *cy-près* application on its own. For example, in *In re British School of Egyptian Archaeology; Murray v Public Trustee*,[96] the distinction between the intent to make an out-and-out gift, and a general charitable intent, was maintained in this statement:

> I am told that, if the court decides that a contributor did not intend to have his money returned in any event, then he must be taken to have had a general charitable intent. I am not sure that the two things are the same. I think that a contributor may well say: 'I parted with my money to the school and did not reserve any right to have it back', without having any positive intention that his contribution should go to an analogous body or, indeed, to some institution to which the court may think proper to devote the money.

---

[92] *Halsbury's Laws of England* (4th edn reissue, Butterworths, London, 1996) vol 5(2), 'Consequences of Failure of Stated Objects'.

[93] *Ibid*, [164] ('If it is shown that the donor intended to part with his whole interest in the property, and therefore to make an outright gift, the question of general charitable intention is irrelevant' [footnote omitted]).

[94] *Ibid*, [157] (listing three exceptions where proof of a general charitable intent is not required; but interestingly, the out-and-out gift theory is not one of the three listed).

[95] HAP Picarda, *The Law and Practice Relating to Charities* (3rd edn, Butterworths, London, 1999) 325, citing, eg: *In re Ulverston and District New Hospital Building Trusts; Birkett v Barrow and Furness Hospital Management Committee* [1956] 1 Ch 622 (CA). More recently, the same principle has also been cited in, eg: *Re Broadbent (decd); Imperial Cancer Research Fund v Bradley* [2001] EWCA Civ 714, [49].

[96] [1954] 1 WLR 546 (Ch) 553.

- some case law cited in support of the out-and-out theory[97] does so in the context of a *surplus in public appeals*, and, as both Picarda[98] and *Halsbury's*[99] note, the out-and-out theory is not cogently supported away from that specific context;
- in Canada, it has judicially been termed a 'line of thought questioning the conditioning of *cy-près* application upon a general pervading charitable intent', and in light of such lack of certainty, the court in this case held that, whichever approach was adopted—an out-and-out gift or a general charitable intention—both were satisfied, permitting a *cy-près* scheme;[100] and
- there is some case law in which the donor clearly did contemplate that the gift may fail and provided a gift-over to cover that eventuality, where that gift-over was void as infringing the rule against perpetuities, where it was certainly *not* an out-and-out gift, yet a *cy-près* scheme was ordered[101]— again denying any equation between an out-and-out gift and a *cy-près* distribution upon failure.

(d) Is a general charitable intent required for left-over surpluses?

Where the donor gives property on trust for a specified charitable purpose, and that has been fully carried out, with a surplus available, is it necessary to find a general charitable intent on the part of the donor before such funds can be applied *cy-près*? This question has elicited contrary indications in the case law, involving monies both given under an instrument, or in response to a public appeal.

On the one hand, it has been held that such an intention *is* required (such that, where it is not to be found, then the surplus must be held on resulting trust for the donor or his estate, rather than be applied *cy-près*).[102] Such a view has been

---

[97] *In re Hillier; Hillier v A-G* [1954] 1 WLR 700 (CA); *In re Ulverston and District New Hospital Building Trusts; Birkett v Barrow and Furness Hospital Management Committee* [1956] 1 Ch 622 (CA); *In re North Devon and West Somerset Relief Fund Trusts; Hylton v Wright* [1953] 1 WLR 1260 (Ch).

[98] HAP Picarda, *The Law and Practice Relating to Charities* (3rd edn, Butterworths, London, 1999) 325.

[99] *Halsbury's Laws of England* (4th edn reissue, Butterworths, London, 1996) vol 5(2), [207]: 'On an initial failure of the stated objects of a charitable gift, the property may only be applied *cy-près* if the donor had a general charitable intention *or, in the case of a surplus, if the donor intended to devote to charity the whole of the property given*' (emphasis added).

[100] *Boy Scouts of Canada, Provincial Council of Newfoundland v Doyle* (Newfoundland CA, 26 Jun 1997) [149]–[150].

[101] *In re Peel's Release* [1921] 2 Ch 218.

[102] *In re Stanford; Uni of Cambridge v A-G* [1924] 1 Ch 73 (£5,000 bequeathed for completion and publication of etymological dictionary; surplus left over; no *cy-près*; resulting trust; no general charitable intent to be found on facts); *Gibson v South American Stores (Gath & Chaves) Ltd* [1950] Ch 177 (CA) (company directors set aside annual sum for employees' health and relief fund; surplus left over; no *cy-près*; sums would revert to the company; no general charitable intent). Cf: *In re Monk; Giffen v Wedd* [1927] 2 Ch 197 (CA) (residue to provide for coal fund and loans for poor inhabitants; surplus left over; applied *cy-près*; a general charitable intent found); *In re Robertson;*

academically supported[103] on the basis that a surplus is truly a case of initial failure, because the donor assessed the amount reasonably required to carry out the specified charitable purpose at the date that the sum was given in *toto* (ie, at the date of vesting), and if that proves to be incorrect, then there was a failure at the date of vesting—the donor mistakenly provided too much for the nominated purpose. In cases of initial failure, of course, a general charitable intent is required. The view is also supportable on the basis that, with only limited exception,[104] the courts have been minded to find a general charitable intention so as to permit a *cy-près* application of the surplus (further illustration of the tendency to favour charity at the expense of lapse, especially with very borderline cases where a specific charitable intention was just as possible on the face of the facts[105]).

On the other hand, other authorities have held that the court does *not* need to find a general charitable intent on the part of the donor to apply a surplus *cy-près*.[106] If a surplus is to be treated as 'analogous to a supervening failure'[107] (in that dedication of part of the fund to charity necessarily entails that all of the fund was so dedicated), then such sentiment is self-explanatory: no general charitable intent is required in cases of subsequent failure. To seek some general charitable intent in surplus cases has also been considered artificial and unnecessary.[108] *Halsbury's* notes that, where money is given for a public appeal that turns out to have a surplus, 'and only at the end of the period does it become

Colin v Chamberlin [1930] 2 Ch 71 (residue for restoration or maintenance of church; surplus left over; applied *cy-près*; general charitable intention found); *In re Royce; Turner v Wormald* [1940] Ch 514 (residue to vicar and church wardens for benefit of choir; left over surplus; *cy-près* scheme ordered; general charitable intention found); *In re Raine (decd); Walton v A-G* [1956] Ch 417 (residue for the 'continuation of the seating' in a church; surplus left over; applied *cy-près*; general charitable intention found). For public appeal cases: *In re Welsh Hospital (Netley) Fund; Thomas v A-G* [1921] 1 Ch 655; *In re North Devon and West Somerset Relief Fund Trusts; Hylton v Wright* [1953] 1 WLR 1260 (Ch).

[103] HA Picarda, *The Law and Practice Relating to Charities* (3rd edn, Butterworths, London, 1999) 345–46. Also supported in: EL Fisch, *The Cy-près Doctrine in the United States* (Matthew Bender & Co, Albany NY, 1950) 195–96. Also noted in: *Halsbury's Laws of England* (4th edn reissue, Butterworths, London, 1996) vol 5(2), [163], but without strong endorsement one way or the other.

[104] *In re Stanford; Uni of Cambridge v A-G* [1924] 1 Ch 73.

[105] HA Picarda, *The Law and Practice Relating to Charities* (3rd edn, Butterworths, London, 1999) 346.

[106] *In re King; Kerr v Bradley* [1923] 1 Ch 243 (residue of £1,094 bequeathed for a stained-glass window in a church; cost of window £800 maximum; surplus applied *cy-près* for a second window, general charitable intent 'irrelevant'); *In re Wokingham Fire Brigade Trusts; Martin v Hawkins* [1951] Ch 373.

[107] As mooted by: P Luxton, *The Law of Charities* (OUP, Oxford, 2001) 561–62. Also favoured by: JE Martin, *Hanbury and Martin Modern Equity* (17th edn, Sweet & Maxwell, London, 2005) 458–59.

[108] A view expressed, eg, in: LA Sheridan, *Keeton and Sheridan's The Modern Law of Charities* (4th edn, Barry Rose Law Publishers, Chichester, 1992) 262; and by the same author: 'The Cy-près Doctrine' (1954) 32 *Can BR* 599, 612; *Halsbury's Laws of Australia* (Butterworths, Sydney, 1991–) [looseleaf] [75–700]; PH Pettit, *Equity and the Law of Trusts* (9th edn, Butterworths, London, 2001) 318; and see also G Dal Pont, *Charity Law in Australia and New Zealand* (OUP, Oxford, 2000) 307, citing similar views of: *Re Tufford* (1984), 6 DLR (4th) 534 (Ont CA) 540.

clear that the purpose is impracticable, the case is one of subsequent failure, for it could not have been said at the moment of each gift that there was no reasonable prospect that the purpose would at some future time be practicable'.[109]

The modern statutory treatment of surpluses raised under public appeal, which seeks to simplify the above uncertainty, is dealt with further in later chapters.

2. What is the Date for Determining Whether Failure was 'Initial' or 'Subsequent'?

(a) Charitable trusts under will

The crucial point for determining whether it is initial or subsequent failure is the date that the property passed to charity.[110] If by *will*, that is the date of the testator's death, according to the principle of *In re Tacon; Public Trustee v Tacon.*[111] If the charitable purpose was possible to carry out for any period following the testator's death, then it is a case of subsequent failure. In that case, the property will be dedicated to charity. There is no question of its resulting back to the donor (or to the donor's estate); nor is there any need to prove that the testator had a general charitable intention.

In each of the following circumstances, the question arose whether the property could be applied *cy-près*:

In re Slevin; Slevin v Hepburn[112]	*In re Wright; Blizard v Lockhart*[113]
14 Feb 1883—testator made will, leaving gift of £200 on trust to St Dominic's Orphanage, Newcastle-on-Tyne	2 Dec 1932—testatrix made will, leaving property on trust to establish a convalescent home, subject to a life interest
24 Feb 1883—testator died	15 Mar 1933—testatrix died
Mar 1883—orphanage closed, before legacy could be paid over to it—impossible to carry out the charitable purpose	15 Feb 1942—life interest came to an end—impracticable at that point to carry out the charitable purpose

---

[109] *Halsbury's Laws of England* (4th edn reissue, Butterworths, London, 1996) vol 5(2), [166].

[110] See, for further discussion, eg: *Halsbury's Laws of England* (4th edn reissue, Butterworths, London, 1996) vol 5(2), [158].

[111] [1958] Ch 447 (CA) 453–54 (Lord Evershed MR) ('the test of . . . impracticability is to be applied at the date of the testator's death; if at that date the disposition is shown to be impracticable . . . that is, incapable for any reason of being practically initiated or administered—then the gift fails altogether and the next-of-kin (or whoever else are entitled in default) take').

[112] [1891] 2 Ch 236 (CA). See also, on this point: *Re Moon's WT; Foale v Gillians* [1948] 1 All ER 300 (Ch); *Williams v A-G (NSW)* (1948) 48 SR (NSW) 505; *Re Moore (decd); Austrust Ltd v United Aborigines Mission and A-G (SA)* (1991) 55 SASR 439; *Re Dunlop (decd)* (1984) 19 *Northern Ireland Judgments Bulletin*, discussed further in: N Dawson, 'Old Presbyterian Persons—A Sufficient Section of the Public?' [1987] *Conv* 114. Cf: *Re Hunter; Genn v A-G of BC* (1973), 34 DLR (3d) 602 (BCSC), and critiqued in: J Hackney, 'Trusts' [1973] *ASCL* 472–73.

[113] [1954] Ch 347 (CA).

Both of these instances constituted cases of subsequent failure. Neither trust was impossible or impracticable at the very moment that the gifts took effect (the date when the testators died), and hence, the property was perpetually dedicated to charity from that moment onwards. A *cy-près* distribution was proper in these circumstances, and there was no need to hunt for a general charitable intent.

The position is similar where there was a 'reasonable prospect', at the date of the testator's death, that it might have been practicable to carry the trusts into execution at some future time[114]—if the court accepts that possibility after undertaking an enquiry, then there is no initial impracticability. If that 'prospect' ultimately did not come to pass, it is a case of subsequent failure, there is consequently no need for a general charitable intention to be manifested, and the next of kin are forever excluded from taking the property.[115] If, however, there was no 'reasonable prospect' at the date of the testator's death of the trust being performed in the future, then there is an initial failure, and the residuary legatee will take the property.

The principles outlined above have been recognised and/or applied in other jurisdictions, such as Australia,[116] Canada[117] and Scotland.[118]

(b) Charitable trusts inter vivos

Where the disposition is by *inter vivos* trust, the situation is not quite so clear. In *In re British School of Egyptian Archaeology; Murray v Public Trustee*,[119] Harman J noted that deciding at what point a subscription or gift *inter vivos* fails is 'not easy to apply'.

Judicially, it has been suggested in *Harris v Sharp*[120] that the crucial date for determining whether it is a case of initial or subsequent failure is the date of the actual instrument evidencing the *inter vivos* trust. The issue, a live one in

---

[114] This wording is derived from the formula adopted by the court in: *In re White's WT; Barrow v Gillard* [1955] Ch 188, 189, which in turn was derived from the earlier decision in: *Re White's Trusts* (1886) 33 Ch D 449, 451. The test was applied subsequently in, eg: *Re Payling's WT; Armstrong v Payling* [1969] 1 WLR 1595 (Ch), where the execution of the trust for a cottage to be used as a home for aged persons was considered practicable, and no failure occurred.

[115] Eg: *Green v Trustees of the Property of the Church of England in Tasmania* (Tas SC, 31 Aug 1992) (endowment for an assistant bishop in northern Tasmania not practicable at the time of the court hearing, but there had been a possibility of that being successfully established at the date of the testator's death; gift administered *cy-près*).

[116] Eg: *A-G (NSW) v Fulham* [2002] NSWSC 629, [21]; *Green, ibid; Re Wilmott (decd); Uniting Church in Australia Property Trust (Vic) v Royal Victorian Institute for the Blind* (SC Vic, 2 Dec 1999) [35]–[40].

[117] Eg: *Wilson Estate v Loyal Protestant Assn* (BCSC, 31 Jan 1986) [8]; *Fidelity Trust Co v St Joseph's Vocational School of Winnipeg* (1984), 27 Man r (2d) 284 (QB) [26]–[27]; *Avalon Consolidated School Board v United Church of Canada* (1983), 42 Nfld & PEIR 8 (Newfoundland SC) [119].

[118] Eg: *Davidson's Trustees v Arnott*, 1951 SC 42 (IH 2 Div) 60.

[119] [1954] 1 WLR 546 (Ch) 552.

[120] CA, 21 Mar 1989, affirming earlier decision of Mervyn Davies J.

that case, can be difficult to resolve. A charity trustee, S, devoted to promoting treatment of heart disease, used trust monies fraudulently, and was imprisoned. Shortly prior to his sentencing hearing, S conveyed £50,000 on trust to his solicitors for a fellowship in paediatric surgery at Liverpool Royal Children's Hospital. Unfortunately, S was unwilling to give an undertaking that the money had not been derived from his fraud. Upon learning of this reluctance, the Liverpool Health Authority purported to disclaim the gift (although this disclaimer was ultimately held not to be legally effective,[121] and the money did eventually pass to the hospital). In that case, the court went on to consider whether, upon disclaimer, a *cy-près* application of the monies would have been possible. As Partington describes the outcome of this case:[122]

> in holding that there had been no initial failure Mervyn Davies J applied *Re White* [1955] 1 Ch 188 and *Re Tacon* [1958] 1 Ch 447 and held that the court must inquire whether at the date of execution of the memorandum there was a reasonable prospect that it would be practicable to carry out the gift at some future time. Since no one could have known that the gift would be rejected at that time it could not have been initially impractical.

In other words, Mervyn Davies J held that there *was* a 'reasonable prospect', and that this constituted an example of subsequent failure. Thus, for the purposes of *cy-près*, it did not matter that there was only a *specific* charitable intention on the part of the donor S on the facts.

This decision has been cogently criticised by Partington on the basis that this should have been construed as a case of initial failure for two reasons: first, the terms of the trust were still to be worked out, and the trustees still to be appointed, at the time that the trust instrument was executed; and secondly, the principle in *Tacon* should not apply to *inter vivos* trusts. Instead, argues this commentator, the donor should be entitled to a reasonable period of time to inquire whether or not his gift is practical and desired:

> if [the] settlor settles money upon a trust to assist teaching Latin at his old school without consulting the school and the next day telephones the news to the governors who—say after a week of deliberation—reject the gift, should the Attorney General be able to apply the money *cy-près*? It is submitted he should not.[123]

Picarda, however, suggests just the opposite—that '[l]ogically there appears to be no good reason for excluding *inter vivos* gifts from the ambit of

---

[121] Upon the reasoning: 'A beneficiary can disclaim a beneficial interest which is given to him by a trust purpose, but neither the hospital nor the Health Authorities were beneficiaries in that sense. The beneficiary of Mr Sharp's disposition was "charity" and there can be no question of the hospital or the Health Authorities disclaiming the benefit of the charitable trust so as to prevent the Attorney General insisting upon the execution of a trust': per Fox LJ.

[122] D Partington, 'Sharp Practice and the Law of Charities' [1988] *Conv* 288, 291.

[123] *Ibid.*

Re Wright.'[124] Unfortunately, the decision in *Harris v Sharp*, however illogical, appears not to have been judicially discussed since it was handed down.

Other scenarios can also create difficulties as to whether they constitute initial or subsequent failure. The example has been given[125] of charitable funds being designated for the building of a new hospital, which sum is payable in instalments. Half-way through construction, a frustrating event occurs that renders completion of the new hospital building impossible. The building has never been used for the purposes intended by the gift, but part of the gift has been spent. Whether this is a scenario of initial failure, because the gift failed before it took effect, or whether it is a case of subsequent failure because part of the fund has been applied for the intended purpose, is unclear—an instance of where, according to the Charity Commissioners, the 'precise moment at which the purposes of the charitable gift actually take[s] effect . . . not [being] fully explored in the legal authorities.'[126]

3. How is a 'General Charitable Intent' Fathomed?

Needless to say, the task of interpreting whether the donor had a general or a specific charitable intent has muddied the evolution of the 'initial failure' *cy-près* doctrine considerably, especially when the donor is, in the usual case, deceased. The vast majority of initial failure *cy-près* cases are likely to be testamentary—there has been a change in circumstances between the making of the will and its taking effect upon the testator's death, such that the charitable purpose can never be carried out as the testator envisaged.[127] It is then left for the court to divine the testator's intention, construing the will as best it can (and usually in the face of a tussle between the charity/s and the residuary beneficiaries[128]). If the testator had no general charitable intention, but only an intention that the income or capital should be used for the particular charitable purpose disclosed in the instrument and no other, the court is simply not in a position to apply the gift *cy-près*. The disputation will then be between the named beneficiary (seeking to establish that there was a valid charitable trust in its favour), and the residuary beneficiary (or, where the charitable disposition was itself the

---

[124] HA Picarda, *The Law and Practice Relating to Charities* (3rd edn, Butterworths, London, 1999) 317.

[125] See: *Funds Raised for and Donated to NHS Hospitals* (1995) 3 Decisions of the Charity Commissioners 35, 38.

[126] *Ibid.*

[127] C Rickett, 'Failure of Charities and the Conundrum of s 32' [2003] *NZLJ* 59, 59; G Moffat, *Trusts Law Text and Materials* (4th edn, CUP, Cambridge, 2005) 906.

[128] As LA Sheridan and VTH Delany, *The Cy-près Doctrine* (Sweet & Maxwell, London, 1959) 103, pragmatically put it, 'usually in cases of initial impossibility the donor or his near relations are at hand trying to get the money'.

residuary clause, the testator's next-of-kin)—with a complete absence of any *cy-près* analysis.[129]

Of course, the process of divination can be sharpened considerably where the draftsperson has specified that the donor had a general charitable intent to support a particular charitable cause, and has chosen a gift to X as one manifestation of that broader charitable intent. Conversely, if the donor has no wish to benefit any other charity than that which is specified in the will, then this can be made plain by the particular drafting adopted.[130]

In the absence of such drafting, however, how is this general charitable intent to be divined? Some judicial tests descend into almost meaningless terminology. Suggestions that the court must consider whether the instrument contains 'a bare intention that the impracticable direction be carried into execution as an indispensable part of the trust declared';[131] or 'the intention is confined to giving effect to the particular plan as the main or essential object in view';[132] or '[a] paramount intention . . . to give the property in the first instance for a general charitable purpose rather than a particular charitable purpose',[133] do not really advance the matter very far. For example, a testator may have had a general charitable intention to relieve poverty in the parish of Shoreditch, and her gift of funds to establish a soup kitchen and a cottage hospital was merely the specific mode of achieving that general intent;[134] but reasonable opinion may differ, and hold that she had the specific intention to establish precisely what she said, a soup kitchen! Furthermore, Fisch points out[135] the artificiality with the doctrine—when testamentary terms that property is to be devoted to a particular purpose 'and no other', or that the property should not be used for any other purpose, were held not to mean what they said, and the doctrine was allowed to apply in any event.

The elicitation of any sort of guidelines has been acknowledged to be a

---

[129]   As occurred, eg, in: *In re Niyazi's WT* [1978] 1 WLR 910 (Ch) 913.

[130]   A point well-emphasised in: EL Fisch, *The Cy-près Doctrine in the United States* (Matthew Bender & Co, Albany NY, 1950) 220 ('Here the lawyer has an exceptional opportunity to make his influence felt. His foresight and his skill will do much to determine whether the gift is to be devoted, and to continue to be devoted, to the public welfare'), 223–24 ('It is incumbent upon the draftsman to make clear beyond controversy that the donor does have this wider purpose').

[131]   *A-G (NSW) v Perpetual Trustee Co Ltd* (1940) 63 CLR 209 (HCA) 225 (Dixon and Evatt JJ).

[132]   *Royal North Shore Hospital of Sydney v A-G (NSW)* (1938) 60 CLR 396 (HCA) 428 (Dixon J). See also, for similar type of wording in English cases: *Mills v Farmer* (1815) 19 Ves 483, 34 ER 595 (Ch) 596; *In re Willis; Shaw v Willis* [1921] 1 Ch 44 (CA) 54; *In re Lysaght (decd); Hill v Royal College of Surgeons* [1966] 1 Ch 191, 202; *In re Rymer; Rymer v Stanfield* [1895] 1 Ch 19 (CA) 35 ('you have to consider whether the mode of attaining the object is machinery or not, or whether the mode is not the substance of the gift').

[133]   *In re Wilson; Twentyman v Simpson* [1913] 1 Ch 314, 320–21.

[134]   As held in: *Biscoe v Jackson* (1887) LR 35 Ch D 460 (CA) (no suitable land could be found for the soup kitchen to operate). The case was followed, in equally dubious circumstances, in Northern Ireland in: *In re Currie; McClelland v Gamble* [1985] NI 299 (Ch).

[135]   EL Fisch, *The Cy-près Doctrine in the United States* (Matthew Bender & Co, Albany NY, 1950) 157–58, putting down such liberal constructions to the policy generally favouring charities.

difficult task, both academically[136] and judicially,[137] with Harman J candidly acknowledging the inconsistency in decision-making:

> It was said by Buckley J in *In re Davis* that the court will lean towards finding a general charitable intent . . . The court has been doing so ever since, and it has leaned so far over that it has become almost prone. I have always had a preference for an upright posture.[138]

The cases are liberally sprinkled with grand statements that the 'terms of this will manifest a general charitable intention', with reference to the fact that it is a charitable bequest and little else. Some courts have even resorted to the dubious justification that it was 'essentially a matter of impression', with little supportive reasoning.[139]

---

[136] Eg: RP Meagher and WMC Gummow, *Jacobs' Law of Trusts in Australia* (6th edn, Butterworths, London, 1997) [1068]; A Hudson, *Equity and Trusts* (4th edn, Cavendish Publishing, London, 2005) 892–94; JG Riddall, *The Law of Trusts* (6th edn, Butterworths, London, 2002) 186–88; G Moffat, *Trusts Law Text and Materials* (4th edn, CUP, Cambridge, 2005) 912, who declares that it is largely dependent upon the discretion of the court to interpret the factual matrix of each case; and even more strongly: D Ong, *Trusts Law in Australia* (Federation Press, Sydney, 1999) 321 ('an exercise in caprice'); G Dal Pont, *Charity Law in Australia and New Zealand* (OUP, Oxford, 2000) 308 ('by no means exact or objective'); EL Fisch, *The Cy-près Doctrine in the United States* (Matthew Bender & Co, Albany NY, 1950) 128 ('has given rise to most of the litigation in *cy-près* cases') 150 ('courts actually make a guess'); *Halsbury's Laws of England* (4th edn reissue, Butterworths, London, 1996) vol 5(2), [159] ('Often . . . the words used give little assistance'), [160].

[137] Eg: *In re Woodhams (decd); Lloyds Bank Ltd v London College of Music* [1981] 1 WLR 493 (Ch) 502 ('To search for such a paramount or dominant charitable purpose or intention is in many cases to follow a will-o' the-wisp'); *A-G (NSW) v Perpetual Trustee Co Ltd* (1940) 63 CLR 209 (HCA) 225, 227 (the distinction, 'however clear in conception, has proved anything but easy of application' and '[a]lmost all charitable trusts expressed with any particularity must tend towards some more general purpose'); *Executor Trustee and Agency Co of South Australia Ltd v Warbey (No 2)* (1973) 6 SASR 336, 345 (the court is 'invited to toss a penny'); *In re the Royal Kilmainham Hospital; A-G v British Legion* [1966] IR 451 (HC) (as to what constitutes a general charitable intent, 'no hard and fast rule can be laid down. Courts have differed much as to what is sufficient to indicate such an intention'); *In re Currie; McClelland v Gamble* [1985] NI 299 (Ch) 306–7 (disclaiming any attempt to conduct a 'consumers' survey' of what the phrase means); *Re Bruce Estate* (PEI SC, 5 Aug 2004) [31] ('essentially a subjective exercise'); *Re Fraser Estate* (2000), 99 ACWS (3d) 525 (PEI SC) [80] ('few guidelines'); *In re Lawton (decd); Lloyds Bank Ltd v Longfleet St Mary's Parochial Church Council* [1940] Ch 984, 985 ('there is no branch of the law so artificial or in which it is so difficult to reconcile conflicting authorities as this question of general charitable intention'); *Re Talbot; Jubb v Sheard* [1933] Ch 895, 902 ('general charitable intent, a thing which is not capable of exact definition'); *Bowman v Secular Society* [1916–17] All ER Rep 1 (HL) (the rule of a general charitable intention 'however admirable in the interest of the public, has, I think, gone further than any other rule or canon of construction in defeating the real intention of testators').

[138] *In re Goldschmidt (decd); Commercial Union Ass Co Ltd v Central British Fund for Jewish Relief and Rehabilitation* [1957] 1 WLR 524 (Ch) 525. For similar sentiments about the keenness of the court to find a general charitable intention, see, eg: *Re Pettit* [1988] 2 NZLR 513, 547; *In re Findlay's Estate; Tasmanian Trustees Ltd v Launceston Girls' Home* (1995) 5 Tas r 333, 342; *A-G (NSW) v Perpetual Trustee Co Ltd* (1940) 63 CLR 209 (HCA) 229–30.

[139] As noted in: *Alacoque v Roache* [1998] 2 NZLR 250 (CA) 255 ('essentially a matter of the impression conveyed by the words used': Somers J), and criticised on this point in: C Rickett, 'The Dead Hand's Grip' [1988] *NZLJ* 335, 336–37. Another notable example of extreme brevity of reasoning occurs in: *Walt Estate v Williams* (1997), 73 ACWS (3d) 558 (BCSC) [40].

Some attempt perhaps should be made, however, to set out those matters that have been considered relevant to this task of construction. The following factors and analysis, drawn from a review of the case law in both England and elsewhere around the Commonwealth, contain some relevant indicia, in cases of initial failure of the trust:[140]

Do the testator's words indicate a limitation to particular people or to that particular place?   Take, for example, a residuary clause which is drafted as follows:

> To pay the income thereof in perpetuity *for charitable purposes only*; the persons to benefit *directly* in pursuance of such charitable purposes are to be only such as *shall* be or shall have been employees of X . . . [or their dependents]

The opening italicised phrase, when considered on its own, may well express a general charitable intention; but the other italicised words indicated to the Supreme Court of Canada[141] that this testator had no such intention. He wished for the income to be used for charitable purposes for the benefit solely of the persons he had stipulated (employees and dependents), and for no one else. Similarly, in another Canadian case,[142] a disposition 'for the *specific* use and benefit of Eurasian children' born of wartime relationships between United States soldiers and Vietnamese women did not evince a general charitable intent—the court had recourse to the dictionary to define 'specific', and hung their decision upon that. The gift lapsed.

The testator may be just as specific about the use of land the subject of the testamentary trust, as the decision in *Fellows v Sarina*[143] demonstrates. A testator provided by will that certain land was not to be sold but was 'to forever remain as a wildlife sanctuary and can be used by all my relations and their friends to picnic or camp thereon'. It was held:[144] that a trust of land for a wildlife sanctuary could be a valid charitable purpose if it was established and maintained so as to be beneficial to the public (whether or not access to the public was permitted); that the trust failed for impracticability due to insufficient funds; and that there was no general charitable intention. Rather, the court considered that the testator had made it plain that he wanted the specific land left by him to become a wildlife sanctuary and that it was 'an integral and essential' part of his gift, because he provided that the property was not to be sold; and that this friends could picnic there—indicating that it was *that* land, and no other, that was to be used to effect the gift. It was thus impermissible to sell the land and apply the proceeds *cy-près*. The gift lapsed, and fell into residue.

---

[140] For various other treatments of lists, and differing authorities in support thereof, see: fn 136 above, and the sources cited therein.

[141] *Reference Re Herbert Coplin Cox* [1953] 1 SCR 94, [35]. This decision was aff'd on appeal: *In re Cox (decd); Baker v National Trust Co* [1955] AC 627 (PC).

[142] *Re Charlesworth Estate* (1996), 62 ACWS (3d) 632 (Man QB) [52].

[143] NSW SC, 9 May 1996. For another case where the identity of the land, the testator's own seaside house, was essential to the trust, such that a general charitable intent could not be found, see: *Re Barry* [1971] VR 395 (Master).

[144] *Fellows, ibid*, 22–23.

The English Chancery court has noted[145] that the easiest cases of a general charitable intent occur where a particular disposition is prefaced by general words which state expressly the object which the donor desires to achieve, and which make it clear that the particular scheme prescribed is only *one* means of achieving that more general end—but that such cases are rare.

How specific and detailed were the testator's instructions?   The more precisely defined are the testator's instructions, the less likely that a general charitable intent will be found.[146]

The decision of *In re Mitchell's WT*[147] provides an excellent example. The testatrix bequeathed part of her residuary estate for 'providing four beds in the Barnsley Beckett Hospital for the use of injured workmen from the Mitchell Main and Darfield Main Collieries'. There was insufficient income from her residuary estate to maintain four beds at the hospital at the date of her death. The evidence was that, had four beds been reserved exclusively for injured workmen in the Main Collieries, they would have been very much under-used. The gift failed and no *cy-près* application was possible. The gift was very particular; and any modification would have frustrated the testatrix's intention to benefit workmen from those pits by providing special facilities at the hospital. Had the testatrix bequeathed the sum on the basis that, although the hospital would not provide four beds for the exclusive use of the workmen, it would nevertheless guarantee that there would always be four beds available, the position (said the court) might have been different.

Where the failed disposition is nestled among other charitable dispositions.[148] Authorities in England[149] and from other jurisdictions[150] demonstrate that

---

[145] *In re Woodhams (decd); Lloyds Bank Ltd v London College of Music* [1981] 1 WLR 493 (Ch) 502–3.

[146] *In re Wilson; Twentyman v Simpson* [1913] 1 Ch 314, 320; *Re Good's WT; Oliver v Batten* [1950] 2 All ER 653 (Ch) 656; *In re Packe; Sanders v A-G* [1918] 1 Ch 437, 442. Also failing to find a general charitable intent on this ground, from other jurisdictions, eg: *Re Tyrie (decd)* [1970] VR 264, 267; *Re Lushington (decd); Manukau County v Wynyard* [1964] NZLR 161 (CA) 172–73; *Executor Trustee and Agency Co of South Australia Ltd v Warbey (No 2)* (1973) 6 SASR 336, 344; *Re Annandale* [1986] 1 Qd R 353, 357–58.

[147] (1966) 110 *Sol Jo* 291 (Ch), as cited and described in: *In re Woodhams (decd); Lloyds Bank Ltd v London College of Music* [1981] 1 WLR 493 (Ch) 502–3.

[148] Called 'charity by association' in: *Re Spence (decd); Ogden v Shackleton* [1979] Ch 483, 494, and noted also in: RA Pearce and J Stevens, *The Law of Trusts and Equitable Obligations* (3rd edn, Butterworths, London, 2002) 548.

[149] *In re Knox; Fleming v Carmichael* [1937] Ch 109; *In re Satterthwaite's WT; Midland Bank Executor and Trustee Co Ltd v Royal Veterinary College* [1966] 1 WLR 277 (CA); and *Guild v Inland Revenue Commissioners* [1991] STC 281, and noted on this point in:—, 'The IHT Exemption for Charities' [1991] June *Trusts and Estates* 66, 67. Earlier authorities, such as *Biscoe v Jackson* (1887) LR 35 Ch D 460 (CA), also support the proposition: see, for discussion of early case law examples: LA Sheridan and VTH Delany, *The Cy-près Doctrine* (Sweet & Maxwell, London, 1959) 75–76.

[150] Eg, in Australia: *Public Trustee of Qld v State of Qld* [2004] QSC 360, [10]; *McLean v A-G (NSW)* [2002] NSWSC 377, [62]; *McCormack v Stevens* [1978] NSWLR 517; and much earlier: *A-G (NSW) v Perpetual Trustee Co Ltd* (1940) 63 CLR 209 (HCA) 219 (Rich J) 225–26 (Dixon and

where the failed charitable disposition is in the same testamentary clause as other charitable dispositions, that is one indicator that the testator had a general charitable intent. One commentator puts it as highly as to say that, in such an instance, there is a deemed general charitable intent.[151]

Nevertheless, the authorities for this factor are questionable. Several cases cited in England in purported support of the factor have had other factors in support of a general charitable intention. In *In re Satterthwaite's WT; Midland Bank Executor and Trustee Co Ltd v Royal Veterinary College*[152] and *In re Knox; Fleming v Carmichael*,[153] the named charities never existed as charities at all; and in *In re Finger's WT; Turner v Ministry of Health*,[154] the testatrix mistakenly believed that she had no next of kin—both factors which support the conclusions in each case that a general charitable intention could be inferred; and in *In re Jenkins's WT; Public Trustee v British Union for the Abolition of Vivisection*[155] and *In re Spence (decd); Ogden v Shackleton*,[156] where the factor could have been invoked to 'flavour' a failed bequest from other dispositions of charitable nature, it was not invoked. Furthermore, the failed charitable bequest was stated by Megarry VC in *Spence* to require an association with 'kindred objects', suggesting that the other dispositions need to be more than charitable— there should be *similarity of purpose*.[157] Additionally, as Luxton points out,[158] not all examples where the charitable disposition at issue was one of many do indeed support a finding of a general charitable intent. For all these reasons, it is submitted that the weight to be attributed to this factor—the association of the failed charitable disposition with others in the same document—is doubtful.

Whether precatory words indicate a general intent. In *Public Trustee of Queensland v State of Queensland*,[159] the testator left one third of his estate to the 'Redcliffe Local Ambulance Committee'. There had never been any committee of that name in existence. By means of a separate clause, the testator continued, 'I express a wish without creating any binding trust or legal obligation

---

Evatt JJ). Eg, in Northern Ireland: *Nesbitt v A G for Northern Ireland* (NI Ch, 17 Apr 1991); *In re Currie; McClelland v Gamble* [1985] NI 299 (Ch) 306–07. Eg, in Canada: *Re Charlesworth Estate* (1996), 62 ACWS (3d) 632 (Man QB) (only charitable bequest; no general charitable intent for that reason).

[151] JG Riddall notes it as a case of 'deemed charitable intention': *The Law of Trusts* (6th edn, Butterworths, London, 2002) 189. In *Halsbury's Laws of England* (4th edn reissue, Butterworths, London, 1996) vol 5(2), [160], the authors note that to find a general charitable intent in such circumstances 'may be relatively easy'.

[152] [1966] 1 WLR 277 (CA) (of the nine named beneficiaries, the one at issue was the 'London Animal Hospital').

[153] [1937] Ch 109.

[154] [1972] 1 Ch 286, 299.

[155] [1966] Ch 249.

[156] [1979] Ch 483.

[157] Noted, eg, in: P Todd and G Watt, *Cases and Materials on Equity and Trusts* (5th edn, OUP, Oxford, 2005) 400.

[158] P Luxton, *The Law of Charities* (OUP, Oxford, 2001) 560, fn 108, citing: *In re Harwood; Colman v Innes* [1936] Ch 285.

[159] [2004] QSC 360.

that The Redcliffe Local Ambulance purchase a new fully equipped ambulance with paramedic equipment.' The court was of the view that this precatory statement was consistent with a general charitable intention to assist in the provision of ambulance services in the Redcliffe area, with the nomination of the Redcliffe Local Ambulance Committee 'merely a means for the fulfilment of that purpose'.[160] The funds were applied *cy-près*.

Similarly, heavy use of the word 'wish' in the will, rather than the more prescriptive word of 'intend', plus a clear anticipation on the face of the will that the property bequeathed by will would not always be used for his 'wish', convinced the court in *Roman Catholic Trusts Corporation for the Diocese of Melbourne v A-G (Vic)*[161] that there was a general charitable intent. The land that was left in trust to establish an agricultural enterprise for 'orphan boys' (for which there was insufficient funds and for which the land was unsuitable) was sold under a *cy-près* scheme, with the proceeds applied for the benefit of disadvantaged children, male and female.

Whether the nominations of the trustees indicate a general charitable intent. Sometimes, the particular trustees nominated by the testator convince the court that a general charitable intent is manifest on the face of the will.

For example, in *Ipswich CC v A-G (Qld)*,[162] property developers conveyed land on trust to the Ipswich City Council 'for town planning purposes' but with the further notation, 'as and when the dedication of such land as reservoir and water resources becomes necessary'. The court was satisfied that the trustee council could use the land for any charitable purposes within its town planning remit. In *obiter*, however, the court noted that the appointment of the Council as trustee indicated a general charitable intent on the part of the developers in any event. A *cy-près* scheme to sell the land and apply funds to construction of a reservoir was approved. The appointment of the Catholic Diocese as trustee held similar sway in finding a general charitable intent in *Roman Catholic Trusts Corporation for the Diocese of Melbourne v A-G (Vic)*.[163]

Is the failed charitable gift to an entity that does not exist? Where the beneficiary institution simply does not exist at the date that the gift takes effect, it comprises an instance of initial impossibility. Broadly speaking, as the court noted in *Aston v Mt Gambier Presbyterian Charge:*[164]

> [i]n most cases when there is failure of the institution, the gift will be a gift direct to that institution, and the question will be whether a general charitable intention exists so that the property can be applied *cy-près* by, for example, directing that it be given to another institution which is engaged in activity compatible with the general charitable intention which is found to exist.

[160] *Ibid*, [10].
[161] [2000] VSC 360.
[162] [2004] QSC 252.
[163] [2000] VSC 360.
[164] (2002) 84 SASR 109, [32]. See also: *In re Harwood; Coleman v Innes* [1936] Ch 285.

There is an apparent distinction in England, however, between a bequest that fails because the institution *never existed*, and one that fails because the institution *once existed* but does not exist any longer.[165] In the former case, the fact that the body never existed indicates of itself that there was a general intention to give to charity in that sector, because the gift could only be defined truly by the purpose of the non-existent (fictitious) institution that the testator (erroneously) had in mind.[166] With rare exception,[167] a general charitable intention will usually be *presumed* in this scenario, and the gift will be applied *cy-près*. Where the body *has* existed, however, there is a tendency to consider that the testator intended to give to that particular body and to no other, and no general charitable intention will be inferred,[168] although again, this rule is not without isolated English exception.[169]

---

[165] See, eg: P Birks (ed), *English Private Law* (OUP, Oxford, 2001), vol I, [4.526]; DG Cracknell (ed), *Charities: The Law and Practice* (Thomson Sweet & Maxwell, London, 1994–) [looseleaf], vol 1, [1.55]; *Halsbury's Laws of Australia* (Butterworths, Sydney, 1991–), 'Cy-près Schemes', [75–600]; G Moffat, *Trusts Law Text and Materials* (4th edn, CUP, Cambridge, 2005) 911–12; JD Davies, 'Trusts' [1972] *ASCL* 261.

[166] Eg, in England: *In re Harwood; Coleman v Innes* [1936] Ch 285, 288 (legacy to the Peace Society of Belfast; no evidence to show that there had ever been a society of that name; a general charitable intention existed; doubted in *Re Koeppler's WT; Barclay's Bank Trust Co Ltd v Slack* [1984] Ch 243 (CA) on the basis that peace societies are political and non-charitable); *In re Satterthwaite's WT; Midland Bank Executor and Trustee Co Ltd v Royal Veterinary College* [1966] 1 WLR 277 (CA) ('London Animal Hospital' had not existed as a charity); *In re Davis; Hannen v Hillyer* [1902] 1 Ch 876 (legacy to 'the Home for the Homeless'; was not, nor ever had been in London, any charitable institution by that name; general charitable intent inferred; legacy applied *cy-près*). Cf: *In re Goldschmidt (decd); Commercial Union Ass Co Ltd v Central British Fund for Jewish Relief and Rehabilitation* [1957] 1 WLR 524 (Ch) ('Fund for the Relief of Distressed German Jews in England' had never existed; no general charitable intent; gift failed).

[167] In *In re Knox; Fleming v Carmichael* [1937] Ch 109, Luxmoore J sought to establish a general charitable intent as a matter of construction, rather than adhere to the usual presumption. VTH Delany notes this to have been an 'anomalous case' amongst the cadre of fictitious institution cases: 'Cy-près Application of Gifts to Fictitious Institutions' (1957) 73 *LQR* 166, 167.

[168] Eg, in England: *In re Harwood; Colman v Innes* [1936] Ch 285, 287 (legacy to Wisbech Peace Society; had existed at one time; no general charitable intent; testatrix meant *that* society and gave it only to it; that gift lapsed); *In re Rymer; Rymer v Stanfield* [1895] 1 Ch 19 (CA) (legacy of £5,000 to the rector of St Thomas' Seminary for the education of priests in the diocese of Westminster; seminary ceased to exist prior to the testator's death; no general charitable intention; gift lapsed); *In re Goldschmidt (decd); Commercial Union Ass Co Ltd v Central British Fund for Jewish Relief and Rehabilitation* [1957] 1 WLR 524 (Ch) (two other bequests to named institutions which had existed but which had folded; no general charitable intention; gifts failed, lapsed into residue); *Re Tharp; Longrigg v The People's Dispensary for Sick Animals of the Poor Inc* [1942] 2 All ER 358 (Ch) (gifts to the Jerusalem Society for the Prevention of Cruelty to Animals of Jerusalem; society became defunct; no general charitable intention; gifts lapsed) rev'd on another point not material for present purposes; *Re Slatter's WT; Turner v Turner* [1964] Ch 512; *In re Spence (decd); Ogden v Shackleton* [1979] Ch 483, 494; *Purday v Johnson* [1886–90] All ER Rep 1111 (Ch). Eg, in Ireland: *In the matter of Prescott (decd); Purcell v Pobjoy* [1990] 2 IR 342, 347.

[169] See: *In re Finger's WT; Turner v Ministry of Health* [1972] 1 Ch 286 (bequest to National Council for Maternity and Child Welfare, which had existed at one time; '[*Harwood*] did not say that it was impossible to find a general charitable intention where there is a gift to an identifiable body which has ceased to exist but only that it would be very difficult . . . In the present case the circumstances are very special'; general charitable intent found; this particular gift applied *cy-près*).

Not all jurisdictions adhere so plainly to this distinction, however. For example, whilst a number of Australasian decisions do suggest that a general charitable intent will be easier to prove in the case of a never-existing institution[170] than a formerly existing one,[171] the New South Wales Court of Appeal has certainly resisted the notion that there is any rule of construction to that effect, deeming it to be illogical.[172] It has been said that, in light of rapid social change, the early law on failed charitable bequests to institutions that do not exist should be approached with some caution.[173] The state of authority in Canada is also decidedly mixed, with some recent decisions supporting the presumptions,[174] and some authority going against.[175]

It must be mentioned for the sake of completeness that if the institution is merely described by the wrong name, and if there is evidence of what the settlor or testator had in mind when he designated an institution incorrectly, then the trust instrument or will can be rectified to ensure that its provisions correspond with that intention.[176] For example, one of the dispositions in *In re Spence's WT; Ogden v Shackleton*[177] constituted a misdescription ('The Blind Home, Scott Street, Keighley' when the correct name was 'Keighley and District Home for the Blind'), which was rectified. No *cy-près* scheme is entailed in this circumstance at all.

[170] Eg, in Australia: *Murdoch v A-G (Tasmania)* (Tas SC, 4 Aug 1992) (non-existent International Red Cross); *Re Constable (decd)* [1971] VR 742, 745 (non-existent Methodist Homes for the Aged at Cheltenham); *Re Pace (decd)* (1985) 38 SASR 336, 341; *Re Daniels (decd)* [1970] VR 72. In New Zealand: *Re Pettit* [1988] 2 NZLR 513, 547 (non-existent Doctors Widows Fund).

[171] Eg, *Re Godfree (decd)* [1952] VLR 353, 358; *Re Mills* [1934] VLR 158; *Re Tyrie (decd) (No 1)* [1972] VR 168, 184–85; *Re Smith* [1954] SASR 151; *Estate of Foran (decd); Mair v A-G for NSW* (NSWSC, 20 Nov 1987). See, for further authorities: GE Dal Pont and DRC Chalmers, *Equity and Trusts in Australia and New Zealand* (LBC Information Services, Sydney, 1996) 408–9.

[172] *A-G (NSW) v Public Trustee* (1987) 8 NSWLR 550 (CA) 554, and followed in, eg: *Public Trustee v A-G (NSW)* (NSWSC, 10 Feb 1994) 12; *A-G (NSW) v Barr* (NSWCA, 11 Oct 1991) 9–10; *Perpetual Trustee Co Ltd v Minister for Health of the State of NSW* (NSWSC, 13 Dec 1990) [no pp].

[173] *A-G (NSW) v Barr* (NSWCA, 11 Oct 1991) 8 (Kirby P).

[174] Eg: *Re Leer Estate* (Sask QB, 13 Jun 2005) [10]; *Re Nakonechny Estate* (2003), ACWS (3d) 620 (Alta QB) [7] (*cy-près* scheme could not be ordered; presumption against a general charitable intent seemingly assumed where two organisations for the education of young priests no longer existed); *British Columbia (Official Administrator) v Ridge Meadows Assn for Community Living* (1999), 86 ACWS (3d) 464 (BCSC) [28]–[45], citing authority to similar effect: *Montreal Trust Co v Richards* (1982) 40 BCLR 114, [1983] 1 WWR 437 (BC SC); *Re Hunter; Genn v A-G (BC)* (1973), 34 DLR (3d) 602 (BCSC).

[175] Eg: *Johnston Estate v Cavalry Baptist Church for Ganaraska Woods Retreat Centre* (2002), ACWS (3d) 752 (SCJ) (bequest to 'Ontario School for Retarded Children'; once existed, but not at the date of the testator's death; yet a general charitable intent found and a *cy-près* scheme ordered); *Weatherhead Estate v Canada* (1995), 57 ACWS (3d) 682 (New Brunswick CA) (intended beneficiary scholarship trust no longer existed; yet a general charitable intent found); *Re Fraser Estate* (2000), 99 ACWS (3d) 525 (PEI SC) (bequest to 'Ethiopian Youth Scholarship Fund'; never existed; no general charitable intent found to exist; no *cy-près* scheme; gift lapsed into residue).

[176] For further discussion and case authorities: AJ Oakley, *Parker and Mellows Modern Law of Trusts* (8th edn, Sweet & Maxwell, London, 2003) 483; GE Dal Pont and DRC Chalmers, *Equity and Trusts in Australia and New Zealand* (LBC Information Services, Sydney, 1996) 406; P Luxton, *The Law of Charities* (OUP, Oxford, 2001) 578; ECE Todd, 'The *Cy-près* Doctrine: A Canadian Approach' (1954) 32 *Can BR* 1100, 1109–1110.

[177] [1979] Ch 483.

Is the charitable gift one of residue (the 'last basket' of the will)?   In *Re Raine (decd); Walton v A-G*,[178] it was suggested that, where a residuary gift is made for a purpose that is charitable, and there is a surplus left after that purpose is fulfilled, 'the overriding intention of a charitable disposition should still prevail, with the result that this surplus must be applied *cy-près*'. An example of a residuary disposition which failed, and that evidenced a general charitable intent, can be found in *In re Woodhams (decd); Lloyds Bank Ltd v London College of Music*.[179] A residuary gift was bequeathed to two colleges of music to found scholarships, to be restricted to orphan boys from children's homes. The colleges refused to accept the gift on those terms. The gift was applicable *cy-près,* discarding that restriction, given that (in the court's view) the provision for orphan boys was not an essential part of the testator's intention. The principle has been noted with approval in other jurisdictions,[180] and influential academic commentary confirms that a general charitable intention may be more willingly discovered where the gift is of the residuary estate.[181]

Have next-of-kin been provided for in other dispositions?   Where the testator expressly states in a recital clause that he has no immediate family and wishes, on that account, to give his estate to charity, or where it is otherwise plain that he had no close relatives for whom he wished to make provision, a general charitable intent may be more willingly inferred[182]—although there are certainly decisions where this factor had absolutely no effect.[183] Similarly, if the testator never married, had no children, and left specific legacies to each one of his brothers and sisters, then the court may conclude that the testator had considered the extent to which he wished to benefit his family and made provisions accordingly, and that he had a general charitable intent with respect to the rest of his estate.[184]

Conversely, where the testator had a close family, the court may be prepared to infer that he would wish the property to fall back into the residue of the

---

[178] [1956] Ch 417, 423.

[179] [1981] 1 WLR 493 (Ch) 505. Also, eg: *In re Royce; Turner v Wormald* [1940] Ch 514.

[180] Eg, in NZ: *Re Waite (decd); Cox v NZ Ins Co Ltd* [1964] NZLR 1034 (CA) 1038. Eg, in Canada: *Weninger Estate v Canadian Diabetes Assn* (1993), 2 ETR (2d) 24 (Ont HC); *Re Buchanan Estate* (1996), 61 ACWS (3d) 841 (BCSC).

[181] Of the many examples, a few will suffice: RP Meagher and WMC Gummow, *Jacobs' Law of Trusts in Australia* (6th edn, Butterworths, Sydney, 1997) [1068] fn 593, citing: *In re Monk; Giffen v Wedd* [1927] 2 Ch 197, and DH McMullen *et al, Tudor on Charities* (6th edn, Sweet & Maxwell, London, 1967) 285–86; P Luxton, *The Law of Charities* (OUP, Oxford, 2001) 560; G Dal Pont, *Charity Law in Australia and New Zealand* (OUP, Oxford, 2000) 315; G Moffat, *Trusts Law Text and Materials* (4th edn, CUP, Cambridge, 2005) 911.

[182] *In re Finger's WT; Turner v Ministry of Health* [1972] Ch 286. Particularly relevant in: *Public Trustee v A-G (NSW)* (NSWSC, 10 Feb 1994) 15–16; *ANZ Executors and Trustee Co Ltd v Trustee for the Presbyterian Church of Australia* (NSWSC, 12 Jun 1990) 28.

[183] Eg: *Adamson Estate v McIntyre* (1997), 70 ACWS (3d) 200 (Ont Gen Div) [27]; *Alacoque v Roache* [1998] 2 NZLR 250 (CA), where the testator provided a specific reason for excluding her relatives, yet a general charitable intent was not found.

[184] *McLean v A-G (NSW)* [2002] NSWSC 377, [62].

estate and devolve to those residuary beneficiaries in the event that the gift failed.[185]

Is the ultimate residuary beneficiary a charity?   Suppose that the charitable gift which fails is contained within a will, the residuary beneficiary of which is a charity.

This factor has assumed some significance since *In re Goldschmidt; Commercial Union Assurance Co Ltd v Central British Fund for Jewish Relief and Rehabilitation*.[186] A testatrix bequeathed, out of her residuary estate, 17 pecuniary legacies—14 of these were to be made to charitable bodies, which did not present a problem; and two bequests were made to institutions which had ceased to exist before the date of her death (those two lapsed). The remaining legacy was 'to the Fund for the Relief of Distressed German Jews in England the sum of £ 5,000'. Finally she directed her trustees to hold any balance of her residuary estate on trust for another charity, 'the Hospital for Sick Children, Great Ormond Street, WC1'. There had never been a fund by the former name in existence, and the question arose as to whether that bequest of £5,000 could be distributed *cy-près* in favour of two organisations with somewhat similar objects. A *cy-près* scheme was rejected, and the legacy fell into residue and passed to the hospital for sick children, the ultimate residuary beneficiary. The court was satisfied that the testatrix had plainly intended to give the £5,000 to a particular institution, which failed; and the final residuary legatee, being a charity, was designed to act as a net, catching whatever charitable objects might fail. Thus, Harman LJ concluded that, given that the final 'net' for the testatrix's money was a charity, there was no room for any finding in favour of a general charitable intent in relation to the specific bequest of the £5,000.

The decision in *Goldschmidt* has not been universally endorsed. It has been both distinguished on its facts,[187] and academically criticised.[188] Ong, for example, suggests[189] that it was wrongly decided, and that the decision goes against earlier Privy Council authority stating that a general charitable intention can be proven, and the *cy-près* doctrine invoked, upon the failure of a specific charitable bequest, 'whether the residue be given to charity or not'.[190] Certainly, the weight to be accorded to this particular factor for determining whether a general charitable intention exists is highly doubtful.

Whether the testator had a particular connection to that particular charitable institution.   If the evidence shows that the testator had a particularly close

---

[185] As expressly found in: *Re Charlesworth Estate* (1996), 62 ACWS (3d) 632 (Man QB) [52].

[186] [1957] 1 WLR 524 (Ch).

[187] *In re Harwood; Coleman v Innes* [1936] Ch 285.

[188] VTH Delany, 'Cy-près Application of Gifts to Fictitious Institutions' (1957) 73 *LQR* 166 (arguing that where the residuary legatee is also a charity, a gift to a fictitious institution should not raise a presumption of general charitable intent, but should be established affirmatively and as a matter of construction, as favoured in *Harwood*).

[189] D Ong, *Trusts Law in Australia* (Federation Press, Sydney, 1999) 320–21.

[190] *Mayor of Lyons v Adv-General of Bengal* (1876) LR 1 App Cas 91 (PC).

connection or affinity with the charitable institution named in the will (which institution was defunct at the date of his death, for example), then a general charitable intention will be difficult to establish. This appeared to motivate the court in *Re Slatter's WT; Turner v Turner*,[191] where the testator gift property to a particular TB hospital at which her daughter had been a longterm patient for over a decade before her death. There was no general charitable intent, no *cy-près* distribution was possible, and the gift lapsed. Other jurisdictions have considered the factor similarly important in negating a general charitable intention.[192] In contrast, the court concluded in *Public Trustee v A-G (NSW)*[193] that, although the gift was to a hospital for the elderly, the testator herself had no connection with it, and a general charitable intention to benefit charitable medical services for the elderly could be inferred.

Miscellaneous other factors.   Given the comprehensive study of the United States' jurisdiction undertaken in the early seminal work by Fisch, it is apposite to note a few further matters that were apparent to that author as relevant to American courts' discretion, but which have not appeared to be significant in English or Commonwealth case law to date. Nevertheless, they are noted for the sake of completeness:

> A general charitable intent has also been implied where the bulk of the donor's fortune is given to charity, and conversely where the bulk of the donor's fortune is given to a private individual no general charitable intent has been found. The fact that the trust was motivated by a desire to perpetuate the memory of the settlor or some other person does not preclude a finding of general intent, although in several cases it has been held to be some evidence of a lack of a general intent.[194]

E   APPLYING THE PROPERTY *CY-PRÈS*

Under the general law *cy-près* doctrine, whatever purposes are substituted by means of a *cy-près* scheme must resemble (under the strict case law position), 'as near as possible', the original purposes designated by the donor.[195] In other words, 'the purposes of the charitable trust are modified to purposes which are similar in theme to the original purposes but allow for modern conditions.'[196]

---

[191]   [1964] Ch 512.
[192]   *Forge v Dorsman* (NSWSC, 10 Jul 1990) 32.
[193]   (NSWSC, 10 Feb 1994) 17–18.
[194]   EL Fisch, *The Cy-près Doctrine in the United States* (Matthew Bender & Co, Albany NY, 1950) 152–53 (footnotes and case citations omitted).
[195]   See, eg: *Da Costa v De Pas* (1754) Amb 228; 27 ER 150; *A-G v Whitchurch* (1896) 3 Ves 114; *A-G v Ironmongers' Co* (1844) 10 Cl & F 908, 922; all noted in *In re The Worth Library* [1994] 1 ILRM 161 (and discussed in 'Casenote', *ILT Digest* (1994) 201, 201). For further early authorities espousing the same view, see: LA Sheridan and VTH Delany, *The Cy-près Doctrine* (Sweet & Maxwell, London, 1959) 39, fn 37.
[196]   *Westminster CC v Duke of Westminster* [1991] 4 All ER 136 (Ch) 142 (Harman J).

Certainly, there have been some notable exceptions to this rule, whereby courts have varied the original charitable purposes to an extent that may have distinctly upset the testator, had he been alive. In one of the most celebrated of these,[197] a trust to provide income for 'the redemption of British slaves in Turkey and Barbary' was applied *cy-près* to 'supporting and assisting charity schools in England and Wales, where the education is according to the Church of England'. Very occasionally, there is some *obiter* to be found in early English case law[198] that supports a wider application of property *cy-près* than the 'as near as possible' mantra usually espoused. However, for the most part, a close analogy between the donor's intention and the *cy-près* scheme 'has been more than a lodestar . . .; it has been the pilot steering the courts'.[199]

Some view the selection of objects 'as near as possible' to the donor's original purposes as a key underpinning of the *cy-près* doctrine. The rationale for a narrow *cy-près* application is four-fold:

- ✓ the court owes a duty to the donor to dispose of the property in accordance with his intentions, given that it is the general charitable intent of the donor (either presumed if subsequent failure or proven if initial failure) to which the court is giving effect;
- ✓ 'keeping faith' with donors is important, because if property is diverted from the original purposes, donors will be deterred from giving to charity;
- ✓ the cost of administering a charity that is close to the original purposes will presumably be less than some differently-focussed scheme;
- ✓ adherence to the donor's wishes prevents whimsical change, 'with every fluctuation of popular opinion' about how the property may be 'better applied';[200] and
- ✓ because a charitable trust must be for the public benefit, by virtue of its legal definition, then choosing analogous purposes also serves a public utility.[201]

---

[197] *A-G v Ironmongers' Co* (1841) Cr & Ph 208, 227. See also: *In re Dominion Students' Hall Trust; Dominion Students' Hall Trust v A-G* [1947] Ch 183; and *Da Costa v De Pas* (1754) Amb 228; 27 ER 150, cited in OLRC, *The Law of Trusts* (1996), vol II, 459, fn 141, another case viewed as 'remarkable', in RP Meagher and WMC Gummow, *Jacobs' Law of Trusts in Australia* (6th edn, Butterworths, Sydney, 1997) [1071].

[198] Most notably: *In re Weir Hospital* [1910] 2 Ch 124 (CA) 132 (Cozens-Hardy MR) ('Where the *cy-près* doctrine has to be applied, it is competent to the Court to consider the comparative advantages of various charitable objects and to adopt by the scheme the one which seems most beneficial').

[199] OLRC, *The Law of Trusts* (1996) vol 2, 459.

[200] EL Fisch, *The Cy-près Doctrine in the United States* (Matthew Bender & Co, Albany NY, 1950) 141, citing: *Harvard College v Soc for Promoting Theological Education*, 3 Gray 280, 301 (Mass 1855) in relation to the ancillary question of how widely the triggers for the *cy-près* jurisdiction should be defined.

[201] These arguments are variously noted, eg, in: S Gardner, *An Introduction to the Law of Trusts* (2nd edn, OUP, Oxford, 2003) 225–26; F Gladstone, *Charity, Law and Social Justice* (Bedford Square Press, London, 1982) 124–25; LA Sheridan and VTH Delany, *The Cy-près Doctrine* (Sweet & Maxwell, London, 1959) 39–44, 47–51.

Against these stands the contention that it ought to be possible to select wider purposes, without reference to the donor's original intention (favouring public welfare over the 'dead hand', as Fisch puts it[202]), for the following reasons:

✓ the *cy-près* scheme could then be drafted with a greater degree of flexibility to achieve an effective and viable project that also has public benefit, to a greater extent than choosing purposes closely associated with the settlor's wishes;

✓ given that 'the role of the doctrine is, in part, to subvert [the settlor's] intention'[203] in any event, it is somewhat artificial to then seek to fasten onto the doctrine the requirement of a very close analogy;

✓ permitting substituted purposes that do not correlate with the donor's favoured application of the property could avoid the wasteful duplication of charitable facilities that are already provided by another charity or by the state;

✓ especially in cases of subsequent failure, why should attention be paid to the donor's original intention, when it was exhausted in the initial absolute gift to charity?

✓ the special treatment that charitable trusts garner (eg, exemption from the rule against perpetuities) has costs for society (*viz*, longterm withdrawal of assets from general use, testators who control their assets from the grave at the expense of the living), and the *quid pro quo* for this is that, when the charitable purpose fails, society ought to obtain its full money's worth by having the property applied so as to realise its best potential;[204]

✓ distributing property with exactitude and as intended 'is less important than other social goals of the law' and that there should be a wide stance adopted in the mis-allocation of property to afford justice;[205] and

✓ a further *quid pro quo* for a wide application of trust property is that, for all the cases where the doctrine is successfully implemented in order to re-direct trust property for substituted purposes, much trust property languishes un-utilised, moribund, and wasted because the doctrine's beneficial operation has not yet been fully applied to those trusts.

As will be discussed in the following chapter, the abovementioned arguments have received legislative attention. In particular, a lesser standard for *cy-près*

---

[202] EL Fisch, *The Cy-près Doctrine in the United States* (Matthew Bender & Co, Albany NY, 1950) 146.

[203] A Hudson, *Equity and Trusts* (4th edn, Cavendish Publishing, London, 2005) 898.

[204] S Gardner, *An Introduction to the Law of Trusts* (2nd edn, OUP, Oxford, 2003) 226. Also see: OLRC, *Report on the Law of Charities* (1996) 406, 428–29; Fisch, *ibid*, 140–44; LA Sheridan and VTH Delany, *The Cy-près Doctrine* (Sweet & Maxwell, London, 1959) 39–44, 47–51; Charity Comm for England and Wales, *Milestones: Managing Key Events in the Life of a Charity* (2003) 33–34.

[205] W Bradford, 'With a Very Great Blame on Our Hearts: Reparations, Reconciliation, and an American Indian Plea for Peace with Justice' (2002) 27 *American Indian L Rev* 1, 91.

application of trust property has been explicitly adopted within some statutory *cy-près* schemes. The philosophy of choosing other purposes 'as near as possible' that has been so evident under the general doctrine of *cy-près* has been partially eroded by Parliamentary, judicial and administrative intervention, and rightly so, in this author's opinion.

4

Charitable Trusts: Statutory Cy-près

A INTRODUCTION

WHEN THE NATHAN COMMITTEE delivered its report in 1952,[1] it concluded that law of charitable trusts *cy-près* was in a poor state. The general law *cy-près* doctrine (especially the threshold triggers of 'impossibility' or 'impracticability') was too limited,[2] and whatever statutory *cy-près* schemes were available had too narrow an application.[3] The Nathan Committee recommended[4] a statutory *cy-près* regime that was wider than the common law version, certainly allowing modification of charitable trusts where the circumstances fell short of impracticability. This was ultimately implemented in the Charities Act 1960. Re-enacted in materially the same terms in s 13 of the Charities Act 1993,[5] the court or the Charity Commissioners are legislatively empowered to alter the original purposes of a charitable trust in defined circumstances. Several other jurisdictions, such as New Zealand,[6] the various State jurisdictions in Australia,[7] Scotland,[8] Ireland,[9] and Northern Ireland,[10] have followed England's lead and have introduced either identical or fairly similar provisions. This chapter will examine and critique the statutory *cy-près* doctrine,[11] by reference to both English and other relevant jurisprudence.

---

[1] *Report of the Committee on the Law and Practice Relating to Charitable Trusts* (Cmd 8710) (HMSO, London, 1952) (*Nathan Committee Report*).

[2] *Ibid*, [104], [110], [118]–[119].

[3] *Viz*, under the Charitable Trusts Act 1853, c 137, the Endowed Schools Acts 1869, and the City of London Parochial Charities Act 1883, cited in: J Warburton, 'The Spirit of the Gift' (1995/96) 3 *Charity Law and Practice Rev* 1, 2.

[4] *Nathan Committee Report*, [365].

[5] Commenced operation 1 Aug 1993. Since enacted as part of the law of the British Virgin Islands by virtue of Trustee (Amendment) Act 2003, discussed further in: J Husbands, 'Charity Trust Reform' (2004) 10(4) *Trusts and Trustees* 26.

[6] Charitable Trusts Act 1957 (NZ), s 32.

[7] Charitable Trusts Act 1993 (NSW), ss 9–11; Trusts Act 1973 (Qld), s 105; Trustee Act 1936 (SA), s 69B; Variation of Trusts Act 1994 (Tas), s 5; Charities Act 1978 (Vic), s 2; Charitable Trusts Act 1962 (WA), s 7.

[8] Law Reform (Miscellaneous Provisions) (Scotland) Act 1990, s 9. This section is not affected in any material respect by the Charities and Trustee Investment (Scotland) Act 2005, which received Royal Assent on 14 Jul 2005.

[9] Charities Act 1961 (Republic of Ireland), s 47.

[10] Charities Act (Northern Ireland) 1964, s 22.

[11] For the purposes of this chapter, this means the powers contained in s 13 of the Charities Act 1993, and its equivalents. For discussion of the court's *cy-près* jurisdiction under s 15 with respect to charitable charter companies, or under s 17 for charities established or regulated by an Act of Parliament, see, eg: P Luxton, *The Law of Charities* (OUP, Oxford, 2001) 546–47.

The relationship between the statutory *cy-près* doctrine and other statutory and general law raises some interesting questions for consideration. For example, does statutory *cy-près* represent a code, ousting and replacing the common law *cy-près* doctrine, or do they run in tandem? This and other issues will be considered in Section B. The English statutory *cy-près* regime, and its various analogues, will comprise the focus of discussion in Section C. In particular, this section will analyse how the 'general charitable intent' requirement is treated under statute, what *cy-près* triggers are specified, and various ancillary matters associated with s 13's terms. Attention will then turn, in Section D, to the important respects in which other jurisdictions have *departed* from England's statutory *cy-près* regime. Such differences in legislative treatment provide a useful basis for comparison and possible future development. The chapter will conclude, in Section E, with some discussion upon procedural aspects of the *cy-près* jurisdiction under statute.

The scope of *cy-près* scheme-making power now permitted by the various statutory schemes, and considered in this chapter, inevitably raises a philosophical tension about the role of the court, as the English Court of Appeal explained in *Varsani v Jesani*:

> potential donors should not be deterred by a belief that their intentions will be overridden by a too ready use of the *cy-près* jurisdiction. . . . but that problem has to be set beside the equal but opposite problem that, in circumstances unforeseen by the donor, his or her bounty may not achieve all that was intended or was reasonably feasible. The balance between those two considerations has to be struck and was struck by Parliament in 1960 [by s 13]. . . . Since then it has been the duty of the court fairly to apply the provisions of that section to the circumstances of each case without any predilection either to making or to refusing to make a scheme.[12]

It should also be noted, before consideration begins of the substantive law underpinning the statutory *cy-près* doctrine, that (contrary to other jurisdictions where the making of *cy-près* schemes remains within the jurisdiction of the courts), most *cy-près* schemes in England are made by the Charity Commissioners,[13] it being observed that the courts have contributed little to the development of the *cy-près* doctrine in England since 1960.[14] It is only for those applications that involve special questions of law (such as whether the bequest was made with a 'general charitable intention), or are otherwise in dispute, that the Commission's jurisdiction is ousted by the court.[15] As far as the English jurisdiction is concerned, general reference to 'court' should be taken to include reference to the 'Charity Commission', as and where appropriate throughout this chapter, unless the context indicates otherwise.

---

[12] [1999] Ch 219 (CA) [29] (Morritt LJ).

[13] Charities Act 1993, s 18(1).

[14] L Sheridan, '*Cy-près* Application of Three Holloway Pictures' (1993/94) 2 *Charity Law and Practice Rev* 181, 182.

[15] See Charities Act 1993, s 16(1), (3), (10).

B RELATIONSHIP BETWEEN STATUTORY *CY-PRÈS* AND OTHER LAW

1. *Cy-près* Doctrine under General Law

The triggers to invoke the general law *cy-près* doctrine and the preconditions that trigger the statutory *cy-près* regime are not identical in scope. The statutory regime, in its various guises around the Commonwealth, does not permit open-slather amendment of trusts purposes, whenever societal or economic conditions dictate that it would be desirable, and in that sense, they are still of 'limited' effect.[16] The regime has been said to preserve the essence of the general law, but to allow a 'certain liberality to a court in seeking to apply trust property *cy-près* ... which it may not have previously been confident in applying'.[17] Both English[18] and Australian[19] courts are in complete agreement that the statutory regimes substantively change the common law by expanding the triggers that enable the court to deal with a *cy-près* application, and that earlier judgments must hence be treated with a degree of circumspection. It is a case of reform, rather than restatement, of what constitutes failure of a charitable purpose— given that it is no longer necessary that actual compliance with the original terms should be impossible or impracticable.[20]

The extended powers conferred by legislation to enable exercise of the *cy-près* jurisdiction, however, do not provide an all-encompassing code. In particular, the general *cy-près* doctrine's requirement of a general charitable intent is still required under the English statutory regime and its equivalents;[21] the property must still be given by the donor for 'exclusively charitable purposes'; and the 'working tests'[22] of obsolescence and impracticability which were judicially developed at general law retain some relevance when matched with a corresponding statutory trigger. All of the learning in respect of these topics

[16] J Warburton, 'Trusts: Still Going Strong 400 Years after the Statute of Charitable Uses' in DJ Hayton (ed), *Extending the Boundaries of Trusts and Similar Ring-Fenced Funds* (Kluwer Law Intl, The Hague, 2002) 174.

[17] *In the matter of Peirson Memorial Trust* [1995] QSC 308 (7 Dec 1995), referring to the Queensland legislation, Trusts Act 1973, s 105, which is in identical terms to the English legislation.

[18] *Varsani v Jesani* [1999] Ch 219 (CA) [16] (Morritt LJ) ('when reading the old cases and considering the applicability today of the principles they embody it is essential to remember the narrowness of the *cy-près* jurisdiction which then existed'). Also: *In re Lepton's Charity; Ambler v Thomas* [1972] 1 Ch 276, 284–85 (s 13 'in part restates the principles applied under the existing law, but also extends those principles'), cited with approval in: *Oldham BC v A-G* [1993] Ch 210 (CA) 221.

[19] *Public Trustee of Qld as trustee of the Anzac Cottages Trusts v A-G (Qld)* [2000] QSC 175 [15]– [16], [18]; *Forrest v A-G (Vic)* [1986] VR 187, 189–90; *Fowler v Geelong College and Kardinia Intl College (Geelong)* (Vic SC, 13 Dec 1996) 17; *Trustees of the Kean Memorial Trust Fund v A-G (South Australia)* (2003) 86 SASR 449; *Aston v Mount Gambier Presbyterian Charge* (2002) 84 SASR 109, 118; *A-G (NSW) v Fulham* [2002] NSWSC 629 (19 Jul 2002) [16].

[20] *Oldham BC v A-G* [1993] Ch 210 (CA) 218. See further: L Sheridan, *Keeton and Sheridan's The Modern Law of Charities* (4th edn, Barry Rose Law Publishers, Chichester, 1992) 221.

[21] But not under all statutory regimes, as discussed in Section D.

[22] So-called by Harman J in: *Westminster CC v Duke of Westminster* [1991] 4 All ER 136 (Ch) 142.

must underpin the statutory regime to make sense of it.[23] In these respects at least, the general law *cy-près* doctrine retains an extremely significant role.

A question arises as to whether the common law doctrine actually runs parallel to the statutory regime, or whether the court *must* consider an application to vary charitable purposes under statute. In other words, can a hopeful charity, for example, seek to invoke the *cy-près* jurisdiction under *either* statute *or* common law?

The issue has been a live one to date in both South Australia and New Zealand, and has given rise to some division of judicial opinion. In respect of the South Australian statutory *cy-près* regime,[24] it was held in *Aston v Mount Gambier Presybterian Charge*[25] that its wording does not exclude the operation of the general *cy-près* doctrine. Instead, it 'provides a further solution to the same or similar problems',[26] so that the terms of a testamentary gift could be varied by either a *cy-près* scheme under the general law or a trust variation under the statute.[27] Not all authority from this jurisdiction concurs, however. In *Trustees of the Kean Memorial Trust Fund v A-G (South Australia)*,[28] the court opined that the statute appeared to encompass the general law principles developed by the equity courts in relation to *cy-près* schemes, 'and it is difficult to see where the section does not at least cover the same area previously covered by those principles.' In New Zealand too, some courts have expressed the view that the statutory regime in that jurisdiction provides the *only* avenue for dealing with failure of charitable purposes[29] (that 'the case must be dealt with in accordance with Part III [of the Charitable Trusts Act 1957] and not under the inherent jurisdiction of the Court'[30]), whilst others have seemingly treated the common law doctrine as an alternative route to a *cy-près* scheme.[31]

[23] For similar comment, see, eg: C Rickett, 'Failure of Charities and the Conundrum of s 32' [2003] *NZLJ* 59, 60; OLRC, *The Law of Trusts* (1996), vol 2, 462; G Dal Pont, *Charity Law in Australia and New Zealand* (OUP, Oxford, 2000) 286.

[24] Contained in: Trustee Act 1936 (SA), s 69B, describing that the charitable purposes 'may be altered by a scheme' in stipulated circumstances.

[25] *Aston v Mount Gambier Presbyterian Charge* (2002) 84 SASR 109 (Duggan J).

[26] *Ibid*, [40].

[27] *Ibid*, [44].

[28] (2003) 86 SASR 449, [56].

[29] *Re Pettit* [1988] 2 NZLR 513, 546 ('In New Zealand, the Court is required to apply s 32(1) if the case falls within that section; to that extent the section has replaced the *cy-près* doctrine'). Also see: *Re Gift for Life Trust* (NZ HC, 9 Nov 2000) [9]; *Re McElroy Trust* [2002] 3 NZLR 99, [15], aff'd: [2003] 2 NZLR 289 (CA); *Re Palmerston North Halls Trust Board* [1976] 2 NZLR 161 (SC) 165. Note that the reasoning utilised in *Palmerston* was criticised in: RJ Smith, 'Trusts' [1977] *ASCL* 298, 299.

[30] *Re Twigger* [1989] 3 NZLR 329, 340; *Re Palmerston North Halls Trust Board* [1976] 2 NZLR 161, 163–65.

[31] *Alacoque v Roache* [1998] 2 NZLR 250 (CA) 255–56 ('During the course of the hearing a reference was made to: *Re Palmerston North Halls Trust Board* [1976] 2 NZLR 161 in which it was held, *inter alia*, that in any case falling within s 32(1) of the Charitable Trusts Act, the property must be disposed of in accordance with Part III of the Act. We would wish to reserve our opinion on that'), and see, on this point: C Rickett, 'Failure of Charities and the Conundrum of s 32' [2003] *NZLJ* 59, 60, and also: 'The Dead Hand's Grip' [1988] *NZLJ* 335, 335, where the author rightly notes that, given the rarity with which these matters reach the CA, it was unfortunate that it was not dealt with.

The reality is that this debate is probably only academic: the court in *Aston* chose to rely upon the statutory power because it was more convenient and easier to do so;[32] there exists no case authority in any jurisdiction, so far as can be ascertained, which utilises the general *cy-près* doctrine in preference to an available statutory regime; and even if the rare case were to arise whereby the general law provided some scope for varying a charitable trust which the statutory regime did not, and that regime were viewed as a code, the court's administrative scheme-making power could probably permit the variation in any event.[33]

2. Administrative Scheme-making Doctrine

The statutory *cy-près* power considered in this chapter does not oust or affect the general administrative scheme-making power of the court under its inherent jurisdiction.[34]

Administrative schemes, of course, do not alter the purposes of a trust but seek to clarify them, or 'fill the gaps'. In contrast, the *cy-près* doctrine is only activated under statute if the 'original purposes' of the charitable trust—the purposes for which the property was originally given—are to be altered.[35] If the alterations in the charitable purposes sought to be made by the trustee 'fall on the administrative side of the line, going, as it does, to the mechanics of how the property devoted to charitable purposes is to be distributed',[36] then there is absolutely no question of any statutory *cy-près* power being invoked.

This point was neatly demonstrated by *In re Laing Trust; Stewards' Co Ltd v A-G*.[37] When the trust was created in 1922 by the settlor's transference of £15,000 worth of shares in his company to the plaintiff trustee, to be held on charitable trust, it was stipulated by memorandum that the capital and income were to be wholly distributed within the settlor's lifetime or within 10 years of his death. The settlor died in 1978, by which time his company had expanded into a large group of public companies. Over these several decades, there was an 'astonishing' increase in the value of the trust fund; by 1982, it was worth approximately £24 million. The settlor had indicated prior to his death that he wished to withdraw the stipulation that the capital should be distributed within

---

[32] In South Australia, the conditions for a *cy-près* distribution under the general law are more onerous than under statute, because of the fact that the latter does away with proof of a general charitable intent, a matter discussed later in the chapter.

[33] This point is also made by: G Dal Pont, *Charity Law in Australia and New Zealand* (OUP, Oxford, 2000) 286, and fn 13.

[34] *City of Burnside v A-G (South Australia) (No 2)* (SC SA, 1 May 1998); *Hunter Region SLSA Helicopter Rescue Service Ltd v A-G (NSW)* [2000] NSWSC 456 (22 May 2000).

[35] *Oldham BC v A-G* [1993] Ch 210 (CA) 219 (Dillon LJ).

[36] *In re J W Laing Trust; Stewards' Co Ltd v A-G* [1984] Ch 143, 153 (Peter Gibson J).

[37] *Ibid*. For a thorough analysis of this case, see, eg: P Luxton, 'In Pursuit of "Purpose" Through Section 13 of the Charities Act 1960' [1985] *Conv* 313, 315–17 ('Although the phrase used "can be altered" in s 13, logically it must follow that the only schemes falling within the section are those in which the original purposes in fact *are* altered').

10 years of his death, but this amendment was never achieved. On the basis that it was expedient to distribute only the income for the designated charitable purposes (Christian evangelism and the relief of poverty), and not the capital, the trustees sought to delete the 10-year stipulation. Being purely administrative (rather than altering an 'original purpose' of the trust), it was held that the stipulation could not be deleted under any *cy-près* scheme, but it was capable of being removed by the court's inherent administrative scheme-making power.

3. Impact of the European Convention on Human Rights

It was stated in *Varsani v Jesani*[38] that, when directing a *cy-près* scheme under s 13 of the Charities Act 1993, the court operates as a 'public authority' under s 6(1) of the Human Rights Act 1998, such that it must take into account the European Convention on Human Rights when exercising its *cy-près* power. Of particular relevance when drafting a scheme for charitable purposes that have failed are: article 9 (protection of religious beliefs) and article 14 (freedom from discrimination on grounds of colour, gender, religion, etc).

As Watt notes, this creates a potential dilemma when the donor's original charitable purpose was discriminatory. The trust may fail, in this scenario, because the trustees refuse to administer the trust in its present form—or it could be argued that such a trust should be deemed to constitute a failed trust *ab initio* if it infringes article 14.[39] Either way, the court's task is to identify an alteration of purpose, 'as near as possible' to the testator's original purpose, bearing in mind the rights and values of the Convention. Traditionally, English courts have creatively circumvented discriminatory trusts, when trustees have refused to act, by declaring that the trustees were integral to the donor's wishes (and hence, it was not a case of finding another trustee who *would* administer the trust); that the trust thereby failed; that it could only be saved by applying the property *cy-près*; that this would require evidence of a general charitable intention; that such an intention existed on the facts; and that a *cy-près* scheme could suitably be drafted, without the discriminatory provision attached, that would honour the testator's intention 'as near as possible'.[40] In so doing, '[t]he reality, of course, is

---

[38] Ch, 31 Jul 2001, [10].

[39] G Watt, *Trusts and Equity* (OUP, Oxford, 2003) 317.

[40] See, eg: *In re Dominion Students' Hall Trust; Dominion Students' Hall Trust v A-G* [1947] Ch 183 (students' hall of residence operated under a charity; constitution contained a colour bar restricting students to those of European origin (hence, white); colour bar deleted under *cy-près* scheme); *In re Lysaght (decd); Hill v Royal College of Surgeons* [1966] 1 Ch 191 (testatrix gave funds to Royal College of Surgeons to establish medical studentships; gift subject to restrictions that recipients were to be male and not of Jewish or Roman Catholic faith; religious disqualification deleted under *cy-près* scheme). For an analogous case: *In re Woodhams (decd); Lloyds Bank Ltd v London College of Music* [1981] 1 WLR 493 (Ch) (testator musician left residuary gifts to music colleges for music scholarships for orphans from named charitable homes; adequate public grants were available for musical education of such orphans; colleges were only prepared to accept gifts if restriction removed; restriction removed under *cy-près* scheme).

that the court quite deliberately by-passed the letter, and probably the spirit, of the donation. The unspoken rule seems to be that malevolent spirits do not count.'[41] The deletion of the discriminatory provision would now also serve to satisfy the court's Convention obligations.

4. Where No Scheme Required Prior to Statute

By virtue of s 29 of the Charities Act 1993, any charitable trustees who hold land as part of the permanent endowment of a charity, or for the purposes of the charity, have the power to sell that land with the consent of the court or of the Charity Commissioners. The relationship between this power of sale and the *cy-près* scheme-making power of s 13 arose for consideration in *Oldham BC v A-G*.[42]

A donor conveyed land to the council on trust to 'preserve and manage it at all times as playing fields for the benefit and enjoyment of the inhabitants of their areas'. This site, the Clayton Playing Fields, came to be very valuable real estate. It was proposed that it be sold to developers for a large sum, and that other land be bought by the council elsewhere to provide a sports-field and improved public facilities. The first legal problem was that if it were part of the 'original purposes' of the charitable trust that the playing fields should be retained, then any sale authorised under s 29 of the Charities Act would inevitably involve an alteration of the original purposes, which would require a *cy-près* scheme. An alteration of the original purposes, however, was only permitted via statutory *cy-près* if at least one of the *cy-près* triggers outlined under statute applied (to be dealt with in more detail in Section C). That was the second problem—the property could still be used for the purposes for which the donor originally gave it, and none of the triggers applied, so there was no room for application of the statutory *cy-près* doctrine.[43] Thus, what was to happen to the Clayton Playing Fields?

The Court of Appeal resolved this potential impasse by holding that, prior to the statutory *cy-près* regime, the mere sale of charitable property and reinvestment of the proceeds in the acquisition of other property to be held for precisely the same charitable purposes, did not require a *cy-près* scheme (power of sale was simply exercised with judicial consent[44]); and the statutory *cy-près* regime was not intended to require a *cy-près* scheme in any circumstances where none

[41] G Watt, *Trusts and Equity* (OUP, Oxford, 2003) 318. For similar doubts as to whether this case was reconcilable with legal principle, see, eg: AJ Oakley, *Parker and Mellows Modern Law of Trusts* (8th edn, Sweet & Maxwell, 2003) 490.

[42] [1993] Ch 210 (CA).

[43] The case was decided under Charities Act 1960, s 13, which contained the same wording for present purposes. The Charities Act 1992, which contained the new version of s 13 eventually consolidated in Charities Act 1993, was not in force at the time of the judgment.

[44] The CA cited the following earlier cases as authority for this proposition: *In re Ashton Charity* (1856) 22 Beav 288; *In re Parke's Charity* (1842) 12 Sim 329; and *In re The North Shields Old Meeting House* (1859) 7 WR 541.

had been required previously. The court concluded of s 13, '[t]hat section is concerned with the *cy-près* application of charitable funds, but sales of charitable lands have, in so far as they have been dealt with by Parliament, always been dealt with by other sections not concerned with the *cy-près* doctrine.'[45] Thus, the trust was not affected by the provisions of s 13.

This conclusion could only apply, however, if the court broadly construed (as it did) that the land itself was not fundamental to the 'original purpose' of the gift.[46] The situation could well be different (explained the court[47]) if the property devoted to a charitable purpose was the essence of the charity. For example, where a particular house once owned by an historical figure was left on trust for the public benefit, then in that circumstance, if the property was to be sold, the original purposes of the charitable trust *would* most certainly be altered, and that could only be permitted if the *cy-près* jurisdiction in s 13 was satisfied. In this case, however, retaining the Clayton Playing Fields was not part of the 'original purposes' of the trust. The charitable purpose was instead construed to be providing playing fields for the inhabitants of the donor's district, which could easily be undertaken at another site altogether. No alteration to the original purposes of the trust was wrought by the proposal to sell the land.

The decision has been judicially approved since,[48] and has been academically mooted[49] to be of significance to many local authorities to whom parks or recreational grounds have been given on trust by benefactors, and where serious upgrade of the facilities could be achieved at another site altogether if the present premises were sold for a sizable sum.

C THE 'ENGLISH VERSION' STATUTORY CY-PRÈS

It may be useful to describe a couple of the most important features of the statutory *cy-près* scheme contained within s 13 and its equivalents, before turning attention to the preconditions, or triggers, for the *cy-près* jurisdiction to apply.

Given for a charitable purpose.   It has previously been observed[50] that, under the general law, the *cy-près* doctrine could not operate where the bequest was not for exclusively charitable purposes. This position is retained by all statutory *cy-près* regimes, prefaced as they are with this or similar wording:

---

[45] [1993] Ch 210 (CA) 222.

[46] It was on this point that the CA and trial judge Chadwick J, reported at [1992] 4 LMELR 97, diverged.

[47] [1993] Ch 210 (CA) 222–23.

[48] Applied by analogy in: *Barnes v Derby Diocesan Board of Finance* [2003] Ch 239, 248.

[49] D Morris, 'Oldham Borough Council v A-G (Casenote)' (1992/93) 1 *Charity Law and Practice Rev* 157, 161;—, 'Civil Proceedings: *Oldham Borough Council v A-G*' (1992) 5(4) LMELR 166, 167.

[50] See pp 54–7.

> in any case where any property . . . is given or held upon trust, or is to be applied, for any **charitable purpose** . . .

It has been judicially reiterated that the regimes simply cannot apply if the property is devoted to a non-charitable purpose.[51]

General charitable intent. It will be recalled[52] that, under the general law, the significant distinction between cases of initial failure of a charitable purpose trust and cases of subsequent failure was that a *cy-près* scheme under the former could not be directed unless a 'general charitable intent' could be discerned. No such general charitable intent was required to be proven in the case of subsequent failure—it was presumed, because once the property is applied to the original charitable purpose, the property is earmarked as a charitable fund for all time, always dedicated to charity.

This legal position has been reproduced under the English statutory *cy-près* regime and in some jurisdictions around the Commonwealth. The categorisation of circumstances which will invoke *cy-près*, stated in s 13(1), extends the availability of *cy-près* far beyond impossibility or impracticability, but in no way affects the general case law pre-requisite that, in cases of initial failure, the charitable gift will lapse unless a general charitable intent can be proven.[53] Hence, s 13(2) states:

> Subsection (1) shall not affect the conditions which must be satisfied in order that property given for charitable purposes may be applied *cy-près* except in so far as those conditions require a failure of the original purposes

Notably, not all statutes have reproduced this English position; this diversity of legal treatment will be discussed later in the chapter.

1. Triggers for the Statutory *Cy-près* Jurisdiction

There are eight separate triggers to enable alteration of a charitable trust's purposes under s 13 (and its analogues in other jurisdictions). The grounds are

---

[51] *Public Trustee v A-G (NSW), Jarrett, Muller and Davies* (1997) 42 NSWLR 600 (Eq) 609 (Santow J). For further discussion on this point, see: C Rickett, 'Politics and *Cy-près*' [1998] *NZLJ* 55, 56 ('The case *[Jarrett]* raised similar issues to *[Re Collier (decd)* [1998] 1 NZLR 81], and in my view, Santow J dealt with them in the correct manner').

[52] See pp 63–4.

[53] *In re JW Laing Trust; Stewards' Co Ltd v A-G* [1984] Ch 143, 149, and further reiterated in, eg: *Halsbury's Laws of England* (4th edn reissue, Butterworths, London, 1996) vol 5(2), [207]; A Hudson, *Equity and Trusts* (4th edn, Cavendish Publishing, London, 2005) 895.

independently drafted; only one needs to be satisfied in any given scenario.[54] Obversely, the grounds are not mutually exclusive, more than one may apply to invoke the *cy-près* jurisdiction.[55] Indeed, some preconditions tend to accompany each other in given fact situations.[56]

There appears to be nothing to preclude the section from applying to either cases of initial failure or to subsequent failure of the charitable trust—the fact that the requirement of a general charitable intent is preserved in s 13(2) adds force to the assertion that cases of initial failure fall within the province of the section. Although some doubt has been cast upon whether s 13 could apply to cases of initial failure,[57] the weight of academic opinion is emphatically that it does;[58] and as will be seen later in this section, trusts which have failed at the outset have certainly been varied under s 13 equivalents in other jurisdictions. Although the previous case law on impossibility or impracticability is still relevant, in that relevant cases can be slotted under one or more of these eight statutory triggers for analogy and distinction with present conundrums, these triggers now codify the circumstances in which the *cy-près* jurisdiction can be invoked.

Having regard to each of these statutory preconditions, and to notable jurisprudence that has arisen in relation to each of them, in turn, they are:

Fulfillment:

> s 13(1)(a)(i): the original purposes of a charitable gift can be altered to allow the property to be applied *cy-près* where the original purposes, in whole or in part, have been as far as may be fulfilled[59]

---

[54] This was plainly indicated by *Varsani v Jesani* [1999] Ch 219 (CA), and noted further in:—, 'Cy-près' [1998] *All ER Ann Rev* 277, 278; and see too: British Columbia LRC, *Report on Non-Charitable Purpose Trusts* (1992) 56, fn 31.

[55] Eg, on identical wording of the relevant provisions in Queensland, in *In the matter of Peirson Memorial Trust* [1995] QSC 308 (7 Dec 1995), s 105(1)(b), (e)(ii), and (c) were satisfied.

[56] Eg, s 13(1)(a)(ii) and (e)(iii) (and their equivalents in other jurisdictions) tend to be grouped together: *Public Trustee of Qld as trustee of the Anzac Cottages Trusts v A-G (Qld)* [2000] QSC 175; *Fowler v Geelong College and Kardinia Intl College (Geelong)* (Vic SC, 13 Dec 1996). Of these two provisions, Sir John Pennyquick noted in *In re Lepton's Charity; Ambler v Thomas* [1972] 1 Ch 276, 285 that (e)(iii) 'appears to be no more than a final writing out large' of (a)(ii).

[57] —, 'Cy-près' [1998] *All ER Ann Rev* 277, 278.

[58] Eg: G Moffat, *Trusts Law Text and Materials* (4th edn, CUP, Cambridge, 2005) 908; DJ Hayton and C Mitchell, *Hayton and Marshall Commentary and Cases on the Law of Trusts and Equitable Remedies* (12th edn, Sweet & Maxwell, London, 2005) 515; M Chesterman, *Charities, Trusts and Social Welfare* (Weidenfeld and Nicolson, London, 1979) 277–78; JG Riddall, *The Law of Trusts* (6th edn, Butterworths, London, 2002) 184–85; PH Pettit, *Equity and the Law of Trusts* (9th edn, Butterworths, London, 2001) 318 and fn 8.

[59] Reproduced in: Trusts Act 1973 (Qld), s 105(1)(a)(i); Variation of Trusts Act 1994 (Tas), s 5(3)(a)(i); Charities Act 1978 (Vic), s 2(1)(a)(i); Charities Act 1961 (Ire), s 47(1)(a)(i); Law Reform (Miscellaneous Provisions) (Scotland) Act 1990, s 9(1)(a)(i). The same effect is obtained in: Trustee Act 1936 (SA), s 69B(1)(a)(i), read together with s 69B(6).

Even in the absence of statutory *cy-près*, this would have constituted a failure of the charitable trust's purpose under the general law *cy-près* doctrine. It would cover, for example, where a surplus of funds given for research into a particular disease remains after a cure has been discovered,[60] or where the body of persons intended to be assisted by the charitable fund can no longer be found.[61]

Impossibility or impracticability:

> s 13(1)(a)(ii): the original purposes of a charitable gift can be altered to allow the property to be applied *cy-près* where the original purposes, in whole or in part, cannot be carried out, or not according to the directions given and to the spirit of the gift[62]

Although the wording of this section may appear as if it only applies to sub-sequent failure—where the trust has been in operation, but cannot be carried out later in time—that construction has not been upheld, at least in Australia. According to *Aston v Mount Gambier Presbyterian Charge*[63] (which concerned equivalent legislation in South Australia[64]), the section can certainly apply to trusts which fail *ab initio*.[65] The wording of the section was wide enough to encompass a charitable trust that suffered an initial failure, where the testator had left part of her residuary estate to the 'Scot's Presbyterian Church Building Fund of Mount Gambier', but there had never been an entity or fund of that name in existence. A *cy-près* scheme was permitted, with the property to be applied to the Presbyterian Church of Mount Gambier for building purposes. Other Australian authorities have similarly held, upon the same wording as

---

[60] Example given in: E Cairns, *Charities: Law and Practice* (3rd edn, Sweet & Maxwell, London, 1997) 176.

[61] Eg, the British slaves in Turkey and Barbary requiring 'redemption' in *A-G v Ironmongers' Co* (1841) Cr & Ph 208, example noted by: A Hudson, *Equity and Trusts* (4th edn, Cavendish Publishing, London, 2005) 896.

[62] Reproduced in: Trusts Act 1973 (Qld), s 105(1)(a)(ii); Variation of Trusts Act 1994 (Tas), s 5(3)(a)(ii); Charities Act 1978 (Vic), s 2(1)(a)(ii); Trustee Act 1936 (SA), s 69B(1)(a)(ii); Charities Act 1961 (Ire), s 47(1)(a)(ii). Somewhat different wording is used in: Law Reform (Miscellaneous Provisions) (Scotland) Act 1990, s 9(1)(a)(ii) (that the purposes 'can no longer be given effect to'). The 'spirit of the gift' requirement is considered later in the chapter.

[63] [2002] SASC 332 (9 Oct 2002) (Duggan J).

[64] Trustee Act 1936 (SA), s 69B(1)(a)(ii).

[65] *Aston v Mount Gambier Presbyterian Charge* [2002] SASC 332 (9 Oct 2002), citing: GE Dal Pont and DRC Chalmers, *Equity and Trusts in Australia and New Zealand* (LBC Information Services, London, 1996) 292. See, also, HA Picarda, *The Law and Practice Relating to Charities* (3rd edn, Butterworths, London, 1999) 310, who argues that to permit it for *ab initio* failure is a sensible result, otherwise 'the trustees would merely need to wait for a token period and then apply to the court, which would say the least, be an odd result').

s 13(1)(a)(ii), that the section embraces initial failure of a charitable trust.[66] As expected, the trigger contained in this section has also permitted a *cy-près* application of trust property—in England[67] and in Victoria[68]—in the case of subsequent failure.

Several of the triggers that were sufficient to establish 'failure' of the charitable trust at general law, considered previously,[69] have equal application under this provision. Notably, the literal wording of the section lends itself to the possible finding that no *cy-près* scheme will be invoked because insufficient time has elapsed to determine whether the original purpose 'cannot be carried out'.[70]

The standard imputed by this phrase 'cannot be carried out' is not one of impossibility. Mere impracticability will suffice. Thus, where a trust was established to provide 'rest homes for ladies', the Victorian Supreme Court[71] agreed that, whilst not impossible to effect, the trust was highly impracticable. The trustees were opposed to any scheme that excluded male residents, and government funding could be jeopardised if the homes were to be conducted for one sex only. Pursuant to (a)(ii), a *cy-près* scheme that permitted a care home for the elderly was ordered. This recent case law mirrors those well-known earlier English authorities in which, the trustees being plainly uncomfortable about certain restrictions imposed by the donor upon those who could benefit from the charitable trust, *cy-près* schemes were permitted because the purposes 'could not be carried out'.[72]

---

[66] See: *Morton v A-G (Vic)* (Vic SC, 23 Dec 1996) (a hospital named in testator's will had ceased to exist as a hospital; property applied *cy-près* to another hospital of similar characteristics to the closed hospital); *Scott v Anti-Cancer Council of Vic* (VSC, 5 Sep 1996) (residuary estate left to Victorian Cancer Research Foundation; no such institution; general intent evinced to devote residuary estate to research of causation, prevention and treatment of cancer; gift applied *cy-près* to the Anti-Cancer Council of Victoria).

[67] Eg: *In re Lepton's Charity; Ambler v Thomas* [1972] 1 Ch 276 (*cy-près* scheme ordered to increase the original £3 annual income payable to a church minister); *Charity of John Haywood, Report of the Ch Comm for England and Wales* (1968) [14]–[19] (restriction of payout to poor Quakers of not more than two guineas to any one person removed); *Royal Holloway and Bedford New College* (1993) 1 Decisions of the Ch Comm 21 (although no reference to s 13 actually occurs in the decision)—discussed and critiqued in: L Sheridan, 'Cy-près Application of Three Holloway Pictures' (1993/94) 2 *Charity Law and Practice Rev* 181.

[68] *Forrest v A-G (Vic)* [1986] VR 187 (*cy-près* scheme ordered to remove restriction that charities eligible for income from the testamentary trust were those in existence in 1965, the date of the testator's death).

[69] See pp 59–62.

[70] As occurred in: *Trustees of the Kean Memorial Trust Fund v A-G (South Australia)* (2003) 86 SASR 449 (25 Jul 2003) (trust's original purpose was provision of grassed playing area for school children; possible zoning alterations of adjoining properties meant that insufficient time had elapsed for conclusion to be drawn that the original purpose could not be fulfilled).

[71] *Roman Catholic Trusts Corp for the Diocese of Melbourne v A-G (Vic)* (Vic SC, 19 Nov 1993). Another case involving the same trustee, wherein a trust was established for 'orphan boys', was widened via a *cy-près* scheme to include needy young males and females: *Roman Catholic Trusts Corp for the Diocese of Melbourne v A-G (Vic)* [2000] VSC 360.

[72] *In re Lysaght (decd)* [1966] 1 Ch 191; *In re Dominion Students' Hall Trust v A-G* [1947] 1 Ch 183; *In re Woodhams (decd); Lloyds Bank Ltd v London College of Music* [1981] 1 WLR 493 (Ch). This point also noted in, eg: P Luxton, *The Law of Charities* (OUP, Oxford, 2001) 565, that the special restriction would be considered under the statute these days to constitute either part of the original purposes or a direction which could be deleted.

Surplus property:

> s 13(1)(b): the original purposes of a charitable gift can be altered to allow the property to be applied *cy-près* where the original purposes provide a use for part only of the property available by virtue of the gift[73]

This section is particularly apposite where the value of the original bequest, or the income derived from it, have significantly increased in value.[74] This scenario has applied, to permit a *cy-près* scheme, in the Queensland case of *In the matter of the Peirson Memorial Trust.*[75] The income generated by the trust exceeded (and would always exceed) what was required for the original purpose, the maintenance of the residential home for underprivileged children. This provision may also have permitted a prompt *cy-près* scheme in respect of an endowment for a French prize at the University of Newcastle,[76] had the NSW legislation[77] been enacted at the time; as it was, the trust was not 'impracticable' at general law, and no *cy-près* order was made.

Amalgamation:

> s 13(1)(c): the original purposes of a charitable gift can be altered to allow the property to be applied *cy-près* where the property available by virtue of the gift and other property applicable for similar purposes can be more effectively used in conjunction, and to that end can suitably, regard being had to the spirit of the gift, be made applicable to common purposes[78]

---

[73] Reproduced in: Trusts Act 1973 (Qld), s 105(1)(b); Variation of Trusts Act 1994 (Tas), s 5(3)(b); Charities Act 1978 (Vic), s 2(1)(b); Charities Act 1961 (Ire), s 47(1)(b); Trustee Act 1936 (SA), s 69B(1)(b). Almost similar wording used in: Law Reform (Miscellaneous Provisions) (Scotland) Act 1990, s 9(1)(b).

[74] E Cairns, *Charities: Law and Practice* (3rd edn, Sweet & Maxwell, London, 1997) 177. According to HL Nathan, this provision would have covered old cases such as *In re King; Kerr v Bradley* [1923] 1 Ch 243 (erection of stained glass window did not use up all the charitable bequest): *The Charities Act 1960* (Butterworths, London, 1962) 76.

[75] [1995] QSC 308, 18 (7 Dec 1995) ('Not only is it increasingly impracticable to give effect to the intention of the settlers of the trusts, but to confine the activities of the trust in that way leads to a surplus of income which will accumulate'). Also the basis for the *cy-près* order in: *Crowther v Brophy* [1992] 2 VR 97.

[76] *Perpetual Trustee Co Ltd v U of Newcastle* (NSWSC, 12 Nov 1991).

[77] Charitable Trusts Act 1993 (NSW), s 9(1), considered later in the chapter.

[78] Reproduced in: Trusts Act 1973 (Qld), s 105(1)(c); Variation of Trusts Act 1994 (Tas), s 5(3)(c); Charities Act 1978 (Vic), s 2(1)(c); Trustee Act 1936 (SA), s 69B(1)(c); Charities Act 1961 (Ire), s 47(1)(c).

Oakley suggests[79] that this section does not involve a *cy-près* scheme at all, given that a consolidation of a number of charities has always been possible without invoking the *cy-près* jurisdiction. The author of the law reform report that prompted the enactment of this provision agrees. Lord Nathan commented[80] that the power contained in this section was not strictly a *cy-près* scheme, and overlapped, to a great extent, with the court's power to make administrative schemes.[81]

By way of an alternative simplified procedure, it should be noted that the Charities Act 1993 provides separately that trustees of a charity with a previous year's income of < £5,000 and no land devoted to charitable purposes may transfer its property to another charity,[82] or amend the charity's purposes so that they become suitable and effective[83]—all without any regard being necessary to the 'spirit of the gift', as s 13(1)(c) requires.

Unsuitability in class or area:

---

s 13(1)(d): the original purposes of a charitable gift can be altered to allow the property to be applied *cy-près* where the original purposes were laid down by reference to an area which then was, but has since ceased to be, a unit for some other purpose, or by reference to a class or persons or to an area which has for any reasons since ceased to be suitable, regard being had to the spirit of the gift, or to be practical in administering the gift[84]

This trigger has been unsuccessfully relied upon for a *cy-près* scheme in Queensland,[85] in circumstances where a church building the subject of the trust was damaged by fire, and the trustees sought to apply the insurance monies to purposes other than the repair of the church. It was argued that the area set aside for the church was no longer appropriate, and would be better devoted to other uses. The court rejected that application on the basis that:

---

[79] AJ Oakley, *Parker and Mellows Modern Law of Trusts* (8th edn, Sweet & Maxwell, London, 2003) 486, citing: *In re Faraker; Faraker v Durell* [1911–1913] All ER Rep 488. Point also noted in: G Watt, *Law of Trusts* (3rd edn, Blackstone Press, London, 2001) 181–82; M Sladen, 'The Charities Act 1985' [1986] *Conv* 78, 83; P Luxton, *The Law of Charities* (OUP, Oxford, 2001) 567; HA Picarda, *The Law and Practice Relating to Charities* (3rd edn, Butterworths, London, 1999) 310.

[80] HL Nathan, *The Charities Act 1960* (Butterworths, London, 1962) 76. Similarly: J Warburton, *Annotated Charities Act 1993* (Sweet & Maxwell, London, 1993) 10–21.

[81] Administrative schemes are contained in Charities Act 1993, s 16(1)(a), authorising 'establishing a scheme for the administration of a charity'.

[82] Charities Act 1993, s 74(2), (3). See generally: Charity Comm for England and Wales, *Small Charities* (2004).

[83] *Ibid*, s 74(5).

[84] Reproduced in: Trusts Act 1973 (Qld), s 105(1)(d); Charities Act 1978 (Vic), s 2(1)(d); Charities Act 1961 (Ire), s 47(1)(d). Somewhat similar wording is used in: Law Reform (Miscellaneous Provisions) (Scotland) Act 1990, s 9(1)(c)(i) and (ii).

[85] *Re Corp of the Synod of the Diocese of Brisbane* [1995] QSC 334 (14 Dec 1995).

[t]here is nothing to suggest that the land and improvements on it may not now and for an indefinite time in the future be used for purposes within the spirit of the trust created in 1887–88 ... the parishioners who donate their time and resources so that the trust property may be used for the purpose for which it was acquired and developed are both willing and able to provide the human and financial resources necessary to enable it to continue to be used, as it has been used for more than 100 years.[86]

Similarly, where an educational charity requires its monies to be used to further education in one London suburb, and the trustees would prefer to apply the funds to support a school in another London suburb, there is no question of any *cy-près* scheme while the former suburb has a continuing and unsatisfied need for education, which the funds would assist in providing.[87]

A *cy-près* order under this section was more successful, however, in England in *Peggs v Lamb*,[88] in which two ancient charitable trusts in favour of the freemen and their widows of the borough of Hungtingdon since 'time immemorial' was inferred. Due to legislative and social changes,[89] by 1991, the class of freemen entitled to benefit had considerably reduced (to 15 only), and the trust income had so increased (to over £500,000) that it was felt that the annual benefit to a freeman (> £30,000) was more than the charitable trust had envisaged. The court approved of a scheme whereby the income was only paid to freemen in need, and the surplus was to be used to help poor and sick inhabitants of the borough.

As Cairns notes,[90] this provision is a useful one by which to delete restrictive conditions that the donor originally stipulated, whether as to geographic area or class of beneficiaries—although even where the trust is widened by a *cy-près* scheme, the court may insist on the trustees giving preference to the members of the original class or location. Indeed, that preferential aspect has been evident in several schemes noted by the Charity Commissioners, from 'patients who belong to the educated middle classes'[91] to pupils wishing to learn English, rather than other languages.[92] Nathan provides further instances of the potential application of the section—where local government boundaries change over time, so that it may be difficult to identify the area mentioned in the original trusts of a charity after the changes have taken place; or where the class of beneficiaries is hard to identify; or is otherwise provided for.[93] Practically speaking, Warburton

---

[86] *Ibid*, Ambrose J (no pp available).

[87] See: *Corp of the Master Wardens and Court of Assistants of the Mystery or Art of Brewers of the City of London v A-G* (Ch, 23 Jul 1999) [13].

[88] [1994] Ch 172, 197.

[89] Under the Municipal Corporations Act 1835, membership of the class of freemen to benefit from this charity was restricted to those who were the sons of freemen and born in the ancient borough.

[90] E Cairns, *Charities: Law and Practice* (3rd edn, Sweet & Maxwell, London, 1997) 178.

[91] See the scheme discussed in: *Report of the Ch Comm for England and Wales* (1985) [36]–[38].

[92] See the scheme discussed in: Ch Comm for England and Wales, *Annual Report—Making a Difference* (2002–03).

[93] HL Nathan, *The Charities Act 1960* (Butterworths, London, 1962) 76.

and Barr postulate that the section can also serve a useful function where two charities provide, say, care for the elderly in the same area, and wish to merge for greater efficiency and utility.[94]

Quite apart from this provision, the English statute also provides some further permissions as to when schemes may be drafted by enlarging the area originally stipulated.[95]

Purposes taken over by others:

> s 13(1)(e)(i): the original purposes of a charitable gift can be altered to allow the property to be applied *cy-près* where the original purposes, in whole or in part, have, since they were laid down, been adequately provided for by other means[96]

This trigger has been applied, for example,[97] to charities for the maintenance of roads or bridges, but where such upkeep was now provided for out of rates or taxes (the property being applied *cy-près* to promote the arts, to provide seats or shelters, to preserve old buildings, or to improve local amenities). This provision, which was an expansion in the law (this trigger not being sufficient for a *cy-près* scheme under the general law[98]) was particularly intended to address the inter-relationship between the public and charitable sectors:

> The Nathan Committee considered that filling the gaps in public services and pioneering in new types of educational, social and cultural work were particularly appropriate to charitable trusts, and this new jurisdiction will be particularly useful in enabling charities who feel that their work overlaps that of a local or national authority to apply for a scheme under which they will be able to devote their funds or part of them to purposes which are not otherwise provided for.[99]

---

[94] J Warburton and W Barr, 'Charity Mergers—Property Problems' [2002] *Conv* 531, 532–34.

[95] See: Charities Act 1993, s 13(4) and Sch 3.

[96] Reproduced in: Trusts Act 1973 (Qld), s 105(1)(e)(i); Variation of Trusts Act 1994 (Tas), s 5(3)(e)(i); Charities Act 1978 (Vic), s 2(1)(e)(i); Trustee Act 1936 (SA), s 69B(1)(e)(i); Charities Act 1961 (Ire), s 47(1)(e)(i); Law Reform (Miscellaneous Provisions) (Scotland) Act 1990, s 9(1)(d)(i).

[97] See: *Report of the Ch Comm for England and Wales* (1968) [67]–[72], which noted that where the objects of a charity for purposes of repair of bridges, sea banks, highways and pavements had become the statutory responsibility of government, *cy-près* schemes would be implemented. Example also noted in: *Report of the Ch Comm for England and Wales* (1972) [50]–[52], and in *Report* (1970) [43].

[98] Noted by: P Luxton, *The Law of Charities* (OUP, Oxford, 2001) 569, citing: *A-G v Day* [1900] 1 Ch 31.

[99] HL Nathan, *The Charities Act 1960* (Butterworths, London, 1962) 77.

Purposes no longer charitable:

> s 13(1)(e)(ii): the original purposes of a charitable gift can be altered to allow the property to be applied *cy-près* where the original purposes, in whole or in part, have, since they were laid down, ceased, as being useless or harmful to the community or for other reasons, to be in law charitable[100]

This section is the 'odd one out' of the *cy-près* triggers listed in s 13, for it contemplates a *cy-près* scheme for a trust that was once charitable but which has lost its charitable status. In other words, the trust has become a *non-charitable purpose trust*, and will remain so until the *cy-près* scheme is devised. The other provisions of s 13 all contemplate that the trust's charitable status remains, but performance of the trust has become inexpedient, frustrated, or extremely difficult—the traditional province of the *cy-près* doctrine.

Academically speaking, this provision has been viscerated. For example, as Jaconelli cogently argues, (e)(ii) suffers from a number of difficulties. The provision 'has extended the scope of *cy-près* beyond its natural habitat' with no further guidance. It is not clear from the drafting whether statutory changes that render something that was charitable and *remains useful and purposeful* (such as an independent school) non-charitable, is covered by the provision, given the reference to purposes 'useless or harmful to the community'. Under the *ejusdem generis* rule of statutory interpretation (queries Jaconelli), should the operation of the section be limited to charitable trusts that are now harmful or useless only? Furthermore, the various difficulties associated with any non-charitable purpose trust (which this trust is, until the *cy-près* power is applied to it) are not dealt with by s 13 at all, leaving a 'lacuna in the legislation in that the legal position has not been rendered entirely clear in regard to the situation between loss of charitable status and the devising of a [*cy-près*] scheme.'[101]

Luxton further argues[102] that the provision has been misunderstood in *Peggs v Lamb*,[103] where Morritt J expressed the *obiter* view that once the class of persons likely to benefit from the charitable purpose shrunk to such a point that the trust could not be considered to be for a 'section of the public', then the trust would

---

[100] Reproduced in: Trusts Act 1973 (Qld), s 105(1)(e)(ii); Variation of Trusts Act 1994 (Tas), s 5(3)(e)(ii) (with slight variation); Charities Act 1978 (Vic), s 2(1)(e)(ii); Trustee Act 1936 (SA), s 69B(1)(e)(ii); Charities Act 1961 (Ire), s 47(1)(e)(ii). Somewhat similar wording is used in: Law Reform (Miscellaneous Provisions) (Scotland) Act 1990, s 9(1)(d)(ii) ('ceased to be such as would enable the trust to become a recognised body').

[101] J Jaconelli, 'Independent Schools, Purpose Trusts and Human Rights' [1996] *Conv* 24, 31–32, where all three points are raised and explored in further detail.

[102] P Luxton, *The Law of Charities* (OUP, Oxford, 2001) 570.

[103] [1994] Ch 172, 197. As noted previously, a *cy-près* scheme was ordered under s 13(1)(d).

cease to be charitable, and the property could be applied *cy-près* under (e)(ii). To the contrary, Luxton submits that, 'once a purpose has been held to be charitable, it does not cease to be so merely because the number of persons to benefit ceases to comprise a sufficient section of the community.'

So far as can be ascertained, no case law authority in any of the jurisdictions under consideration has turned upon this provision. Assuming that the provision *does* cover statutory or common law changes from charitable to non-charitable status, some examples indicate that the provision may have some work to do in the future. One illustration is the decision of the English Charity Commissioners to rule that the purposes of rifle and pistol clubs could no longer be construed as charitable (as they once were[104]), given the 'radical change in circumstances' over the last century.[105] Other trusts that could well have been charitable at law once, but which would not now be so, include trusts that promote smoking[106] or anti-vivisection.[107] Presumably, then, the courts or Commissioners would be able to draft a *cy-près* scheme in respect of any trusts in favour of these sorts of purposes that have become legally frustrated.[108] By way of further example, academic commentary has suggested that the section could potentially apply: if an independent school was ever to have its charitable status withdrawn;[109] if some charity that was registered as a charity (and thus, conclusively presumed to be charitable[110]) was removed from the register[111] because the Commissioners considered its purpose no longer to

---

[104] *Re Stephens; Giles v Stephens* (1892) 8 TLR 792.

[105] (1993) 1 Decisions of the Ch Comm 10, and this example also cited in: J Jaconelli, 'Independent Schools, Purpose Trusts and Human Rights [1996] *Conv* 24, 31 and fn 19.

[106] Cracknell provides the example of a trust for the provision of tobacco for residents in aged homes, established before the harmful effects of tobacco were known: DG Cracknell (ed), *Charities: The Law and Practice* (Thomson Sweet & Maxwell, London, 1994–) [looseleaf] [I.64].

[107] See, eg: JE Martin, *Hanbury and Martin Modern Equity* (17th edn, Sweet & Maxwell, London, 2005) 462, who cites the example of trusts against vivisection, which were charitable under *In re Foveaux* [1895] 2 Ch 501, and then were declared not to be so in *National Anti-Vivisection Society v IRC* [1948] AC 31 (HL) because *Foveaux* was held to have been wrongly decided.

[108] Cf Luxton's argument that the provision should only apply to those purposes that have *ceased* to be charitable, as the wording provides, and not to those that were *never* charitable at law: P Luxton, *The Law of Charities* (OUP, Oxford, 2001) 571 (for this reason, Luxton argues that an anti-vivisection trust would not fall within the province of (e)(ii)). Of similar view: HA Picarda, *The Law and Practice Relating to Charities* (3rd edn, Butterworths, London, 1999) 313; GW Keeton, *Modern Developments in the Law of Trusts* (Faculty of Law, Queen's University, Belfast, 1971) 310.

[109] Eg: AJ Oakley, *Parker and Mellows Modern Law of Trusts* (8th edn, Sweet & Maxwell, London, 2003) 487; JE Martin, *Hanbury and Martin Modern Equity* (17th edn, Sweet & Maxwell, London, 2005) 462; Luxton, *ibid*, 570; J Jaconelli, 'Independent Schools, Purpose Trusts and Human Rights' [1996] *Conv* 24, 30–32. If this were to happen, a further conundrum arises—what would happen to its property? Should that be applied *cy-près*? See, on this point: J Burchfield, 'Private Action, Public Benefit' (2003) 2 *PCB* 110, 113–14.

[110] Charities Act 1993, s 4(1).

[111] As obliged under Charities Act 1993, s 3(4).

be charitable at law;[112] or if a charity ceased to be a trust for a 'section of the public'.[113]

Although (e)(ii) does not expressly say so, the *cy-près* scheme devised by the court must surely be for charitable purposes, rather than for any purposes 'as near as possible' to the original intention of the donor which has itself become non-charitable. This is supportable on the basis that courts have been averse in the past to ordering any *cy-près* scheme, the charitable lawfulness of which is open to question. For example, in *A-G (NSW), v Fulham*,[114] the court declined an invitation to direct that a part of the trust funds be set aside for the maintenance of war memorials. Whilst it was submitted that a war memorial is a work of public utility under the fourth head of *Pemsel's* categorisation,[115] Bryson J held that 'provision of a memorial may well fall outside the relevant concept of public benefit, and it would not be appropriate for me to include a provision the lawfulness of which was doubtful in a scheme ordered by the Court.'[116] Elsewhere, it has also been reiterated that the substituted scheme must be legally charitable, or approval will be refused.[117]

Ineffectiveness:

> s 13(1)(e)(iii): the original purposes of a charitable gift can be altered to allow the property to be applied *cy-près* where the original purposes, in whole or in part, have, since they were laid down, ceased in any other way to provide a suitable and effective method of using the property available by virtue of the gift, regard being had to the spirit of the gift[118]

This trigger for *cy-près* represents a considerable liberality upon the common law doctrine, allowing a court to apply property to other charitable purposes in

---

[112] Suggested by: HL Nathan, *The Charities Act 1960* (Butterworths, London, 1962) 77–78; HA Picarda, *The Law and Practice Relating to Charities* (3rd edn, Butterworths, London, 1999) 313; GW Keeton, *Modern Developments in the Law of Trusts* (Faculty of Law, Queen's University, Belfast, 1971) 310.

[113] Suggested by: JE Martin, *Hanbury and Martin Modern Equity* (17th edn, Sweet & Maxwell, London, 2005) 462, as a possible ground for alteration of the trust's purpose under *Peggs v Lamb* [1994] Ch 172, although reliance on this ground was ultimately unnecessary. Note, though, the rebuttal of this argument by Luxton, cited above, fn 102 above.

[114] [2002] NSWSC 629 (19 Jul 2002).

[115] *Commissioners for the Special Purposes of the Income Tax v Pemsel* [1891] AC 531 (HL) 583 (Lord Macnaghten).

[116] [2002] NSWSC 629, [87].

[117] *Re Tennant* [1996] 2 NZLR 633, 636.

[118] Reproduced in: Trusts Act 1973 (Qld), s 105(1)(e)(iii); Variation of Trusts Act 1994 (Tas), s 5(3)(e)(iii); Charities Act 1978 (Vic), s 2(1)(e)(iii); Charities Act 1961 (Ire), s 47(1)(e)(iii); Trustee Act 1936 (SA), s 69B(1)(e)(iii). Somewhat similar wording is used in: Law Reform (Miscellaneous Provisions) (Scotland) Act 1990, s 9(1)(d)(iii).

circumstances falling well short of impossibility.[119] The provision has variously been judicially endorsed as a usefully 'broad criterion'[120] and as a 'significant change' in the general law,[121] 'very much wider than [the jurisdiction] which existed under the old law'.[122]

Of course, defining *cy-près* triggers with greater liberality inevitably poses significant policy dilemmas. For example, Hudson puts the position[123] that the wide drafting evident in this provision mirrors an understanding that the charity sector often mimics the work of the welfare state, and that it would be preferable to apply charitable funds *cy-près*, for uses not provided for by the state, rather than persist with unwanted and wasteful duplication. It also tends to place an emphasis upon 'society as a whole', with the promotion of the public good to be all-important; and avoids repetitive applications to the court to re-structure the trust, sometimes brought years apart with little successful application of the trust property in between court visits.[124] Indeed, the same pro's and con's of a wide definition of *cy-près* triggers are reflected in just how widely the courts should scour for substituted purposes when those triggers are indeed activated. These differences of view are outlined later.[125]

On the face of the wording, the provision may appear sufficiently broad to enable a court to substitute a beneficial and useful purpose for an original purpose which is complained of to be useless—a mere whimsy on the part of the donor—or which is simply not as expedient and desirable as another use to which the property could be applied. That possibility has certainly caught the attention of some judiciary, although it has not been embraced. A change of the trust's purposes under (e)(iii) 'merely because it is expedient or because it involves the use of trust property for purposes considered more useful or beneficial' has been considered by, for example, South Australian[126] and

---

[119] See comments in: *A-G (NSW) v Fulham* [2002] NSWSC 629 (19 Jul 2002) [17]; *In the matter of the Peirson Memorial Trust* [1995] QSC 308 (7 Dec 1995) 16 (the provision 'allows a certain liberality to a court in seeking to apply trust property *cy-près* where the original purposes may no longer be effected, which it may not have previously been confident in applying'). Also, see: *Bahamas District of the Methodist Church in the Caribbean and the Americas v Methodist Church of The Bahamas* (PC, 26 Jul 2000) ('In the nineteenth century the courts interpreted this jurisdiction restrictively by giving impossibility and impracticability a narrow definition. In England this over-rigid approach was relaxed by statutory intervention': Lord Nicolls of Birkenhead, no pp available).

[120] *Trustees of the Kean Memorial Trust Fund v A-G (South Australia)* (2003) 86 SASR 449, [68].

[121] *Fowler v Geelong College and Kardinia Intl College (Geelong)* (Vic SC, 13 Dec 1996) 19. See also: OLRC, *Law of Trusts* (1996), vol 2, 462 (the section's 'wisest' provision, 'the limits [of which] have yet to be discovered').

[122] HL Nathan, *The Charities Act 1960* (Butterworths, London, 1962) 77.

[123] A Hudson, *Equity and Trusts* (4th edn, Cavendish Publishing, London, 2005) 897.

[124] Both points are made by: EL Fisch, *The Cy-près Doctrine in the United States* (Matthew Bender & Co, Albany NY, 1950) 142–43, citing as two cases years apart concerning the same trust, the first unsuccessful in its application to use the doctrine: *St Louis v McAllister*, 218 SW 312 (1920) and *Thatcher v Lewis*, 76 SW (2d) 677 (1934).

[125] See pp 128–39.

[126] Discussing the identically-worded South Australia provision in s 69B(1)(e)(iii) of the Trustee Act 1936, in: *Trustees of the Kean Memorial Trust Fund v A-G (South Australia)* (2003) 86 SASR 449, [68] (*cy-près* scheme denied).

Scottish[127] courts, and by the English Charity Commissioners,[128] to be impermissible. Another court noted, of the Victorian equivalent, that to overrule some 'useless purpose' may be within the remit of the section, but that a caveat upon that power would apply in any event:

> it may be thought that Parliament has, arguably, enabled the court to interfere with, and to vary, gifts which had been made to what Farwell LJ in *Re Weir Hospital*[129] called 'the instances of charities of the most useless description'. Even if the court has been given an expanded role in this way, then in my opinion, the court would nonetheless still seek to obey the wishes of the testator. . . . the task of the court is to abide by the intention of the testator, rather than to impose its own belief as to whether more beneficial gifts could be made than those chosen by the testator.[130]

The fact that the court must again have regard to the 'spirit of the gift' under this sub-section also tends to put a brake upon the ability to alter the purposes *cy-près*, simply because the original purposes stipulated by the donor are less effective than some other application of the property.[131]

The reality remains that (e)(iii) creates something of a tension. Some of the aforementioned judicial statements tend to hark back to the requirement at common law that the trust had to be 'impracticable' as a minimum; but clearly the trust may be 'unsuitable and ineffective' and trigger *cy-près* under the statute's plain wording. Until this lower threshold is embraced to revamp those charities 'of the most useless description', full effect will not be given to (e)(iii). Having said that, however, numerous examples do exist, both in England[132]

---

[127] Discussing the identically-worded Scottish provision in s 9 of the Law Reform (Miscellaneous Provisions) (Scotland) Act 1990, in: *Smart (Trustee of the Mining Institute of Scotland Benevolent Fund and of the Mining Institute of Scotland Educational Trusts)* 1994 SLT 785 (Court of Session, Outer House) (*cy-près* scheme to amalgamate two trusts denied).

[128] See, eg: Ch Comm for England and Wales, *Ch Comm Origin and Functions* (CC1, 1992) 11.

[129] *In re Weir Hospital* [1910] 2 Ch 124 (CA) 136.

[130] *Fowler v Geelong College and Kardinia Intl College (Geelong)* (Vic SC, 13 Dec 1996) 19.

[131] AJ Oakley, *Parker and Mellows Modern Law of Trusts* (8th edn, Sweet & Maxwell, London, 2003) 486, citing: *In re Lepton's Charity; Ambler v Thomas* [1972] 1 Ch 276; J Warburton, 'The Spirit of the Gift' (1995/96) 3 *Charity Law and Practice Rev* 1, 5.

[132] In the courts: *Varsani v Jesani* [1999] Ch 219 (CA) 232 (split occurred in a Hindu sect upon religious grounds; Morritt LJ admitted that '[i]t could not be said that it was either impossible or impractical to carry out the purposes of the charity so long as either or both of the groups professed the faith of Swaminarayan according to the teaching and tenets of Muktajivandasji'; *cy-près* scheme directed); *In re Lepton's Charity; Ambler v Thomas* [1972] 1 Ch 276 (testator's will of 1715 provided payment to minister of £3 per year, and the rest to the aged and needy of the district; trust property increased in value such that, by 1967, yearly income was about £792, compared with £5 in 1715; £3 could have been paid to minister on an ongoing basis, and needy would have absorbed the rest; but a *cy-près* scheme directed to enable minister to be paid £100 per year from the fund). By the Charity Commissioners: Ch Comm for England and Wales, *Annual Report* (1999–2000) 7, *St Dunstan's* (charity established in 1915 to care for ex-Service personnel blinded in 'war or warlike' conflict; limitations meant that many ex-Service personnel could not receive help because their condition was not service-related; in 1999, charity's objects widened to benefit all blind ex-Service personnel, irrespective of the cause of their visual impairment).

and in other jurisdictions,[133] whereby, pursuant to this ground, another more effective way could be devised for the trust property—in circumstances where to carry on the charitable trust according to the intention of the donor would certainly not have been 'impossible' or 'impracticable', as those terms of art were interpreted under general law. The case law amply illustrates that statutory *cy-près* schemes have gone further than the general law *cy-près* would ever have permitted.

As a final note on (e)(iii), the statutory phrase, 'method of using the property', does not encompass a direction in a charitable trust to distribute the capital by a stipulated date. Thus, in *In re Laing Trust; Stewards' Co Ltd v A-G*,[134] that direction could not be deleted pursuant to this statutory *cy-près* trigger.

2. The 'Spirit of the Gift' Requirement

Several of the statutory triggers[135] discussed above expressly require that the court have regard to the 'spirit of the gift' when determining whether the original charitable purposes of the trust have failed and should be altered.

The phrase is not statutorily defined, and even at the outset of its statutory use in the English charities legislation, Viscount Simonds declared that he had difficulty in saying what it meant.[136] It was derived from a Scottish statute,[137] but with a significant difference. Whereas in Scotland, regard had to be made to the spirit of the intention of the donor in framing a *cy-près* scheme and applying the property to substituted purposes, the spirit of the gift has to be considered much earlier under s 13, in order to decide whether any of the triggers have occurred in the first place.[138]

It has been judicially defined in England (and cited with approval else-where[139]) to mean 'the basic intention underlying the gift or the substance of the gift rather than the form of the words used to express it or conditions imposed to effect it'.[140] It requires the court 'to look beyond the original purposes as defined

---

[133] *Cy-près* schemes ordered on this basis in Australia in, eg: *Ipswich CC v A-G (Qld)* [2004] QSC 252; *Re Banyo Seminary Trust* [2000] QSC 215; *Forrest v A-G (Vic)* [1986] VR 187. In Ireland: *Representative Church Body v A-G* [1988] IR 19, 22; *Re Royal Kilmainham Hospital; A-G v The British Legion* [1966] IR 451, 469, 472–73. In Northern Ireland: *Re Steele; Northern Bank and Trustee Co Ltd v Linton* [1976] NI 66, 71–72.

[134] [1984] Ch 143.

[135] Charities Act 1993, s 13(1)(a)(ii), (c), (d), and (e)(iii).

[136] 221 *Hansard Debates* (Official Report) 601, as cited in: HL Nathan, *The Charities Act 1960* (Butterworths, London, 1962) 75, fn 13.

[137] From the Education (Scotland) Act 1946, 9 and 19 Geo 6, c 72, s 116(2).

[138] Noted in: HL Nathan, *The Charities Act 1960* (Butterworths, London, 1962) 75.

[139] Eg: *Fowler v Geelong College and Kardinia Intl College (Geelong)* (Vic SC, 13 Dec 1996) 17, citing: *In re Lepton's Charity; Ambler v Thomas* [1972] 1 Ch 276, 284–85; *Forrest v A-G (Vic)* [1986] VR 187, 190; *Public Trustee of Queensland as Trustee of the Anzac Cottages Trusts v A-G (Queensland)* [2000] QSC 175, [19].

[140] *In re Lepton's Charity; Ambler v Thomas* [1972] 1 Ch 276, 285, and cited with approval in: *R v York Health Authority; ex p Nicholas* (QB, 1 May 1992) [no pp]; *Peggs v Lamb* [1994] Ch 172, 197; *Varsani v Jesani* [1999] Ch 219 (CA) 234 (Morritt LJ).

by the objects specified in the declaration of trust and to seek to identify the spirit in which the donors gave property upon trust for those purposes.'[141] This has been expressed by a Victorian court, which has had cause to consider the phrase, as follows:

> ['spirit of the gift'] effects a shift in emphasis in the application of the *cy-près* doctrine; that is, away from the common law position of requiring the impossibility or impracticality of the testator's original objective being achieved to those circumstances which frustrate the purposes . . . being attained. The spirit of the gift is . . . directed to such matters as the nature of the class or classes of recipients, the location or times at which gifts are to be made or the age, sex or status of the recipients. The list of frustrating circumstances can never be closed.[142]

In *Varsani v Jesani*,[143] Morritt LJ of the English Court of Appeal made two further significant observations about the phrase, *viz*, that it is only used in those statutory paragraphs that 'require the court to make a value judgment', and that '[t]he court is not *bound* to follow the spirit of the gift but it must pay regard to it when making [those] value judgment[s].'

The phrase has the potential to curtail, rather than expand, s 13's *cy-près* doctrine, a position put by Warburton, who contends[144] that both the original objective of the Nathan Committee,[145] and legislative developments since,[146] confirm that the need to have regard to the 'spirit of the gift' is capable of acting as a restriction on the application of the statutory *cy-près* doctrine. The statutory *cy-près* regime does not provide explicit guidance as to how the court is to select alternative purposes (or more usually, alternative charitable organisations by which to carry out that purpose[147]). Recourse must be had to the general law (and to Charity Commissioner guidelines) for that. As Chesterman observes,[148] the trustees must surely ensure that any newly-selected purposes under a *cy-près* scheme should not themselves be unsuitable or ineffective or otherwise 'fail' under s 13. Hence, for this reason too, the court will seek to give effect to the 'spirit of the trust' when drafting a substituted scheme.

The following factors, derived from a consideration of case law, are significant touchstones when determining the combined question of whether the original purposes should be altered, and if so, what scheme should be appropriately determined so as to give effect to the 'spirit of the gift':

---

[141] *Varsani, ibid*, 238 (Chadwick LJ).

[142] *Forrest v A-G (Vic)* [1986] VR 187, 190 (Nathan J).

[143] [1999] Ch 219 (CA) 234 (author's emphasis in second quotation).

[144] J Warburton, 'The Spirit of the Gift' (1995/96) 3 *Charity Law and Practice Rev* 1, 5.

[145] *Ibid*, 2–3, and see especially, the *Nathan Committee Report*, [365] and item (c) therein.

[146] *Ibid*, 4. The requirement was removed from the provisions relating to small charities, which are governed by ss 74, 75 of the Charities Act 1993.

[147] Note the comments in: *Gray v Australian Cancer Foundation for Medical Research (No 2)* [1999] NSWSC 725, [18] that 'a *cy-près* scheme is a method of carrying out a charitable purpose. It may be that particular bodies are selected to carry out the charitable purpose, but that is really incidental'.

[148] M Chesterman, *Charities, Trusts and Social Welfare* (Weidenfeld and Nicolson, London, 1979) 273.

Seeking to avoid continuing dispute and hostilities.   Where a change of charitable purpose is sought, and where one of the triggers for invoking the *cy-près* jurisdiction exists, the court will seek to obtain a practicable and expedient outcome—which may entail pragmatically formulating a scheme that will avoid the bitter disputes that have afflicted that charitable trust in the past. In *A-G (NSW) v Fulham*,[149] Bryson J unhappily noted of one *cy-près* scheme put to that court:

> If I set processes like those going I would be fairly certain to generate expense, delay, bad feeling and litigation, with diversion of energy and diminution of resources away from attainment of charitable objects; whereas under the plaintiff's scheme the funds pass immediately to worthy charitable objects. If the funds were left under the control of the Hall Trust, disputes and litigation would in my view be a fair certainty, and would continue the Hall Trust's long history of engagement in such troubles. Claims of practicality appear to me to require a course which will bring the unhappy history of the Hall Trust to a relatively early close with its funds in the hands of worthy charities.[150]

Similar considerations justified, in part, the *cy-près* scheme formulated in *Varsani v Jesani*,[151] where a charity was established with the purpose of promoting the faith of a Hindu sect. Upon the death of the leader, the sect split into two factions as a result of allegations of misconduct made against the successor. The majority did not believe the allegations, and continued to recognise the successor as leader, but the minority believed that the successor had lost divine status. In light of this impasse, the main asset of the charity, a temple in London, was only being used by one faction, to the exclusion of the other. It was held that the assets of the charity should be divided and held upon separate trusts for the two groups under a *cy-près* order (although how that was to be managed was not explained in the report). With a dose of pragmatism, Morritt LJ declared, 'either or both groups often litigate in preference to permitting a benefit to be conferred on the other. But the spirit of the gift to which the court is to have regard [when directing a *cy-près* scheme] is that which prevailed at the time of the gift when the two groups were in harmony.'[152]

Taking account of social, historical, economic and political changes since the original purpose was conceived.   Where the passing of time, and changing social or political conditions, mean that the original purpose retains no utility, then a *cy-près* scheme will be ordered that more closely adheres to the 'spirit of the gift'; and further, when formulating the *cy-près* application in these circumstances, the court may deliberately avoid any close analogy between the *cy-près* scheme and the original purpose.

As judicially remarked in *In the Matter of the Peirson Memorial Trust*,[153] where a property was left on trust for the provision and maintenance of appropriate accommodation for disadvantaged children:

[149] [2002] NSWSC 629 (19 Jul 2002).
[150] *Ibid*, [83].
[151] [1999] Ch 219 (CA).
[152] *Ibid*, 234.
[153] [1995] QSC 308 (7 Dec 1995).

a combination of factors has made it impracticable to continue to pursue the aim of the settlers. Social and economic conditions have changed greatly since the trust was first established nearly half a century ago. As well there has been a change in policies and perceptions both in the community and by governments about how disadvantaged children should be cared for. . . . [and additionally] the major social problem in the Wide Bay District at the present day [is] caring for adolescent and younger children from broken homes and from families under stress.[154]

On this basis, *cy-près* schemes have been permitted where trusts were originally established: to ameliorate the destitution suffered by families of those killed in war, but government pensions and compensation now exist to reduce the financial hardship of widows and children of the deceased;[155] to provide housing for one sex only, but where changed social conditions dictated that both men and women could and should now benefit;[156] and to build a meeting hall for returned servicemen, but where the passage of time and other social changes meant that such a scheme was no longer useful.[157] The 'spirit of the gift' was protected by a suitable *cy-près* scheme in each instance.

Not spreading the charitable trust fund too thinly among a wider class of persons or purposes.   On the one hand, the class of persons and purposes who may benefit from the *cy-près* scheme may have to be widened in order to take account of changing attitudes. On the other hand, the trust fund must not be spread too thinly so as to reduce its beneficial effect. It can be a difficult balancing act, as a couple of contrasting Australian cases illustrate:

In *Re Anzac Cottages Trust*,[158] the 'spirit of the trust' was judicially defined to be the acquisition of land, and the building of housing, for those dependants whose spouse or parent had died as a result of war service in the armed services of Australia and who were in necessitous circumstances. One draft scheme proposed to provide for 'widows of service men who enlisted in Queensland and who died while on active service with the Australian Defence Forces'. It was rejected: '[i]t is too wide because it covers many more people than widows and widowers, and too narrow because it applies only to the air force and not all the armed services.'[159]

In *Penny v Cancer & Pathological Research Institute of Western Australia*,[160] the testator's bequest in favour of the Cancer and Pathological Research Institute of Western Australia failed because the institute was not in existence at the date of the testator's death. A *cy-près* scheme in favour of the defendant research institute was approved on

---

[154]   *Ibid*, 10–11 (White J).
[155]   *Public Trustee of Qld as trustee of the Anzac Cottages Trusts v A-G (Qld)* [2000] QSC 175, [22], [24] ('Government provision of pensions and benefits has ameliorated to some extent the economic destitution that once followed the death of the family income earner. In order to give effect to the "spirit of the trust", those changes must be taken into account').
[156]   *Anzac Cottages Trusts, ibid* (trust originally intended for returned army servicemen's families; both men and women now enlisted in those services, and in other naval and other military sectors).
[157]   *A-G(NSW) v Fulham* [2002] NSWSC 629 (19 Jul 2002).
[158]   [2000] QSC 175.
[159]   *Ibid*, [29].
[160]   (1994) 13 WAR 314.

the basis that, '[e]ven if it is accepted that the original trust did not intend to promote cancer education, as distinct from cancer research, the scheme makes it clear that the purpose of the substituted trust is, specifically, cancer research. The mere fact that the proposed beneficiary has wider objects and engages in wider activities, seems to be beside the point once it is appreciated that the scheme requires that the bequest be devoted to the same charitable purposes as in the old trust'.[161]

As Cairns observes,[162] it is a good rule of thumb to assume that, to satisfy the spirit of the testator's intention, the substituted scheme should at least include the geographical area or class of persons that were originally stipulated for, even to the extent that the scheme may direct that the originally benefited persons obtain preferential treatment under the scheme.

Taking account of legal changes since the disposition took effect. It will be recalled[163] that English courts have been prepared to delete a restriction on race or religion that appeared in the donor's original disposition, in circumstances where the trustees refused to accept the gift with the restriction in place. Such restrictions these days would contravene anti-discrimination laws, for which reasons those trusts would fail in any event.

A different sort of legal change that adversely affected the disposition was also evident in the Australian case of *Forrest v A-G (Victoria).*[164] The testator directed that the income of his residuary estate be applied to charities that were exempt from probate or estate duty 'at the date of my death'. After his death in 1965, and due to changing tax laws, many charities came into existence that were (but for the words, 'at my death') eligible, whilst others had been changed by legislation and were no longer eligible. The trustees successfully applied for the settlement of a *cy-près* scheme to enlarge the class of possible beneficiaries to include charitable institutions which were not in existence at the testator's death. The 'spirit of the gift' was to benefit all Victorian charities, not merely that band that was diminishing in number due to changes of law. The fact that, in this case, there were a number of charities to which distributions *could* still be made in accordance with the will has prompted Sheridan to remark that a *cy-près* scheme was therefore 'surprising'.[165]

The financial 'health' of alternative charitable organisations may be relevant. In *Re Anzac Cottages Trust*, the court refused to make a *cy-près* order in favour of the Returned Services League charity on the basis, *inter alia*, that it was already well provided for.[166] Although that factor has not been oft-cited, it finds

---

[161] *Ibid*, [10] (Anderson J).

[162] E Cairns, *Charities: Law and Practice* (3rd edn, Sweet & Maxwell, 1997) 180–81. Also see: DG Cracknell (ed), *Charities: The Law and Practice* (Thomson Sweet & Maxwell, London, 1994–) [looseleaf] [I.66], and the guidelines contained therein.

[163] See pp 96–7.

[164] [1986] VR 187.

[165] LA Sheridan, *Keeton and Sheridan's The Modern Law of Charities* (4th edn, Barry Rose Law Publishers, Chichester, 1992) 224.

[166] [2000] QSC 175, [28].

a parallel in the Charities Bill 2004[167] that was proposed for England, but which has not been implemented to date.[168] In that Bill, it was stated that the court and Charity Commissioners should no longer be guided only by the 'spirit of the gift' but by 'appropriate considerations', which are defined to include 'social and economic circumstances prevailing at the time'.[169] These proposed amendments (which, at the time of writing, remain intact but are still under debate[170]) have been academically welcomed on the basis that they seek to give to the Charity Commission 'a wider role and perspective'.[171]

Taking account of the charitable trust as a whole.   Where a charitable trust contains more than one charitable purpose, the court, when asking itself whether the 'original purposes' of the trust have ceased to be suitable or effective, must construe whether the *entire* charitable trust now suits the donor's original purpose. The 'spirit of the gift' is to be determined by having regard to the entire trust, not to each individual charitable disposition within the trust.

This principle was decided, and applied, in *In re Lepton's Charity; Ambler v Thomas*,[172] where a will of 1715 provided for the payment of £3 to the minister (one trust), and the residual amount from the trust fund to be paid to the poor, aged and needy of the parish (a separate trust). At the time, the trust fund income was about £5 per year. By 1967, the trust fund income had increased to about £760 per year, but the minister's payment was restricted to the originally-worded £3 a year. Could that latter sum be increased by *cy-près* order, on the basis that the charitable trust as a whole had ceased to provide a suitable and effective method of using the trust fund income? The court allowed an adjusted amount to be substituted, satisfied that the intention underlying the gift was to divide the trust fund in such a manner that the minister took a clear three-fifths of it.[173]

Thus, a distillation of case law, statutory provisions, and academic observations referenced above in this section suggest that, when seeking to divine the 'spirit of the gift' (in order to assess both whether a *cy-près* trigger has occurred, and if so, how the property would be most suitably applied *cy-près*), the following principles have guided the courts to date:

- it is important to resolve the failed trust in a way that mitigates against disputes arising, and/or brings any ongoing disputes to a halt;
- any changes in history, economic policy, social policy, and the political landscape, need to be taken into account;

---

[167] In particular, ch 4 of the Bill, 'Application of Property *Cy-près*'.

[168] Introduced Dec 2004, but did not receive Royal Assent before the General Election on 5 May 2005. Hence, the Bill was re-introduced in the HL on 18 May 2005.

[169] See ss 15(2), (3).

[170] See: Charities Bill 2005 [HL] (as amended on report) (HL Bill 27, 54/1, ordered to be printed 18 October 2005) 17.

[171] J Burchfield, 'The Draft Charities Bill' (2004) 5 *PCB* 310, 315.

[172] [1972] 1 Ch 276.

[173] *Ibid*, 285–86.

- the trust cannot be spread too thinly amongst too large an area or class of persons, or else it could lose its beneficial effect;
- any changes in the law must be taken into consideration;
- the financial well-being of other charitable organisations may determine whether or not they receive any property via a *cy-près* scheme; and
- the entire charitable trust must be assessed to determine whether the 'spirit of the gift' is being satisfied, and if not, how it should be amended.

D VARIATIONS UPON THE ENGLISH STATUTORY THEME

Statutory reform of the *cy-près* doctrine has not followed uniform paths. Some jurisdictions have chosen to discard some of the general *cy-près* doctrine, and in doing so, their enactments manifest some significant variations from the English statutory regime. In particular, as demonstrated in the following discussion, the legislatures of New Zealand and Western Australia have implemented the widest of the statutory *cy-près* regimes—as evidenced by their treatment of the requirement of a general charitable intent, the triggers for the *cy-près* jurisdiction, and the application of trust property once the *cy-près* jurisdiction is invoked.

1. The Requirement of a General Charitable Intent

The general law, and the statutory provisions considered in the previous section, all require that the donor had a general charitable intent when giving property on trust to the charitable purpose before any *cy-près* direction can occur. In cases of subsequent failure, that intent will be presumed; but in cases of initial failure, it must be proven.

Some statutes, however, have sought to distance themselves from the general *cy-près* doctrine by either doing away with the general charitable intent requirement altogether, or statutorily putting in place a presumption that one exists in *all* cases. Any relaxation of this technical and difficult requirement[174] has the considerable benefit of avoiding protracted and costly litigation to determine the question as to whether a particular testator had a general or a specific charitable intent.[175] The statutory attempts to do away with the requirement have not, however, always progressed smoothly.[176]

---

[174] See previous chapter 3 for the technical difficulties associated with this requirement.

[175] The OLRC recommended that the requirement be abolished in its proposed statutory *cy-près* scheme for this very reason: *The Law of Trusts* (1996), vol 2, 471.

[176] For an interesting criticism of an early Pennsylvania statute that sought to eliminate the requirement, see: EL Fisch, *The Cy-près Doctrine in the United States* (Matthew Bender & Co, Albany NY, 1950) 159–162. This author's comment that '[t]he wording of the statute . . . appears to be contradictory' is, coincidentally enough, most apposite to the statutes considered in this section.

(a) Abolishing the requirement

The operative scheme in South Australia[177] expressly does away with any proof of a general charitable intent whatsoever. This can be particularly beneficial where the entity or purpose to which the testator left her money *no longer exists* at the date of the testator's death—an instance of initial failure of the charitable trust—as the facts of *Aston v Mount Gambier Presbyterian Charge*[178] demonstrate. The testator included in her will a bequest to the 'Scot's Presbyterian Church Building Fund', but at the date of her death, there was no such fund. The new church had already been constructed and paid for, and the building fund bank account closed. It will be recalled[179] that it is notoriously difficult to find a general charitable intent at general law, where the beneficiary did once exist, but does not any longer (the intent is then more likely to be construed as specific). Noting that its task was easier under statute than under the general law because it did not have to find a general charitable intent,[180] the court approved of a *cy-près* application of the monies toward the construction of buildings or extensions associated with the new church, or for their maintenance.

It is also apparent that, under the Western Australian and New Zealand statutory schemes, it was intended that it should be unnecessary to find a general charitable intent. Some believe that, as a result, the distinction between specific and general charitable intent has lost its relevance for these two jurisdictions.[181] The legislation in both jurisdictions, however, suffers from an unfortunate internal inconsistency, as the following provisions demonstrate:

---

(1) Subject to the provisions of subsection (3) of this section, where any property or income is given or held upon trust, or is to be applied, for any charitable purpose, and [various preconditions are stated] then (**whether or not there is any general charitable intention**) the property and income . . . shall be disposed of for some other charitable purpose . . . in the manner directed . . .

(3) This section shall not operate to cause any property or income to be disposed of as provided in subsection (1) . . .

  (a) if, in accordance with any rule of law, the intended gift thereof would otherwise lapse or fail and the property or income would not be applicable for any other charitable purpose[182]

---

[177] Trustee Act 1936 (SA), s 69B(3).

[178] (2002) 84 SASR 109.

[179] See p 82.

[180] (2002) 84 SASR 109, [44].

[181] RP Meagher and WMC Gummow (eds), *Jacobs' Law of Trusts in Australia* (6th edn, Butterworths, Sydney, 1997) [1068], fn 590, [1077].

[182] See: Charitable Trusts Act 1962 (WA), s 7(1), (3); Charitable Trusts Act 1957 (NZ), s 32(1), (3). The former was adopted from the latter.

As some commentators have pointed out,[183] (3)(a) appears to re-introduce the requirement of a general charitable intent where the trust suffers from initial failure, for that is the 'rule of law' that applies in cases of initial failure. The drafting is odd, for why would the respective Parliaments of Western Australia and New Zealand specifically negate the requirement for a general charitable intent in (1), only to bring it back in via (3)(a), which is expressed to be in paramount terms to (1)?

Judicial commentary in New Zealand indicates a further degree of confusion. On the one hand is authority that the practical effect of the section is to supersede, and entirely supplant, the *cy-près* doctrine by doing away with a general charitable intent in *all* situations, whether of initial or subsequent failure[184]—so as to 'remove the limitation which applied to the old *cy-près* doctrine.'[185] In that case, there is a good case to be made for reading down (3)(a) as simply requiring that, for *cy-près* to apply, the purposes of the trust must be exclusively charitable—another carry-over from the general law. That construction would make sense of (3)(a), whilst ensuring that it is unnecessary to hunt for any general charitable intent on the donor's part as (1) suggests. On the other hand is judicial opinion that, if there is no general charitable intention discernible at all on the part of the testator, and if the gift fails *ab initio*, then the gift cannot be applied *cy-près* and shall lapse, just as it would at general law.[186] The New Zealand Court of Appeal explained its reasoning on this basis:

> the provisions of s 32(3) clearly preserve the law about lapse. The whole of s 32(1) is subject to the preservation of the general law about lapse which applies to the case of charitable gifts where the stated purposes or objects are an indispensable part of the trust to which effect cannot be given—where, in short, there is no discernible general charitable intention.[187]

On that rationale, s 32(3) would have paramount 'bite' and bring the general law and statutory *cy-près* into line with each other—but what, then, is the point of (1)'s phrase, 'whether or not there is any general charitable intention'? The section's drafting unfortunately obfuscates rather than clarifies.

It is perhaps also prudent to reiterate that the provisions reproduced in the box above in no way negate the requirement that the trust property must have been given for charitable purposes—Rickett explains this point succinctly:

---

[183] D Ong, *Trusts Law in Australia* (Federation Press, Sydney, 1999) 330; OLRC, *Law of Trusts* (1996) vol 2, 465; *Halsbury's Laws of Australia* (Butterworths, Sydney, 1991–), 'Cy-près Schemes', [75–800]; C Rickett, 'Failure of Charities and the Conundrum of s 32' [2003] *NZLJ* 59, 60; G Dal Pont, *Charity Law in Australia and New Zealand* (OUP, Oxford, 2000) 327.

[184] See: *Re Palmerston North Halls Trust Board* [1976] 2 NZLR 161 (SC) 164. This is the academic viewpoint expressed in C Rickett, 'Politics and Cy-près' [1998] *NZLJ* 55, 57; in GE Dal Pont and DRC Chalmers, *Equity and Trusts in Australia and New Zealand* (LBC Information Services, Sydney, 1996) 411; and in MFL Flannery, 'The Variation of the Charitable Trust' [1977] *NZLJ* 368, 368.

[185] *A-G, ex rel Rathbone and McKay v Waipawa Hospital Board* [1970] NZLR 1148 (SC) 1153.

[186] *Re Collier (decd)* [1998] 1 NZLR 81, 96.

[187] *Alacoque v Roache* [1998] 2 NZLR 250 (CA) 256 (discussed further, and expansively critiqued, in: C Rickett, 'Failure of Charities and the Conundrum of s 32' [2003] *NZLJ* 59, 60).

[the section] is not a panacea for the salvation of gifts for non-charitable purposes as charitable. In that context, all that s 32 does is to avoid the difficulty of divining a general charitable intention where a particular charitable purpose already exists, but where that purpose cannot be achieved for some reason.[188]

(b) Presuming the requirement

The statutory *cy-près* schema in New South Wales's legislation, the Charitable Trusts Act 1993, is also somewhat peculiarly drafted:

s 10(1) This Part does not affect the requirement that trust property cannot be applied *cy-près* unless it is given with a general charitable intention.

(2) However, **a general charitable intention is to be presumed** unless there is evidence to the contrary in the instrument establishing the charitable trust.

On the one hand, 10(1) provides that its categorisation of triggering *cy-près* conditions[189] must still be accompanied by a general charitable intent (seemingly preserving the general law and English statutory position), but then goes on to 'almost eviscerate'[190] that provision by 10(2)'s presumption.

Judicially, various significant points about the presumption should be noted. By its terms, it overturns the general law position, stated by the High Court of Australia in 1940, that 'no definite presumption has been established in favour of a general charitable intention.'[191] This provision is not concerned with whether the intention is charitable, but rather whether it is *general* (the court must still be satisfied according to the usual common law principles that the trust purpose was charitable).[192] It simply supports and reflects the proposition that, even when a general intention of charity is required, in cases of initial failure of the charitable trust, this requirement is undemanding;[193] and it is extremely unlikely to be displaced by any contrary intention in the terms of the trust or will.[194] If there was a gift-over to another non-charitable purpose, in default of

---

[188] C Rickett, 'Politics and *Cy-près*' [1998] *NZLJ* 55, 56, criticising the court's reasoning on this point in: *Re Collier (decd)* [1998] 1 NZLR 81.

[189] As outlined in Charitable Trusts Act 1993 (NSW), s 9(1).

[190] As concluded by: D Ong, *Trusts Law in Australia* (Federation Press, Sydney, 1999) 330. Cf: S Srivastava, 'Administrative Efficiency in Charitable Trusts' (1994) *LSJ* 31, 31 (presumption 'retain[s] the requirements of a soundly tested legal principle').

[191] *A-G (NSW) v Perpetual Trustee Co Ltd* (1940) 63 CLR 209 (HCA) 228 (Dixon and Evatt JJ).

[192] Stated in: *Public Trustee v A-G (NSW), Jarrett, Muller and Davies* (1997) 42 NSWLR 600, 609, which was cited and applied in: *McLean v A-G (NSW)* [2002] NSWSC 377, [53], [60]–[67] (bequest of residuary estate for school at Cessnock; at time of testator's death, school had ceased to operate; *cy-près* application ordered).

[193] *A-G (NSW) v Fulham* [2002] NSWSC 629, [22], citing: *A-G (NSW) v Perpetual Trustee Company Ltd* (1940) 63 CLR 209 (HCA) 225 (Dixon and Evatt JJ). Also: M Evans, *Outline of Equity and Trusts* (3rd edn, Butterworths, Sydney, 1996) 295.

[194] D Ong, *Trusts Law in Australia* (Federation Press, Sydney 1999) 330; G Dal Pont, *Charity Law in Australia and New Zealand* (OUP, Oxford, 2000) 323.

a charitable purpose for a specific institution, that may perhaps be sufficient to displace the presumption,[195] but there has been no authority to date, so far as can be ascertained, in which the presumption has been displaced.[196]

Clearly, the NSW provision is not intended to go as far as the New Zealand and Western Australian provisions, which abolish the requirement of a general charitable intent altogether.

2. Other Triggers for the *Cy-Près* Jurisdiction

It is notable that some statutes define a '*cy-près* event', the trigger for a *cy-près* application of trust property, even more widely than does the English statutory regime.

For example, the South Australian statute permits the court to invoke its *cy-près* jurisdiction:

> where it is not reasonably practicable having regard to:
>
> (i)   the **value of the trust property**; or
> (ii) **changes in circumstances** that have taken place since the constitution of the trust; or
> (iii) **any other relevant factor**,
>
> to apply the trust property in accordance with the original purposes.[197]

The 'catch all' phrase in (iii) is very wide. It could conceivably cover the useless or capricious charitable purpose trust, although there is no authority yet on the meaning of this phrase. One can only ponder whether (iii) would embrace the wider definition of *cy-près* which the American Law Institute postulated in 2001, where 'it is or becomes wasteful to apply all of the property to the designated purpose'.[198] Such wording is a *carte blanche* to rewrite the donor's intention; invokes the subjective intent of what is 'wasteful'; and takes the doctrine considerably further than it has been treated in England, at least.

---

[195] Ong, *ibid*. Also: M Chesterman, *Charities, Trusts and Social Welfare* (Weidenfeld and Nicolson, London, 1979) 277.

[196] For cases where the presumption was upheld, see: *McLean v A-G (NSW)* [2002] NSWSC 377; *Permanent Trustee Co Ltd v A-G (NSW)* [1999] NSWSC 288 (9 Apr 1999).

[197] Trustee Act 1936 (SA), s 69B(1)(d), to be read in conjunction with s 69B(6), the 'spirit of the gift' provision. See, for similar wording: Tasmania's Variation of Trusts Act 1994, s 5(3)(d).

[198] See: ALI, *Restatement of the Law (Third), Trusts (Tentative Draft No 3)* (ALI Publishers, St Paul Minn, 5 Mar 2001) § 67, p 189–90.

Meanwhile, provision (ii) of the above-cited legislation has been relied upon successfully to invoke a *cy-près* scheme.[199]

Of all the legislative provisions considered to date, the legislation in Western Australia and New Zealand contain probably the most widely-worded triggers for the court to invoke its *cy-près* jurisdiction:

where . . .

    (a) it is impossible, impracticable or **inexpedient** to carry out that purpose; or

    (b) the amount available is inadequate to carry out that purpose; or

    (c) that purpose has been effected already; or

    (d) that purpose is illegal or **useless or uncertain**[200]

On the Canadian scene, although the OLRC declared that it was unable to find any legislation that was 'prepared to allow variation of charitable trust objects wherever and whenever the court considers it necessary or desirable, and to leave it at that',[201] the abovementioned provision certainly approaches that degree of liberality on its face. On its terms, 'inexpedient' or 'useless' purposes can be changed. This would appear to permit the court to replace an unproductive charitable purpose with another scheme that is (in the trustees' opinion) more publicly beneficial or desirable. However, that liberal view was expressly ruled out by the New Zealand Court of Appeal, in *Trustees of the McElroy Trust*.[202] Whilst prepared to give 'inexpedient' its natural meaning[203]

---

[199] *City of Burnside v A-G (SA)* (SC SA, 1 May 1998) (Council held land for benefit of its residents to use as a public recreation ground; land leased to adjoining school and used as sports arena and indoor recreation centre by school; exclusive use by school in school hours was held to be inconsistent with charitable intentions; *cy-près* scheme ordered). Also see: *General Assembly (Clare Trust) Inc v A-G (South Australia)* [1991] SASC 2832 (24 Apr 1991) (although here, the purposes of the trust were not changed, giving rise to an administrative rather than a *cy-près* scheme).
[200] Charitable Trusts Act 1962 (WA), s 7(1); Charitable Trusts Act 1957 (NZ), s 32(1). In subsection (2) of these respective sections, it is provided that any surplus of a charitable trust may be disposed of for some other charitable purpose. For a study of the statutory drafting of this sub-section, see: MFL Flannery, 'The Variation of the Charitable Trust' [1977] *NZLJ* 368. Tasmania's legislation also refers to the requirement that it 'has become impossible, impracticable or inexpedient to carry out the original purposes of a trust for charitable purposes': Variation of Trusts Act 1994, s 5(2).
[201] OLRC, *The Law of Trusts* (1996), vol 2, 468.
[202] *Re McElroy Trust* [2003] 2 NZLR 289 (CA, 20 Feb 2003). Discussed further in: C Rickett, 'Failure of Charities and the Conundrum of s 32' [2003] *NZLJ* 59, 60).
[203] *Ibid*, [11], [14] ('inexpedient' means 'the original charitable purpose or purposes having become unsuitable, inadvisable or inapt. . . . Clearly Parliament wished to give the Courts power to approve a scheme of variation in circumstances beyond those where the original purpose could no longer be carried out. The concept of inexpediency introduced a value judgment rather than simply an assessment of feasibility. . . . the question is not whether the scheme carries out the purposes of the trust better. Rather it is whether it is now inexpedient to carry them out'). See at first instance: [2002] 3 NZLR 99, 105 (O'Regan J) ('inexpedient' was not to be 'coloured by its collocation with the terms "impossible" and "impracticable" ').

(which, of course, renders it wider than 'impossible' or 'impracticable'), a *cy-près* scheme was rejected in this case. The testator's original intention (it was held) was to provide homes for the elderly; changing social conditions, government subsidising of elderly accommodation, and the trustees' inability to provide the accommodation on farming land left on trust by the testator, did not combine to make it 'inexpedient' to carry on the trust that was originally established.

The New South Wales legislation is drafted differently again, opting to state only one ground for *cy-près*, but on an inclusive (and therefore extremely wide) basis:

> s 9(1) The circumstances in which the original purposes of a charitable trust can be altered to allow the trust property or any part of it to be applied *cy-près* **include** circumstances in which the original purposes, wholly or in part, have since they were laid down **ceased to provide a suitable and effective method of using the trust property, having regard to the spirit of the trust**[204]

The OLRC approached the matter on yet another footing, opting to state the triggers for its proposed legislation very briefly and broadly: 'impracticability, impossibility, or **any other difficulty**'.[205] The intention of the OLRC was to release the court from any restricted interpretation that case law had placed upon the other two words. This proposal has not been enacted to date.

However, in contrast to the OLRC proposal, an articulation of these so-called 'difficulties' has been the preferred course of other legislatures, an approach which endorses itself to this author. The triggers for the operation of a *cy-près* scheme are vitally important for the coherent development of this area of jurisprudence. If they are to be broadened by statute, then their clear delineation, as the English statute has enacted, would seem to be the optimal solution. Further, it is this author's contention that adherence to the donor's wishes so far as possible, by adopting a 'narrow gate' view of what constitutes appropriate triggers for the exercise of the *cy-près* jurisdiction, is the most effective manner by which to encourage charitable giving. For this reason, the OLRC's trigger of 'difficulties', the ALI's trigger of 'wasteful', and the South Australian legislature's reference to 'other relevant factors', are arguably not the 'best practice' drafting solutions for this most important first stage of the *cy-près* analysis.

---

[204] Charitable Trusts Act 1993 (NSW), s 9(1).
[205] OLRC, *The Law of Trusts* (1996), vol 2, 470 and Draft Bill, s 76(1)(a).

E APPLYING THE PROPERTY *CY-PRÈS*

It will be recalled from the previous chapter that there is a distinct dichotomy of view between those who consider that property should be applied 'as near as possible' to the donor's original purpose, in order not to discourage donors from giving to charity; and those who favour the view that the property ought to be applied to the 'next best' use, maximising public benefit wherever possible. This has proven to be a particularly thorny issue. The various options of how property should be applied *cy-près* will be considered shortly, after a couple of preliminary questions are postulated.

1. What is the Original Reference Point for the Donor's Intention?

There are two possible (and possibly competing) reference points against which to devise a *cy-près* scheme.

Under the first one, the court will construe what the testator stated in his will—the precise terms of the disposition—and select an analogous scheme to that. This will entail an analysis of the 'essential elements of the original trust', a scrutiny of the terms of the will or trust deed, and nothing more. There are numerous examples of this approach,[206] but a neat illustration is that provided in *Re Twigger*.[207] The testator's intention, in bequeathing certain property to the Canterbury Orphanage, could be broken down into the following elements of intention: to benefit (a) children, (b) in Canterbury, (c) on a non-denominational basis, (d) by means of residential care, (e) not necessarily for a permanent or long period per child's stay, (f) where the parents could not provide care to the child for whatever reason. After evidence was called from the Cholmondeley Children's Home as to its objects, purposes and operational day-to-day running, the court was satisfied that these elements were well-matched to that institution.[208]

---

[206] Eg, in Australia: *A-G (NSW) v Perpetual Trustee Co Ltd* (1940) 63 CLR 209 (HCA) (the disposition of Milly Milly, the farm, had four elements: (a) the training, (b) of orphan (c) lads (d) in farming techniques; *cy-près* scheme permitted by majority); *Perpetual Trustees Tasmania Ltd v A-G (Tas)* (SC, 12 Apr 2002) (bequest to 'Australian Anti-Cancer Society/Research'; no such institution existed; the bequest broken down into the elements: (a) cancer of any sort, (b) for research activities, (c) with a national, not state, perspective; *cy-près* scheme permitted); *Mother Theresa Celine v Union Fidelity Trustee Co of Aust Ltd* (VSC, 14 Apr 1987) (breaking the bequest to St Joseph's Homes (defunct) into three elements; *cy-près* scheme permitted). In Canada, eg: *Johnston Estate v Cavalry Baptist Church for Ganaraska Woods Retreat Centre* (2002), ACWS (3d) 752 (SCJ) (breaking the bequest into (a) school for educational needs, (b) in Ontario, (c) for developmentally delayed, (d) children, (e) also providing for daily living needs; *cy-près* scheme ordered in favour of two institutions).
[207] [1989] 3 NZLR 329.
[208] *Ibid*, 342.

Under the second reference point, the courts seek to determine, by recourse to extrinsic evidence (eg, affidavits from witnesses who knew the testator), what the testator would have done with the property, had he known that the purpose was impossible when he made the will. This approach envisages that the testator may not have bequeathed his property to the original institution or anything like it, but for some quite diverse purpose. For example, had he known that an educational facility for female orphans would be held to be discriminatory, and that his property would be applied for both male and female students at that facility, he may well have chosen to direct his gift to a soup kitchen for the itinerant and homeless instead.

As Eames J noted in *Fowler v Geelong College & Kardinia International College (Geelong)*,[209] the two aforementioned reference points may not result in the same answer to the question of which competing *cy-près* scheme is 'as near as possible' to the settlor's intention to benefit charity.

There is judicial division in Australia about which reference point should be used, with some opinion favouring the second approach,[210] and other opinion suggesting that the relevant question must be whatever scheme most 'closely accords' with the scheme articulated in the will.[211] The first reference point appears far more supportable on the basis that the statute refers to the 'spirit of the gift'—the gift being that which was expressed in the will or the trust ('the *spirit of the document*', in other words). This also upholds a consistent approach with much earlier equity cases which held, similarly, that '*cy-près*' meant the closest to that which had failed, not the closest to other charitable purposes which may have been provided for by the testator, had he known that the bequest would fail.[212]

2. Can Extrinsic Evidence be Relied Upon?

Another question is how the court is permitted to determine whether the testator had a general charitable intention when making the bequest, and whether the proposed *cy-près* scheme would have accorded with the testator's intentions. As noted above, some courts have concentrated upon the terms of the will, and the will alone. The use of extrinsic evidence—such as conversations that the testator had with relatives or friends, whether relatives were close or whether the testator saw no need to provide for them, indications that the testator had the welfare

---

[209] (Vic SC, 13 Dec 1996) 17.

[210] *Gray v Australian Cancer Foundation for Medical Research* [1999] NSWSC 492, [22] ('In working out the *cy-près* scheme the Court has to move away from construing what the testator said in it and work out how best to effectuate his general charitable intention'); *Forrest v A-G (Vic)* [1986] VR 187, 189.

[211] *Fowler v Geelong College and Kardinia Intl College (Geelong)* (Vic SC, 13 Dec 1996) 6–7.

[212] LS Bristowe and WI Cook, *The Law of Charities and Mortmain* (Reeves and Turner, London, 1889) 144, citing, at fn (a): *A-G v Ironmongers' Co* (1844) 10 Cl & F 908, 922.

of say, the elderly, in mind when framing the will and would have wished to benefit the elderly in some form, no matter what[213]—remains a point of some controversy.

Some judges have rejected extrinsic evidence as inappropriate,[214] preferring the view that the testator's intention must be construed from the document alone. This has academically been supported: 'to seek the intention of a testatrix regarding schemes which replace her own trust is to go too far'.[215]

However, the use of extrinsic evidence has been strongly endorsed judicially, both in England and elsewhere, on three counts. First, extrinsic evidence has always been admissible to determine what institutions the testator may have intended, to make sense of the institution referred to in the will.[216] When construing a will, the 'armchair principle' permits a court, by means of extrinsic evidence, to have regard to the circumstances in which the will was made.[217] Secondly, when settling a scheme, the court is engaged in an administrative task, for which it is bound to observe the rules in which evidence is presented, but not to limit the content of that evidence.[218] On that basis, it would be 'extraordinary' if extrinsic evidence was admissible for an administrative scheme (as it is), yet not be admissible for a *cy-près* scheme.[219] Thirdly, the statutory direction to consider the 'spirit of the gift' invites the use of extrinsic evidence:

> evidence of the sympathies, prejudices, approach to life, and attitudes of the testatrix at the time she made her will are all capable of adding to the court's understanding of her intention and/or the spirit of the Will as she intended to embody that spirit by this gift. If the Court is primarily concerned to adopt a *cy-près* approach which meets the spirit with which the testatrix imbued her gift in the Will, it seems to me that it would be an absurd result if the court, which has no personal knowledge of the testatrix, might adopt a *cy-près* scheme whilst refusing to consider evidence of those who knew the

---

[213] This sort of evidence was adduced from the solicitor of the deceased, to assist the court's task, eg, in: *In re Bianco (decd); Cox v A-G (Vic)* (SC Vic, 23 Sep 1997).

[214] See: *Phillips v Roberts* [1975] 2 NSWLR 207 (CA) 224–25 (Mahoney JA). See also: *In re Currie; McClelland v Gamble* [1985] NI 299 (Ch), where it was noted that, although extrinsic evidence had been admitted in other decisions, 'I am inclined to approach [the task] as one to be decided . . . on the construction of the particular instrument'.

[215] RJ Smith, 'Trusts' [1977] *ASCL* 298, 300.

[216] *Fowler v Geelong College and Kardinia Intl College (Geelong)* (Vic SC, 13 Dec 1996) 18, citing: *Re Pace (decd)* (1985) 38 SASR 336, 339. Also noted in: *A-G (NSW) v Perpetual Trustee Co Ltd* (1940) 63 CLR 209 (HCA) 227 ('No doubt the terms of the document, together with any extrinsic circumstances admissible in aid of construction, form the materials for ascertaining whether the specific directions were animated by a wider charitable purpose which amounted to the true or substantial object of the trust') (Dixon and Evatt JJ). See also, for approval of the use of extrinsic evidence in Canada: *Re Charlesworth Estate* (1996), 62 ACWS (3d) 632 (Man QB) [50]; *Re Bruce Estate* (PEI SC, 5 Aug 2004) [30]; *Lund Estate v BC (A-G)* (1995) 59 ACWS (3d) 811 (BCSC) [20].

[217] *Perrin v Morgan* [1943] AC 399 (HL) 420 ('To understand the language employed the court is entitled . . . to sit in the testator's armchair': Lord Romer).

[218] *Phillips v Roberts* [1975] 2 NSWLR 207 (CA) 211 (Hutley JA), cf Mahoney JA, cited above. The third member of the CA, Samuels JA, did not decide the point.

[219] RP Meagher and WMC Gummow, *Jacobs' Law of Trusts in Australia* (6th edn, Butterworths, Sydney, 1997) [1073]. When referring to *Phillips, ibid*, these authors prefer the view of Hutley JA to that of Mahoney JA.

testatrix, intimately, throughout her long life, and where those witnesses would swear that the scheme favoured by the Court was contrary to the intentions and spirit of the gift in her Will, as they knew the attitudes and interests of the testatrix at the time when she made the Will … The evidence of witnesses might in some cases prove unpersuasive, but that is no reason … why the court should be confined to examining other, possibly more nebulous, evidence gleaned from the terms of the Will.[220]

Thus, it is plain that the weight of judicial opinion and reasoning certainly favours the use of extrinsic evidence when the court is faced with drafting a *cy-près* scheme.

3. How Close Must the *Cy-près* Application Be?

Under the general doctrine of *cy-près*, where one or more of the *cy-près* conditions is fulfilled so that the court's jurisdiction to make a scheme is invoked, then the trust property is to be applied on analogous purposes ('as near as possible') with those which the testator/settlor originally stipulated. The definitions of the general *cy-près* doctrine[221] commonly indicate the selection of some purpose 'as near as possible' to the original purpose of the settlor. In Canada, where the general doctrine continues to apply without statutory invocation, topical examples demonstrate that this standard has been adhered to.[222]

One of the more poignant examples of the general doctrine in operation occurred in New South Wales in *Perpetual Trustee Co Ltd v Braithwaite*.[223] The testator bequeathed her residential property in Sydney to establish a home, called the 'Shelter Wing of Camelot'. It was intended as a convalescent home, and had this signage outside it: 'The Shelter Wing for the Use of Travelling Unemployed—Come in and Rest Awhile—but After 48 Hours, Make Room for

---

[220] *Fowler v Geelong College and Kardinia Intl College (Geelong)* (Vic SC, 13 Dec 1996) 16, citing as support for this approach: *Re Twigger* [1989] 3 NZLR 329, 342. Also see: *Varsani v Jesani* [1999] Ch 219 (CA) 238 (Chadwick LJ) (the need to construe the 'spirit of the gift' can be done 'with the assistance of the document as a whole and any relevant evidence as to the circumstances in which the gift was made'); *In re Lepton's WT; Ambler v Thomas* [1972] 1 Ch 276, 285 (spirit, equivalent to the donor's intention, is 'ascertainable from the terms of the relevant instrument read in the light of admissible evidence').

[221] See pp 1–2.

[222] Eg: *Johnston Estate v Cavalry Baptist Church for Ganaraska Woods Retreat Centre* (2002), ACWS (3d) 752 (SCJ) [10] ('The question as to which of the claimants should receive the gift must be answered by the court so as to donate the proceeds to charitable purposes as near as may be to what the testatrix intended'); *Re Fraser Estate* (2000), 99 ACWS (3d) 525 (PEI SC) [4]. Also: *Weninger Estate v Canadian Diabetes Assn* (1993), 2 ETR (2d) 24 (Ont HC) (bequest to Assn 'for the purpose of providing insulin to the needy'; *cy-près* scheme permitted to apply funds to ongoing insulin research projects, even though both needy and wealthy would benefit from research). See also, eg: *NS Rajabathar Mudaliar v MS Vadivelu Mudaliar* (1970) 1 SCC 12 ('the court applies the property *cy-près, viz,* to some other charities as nearly as possible resembling the original trust').

[223] (NSWSC, 29 May 1992).

the Next Weary Wayfarer—As Men of Honour, Please Leave All Tidy'. The use of convalescent homes disappeared with the onset of advanced medical and outpatient care, the Sydney property was not needed for that purpose any longer, and a *cy-près* scheme of the property was ordered. The property was sold, and the proceeds applied to improving an aged and disabled care facility nearby. Upon argument that this was too narrow a band of beneficiaries, compared with the testator's original intention, the court held that it was not so disproportionately in favour of the aged as to be at the expense of the rest of the local community who may require convalescence. It is plain that finely balanced, even 'knife-edge', judgments arise in this area of the *cy-près* doctrine.

On a pragmatic level, it has also been reiterated that the court's role in this respect is a purely administrative one, with some relaxation and 'best practice' permitted at the expense of strict logic, as the following passage from *A-G (NSW) v Fulham* demonstrates:

> It is not . . . required that the Court search for a new definition of the charitable purpose which in rigorous logic is as nearly as possible the same as the one which failed. The Court acts administratively, makes choices and has regard to practical considerations in a search for an appropriate analogous application of charitable property, in a context where it is impossible to achieve the original purpose, no existing charity can exactly qualify and no existing charity has any rights. If existing charities had any actual entitlement there would be no need for a scheme. The Court is not bound by all ordinary judicial processes including adherence to evidence law and need not extend procedural justice to all charities which may conceivably have some expectations. . . . contests as to the form of *cy-près* schemes are rare, they are free from technicality and the Court is in uncharted territory.[224]

It is evident that there are four different standards that can apply to the application of property in these circumstances. Each has derived some support among the jurisdictions.

Match the cy-près application as closely as possible.   This is the narrowest and least flexible form of scheme-making power. This has certainly been favoured under the current English statute (and its equivalents), which simply provide that, where one or more of the triggers is satisfied, the property can be 'applied *cy-près*'.[225] No further guidance is given in the statute.

It has been said that this 'modest' enactment was deliberate, in order to avoid discouraging donors who might be put off by the thought that the property would no longer be designated for the purpose preferred by the donor.[226] Indeed, it could be said that the scope for *cy-près* application of property is rather

---

[224] [2002] NSWSC 629 (19 Jul 2002) [18], citing, in part: *Phillips v Roberts* [1975] 2 NSWLR 207 (CA) 211.
[225] See, eg, the opening words of Charities Act 1993, s 13(1).
[226] J Warburton, 'Charitable Companies and the *Ultra Vires* Rule' [1988] *Conv* 275, 282 (for this reason, 'any modifications in the *cy-près* doctrine . . . have always been modest').

constrained under the very statutory wording that the English legislature chose. First, the phrase, 'property . . . to be applied *cy-près*', ties the statutory power to distribute property to other purposes to the cautious, 'as near as possible'; and secondly, the reference to the need to have regard to the 'spirit of the gift' in s 13 does act as a restriction, when new schemes are devised and new purposes formulated.[227]

Certainly, much of the language of the English Charity Commissioners' Reports does not demonstrate any far-flung intentions with respect to the *cy-près* application of property.[228] Some of the more interesting examples of the Charity Commissioners' approach are illustrative of the narrow approach:

The case and the original charity	The *cy-près* trigger	The *cy-près* application
Bequest to Highgate School:[229] Thirty Greek manuscripts were given to a London school in 1872 for teaching the students classical Greek. The manuscripts were each between 300–600 years old. They were stored away from 1938, forgotten, and only rediscovered when offices were being moved in 1986.	The manuscripts were not suitable for teaching A-level classical Greek; and were costly to insure, being valued at up to £60,000.	The Charity Commissioners authorised their sale, but given that they were given for the purposes of teaching and study, the proceeds of sale were to be applied as follows: to pay for conversion of a chapel to the school library; and to provide books and equipment for the school library.

---

[227] Noted in: M Chesterman, *Charities, Trusts and Social Welfare* (Weidenfeld and Nicolson, London, 1979) 277 (some 'may have paid too little heed to the phrase "the spirit of the gift" . . . and thereby overstated the cases for crossing the boundaries between different categories of charitable purpose'); DG Cracknell (ed), *Charities: The Law and Practice* (Thomson Sweet & Maxwell, London, 1994–) [looseleaf] [I.65]; AJ Oakley, *Parker and Mellows Modern Law of Trusts* (8th edn, Sweet & Maxwell, London, 2003) 486; J Warburton, 'The Spirit of the Gift' (1995/96) 3 *Charity Law and Practice Rev* 1, 5.

[228] See various *Reports of the Ch Comm for England and Wales*: acknowledging their duty to 'keep faith with the spirit of the [the] original trusts': (2000–01) 11; 'we must as an arm of the Court be bound by the principles of *cy-près*': (1987) 11; 'It is often suggested that both the doctrine itself and the Commissioners' application of it are unnecessarily restricted. In our experience, these criticisms are usually made by those who wish to see funds diverted to some worthy but quite different purpose, or to an area of benefit markedly different from that intended by the founder. There is a good deal of (understandable) misapprehension on this matter. We fear it will always be so': (1984) [28]; also (1988) [53]; 'we are constrained by law to make sure that the new purposes remain consonant with the old ones': *Annual Report* (1998) 10.

[229] *Report of the Ch Comm for England and Wales* (1987) [48]. For a somewhat similar instance, where three Stradivarius instruments, costly to insure and impracticable for day-to-day use, were sold and proceeds applied closely to the original purpose, see: *The Royal Academy of Music case*, in *Report of the Ch Comm for England and Wales* (1986) App B.

The case and the original charity	The *cy-près* trigger	The *cy-près* application
The Haycraft Trust:[230] This trust had, as its purpose, the teaching of English in the UK. It had worked with other charities since the 1960s to teach, through affiliates, worldwide.	Haycraft wished to apply its assets to make English training accessible to people in jurisdictions abroad where travel to the UK was not a possibility. It was unable to work effectively with other charities to achieve this aim unless its purposes were widened.	A *cy-près* scheme was ordered to allow Haycraft's assets to be used for teaching of any language, with a preference for English, anywhere in the world.
The Home of Rest for Horses:[231] The original purpose of this charity was to care for poor people's horses.	The Report only records that the charity wished to widen its purposes to benefit more disadvantaged persons.	The approval of a *cy-près* scheme was foreshadowed so that the charity could also assist those charities that provided pony riding for the disabled.
Royal School for Deaf Children, Birmingham:[232] Residential school founded for the education of deaf children.	Educational policy changed; such children were to be integrated into the ordinary school system, and the number of pupils at the school significantly reduced.	Trust property was to be used for a resource centre for children and adults who suffered from a hearing impairment and from some other disability.
Hermitage Lands Highway Charity:[233] This charity provided for the repair and support of a particular causeway or pavement.	The Ministry of Transport then took over the maintenance of this property.	The funds were applied *cy-près* for the inhabitants of the town for a public clock, beautifying the neighbourhood, providing a recreation ground or village hall or bus shelter.
St Dunstans:[234] This charity was established during WWI to care for ex-service members blinded in 'war or warlike' conflict.	A number of ex-service members urgently needed treatment and care, but could not prove that their condition was directly caused by their war service.	The objects were changed to allow application of the funds to all blind ex-service members, regardless of how their visual impairment was caused.

[230]   Ch Comm for England and Wales, *Annual Report—Making a Difference* (2002–3).
[231]   *Report of the Ch Comm for England and Wales* (1971) [26].
[232]   *Report of the Ch Comm for England and Wales* (1985) [39]–[42].
[233]   *Report of the Ch Comm for England and Wales* (1972) [50]–[52].
[234]   Ch Comm for England and Wales, *Annual Report* (1999–2000) 7.

The case and the original charity	The *cy-près* trigger	The *cy-près* application
The Maharajah's Well, Stoke Row:[235] Charity for sinking of a Well, and laying out land as a pleasure garden and as an income-producing cherry orchard for the upkeep of the Well.	Income from the cherry orchard insufficient to maintain Well; the Well was no longer needed for the cherry orchard; and special licence required to use water in any event.	The funds were applied for the maintenance of the Well and the land as places of historic and architectural interest and natural beauty.

Examples of this restrictive approach abound around other jurisdictions. The Irish High Court stated, of equivalent provisions in its jurisdiction,[236] that although the section—

> has caused substantial inroads to be made into the restrictive common law approach to the *cy-près* doctrine, it is still desirable and necessary to have due regard for the wishes of the donor so as to avoid the threat of making the practice of donating to charity a veritable shot in the dark.[237]

The New South Wales Supreme Court cast precisely the same restriction over the *cy-près* power under that jurisdiction's equivalent statutory regime:

> the court does not have a free hand to re-cast the provisions of the will in whatever way seems to it to be desirable. The scheme which is being settled is a *cy-près* scheme— that means that the scheme must be one which carries into effect, as closely as is now possible, the intention which the testator had.[238]

In another case, the New South Wales Court of Appeal,[239] unusually of its own volition (without the point being raised by the appellant), decreed that a *cy-près* scheme devised by the trial judge did not sufficiently preserve the donor's intention of keeping the capital of the trust intact. It reiterated that 'although the settling and approval of *cy-près* schemes has never been subject to a technical approach, the court's prime responsibility is to give effect as closely as possible to what the founder of the trust wanted.'[240]

Sheridan's discussion of the English Charity Commissioners' decision in the *Royal Holloway and Bedford New College Application*[241] is also on point.[242]

---

[235] *Report of the Ch Comm for England and Wales* (1983) [53]–[56].

[236] Charities Act 1961, s 47.

[237] *Magee v A-G* (Irish HC, 25 Jul 2002) [no pp].

[238] *McLean v A-G (NSW)* [2003] NSWSC 853, [4].

[239] *Lovett v Permanent Trustee Co Ltd* (NSWCA, 24 Mar 1987).

[240] *Ibid*, [19].

[241] Reported as: *Royal Holloway and Bedford New College* (1993) 1 Decisions of the Ch Comm 21, and also see: Ch Comm for England and Wales, *Annual Report* (1992) [41]–[45].

[242] L Sheridan, '*Cy-près* Application of Three Holloway Pictures' (1993/94) 2 *Charity Law and Practice Rev* 181. Also see, for further commentary upon this case by the same author: LA Sheridan, *The Barry Rose Charity Statutes* (Barry Rose Law Publishers, Chichester, 1998) 109–10.

The founder of Royal Holloway College donated a collection of art for the picture gallery of the College, which included three particular pictures—a Turner, a Constable, and a Gainsborough. By 1991, several problems had manifested: the College had a deficit of some £1.4 million, buildings could not be maintained without compromising academic standards, there were no funds to provide for the care, maintenance and security of the pictures, and their very high value meant that they were difficult to insure and to store or to leave on public display. The trustees sought, via a *cy-près* scheme, to sell these three pictures and apply the proceeds towards reducing the deficit. This was permitted, which drew the following criticism by Sheridan:

> It is unusual for a *cy-près* scheme to convert the capital of a trust into money available for expenditure on purposes of the trustee which are not closely related to the purposes of the trust which is being altered. . . . it is a matter of public concern, that potential benefactors may be deterred from generosity . . . by foreseeing the authorised use, by trustees short of cash, of property meant as a permanent endowment, for purposes other than those for which the gift of the property was intended.[243]

(This is to be contrasted with the sale of Greek manuscripts and the *cy-près* application of the funds for other educational purposes discussed above.[244]) Such critiques bring into sharp relief the tension that *cy-près* schemes constantly generate—trying to ensure that the trust fund is used for the greater good, whilst not discouraging donors from giving to their favourite charitable causes without fear that their property will be diverted to that which would not have won their endorsement.

As a final point of significance, it is evident from the Charities Bill 2005 (which, at the time of writing, is presently under debate[245]) that a fairly close correlation between original and *cy-près* purposes is likely to be statutorily countenanced in the future, should this Bill be passed intact. Section 14B(3), if passed, would state that a *cy-près* scheme must have regard to the following matters:

(a) the spirit of the original gift;
(b) the desirability of securing that the property is applied for charitable purposes which are close to the original purposes, and
(c) the need for the relevant charity to have purposes which are suitable and effective in the light of current social and economic circumstances.[246]

During Parliamentary Debates, Lord Bassam of Brighton described the content of this sub-section as intending to change the law in some respect, in that it—

---

[243] Sheridan, *ibid*, 184; and 'The scheme appears perilously close to cutting across the doctrine that preference of the trustees for some other object than that of the settlor is no ground for *cy-près* application': Sheridan, *The Barry Rose Charity Statutes, ibid*, 110.

[244] See p 130.

[245] Charities Bill [HL] (as amended on report) (HL Bill 27, 54/1, ordered to be printed 18 October 2005) 19.

[246] Section 14B(3), as inserted by s 18 of the Charities Bill, *ibid*.

would slightly alter the way the *cy-près* rule can be applied. It will allow the commission to take into account not only the need to find a new purpose that is close to the failed purpose but the spirit of the original gift and the need to ensure that the charity can make a significant social or economic impact. In other words, proximity of purpose would not be the overriding imperative; equal consideration would be given to the spirit of the gift and the social or economic impact imperative.[247]

Despite the implication that the *cy-près* requirement would be 'relaxed' by insertion of the abovementioned provision,[248] it is this author's view that the conjunctive requirements, and the presence of pre-requisite (b) 'close to the original purposes', do not embrace a particularly wide view of the *cy-près* scheme-making power. This is especially so, when the drafting is compared to the wider possibilities which are discussed below.

Application of trust property to some other charitable purpose within the same head of charity *as that which the donor nominated.* This option closely approximates the recommendation of the OLRC that 'for the purpose of a variation, the court should be required to approve or select one or more purposes as close as is practicable or reasonable to the original ... purpose or purposes'.[249]

On the one hand, that Commission was concerned about *cy-près* applications that would shift the trust property from one head of charity to another and cause possible apprehension to would-be donors, but on the other hand, considered that the court should be given some leeway by not having to search for purposes that would come 'as near as possible' to purposes that were out of date.[250] Something else that was within the same head of charity was considered to be acceptable.

Interestingly, it is also evident that this particular *cy-près* standard has also been considered appropriate by the English Charity Commissioners under s 13 where the original charitable purpose was charitable under the fourth *Pemsel* head. The use of land for a pig market (the land had been purchased by public subscription, and it was not run as a commercial venture) was held to be charitable. The Council owner wished to sell the land and acquire, in its place, land to be used as a public car park. A *cy-près* scheme would be necessary to effect this change of purpose, and it was permitted as sufficiently 'analogous'.[251] On a similar note, the disposition of land on trust for the poor to take fuel for

---

[247] House of Lords, *Hansard*, 14 Mar 2005, col GC 417–18.

[248] Mooted, eg, in: DJ Hayton and C Mitchell, *Hayton and Marshall Commentary and Cases on the Law of Trusts and Equitable Remedies* (12th edn, Sweet & Maxwell, London, 2005) 510.

[249] See OLRC, *Law of Trusts* (1996) vol 2, 472, and Draft Bill, s 76(2)(b).

[250] The Commission cites (*ibid*, 461) the well-known example of *A-G v Ironmongers' Co* (1841) Cr & Ph 208, 41 ER 469, aff'd (1844) Cl & Fin 908, 8 ER 983 (property held 'for the redemption of British slaves in Turkey or Barbary').

[251] *Report of the Ch Comm for England and Wales* (1980) [126]–[134], *Saffron Walden Pig Market, Essex*.

their use was converted, via a *cy-près* scheme, into a trust for relieving poverty in the same region, by providing recreational and sports facilities and relieving sickness and old age—within the same *Pemsel* head, but reasonably different in character.[252]

Application of trust property to some other charitable purpose *(whether or not under the same head of charity as that which the donor nominated).*   Reasonably early on, in 1976, the Goodman Committee had also considered that moving between charitable heads would be an attractive feature of a revamped *cy-près* doctrine, 'so that the funds might be used for objects satisfying existing local needs, which might well be of a quite different nature to the original trusts'.[253] A decade later, again the Charity Commissioners received the same type of urging. The authors of the Woodfield Report criticised the Commissioners[254] for adopting too narrow an approach when settling *cy-près* schemes, by not straying too far from the donor's original intentions. Certainly, the Commissioners were on record as strongly disproving of changing the purpose to another head or field of charitable activity.[255]

In light of all of this, the Charity Commissioners published guidelines in 1989 concerning the selection of *cy-près* purposes.[256] It was a pragmatic development. The revised guidelines, in particular:[257]

- contemplated applying charitable trust funds for another purpose altogether—'the proceeds of an almshouse or a school might not be appropriated solely for the relief of poverty or for educational purposes respectively if the area of benefit were already adequately provided with poor or educational charities'; and
- did not require a 'near as possible' approach; in fact, the guidelines specifically note that '[i]f the view is taken that the nearest practical purpose is not suitable or effective, then other purposes may be selected'.

Although this would appear to be a considerable relaxation on the *cy-près* principle of 'as near as possible', various academic commentary has since

---

[252] *Ibid*, [113]–[115], *Fuel Allotment, Sunninghill, Berkshire*.

[253] National Council of Social Service, *Charity Law and Voluntary Organisations* (Lord Goodman Report) (1976) [189]–[191], and recommending in [192(c)] that the doctrine move away from its traditional perspective, 'to make it clear that, in appropriate cases a fundamental change in the objects of the charity can be authorised'.

[254] Sir Philip Woodfield *et al*, *Efficiency Scrutiny of the Supervision of Charities* (1987) (Woodfield Report) [84]– [85], and recommendation no 27; M Sladen, 'The Charities Act 1985' [1986] *Conv* 78, 82–84; M Chesterman, *Charities, Trusts and Social Welfare* (Weidenfeld and Nicolson, London, 1979) 277.

[255] Note the Commissioners' strong reproach of that course in: *Report of the Ch Comm for England and Wales* (1970) [41].

[256] See: *Report of the Ch Comm for England and Wales* (1989) [73]–[75].

[257] *Ibid*, [74].

noted[258] that this is the *exceptional* approach of the Charity Commissioners. Certainly, the case law sampled in the *Annual Reports* indicates that the Commissioners will prefer to ensure that property devoted to one head of charity is retained for that head of charity. Simply choosing a more beneficial use of the property would appear not to have been embraced as part of England's current *cy-près* law. Prior to the Charities Bill 2005 mentioned above, recent reviews of the charity jurisdiction did not give rise to any further guidelines from the Commission as to the exercise of the *cy-près* jurisdiction.[259]

One might be tempted to think that the Charity Commissioners would be assisted in their task if the particular *cy-près* standard in the heading, permitting 'some other charitable purpose', were to be statutorily enacted. However, experience elsewhere dictates that this has been singularly unsuccessful in achieving a flexible *cy-près* standard. The statutory regimes of Western Australia[260] and New Zealand[261] expressly allow for the trust property to be applied 'for some other charitable purpose'. Both academic[262] and judicial[263] opinion have remarked that, under the wording adopted by the respective legislatures, the substituted scheme definitely need not be *cy-près* at all, nor for a purpose 'as near as possible' to the original, and could be applied under another *Pemsel* head entirely.

Although the OLRC has opined that, in drafting their *cy-près* schemes in this way, the Western Australian and New Zealand legislatures 'make a determined effort to discard the technicalities of the *cy-près* power',[264] that assessment tends to overstate the reality. Whatever scope the respective Parliaments may have intended for the *cy-près* application of property under these provisions, they have been substantially tightened by 'judicial re-drafting'. In *Re Twigger*, Tipping J opined that, in formulating or deciding upon any *cy-près* scheme, and notwithstanding that 'Part III does not make a *cy-près* approach mandatory':

[258] E Cairns, *Charities: Law and Practice* (3rd edn, Sweet & Maxwell, 1997) 180. For similar sentiments, see also: J Warburton, 'The Spirit of the Gift' (1995/96) 3 *Charity Law and Practice Rev* 1, 10; DG Cracknell (ed), *Charities: The Law and Practice* (Thomson Sweet & Maxwell, London, 1994–) [looseleaf] [I.66]; HA Picarda, *The Law and Practice Relating to Charities* (3rd edn, Butterworths, London, 1999) 309.
[259] The doctrine warranted brief mention only in, eg: Cabinet Office, Strategy Unit, *Private Action, Public Benefit. A review of Charities and the Wider Not-For-Profit Sector* (2002) p 47. A further review, and potential for relaxing the doctrine's triggers and application, were foreshadowed in the accompanying discussion paper of the Cabinet Office, *Providing Flexibility for Charities to Evolve and Merge* (2002) 8.
[260] Charitable Trusts Act 1962 (WA), s 7(1).
[261] Charitable Trusts Act 1957 (NZ), s 32(1).
[262] HAJ Ford and WA Lee, *Principles of the Law of Trusts* (3rd edn, LBC Information Services, Sydney, 1996) [2068]; OLRC, *Law of Trusts* (1996) vol 2, 464; *Halsbury's Laws of Australia* (Butterworths, Sydney, 1991–), 'Cy-près Schemes', [75–800]; G Dal Pont, *Charity Law in Australia and New Zealand* (OUP, Oxford, 2000) 326; C Rickett, 'Failure of Charities and the Conundrum of s 32' [2003] *NZLJ* 59, 60; N Richardson, 'Modern Problems for Ancient Charities' (2001) 15 *Trust Law Intl* 159, 160.
[263] *Penny v Cancer & Pathological Research Institute of Western Australia* (1994) 13 WAR 314, 318.
[264] OLRC, *Law of Trusts* (1996) vol 2, 468.

the court owes a duty to the settlor of the trust property to dispose of it as nearly as possible in accordance with the intention of the settlor. It also owes a duty to those proposed to be benefited by the trust and to the public generally to dispose of the fund or property, as nearly as possible in accordance with the charitable purposes of the trust and in such a way as will best serve the interests of those intended to be benefited.[265]

Other more recent New Zealand authority[266] has followed a similar line of reasoning. This is in spite of the fact that the present legislation, and its similarly-worded predecessor,[267] do not seem to require anything like that degree of adherence to the original purpose, and in spite of the fact that other (earlier) authority does exist to support the view that the application of the property to any charitable purpose, 'without regard to its resemblance to the old purpose', is permissible.[268]

Such confusion, whilst not atypical of the *cy-près* doctrine, is unfortunate. As Flannery notes, '[a] differentiation is necessary between deference to and dictation by the [donor]';[269] and however widely the New Zealand legislation may be worded, the courts have opted for the latter interpretation of it. To add further to the debate, the Western Australian judiciary has interpreted that jurisdiction's similar legislation in precisely the same manner. In *Penny v Cancer and Pathological Research Institute of Western Australia*,[270] Anderson J held the New Zealand approach to be correct: 'the court would not readily approve a scheme which did not have that degree of resemblance, even although a *cy-près* approach is not mandatory'.[271]

Application of trust property to some purpose, charitable or non-charitable, *that would maximise the 'public benefit' derived from the trust property.* This widest option has not been implemented by statute to date. The contention that trustees should be permitted to use trust assets in *whatever* manner they consider

---

[265] [1989] 3 NZLR 329 (HC) 341, citing with approval: *Re Goldwater (decd)* [1967] NZLR 754, 755 ('The substituted trust under any scheme must, in my view, accord as closely as is reasonably possible in the changed circumstances to the terms of the original trust'), and *Re the Door of Hope* (1905) 26 NZLR 96, 100 ('the fund should be administered by some existing institution closely corresponding to the Auckland Women's Home').

[266] *Re Tennant* [1996] 2 NZLR 633, 636; *Re Wilson Home Trust* [2000] 2 NZLR 222, 225; *Re Centrepoint Community Growth Trust* [2000] 2 NZLR 325, 336–37. See earlier, also: *Re Goldwater (decd)* [1967] NZLR 754, 757; *In re Amelia Bullock-Webster (decd)* [1936] NZLR 814, 824.

[267] *Viz,* the Religious, Charitable and Educational Trusts Act 1908.

[268] Eg: *Public Trustee v A-G* [1923] NZLR 433, 442 (where the court drew a distinction between, on the one hand, the wider approach which it considered was permitted under s 15 of the Religious Charitable and Educational Trusts Act 1908 and, on the other hand, the common law doctrine of *cy-près*), cited with approval in: *In re Palmer (decd); White v Feltham Children's Home Trust Inc* [1939] NZLR 189, 193. Also: *In re Harding (decd); Dixon v A-G* [1960] NZLR 379, 384; *Re Martin (decd)* [1968] NZLR 289, 290 ('The Court, in my view, is given a wide and general discretion to dispose of [the property] for some other charitable purpose. The section . . . certainly does not expressly limit that discretion . . . the section gives power to distribute the proceeds of sale for the charitable purposes set out in the will or for other charitable purposes approved by the Court').

[269] MFL Flannery, 'The Variation of the Charitable Trust' [1977] *NZLJ* 368, 368, 373.

[270] (1994) 13 WAR 314.

[271] *Ibid*, 318.

would most advance the public interest has, however, received strong academic support in the United States, for example[272] (although, notably, one United States Court considered 'such a promiscuous resort to the *cy-près* power' to be 'unsettling'[273]).

When reviewing the operation of charities law in 1989, the Home Office declared that the strict view of *cy-près*, matching the charity's new objects as closely as possible with the old, could 'stifl[e] new initiatives and inhibit desirable changes to the objects, especially of parochial charities.'[274] However, no further changes to the *cy-près* statutory doctrine were recommended. It was merely said that the Charity Commission would review its precedent systems and update the guidance given to its staff. Subsequently, the Cabinet Office foreshadowed a possible relaxation in the strict view of the *cy-près* doctrine in England that new purposes as near as possible must be chosen,[275] but as noted above, the Charities Bill 2005, as the most recent development of note in this jurisdiction, certainly does not encourage a wide *cy-près* application of property.

Overall assessment. The policy behind the liberal statutory direction of 'some other charitable purpose' (the third option explored above) is primarily supportable on the basis that it offers flexibility. As the OLRC approved, 'the necessity of selecting varied objects that are as close as possible to the donor's own purposes can hamper the application of charitable funds to contemporary needs.'[276] Indeed, even restricting the substituted scheme to 'charitable purposes' can exclude from *cy-près* consideration many purposes that are benevolent and laudable, but not charitable at law. However, against this is the dual conundrum of wishing to remain as true as possible to the settlor's wishes, and not wishing to put off would-be donors who may baulk at the possibility, for example, of their bequests for the relief of poverty being used for the advancement of religion.

In this author's view, the solution proffered by the New Zealand and Western Australian statutes, in permitting *any* other charitable purpose to be selected, is the optimal one. It is liberal and flexible. By plain drafting, it seeks to displace the general law's 'as close as possible' mantra where appropriate (and in that

---

[272] Eg: R Atkinson, 'Reforming *Cy-près* Reform' (1993) 44 *Hastings LJ* 1111, 1156 ('the need for charity to respond rapidly to social change has become increasingly clear; the tradition of rigid dead hand control is in conflict with this need. If we come to see charities as living altruistic communities acting in their own right, rather than as servants of two competing masters, individual donors on the one hand and the state on the other, the traditional doctrine of *cy-près* will have no role'). Also mooted in: M Chesterman, *Charities, Trusts and Social Welfare* (Weidenfeld and Nicolson, London, 1979) 224–27.

[273] *Board of Trustees of the Museum of the American Indian v Board of Trustees of the Huntington Free Library and Reading Room*, 610 NYS 2d 488, 499 (NY App Div 1994).

[274] Secretary of State for the Home Department, *Charities: A Framework for the Future* (1989) Cm 694, 37, picking up on an earlier suggestion to this effect: Sir Philip Woodfield *et al*, *Efficiency Scrutiny of the Supervision of Charities* (1987) (Woodfield Report) [84]–[85].

[275] Cabinet Office Strategy Unit, *Providing Flexibility for Charities to Evolve and Merge* (2002) 8.

[276] OLRC, *The Law of Trusts* (1996) vol 2, 471.

regard, this author agrees with other commentary that it is unfortunate that general law notions have been permitted to restrict that plainly worded statutory power[277]). Putting the position in these jurisdictions in its most positive light, the concern that the testator's intention may be discarded has been tempered by judicial caution to honour that intent wherever possible. That caveat against straying too far from the testator's wishes should, in this author's view, be left to the courts to invoke, rather than be implemented by legislative direction of the type contained in the English (and equivalent) statutes. The problem with the widest (fourth) option is that the framework provided by the definition of charity and the donor's original charitable purposes would be jettisoned, making the drafting of a substituted scheme potentially quite arbitrary. As will be discussed in a later chapter, a similar problem has arisen in the context of non-charitable purpose trusts.[278]

F SOME PROCEDURAL ASPECTS OF THE *CY-PRÈS* JURISDICTION

Although this chapter does not presume to equate to a manual of the statutory *cy-près* doctrine,[279] a few of the more controversial procedural aspects will be briefly considered in this section.

Under the English statutory *cy-près* regime, the trustees cannot apply trust property *cy-près* of their own volition. An application to the court or the Charity Commissioners is always necessary. The statutory regime does, however, place the trustee under a duty to apply for the authorisation of a scheme if it appears appropriate to do so.[280] This appears to do no more than to restate the common law position, as stated in *National Anti-Vivisection Society v Inland Revenue Commissoners*,[281] and is a duty which other courts have since reiterated.[282] Thus, in any situations where the trust fund devoted to charity is too large or too small, or overtaken by developments that render it ineffective or obsolete, the

---

[277] G Dal Pont, *Charity Law in Australia and New Zealand* (OUP, Oxford, 2000) 326.

[278] See ch 6.

[279] Comprehensive details of procedural matters are contained, eg, in: *Halsbury's Laws of England* (4th edn reissue, Butterworths, London, 1996) vol 5(2), [174] ff; LA Sheridan and VTH Delany, *The Cy-près Doctrine* (Sweet & Maxwell, London, 1959) chh 9, 10; G Dal Pont, *Charity Law in Australia and New Zealand* (OUP, Oxford, 2000) 253–56, 266–84.

[280] Charities Act 1993, c 10, s 13(5). The Charity Commissioners note that the provision guards against 'lethargy or of unthinking satisfaction with their present trusts': *Report of the Ch Comm for England and Wales* (1970) [45].

[281] [1948] AC 31 (HL) 66 (Lord Russell) 74 (Lord Simonds), and noted in: J Warburton, 'Charitable Trusts—Unique' [1999] *Conv* 20, fn 24, and by the same author: *Annotated Charities Act 1993* (Sweet & Maxwell, London, 1993) 10–22; and in HL Nathan, *The Charities Act 1960* (Butterworths, London, 1962) 13, 80. Also: C Baxter, 'Trustees' Personal Liability and the Role of Liability Insurance' [1996] *Conv* 12, fn 5, citing also: *Annual Report of the Charity Commissioners* (1992) 25.

[282] Eg: *Re Anzac Cottages Trust* [2000] QSC 175, [13] ('the trust was at a stage where the Public Trustee was under a duty to make an application for the property, subject to the Anzac Cottages Trust, to be applied *cy-près*').

trustee *must* take steps to ensure that the property is applied *cy-près*. If the trustee refuses to apply for a scheme, the Charity Commissioners, the Attorney-General, and individuals who are 'interested in the charity' or people who are 'inhabitants of the charity, if it is a local charity', have powers to instigate *cy-près* proceedings.[283]

Whilst appearing to give the *cy-près* jurisdiction 'teeth', the trustees' duty has been academically criticised as being too loosely drafted.[284] These criticisms have included the following: what triggers the trustees' duty, and how serious must the trust's failure be to compel the trustees to apply for a *cy-près* scheme; how is the duty enforced, and what are the sanctions for trustees' non-performance; what steps must the alternative parties take if the trustees do not act; do the Charity Commissioners have a duty to frame a *cy-près* scheme at all, or merely a power; does the obligation on the trustees to apply for a *cy-près* scheme in respect of a 'trust for charitable purposes' actually mean a duty in respect of 'a trust for purposes that were originally charitable', to make proper sense of s 13(1)(e)(ii)? None of these matters is addressed on the face of the English legislation; nor are they tackled in the relevant Charity Commission guidelines.[285]

To take the obverse position, the South Australian statutory *cy-près* regime does not oblige the trustees to apply for a *cy-près* scheme, but merely empowers them to do so.[286] The OLRC, in rejecting the English provision,[287] also supported this approach for the province of Ontario, on the bases that the trustees are already under a fiduciary duty to act in the best interests of the trust, that there was no need to buttress that equitable duty with a statutory duty where there was no evidence that trustees were ignoring their fiduciary obligations, and that the Attorney-General already had an inherent authority to ensure that trustees' duties were discharged according to law.[288] To this may be added the suggestion that, in circumstances where 'a statute authorises the doing of a thing for the sake of justice or the public good, the word "may" means "shall" '.[289] In *A-G, ex rel Rathbone and McKay v Waipawa Hospital Board*,[290]

---

[283]   Charities Act 1993, ss 18, 28, but rarely used, notes R Venables, 'Cy-près and Yet So Far Away' [May, 2002] *Legal Executive Journal* 54, 54.

[284]   M Chesterman, *Charities, Trusts and Social Welfare* (Weidenfeld and Nicolson, London, 1979) 278–82; P Luxton, 'Whither Cy-près? An Anglo-American Analysis of Practical Problems' [1987] *NLJ Annual Charities Review* 34, 42; J Jaconelli, 'Independent Schools, Purpose Trusts and Human Rights' [1996] *Conv* 24, 32. For criticisms of the duty contained in Charities Act (Northern Ireland) 1964, s 22(6), see: N Dawson, 'Cy-près: Means, Motive and Opportunity—and Other Matters' (1988) 39 *NILQ* 177, 183–84.

[285]   Ch Comm for England and Wales, *Making a Scheme* (CC36, 1992).

[286]   Trustee Act 1936 (SA), s 69B(3).

[287]   OLRC, *Law of Trusts* (1996) vol 2, 462, calling this 'perhaps the most interesting provision of s 13'.

[288]   *Ibid*, 474.

[289]   *Craies on Statute Law* (6th edn, 285), cited in: *A-G, ex rel Rathbone and McKay v Waipawa Hospital Board* [1970] NZLR 1148 (SC) 1154.

[290]   *Ibid*.

the New Zealand Supreme Court had to consider the effects of a provision[291] which stated that the trustees 'may prepare or cause to be prepared . . . a scheme for the disposition of the property'. It concluded that the provision was not expressed in mandatory terms, for the trustees were under a duty to apply in any event.[292]

As noted previously, in England, the responsibility for making a *cy-près* scheme rests with either the courts or the Charity Commission. As an alternative, England's draft Charities Bill 2005 provides that, when making a *cy-près* scheme, the Charity Commission could impose on a transferee charity (via the scheme) an obligation to ensure that the trust property 'is applied for purposes which are, so far as is reasonably practicable, similar in character to the original purposes'.[293] Ridout observes[294] that this raises the spectre of the Commission delegating to the charities themselves the determination of the *cy-près* distribution—not, that author suggests, a 'best practice' outcome.

The Nathan Committee originally considered that there should ideally be some time period during which a charitable trust should be immune from *cy-près* alteration, in order to prevent would-be donors from being discouraged. It recommended a period of 35 years from foundation of the charitable trust if the donor was not living when the *cy-près* application was made (otherwise, if the trustees and donor agreed the *cy-près* scheme, there should be no time limit).[295] That recommendation made no appearance in s 13 of the Charities Act 1993, nor in any of the other statutory enactments considered in this section. Interestingly, in *Forrest v A-G (Victoria)*,[296] a *cy-près* scheme was ordered some 20 years from the date of the testator's death. In the Northern Ireland case of *Re Steele*,[297] the time between the will's taking effect and the *cy-près* scheme being implemented was even shorter, a mere decade. The lack of any period of immunity has been noted to enhance the widest possible use of statutory *cy-près*.[298]

Finally, when the court is called upon to amend a trust that is already subject to a *cy-près* scheme, regard must be primarily had to the donor's *original* intention, and not to the intention evident in the *cy-près* scheme now in force.

---

[291] Charitable Trusts Act 1957, s 34.

[292] [1970] NZLR 1148 (SC) 1153.

[293] Charities Bill 2005, s 18, inserting s 14B(4), and, at the time of writing, the draft section remains in place: Charities Bill [HL] (as amended on report) (HL Bill 27, 54/1, ordered to be printed 18 October 2005) 19.

[294] P Ridout, 'From 1601 to 2004 and onwards' July/August (2004) *Trusts and Estates Law and Tax Journal* 16, 18.

[295] *Nathan Committee Report*, [365] and item (d) therein.

[296] [1986] VR 187.

[297] [1976] NI 66 (Murray J).

[298] J Warburton, 'The Spirit of the Gift' (1995/96) 3 *Charity Law and Practice Rev* 1, 7; LA Sheridan, *Keeton and Sheridan's The Modern Law of Charities* (4th edn, Barry Rose Law Publishers, Chichester, 1992) 223–24, both citing *Forrest* as illustrative of this point.

This position has been supported both judicially[299] and academically[300]—notwithstanding that the relevant legislation seems to suggest otherwise[301]—on the basis that this sort of legislation effects only administrative changes, but was not 'generally intend[ed] to alter the substantive law of charities.'[302]

[299] *Permanent Trustee Co Ltd v A-G (re Byrne's Estate) (No 2)* (NSWSC, 1 Mar 1995) 3, and earlier (NSWSC, 12 Dec 1994) 4, both citing: LA Sheridan and VTH Delany, *The Cy-près Doctrine* (Sweet & Maxwell, London, 1959) 44; and *Re Lambeth Charities* (1853) 22 LJ Ch 959; and *A-G v Bishop of Worcester* (1851) 9 Hare 328; 68 ER 530.

[300] Sheridan and Delany, *ibid*; J Warburton, *Annotated Charities Act 1993* (Sweet & Maxwell, London, 1993) 10–21.

[301] Eg, Charities Act 1993, s 13(3) provides that references to the 'original purposes of a gift shall be construed, where the application of the property given has been altered or regulated by a scheme . . ., as referring to the purposes for which the property is for the time being applicable.'

[302] *Permanent Trustee Co Ltd v A-G (re Byrne's Estate) (No 2)* (NSWSC, 1 Mar 1995) 3.

5

Charitable Public Appeal Funds

A INTRODUCTION

WHERE AN APPEAL for public donations is issued to fulfill a specific charitable purpose, the fund into which the donations are placed is generally subject to trust. The donors, as settlors, give their money to the fund-raising committee/appeal organisers as trustees, and the charitable purposes for which the donations are to be applied are the valid objects of the trust.[1] Significantly, 'the fund-raiser is a trustee of the funds which he collects, despite the absence of any formal appointment as trustee, and despite any lack of awareness on his part that he is a trustee.'[2] The trust will be charitable at law where it is of a public nature (that is, beneficial to the community, or a defined section of the community) rather than of a private and personal nature (where donors provide for themselves, out of monies subscribed by themselves, some kind of relief)[3] and where it satisfies the *Pemsel* four-prong test of charity[4] (disaster funds do not always fall within one of these four prongs[5]).

Of course, in many cases of periodic fundraising for charitable purposes, donations are made to an incorporated body (which owns property conveyed to it absolutely), or to an unincorporated body, the constitution of which permits that donations can be used for general purposes if, for whatever reason, the donation is unable to be applied to the specific purpose for which it was

---

[1] See British Columbia LRC, *Informal Public Appeal Funds* (1993) 4, citing: *In re Trusts of the Abbott Fund; Smith v Abbott* [1900] 2 Ch 326, 331.

[2] *Jones v A-G; R v Wain* (1994) 2 Decisions of the Ch Comm 33–35. Point also forcefully made in: E Cairns, 'Appeals and Fund Raising' (1994) 2 *PCB* 126, 126 ('It is seldom appreciated that a person who solicits funds from members of the public for a particular purpose is a trustee of the funds he collects and holds them upon trust for those purposes. If he applies those funds for another purpose he may be guilty of obtaining money by deception').

[3] The distinction noted and applied, in favour of a public charitable trust, in, eg: *In re North Devon and West Somerset Relief Fund Trusts; Hylton v Wright* [1953] 1 WLR 1260 (Ch) 1265 (fund for flood relief); *In re Hobourn Aero Components Ltd's Air Raid Distress Fund* [1946] Ch 194 (CA) 209 (fund for air-raid distress in Coventry).

[4] *Commissioners for Special Purposes of the Income Tax v Pemsel* [1891] AC 531 (HL) 583 (' "Charity" in its legal sense comprises four principal divisions: trusts for the relief of poverty; trusts for the advancement of education; trusts for the advancement of religion; and trusts for other purposes beneficial to the community, not falling under any of the preceding heads').

[5] Eg: *In re Gillingham Bus Disaster Fund; Bowman v Official Solicitor* [1958] Ch 300, concerned a memorial fund to aid the expenses and care of the families of the deceased cadets and the injured cadets who were hit by an omnibus while marching on a dark foggy night; this fund was not charitable in the legal sense. For an interesting insight into a charitable appeal, see: RW Suddards, *Bradford Disaster Appeal: The Administration of an Appeal Fund* (Sweet & Maxwell, London, 1986).

canvassed.[6] In other cases, direct grants from governmental agencies have replaced public collections as the primary source of funds for public appeals,[7] with attached conditions upon their use. Alternatively, the rules of the public appeal are usually carefully drafted, and the ultimate destination of the unused donations (to another nominated charity, for example) is clearly explained[8] (although there are notable instances where this did not occur, causing legal headaches[9]). In yet other circumstances, an Act of Parliament may be passed to authorise the proposed *cy-près* application of the entire fund raised by public appeal.[10] Interestingly, dormant funds resulting from public charitable appeals were applied, by virtue of a special Act of Parliament,[11] to fund the construction of the Law Courts in London.[12] This chapter is not concerned with those more straightforward scenarios.

Instead, it considers the position where donations are made to an unincorporated body, the trustees are faced with the fact that they cannot spend any or all of the monies on the purpose for which the fund was established, and the rules are silent (typically where the public appeal is launched within a few days of a deserving event upon both a wave of goodwill and an absence of legal advice[13]). There are three possible destinations for such unused donations: either revert to the donors, apply *cy-près*, or pass as *bona vacantia*. In a concerted effort to avoid the monies either languishing in court or being subsumed into general revenues of the Crown as *bona vacantia*, both the general law and statutory enactments have attempted to offer solutions to this dilemma—

---

[6] British Columbia LRC, *Informal Public Appeal Funds* (1993) 5–6.

[7] See GE Dal Pont and DRC Chalmers, *Equity and Trusts in Australia and New* Zealand (LBC Information Services, Sydney, 1996) 405.

[8] As urged in, eg, E Cairns, 'Appeals and Fund Raising' (1994) 2 *PCB* 126, and in the publications of the Ch Comm for England and Wales, *Fundraising and Charities* (CC20) 2–3; *Disaster Appeals, Attorney General's Guidelines* (CC40, 1992) 2–3.

[9] Eg, in Australia: *Re Trust Deed Relating to the Darwin Cyclone Tracy Relief Trust Fund; Adermann v Corp of the City of Darwin* (1979) 39 FLR 260 (NTSC), where the terms of the trust deed governing the charitable appeal funds permitted the trustees to transfer any surplus to various institutions nominated in s 78(1)(a) of the Income Tax Assessment Act 1936 (Aus). Some of those institutions were not charitable at law; the trustees' powers under the trust deed were judicially read down to mean that the surplus could be distributed to other institutions under s 78(1)(a) that were charitable at law, and which were connected to the city of Darwin. Eg, in England: see the public appeal to rescue sea birds affected by oil from the sinking of the Torrey Canyon, discussed in: *Report of the Ch Comm for England and Wales* (1971) [41], and the example of the disaster fund that lead to 'bad feeling' cited in: Charity Comm for England and Wales, *Milestones: Managing Key Events in the Life of a Charity* (2003) 21.

[10] Eg, as occurred, following the decision in *Beggs v Kirkpatrick* [1961] VR 764: Ripon Peace Memorial Trust Act 1961 (Vic).

[11] Courts of Justice Building Act 1865, c 48.

[12] Noted in: HL Nathan, *The Charities Act 1960* (Butterworths, London, 1962) 13.

[13] Noted to be the case in, eg: *In re North Devon and West Somerset Relief Fund Trusts; Hylton v Wright* [1953] 1 WLR 1260 (Ch) 1263. Also see the comments of the Charity Commissioners upon the less-than-carefully worded public appeal launched in: *In re Gillingham Bus Disaster Fund; Bowman v Official Solicitor* [1958] Ch 300, cited in: LA Sheridan, *Keeton and Sheridan's The Modern Law of Charities* (4th edn, Barry Rose Law Publishers, Chichester, 1992) 264.

although, as will be discussed in this chapter, their efforts have often been criticised as complicated, artificial, and even unnecessary.

The ways in which *over-subscribed* public charitable appeals have been dealt with in general law and under English statute are examined in Section B, before turning attention to the legal treatment accorded to *under-subscribed* public charitable appeals in Section C. Both scenarios require an analysis as to whether there is an initial or subsequent failure of the trust. It will be evident from the several English decisions canvassed in the two sections that the courts' determinations are complex, inconsistent, and at times difficult to reconcile.[14] This chapter is devoted to consideration of public appeals which are conducted for *charitable* purposes; non-charitable public appeals will be considered in the following chapter.

B OVER-SUBSCRIBED PUBLIC CHARITABLE APPEALS

1. Initial Failure or Subsequent Failure?

The amount of donations realised by public appeal for a specific purpose may exceed that which was required for the charitable purpose, and the trustees have to distribute that excess. The charitable purpose may be completely met out of the donations, leaving a surplus, for example: where the fund has been amalgamated with other entities, and the trust is to be disbanded;[15] where money is collected for a war hospital which becomes redundant when peace returns[16] or for a school which closes down;[17] where the money to provide for a fire brigade and equipment was no longer required when the brigade and assets were sold

---

[14] British Columbia LRC, *Informal Public Appeal Funds* (1993) 10–11 ('courts have been less consistent in their application of *cy-près* principles to public appeal funds than with other charitable trusts'); GW Keeton, *Modern Developments in the Law of Trusts* (Faculty of Law, Queen's University, Belfast, 1971) 310 ('[i]n a series of unfortunate decisions, the courts [have] made this a subject of almost intolerable complexity'). For detailed consideration of the English cases canvassed herein, see, in particular: See: D Wilson, 'Section 14 of the Charities Act 1960: A Dead Letter?' [1983] *Conv* 40; R Thompson, ' "Public" Charitable Trusts Which Fail: An Appeal for Judicial Consistency' (1971) 36 *Saskatchewan L Rev* 110, 122 ('In the interest of consistency, the courts should treat cases arising out of public appeals in the same way as they treat bequests ... A great benefit of this consistent approach is that it would avoid some peculiarly inconsistent judgments').

[15] *In re West Sussex Constabulary's Widows, Children and Benevolent (1930) Fund Trusts; Barnett v Ketteringham* [1971] Ch 1 (Fund was established to provide for widows and orphans of deceased members of the West Sussex Constabulary; this was amalgamated with other police forces in Sussex to form a single force; fund had to be distributed).

[16] *In re Welsh Hospital (Netley) Fund; Thomas v A-G* [1921] 1 Ch 655 (appeal launched for subscriptions to fund for establishing hospital for sick and wounded Welsh soldiers; donations received from private individuals, street collections, etc; in March 1919, the hospital, being no longer required for the object for which it had been built, was disposed of and staff disbanded). For another war case where a surplus was held: *In re British Red Cross Balkan Fund; British Red Cross Society v Johnson* [1914] 2 Ch 419.

[17] *Braithwaite v A-G* [1909] 1 Ch 510.

on;[18] where no further persons came forward to claim from a disaster relief fund,[19] or where the founding member, or those to be benefited by the appeal, have died.[20] In all of these scenarios, the purpose for which the money was given cannot be achieved. (Of course, where the purpose can still be achieved, that money cannot and should not be put to any other use, a matter that the English Charity Commissioners reiterated in the East Pakistan Cyclone Fund Appeal[21]).

In the case of over-subscriptions, case law indicates that this is an example of subsequent failure: that following the application of contributions to the charitable purpose, 'the identity [of the fund] is lost',[22] that where the charitable purpose has been 'in operation for a number of years ... That purpose being no longer practicable ... the charitable trusts do not fail [*ab initio*]'.[23] In *In re Monk; Giffen v Wedd*, it was said: '[i]f there should be any failure here it would be in the nature of a partial failure by matter subsequent, not ... a total failure through failure of a condition precedent.'[24]

It has been suggested by some commentators that this issue is not entirely settled, so that unexpended donations made to a charitable appeal that is being wound up after its purpose has been fulfilled *may* constitute initial failure of those particular donations.[25] Nevertheless, the weight of judicial (and academic[26]) opinion is that this constitutes a *subsequent* failure, and rightly so, in this author's opinion.

2. Application of *Cy-près* at General Law

In the case of subsequent failure of a charitable trust appeal, a resulting trust in favour of the donors cannot occur. According to Jenkins LJ in *In re Ulverston*

---

[18] As in: *In re Wokingham Fire Brigade Trusts; Martin v Hawkins* [1951] Ch 373.

[19] As in: *Re Trust Deed Relating to the Darwin Cyclone Tracy Relief Trust Fund; Adermann v Corp of the City of Darwin* (1979) 39 FLR 260 (NT SC).

[20] *In re British School of Egyptian Archaeology; Murray v Public Trustee* [1954] 1 WLR 546 (Ch) (set up at the behest of Sir Flinders Petrie); *In re Trusts of the Abbott Fund; Smith v Abbott* [1900] 2 Ch 326 (resulting trust for the donors to the Abbott Fund established for two deaf and dumb ladies; after ladies died, fund distributed).

[21] *Report of the Ch Comm for England and Wales* (1971) [40].

[22] *In re West Sussex Constabulary's Widows, Children and Benevolent (1930) Fund Trusts; Barnett v Ketteringham* [1971] Ch 1.

[23] *In re Wokingham Fire Brigade Trusts; Martin v Hawkins* [1951] Ch 373.

[24] [1927] 2 Ch 197 (CA) 211–12.

[25] See pp 70–2.

[26] See, eg: D Wilson, 'Section 14 of the Charities Act 1960: A Dead Letter?' [1983] *Conv* 40, 45; DJ Hayton and C Mitchell, *Hayton and Marshall Commentary and Cases on the Law of Trusts and Equitable Remedies* (12th edn, Sweet & Maxwell, London, 2005) 513; G Moffat, *Trusts Law: Text and Materials* (4th edn, CUP, Cambridge, 2005) 913; OLRC, *Law of Trusts* (1996) vol 2, 458; LA Sheridan, *Keeton and Sheridan's The Modern Law of Charities* (4th edn, Barry Rose Law Publishers, Chichester, 1992) 251, 261; JE Martin, *Hanbury and Martin Modern Equity* (17th edn, Sweet & Maxwell, London, 2005) 458; DWM Waters, *Law of Trusts in Canada* (2nd edn, Carswell, Toronto, 1984) 625, 629; HAP Picarda, *The Law and Practice Relating to Charities* (3rd edn, Butterworths, London, 1999) 354–55; JG Riddall, *The Law of Trusts* (6th edn, Butterworths, London, 2002) 194.

and District New Hospital Building Trusts; Birkett v Barrow and Furness Hospital Management Committee:

> The intention of a subscriber might well be that his contribution should be returned in the event of a total failure *ab initio* of the purpose for which he made it, but that, in the event of a surplus being left over after that purpose had been duly fulfilled, any share in such surplus which might be regarded as representing his subscription or some part thereof should be permanently devoted to charity. In forming his intention as to the fate of his contribution in the latter event (if, indeed, he formed one at all), he might well be influenced by the fact that the inclusion of contributions from anonymous sources, and the indiscriminate spending of a mixture of anonymous contributions and contributions from named subscribers, would make it impossible to ascertain whether the whole or any and, if so, what part of any particular contribution had been spent. . . . [and that] I think it might well have been held [in *Welsh Hospital*] that, once the charity for which the fund was raised had been effectively brought into action, the fund was to be regarded as permanently devoted to charity to the exclusion of any resulting trust.[27]

Apart from the reference to *In re Welsh Hospital (Netley) Fund; Thomas v A-G*[28] in the abovementioned passage, other authorities have held that, where publicly raised monies were put to charitable use, with a surplus over, then in light of the subsequent failure of the charitable purpose with which those donations were infused, no resulting trust could be found; the donors must be construed to have had no expectation of being repaid.[29]

Additionally, given that over-subscribed appeals are treated as instances of subsequent failure, no general charitable intent on the part of the donor is hence required to be proven. The gift on trust, upon being applied for charitable purposes, is taken to have been applied to charity in perpetuity, and is to be applied *cy-près* where application of those funds becomes impossible or impracticable.[30] Certainly, the weight of authority in England supports the view that the donor of a contribution to a charitable public appeal in which the purpose has been met need not have any general charitable intention in order for a *cy-près* application of the unused donation to occur. For example, in *In re Wokingham Fire Brigade Trusts*,[31] subsequent failure of the charitable appeal occurred when funds were

[27] [1956] Ch 622 (CA) 636.
[28] [1921] 1 Ch 655.
[29] *In re Monk; Giffen v Wedd* [1927] 2 Ch 197 (CA) 212 ('Counsel for the respondents were not able to cite any case in which, a charity having actually been put into operation and having afterwards proved incapable of exhausting the whole charitable fund, it had then been held that there was a resulting trust for the donor, or in the case of a will for his next-of-kin'); *In re Wokingham Fire Brigade Trusts; Martin v Hawkins* [1951] Ch 373; *In re North Devon and West Somerset Relief Fund Trusts; Hylton v Wright* [1953] 1 WLR 1260 (Ch) 1267; *Re Trust Deed Relating to the Darwin Cyclone Tracy Relief Trust Fund; Adermann v Corp of the City of Darwin* (1979) 39 FLR 260 (NTSC). In the context of a non-charitable trust, see: *West Sussex Constabulary's Widows, Children and Benevolent (1930) Fund Trusts, In re; Barnett v Ketteringham* [1971] Ch 1.
[30] *In re Cooper's Conveyance Trusts; Crewdson v Bagot* [1956] 1 WLR 1096 (Ch) 1104, citing: *In re Slevin; Slevin v Hepburn* [1891] 2 Ch 236 (CA) and *In re Wright; Blizard v Lockhart* [1954] Ch 347(CA).
[31] [1951] Ch 373.

requested to purchase and maintain a local fire brigade, which was ultimately disbanded. Danckwerts J considered that the trust created by the charitable appeal had been in place for several years, that the donations were made out-and-out for a charitable purpose, and that it was 'not necessary to consider whether there was any general charitable intention' on the part of the donors to the fire brigade's equipment and upkeep.[32] The unexpended fund was applied *cy-près*. In *Ulverston*, Jenkins LJ considered that this view was correct.[33] Further concurrence may be found in both Australian[34] and Canadian[35] authorities.

Thus, where a charitable purpose has been met by public appeal and a surplus of funds is left over, attempts by the court (whether in England[36] or elsewhere[37]) to satisfy itself that the donors did indeed have a general charitable intent must arguably be considered to have been unnecessary and wrongly decided.

3. Effect of Charities Act 1993, s 14

The statutory enactment in s 14, governing charitable collections which fail, does not apply where an unexpended surplus of donations is left after the charitable appeal is fulfilled. In other words, it has no application to

---

[32] *Ibid*, 377, although Danckwerts J did opine that the original donors had donated their monies with the specific intention of establishing a fire brigade.

[33] See also: *In re British School of Egyptian Archaeology; Murray v Public Trustee* [1954] 1 WLR 546 (Ch) (donations given to The British School of Egyptian Archaeology, founded in 1905 by Sir Flinders Petrie and applied towards the school's purposes; outbreak of war in 1939 put an end to the school's main activities; after Sir Flinders' death in 1942, never a going concern; held that it was not necessary to consider whether there was any general charitable intention; trust funds applied *cy-près*).

[34] *Perpetual Trustees Tasmania Ltd v A-G (Tas)* (SC, 18 Nov 1993) 8, following: *Beggs v Kirkpatrick* [1961] VR 764, 767.

[35] *Re Northern Ontario Fire Relief Fund Trusts* (1913), 4 OWN 1118, 11 DLR 15 (HC) (appeal for sufferers from a Northern Ontario forest fire; surplus remained; held that surplus should be applied *cy-près* towards establishment of hospitals at two localities; no reference to general charitable intention being required; of which Waters terms this, 'judicial silence is golden': DWM Waters, *Law of Trusts in Canada* (2nd edn, Carswell, Toronto, 1984) 631.

[36] Eg: *In re North Devon and West Somerset Relief Fund Trusts; Hylton v Wright* [1953] 1 WLR 1260 (Ch) (fund for flood relief; surplus left over after purpose of assisting flood victims acquitted; the court found a general charitable intent; 'main underlying object' was to 'benefit the people of the district in question': at 1267, 1269); relying upon: *In re Welsh Hospital (Netley) Fund; Thomas v A-G* [1921] 1 Ch 655, 661 (an appeal to the inhabitants of Wales for subscriptions to a Welsh wartime hospital at Netley; 'main underlying object' of donors 'was to provide money for the comfort of sick and wounded Welshmen, and that all the subscribers intended to devote their contributions not only to the particular object, but generally to the benefit of their sick and wounded countrymen'). In *In re Ulverston and District New Hospital Building Trusts, Birkett v Barrow and Furness Hospital Management Committee* [1956] 1 Ch 622 (CA) 634, Jenkins LJ considered that it was unnecessary in *Welsh Hospital* to find a general charitable intent. Also agreeing that 'the better opinion seems to be that these authorities are incorrect', see: DWM Waters, *Law of Trusts in Canada* (2nd edn, Carswell, Toronto, 1984) 629. Cf: OLRC, *Law of Trusts* (1996) vol 2, 458, which expresses preference for the *North Devon* view.

[37] *Re Trust Deed Relating to the Darwin Cyclone Tracy Relief Trust Fund; Adermann v Corp of the City of Darwin* (1979) 39 FLR 260 (NTSC) 263 ('I consider further that the persons who subscribed to that trust must be taken to have expressed a general charitable intent', citing *North Devon*).

over-subscribed charitable appeals. The reason for this conclusion is contained in s 14(7): charitable purposes are only deemed to fail, for the purposes of the section, where any difficulty in applying the property to those purposes makes it available for return to the donors (by way of a resulting trust).[38] In the case of subsequent failure/oversubscriptons, a resulting trust is simply not available. The donations are forever dedicated to charity. As Wilson explains,[39] if any of the donated funds have been actually applied to the charitable purpose, then on the view of Jenkins LJ in *Ulverston*, the failure is subsequent and a *cy-près* distribution would be ordered—leaving no room for s 14 to apply. On this basis, the general law position (described in sections 1 and 2 above) would continue to apply to failed charitable appeals that result from a surplus, unamended by statute.[40]

C UNDER-SUBSCRIBED PUBLIC CHARITABLE APPEALS

1. Initial Failure or Subsequent Failure?

A public appeal, whilst canvassed with the best of intentions, may prove disappointing and/or undersubscribed. For instance, it may fail to reach the scale of subscriptions required to do anything useful for the intended project;[41] policy changes introduced after the appeal may induce abandonment of the project altogether before any donations have been expended towards its purpose;[42] the

---

[38] Interestingly, this sub-section, governing what is meant by a gift 'failing' in this context, also applies to the new s 14A, which has been foreshadowed by the Charities Bill [HL] (as amended on report) (HL Bill 27, 54/1, ordered to be printed 18 October 2005) 19 (of which see s 17, which inserts the new s 14A). Section 14A would apply to property given for specific charitable purposes in response to a solicitation which contained a statement that property given in response to it would, if the purposes fail, be applicable *cy-près* unless the donor made a relevant declaration at the time of making the gift. For further details of this proposed amendment, see: Memorandum by the Home Office, *Charities Bill [HL]* (May 2005).

[39] S Wilson, *Todd and Wilson's Textbook on Trusts* (7th edn, OUP, Oxford, 2005) 311–12.

[40] JE Martin, *Hanbury and Martin Modern Equity* (17th edn, Sweet & Maxwell, London, 2005) 463; DJ Hayton and C Mitchell, *Hayton and Marshall Commentary and Cases on the Law of Trusts and Equitable Remedies* (12th edn, Sweet & Maxwell, London, 2005) 514; JG Riddall, *The Law of Trusts* (6th edn, Butterworths, London, 2002) 17; DWM Waters, *Law of Trusts in Canada* (2nd edn, Carswell, Toronto, 1984) 630; HAP Picarda, *The Law and Practice Relating to Charities* (3rd edn, Butterworths, London, 1999) 355 ('Given that in the case of a supervening failure there can never be a resulting trust, s 14 of the Charities Act 1993 does not appear to affect the [general] law').

[41] As in: *In re Ulverston and District New Hospital Building Trusts, Birkett v Barrow and Furness Hospital Management Committee* [1956] 1 Ch 622 (CA) (insufficient monies to build a new hospital to replace the existing cottage hospital); *In re Henry Wood National Memorial Trust; Armstrong v Moiseiwitsch* [1966] 1 WLR 1601 (Ch) (insufficient monies to build a new concert hall to replace that which was destroyed during war); *Beggs v Kirkpatrick* [1961] VR 764 (donation to construct a sanctum at a Hindu educational facility that was not built).

[42] As in: *In re Uni of London Medical Sciences Institute Fund; Fowler v A-G* [1909] 2 Ch 1 (CA) (legacy of £25,000 to the Institute of Medical Sciences Fund, University of London; scheme to establish the institute launched in 1902, but abandoned in 1907 because of lack of funds and a change of opinion by medical school).

intervention of war and national reorientating of health policy may mean that the appeal was the wrong idea for the wrong time;[43] the increased costs of travelling may mean that it would be several years before a travelling scholarship would net enough to prove useful;[44] or none of the donations may be required because, say, a government relief package or insurance policy payout becomes available to redress the need for public aid.[45]

The weight of judicial opinion indicates that these are instances of *initial*, not subsequent, failure of the trust. Various authorities have referred, in such circumstances, to 'a total failure *ab initio* of the purpose for which he made [the donation] . . . there has been no effective application of it for the purpose for which it was raised';[46] that 'apart from expenses [of administration, etc], the fund is intact',[47] and that in the event of under-subscriptions, it is 'an initial failure of the charitable purpose'.[48]

It has occasionally been academically argued[49] that these cases are truly examples of subsequent failure, because at the time that the donation was given and the gift was effective, the purpose of the public appeal was not impossible nor impracticable, and it could not be said at that point that there was no reasonable prospect that the purposes would be possible at some future date— it became so thereafter—so that there was no failure *ab initio*. However, such views have not received much widespread support in either the cases or the literature.

2. At General Law: The Identifiable and Traceable 'Named Donors'

The case law discussed in this section draws distinctions between donations made by identifiable donors, and anonymous donations of the type frequently raised via raffles, show entertainments, sweepstakes, church-giving plates, and proceeds of collecting boxes. The firstmentioned of these categories is con-

---

[43] *In re Hillier's Trusts; Hillier v A-G* [1954] 1 WLR 700 (CA) (appeal launched for erection and maintenance of new hospital at Slough; contributions from both named subscribers and anonymous donors; never became possible to build the proposed hospital at Slough because of war conditions and because National Health Service Act 1946 precluded erection of new voluntary hospitals).

[44] *Re Ethel Pedley Memorial Travelling Scholarship Trust* (1949) 49 SR (NSW) 329 (Eq).

[45] Point made in OLRC, *Law of Trusts* (1996) vol 2, 458.

[46] *In re Ulverston and District New Hospital Building Trusts; Birkett v Barrow and Furness Hospital Management Committee* [1956] 1 Ch 622 (CA) 636 (Jenkins LJ). Similar comment made in: *In re British School of Egyptian Archaeology; Murray v Public Trustee* [1954] 1 WLR 546 (Ch) 554.

[47] *In re West Sussex Constabulary's Widows, Children and Benevolent (1930) Fund Trusts; Barnett v Ketteringham* [1971] Ch 1, 14.

[48] *In re Hillier's Trusts; Hillier v A-G* [1954] 1 WLR 9 (first instance) (Upjohn J), approved by Goff J in: *Re West Sussex Constabulary's Widows, Children and Benevolent (1930) Fund Trusts, Barnett v Ketteringham* [1971] Ch 1, 12.

[49] R Thompson, ' "Public" Charitable Trusts Which Fail: An Appeal for Judicial Consistency' (1971) 36 *Saskatchewan L Rev* 110, 120–22. Also referred to in P Luxton, *The Law of Charities* (OUP, Oxford, 2001) 584; HAP Picarda, *The Law and Practice Relating to Charities* (3rd edn, Butterworths, London, 1999) 347.

sidered in this section, whilst the 'anonymous donors' will be discussed later in section 3.

(a) Presumption of a resulting trust/conditional gift

Where the donors, or subscribers, to the public appeal are identifiable (including where their donations are legacies by will), then at common law, it is presumed that the trustees hold those particular donations on resulting trust for the identifiable donors.

> *Prima facie*, the subscriber who gives his name intends to subscribe for the particular and exclusive purpose for which his subscription has been solicited and none other, and there will be a resulting trust in his favour if that purpose fails.[50]

The leading English illustration of this is the case of *In re Ulverston and District New Hospital Building Trusts; Birkett v Barrow and Furness Hospital Management Committee.*[51] Between 1924–42, appeals were made for contributions to the Ulverston and District New Hospital Building Fund for the replacement of the Ulverston cottage hospital with a new hospital. Contributions were forthcoming from named and anonymous donors; contributions dwindled to less than £8 in 1937, ceased in 1942, and were totally insufficient to finance the building of a new hospital. It was held that so much of the fund as represented the contributions of identifiable donors was subject to a resulting trust in favour of those donors. Similarly, in *In re West Sussex Constabulary's Widows, Children and Benevolent (1930) Fund Trusts; Barnett v Ketteringham,*[52] the identifiable donations and legacies given to a police widows' fund were to be held on resulting trusts for the donors and their estates, the gifts having been made for a particular purpose which had failed.

The Australian authority of *Beggs v Kirkpatrick*[53] follows the *Ulverston* approach. Donations were made toward the construction of a new hospital, monies coming from living donors and from bequests from testators, and also from contributions from local organisations, either directly out of their funds or from the proceeds of various social and public functions. The appeal generated only one-third of the funds sought. The identifiable donors were held to be entitled to their donations back on resulting trusts.

Occasionally, courts have reached the same result (the money goes back to the donors) via a different line of reasoning, that of conditional gift. It has been

[50] *In re Ulverston and District New Hospital Building Fund; Birkett v Barrow and Furness Hospital Management Committee* [1956] Ch 622 (CA) 634 (Jenkins LJ), following: *In re Trusts of the Abbott Fund; Smith v Abbott* [1900] 2 Ch 326.
[51] *Ibid.* See also: *In re Uni of London Medical Sciences Institute Fund; Fowler v A-G* [1909] 2 Ch 1 (CA) (especially Kennedy LJ; the other members of the court found in favour of the donor on a different basis); *In re Henry Wood National Memorial Trust; Armstrong v Moiseiwitsch* [1966] 1 WLR 1601 (Ch).
[52] [1971] Ch 1.
[53] [1961] VR 764.

reasoned that a gift by the donor was conditional upon there being a sufficient fund for the charitable purpose, and where fulfilment of that purpose is impossible (lack of funds, change of policy, etc), then the gift must fail and the property revert to the donor. Such a view was expressed by the majority of the Court of Appeal in *In re University of London Medical Sciences Institute Fund; Fowler v A-G*,[54] who considered the testator's legacy of £25,000 to be a conditional gift only for the establishment of the medical institute because he had made it clear that should that main purpose become impossible, he would want his money to come back to himself or his estate. The *Medical Sciences* view of a conditional gift has been called an 'exceptional case' by Denning LJ,[55] and has not been followed in Australia,[56] although academically, the tactic has been endorsed.[57]

(b) Rebutting the presumption of a resulting trust

A resulting trust may only operate, pursuant to which the surplus is held on trust for the donors in proportion to the quantum of each donor's contribution to the entire fund, if the donor intended his contribution to be conditional upon the fulfilment of the specific charitable purpose.[58] Of course, any resulting trust is based upon the presumed intent of the parties. Ultimately, then, it depends upon what the court infers to have been the true intention of the donors when they gave their subscriptions to the public appeal,[59] with the caveat that the court will not infer an intent 'that would be absurd on the face of it.'[60] The task of construing donors' intents has been judicially chastised to be a complicated and uncertain one.[61]

In practice, as the following discussion demonstrates, the presumption of a resulting trust has been frequently rebutted in cases of donations from identifiable subscribers, such that no resulting trust has eventuated, and the unused donations have been applied *cy-près*. Significant indicators by which to rebut the presumption, as derived from English and Commonwealth case law, include the following:

---

[54] [1909] 2 Ch 1 (CA) (especially Vaughan Williams LJ at 7 and Farwell LJ at 8 in separate judgments). Also suggested in: *In re Hillier's Trusts; Hillier v A-G* [1954] 1 WLR 700 (CA) 714 by Lord Evershed MR, that 'it clearly remains possible that some individual donor may have attached to his gift such special terms as would enable him, distinguishing himself from his fellow contributors, to claim now a return of his money', in which case resulting trusts would ensue.
[55] *In re Hillier's Trusts; Hillier v A-G* [1954] 1 WLR 700 (CA) 717.
[56] *Misra v Hindu Heritage Research Foundation Ltd* (NSW SC, 21 Jun 1996) 11–13.
[57] Eg: G Dal Pont, *Charity Law in Australia and New Zealand* (OUP, Oxford, 2000) 304–5.
[58] *In re Trusts of the Abbott Fund; Smith v Abbott* [1900] 2 Ch 326.
[59] *In re Welsh Hospital (Netley) Fund; Thomas v A-G* [1921] 1 Ch 655, 658.
[60] *In re West Sussex Constabulary's Widows, Children and Benevolent (1930) Fund Trusts; Barnett v Ketteringham* [1971] Ch 1, 12.
[61] *In re North Devon & West Somerset Relief Fund Trusts; Hylton v Wright* [1953] 1 WLR 1260 (Ch) 1267. See also, the comments of Young J in *Misra v Hindu Heritage Research Foundation Ltd* (NSW SC, 21 Jun 1996) 7–8.

Has the donor obtained any (even slight) benefit from the donation?   Where donations have been made by donors to public appeals for good causes, via the media of raffles, sweepstakes, amateur concerts or fashion soirées, the generally held view is that no resulting trust can be presumed.[62]

Certain 'benefits' may accrue to the donor. First, the donor who purchased his ticket has entered into a contract, for which he has received his consideration—the pleasure and entertainment derived from the concert, the thrill of the raffle competition—and which stand over and above any motivation of assisting the public appeal. If the donor is to obtain a benefit, even a slight benefit, then the usual presumption will be that no resulting trust can occur. Consequently, it has been said that a resulting trust cannot exist where there is a contract.[63] On the same principle, if the donor makes a claim for income tax deduction in respect of the donation, that indicates that it was intended as an absolute gift and that any interest in the money is abandoned, because that is the basis upon which to claim such a deduction.[64] Secondly, where raffles or concerts are put on for a public appeal, only the profit from the endeavour accrues to the fund, and there may be none of that—the donor makes no direct contribution to the public appeal fund (he has 'gotten something for nothing', in that case), so does not directly fulfil the role of settlor for a resulting trust.[65]

Difficulties in quantification or identification not a bar.   A resulting trust in favour of the donors will not be denied, simply because it would be a difficult accounting exercise to determine which donors were entitled to which amount. Equity will, apparently, be up to the task of 'cut[ting] the gordian knot by simply dividing the ultimate surplus in proportion to the sources from which it has arisen',[66] a view with which Australian courts have concurred.[67] However,

[62] The most oft-cited and illustrative authority for this proposition is that of: *In re West Sussex Constabulary's Widows, Children and Benevolent (1930) Fund Trusts; Barnett v Ketteringham* [1971] Ch 1, wherein no resulting trust applied to moneys raised by entertainments, raffles and sweepstakes, and proceeds of collecting tins; but moneys representing identifiable donations/legacies were to be held on resulting trusts for the donors and their estates.

[63] *In re West Sussex Constabulary's Widows, Children and Benevolent (1930) Fund Trusts; Barnett v Ketteringham* [1971] Ch 1, 10–11 (Goff J), citing: *In re Gillingham Bus Disaster Fund; Bowman v Official Solicitor* [1958] Ch 300, 314, with some suggestion of similar reasoning (certainly the same result) in: *In re Welsh Hospital (Netley) Fund* [1921] 1 Ch 655, 660. The contractarian theory also received *obiter* support by Vinelott J in: *Conservative and Unionist Central Office v Burrell (Inspector of Taxes)* [1980] 3 All ER 42 (Ch) 63; and by Brightman J in: *In re William Denby & Sons Ltd Sick and Benevolent Fund; Rowling v Wilks* [1971] 1 WLR 973 (Ch) 979.

[64] *Misra v Hindu Heritage Research Foundation Ltd* (NSW SC, 21 Jun 1996) (donation of $50,508 for the building of a sanctum; tax deduction claimed by the donor in respect of the donation; sanctum not constructed; donation held to be an out-and-out gift, not a conditional gift), citing: *Re Australian Elizabethan Theatre Trust* (1991) 30 FCR 491.

[65] *In re West Sussex Constabulary's Widows, Children and Benevolent (1930) Fund Trusts; Barnett v Ketteringham* [1971] Ch 1, 9–10 (Goff J); also citing: *In re Gillingham Bus Disaster Fund; Bowman v Official Solicitor* [1958] Ch 300, 314, and *Cunnack v Edwards* [1896] 2 Ch 679 (CA).

[66] *In re West Sussex Constabulary's Widows, Children and Benevolent (1930) Fund Trusts; Barnett v Ketteringham* [1971] Ch 1, 11.

[67] *Misra v Hindu Heritage Research Foundation Ltd* (NSW SC, 21 Jun 1996); *Beggs v Kirkpatrick* [1961] VR 764.

where the donations have been made over many years with less than ideal record-keeping,[68] or where the identification of original donors is extremely difficult and timeconsuming,[69] it should be possible to rebut the presumption of a resulting trust in those circumstances.[70] Where the donors are truly anonymous and always will remain so, giving via raffles, collecting tins and the like, a resulting trust is a nonsense, as will be discussed shortly.[71]

External indicators rebutting a resulting trust.   Where an identified donor makes a donation to a charitable public appeal, and expressly disclaims any right to the money thereafter;[72] or where statute provides that any money given for charitable public appeal to a society becomes the absolute property of the society,[73] then the donors must be taken to have parted with all interest in the sums so given, and there can be no resulting trust in their favour.

Where no donors come forward to claim.   It has been suggested, under the general law, that where no donors come forward to claim their monies back following advertisement of the surplus, that indicates that no resulting trusts should be presumed generally.[74] In *In re Hillier's Trusts; Hillier v A-G*,[75] no resulting trusts of the donations were found to exist; and Lord Evershed MR later explained[76] that his conclusion in that case was influenced by the fact that, notwithstanding extensive advertisement, no single contributor had come forward to reclaim his contribution.

Not all judicial opinion agrees, however. Such inactivity has been explained away as perhaps the consequence of embarrassment[77] or the nervousness of 'playing Shylock',[78] to which no great importance should be attached. In any event, the factor appears equivocal at best. The Supreme Court of Victoria held, in *Beggs v Kirkpatrick*,[79] that the fact that named donors did not come forward to object to a proposed *cy-près* scheme or to claim their monies back did not bar a resulting trust of their donations. Adam J played down the factor in this way:

> In the result, then, I consider that those whom I have described as the individual donors to the appeal are entitled to be repaid their donations. . . . I have not overlooked the fact

---

[68] *Cunnack v Edwards* [1895] 1 Ch 489, 497, 498.

[69] *In re Trusts of the Abbott Fund; Smith v Abbott* [1900] 2 Ch 326 (resulting trust held); *In re Gillingham Bus Disaster Fund; Bowman v Official Solicitor* [1958] Ch 300 (resulting trust held).

[70] Noted as *obiter* in: *In re Hillier's Trusts; Hillier v A-G* [1954] 1 WLR 700 (CA) 714–15 (Denning LJ).

[71] See Section 3, pp 158 ff.

[72] As occurred with many donors in *Beggs v Kirkpatrick* [1961] VR 764.

[73] *Braithwaite v A-G* [1909] 1 Ch 510, 516 (concerning Friendly Societies Act of 1793 (33 Geo 3, c 54) s 14).

[74] *In re Hillier's Trusts; Hillier v A-G* [1954] 1 WLR 700 (CA) 716–17 (Denning LJ).

[75] [1954] 1 WLR 700 (Lord Evershed MR and Denning LJ; Romer LJ dissenting).

[76] *In re Ulverston and District New Hospital Building Trusts; Birkett v Barrow and Furness Hospital Management Committee* [1956] Ch 622 (CA) 642–43.

[77] *In re Hillier's Trusts; Hillier v A-G* [1954] 1 WLR 700 (CA) 714 (Lord Evershed MR).

[78] *Ibid*, 721 (Romer LJ).

[79] [1961] VR 764.

that no person came forward to object to the diversion of the funds raised to another purpose. In a case where it was doubtful for what precise purpose moneys were raised, this might, I think, be of some assistance in resolving doubts, but where the intention is clear, I find little, if any, help from this circumstance.[80]

Where the donation was accompanied by a general charitable intent. If the court is prepared to deduce from the facts and surrounding circumstances that, by making the particular donation, the donor was actually advancing a wider charitable purpose, then the court will impute to that donor a general charitable intent. In other words, it must be found that a subscriber did not necessarily intend to limit his bounty to that one particular object the subject of the charitable appeal, but merely intended to indicate that object as the preferred object of his bounty, without any intention of excluding other analogous charitable purposes in the event of the preferred object failing. No matter how 'long a stretch of the imagination' a general charitable intent in these circumstances may be,[81] such a finding will rebut the presumption of a resulting trust, and will permit the donation to be applied *cy-près*.

The terms of the appeal itself must be closely studied. If the public appeal documents (public notices, circulars, brochures, etc) refer to some other charitable purpose as well, distinct from the actual purpose for which donations are being sought, that may influence the finding of a general charitable intent on the part of those who donated. This factor, though, is very fact-specific. On the one hand, in *Ulverston*,[82] the chairman's published letter of invitation referred to the need to provide medical care in the Ulverston district, quite apart from the actual building and maintenance of the new hospital. Thus, it was argued that the appeal itself indicated a general charitable intention to secure the improvement of the facilities for medical and surgical treatment in the districts served by the Ulverston cottage hospital, the project of building a new hospital being merely a mode—though, no doubt the primary mode—of carrying out that general intention. However, the letter's terms were held to be insufficient to indicate that there was any general charitable intent on the part of the donors who responded to that letter. The building of a new hospital at Ulverston and its maintenance remained at all times the 'sole objective'.

On the other hand, in *Hillier*,[83] where a fund was created to build a new

---

[80] *Ibid*, 770.

[81] Note, eg, the comments in DWM Waters, *Law of Trusts in Canada* (2nd edn, Carswell, Toronto, 1984) 630 ('if the public respond to an appeal for a specific charitable purpose, for instance to provide clothing, food, and shelter for flood or fire victims, it is only by a long stretch of the imagination that one can infer an intention on the part of anonymous donors to contribute for other purposes').

[82] *In re Ulverston and District New Hospital Building Trusts; Birkett v Barrow and Furness Hospital Management Committee*[1956] 1 Ch 622 (CA).

[83] *In re Hillier's Trusts; Hillier v A-G* [1954] 1 WLR 700 (CA). Note that the terms of the respective appeals were also closely studied in the *Welsh Hospitals* case and the *North Devon and West Somerset Relief Fund Trusts* to ascertain a general charitable intent—although without good reason, given that both were subsequent failure cases, and a general charitable intent is presumed. In both cases, a *cy-près* distribution was permitted.

Slough hospital which never eventuated, the terms of the several documents which comprised the appeal indicated the opposite. One subscription form allowed donors to subscribe towards the augmentation of the income or capital of existing hospitals, even those that the donor might nominate. A brochure emphasised 'the truly British characteristic of making provision, without force, for those in need of medical care' in voluntary hospitals. All in all, the court considered that it was not crucial to the donors' intentions that the Slough hospital the subject of the appeal should be a voluntary hospital. A general charitable intention was found, and a *cy-près* scheme to apply the unused fund to an existing Slough hospital was approved.

Equating an out-and-out gift with a general charitable intention. Some authorities, both in England[84] and elsewhere,[85] indicate that if the donors intended to make a perpetual out-and-out gift to the charity, without expecting their money back under any circumstances, then they *must* have had a general charitable intention—that one must necessarily impute the other:

> If they have parted with their money out-and-out, they must be taken to have done so with a general charitable intention, or, in other words, to have devoted their money irretrievably to charity.[86]

As the OLRC has noted, this judicial reasoning hints at a separate doctrine, applicable to charitable public appeals only, whereby there is no need to find a general charitable intention, and that the mere intent to part with the property out-and-out is sufficient to attract the application of the *cy-près* doctrine.[87]

Not all agree, however. Other commentary suggests that the existence of any such equation is unsettled at best.[88] Furthermore, some English judgments make it plain that an out-and-out gift is not the same thing as a general charitable intent. For example, in *In re British School of Egyptian Archaeology; Murray v Public Trustee*, it was said:

---

[84] *In re Hillier's Trusts; Hillier v A-G* [1954] 1 WLR 700 (CA) 711 (Lord Evershed MR) ('persons giving to such collections must be taken to have intended to part, out-and-out, with their money in any event—an inference inconsistent with an intention to benefit a limited and exclusive purpose, or with any but a general charitable intention'). Also: *In re Uni of London Medical Sciences Institute Fund; Fowler v A-G* [1909] 2 Ch 1 (CA). The point is also discussed, by reference to other authorities, in LA Sheridan, *Keeton and Sheridan's The Modern Law of Charities* (4th edn, Barry Rose Law Publishers, Chichester, 1992) 261–62; G Dal Pont, *Charity Law in Australia and New Zealand* (OUP, Oxford, 2000) 305.

[85] *Halifax School for the Blind v A-G* [1935], 2 DLR 347, cited on this point by R Thompson, ' "Public" Charitable Trusts Which Fail: An Appeal for Judicial Consistency' (1971) 36 *Saskatchewan L Rev* 110, 118; and in DWM Waters, *Law of Trusts in Canada* (2nd edn, Carswell, Toronto, 1984) 631, fn 54.

[86] *In re Ulverston and District New Hospital Building Trusts; Birkett v Barrow and Furness Hospital Management Committee* [1956] Ch 622 (CA) 632 (Jenkins LJ).

[87] OLRC, *Report on the Law of Charities* (1996) 447, fn 28.

[88] DWM Waters, *Law of Trusts in Canada* (2nd edn, Carswell, Toronto, 1984) 630; LA Sheridan, *Keeton and Sheridan's The Modern Law of Charities* (4th edn, Barry Rose Law Publishers, Chichester, 1992) 224–25, 255.

I think that a [contributor] may well say: "I parted with my money to this society; I do not reserve any right to have it back", without having any positive intention that it should go to an analogous society or, indeed, to [some institution] to which the court might think proper to devote the money.[89]

Given that this was a case of subsequent, not initial, failure, however, this is merely *obiter*, but the sentiment is one that has been repeated elsewhere.[90]

(c) The backstop position: bona vacantia

Strictly speaking, where a charitable public appeal suffers an initial failure (as in the case of under-subscriptions), and where it is construed that the donor made the contribution with no expectation of ever receiving it back, but with no general charitable intention, the property is 'ownerless' and should pass as *bona vacantia* to the Crown. In *Westdeutsche Landesbank Girozentrale v Islington LBC*, Lord Browne-Wilkinson set out the position thus:

If the settlor has expressly, or by necessary implication, abandoned any beneficial interest in the trust property, there is in my view no resulting trust: the undisposed-of equitable interest vests in the Crown as *bona vacantia*: see *In re West Sussex Constabulary's Widows, Children and Benevolent (1930) Fund Trusts* [1971] Ch 1.[91]

In reality, however, the 'usual practice' in England appears to dictate otherwise. In *Ulverston*, Jenkins LJ noted that the Attorney-General often waives the claim of *bona vacantia* and brings in a *cy-près* scheme for that part of the donated fund.[92] Where that occurs, there is, of course, as Jenkins LJ noted, 'little practical importance' in seeking to find a general charitable intention. Interestingly, such waiver has also been recognised in Australia to permit anonymous donations that would otherwise pass *bona vacantia* to be applied *cy-près*.[93]

It follows from the above discussion that, as a matter of logic, unused donations are properly to be treated as *bona vacantia*, for the purposes of English law, only where the following conditions are met:

♦ the court is prepared to infer that the donor intended to part with the money absolutely and did not intend to keep any part of the money for himself; and

♦ the monies cannot be applied *cy-près*, either because

---

[89] [1954] 1 WLR 546 (Ch) 553 (donations given to The British School of Egyptian Archaeology, founded in 1905 by Sir Flinders Petrie; outbreak of war in 1939 put an end to the school's main activities; after Sir Flinders' death in 1942, never a going concern; held that it was not necessary to consider whether there was any general charitable intention; trust funds applied *cy-près*). On this point, see also: *In re Wokingham Fire Brigade Trusts; Martin v Hawkins* [1951] Ch 373.

[90] *In re Ulverston and District New Hospital Building Trusts; Birkett v Barrow and Furness Hospital Management Committee* [1956] 1 Ch 622 (CA) 633–34.

[91] [1996] AC 669 (HL) 708.

[92] [1956] 1 Ch 622 (CA) 634. However, that appears not to have occurred in *Ulverston* itself, for Oakley notes that the donations of unidentifiable donors in this case were paid into Treasury to await the possibility of donors claiming it: AJ Oakley, *Parker and Mellows Modern Law of Trusts* (8th edn, Sweet & Maxwell, London, 2003) 488.

[93] As occurred in respect of the anonymous donations in: *Beggs v Kirkpatrick* [1961] VR 764, 770.

– it was a charitable bequest infused with a specific charitable intention,[94] or
– it was non-charitable;[95] and

♦ the Crown is not prepared to waive its claim to the property.[96]

(d) Conclusion: Identifiable donors under general law

It is manifestly plain from the above discussion that the presumption of a resulting trust in favour of identifiable donors, with respect to any unused donations, is very weak. The presumption is easily rebutted on several fronts, and the authorities that support the finding of a resulting trust are infrequent. In the absence of a resulting trust, the question for the court is whether the donation was given with a general charitable intent—if it was, the unused donation can be applied *cy-près*, if it was not, then the donation passes to the Crown as *bona vacantia*.

3. At General Law: The Anonymous Donors

Having canvassed the manner in which identifiable and traceable donors to public charitable appeals are treated under general law, it is now necessary to consider the contrasting, and even more complicated, status of those donors whose identities remain unknown.

(a) No resulting trust

Where anonymous donations are made via collecting boxes, street collections, raffles, church plate, etc, for a specific purpose, then the overwhelming view is that no resulting trust will ensue. These donors must be presumed to have parted with their money out-and-out, with no intention of having the sums returned to them, whether the specific purpose is carried out and a surplus left over,[97] or is not carried out at all.[98] The courts will not presume that they wished for the

---

[94] As held, with respect to anonymous donations, in *Ulverston*, per Jenkins LJ (at 632–33).

[95] As in: *In re West Sussex Constabulary's Widows, Children and Benevolent (1930) Fund Trusts; Barnett v Ketteringham* [1971] Ch 1 (non-charitable trust; monies raised by entertainments, raffles and sweepstakes and proceeds of collecting boxes; intention on part of donors to part with their money out-and-out in all circumstances; donations were *bona vacantia*).

[96] With respect to *Ulverston*, see 634.

[97] *In re Welsh Hospital (Netley) Fund; Thomas v A-G* [1921] 1 Ch 655, 660–61, approved and applied in *In re West Sussex Constabulary's Widows, Children and Benevolent (1930) Fund Trusts; Barnett v Ketteringham* [1971] Ch 1, 11–13 in the context of a non-charitable trust.

[98] *In re Hillier's Trusts; Hillier v A-G* [1954] 1 WLR 9 (Upjohn J) 22, approved in: *In re West Sussex Constabulary's Widows, Children and Benevolent (1930) Fund Trusts; Barnett v Ketteringham* [1971] Ch 1. This part of Upjohn J's decision was not overruled on appeal. Also approved in Australia in: *Beggs v Kirkpatrick* [1961] VR 764, 770 ('think I may properly conclude that all contributions from other sources [not identifiable legacies and contributions] were given out-and-out').

donations back if the charitable purpose is not fulfilled; nor is a conditional gift-type construction that was evident in *In re University of London Medical Sciences Institute Fund; Fowler v A-G*[99] likely. Rather, each anonymous donation was intended as one perpetually dedicated to charity: 'the law gives him credit for the best of intentions'.[100] It has been said that to suggest otherwise is 'absurd on the face of it'.[101]

Nevertheless, there is limited judicial authority in *Ulverston* to the effect that even a small anonymous donor may possess an intent to return of his money (thus creating a resulting trust) if the charitable purpose fails and if he can *prove* that he put a specified sum in a collecting box.[102] It was similarly stated in *Gillingham Bus Disaster Fund* (a non-charitable public appeal) that, whether the donor be the identifiable large giver or the anonymous coin giver to a collecting box, '[t]hey all give for the one object. If they can be found by inquiry, the resulting trust can be executed in their favour.'[103] The suggestion of a resulting trust in these circumstances has been criticised both judicially[104] and academically[105] as unrealistic and highly inconvenient, as it would entail that

[99] [1909] 2 Ch 1 (CA) (especially Vaughan Williams LJ at 7 and Farwell LJ at 8 in separate judgments), as discussed above, p 152.

[100] *In re Hillier's Trusts; Hillier v A-G* [1954] 1 WLR 700 (CA) 715 (Denning LJ); *In re Welsh Hospital (Netley) Fund; Thomas v A-G* [1921] 1 Ch 655, 661.

[101] *In re Welsh Hospital (Netley) Fund; Thomas v A-G* [1921] 1 Ch 655, 661 (P O Lawrence J).

[102] *In re Ulverston and District New Hospital Building Fund; Birkett v Barrow and Furness Hospital Management Committee* [1956] 1 Ch 622 (CA) 314 (Jenkins LJ) ('If the organisers of a fund designed exclusively and solely for some particular charitable purpose send round a collecting box on behalf of the fund, I fail to see why a person who had put £ 5 into the box, and could prove to the satisfaction of the court that he had done so, should not be entitled to have his money back in the event of the failure of the sole and exclusive charitable purpose for which his donation was solicited and made'). Also: *In re British Red Cross Balkan Fund, British Red Cross Society v Johnson* [1914] 2 Ch 419, and that also seems to have been the view adopted in *In re Henry Wood National Memorial Trust; Armstrong v Moiseiwitsch* [1966] 1 WLR 1601 (Ch), although the report is brief and rather unhelpful, with no reasoning to support that view.

[103] *In re Gillingham Bus Disaster Fund; Bowman v Official Solicitor* [1958] Ch 300, 314 (Harman J) (£7,300 surplus held on resulting trust for donors, and enquiry ordered to identify donors).

[104] Jenkins LJ's suggestion in *Ulverston* was called 'somewhat fanciful and unreal' in *In re West Sussex Constabulary's Widows, Children and Benevolent (1930) Fund Trusts; Barnett v Ketteringham* [1971] Ch 1, 13 by Goff J. Also, in *In re Welsh Hospital (Netley) Fund; Thomas v A-G* [1921] 1 Ch 655, it was noted that *In re British Red Cross Balkan Fund; British Red Cross Society v Johnson* [1914] 2 Ch 419 was a case in which a resulting trust in favour of subscribers was admitted, not argued. The *British Red Cross* case was also considered to be 'questionable' in *Barlow Clowes Intl Ltd v Vaughan* [1992] 4 All ER 22 (CA), where Dillon LJ preferred the view that the surplus funds ought to have been applied *cy-près*.

[105] G Moffat, *Trusts Law Text and Materials* (4th edn, CUP, Cambridge, 2005) 912; AJ Oakley, *Parker and Mellows Modern Law of Trusts* (8th edn, Sweet & Maxwell, London, 2003) 301; D Wilson, 'Section 14 of the Charities Act 1960: A Dead Letter?' [1983] *Conv* 40. *British Red Cross* also criticised, on the basis that the funds ought to have been applied *cy-près*, in: G McCormack, 'The Eye of Equity: Identification Principles and Equitable Tracing' [1996] *JBL* 225, 232; that the case was probably wrongly decided: P Luxton, *The Law of Charities* (OUP, Oxford, 2001) 584, and 'an aberration': HAP Picarda, *The Law and Practice Relating to Charities* (3rd edn, Butterworths, London, 1999) 354. *Halsbury's Laws of England* (4th edn reissue, Butterworths, London, 1996) vol 5(2), [167] fn 4 notes with apparent relief that Jenkins LJ's view may now be 'left out of account by reason of the statutory provisions [in s 14]').

part of the surplus that represents the contributions from unidentified donors being paid into court to await claims by them[106]—with associated delays, uncertain timeframes, difficulties of proof and unclaimed monies simply languishing.

(b) Anonymous donations 'cross-infecting' identifiable donations

According to one significant body of opinion, *all* donations will be cross-infected with an intent on the part of anonymous donors to make a perpetual, out-and-out gift.

One Australian court has noted that, 'if to everybody's knowledge the money is put in a trust account this will tend to suggest that there is a trust or a conditional gift. Contrarywise, if the money is put into a mixed fund and is administered together with other monies, then the facts will point in the opposite direction [an out-and-out gift]'.[107] In that case, a donation of $50,508 was made for the building of a Hindu temple sanctum in Sydney, which was to comprise part of an educational centre. Relations between the donor and the Hindu organisation which received the monies soured, the temple was never built, and the question arose as to whether such a donation (conducted as part of a public appeal) was an out-and-out or a conditional gift. Young J held it to be an absolute gift:

> The material seems to indicate there was no separate trust fund. Moneys were being paid to . . . the builder, out of the general donations which had been collected. It would seem that the plaintiff must have known that his particular $50,000 was not being kept aside in some separate fund to pay for the sanctum when the temple or educational centre got to that stage, but rather donations were being used as they came in for production of the whole building. This is not uncommon. Very often church and school bodies have building funds and sell bricks or seats or something else as a fund raising gimmick and no one ever for a moment intends that any particular donation is to be held in trust and only applied to a particular brick or a particular seat.[108]

Leading English authorities accord with this view. In *In re Hillier's Trusts; Hillier v A-G*, Denning LJ held that all donors should be treated alike, and that if the poor widow contributing coins on a church plate did not expect her money back, nor would the large industrialist contributing via deeds of covenant or cheque—any presumption of a resulting trust would be rebutted for *all* donors.[109] In that same case, Evershed MR held similarly,[110] as did the earlier authority of *Welsh Hospital*.[111]

---

[106] Pursuant to Trustee Act 1925, c 19, s 63.
[107] *Misra v Hindu Heritage Research Foundation Ltd* (NSW SC, 21 Jun 1996).
[108] *Ibid*, 12.
[109] [1954] 1 WLR 700 (CA) 715–16.
[110] *Ibid*, 712. Romer LJ dissented. Earlier, the trial judge Upjohn J had held that such contributions specially earmarked for the proposed hospital must be paid back to the donors on a resulting trust: [1954] 1 WLR 9 (Ch).
[111] [1921] 1 Ch 655, 661 (PO Lawrence).

In *Ulverston*,[112] however, Jenkins LJ disagreed with this result. He distinguished *Welsh Hospital* on the basis that it concerned a surplus derived from an over-subscription, where (in his view) a resulting trust of any unused donations was much more difficult to establish.[113] In *Ulverston*, however, the charitable appeal failed due to insufficiency of funds, an under-subscription. In these circumstances, Jenkins LJ considered that, where the one fund for the establishment of a new cottage hospital at Ulverston included contributions from anonymous sources *and* identified contributions, the latter were to be held on resulting trust for the donors. In other words, there was no cross-infection.

The lack of satisfactory guidance provided under the general law in this respect has been academically rued.[114]

(c) Are anonymous donors always fixed with a general charitable intent?

With the exception of Jenkins LJ in *Ulverston*, who considered it arguable that anonymous donors intended to contribute only to a specific charity with no general charitable intent,[115] the authorities collectively appear to consider[116] that anonymous donations via sweepstakes, raffles, collecting boxes and the like exhibit both an intention to make an out-and-out gift, *and* a general charitable intention. Accordingly, *cy-près* applications of the unused anonymous donations have been permitted in such cases. In *Hillier*, Denning LJ opined that the law 'presumes that those who gave the money would wish that any surplus should be devoted to a charitable purpose as near as may be to the original purpose'.[117]

Under the *Ulverston* view, however, anonymous donations (assuming them to have been made as out-and-out gifts) must pass *bona vacantia*, in the absence of any general charitable intent.

(d) Are identifiable donors 'infected' with a general charitable intent by anonymous donors?

The same authorities that believe cross-infection to rebut any resulting trust (such as *Hillier*[118]) also dictate that a general charitable intention will be found on the part of *all* donors, anonymous and identifiable. In other words, the inclusion in the fund of contributions from anonymous sources has the effect of

---

[112] *In re Ulverston and District New Hospital Building Fund; Birkett v Barrow and Furness Hospital Management Committee* [1956] 1 Ch 622 (CA).

[113] *Ibid*, 635–36.

[114] HAP Picarda, *The Law and Practice Relating to Charities* (3rd edn, Butterworths, London, 1999) 348–50.

[115] [1956] 1 Ch 622 (CA) 633–34. Expressly approved in: *Beggs v Kirkpatrick* [1961] VR 764.

[116] In *Beggs, ibid*, the court ultimately held that the anonymous donations were given with a general charitable intent and could thus be applied *cy-près*.

[117] [1954] 1 WLR 700 (CA) 716.

[118] *In re Hillier's Trusts; Hillier v A-G* [1954] 1 WLR 700 (CA) 716–17. Also: *In re Welsh Hospital (Netley) Fund; Thomas v A-G* [1921] 1 Ch 655, 660–61.

fixing named subscribers with a general charitable intention, so as to make the entire fund a proper subject of *cy-près* application.

Ulverston, of course, stands apart on this point also, with Jenkins LJ opining that:

> I entirely fail to see why the imputation of a general charitable intention to anonymous contributors (if rightly made) should afford any ground for imputing a general charitable intention to subscribers who give their names. . . . Even if a general charit-able intention is rightly to be attributed to the anonymous contributors to collection boxes, neither the fact that they have chosen to contribute in that way, nor the named subscriber's knowledge that anonymous contributions have been made in that way, seems to me to have any bearing on the intention of the named subscriber.[119]

At its highest, Jenkins LJ was prepared to concede that the mixing of identifiable and anonymous contributions was a factor which *could be* taken into account for the purpose of resolving the doubt in favour of a general charitable intention for the named donors (ultimately, no general charitable intent was found).

Faced with these competing views, the *Ulverston* approach has been explicitly preferred in Australia in *Beggs v Kirkpatrick*.[120] When the construction of a proposed new hospital proved impracticable due to insufficiency of funds, it was decided by the committee to devote the fund towards enlarging the existing hospital. This plan proved legally flawed. In respect of the donations from named, identifiable individual donors or testators, it was held that their donations were (a) held on a resulting trust for those donors, and (b) made for a particular purpose only (the building of the new hospital). No gen-eral charitable intent could be imputed to them, notwithstanding the knowledge that such donations would be mixed with contemporaneous anonymous gifts from the various social and public fund-raising activities.[121] Only the anonymous donations could be applied *cy-près* toward enlarging the existing hospital.

(e) Conclusion: Anonymous donors

The donations of donors who give anonymously to charitable public appeals will always be applied *cy-près*, according to the bulk of authority in England and elsewhere. No resulting trust of those donations will be held. The 'cross-infection' problem, where anonymous and named donations are mixed, has given rise to a weave of inconsistency among the authorities. Under the *Hillier* approach, the entire mixed fund should be applied *cy-près*; under the *Ulverston* and *Beggs* viewpoint, the named donations can revert under a resulting trust, whilst the anonymous donations must be applied *cy-près*.

---

[119] [1956] Ch 622 (CA) 634.
[120] [1961] VR 764.
[121] *Ibid*, 770.

4. Effect of Charities Act 1993, s 14

Not surprisingly, given the utterly confusing signals from highest level authorities, as canvassed in the foregoing discussion, courts have occasionally adverted to the benefit of simplicity which a change in the law might bestow upon the topic:

> It may or may not be desirable for the law to be altered so as to make all funds subscribed for charitable objects which fail applicable *cy-près* for other charitable purposes to the exclusion of any resulting trust in favour of the donors; but I cannot agree that the law as it stands is to that effect.[122]

and:

> It must not be thought that I feel much satisfaction with the state of the law which I consider obliges me to make declarations [of resulting trusts instead of *cy-près* scheme] which may prove administratively inconvenient and costly to a fund raised for charitable purposes, but the remedy, if desirable, would appear to be with the Legislature.[123]

(a) Seeking simplification

In an apparent effort to simplify the law with respect to monies given to 'charitable purposes which fail'[124] (and to preserve more unused donations for charitable uses), s 14 of the Charities Act 1993 (re-enacting a previous version of the provision[125]) was introduced. Similar legislation has been enacted elsewhere.[126]

Broadly speaking, s 14 reverses the general law by the 'simple expedient'[127] of providing that donors, in nominated circumstances, shall be deemed to have a general charitable intention—thus obviating any refund of those donations, and ensuring that they are applied to charitable purposes. Having regard to s 14(1)–(7) of the Charities Act, the following types of donations are now applicable *cy-près*:[128]

- donations from all anonymous donors who cannot be identified or found after reasonable advertisements and inquiries;

---

[122] *In re Ulverston and District New Hospital Building Fund; Birkett v Barrow and Furness Hospital Management Committee* [1956] 1 Ch 622 (CA) 641 (Jenkins LJ).

[123] *Beggs v Kirkpatrick* [1961] VR 764, 771.

[124] The provision only applies to charitable public appeals, and has no application to cases such as *Gillingham* or *West Sussex.*

[125] Charities Act 1960, s 14, amended by Charities Act 1992, s 15. See also: Charities (*Cy-près* Advertisements, Inquiries and Disclaimer) Regulations 1993.

[126] Eg: Variation of Trusts Act 1994 (Tas), s 11; Charities Act 1978 (Vic), s 3; Charities Act 1961 (Ire), s 48; Charities (Northern Ireland) Act 1964, s 23; Charities Act 1984 (Singapore), s 22.

[127] As described with approval in: DB Parker and AR Mellows, *The Modern Law of Trusts* (Sweet & Maxwell, London, 1983) 233.

[128] Derived from: DG Cracknell (ed), *Charities: The Law and Practice* (Thomson Sweet & Maxwell, London, 1994–) [looseleaf], vol 1, [I.58].

- donations from identifiable donors who have signed written disclaimers to have the property returned;
- donations from all donors who contributed to appeals via cash collections, lotteries, sales of work or other fundraising activities which do not distinguish between individual donors, and of whom it is presumed that they cannot be identified or found;
- donations from identifiable donors, where it appears to the court that it would be unreasonable, having regard to the amounts likely to be returned to the donors, to incur expense with a view to returning the property, or that it would be unreasonable, having regard to the nature, circumstances and amount of the gifts, for the donors to expect the property to be returned—the court may direct that the donations be treated as belonging to unidentifiable donors.

To reiterate, a general charitable intention on the part of all of the above-mentioned donors is now statutorily presumed, thus obviating the need to prove this on the facts:[129]

Given the extent of 'cross-infection' that pervades the general law where contributions from identified and anonymous donors are mixed, it perhaps comes as no surprise that this continues under s 14's provisions. Anonymous donors are presumed to give with a general charitable intention under s 14(3)—Picarda notes that identifiable donors who make gifts toward a mixed fund will be cross-infected by that general charitable intent as well, unless, at the time of making the gift, the identifiable donor expresses a specific charitable intent.[130]

It is also apparent that any *cy-près* application of the charitable appeal funds must be closely analogous to the original purpose. It has been judicially emphasised, with respect to the similar Irish provision,[131] that there remains an overriding requirement that, corresponding with the position at general law, the application of the fund should be *cy-près*, 'as near as possible'.[132]

(b) Criticisms of the provisions

In spite of the provisions in s 14 being academically regarded as 'sensible',[133] 'long overdue',[134] and 'eliminat[ing] a wild goose chase for a general charitable

---

[129] Note the observation of LA Sheridan, *Keeton and Sheridan's The Modern Law of Charities* (4th edn, Barry Rose Law Publishers, Chichester, 1992) 253, that if anonymous donations were to pass as *bona vacantia* under the Jenkins LJ view in *Ulverston*, they would now be applied *cy-près*.

[130] HAP Picarda, *The Law and Practice Relating to Charities* (3rd edn, Butterworths, London, 1999) 354.

[131] Charities Act 1961 (Ire), s 48.

[132] *In re Olivia Fund Committee; Doyle v A-G* (Irish HC, Ch, 22 Feb 1995) [no pp].

[133] JE Martin, *Hanbury and Martin Modern Equity* (17th edn, Sweet & Maxwell, London, 2005) 463.

[134] AJ Oakley, *Parker and Mellows Modern Law of Trusts* (8th edn, Sweet & Maxwell, London, 2003) 488. Also considered positively in: JG Riddall, *The Law of* Trusts (6th edn, Butterworths, London, 2002) 194.

intent',[135] they have not met with universal approval. Three criticisms are of particular note.

Provisions are superfluous. It has been alleged by Wilson[136] and others[137] that their operation appears to be, at best, very limited, and at worst, superfluous. The reason for this is that charitable purposes are deemed to have failed, for the purposes of s 14, 'where any difficulty in applying the property to those purposes makes that property or the part not applicable *cy-près, available to be returned to the donors.*'[138] The emphasised text is the nub of the difficulty with s 14. For s 14 to 'bite' so as to allow the unused donations to be applied *cy-près* under its umbrella, those donated monies must be available to revert to the donors on a resulting trust under general law. The reality under general law, however, is that very rarely will donations be held on resulting trust for the donors. The more likely scenarios under the general law of where property is applicable *cy-près*, or where the property passes to the Crown as *bona vacantia*, are not covered by the terms of s 14. This leaves little scope for the operation of this provision.[139]

An over-emphasis upon returning donations. Falling in between the anonymous donors who cannot be identified, and the donors who are identified and who have disclaimed (refuted any wish to have the monies returned to them)—both classes of whom were presumably intended to fall within s 14's terms and have their donations applied *cy-près*—are all the *identifiable donors who have not disclaimed.* This category of donors would appear not to be caught by s 14, so that their donations are not distributed *cy-près* under the provision. Instead, a presumed resulting trust of their monies continues, unchanged from the general law, and the money must be returned to those identifiable donors if the resulting trust is not rebutted.[140]

In noting that s 14 clearly intends that those who are identifiable donors should have their donations returned to them, the OLRC was provoked to make the following disapproving statement:

> we have not been persuaded that Ontario should adopt provisions modelled upon [section 14] . . . It seems to us that, although the English provision simplifies matters by abolishing the need for proof of a general charitable intent, it then carries the right of

---

[135] LA Sheridan, *Keeton and Sheridan's The Modern Law of Charities* (4th edn, Barry Rose Law Publishers, Chichester, 1992) 251.

[136] See: D Wilson, 'Section 14 of the Charities Act 1960: A Dead Letter?' [1983] *Conv* 40, 40–44, and at 49: 'One might, then, conclude that s 14 . . . (at least with regard to anonymous donors), is a dead letter of English law.'

[137] Eg: DJ Hayton and C Mitchell, *Hayton and Marshall Commentary and Cases on the Law of Trusts and Equitable Remedies* (12th edn, Sweet & Maxwell, London, 2005) 514; G Moffat, *Trusts Law Text and Materials* (4th edn, CUP, Cambridge, 2005) 912, citing Wilson, *ibid.*

[138] Charities Act 1993, s 14(7).

[139] Note the similar sentiment in, eg: DJ Hayton, *Underhill and Hayton Law Relating to Trusts and Trustees* (16th edn, Butterworths, London, 2003) 342, that, due to the rarity of finding a resulting trust in cases of charitable appeal donations, the superfluousness of s 14 'scarcely matters'.

[140] Also noted in: JG Riddall, *The Law of Trusts* (6th edn, Butterworths, London, 2002) 194.

contributors to the return of their gifts to such a length that this appears to become the principal concern of the provision.[141]

To redress this, the OLRC recommended[142] that, in the event of any public appeal that fails (either initial or subsequent failure), then the only donors who should be entitled to return of their monies are those that expressly requested a refund. The Commission therefore indicated that any resulting trust should be express, never implied. In all other cases, unused donations should be available for application *cy-près* for other charitable purposes.

Scant judicial consideration.   In England, as in other jurisdictions in which it has been equivalently enacted, the provision has received little judicial treatment. In the brief case of *In re Henry Wood National Memorial Trust; Armstrong v Moiseiwitsch*,[143] with respect to an appeal to raise money for the construction of a new concert hall which accrued insufficient monies, Stamp J found that the identifiable donations (the donors did not disclaim) should be held on resulting trust for the donors; and that those from donors who were not identifiable by any reasonable enquiries or advertisements were not returnable (presumably, these were applied *cy-près*).

Perhaps the most important point actually, about s 14 is that made by Luxton[144]—that, regardless of how 'dead letter' the provisions may strictly appear to be, the courts and Charity Commissioners have proceeded on the assumption that the section *is* applicable to donations from unidentifiable and anonymous donors. For example:

> *The South Petherton Swimming Pool Fund, Somerset*: A group of people in Petherton wished to build a swimming pool so that young people could be taught to swim; insufficient monies to build a pool were raised by public subscription, all identified donors (bar one) disclaimed; £300 was set aside to meet any claims made within 12 months by donors who could not be identified or found; and the rest of the funds were applied *cy-près* to meet the costs of taking children to a close town for swimming lessons.[145]

Statutory variations upon the theme of applying excess donations raised by charitable public appeal exist around the Commonwealth, with different provisions having been enacted in Queensland,[146] New South Wales,[147]

---

[141] OLRC, *Law of Trusts* (1996) vol 2, 472.

[142] *Ibid*, 472–73.

[143] [1966] 1 WLR 1601 (Ch).

[144] P Luxton, *The Law of Charities* (OUP, Oxford, 2001) 588, and see the detailed discussion of the provisions and accompanying regulations at 588–94.

[145] As described in: *Report of the Ch Comm for England and Wales* (1982) [62]–[63]. Also see *Report* (1970) [46]. For a further example, re the Mile End Memorial Hall Fund, see: PH Pettit, *Equity and the Law of Trusts* (9th edn, Butterworths, London, 2001) 317.

[146] See: Charitable Funds Act 1958 (Qld), s 5, which permits alteration of purposes and appropriation of charitable funds per *cy-près* schemes; and separately, for *cy-près* schemes for disaster appeals: Collections Act 1966 (Qld), ss 35B–35D.

[147] See: Dormant Funds Act 1942 (NSW), s 2(1) which permits *cy-près* schemes for dormant funds donated to or collected 'for any charitable purpose or any purpose of a public character'.

Tasmania,[148] South Australia,[149] Victoria,[150] Western Australia,[151] and New Zealand.[152] Detailed studies of the differences between these various regimes are to be found in academic literature elsewhere,[153] and some pertinent provisions will be considered further in chapter 6[154] (given that many of these statutes cover public appeals for purposes that are wider than those which are strictly charitable in law).

[148] See: Variation of Trusts Act 1994 (Tas), s 11.

[149] See: Collections for Charitable Purposes Act 1939 (SA), s 16.

[150] See: Charities Act 1978 (Vic), s 3.

[151] See: Charitable Collections Act 1946 (WA), s 16.

[152] See: Charitable Trusts Act 1957 (NZ), Pt IV, 'Schemes in Respect of Charitable Funds Raised by Voluntary Contribution'. The subtleties of drafting of this Part are explored in greater detail in: MF Flannery, 'The Variation of the Charitable Trust' [1977] *NZLJ* 368, 371–72.

[153] For further detail of the Australian and New Zealand provisions, see especially: G Dal Pont, *Charity Law in Australia and New Zealand* (OUP, Oxford, 2000) 301, 330–44.

[154] See pp 207–10.

6

Non-charitable Trusts

T RADITIONALLY, THE CY-PRÈS doctrine has been a privilege associated with charitable trusts jurisprudence. Many definitions of the doctrine manifest this view.[1] The purpose of this chapter, however, is to consider to what extent (if any) the *cy-près* doctrine has been recognised and applied in the context of *non-charitable* trusts.

The main subject of consideration in this chapter is the non-charitable *purpose trust*. These creations can *validly* exist in three circumstances: as anomalous trusts for the upkeep of monuments and animals; as mixed persons/purposes trusts; and as statutorily-authorised non-charitable trusts. In more than one of these categories, there have been some judicial or statutory suggestions among various common law jurisdictions that an alteration in the application of property 'as near as possible' to the original purpose is permissible. The treatment of the *cy-près* doctrine in the context of the three circumstances referred to above—all under the banner of non-charitable trusts—will be considered in Section B. Attention will turn, in Section C, to the vexed issue of applying donated monies *cy-près* in the case of *non-charitable public appeals*, in circumstances where either insufficient monies are raised from donors, or the appeal is oversubscribed.

B NON-CHARITABLE TRUSTS

Trusts which are created for non-charitable purposes are difficult creatures of equity, and occupy a peculiar position in English law. Standing apart from private trusts (for the benefit of named persons or an ascertainable class of persons) and charitable trusts, non-charitable purpose trusts are created to promote nominated purposes which fall outside *Pemsel's* legal definition of charity.[2] In other words, such a trust is not for the relief of poverty, nor for the advancement of education, nor for the advancement of religion, nor for any other purpose beneficial to the community. For example: trusts to contribute to the

---

[1] See ch 1, pp 1–2.
[2] *Commissioners for Special Purposes of the Income Tax v Pemsel* [1891] AC 531(HL) 583 (Lord Macnaghten), 571 (Lord Herschell) 556 (Lord Watson) agreeing.

nursery fund of the Sussex Cricket Club;[3] to fund an annual award for a 'lyric beautiful in form';[4] to fund the maintenance of good relations between nations;[5] for public purposes in the parish of X;[6] for creating a new alphabet for the English language;[7] for patriotic purposes;[8] or to provide a war memorial,[9] may each be imbued with laudable and benevolent motivations—but none of them is charitable at law.

Beyond the 'ring-fence' of anomalous cases, mixed persons/purposes and statutory purpose trusts, trusts which are created with a view to furthering some non-charitable purpose are void.[10] Whilst some allege that non-charitable purpose trusts used to be permitted more than a century ago—and the fact that they are not today truly stems from a judicial misreading of these early cases that has never been corrected[11]—non-charitable trusts are not easily supportable under modern trusts law for four key reasons.

The first problem is one of enforcement. There is, allegedly, no designated party to ensure that the trustees comply with the directions contained either within the trust instrument or in statute. Private trusts are enforceable at the suit of the beneficiaries,[12] and charitable trusts by the intervention of the Crown (or, more specifically, the Attorney-General, for 'there is no one else to represent charity ... the Attorney-General, as representing the Crown, has to represent charities in all senses'[13]). No strict equivalent, however, exists for the non-charitable trust.[14] Whilst in charitable cases, the Attorney-General can help to devise *cy-près* and administrative schemes and can be charged with the duty of enforcing such schemes and preventing their maladministration, the absence of any such 'custodian' in non-charitable trust cases supposedly renders the

[3] *In re Patten; Westminster Bank Ltd v Carylon Sussex* [1929] 2 Ch 276, 289–90.
[4] *Re Millen* (1986), 30 DLR (4th) 116 (BCSC).
[5] As in *In re Astor's ST; Astor v Scholfield* [1952] Ch 534.
[6] *Obiter* example given by Harman LJ in: *In re Endacott (decd); Corpe v Endacott* [1960] Ch 232 (CA).
[7] *In re Shaw (decd); Public Trustee v Day* [1957] 1 WLR 729 (Ch).
[8] A further *obiter* example given by Harman LJ in: *In re Endacott (decd); Corpe v Endacott* [1960] Ch 232 (CA) 250.
[9] Noted in: *A-G (NSW) v Fulham* [2002] NSWSC 629 (19 Jul 2002) [87].
[10] *Re Astor's ST; Astor v Scholfield* [1952] Ch 534. Or 'voidable', as some commentators would prefer to argue: J Jaconelli, 'Independent Schools, Purpose Trusts and Human Rights' [1996] *Conv* 24, 27.
[11] This is the thesis of the work of P Baxendale-Walker, *Purpose Trusts* (Butterworths, London, 1999), esp ch 1, and also noted, eg, by: JE Martin, *Hanbury and Martin Modern Equity* (17th edn, Sweet & Maxwell, London, 2005) 371; G Thomas, 'Purpose Trusts' in J Glasson (ed), *International Trust Laws* (Jordan Publishing Ltd, Bristol, 1992) vol 1, ch 4, B4–5; RBM Cotterrell, 'Some Sociological Aspects of the Controversy Around the Legal Validity of Private Purpose Trusts' in S Goldstein (ed), *Equity and Contemporary Legal Developments* (Hebrew University, Jerusalem, 1992) 303.
[12] Note Brightman J's comment in *In re Recher's WT; National Westminster Bank Ltd v National Anti-Vivisection Society Ltd* [1972] Ch 526, 538 ('a trust for non-charitable purposes, as distinct from a trust for individuals, is clearly void because there is no beneficiary').
[13] *Thomas v A-G* [1936] 2 All ER 1325 (Ch) 1328.
[14] See discussion in, eg: Manitoba LRC, *Non-Charitable Purpose Trusts* (1982) 9–11; OLRC, *Law of Trusts* (1996) vol 2, 431.

court's task of re-allocating the trust property an impossible one.[15] Essentially, trusts depend for their existence on a court of equity acting against the person of the trustee—and no valid trust can exist if there is no person who can bring the trustee before the court.[16] The so-called 'beneficiary principle' is contravened because, to adapt the words of Sir William Grant MR in *Morice v Bishop of Durham*,[17] there is nobody in whose favour the court can decree performance. Plainly put, the purpose cannot sue;[18] a purpose 'is not corporeal and cannot appear before the court'.[19]

Interestingly, some academic commentary contends that the enforcement problem for non-charitable trusts is overstated or is just plain wrong. It has variously been argued that:

- trustees are answerable for their (mis)conduct, not to the beneficiaries, but to the court;[20]
- even private trusts in favour of the unborn can be valid, rendering lack of enforcement by a beneficiary in the context of non-charitable trusts somewhat non-sensical;[21]
- large private trust funds can be difficult to enforce too, especially where the class of a discretionary trust may be huge, fluctuating, and entirely unknown to the trustees, yet those types of private trusts are validated time and again;[22]
- the so-called enforcement arm of the Attorney-General in respect of charitable trusts is tempered by the realism that the Attorney-General hardly ever intervenes;[23]
- just because the settlor's intention under a non-charitable purpose trust may be subverted without redress only means that 'half a loaf is better than the no bread of invalidity';[24]

---

[15] *In re Astor's ST; Astor v Scholfield* [1952] Ch 534, 547–48 (Roxburgh J).

[16] Cited by counsel, Browne-Wilkinson QC, in argument, in: *Town Investments Ltd v Dept of the Environment* [1978] AC 359 (HL) 376.

[17] (1805) 10 Ves 522; [1803–13] All ER Rep 451 (Ch) 454.

[18] *Leahy v A-G for NSW* [1959] AC 457 (PC) 484.

[19] As colourfully expressed by: JA Dash, 'Purpose Trusts: The Nevis Perspective' (2003) 9(8) *Trusts and Trustees* 8, 8.

[20] JE Martin, *Hanbury and Martin Modern Equity* (17th edn, Sweet & Maxwell, London, 2005) 371.

[21] Martin, *ibid*.

[22] HAJ Ford, 'Dispositions for Purposes' in PD Finn (ed), *Essays in Equity* (Law Book Co, Sydney, 1985) 172; RBM Cotterrell, 'Trusting in Law: Legal and Moral Concepts of Trust' in MDA Freeman and BA Hepple (eds), *Current Legal Problems, Collected Papers (Vol 46, Pt 2)* (OUP, Oxford, 1993) 90 ('Ability to accumulate and to hold funds dedicated to abstract purposes rather than defined by reference to individual or collective beneficial entitlements may also seem increasingly important').

[23] GE Dal Pont and DRC Chalmers, *Equity and Trusts in Australia and New Zealand* (LBC Information Services, Sydney, 1996) 320–21; M Pawlowski, 'Purpose Trusts: Obligations without Beneficiaries?' (2002) 9(1) *Trusts and Trustees* 10, 10; S Hepburn, *Principles of Equity and Trusts* (Cavendish Publishing (Australia), Sydney, 1997) 340.

[24] S Gardner, *An Introduction to the Law of Trusts* (2nd edn, Clarendon Law Series, OUP, Oxford, 2003) 261.

- whether there are beneficiaries to enforce the trust is practically irrelevant when conscientious trustees are the norm in any event—'compliant trustees regard their legal duties . . . and try to perform them properly, irrespective of their enforceability . . . [and] most trustees seem to be compliant';[25]
- any equitable right to sue to enforce a non-charitable trust is simply 'the product of the tribunal's willingness to listen to a claimant [such that if] a court had been willing to listen to a person with a special interest in the preservation of the independence of newspapers [in *Re Astor's Settlement*] . . . he would then have had equitable rights' sufficient to enforce the trust;[26]
- the 'enforcer' need not be a beneficiary, and that provided that the settlor has expressly provided for *some* 'enforcer', there is a mechanism for the 'positive enforcement of the trust', thus satisfying the ethos behind the beneficiary principle;[27]
- 'settlor-enforced trusts' have been successfully enacted in statutory non-charitable purpose trust regimes (considered later in the chapter[28]);
- in any event, if not the settlor, it has been postulated that the residuary legatee, or those entitled on intestacy, may have standing to apply to the court to compel the performance of the trust, should the trustee fail to do so[29]—although it has been equally postulated that the residuary beneficiary has a distinct interest *not* to enforce the trust, since the property would then pass to him;[30]
- the lack of enforcement by a beneficiary has not been consistently treated as a fundamental obstacle to the validity of purpose trusts—instead, 'the

[25] Gardner, *ibid*, 263, who proposes the recognition of valid but unenforceable trusts. The same proposition is noted, with some reservations, in G Moffat, *Trusts Law Text and Materials* (4th edn, CUP, Cambridge, 2005) 251.
[26] HAJ Ford, 'Dispositions for Purposes' in PD Finn (ed), *Essays in Equity* (Law Book Co, Sydney, 1985) 173–74. It has been suggested that 'the Press Council would have an interest in implementing many of the purposes in question in [*Re Astor*]': R O'Malley, 'Charitable Status and Fiscal Privileges: Two Separate Issues?' (2003) 4 *Hibernian LJ* 177, fn 153.
[27] DJ Hayton, 'Developing the Obligation Characteristic of the Trust' (2001) 117 *LQR* 96, 99 (the Mother Superior of a contemplative order of nuns, for example). Hayton also draws an analogy (at 101) with the Quistclose trust, where the payer has a right to restrain misappropriation of the money—a short step, then, to the settlor giving property to a non-charitable purpose. Also see: J Hackney, *Understanding Equity and Trusts* (Fontana Press, London, 1987) 70.
[28] See pp 194 ff.
[29] See, eg: J Mowbray *et al, Lewin on Trusts* (17th edn, Sweet & Maxwell, London, 2000) 4–40; G Watt, *Trusts* (OUP, Oxford, 2004) 146; RBM Cotterrell, 'Some Sociological Aspects of the Controversy Around the Legal Validity of Private Purpose Trusts' in S Goldstein (ed), *Equity and Contemporary Legal Developments* (Hebrew University, Jerusalem, 1992) 306. As held in: *In re Thompson; Public Trustee v Lloyd* [1934] Ch 342, 344 (£1,000 for promotion of foxhunting; residue to Trinity Hall, Cambridge; bequest valid). Also see: *In re Astor's ST; Astor v Scholfield* [1952] Ch 534, 544–46, in which Roxburgh J cited a number of cases in which 'there was a residuary legatee to bring before the court any failure to comply with the directions'.
[30] Noted, eg, in: M Pawlowski, 'Purpose Trusts: Obligations without Beneficiaries?' (2002) 9(1) *Trusts and Trustees* 10, 11; L McKay, 'Trusts for Purposes—Another View' (1973) 37 *Conv* 420; DJ Hayton, *Hayton and Marshall Commentary and Cases on the Law of Trusts and Equitable Remedies* (11th edn, Sweet & Maxwell, London, 2001) 211.

few reported cases suggest that such trusts might also be held invalid on one or more of many other grounds', eg, it failed for uncertainty of objects, or it was capricious, useless or wasteful, or it was contrary to public policy, or it offended the rule against perpetuities;[31]

- and most controversially of all, there is indeed no rule against non-charitable purpose trusts in English law, and that the so-called 'beneficiary principle' is erroneous, based upon a misreading of early authorities by judges and lawyers:

> The Purpose Trust was a fine, robust thing. . . . Yet, with a few strokes of the judge's pencil in a few latter day cases, the Purpose Trust together with 600 years of English legal history, were consigned to a dusty receptacle labelled 'anomalous exceptions', never again to be opened. Or were they?[32]

This constitutes an impressive list of reasons as to why the lack of an 'enforcer' should not necessarily be detrimental to the validity of a non-charitable purpose trust. Despite these myriad arguments, however, the perceived lack of any person to enforce such a trust remains its key stumbling block. As Thomas pragmatically notes, 'it is difficult to avoid the conclusion that . . . English law today is wedded to the beneficiary principle and that it is this principle that poses the main obstacle to the creation of non-charitable purpose trusts in England.'[33]

The second problem countenancing against recognition of the non-charitable purpose trust pertains directly to the variation of the trust purposes. It has been said[34] that the lack of any *cy-près* doctrine is crucial, because whilst some non-charitable purpose trusts may state their purposes precisely and succinctly, the court will be at a loss to proceed where the purpose is impossible or impracticable or the mode of operation of the trust is unclear. A lack of certainty within *charitable* trusts can be remedied by either the initial or subsequent *cy-près* doctrines, or by an administrative scheme. None of these options, however, appears at first sight to be available for a non-charitable trust under general law.

---

[31] G Thomas, 'Purpose Trusts' in J Glasson (ed), *International Trust Laws* (Jordan Publishing Ltd, Bristol, 1992) vol 1, ch 4, B4–10; JE Martin, *Hanbury and Martin Modern Equity* (17th edn, Sweet & Maxwell, London, 2005) 371. Also see: P Baxendale-Walker, *Purpose Trusts* (Butterworths, London, 1999) 122–23, who notes *In re Wood; Barton v Chilcott* [1949] Ch 498, *In re Astor's ST; Astor v Scholfield* [1952] Ch 534, and *In re Endacott (decd); Corpe v Endacott* [1960] Ch 232 (CA) as examples of cases which are commonly cited for the beneficiary principle, but which actually failed for want of certainty of object. Also see: RBM Cotterrell, 'Some Sociological Aspects of the Controversy Around the Legal Validity of Private Purpose Trusts' in S Goldstein (ed), *Equity and Contemporary Legal Developments* (Hebrew University, Jerusalem, 1992) 323 ('In many of the nineteenth century decisions, the judges emphasise that the vagueness of the trust creator's expressed purposes makes it impossible for the court to enforce the trust. There is no hint that the absence of identifiable beneficiaries is, itself, a problem').

[32] Baxendale-Walker, *ibid*, 64–65.

[33] G Thomas, 'Purpose Trusts' in J Glasson (ed), *International Trust Laws* (Jordan Publishing Ltd, Bristol, 1992) vol 1, ch 4, B4–10.

[34] S Bright, 'Charity and Trusts for the Public Benefit—Time for a Re-think?' [1989] *Conv* 28, 29.

Thirdly, a non-charitable trust is generally (except for pension funds[35] and notwithstanding occasional indications to the contrary[36]) to adhere to the rule against perpetuities. In fact, where non-charitable purpose trusts are concerned, this has encompassed two rules under the general law (statutes have amended the position in some respects). First, the rule means that a trust is only valid if it vests within a reasonable timeframe, which under the general law usually meant a life in being plus a further 21 years. Secondly, the rule means that non-charitable purpose trusts cannot last forever, they must end within the perpetuity period (charitable trusts, on the other hand, can be of perpetual duration, yet a further signal of the policy to encourage charitable giving). The policy of these rules is to preclude property being tied up for too long a period, and to counterbalance the settlor's right to control economic resources and to deprive the community/his family of control over those assets.[37] Due to the advantage of perpetuity which the charitable trust enjoys and which is denied to the non-charitable purpose trust, the courts frequently confront the task of trying to find a trust charitable and valid, rather than non-charitable and perpetuitous.[38]

The fourth problem relates to the human nature of settlors who may wish to settle property upon non-charitable trusts. Not being strait-jacketed by the four heads of charity which are, by statute[39] and longstanding acceptance, deemed to be socially useful, settlors may use non-charitable purpose trusts for a whole spectrum of objects—from those that are benevolent, well-meaning and falling just short of legally charitable,[40] to those that are purely self-indulgent and frustratingly whimsical. Any vehicle that removes from the community the beneficial use of capital, because a settlor invoked an eccentric and useless

---

[35] See: JE Martin, *Hanbury and Martin Modern Equity* (17th edn, Sweet & Maxwell, London, 2005) 373 and fn 41; G Thomas, *Thomas on Powers* (Sweet & Maxwell, London, 1998) 148, and Pension Schemes Act 1993, c 48, s 163.

[36] *In re Dean; Cooper-Dean v Stevens* (1889) 41 Ch D 552, critiqued, eg, in Martin, *ibid*.

[37] RH Maudsley, *The Modern Law of Perpetuities* (Butterworths, London, 1979) 232 ('We do need some perpetuity rule which is intended to hold a balance between the control by the dead hand and control by the living'); JHC Morris and WB Leach, *The Rule Against Perpetuities* (2nd edn, Stevens, London, 1962) 167–69, 183; OLRC, *Report on the Law of Charities* (1996) 438.

[38] For a very recent example, see: *Ulrich v Treasury Solicitor* [2005] 1 All ER 1059 (Ch). For a much earlier example: *In re Church Patronage Trust; Laurie v A-G* [1904] 2 Ch 643 (CA) ('The whole question which we have to decide in this case is whether certain dispositions made by the codicil of the testatrix, which clearly would be invalid as being against the law regarding perpetuities unless they can be brought within the exception in favour of charitable trusts, fall within this exception'; the trust was not charitable).

[39] The preamble to the Charitable Uses Act 1601 (Eng), 43 Eliz 1, c 4 (commonly known as the Statute of Elizabeth).

[40] As stated in *Trustees of the Londonderry Presbyterian Church House v IRC* [1946] NI 178 (CA), 'The objects of a trust may be in every way admirable and worthy and may be such as to conduce to the benefit of the public or of a substantial section of the public or of the inhabitants of a certain district and yet the trust may not in law be a charitable trust'; no charitable trusts in this case.

purpose to which to put his money, requires cautionary treatment.[41] Moffat, for example, states that it is 'improbable' that a court would validate any purpose trust, no matter how capricious.[42] A variety of non-charitable purpose trusts have been judicially rejected as invalid in the past as being overly eccentric— from a trust to board up the rooms of a house for 20 years,[43] to trusts to erect bronzed monuments around Scotland,[44] to a trust to 'provide holidays in the south of France for labradors'.[45] The prospect that upholding non-charitable purpose trusts might see the validation of 'a trust for the maintenance of my ant collection', for example, prompted the OLRC to recommend against their statutory recognition. The Commission was particularly anxious to avoid 'engaging the state or the courts unduly in the execution of the idiosyncratic intention of disponers.'[46] There is, of course, a policy dimension to this ground of objection as well. The very fact that the donor removes property from commercial circulation or from family members, via the vehicle of a non-charitable trust, would also remove the property from the auspices of others' control—it 'raise[s] the spectre of large amounts of capital being dedicated to purposes which escape both the judicial and administrative policing of private initiatives which is provided by charity law, and the state direction, co-ordination and supervision of public purposes established by the modern welfare state.'[47]

Thus, because they have to be enforceable, sufficiently certain and sufficiently finite, and because of policy concerns about their possibly eccentric character, non-charitable trusts have rarely been recognised as valid at law, except for those previously mentioned categories, *viz*, anomalous cases, mixed persons/

---

[41] Noted, eg, by: JE Martin, *Hanbury and Martin Modern Equity* (17th edn, Sweet & Maxwell, London, 2005) 389–90; S Gardner, *An Introduction to the Law of Trusts* (2nd edn, Clarendon Law Series, OUP, Oxford, 2003) 103–4, and by the same author, see: 'New Angles on Unincorporated Associations' [1992] *Conv* 41, 52; JD Heydon and PL Loughlan, *Cases and Materials on Equity and Trusts* (5th edn, Butterworths, Sydney, 1997) 543; Manitoba LRC, *Non-Charitable Purpose Trusts* (1992) 12.

[42] G Moffat, *Trusts Law Text and Materials* (4th edn, CUP, Cambridge, 2005) 251.

[43] *Brown v Burdett* (1882) 21 Ch D 667 (house left on trust, with direction that most of the rooms be sealed up for 20 years; invalid).

[44] *McCaig's Trustees v Kirk-session of United Free Church of Lismore*, 1915 SC 426, 434 ('[t]he prospect of Scotland being dotted with monuments to obscure persons cumbered with trusts for the purpose of maintaining these monuments . . . appears to me to be little less than appalling'). Several related *McCaig* cases are referenced, eg, in JE Martin, *Hanbury and Martin Modern Equity* (17th edn, Sweet & Maxwell, London, 2005) 390.

[45] *Obiter* example of an invalid non-charitable purpose trust given in: *Perpetual Trustees Ltd v State of Tasmania* [2000] Tas SC (6 Jun 2000).

[46] OLRC, *Report on the Law of Charities* (1996) 438. For an analogous, tongue-in-cheek example of 'a statue of a jumped-up politician in every town square', see: J Hackney, *Understanding Equity and Trusts* (Fontana Press, London, 1987) 69.

[47] RBM Cotterrell, 'Some Sociological Aspects of the Controversy Around the Legal Validity of Private Purpose Trusts' in S Goldstein (ed), *Equity and Contemporary Legal Developments* (Hebrew University, Jerusalem, 1992) 331, arguing that this policy reason probably best explains the reasoning behind the court's refusal to recognise the validity of the *Re Astor* trust.

purposes trusts, and non-charitable trusts that are statutorily authorised as valid.

Interestingly, the relationship between the *cy-près* doctrine and non-charitable trusts has been rarely considered. Both academic literature and case law concerning non-charitable trusts have tended to concentrate upon the first and the third of the abovementioned problems, *viz*, finding 'an enforcer' for the non-charitable purpose, and how the rule against perpetuities can be resolved to prevent voiding of the trust. As the Manitoba Law Reform Commission intimated,[48] the certainty of non-charitable trusts, as an issue, has rarely been litigated because a lack of enforceability invalidated them well before the matter could be canvassed. These problems of enforcement and perpetuities will not be explored further in any detail. Instead, the following sections will examine to what extent (if any) the *cy-près* doctrine may be invoked to permit judicial alteration of the non-charitable purpose if such purpose becomes impossible or impracticable.

1. Anomalous Cases[49]

The upkeep of animals or monuments represents an 'extraordinary exception'[50] to the general rule of the invalidity of purpose trusts—or, as Harman LJ colourfully put it, indicate 'mere occasions when Homer nodded'.[51] The following bequests on trust have been upheld, for example: to provide for the care and upkeep of certain graves, a vault and monuments;[52] to feed the testator's horses and hounds;[53] and to provide a monument to the testator's wife's first husband.[54]

Various reasons have been provided for their legal recognition: that the trust objects, whilst non-charitable, are stated with absolute certainty and hence are usually unproblematical;[55] that these anomalous cases are, whilst

---

[48]   *Non-Charitable Purpose Trusts* (1992) 29.

[49]   Note the five-fold classification of these by JHC Morris and WB Leach, *The Rule Against Perpetuities* (2nd edn, Stevens, London, 1962) 310, which was adopted by Lord Evershed MR in *In re Endacott (decd); Corpe v Endacott* [1960] Ch 232 (CA) 246.

[50]   GE Dal Pont and DRC Chalmers, *Equity and Trusts in Australia and New Zealand* (LBC Information Services, Sydney, 1996) 319.

[51]   *Re Endacott (decd); Corpe v Endacott* [1960] Ch 232 (CA).

[52]   *In re Hooper; Parker v Ward* [1932] 1 Ch 38. Also, eg: *Pirbright v Salwey* [1896] WN 86; *Trimmer v Danby* (1856) 25 LJ Ch 424.

[53]   *In re Dean; Cooper-Dean v Stevens* (1889) 41 Ch D 552. Also: *Pettingall v Pettingall* (1842) 11 LJ Ch 176; *In re Thompson; Public Trustee v Lloyd* [1934] Ch 342.

[54]   *Mussett v Bingle* [1876] WN 170.

[55]   *In re Catherall (decd); Lloyds Bank Ltd v Griffiths* (Ch, 3 Jun 1959) ('Purpose must embody a definite concept, and means to attain it must be described with sufficient certainty. In this case I should have no difficulty in deciding what would be a suitable memorial'), cited in: *In re Endacott (decd); Corpe v Endacott* [1960] Ch 232 (CA) 248–49. Also: JE Martin, *Hanbury and Martin Modern Equity* (17th edn, Sweet & Maxwell, London, 2005) 374.

non-charitable, generally of a 'public character' that deserve recognition;[56] that such trusts are a concession to human frailty;[57] that they are 'located in the culture of the family . . . untidy, but in broad terms far from indefensible';[58] or that they are a product of a class-conscious society, an example of 'judicial tenderness to that section of the table above the salt'.[59] Notwithstanding the multitude of reasons provided for their validity, their expansion has not been judicially endorsed, either in England[60] or elsewhere.[61]

The question for present purposes is as follows: what if the purpose is impossible, impracticable or infeasible to carry out, either initially or subsequently? For example, the type of monument may be banned as racially offensive; or the animal for whose upkeep a sum of money is left on trust may die before the trust fund is expended. To date, no *cy-près* application of the fund to another similar purpose has ever been countenanced, so far as can be ascertained.

Plainly, any lack of certainty in the disposition of a 'monuments trust' cannot be cured by a *cy-près*, or even by an administrative, scheme. Instead, the trust will fail. This was the outcome in *In re Endacott (decd); Corpe v Endacott*,[62] where a residuary gift of £20,000 was left 'to the North Tawton Devon Parish Council for the purpose of providing some useful memorial to myself'. The disposition could not be upheld under any one of several arguments. It was not an absolute gift to the Council, but was conveyed on trust. Whilst intended to be 'useful', the fact remained that just because it would serve a public interest of some kind did not render it charitable. The mere fact that the gift was to the parish council also did not make it charitable, as several activities of the council were not charitable at law. Nor did the gift fall within the public character of these anomalous cases. Therefore, since the gift was one of residue and the gift failed, it passed according to the rules of intestacy.

Where an animal dies before the trust fund that was designated for its care is expended, no *cy-près* application of the balance by reason of subsequent failure has been discussed in the limited case law to date. Rather, it has been suggested that either the fund is properly claimable by the person who now owns the

---

[56] *Endacott, ibid*, 245 ('a trust of a public character, but not a charitable trust').
[57] GE Dal Pont and DRC Chalmers, *Equity and Trusts in Australia and New Zealand* (LBC Information Services, Sydney, 1996) 319.
[58] S Gardner, *An Introduction to the Law of Trusts* (2nd edn, Clarendon Law Series, OUP, Oxford, 2003) 258.
[59] J Hackney, *Understanding Equity and Trusts* (Fontana Press, London, 1987) 70.
[60] *In re Endacott (decd); Corpe v Endacott* [1960] Ch 232 (CA) 250–51 ('these cases stand by themselves and ought not to be increased in number, nor indeed followed, except where the one is exactly like another. Whether it would be better that some authority now should say that those cases were wrongly decided, this perhaps is not the moment to consider [but] . . . the case of providing outside a church an unspecified and unidentified memorial [is not] the kind of instance which should be allowed to add to those troublesome, anomalous and aberrant cases').
[61] Eg, in Australia: *Pedulla v Nasti* (1990) 20 NSWLR 720, 722–23; *Perpetual Trustee Co Ltd v John Fairfax & Sons Pty Ltd* (1959) 76 WN(NSW) 226, 228.
[62] [1960] Ch 232 (CA).

animal as a residuary legatee;[63] or the trust fund should result back to the testator's estate.[64]

In fact, there has never been any upholding of an anomalous case that was, in *any* sense, uncertain, much less unworkable, impossible or impracticable. Thomas states the position thus:

> In view of the fact that English law has traditionally not recognised the validity of non-charitable purpose trusts, other than a few anomalous cases, it has never had to work out the implications of such trusts. The test of certainty of objects of a non-charitable purpose trust has never been determined. If a non-charitable purpose trust can exist at all, the definition or description of the purpose must be sufficiently certain. Conceptual certainty would seem to be essential.[65]

Another of those so-called 'implications' that has remained unconsidered is the ramification of an anomalous case that is, not so much uncertain as *impossible* to carry out.

Furthermore, if the better view[66] is that the anomalous cases are, properly-speaking, not trusts at all, but only *powers* (whereby the trustee may perform the terms of the trust to care for the animal or provide the monument if he so wishes, but the court will not oblige him to do so), then to talk of a *cy-près* application of the trust property is not cogent. The disposition will be valid but unenforceable, and if it is impossible to carry out, then the property must revert back to the testator's residuary estate upon a resulting trust.

Given the lukewarm reception afforded to the anomalous cases, the lack of any precedent, and the likely construing of such cases as powers only, the *cy-près* doctrine is unlikely ever to have any role to play in validating an anomalous trust that is, or becomes, impossible or impracticable to carry out.

2. Mixed Persons/Purposes Trusts

A settlor may frame the objects which he wishes to benefit as persons (in which case, the trust will be *prima facie* a valid private trust) or as purposes (in which case, the trust will only be *prima facie* valid if those purposes are legally charitable). Where the purposes framed within the trust instrument are non-charitable, the trust may nevertheless be 'saved' if the trust is re-oriented as a

---

[63] P Matthews, 'Trusts to Maintain Animals' (1983) 80 *LS Gaz* 2451, 2452, and also cited in: JE Martin, *Hanbury and Martin Modern Equity* (17th edn, Sweet & Maxwell, London, 2005) 376.

[64] British Columbia LRC, *Non-Charitable Purpose Trusts* (1992) 47, noting that outcome to be a 'fair inference', but citing no authority in support of the contention.

[65] G Thomas, 'Purpose Trusts' in J Glasson (ed), *International Trust Laws* (Jordan Publishing Ltd, Bristol, 1992) vol 1, ch 4, B4–14.

[66] M Pawlowski, 'Purpose Trusts: Obligations without Beneficiaries?' (2002) 9(1) *Trusts and Trustees* 10, 10. Also argued in: RBM Cotterrell, 'Some Sociological Aspects of the Controversy Around the Legal Validity of Private Purpose Trusts' in S Goldstein (ed), *Equity and Contemporary Legal Developments* (Hebrew University, Jerusalem, 1992) 306–9.

private trust, such that the trust is properly viewed as for the benefit of an ascertainable class of beneficiaries. It is a question of construction to assess whether the trust is for (valid) persons or for (invalid) purposes,[67] and is not without difficulty.

(a) A question of construction

The case of *In re Denley's Trust Deed; Holman v HH Martyn & Co Ltd*[68] is the seminal authority for this approach. H Martyn & Co Ltd transferred land on trust to be maintained and used 'for the purpose of a recreation or sports ground primarily for the benefit of the employees of the company and secondarily for the benefit of such other person or persons (if any) as the trustees may allow.' There was no question of this being a charitable trust—the running of a sports ground is non-charitable,[69] and in any event, this was not a trust for 'a section of the public', given that it was set up to benefit the company's employees. The trust was seemingly for the *non-charitable purpose* of running a sports facility, but Goff J held otherwise. His Lordship validated the trust on the basis that it was 'directly or indirectly for the benefit of ascertainable beneficiaries', *viz*, the company employees and others who were granted permission to use the facilities.[70]

In other words, Goff J looked through the gauze screen of the stated purpose, to the group of beneficiaries standing behind that gauze, so as to construe the trust as having beneficiaries who were capable of bringing an action to enforce the trust. He contrasted the case before him to the type of purpose trust, 'the carrying out of which would benefit an individual or individuals, where that benefit is so indirect or intangible or which is otherwise so framed as not to give those persons any *locus standi* to apply to the court to enforce the trust'.[71] The trust deed expressly stated that the company employees were entitled to the use and enjoyment of the land, and hence there were beneficiaries to enforce it.

Was this predominantly a purpose or a persons trust? Opinions differ. The emphasis placed by Goff J upon the *locus standi* of the employees to enforce the trust strongly indicates that it was predominantly viewed as a private (persons) trust. That view draws support from Vinelott J's later analysis of *Denley*:

---

[67] JE Martin, *Hanbury and Martin Modern Equity* (17th edn, Sweet & Maxwell, London, 2005) 368 (noting, for example, that a trust to promote fox-hunting could be for that purpose, or for the benefit of sportspersons); P Hargreaves, 'Charitable, Purpose and Hybrid Trusts: A Jersey Perspective' [2002] *PCB* 30, 36.

[68] [1969] 1 Ch 373.

[69] Eg: *In re Nottage; Jones v Palmer* [1895] 2 Ch 649 (CA) 656 ('a gift, the object of which is the encouragement of a mere sport or game primarily calculated to amuse individuals apart from the community at large, cannot upon the authorities be held to be charitable, though such sport or game is to some extent beneficial to the public'; in this case, a trust to provide a winner's trophy for a yacht race was void). See also, for non-charitable trusts: *In re Clifford; Mallam v McFie* [1912] 1 Ch 29 (bequest to an angling society); *Royal Agricultural and Industrial Assn v Chester* (1974) 48 ALJR 304 (HCA) (trust to improve breeding and racing of homer pigeons).

[70] [1969] 1 Ch 373, 383.

[71] *Ibid*, 382–83.

That case on a proper analysis, in my judgment, falls altogether outside the categories of . . . purpose trusts . . . . the benefit to be taken by any member of the class is at the discretion of the trustees, but any member of the class can apply to the court to compel the trustees to administer the trust in accordance with its terms.[72]

In similar vein, Thomas argues that the classification was not clear, but that Lord Goff's 'concern that the employees to be benefited should be ascertained or ascertainable at any given time suggests that it was a trust for individuals, and not a purpose trust at all.'[73] Gardner also appears to consider the trust a private one in the main, remarking that the *Morice* principle that there must be 'somebody in whose favour the court can decree performance' is satisfied in the *Denley* scenario by '[a]ccepting *de facto* benefit as a substitute for status as a beneficiary'.[74] At odds with this view, however, stands Duckworth, who laments that 'the debate was never concluded over whether the judge in *Re Denley* was right to treat that trust as a purpose trust.'[75] Ford also does not favour the view that the trust was one for persons.[76]

This *Denley* approach of re-orienting a non-charitable purpose trust as a *private* trust, has been followed since, as instanced by the following notable cases—

in England:

> *In re Lipinski's WT; Gosschalk v Levy*[77]—a residuary estate was conferred upon trustees by will on trust, one half for the Hull Judeans (Maccabi) Association 'in memory of my late wife to be used solely in the work of constructing the new buildings for the association and/or improvements to the said buildings'—the purposes of the Association were non-charitable, but the testator clearly intended to benefit the members of the association, by allowing the association to build something new by way of accommodation, or to improve or convert some other existing premises— 'accordingly the case appears to me to be one of the specification of a particular purpose for the benefit of ascertained beneficiaries, the members of the association for the time being'.[78]
>
> *Wicks v Firth (Inspector of Taxes)*[79]—a company executed a trust deed settling funds on trustees to make discretionary awards to the children of employees of the company to assist them in their further education by way of scholarships. The trusts were non-charitable (the beneficiaries were linked by employment, and hence, it was not for the

---

[72] *In re Grant's WT; Harris v Anderson* [1980] 1 WLR 360 (Ch) 371–72. For discussion of Vinelott J's views, see, eg: G Moffat, *Trusts Law Text and Materials* (4th edn, CUP, Cambridge, 2005) 249–50.

[73] G Thomas, 'Purpose Trusts' in J Glasson (ed), *International Trust Laws* (Jordan Publishing Ltd, Bristol, 1992) vol 1, ch 4, B4–11.

[74] S Gardner, *An Introduction to the Law of Trusts* (2nd edn, Clarendon Law Series, OUP, Oxford, 2003) 254, fn 30.

[75] A Duckworth, 'STAR Wars: The Colony Strikes Back' (1998) 12 *Trust Law Intl* 16, 23.

[76] HAJ Ford, 'Dispositions for Purposes' in PD Finn (ed), *Essays in Equity* (Law Book Co, Sydney, 1985) 174.

[77] [1976] 1 Ch 235 (Oliver J).

[78] *Ibid*, 249.

[79] [1983] 2 AC 214 (HL), and earlier: [1982] Ch 355 (CA).

public benefit). However, '[i]n the few short years of its existence it has brought welcome financial relief to many young students who exist on government grants'.[80] The trust was a valid non-charitable trust.

and in Canada:

> *Keewatin Tribal Council Inc v Thompson*[81]—three residential properties were conveyed on trust for the housing of children of the northern and northeastern Manitoba Indian bands who were attending high school in Thompson, away from the Indian reserves. The purposes of the trust, to provide housing, were non-charitable. However, the band children and the bands themselves derived direct benefit from the trust, and had sufficient interest to enforce the trust, if necessary.

but, interestingly enough, *Denley* has received a rather lukewarm reception in Australia:[82]

> *Strathalbyn Show Jumping Club Inc v Mayes*[83]—land was conveyed on trust for use 'as a polo ground and subject to such use by any polo club to permit the said land to be used as a recreation ground, [etc]'. The trust was construed as a purpose, and not as a private, trust. Bleby J noted that, '[i]t is difficult to avoid the conclusion that Goff J [in *Denley*] was sanctioning the creation of a non-charitable purpose trust. In doing so, the case has not escaped criticism'. It was further stated that 'even if *Re Denley* can properly be said to be a broad application of the beneficiary principle, it is clear that there must still be an identifiable class of persons who would have standing to enforce the trust', which there was not in this case, given the term, 'any polo club'.[84]

It has been suggested that some earlier or contemporaneously decided English cases in which a valid trust was found, fit within the *Denley* mixed persons/purposes analysis.[85] It is fair to note, however, that in one instance, the Privy Council, which may have reoriented a bequest in *Denley* fashion to find a class

---

[80] *Ibid*, 372 (quote by Denning and Watkins LJJ), although *Re Denley* was not referred to in this case at either trial or appellate level.

[81] (1989), 61 Man R (2d) 241 (QB), and cited with approval in Manitoba LRC, *Non-charitable Purpose Trusts* (1992) 10–12. Note, however, the reservation about *Re Denley* expressed by the OLRC, *The Law of Trusts* (1996) vol 2, 433.

[82] For a very recent endorsement and application in Queensland, see: *Yeomans v Yeomans* [2005] QSC 85 (19 Apr 2005) [9]–[10].

[83] [2001] SASC 73.

[84] *Ibid*, [49]–[50]. Bleby J cited other instances of Australian judicial criticism of the *Denley* principle, *viz*: *Tidex v Trustees Executors and Agency Co Ltd* [1971] 2 NSWLR 453, 465; *Re Australian Elizabethan Theatre Trust; Lord v Commonwealth Bank of Australia* (1991) 30 FCR 491, 502. See subsequently, also: *Edwards v A-G (NSW)* [2004] NSWCA 272, [96] ('even if [*Denley*] is part of Australian law (a proposition that most equity lawyers would deny; see eg *Jacobs on Trusts*, 6th edn [1008], footnote 46(2)').

[85] Eg: *In re Aberconway's ST; McLaren v Aberconway* [1953] Ch 647 (CA) (trust for the upkeep and development of gardens); *In re Trusts of the Abbott Fund; Smith v Abbott* [1900] 2 Ch 326 (trust to benefit two old ladies during their lives); *In Re Andrew's Trust* [1905] 2 Ch 48 (gift for education of a deceased clergyman's children); *In re Osoba (decd); Osoba v Osoba* [1979] 1 WLR 247 (CA) (trust for daughter's education and mother's maintenance); *Barclays Bank Ltd v Quistclose Investments Ltd* [1970] AC 567 (HL) (trust in favour of both persons, the company's shareholders, and for the purpose of a dividend payment).

of beneficiaries standing behind the gauze purpose, declined to so do, indicating that the trust was dominantly purpose-framed, and being a non-charitable purpose, was invalid.[86] Certainly, the decision in *Denley* does not apply as to validate non-charitable purpose trusts where either the benefit to the individuals is perceived as too indirect to confer upon them any *locus standi* to apply to the court to enforce the trust,[87] or where there is no class of ascertainable beneficiaries that would be benefited by the trust, thus rendering the trust administratively unworkable.[88]

(b) What if the purpose is impossible or impracticable to fulfil?

To now return to the key question: what should occur if the purposes described in the abovementioned examples become impossible or impracticable (eg, the sporting ground is no longer required, or onsite accommodation is provided for the school children on campus, rendering further housing unnecessary)? Does the court have the power to invoke the *cy-près* doctrine in order to apply the trust property for some other purpose?

So far as can be ascertained, this question has never been expressly addressed in mixed persons/purposes trusts, because any scope for operation of the doctrine has been effectively ousted by other means:

An express gift-over provision.   For example, in *Denley* itself, the settlor carefully specified what was to happen if the object of the trust could not be fulfilled. Clause 2(j) of the trust deed stated that if, at any time, the land ceased to be required or used by the employees as a sports ground, then the trustees were required to convey the land to the General Hospital at Cheltenham. This is precisely the manner in which any *cy-près* jurisdiction (if it exists at all in the *Denley* scenario) is effectively ousted.[89] Due to the difficulties to which failed purposes can give rise in the non-charitable context, Baxendale-Walker reiterates that it is essential, as a matter of practicality, that—

---

[86] See, eg: *Leahy v A-G for NSW* [1959] AC 457 (PC) (residuary gift for construction of new convent; trust's performance would have benefited individuals of religious order; however, construed as a non-charitable purpose trust). Also see, for similar point: *Bacon v Pianta* (1966) 114 CLR 634 (HCA).

[87] As applied in, eg: *Twinsectra Ltd v Yardley* [2002] UKHL 12, 2 AC 164 [88] ('it seems unlikely that the banks' object was to benefit the creditors (who included the Inland Revenue) except indirectly. The banks had their own commercial interests to protect by enabling the subsidiary to trade out of its difficulties. If so, then the primary trust cannot be supported as a valid non-charitable purpose trust'). Note the suggestion in JD Heydon and PL Loughlan, *Cases and Materials on Equity and Trusts* (5th edn, Butterworths, Sydney, 1997) 543 that the benefit of developing gardens may have been too indirect to warrant a valid trust in: *In re Aberconway's ST* [1953] Ch 647.

[88] Eg: *R v District Auditor No 3, Audit District of West Yorkshire Metropolitan CC; ex p West Yorkshire Metropolitan CC* [1986] RVR 24 (QB) (with respect to the class of beneficiaries described as the 'inhabitants of West Yorkshire', it was said that this could not be brought within the scope of *Denley* or *Lipinski* because there were 'no ascertained or ascertainable beneficiaries'; there were approximately 2,500,000 so-called inhabitants).

[89] Also noted by: OLRC, *Report on the Law of Charities* (1996) 445.

in drafting a Purpose Trust, express default provision should always be made for frustration of the purpose. The gift over could be to another Purpose Trust, a Beneficiary [private] Trust or by way of express resulting trust. However, if the draftsman omits such provision the Courts may disappoint the expectations of the settlor. There is nothing unique to Purpose Trusts about this.[90]

Winding up the association. In *Lipinski*, significance was attached to the fact that, under the constitution of the association, a majority of the members could alter the constitution and thereby provide for the division of the association's assets among themselves. Thus, the members of the association could be entitled not to enforce the purpose, or to vary it, by suitable amendment to the constitution.[91] This raises the prospect that, by virtue of the contract between them, members of an association could change the purpose for which the fund was given—which, if true, would also provide an alternative course of action where the purpose becomes impossible or impracticable to fulfill. Distinct reservations, however, have been raised as to whether that was ever the result that *Lipinski* intended: 'if there is a purpose trust, and it is variable, it is clear that the power to do so must come from the general law and cannot come from any contractual arrangement between the members as is suggested in this case.'[92]

***Reliance upon the rule in* Saunders v Vautier.** If the purposes of the trust appear impracticable, could the beneficiaries (employees of the company, for example) rely upon the rule in *Saunders v Vautier*?[93] This rule provides that where there is more than one beneficiary, provided that they are all of age of majority, legally capable and absolutely entitled, they can agree to call upon the trustee to transfer the property to them.

On the one hand, Moffat has remarked that it is very doubtful whether Goff J would have intended that the class of persons under a *Denley* trust could all be permitted to act together, pursuant to the rule, to defeat the purpose of the trust and claim the trust property for themselves.[94] On the other hand, Hackney has suggested that one consequence of *Denley* is that the beneficiaries (assuming that they could all find each other) could demand the trust property from the trustees, and defeat both the donor's intentions and also, if the purpose happened to be charitable, 'the legitimate expectations of the charity.'[95]

---

[90] P Baxendale-Walker, *Purpose Trusts* (Butterworths, London, 1999) 206.

[91] [1976] 1 Ch 235, 249–50. The court cited: *In re Bowes; Earl Strathmore v Vane* [1896] 1 Ch 507. Cf: *Radmanovich v Nedeljkovic* [2001] NSWSC 492, [129] ('in the present case Rule 50 of 1950 shows that the members can never divide up the property between them beneficially but once the association comes to an end the property must be transferred to the Serbian Orthodox Church. Accordingly, the trust can never take effect under the *Denley* principle').

[92] J Hackney, 'Trusts' [1976] *ASCL* 412, 422.

[93] (1841) 4 Beav 115, as expanded in *Gosling v Gosling* (1859) Johns 265; 70 ER 423.

[94] G Moffat, *Trusts Law Text and Materials* (4th edn, CUP, Cambridge, 2005) 249 ('It is at least open to doubt whether that outcome would have been envisaged by Goff J as a corollary of his decision').

[95] J Hackney, *Understanding Equity and Trusts* (Fontana Press, London, 1987) 71–73.

So far as can be ascertained, the point has never fallen for decision. Whilst none of this precisely answers the question as to whether the *cy-près* doctrine applies to *Denley* trusts, it is some evidence that other avenues to vary the purposes may be open, apart from the *cy-près* doctrine, if the purposes became impracticable to carry out.

Treating the trust as a private trust, with purpose as a mere motive.   Another option, where the purposes of the trust fail, is to treat the trust as one for the conveyance of the property to the beneficiaries as gifts, with the purpose merely construed as a motive for the gift, rather than to construe it as a purpose trust which has failed.

This approach has occurred in some notable English cases. Early examples occurred in *In re Andrew's Trust; Carter v Andrew*[96] and *In re Bowes; Earl Strathmore v Vane*.[97] In the former, a gift for the education of a deceased clergyman's children was unable to be carried into effect once their education was completed; and in the latter, a bequest to plant an estate with trees, for the sum of 5000*l*, was impossible to carry out because the estate would only support the planting of trees to the cost of 800*l*. In both cases, the trusts were held to convey the beneficial entitlement to the trust property to the human beneficiaries, the children and the owners of the estate. The purposes were discarded, and the beneficiaries took the property. A more recent example occurred in *In re Osoba (decd); Osoba v Osoba*,[98] in which a gift for the maintenance of the testator's wife and mother and for the training of his daughter to university level failed because both wife and mother had died and the daughter's university education had also been completed. In both cases, the trusts were held to convey the absolute entitlement to the trust property to the human beneficiaries, even after the purposes had been completed or frustrated—in Goff LJ's words in *Osoba*, 'a gift to all three [daughter, widow and mother] . . . in which case the expressed purposes are no more than purpose or motive'.[99]

Academically, it has been noted that these decisions achieve (by orienting the trusts as private rather than purpose trusts) the outcome of avoiding either a resulting trust or the Crown taking the property as *bona vacantia*, where the purpose of the trust is frustrated.[100] They certainly provide a further avenue for recognising a trust for non-charitable purposes. They do not, however, authorise any *cy-près* application of the trust property in the event of failure of the trust purpose.

[96] [1905] 2 Ch 48.
[97] [1896] 1 Ch 507.
[98] [1979] 1 WLR 247 (CA).
[99] *Ibid*, 254.
[100] P Baxendale-Walker, *Purpose Trusts* (Butterworths, London, 1999) 203–6; HAJ Ford and IJ Hardingham, *Trusts Commentary and Materials* (6th edn, Law Book Co, Sydney, 1990) 687.

(c) The application of cy-près

What *cy-près* powers rest with the court to alter a mixed persons/non-charitable purpose trust that has become impossible or impracticable to execute?

The question remains, to date, unanswered by the judiciary. In the immediate aftermath of *Denley*, Hackney noted that the capacity to vary the purposes stipulated in the trust deed was far from clear: '[w]e await with interest the first group of employees seeking to turn their "sports ground" purpose trust into an "open air theatre" purpose trust'.[101] The wait continues. Several years later, when briefly considering the interrelationship between the *cy-près* doctrine and *Denley*-type trusts, the OLRC stated that, in its opinion, it was 'not clear' whether the doctrine applied, but that it was likely not to.[102] In this author's opinion, the application of the *cy-près* doctrine to these trusts is most improbable for three reasons.

First, notwithstanding their hybrid nature, it seems clear that, in one key respect, *Denley* trusts veer further in the direction of private than purpose trusts. Goff J explicitly stated that the relevant test for certainty of objects in these types of trusts was whether there was an 'ascertainable' class of beneficiaries.[103] Significantly, the court did not refer to what test of certainty ought to apply to this as a *purpose* trust.[104] Bearing this in mind, no *cy-près* doctrine can sensibly apply to private trusts. Either the persons to benefit from the trust are ascertainable, or they are not. There is no question of substituting one purpose to which the property may be applied for another. This view that *Denley* trusts are more private- than purpose-oriented is buttressed by the opinion expressed in *R v District Auditor, ex p West Yorkshire Metropolitan CC*[105] that the 'administrative workability' test of certainty is to be applied to *Denley*-type trusts (that the class of beneficiaries must not be too wide). Again, to apply the *cy-près* doctrine in these circumstances, were the nominated purpose to be impossible or impracticable, appears inconsistent and incongruous.

Secondly, Goff J expressly remarked that he would have no power to settle a scheme in the event that some employees wished to use the sports facilities for one purpose and where some employees postulated another, and incompatible, purpose. If there was an impasse, his Lordship considered that the court could not resolve it, 'because it clearly could not either exercise the trustees' power to make rules or settle a scheme, this being a non-charitable trust.'[106] However, his Lordship continued: 'it would not be right to hold the trust void on this ground.

---

[101] J Hackney, 'Trusts' [1976] *ASCL* 412, 422.
[102] OLRC, *Report on the Law of Charities* (1996) 445 ('an open question what becomes of the property').
[103] [1969] 1 Ch 373, 386.
[104] This point is also suggested in: Manitoba LRC, *Non-Charitable Purpose Trusts* (1992) 11, fn 34.
[105] [1986] RVR 24 (QB).
[106] [1969] 1 Ch 373, 387.

The court can, as it seems to me, execute the trust both negatively by restraining any improper disposition or use of the land, and positively by ordering the trustees to allow the employees and such other persons (if any) as they may admit to use the land for the purpose of a recreation or sports ground.'[107] These solutions do not, of course, equate to changing the purposes of the trust. If Goff J was not prepared to countenance that the court's inherent scheme-making power could be used for the *Denley* trust, it is farfetched to believe that the *cy-près* doctrine could be invoked if, say, the land could not be practicably used as a sportsground.

Thirdly, there is the problem of a missing framework. The application of the *cy-près* doctrine to charitable trusts is achieved against a backdrop of a general charitable intent, whether established (in the case of initial failure of the charitable purpose) or presumed (in the case of subsequent failure). The definition of charity, per the four heads of *Pemsel's* case, provides the necessary framework for the court (or the Charity Commissioners) to devise substitute purposes. Where no general charitable intent is present whatsoever in a *Denley*-type trust, then that framework against which to apply the assets to like-minded purposes, falls away. This is an issue with which law reform commissions have especially grappled when seeking to statutorily authorise non-charitable purpose trusts (also known as the 'pure purpose trust'). These conundrums are examined in the next section.

Before doing so, however, it is useful to briefly recap on the two non-charitable trusts considered to date. The better view appears to be that the *cy-près* doctrine has no application to *Denley* trusts or to the anomalous cases. This position is unlikely to change, given the relative paucity with which *Denley* has been applied, the other solutions for impracticable purposes which relevant *Denley*-type cases have outlined, and the severe strictures placed upon any expansion of the anomalous cases.

3. Non-charitable Purpose Trusts

Having dealt with the other two categories of non-charitable trusts, that is, the anomalous and mixed persons/purposes trusts, it is now apposite to turn attention to the third (and most interesting) category, the non-charitable purpose trust, which stands apart from the aforementioned categories as a creature of statute.

(a) *Why should non-charitable purpose trusts be recognised?*

There is a strong sense among some commentators that to restrict purpose trusts 'to charity and fox-hunting' is one of the more quaint and outdated semblances

---

[107] *Ibid*, 388.

of English trust law.[108] However, whilst there is some sporadic support amongst English commentators for the recognition/validation of pure purpose trusts, the topic has been patently marked by an absence of any statutory or law reform interest to date. The reasons which have been postulated as to why non-charitable purpose trusts should be permitted include the following:

- non-charitable trusts are not devices that inherently violate public policy (if they did, they would be struck down, as would any trust);[109]
- trusts of this type act as a cogent device for gifting assistance to the public or to some section of it, frequently providing for purposes that are beneficial to the community,[110] or advancing useful 'social experiments';[111]
- they enable stable and enduring funding for lawful non-profit activities,[112] so much so that 'it is difficult to conceive of any significant reason why the law should not assist non-charitable purposes in overcoming the obstacles to validity';[113]
- non-charitable purpose trusts *are* enforceable (as detailed in arguments outlined above[114]);
- in a free capitalist society, 'a settlor should be permitted to dispose freely of his own property subject to acceptable restrictions (such as tax or the requirement that valid purpose shall not promote activities which are contrary to law).. .. a settlor ought to be able to do what he wishes with his own assets';[115]

[108] Eg: A Duckworth, 'Trust Law in the New Millennium: Part I—Retrospective' (Nov 2000) *Trusts and Trustees* 12, 13.

[109] Manitoba LRC, *Non-Charitable Purpose Trusts* (1992) 12; also argued in: S Bright, 'Charity and Trusts for Public Benefit—Time for a Re-Think?' [1989] *Conv* 28.

[110] DJ Hayton, 'Modernising the Trustee Act 1925' in DJ Hayton (ed), *Modern International Developments in Trust Law* (Kluwer Law Intl, The Hague, 1999) 279 ('many socially desirable purposes'); and in the same volume, also by Hayton, 'Exploiting the Inherent Flexibility of Trusts', 331; OLRC, *Report on the Law of Charities* (1996) 438. For further strong support for the non-charitable purpose trust by Hayton, see: 'Developing the Obligation Characteristic of the Trust' in DJ Hayton (ed), *Extending the Boundaries of Trusts and Similar Ring-Fenced Funds* (Kluwer Law Intl, The Hague, 2002) 189, reproduced in: (2001) 117 *LQR* 96. Also argued in Bright, *ibid*, 38 (decrying the denial of tax etc advantages to 'other meritorious but non-charitable organisations').

[111] L McKay, 'Trusts for Purposes—Another View' (1973) 37 *Conv* 420, 434. Also: M Pawlowski, 'Purpose Trusts: Obligations without Beneficiaries?' (2002) 9(1) *Trusts and Trustees* 10, 10 ('testator ... may want to benefit a legitimate public object or useful social experiment'); R O'Malley, 'Charitable Status and Fiscal Privileges: Two Separate Issues?' (2003) 4 *Hibernian LJ* 177, 210–11; OLRC, *Report on the Law of Charities* (1996) 438.

[112] British Columbia LRC, *Non-Charitable Purpose Trusts* (1992) 56.

[113] Manitoba LRC, *Non-Charitable Purpose Trusts* (1992) 12, and cited with approval in: KA Beauchamp, 'Law Reform in Canada: The Proposed Introduction of the Non-Charitable Purpose Trust into Canada' in DWM Waters (ed), *Equity, Fiduciaries and Trusts* (Carswell, Toronto, 1993) 124–25.

[114] See pp 171–3.

[115] AR Anderson, 'The Statutory Non-Charitable Purpose Trust: Estate Planning in the Tax Havens' in DWM Waters (ed), *Equity, Fiduciaries and Trusts* (Carswell, Toronto, 1993) 101–2. Also put forcefully in: British Columbia LRC, *Report on Non-Charitable Purpose Trusts* (1992) 22, and noted by OLRC, *Report on the Law of Charities* (1996) 438, but not ultimately persuasive for that Commission, as it rejected the recognition of a non-charitable purpose trust: at 439.

- if charitable trusts are exempt from the rule against perpetuities because of the benefits upon the community that they bestow, and if non-charitable purpose trusts should not be recognisable unless they also purport to provide a benefit to an appreciable section of the public, then a non-charitable trust that is perpetuitous should be no reason, of itself, to deny its validity;[116]
- the proliferation of the non-charitable purpose trust in offshore jurisdictions has resulted, in reality, not from any desire to supplement the law of charity or to validate trusts for matters which the English law considers uncharitable (such as anti-vivisection), but rather, for purely commercial transactions.[117] Advantages emerge from establishing trusts for which there are no detectable beneficiaries, where the trust property cannot, in the strict sense, belong to anyone—arranging commercial transactions that are 'invisible to regulators, creditors and competitors alike'.[118] In so doing, offshore jurisdictions have simply responded to a demand for a product, something which the law of trusts has always been adept at providing, and which should be encouraged;[119]
- the fact that the concept of the non-charitable purpose trust may have been the subject of 'mutations . . . in certain tax havens . . . should not be used as an argument against its proper use. These curious trusts are allowed to exist because the legislatures of these tax havens allow them to exist . . . Such trusts would wither on the vine if legislatures were to deprive them of tax advantages';[120]
- charitable trusts should be construed as trusts for purposes (rather than as trusts for a class of persons who will benefit from the charitable donation), and it is not such a large step to hold that non-charitable purpose trusts

---

[116] R O'Malley, 'Charitable Status and Fiscal Privileges: Two Separate Issues?' (2003) 4 *Hibernian LJ* 177, 206–7, 210–11.

[117] Noted by many commentators, eg: A Duckworth, 'Trust Law in the New Millennium: Part I — Retrospective' (Nov 2000) *Trusts and Trustees* 12, 13; S Moerman, 'Non-Charitable Purpose Trusts' (2000 Jan) *Trusts and Trustees* 7 (providing numerous scenarios); P de Pourtales, 'Purpose Trusts in the Bahamas' (2001 Oct) *Trusts and Trustees* 17, 18. A very interesting account of precisely how STAR trusts have been used under the Cayman Islands regime is contained in: GJR Stein, 'Cayman STAR Trusts: Three Years On' (2000 Nov) *Trusts and Trustees* 28.

[118] G Moffat, *Trusts Law Text and Materials* (4th edn, CUP, Cambridge, 2005) 252–53, who cites, for further relevant discussion: P Matthews, 'The New Trust: Obligations without Rights?' in AJ Oakley (ed), *Trends in Contemporary Trust Law* (Clarendon Press, Oxford, 1996) ch 1, and DWM Waters, 'The Protector: New Wine in Old Bottles' in AJ Oakley (ed), *Trends in Contemporary Trust Law* (Clarendon Press, Oxford, 1996) ch 4.

[119] Moffat, *ibid*, 252. Also forcefully put in, eg: JA Dash, 'Purpose Trusts: The Nevis Perspective' (2003) 9(8) *Trusts and Trustees* 8, 12–13; P Matthews, 'The New Trust: Obligations without Rights' in AJ Oakley (ed), *Trends in Contemporary Trust Law* (Clarendon Press, Oxford, 1996) 30–31 ('client-driven' practices abound in modern trust law).

[120] P Parkinson, 'Review Essay: *Trends in Contemporary Trust Law* by A Oakley' (1998) 20 *Sydney L Rev* 348 (accessed online, no pp available).

(with, perhaps, no identifiable beneficiaries) ought to be valid as well (although case law does tend to the contrary view[121]);

- the 'dramatically different treatment we afford to trusts for charitable purposes and those for non-charitable purposes' is increasingly difficult to justify;[122] and
- by disallowing non-charitable purpose trusts, it is not as if English law does not recognise them in another guise—various artificial approaches have been used to apply property for non-charitable purposes, such as construing a gift for purposes as a gift for the members of an unincorporated association, or by construing gifts as being conditional upon the recipient carrying out a stated (non-charitable) purpose.[123]

Nevertheless, despite this wealth of support, it seems unlikely that the introduction of the non-charitable purpose trust into English law will occur in the near future.

A reform proposal[124] by the Goodman Committee in 1976, that trusts for non-charitable purposes should be validated, has never been judicially or legislatively embraced. Why not? Undoubtedly, this reluctance is motivated by practical concerns, rather than by doctrinal considerations of how to, for example, draft appropriate *cy-près* provisions! Hayton notes that 'there is a feeling that pure purpose trusts may be hijacked for shady dealings involving hiding beneficial ownership.'[125] Moffat points out that the reluctance may stem from efforts to widen the definition of 'charity'—'[c]ontemporary liberalisation of the definition of charitable purposes ... in the direction of recognising as charitable many, perhaps most, non-contentious purposes of a beneficial nature could paradoxically reinforce the adoption by the courts of a restrictive approach [toward non-charitable purpose trusts].'[126] (Interestingly, the OLRC

---

[121] Especially: *In re Church Patronage Trust; Laurie v A-G* [1904] 2 Ch 643 (CA) ('If there is a trust at all in this case it is a trust without a *cestui que trust*. It seems to me that those grounds are sufficient to shew that in this particular case there is great difficulty in saying there is a charitable trust': Vaughan Williams LJ). The author is indebted to Professor Geraint Thomas for drawing her attention to this case.

[122] KA Beauchamp, 'Law Reform in Canada: The Proposed Introduction of the Non-Charitable Purpose Trust into Canada' in DWM Waters (ed), *Equity, Fiduciaries and Trusts* (Carswell, Toronto, 1993) 113–14.

[123] M Pawlowski, 'Purpose Trusts: Obligations without Beneficiaries?' (2002) 9(1) *Trusts and Trustees* 10, 11–12.

[124] Lord Goodman (Chair), *Charity Law and Voluntary Organisations* (1976) 181.

[125] DJ Hayton, 'Modern Trust Law Reform in the United Kingdom' in DJ Hayton (ed), *Modern International Developments in Trust Law* (Kluwer Law Intl, The Hague, 1999) 305, and also cited in JE Martin, *Hanbury and Martin Modern Equity* (17th edn, Sweet & Maxwell, London, 2005) 394–95.

[126] G Moffat, *Trusts Law Text and Materials* (4th edn, CUP, Cambridge, 2005) 251. This author also notes that the beneficiary principle is probably too firmly entrenched: '[it] could only be overturned by legislation or the House of Lords': at 251. Note the drafting of the new 10-pronged definition of charity in: *Review of Charities and the Wider Not-For-Profit Sector* (Sep 2002): 1. the prevention and relief of poverty; 2. the advancement of education; 3. the advancement of religion; 4. the advancement of health (including the prevention and relief of sickness, disease or of human suffering); 5. social and community advancement (including the care, support and protection of the

was also of the view that a widening of the definition of 'charitable purpose' would provide a better course of reform than to validate the non-charitable purpose trust.[127]) Matthews adds to this that the role of the Attorney-General in the province of charitable trusts point to the countervailing 'public benefit' which those trusts provide, and which the non-charitable purpose trust, as an entity of private law, cannot match.[128]

Whatever the true reason, the statutory innovations evident in offshore jurisdictions, shortly to be considered, find no counterpart yet in English law.

(b) If they are recognised, should the cy-près doctrine apply to them?

If the non-charitable purpose trust is to be permitted, and if that purpose is, or becomes, impossible or impracticable, should substitution of another purpose be permitted, or should the trust fail?

Non-charitable trusts (if they are to be validated) are no different from any other trust—'[p]urpose must embody a definite concept, and means to attain it must be described with sufficient certainty.'[129] In the vast majority of cases, the purposes of a non-charitable purpose trust could be carried out, with no spectre of impossibility or impracticability arising. Bright gives the example[130] of the 40-letter alphabet trust in *In re Shaw (decd); Public Trustee v Day*[131] as comprising a precisely stated non-charitable purpose trust. Others, such as the gifts to ensure the integrity and independence of newspapers and journalistic freedom in *In re Astor's ST; Astor v Scholfield*,[132] were not in that category, unfortunately.

---

aged, people with a disability, children and young people); 6. the advancement of culture, arts and heritage; 7. the advancement of amateur sport; 8. the promotion of human rights, conflict resolution and reconciliation; 9. the advancement of environmental protection and improvement; and 10. other purposes beneficial to the community. This has not passed into legislation as yet.

[127] OLRC, *Report on the Law of Charities* (1996) 439.

[128] P Matthews, 'From Obligation to Property, and Back Again? The Future of the Non-Charitable Purpose Trust' in DJ Hayton (ed), *Extending the Boundaries of Trusts and Similar Ring-Fenced Funds* (Kluwer Law Intl, The Hague, 2002) 231.

[129] *In re Catherall (decd); Lloyds Bank Ltd v Griffiths* (Ch, 3 Jun 1959), and see also: *In re Astor's ST; Astor v Scholfield* [1952] Ch 534, 547 ('If . . . an enumeration of *purposes outside the realm of charities* can take the place of an enumeration of beneficiaries, the purposes must . . . be stated in phrases which embody definite concepts and the means by which the trustees are to try to attain them must also be prescribed with a sufficient degree of certainty').

[130] S Bright, 'Charity and Trusts for the Public Benefit—Time for a Re-think?' [1989] *Conv* 28, 39. Also see the assessment in: P Baxendale-Walker, *Purpose Trusts* (Butterworths, London, 1999) 124. Cf, though: A Duckworth, *STAR Trusts* (Gostick Hall Publications, 1998) 21 (contending that 'many purpose trusts' would present purposes that were insufficiently defined).

[131] [1957] 1 WLR 729 (Ch), under which playwright George Bernard Shaw sought to establish, by testamentary trust, a detailed plan of research into the merits of a proposed alternative alphabet.

[132] [1952] Ch 534. The specified objects included the following: '1. The establishment maintenance and improvement of good understanding . . . between nations . . . and also between different sections of people in any nation or community. 2. The preservation of the independence and integrity of newspapers and the encouragement of the adoption and maintenance by newspapers of fearless educational and constructive policies. 3. The promotion of the freedom independence and integrity of the Press . . . 5. The protection of newspapers . . . from being absorbed or controlled by combines . . .

It has been academically accepted that there has never been any comparable attempts under the general law to transpose the *cy-près* doctrine to non-charitable purpose trusts.[133] A reason for this reluctance is explained by the Manitoba Law Reform Commission in these terms:

> In *cy-près*, the finding of a general charitable intent allows the court to use the definition of charity as the frame of reference to establish the variation scheme. The remedy is workable because the definition of charity has a definite boundary. . . . However, the *cy-près* doctrine itself cannot easily be applied to non-charitable purpose trusts. The doctrine requires that a general charitable intent be found; a corresponding requirement that a general non-charitable intent be found would be meaningless, since the court would have no recognized framework within which to find it. The boundaries of the legal definition of charity are known; the boundaries of 'non-charity' are not.[134]

On point, as the British Columbia Law Reform Commission observed, to rely upon the framework of a 'general dispositive intent' would be 'to add an undue element of mysticism to the exercise.'[135]

What alternatives exist for non-charitable purpose trusts *if* they are to be validated at general law, and *if* the *cy-près* doctrine cannot be invoked? Three answers to this thorny question have been postulated over the years:

- *Trust property results to the donor.* Swadling has suggested[136] that, where a non-charitable purpose trust fails for impossibility or impracticability, it would be feasible to 'utilize the sort of trust which arose in *Vandervell*, using the (slightly dubious) argument that funds not spent before the purpose failed were simply funds over which no valid trust had been declared',[137] giving rise to a resulting trust back to the settlor (or his estate). In other words, the donor of the property may convey property on trust for a non-charitable purpose, but find that there has been a failure to exhaust the beneficial interest—the property will be construed as having been left with the donor. Hackney has similarly posited that if a non-charitable purpose trust was to be validated, if the trust's purpose failed, and 'where the failure is initial, it seems that the beneficial interest remains with the

6. The restoration . . . protection and maintenance of the independence of . . . writers in newspapers . . . 7. The establishment . . . or support of any charitable public or benevolent schemes . . . for or in connection with (a) the improvement of newspapers or journalism or (b) the relief or benefit of persons . . . engaged in journalism.'

[133] PA Lovell, 'Non-charitable Purpose Trusts—Further Reflections' (1970) 34 *Conv* 77, 95, cited in: Manitoba LRC, *Non-Charitable Purpose Trusts* (1992) 11, fn 36; KA Beauchamp, 'Law Reform in Canada: The Proposed Introduction of the Non-Charitable Purpose Trust into Canada' in DWM Waters (ed), *Equity, Fiduciaries and Trusts* (Carswell, Toronto, 1993) 122–24.
[134] Manitoba LRC, *Non-Charitable Purpose Trusts* (1992) 31–32.
[135] British Columbia LRC, *Non-Charitable Purpose Trusts* (1992) 51. Note also, the concerns of the OLRC in this regard in: *Report on the Law of Charities* (1996) 446.
[136] W Swadling, 'Orthodoxy' in W Swadling (ed), *The Quistclose Trust: Critical Essays* (Hart Publishing, Oxford, 2004) 37; see also: W Swadling, 'Quistclose Trusts and Orthodoxy' (2004) 11 *Journal of Intl Trust and Corporate Planning* 121 [accessed online].
[137] Citing: *Vandervell v Inland Revenue Commissioners* [1967] 2 AC 291 (HL).

settlor.'[138] In the case of subsequent failure, Hackney also proposed a resulting trust, as the following example demonstrates:

> If we return to the example of a trust to educate children, . . . and where our settlor makes it crystal clear that education is not the motive, but the fundamental and sole purpose of the gift, there are two possible failure scenarios. The first is that the education is successfully completed and there is a balance. The second is where the purpose is frustrated, . . . (the child's university is closed down, say). In both cases, if the purpose is integrated into the gift, if it is part of the disposition, the balance should go on resulting trust to the estate . . . or to residuary legatees.[139]

Notably, neither of these commentators suggested a *cy-près* application of the property in these circumstances.

- *Apply for charitable purposes.* The British Columbia Commission outlined[140] two other possible options for distribution of the property where a non-charitable purpose trust could not be fulfilled, and where the settlor did not provide directions. The first of these was to apply the property to a strictly charitable purpose. This avenue did not, however, appeal to the Commission.

- *Transfer of trust property to the Crown.* Treating the trust property as *bona vacantia* to be passed to the Crown was another of the options postulated by the British Columbia Commission, but this did not find favour either. Ultimately, the Commission endorsed a non-charitable *cy-près* distribution instead.

It is true to say that a case can be mounted by which to argue that the use of the *cy-près* doctrine in the context of non-charitable trusts should be both proper and encouraged.

For one thing, a *cy-près* power has important policy justifications in respect of any type of purpose trust. It has been suggested by Gardner[141] that the *cy-près* doctrine is simply 'a matter of the public getting its money's worth for the costs which such trusts entail, in the form of tax loss and the long-term withdrawal of assets from the economy'. In other words, to be permitted to alter a trust's objects to achieve a more socially useful outcome than the present impracticable object is a benefit that acts as the *quid pro quo* for the social costs of setting up trusts. This reasoning accords with the sentiments of Martin: '[r]esources are scarce, and need to be put to good use.'[142] The application of *cy-près* upon this reasoning, so as to ensure that funds are not tied up for impossible or

---

[138] J Hackney, *Understanding Equity and Trusts* (Fontana Press, London, 1987) 154.
[139] *Ibid*, 155.
[140] British Columbia LRC, *Non-Charitable Purpose Trusts* (1992) 46–49.
[141] S Gardner, 'New Angles on Unincorporated Associations' [1992] *Conv* 41, 52.
[142] JE Martin, *Hanbury and Martin Modern Equity* (17th edn, Sweet & Maxwell, London, 2005) 394.

impracticable purposes but are used for the benefit of the public, would thereby embrace both charitable and non-charitable trusts alike.

Secondly, the court's scheme-making powers extend well beyond the charitable trust scenario now in any event. Since the decision in *McPhail v Doulton*,[143] a court can exercise its inherent scheme-making power so as to ensure that the settlor's intentions be given effect to under a private trust. Lord Wilberforce stated that the court:

> may authoris[e] or direct representative persons of the classes of beneficiaries to prepare a scheme of distribution, or even, should the proper basis for distribution appear, by itself directing the trustees so to distribute. The books give many instances where this has been done, and I see no reason in principle why [the courts] should not do so in the modern field of discretionary [private] trusts.[144]

The Manitoba Law Reform Commission noted[145] that, prior to this decision, it was thought that schemes could only be drafted for charitable trusts, not for private trusts, but in this case, the only pre-condition to the scheme was that the court must have a clear understanding of the settlor's intentions.[146] Thus, said the Commission, it is not such a large step to endorse the creation of a *cy-près* scheme for non-charitable purpose trusts—just as for private trusts—where the settlor's intent is obvious. The analogy between the type of power expressed in *McPhail*, and its potential application to support a power to vary non-charitable purpose trusts, has been noted elsewhere—termed, in fact, 'in effect, a non-charitable *cy-près*.[147]

Thirdly, application of the *cy-près* doctrine encourages a finding that the trust is valid and should not fail. It has been strongly suggested[148] that the equitable principle of paying the utmost respect to the settlor's intention demands that a trust should be upheld unless there are convincing and overwhelming reasons for not doing so. As Bright notes, '[i]t is not as though by striking down a trust we are ensuring that the money will be put to a better cause; indeed frequently the opposite may well be true.'[149] The British Columbia Law Reform Commission made the ancillary point that the alternatives to a *cy-près* application of property, when a non-charitable purpose trust is incapable of fulfillment, will counter the settlor's wishes in most cases. If one takes the resulting trust

---

[143] [1971] AC 424 (HL).

[144] *Ibid*, 457.

[145] Manitoba LRC, *Non-Charitable Purpose Trusts* (1992) 30, fn 3.

[146] [1971] AC 424 (HL) 457.

[147] Eg: P Baxendale-Walker, *Purpose Trusts* (Butterworths, London, 1999) 129, 271 (quote); JD Heydon and PL Loughlan, *Cases and Materials on Equity and Trusts* (5th edn, Butterworths, Sydney, 1997) 518. Earlier, LA Sheridan and VTH Delany, *The Cy-près Doctrine* (Sweet & Maxwell, London, 1959) 50, suggested a similar *cy-près* doctrine by analogy, given that some of the miscellaneous applications of the doctrine, such as the rule against *Whitby v Mitchell*, concerned private trusts.

[148] JW Harris, 'Trust, Power and Duty' (1971) 87 *LQR* 31, 38–39, cited with approval in: Manitoba LRC, *Non-Charitable Purpose Trusts* (1992) 12.

[149] S Bright, 'Charity and Trusts for the Public Benefit—Time for a Re-think?' [1989] *Conv* 28, 35.

option, then the property may end up being distributed among next-of-kin whom the settlor never intended to benefit.[150] If one applies the trust property to some charitable purpose instead of the failed non-charitable one, then that goes directly against the wishes of the settlor who could, after all, surely have selected a charitable purpose himself. If one turns over the property to the Crown as *bona vacantia*, that would enable the government to use the property in accordance with its own priorities, regardless of whether the settlor may have approved. For these reasons, that Commission preferred the *cy-près* approach.[151]

Be this as it may, English equity is hard-pressed to recognise non-charitable purpose trusts, let alone to apply the *cy-près* doctrine to them. Legislatures elsewhere have been far more proactive.

(c) Legislative enactments permitting pure purpose trusts

From the British Virgin Islands to Brunei, offshore jurisdictions have not been backward in statutorily validating non-charitable purpose trusts. Such regimes have several common features. Typically, the purposes must (variously expressed) be specific, reasonable, possible, capable of fulfillment, not immoral, nor contrary to public policy, nor unlawful. Sometimes, it is explicitly provided that at least one trustee must be a lawyer or other designated (official) person, and that the trust must be in writing. Unanimously, these trusts must have an 'enforcer' or 'protector' (a 'stooge', their critics have said[152]), a person who is occasionally required to have consented in writing or be a party to the trust instrument. Typically it is provided that the trust must specify those events which will terminate the trust; and most statutes exempt such trusts from the rule against perpetuities. A *cy-près* mechanism can prove very useful where the purpose trust is perpetual.[153]

However, the degree to which the respective statutes stipulate that, where the purposes of the trust become impossible or impracticable, a *cy-près* power may be invoked, differs enormously. On a sliding scale of draftsmanship, some jurisdictions' provisions specify the triggers for *cy-près*, and how the property is then to be applied, with laudable particularity; some appear to contemplate a *cy-près* distribution but leave the matter unsatisfactorily unclear;

---

[150] A point also made in favour of a *cy-près* approach being adopted in non-charitable purpose trusts in: DJ Hayton, 'Anglo-Trusts, Euro-Trusts and Caribbo-Trusts: Whither Trusts?' in DJ Hayton (ed), *Modern International Developments in Trust Law* (Kluwer Law Intl, The Hague, 1999) 8–9. Or, as LA Sheridan and VTH Delany, *The Cy-près Doctrine* (Sweet & Maxwell, London, 1959) 51, put it: 'A person who makes a gift for "charitable or benevolent purposes" would doubtless prefer it to go to non-benevolent charity than to his remote unheard-of relation in the antipodes, and public policy would be served by so applying it').

[151] British Columbia LRC, *Non-Charitable Purpose Trusts* (1992) 48.

[152] P Matthews, 'The New Trust: Obligations without Rights?' in AJ Oakley (ed), *Trends in Contemporary Trust Law* (Clarendon Press, Oxford, 1996) 27.

[153] Noted by: S Moerman, 'BVI Purpose Trusts' (2004) 10(3) *Trusts and Trustees* 18, 24.

and others ignore the possibility of *cy-près* altogether. Key international legislation (with the exception of provisions in Liechtenstein[154] and North America[155]) will comprise the focus of discussion in this section.[156] Notably, the *cy-près* provisions of these statutes have merited very little academic analysis to date,[157] with key debates concentrating upon the general efficacy of this type of legislation.[158]

The clearest cy-près provisions. The non-charitable purpose trust regimes established in the Bahamas,[159] the Cayman Islands[160] (the 'boldest'[161] and 'most

---

[154] The Law of Trust Enterprises, enacted 10 Apr 1928. Note the contention by AJ Oakley, *Parker and Mellows Modern Law of Trusts* (8th edn, Sweet & Maxwell, London, 2003) 80, fn 10 that to permit the creation of purpose trusts was probably unintentional in the case of Liechenstein, and by Matthews that it is a 'special case': P Matthews, 'The New Trust: Obligations without Rights?' in AJ Oakley (ed), *Trends in Contemporary Trust Law* (Clarendon Press, Oxford, 1996) 23.

[155] See: Civil Code of Quebec, art 1268 ('A private trust is a trust created for the object of erecting, maintaining or preserving a thing or of using a property appropriated to a specific use, whether for the indirect benefit of a person or in his memory, or for some other private purpose'); art 1270 ('A social trust is a trust constituted for a purpose of general interest, such as cultural, educational, philanthropic, religious, or scientific purpose'). For the Californian equivalent: Californian Probate Code, s 15203 ('A trust may be created for any purpose that is not illegal or against public policy), s 15204 ('A trust created for an indefinite or general purpose is not invalid for that reason if it can be determined with reasonable certainty that a particular use of the trust property comes within that purpose'). For interesting discussion of the limited purpose trusts permitted by code in various US States, see: AA Bove, 'The Use of Purpose Trusts in the United States' (2004) 10(8) *Trusts and Trustees* 6, 7–8.

[156] All of the relevant statutory material referred to in this section is taken from the copies of relevant legislation conveniently reproduced at: J Glasson (ed), *International Trust Laws* (Jordan Publishing Ltd, Bristol, 1992) vol 2, 'Source Material' tab; and from the 'ILS Corporate Downloads' website, located at: <www.ils-world.com/library/index.shtml>.

[157] The legislation is generally discussed in, eg: P Baxendale-Walker, *Purpose Trusts* (Butterworths, London, 1999) 243–308; AR Anderson, 'The Statutory Non-Charitable Purpose Trust: Estate Planning in Tax Havens' in DWM Waters (ed), *Equity, Fiduciaries and Trusts* (Carswell, Toronto, 1993) 99; P Matthews, 'The New Trust: Obligations without Rights?' in AJ Oakley (ed), *Trends in Contemporary Trust Law* (Clarendon Press, Oxford, 1996) 23.

[158] Eg, the efficacy of the Cayman Islands 'STAR' trust device was debated in: P Matthews, 'Shooting STAR: The New Special Trusts Regime from the Cayman Islands' (1997) 11 *Trust Law Intl* 67; A Duckworth, 'STAR Wars: The Colony Strikes Back' (1998) 12 *Trust Law Intl* 16; P Matthews, 'STAR: Big Bang or Red Dwarf' (1998) 12 *Trust Law Intl* 98; A Duckworth, 'STAR Wars: Smiting the Bull' (1999) 13 *Trusts Law Intl* 158; but the *cy-près* provisions contained in the regime did not feature in that debate.

[159] Purpose Trusts Act 2004 (No 17 of 2004, assented to 17 Aug 2004). Section 3 recognises 'authorised purpose trusts' for non-charitable purposes. Discussed further in, eg: 'Purpose Trusts introduced in The Bahamas' (2004) 11(1) *Trusts and Trustees* 20.

[160] Special Trusts (Alternative Regime) Law 1997 (No 18 of 1997 (STAR Law)), s 6(3), and now (Cayman Islands) Trusts Law (2001 Revision), s 104(1), which recognises STAR trusts (called in s 391, 'special trusts'). Section 11 of the Special Trusts (Alternative Regime) Law 1997 contains the *cy-près* provision; but if the trust cannot be reconstituted consistently with the general intent of the trust, the trustees must dispose of the property as if the trust had failed. For further mention of the *cy-près* provisions in this legislation, see, eg: G Thomas and A Hudson, *The Law of Trusts* (OUP, Oxford, 2004) [40.07].

[161] A Huxley, 'Rhodes, Arakan, Grand Cayman: Three Versions of Offshore' in I Edge (ed), *Comparative Law in Global Perspective* (Transnational Publishers, London, 2001) 147.

sophisticated'[162] of the 'designer trusts') and Brunei,[163] contain *cy-près* provisions that are unusual in their explicitness. The provisions—similar to each other, but not identical—define the triggers for the application of the *cy-près* jurisdiction to the non-charitable purpose, *and* provide some guidance as to how the property is to be applied *cy-près*. The Bahamas provision provides a useful illustration:

8(2) If the execution of an authorised purpose trust in accordance with its terms is or becomes (otherwise than by the fulfillment of any purpose) in whole or in part

(a) impossible or impracticable;
(b) unlawful or contrary to public policy, or
(c) obsolete in that, by reason of changed circumstances it fails to achieve the general intent of the trust,

the trustees of the trust shall, and any authorised applicant may, unless the trust is reformed pursuant to its own terms, apply to the Court to reform the trust *cy-près*.

(3) On such application, the court may reform the trust in accordance with the general intent of its trust instrument . . .

The *cy-près* statutory regime enacted in the Seychelles[164] is briefer, but clearly the draftsman has considered the *cy-près* doctrine in totality (both triggers and application) for a non-charitable 'purpose international trust':

Where the trust property is held for a charitable or other purpose, the court . . . may approve an arrangement which varies . . . the purpose . . . of the trust . . . if it is satisfied that the arrangement is

(a) suitable or expedient, and
(b) consistent with the original intention of the settlor and the spirit of the settlement.[165]

The provisions of the Jersey Islands' regime[166] and St Kitts[167] similarly consider

---

[162] DJ Hayton, 'STAR Trusts' (1998) 4 *Amicus Curiae* 13, 13, and by the same author: 'Preface to STAR Trusts' in A Duckworth, *STAR Trusts* (Gostick Hall Publications, 1998) i. The reasoning behind and implementation of the legislation is explained by the draftsman himself, A Duckworth, in the aforementioned book.

[163] International Trusts Order 2000, Constitution of Brunei Darussalam. Section 75 recognises 'special trusts', which under s 77(3) may have purposes that are 'either charitable or non-charitable'. Section 84 contains the *cy-près* provisions.

[164] International Trusts Act 1994 (No 26 of 1994), s 14(1) recognises a 'purpose international trust' which may be non-charitable (charitable international trusts are provided for separately in s 13).

[165] *Ibid*, s 65. There is a separate *cy-près* variation power for charitable trusts contained in s 64, with more specific triggers for that context.

[166] Trusts (Amendment No 3) (Jersey) Law 1996 (assented to 24 Apr 1996) art 7, amending art 38 of the Trusts (Jersey) Law 1984 by insertion of new arts 10A–10C, which recognise non-charitable purpose trusts. For further discussion of this legislation, see: P Hargreaves, 'Charitable, Purpose and Hybrid Trusts: A Jersey Perspective' [2002] *PCB* 30. See now, Trusts (Jersey) Law 1984 (revised edn 2004), art 42(2).

[167] Trusts Act 1996 (No 23 of 1996, assented to on 22 Jan 1997), s 13, recognising the 'common trust' which can be a non-charitable purpose trust.

the *cy-près* doctrine from both angles, almost matching the Seychelles' regime with their brevity.[168]

The most elegantly drafted (and widest) *cy-près* provision is that appearing in the non-charitable purpose trust regime of Barbados[169] (and repeated elsewhere[170]). It simply transposes the *cy-près* doctrine from the charitable arena to the non-charitable purpose trust, but does not insist upon a strict *cy-près* application at all:

14(1) Where a trust is created for a non-charitable purpose, the terms of the trust may provide that the doctrine of *cy-près* is, *mutatis mutandis*, applicable thereto.

(2) For the purpose of subsection (1), where a purpose that is reasonably similar to the original purpose cannot be found, a purpose that is not contrary to the spirit and meaning of the settlement may be substituted for the original purpose.

Sub-section (2) does truly render this a 'liberal *cy-près*' provision.[171]

Some notable points emerge from these provisions. Several of the enactments do not precisely duplicate the triggers prescribed by either the common law or statutory charitable trusts *cy-près* doctrine. By requiring impossibility of the purpose, rather than impracticability or mere obsolescence of the original purpose, the Jersey Islands provision, for example, is far narrower in its scope.[172] Under all of the schemes noted above, the substituted schemes need not have any public benefit. It would appear that they can be just as idiosyncratic as the original non-charitable purpose devised by the settlor (always bearing in mind that most statutes require that the non-charitable purpose itself must be 'reasonable'—this may well obviate any recognition of whimsical and quite useless aims by the settlor in the first place). It is also unnecessary for the substituted application of the trust property to have any charitable aspect under any of the regimes (notwithstanding the judicial involvement in its design).

Half the equation. Somewhat less explicit are the provisions of the British Virgin Islands,[173] which provide that the court may 'vary any of the purposes of the trust',[174] and in exercising that power, the court shall have regard to 'such factors as the Court thinks material, which may include such changes in

[168] Under Trusts (Jersey) Law 1984 (revised edn 2004), art 42(2), 'Where an interest or property is held by the trustee for a [charitable or non-charitable] purpose which has ceased to exist or is no longer applicable, that interest property shall be held for such other charitable [or non-charitable] purpose as the court may declare to be consistent with the original intention of the settlor.' St Kitts' Trusts Act 1996, s 58(2) is in materially similar terms.

[169] International Trusts Act 1995, s 10, c 245, recognises non-charitable purpose trusts.

[170] See, eg: St Vincent and the Grenadines' International Trusts Act 1996, s 15 (a non-charitable 'international trust' is validated under s 12); Montserrat's Trust Act 1998, s 25. Grenada's International Trusts Act 1996, s 18 omits (2) from its provision.

[171] P Baxendale-Walker, *Purpose Trusts* (Butterworths, London, 1999) 285.

[172] P Hargreaves, 'Charitable, Purpose and Hybrid Trusts: A Jersey Perspective' (2002) 1 *PCB* 30, 32.

[173] By virtue of the Trustee Ordinance 1961, c 303, s 84, assented to on 24 Aug 1961, as amended by: Trustee (Amendment) Act 2003, ss 11, 12, inserting, *inter alia*, a new ss 84A.

[174] *Ibid*, s 84(15). See also: 2003 Amending Act, *ibid*, s 84A(22).

circumstances since the trust was created'.[175] Those 'changes in circumstances' are further defined inclusively to encompass:

> where the execution of the trust has become
>
> (a) impossible or impracticable,
> (b) unlawful or contrary to public policy, or
> (c) obsolete in that, by reason of changed circumstances, it fails to achieve the intention of the settlor and the spirit of the gift.[176]

The British Virgin Islands provision has been praised[177] for its comprehensive coverage in comparison with other offshore statutes, although notably, no guidelines are provided as to how the property is to be applied under the substituted arrangements.

Provisions entirely lacking in clarity.   Even less satisfactory are the provisions of Bermuda's[178] non-charitable trusts statutory regime. Whilst this regime appears to contemplate the use of a *cy-près* power to vary the purposes of the non-charitable trust, the provisions are less than explicit about the triggers for the jurisdiction to be invoked, and how the property should then be applied. On application by the settlor, trustee, or person appointed to enforce the trust, the court 'may, if it thinks fit approve a scheme to vary any of the purposes of the trust'.[179] No further details are given. A similar *cy-près* formula appears in the statutory regime of Anguilla.[180] Equally as terse, the recognition of the 'purpose international trust' in St Lucia[181] is accompanied by the provision[182] that its terms 'may provide that the doctrine of *cy-près* is applicable' to it—with no further elucidation.

Thomas regards the Bermuda provision as one which 'has yielded simplicity at the expense of certainty and clarity', and provides the following example of how little guidance the legislature has seen fit to give:

> The intention may be to confer authority on the court to make a kind of *cy-près* scheme in respect of a purpose trust [but] . . . Suppose, for example, that the purpose of the trust is to retain shares in a private family company, but the value of those shares is suddenly in danger of falling drastically. Can the court vary the purpose in such a case? If so, by reference to what criteria would it be able to do so?[183]

---

[175]   *Ibid*, s 84(16)(a), and see also, since the 2003 Amending Act, *ibid*, s 84A(23)(a).

[176]   *Ibid*, s 84(17), and, since the 2003 Amending Act, *ibid*, s 84A(24).

[177]   S Moerman, 'BVI Purpose Trusts' (2004) 10(3) *Trusts and Trustees* 18, 25.

[178]   Trusts (Special Provisions) Amendment Act 1998 (assented to 24 Jun 1998), substituting a new ss 12A–12D into the Trusts (Special Provisions) Act 1989 (No 62 of 1989, assented to 28 Dec 1989). These sections recognise 'purpose trusts' of non-charitable nature.

[179]   *Ibid*, s 12B(2).

[180]   Trusts Ordinance 1994, s 15(1), recognises non-charitable purpose trusts, and s 49 contains wording similar to s 12B(2), *ibid*.

[181]   International Trust Act 2002 (No 15 of 2002), s 21.

[182]   *Ibid*, s 22.

[183]   G Thomas, 'Purpose Trusts' in J Glasson (ed), *International Trust Laws* (Jordan Publishing Ltd, Bristol, 1992) vol 1, ch 4, B4–53.

Anderson makes the point that the Bermuda legislation requires that the trust shall provide for terms dealing with the disposition of surplus assets when the trust terminates, such that it would be 'unlikely that a *cy-près* scheme would ever be necessary' under that regime.[184] Nevertheless, even Anderson admits that an amendment to the Bermuda statute to provide for *cy-près* schemes for non-charitable purpose trusts would be 'an appropriate improvement'—a view with which this author concurs.

Complete omission of cy-près provisions. The vehicle of a non-charitable purpose trust is also recognised by statutory regimes in Nauru,[185] the Cook Islands,[186] Cyprus,[187] Niue,[188] and Isle of Man,[189] but none of these regimes contains any provisions dealing with varying the trust's purposes, should the original purpose be, or become, impossible or impracticable. Jurisdictions such as Belize,[190] Mauritius,[191] Nevis,[192] Labuan (Malaysia),[193] which also make explicit provision for non-charitable purpose trusts, extensively set out the *cy-près* triggers for *charitable* trusts,[194] but then do not extend those provisions to authorise a court to make a *cy-près* scheme in respect of non-charitable purpose trusts. Presumably, it is not open to the court in these jurisdictions to vary the purposes of the non-charitable purpose trust, should the originally stipulated purpose become impossible or impracticable. The trust will fail in those circumstances.

(d) *Canadian proposals for reform*

In addition to these statutory purpose trusts, there have been significant proposals for reform elsewhere. For example, law reform commissions in

---

[184] AR Anderson, 'The Statutory Non-Charitable Purpose Trust: Estate Planning in the Tax Havens' in DWM Waters DWM (ed), *Equity, Fiduciaries and Trusts* (Carswell, Toronto, 1993) 106.

[185] Foreign Trusts, Estates and Wills Act 1972 (assented to on 17 Feb 1972). Section 6 recognises a non-charitable purpose trust, provided that it complies with the requirements of validity in s 6(2).

[186] International Trusts Act 1984 (No 14 of 1984, assented to 27 Dec 1984). Section 12(2) recognises 'international trusts' which can be non-charitable purpose trusts.

[187] International Trusts Law 1992 (No 69(1) of 1992, assented to 24 Jul 1992). Sections 2, 7(3), recognise 'international trusts' which are non-charitable purpose trusts.

[188] Trusts Act 1994, s 16.

[189] Purpose Trusts Act 1996.

[190] Trusts Act (revised edn 2000), c 202, s 15.

[191] Trusts Act 2001, s 19. The limitation of the *cy-près* provisions to cover only charitable purpose trusts is further noted in: S Moerman, 'The Mauritius Purpose Trust' (2003) 9(4) *Trusts and Trustees* 21, 23.

[192] International Exempt Trust Ordinance 1994, s 8. The limitation of the *cy-près* provisions to cover only charitable purpose trusts further noted in: JA Dash, 'Purpose Trusts: The Nevis Perspective' (2003) 9(8) *Trusts and Trustees* 8, 10.

[193] Labuan Offshore Trusts Act 1996, s 4(3), recognises offshore trusts for a particular purpose, 'whether charitable or not'.

[194] See, eg: Trusts Act (revised edn 2000) (Belize), c 202, s 45(1), which sets out 8 separate triggers, (a)–(h). Similarly, see Trusts Act 2001 (Mauritius), s 59; International Exempt Trust Ordinance 1994 (Nevis), s 11. Also see the two triggers in Labuan Offshore Trusts Act 1996, s 18(2), which again is stated to apply to trust property held for a charitable purpose.

Canada[195] have suggested the statutory recognition of non-charitable purpose trusts, although these law reform recommendations have not been legislatively implemented to date. The *cy-près* provisions of the British Columbia draft Bill are most interesting:

44(5). Subject to subsection (9), if, in the opinion of the court, a non-charitable purpose trust is or has become impossible to perform or incapable of effectively fulfilling the purpose intended by the settlor, the court may at any time:

a. approve a scheme substituting a purpose for the non-charitable purpose trust that is as similar to the original purpose as is reasonably practicable, or

b. if the court is unable to find a purpose that is reasonably similar to the original purpose of the trust, approve a scheme substituting a purpose that is not contrary to the spirit of the original settlement.

(6) Subject to subsection (9), the court may vary a non-charitable purpose trust by approval of a scheme substituting a new purpose for the trust that is not contrary to the spirit of the original settlement if the court is of the opinion that the purpose of the trust is obsolete, or no longer useful or expedient, due to a change in circumstances since the creation of the trust.

(7) In exercising the power to vary a non-charitable purpose trust under subsection (6), the court must consider the views, if any, of the settlor and the trustees concerning the continued usefulness or relevance of the trust and the proposed variation.

(8) If the court finds it is unable to approve a scheme to substitute a purpose for a non-charitable purpose trust under subsections (5) and (6), it may order that the trust property be returned to the settlor or to the settlor's personal representative.

(9) Subsections (5) and (6) do not apply if:

a. the trust document or declaration contains a legally valid direction concerning the ultimate disposition of the trust property, or

b. the intention of the settlor concerning the ultimate disposition of the trust property can be inferred from the trust document or declaration and is legally valid.[196]

The draft legislation posits, in s 44(5)(a) and (b), two different standards of similarity between the original non-charitable purpose and the substituted purpose. It suggests that, where the purpose of the settlor is narrowly conceived, another purpose broadly consistent will be acceptable. The lower threshold of similarity—choosing a purpose 'not contrary to the spirit of the original settlement'—was considered by the Commission to be particularly valuable in allowing the court to avoid the 'rather undignified position' of having to match

[195] Manitoba LRC, *Non-Charitable Purpose Trusts* (1992); British Columbia LRC, *Non-Charitable Purpose Trusts* (1992), and earlier: *Non-Charitable Purpose Trusts* (Working Paper No 66, 1991).

[196] This provision was intended to be a new s 44 of the Law and Equity Act, RSBC 1979, c 224, but it has not been implemented in new version of that Act. See also: art 103 of the Manitoba LRC proposal.

the settlor's capricious purpose with another equally as useless project—'[a]llowing the court to substitute any useful purpose except one that is diametrically opposed to the spirit of the settlement ... would avoid an unseemly exercise in whimsy'.[197] The possibility of a resulting trust was preserved in this proposed Bill, in s 44(8), in the unlikely event that the court found it impossible to substitute a new purpose for the settlor's original purpose. If, as in *Re Denley*, the settlor explicitly provides a gift-over in default of the purpose being possible or practicable, that must be observed under the terms of the Bill. A *cy-près* application of the property will then be excluded. As a further boundary around the donor's intention in the context of non-charitable trusts (especially given the absence of a general charitable intent and definition of charity which ring-fences that intention for charitable trusts *cy-près*), the court is compulsorily directed to consider the views of the settlor and the trustees.

It should be noted in passing that, in order to allow non-charitable purpose trusts to take effect in *some* fashion, one approach that has been adopted in Ontario[198] (and followed in other Canadian provinces[199]) has been to treat a non-charitable purpose trust as a *power*, rather than as a trust. A power only *enables*, but does not oblige, the holder of the power to deal with the property; it follows that if a nominated non-charitable purpose is, or becomes, impossible or impracticable, the property does not have to applied in any event. This supposedly circumvents any *cy-près* problems. There will simply be a resulting trust for those persons entitled in default of appointment. However, these enactments have been considered to be problematical at best,[200] and English courts have declined to follow the approach of treating a purpose trust as a power.[201]

Leaving that possibility to one side, as the enactments from offshore jurisdictions, and the proposals of British Columbia, clearly demonstrate, it is possible to successfully draft a version of the *cy-près* doctrine for non-charitable trusts.

---

[197] British Columbia LRC, *Non-Charitable Purpose Trusts* (1992) 53. See, especially, the explanatory notes accompanying the Draft Bill in this report: 'still allows the court to supply a new purpose, rather than let the trust fail. The new purpose must not defeat the settlor's original intention, however, or else no one would set up a non-charitable purpose trust'.

[198] Perpetuities Act, RSO 1990, c P9, s 16.

[199] See, for further discussion, OLRC, *Report on the Law of Charities* (1996) 442, fn 18.

[200] OLRC, *ibid*, 441–44, identifying seven distinct problems with the Ontario provision; nor did the BC Commission consider its jurisdiction's equivalent provision in s 21 satisfactory, as discussed in: *Report on Non-Charitable Purpose Trusts* (1992) 34–38. Problems also noted in: JA Dash, 'Purpose Trusts: The Nevis Perspective' (2003) 9(8) *Trusts and Trustees* 8, 8.

[201] *In re Astor's ST; Astor v Scholfield* [1952] Ch 534, 546–47; *In re Endacott (decd); Corpe v Endacott* [1960] Ch 232 (CA) 246; *Inland Revenue Commissioners v Broadway Cottages Trust* [1955] Ch 20 (CA) 36 ('a valid power cannot be spelt out of an invalid trust'). Cf: J Mowbray *et al*, *Lewin on Trusts* (17th edn, Sweet & Maxwell, London, 2000) 4–43, who suggest that an *express* power for the trustees to devise a method of achieving a non-charitable object would be valid, and also: *Lewin on Trusts: First Supplement to the Seventeenth Edition* (Sweet & Maxwell, London, 2003) 4–43, citing: *Twinsectra Ltd v Yardley* [2002] UKHL 12, 2 AC 164 in support of that proposition.

The best of these have some key hallmarks. They specify that the original purposes must be reasonable (so as to exclude purely self-indulgent purposes); define the triggers for implementation of a *cy-près* scheme; require some degree of similarity between the original and the substituted purposes; and permit evidence to be drawn from the settlor or trustees when determining that substituted purpose.

C NON-CHARITABLE PUBLIC APPEALS

The difficulties associated with undersubscribed (or oversubscribed) charitable public appeals have been previously considered.[202] Where the public appeal is non-charitable, the primary question remains (as was the case for the charitable appeals): are the donations held on resulting trust for the donors? If they are not (and if the appeal itself or its governing rules are silent about the destination of the funds, should the purpose fail), then the only destination available for the unused monies is to pass as *bona vacantia*.

The competing tensions between a resulting trust of donations and their devolving to the Crown are discussed in section 1. Notwithstanding occasional indications to the contrary,[203] the general law position is that a *cy-près* scheme is not appropriate where a public appeal fails as a trust for non-charitable purposes. The extent to which this position has been relaxed or overturned is discussed in section 2.

1. Resulting Trust Back to the Donor

The manifest difficulties of finding that donations to a public appeal were to revert on resulting trust to the donors emerged in *In re Gillingham Bus Disaster Fund; Bowman v Official Solicitor*.[204] In December, 1951, a bus ran into a column of cadets who were marching along a road in Gillingham, killing 24 and injuring others. The mayors of Gillingham, Rochester and Chatham decided to open a memorial fund, and the town clerk of Gillingham wrote a letter to a daily newspaper, stating that the fund was 'to be devoted, among other things, to defraying the funeral expenses, caring for the boys who may be disabled, and then to such worthy cause or causes in memory of the boys who lost their lives, as the mayors may determine'. The appeal was very successful, and raised

---

[202] See ch 5.

[203] As held in *Sheppard v Bradshaw* (1921) 50 OLR 626, 64 DLR 624 (Ont HC), cited further as an example of incorrect law in: DWM Waters, *Law of Trusts in Canada* (2nd edn, Carswell, Toronto, 1984) 631, fn 57.

[204] [1958] Ch 300 (Harman J), aff'd, on other points, in: [1959] Ch 62 (CA).

almost £9,000; and the trust so created was non-charitable.[205] Following application of the funds raised by individual donations and street collections (and
other sources, possibly whist drives and concerts[206]), a surplus of £7,300 was
held (the small sum spent was attributable to admission of legal liability and
payment of compensation by the bus company).

Harman J considered that a resulting trust of the surplus was appropriate:

> the settlor or donor did not part with his money absolutely out-and-out but only
> sub modo to the intent that his wishes as declared by the declaration of trust should
> be carried into effect. When, therefore, this has been done any surplus still belongs to
> him. This doctrine does not, in my judgment, rest on any evidence of the state of mind
> of the settlor, for in the vast majority of cases no doubt he does not expect to see his
> money back . . . The resulting trust arises where that expectation is for some unforeseen
> reason cheated of fruition, and is an inference of law based on after-knowledge of the
> event.[207]

Harman J rejected the Crown's argument that the donated monies should be
treated as *bona vacantia*, based upon the following reasoning:

> I see no reason myself to suppose that the small giver who is anonymous has any wider
> intention than the large giver who can be named. They all give for the one object. If they
> can be found by inquiry the resulting trust can be executed in their favour. If they
> cannot, I do not see how the money could then . . . change its destination and become
> *bona vacantia*. It will be merely money held upon a trust for which no beneficiary can
> be found. Such cases are common and where it is known that there are beneficiaries the
> fact that they cannot be ascertained does not entitle the Crown to come in and claim.
> The trustees must pay the money into court like any other trustee who cannot find his
> beneficiary.[208]

The monies were duly paid into court,[209] and an inquiry was ordered to identify
the donors to enable return of the monies. The result was highly unsatisfactory.
Most donors were never traced, the money remained in Treasury for over three

---

[205] Some of the purposes were conceded not to be charitable, some (such as 'other worthy causes')
were not necessarily charitable, and the provision could not be validated under the Charitable Trusts
(Validation) Act 1954, c 58. The purpose of this Act was to restrict to charitable objects certain
instruments taking effect before 16 Dec 1952 which provided 'for property to be held or applied for
objects partly but not exclusively charitable'. This lastmentioned aspect of *Gillingham*, whilst applied
in: *In re Atkinson's WT; Atkinson v Hall* [1978] 1 WLR 586 (Ch), has not been followed in later
English decisions: *In re Wykes' (decd); Riddington v Spencer* [1961] Ch 229; *Ulrich v Treasury
Solicitor* [2005] 1 All ER 1059 (Ch) [28].

[206] These were mentioned in argument but not in the judgment itself. Harman LJ simply referred to
'street collections and so forth', a point of some significance noted in: *In re West Sussex Constabulary's Widows, Children and Benevolent (1930) Fund Trusts; Barnett v Ketteringham* [1971] Ch 1,
11.

[207] *Re Gillingham Bus Disaster Fund* [1958] Ch 300, 310. The court followed: *In re Hobourn Aero
Components Ltd's Air Raid Distress Fund* [1946] Ch 86, and distinguished: *Cunnack v Edwards*
[1896] 2 Ch 679 (CA).

[208] *Ibid*, 314.

[209] Under s 63 of the Trustee Act 1925, c 19. Payment into court means that the trustees obtain a
discharge of further responsibility for the trust monies.

decades, and in 1993, was finally distributed to 17 survivors of the disaster—
garnering them £400 each.[210]

The type of legal tussle evident in *Gillingham*—between resulting trust and
bona vacantia—has since arisen in the analogous context of company pension
schemes (where a contributory pension scheme is established for employees
on trust, where contributions from employers and employers are made, and a
surplus results);[211] and with respect to the appropriate destination of the funds
of defunct voluntary associations.[212]

Whilst *Gillingham* has been followed in Canada[213] and cited with approval
in Australia,[214] several factors indicate that its resulting trust approach has
lost judicial favour. The later authority of *In re West Sussex Constabulary's
Widows, Children and Benevolent (1930) Fund Trusts*[215] expressly declined
to follow *Gillingham*. Instead, it held that there was an intention on the part
of each anonymous donor to a non-charitable public appeal to part with
his money absolutely, and not just for the nominated purpose (which, in that
case, was to provide for the widows and orphans of deceased members
of the West Sussex Constabulary and other benevolent purposes). Consequently, where the original purpose could not be met, donations to collecting
boxes and the like were *bona vacantia*. (That portion attributable to known
donations and legacies was held on a resulting trust for the donors/testators
or their estates.)

Other authorities have also rejected the resulting trust approach. As has been
noted previously,[216] Upjohn J's decision in *In re Hillier's Trusts; Hillier v A-G*[217]
endorsed the absolute gift (out-and-out) approach, at least so far as anonymous
donations are concerned.[218] As Oakley notes,[219] however, any statements which
are made in the context of *charitable* appeals, are merely *obiter*. In the view of
that author, the question of whether anonymous donations for non-charitable
purposes which fail are held on resulting trust or are *bona vacantia* remains to be

---

[210] G Moffat, *Trusts Law Text and Materials* (4th edn, CUP, Cambridge, 2005) 875, citing *The
Guardian*, 4 Dec 1993.

[211] See, especially: *Davis v Richards & Wallington Industries Ltd* [1990] 1 WLR 1511 (Ch)
1543–44; *Air Jamaica Ltd v Charlton* [1999] 1 WLR 1399 (PC).

[212] As discussed in, eg: MA Hickling, 'The Destination of the Funds of Defunct Voluntary
Associations' (1966) 30 *Conv* 117.

[213] *Re Canada Trust Co v Cantol Ltd* (1980), 103 DLR (3d) 109 (BCSC) [14] (pension trust).

[214] *Radmanovich v Nedeljkovic* [2001] NSWSC 492 (15 Jun 2001).

[215] [1971] Ch 1, 13 (Goff J).

[216] See pp 158, 204.

[217] [1954] 1 WLR 9 (Ch) 21–22.

[218] On appeal in *In re Hillier's Trusts; Hillier v A-G* [1954] 1 WLR 700 (CA) 715, Denning LJ
contrasted the views of Harman J in *Gillingham* and Upjohn J in *Hillier* and expressly approved of the
latter. Also endorsing the *Hillier* approach: *In re Welsh Hospital (Netley) Fund; Thomas v A-G* [1921]
1 Ch 655, 659–60 (PO Lawrence J); *In re North Devon and Somerset Relief Fund Trusts; Hylton v
Wright* [1953] 1 WLR 1260 (Ch) 1266–67 (Wynn-Parry J).

[219] AJ Oakley, *Parker and Mellows Modern Law of Trusts* (8th edn, Sweet & Maxwell, London,
2003) 301–2.

settled in English law, given the opposing views adopted in *Gillingham* and in *West Sussex Constabulary*.[220]

The contractarian theory has also been used to deny a resulting trust in pension funds,[221] defunct societies,[222] and public appeal[223] cases. According to this theory, where the donors paid for a reciprocal benefit, they were entitled only to what they contracted for, and once they had obtained it, there was no intention on the part of the donors to retain any beneficial ownership. Finally, to further dent the resulting trust approach, it has been held[224] that, whilst the clearest indication will be required to rebut such a trust, that rebuttal can be either by an express provision or by implication.

It is true that, whilst rejecting the *Gillingham* approach avoids the hassles of a resulting trust, a finding of 'ownerless' property passing as *bona vacantia* entails some problems of its own. It has been judicially stated to be 'a result which should not lightly be imputed to any transferor.'[225] It is plain that, on occasion, courts would prefer to find *some* owner for an unexhausted donation rather than none, to avoid the property passing to the Crown.[226] As Martin notes, there is a suggestion that to treat the donated monies as *bona vacantia* is to 'tak[e] the line of least resistance in a manner unauthorised by law.'[227]

Some law reform opinion,[228] however, has favoured the *bona vacantia* approach over any purported *cy-près* application of unused donations (were

---

[220] *Ibid*, 305.

[221] *Palmer v Abney Park Cemetery Co Ltd* (Ch, 4 Jul 1985), cited, although not necessarily endorsed, in: *Davis v Richards & Wallington Industries Ltd* [1990] 1 WLR 1511 (Ch) 1540. Scott J considered that the fact that employee contributors to a pension fund had obtained everything that they had contracted for did not necessarily prevent there being a resulting trust in their favour. On this point, see: S Gardner, 'New Angles on Unincorporated Associations' [1992] *Conv* 41.

[222] *Cunnack v Edwards* [1896] 2 Ch 679 (CA) (fund established by subscriptions to provide for widows of deceased members; surplus remained in fund after death of last widow; funds passed *bona vacantia*; it was never contemplated that the fund would end, so subscribers presumed to have intended to abandon any interest in the monies when making the donation; members of the society had received all that they contracted for pursuant to the subscription). Also: *Braithwaite v A-G* [1909] 1 Ch 510, 519.

[223] Eg: *In re West Sussex Constabulary's Widows, Children and Benevolent (1930) Fund Trusts* [1971] Ch 1.

[224] *Davis v Richards & Wallington Industries Ltd* [1990] 1 WLR 1511 (Ch). A resulting trust of employees' contributions to a pension fund was excluded in this case, and the property was treated as *bona vacantia*.

[225] *Jones v Williams* (Ch, Knox J, 15 Mar 1988), cited in: *Davis, ibid*, 1541.

[226] Eg, as in the case of what is to happen to the funds of a dissolved society: *In re Bucks Constabulary Widows' and Orphans' Fund Friendly Society (No 2)* [1979] 1 WLR 936 (Ch); *In re GKN Bolts and Nuts Ltd (Automotive Division) Birmingham Works, Sports and Social Club* [1982] 1 WLR 774 and *In re Sick and Funeral Society of St John's Sunday School, Golcar* [1973] 1 Ch 51. Nor did the Privy Council favour *bona vacantia* in the case of pension contributions in: *Air Jamaica Ltd v Charlton* [1999] 1 WLR 1399 (PC).

[227] JE Martin, *Hanbury and Martin Modern Equity* (17th edn, Sweet & Maxwell, London, 2005) 245, citing Harman J in *In re Gillingham Bus Disaster Fund* [1958] Ch 300.

[228] OLRC, *Report on the Law of Charities* (1996) 448 ('if the donor no longer takes an interest in the disposition of the property, then state purposes supported by the consolidated revenue fund are as valid as any *cy-près* charitable purpose').

that to be authorised by statute). It is argued that an intent to abandon the monies as an out-and-out gift (which must be found if the property is to devolve to the Crown) is rather removed from an intention on the part of the donor to benefit analogous purposes. The mere fact that the donor abandoned the beneficial interest in the monies does not impute that the donor intended them to be applied *cy-près*. Furthermore, given the difficulties with framing a *cy-près* doctrine in the absence of a general charitable intent and a definition of charity, the *bona vacantia* approach is arguably preferable in cases of non-charitable public appeals.

In spite of such misgivings, the *cy-près* application of donated monies for non-charitable public appeals has been favoured and/or encouraged in several key instances, a matter to which attention will now turn.

2. *Cy-près* Applications of Donated Monies

(a) The available options

Clearly, a *cy-près* application of unused donations raised for a non-charitable appeal, whilst impossible to achieve at general law, has the benefit of both convenience and appeasement. There is no question of publicly-raised funds languishing in court whilst the almost impossible effort of identification of original donors is carried out; and there is no threat of property passing to the Crown to be used for governmental policies with which the settlor may have disagreed. That this issue is contentious, however, is illustrated by the fact that *cy-près* application of unused donations for non-charitable appeals has received law reform approval,[229] disagreement,[230] and turnaround of opinion.[231] There are, in practice, three possible mechanisms by which a *cy-près* application in this context may occur.

First, the Crown itself may endorse it. As mentioned in the previous chapter,[232] where public appeal monies remain unexpended, where a resulting trust is denied, and where the Crown takes the property as *bona vacantia*, it is always open to the Crown to waive its right to the property and seek application of the property via a *cy-près* scheme. In England, this has been judicially said to be the 'usual approach',[233] which may be taken to comprise some form of encouragement for the practice. The Crown's willingness to seek a *cy-près* distribution in

---

[229] British Columbia LRC, *Report on Informal Public Appeal Funds* (1993) 19–20 ('Surpluses in both charitable and non-charitable funds should be available to meet other valid needs').

[230] OLRC, *Report on the Law of Charities* (1996) 447–48.

[231] Note the change in view between *ibid*, and OLRC, *Report on the Law of Trusts* (1984) 472, where a *cy-près* application of non-charitable public appeal monies was recommended.

[232] See p 157.

[233] *In re Ulverston & District New Hospital Building Fund; Birkett v Barrow and Furness Hospital Management Committee* [1956] 1 Ch 622 (CA) 630.

this regard has been said to have a certain analogy to its prerogative *cy-près* power, which must be invoked where outright gifts to charity fail.[234]

Secondly, the terms of the appeal may permit a *cy-près* distribution. In England, guidelines prepared by the Charity Commission recommend that the terms of the non-charitable appeal itself clearly indicate the destination of any surplus, and that analogous purposes should be permitted under the appeal.[235] Other law reform opinion has similarly urged the wording of the appeal 'to make it clear to donors at the outset that if any money is not needed for the primary purpose of the fund, it will be used in other specified ways.'[236] In other words, the rules of the public appeal themselves may permit a *cy-près* application of monies raised for non-charitable public appeals.

Thirdly, some statutes permit donations for public appeals to be applied *cy-près*, in circumstances where these public appeals are for purposes which are defined by the statute far more widely than what would be strictly charitable at law. Certain State legislatures in Australia (discussed in the following section), and provincial legislatures in Canada,[237] have adopted this initiative. It tends to follow from the very nature of public appeals that any *cy-près* application permitted by these statutes will impute a public benefit.[238] The particularly interesting issues for the Australian State legislatures, at least, have concerned whether a resulting trust should arise where donors are identifiable, and what degree of similarity should exist between the appeal's original purpose and the new application. Opinion has differed on these points.

The following three Australian State jurisdictions provide a convenient sample of the inconsistent ways in which the *cy-près* application of non-charitable public appeals have been legislatively handled.[239]

(b) Some statutory examples

In Queensland, the legislature has specifically provided, in the Collections Act 1966, for what is to happen if donors give money to a 'disaster relief fund' (which may include non-charitable purposes), and that money is not used for the purpose for which it was given. These disaster funds are defined as 'raised by or resulting from any appeal for support for the purpose of assisting persons suffering distress, whether physical, mental or financial, as a result of any

---

[234] OLRC, *Report on the Law of Charities* (1996) 448. See, on this topic, pp 23–6.

[235] Ch Comm for England and Wales, *Disaster Appeals, Attorney General's Guidelines* (CC40, 1992) especially the forms of appeal reproduced in section 3.

[236] British Columbia LRC, *Report on Informal Public Appeal Funds* (1993) 16.

[237] Eg, from Nova Scotia: Trustee Act, RSNS 1989, c 479, s 52(3). This legislation was substantially endorsed in the BC *Report, ibid*, 20–21.

[238] OLRC, *Report on the Law of Charities* (1996) 447.

[239] See, for further detailed discussion, eg: D Ong, *Trusts Law in Australia* (Federation Press, Sydney, 1999) 327–31; G Dal Pont, *Charity Law in Australia and New Zealand* (OUP, Oxford, 2000) 330–44.

catastrophe or disaster arising from natural causes, inevitable accident, wilful act or negligence'.[240]

The preconditions for the operation of the legislation do not duplicate the *cy-près* doctrine—instead, if there has been no payment from that fund for a year or more, or if the disaster relief fund has ceased to operate, or was never set up,[241] then the donations are to be transferred to a statutorily created and overarching 'disaster appeals trust fund',[242] whereupon other disaster relief funds can be supplemented with funds from this overarching fund, as required.[243] There is no requirement that this alternative application of the donated monies be for a charitable purpose, but only for another disaster scenario.

By separate legislation, the Charitable Funds Act 1958 (Qld), a *cy-près* scheme can be effected whenever a trust of a fund which was raised by public collection fails, and where those public collections were made for 'benevolent or philanthropic purposes' or 'public purposes'[244] (ie, non-charitable purposes can be included). The fund will 'fail' in circumstances which traverse much wider territory than the traditional *cy-près* doctrine, *viz*:[245]

(a) it becomes impossible or impracticable or inexpedient to carry out the purpose or all or any of the purposes for which a fund was established or is held; or
(b) the property available in the fund proves inadequate to carry out such purpose or all or any of such purposes; or
(c) such purpose or all or any of such purposes has or have been already effected; or
(d) the property available in the fund is more than sufficient to meet all reasonable requirements for such purpose or all or any of such purposes; or
(e) such purpose has or all or any of such purposes have ceased to exist; or
(f) such purpose is or all or any of such purposes are uncertain or cannot be identified or is or are not sufficiently defined; or
(g) such purpose is or all or any of such purposes are illegal

Any *cy-près* application of the donated monies must be made in favour of other charitable purposes (as that term is defined widely in the Act). Importantly, where contributions to public collections from identifiable donors have occurred, then unless there is some contrary intention expressed by the donor, a resulting trust in their favour arises. The legislation states that the donation shall be taken to have been contributed for the 'particular and exclusive purpose for which [it] was solicited'.[246] The donor, who can be identified either at the time of the donation or thereafter, may, within a specified period, demand the return of his donation from the trustees of the fund.

---

[240] Collections Act 1966, s 35B(1).
[241] *Ibid*, ss 35B(2), 35C(4).
[242] *Ibid*, s 35A(1).
[243] *Ibid*, s 35B(10).
[244] Charitable Funds Act 1958, s 2 'Definitions'.
[245] *Ibid*, s 5.
[246] *Ibid*, s 20(1).

In New South Wales, the legislation[247] is differently drafted. Any so-called 'dormant funds' can be used for some purpose other than that for which the fund was acquired. The relevant donated funds include those which have been collected for any 'charitable purpose' or for any 'purpose of a public character'. The latter is defined[248] beyond what is strictly charitable at law, to mean any fund 'which is directed to the benefit of the public or a section of the public', including for parks and gardens, war and public memorials, or for relief of war.

The circumstances in which the fund will be regarded as 'dormant' are described[249] in far wider terms than the traditional *cy-près* doctrine:

(1) The Commissioner may determine a fund to be a dormant fund if satisfied that:

(a) for at least the immediately preceding 6 years, the trustees have not used the fund genuinely for the purposes for which it was donated, collected or otherwise acquired, or
(b) it is not practicable to use the fund for those purposes, or
(c) it is unlikely that those purposes will be achieved within a reasonable time, or
(d) the trusts, or the objects of the trusts or the purposes, for which the fund was donated, collected or otherwise acquired are uncertain or cannot be ascertained . . .

In that event, the Commissioner is to give due consideration to any representations made by trustees or other interested parties, and then formulate proposals for the application of the dormant fund,[250] which must be approved by either the Attorney-General or by a committee of referees, depending upon the size of the fund.[251]

The newly formulated purposes do not necessarily have to be the same or analogous to the original purpose of the donations.[252] The legislation explicitly provides that referees are not bound to follow the *cy-près* principle when formulating proposals.[253] This leeway contrasts with the cautionary note of the British Columbia Law Reform Commission which stated on this issue, '[i]n order for the public to accept re-allocation readily, the purpose to which the surplus is directed should be similar enough to the original one for donors to think their intentions are being respected.'[254] No resulting trust is stated to apply in respect of identifiable donations, unlike the abovementioned Queensland legislation.

A third variation upon the statutory theme is provided by Western Australia's Charitable Collections Act 1946. This statute provides that where property is collected for a war fund, and such property is not or will not be required for that original purpose, then such property 'shall be applied to purposes connected

---

[247] The Dormant Funds Act 1942 (NSW).
[248] *Ibid*, s 2.
[249] *Ibid*, s 5A.
[250] *Ibid*, s 11.
[251] *Ibid*, ss 12, 13.
[252] *Ibid*, s 11(2).
[253] *Ibid*, s 18.
[254] *Report on Informal Public Appeal Funds* (1993) 20.

with the present war' unless the Minister directs otherwise[255] (presumably, if there was no relevant war, then the funds would be diverted to 'any other charitable purpose' as permitted for other types of public appeal). This statute represents an unusual example of the legislature dictating a very close *cy-près* application of unused donations which are garnered via public appeal.

3. Public Appeals for Private Persons

To close this section, it is appropriate to briefly consider the scenario where a public appeal is mounted on behalf of specific person/s (hereafter, X) for their care and maintenance, and the monies collected for the appeal are not expended for that purpose. For example, the purpose may become impossible, either due to X's death or cure. The trust created by the public appeal may be construed as a trust for non-charitable purposes (given that it is not for the *public* benefit and hence, cannot be charitable[256]), or it may be construed as a private trust for X as beneficiary, where the enunciated purpose is merely a motive, but does not import a purpose trust. In either event, the same question arises: what happens to the surplus when the purpose for which the appeal was raised can no longer be fulfilled?

Under the general law, two different outcomes have occurred. In *In re Trusts of the Abbott Fund*,[257] it was held that the donors who subscribed to a fund for the maintenance of two deaf and dumb ladies must have intended the fund to be used only for those costs associated with their care, and following their deaths, the surplus was to be held on resulting trust for the donors. This result has been described variously as 'unusual',[258] and 'unfortunate' for possibly giving rise to the *Gillingham* scenario.[259] On the other hand, in *In re Andrew's Trust; Carter v Andrew*,[260] where an appeal was raised for the education of the children of a deceased clergyman, the court held that the surplus in the fund (following the completion of their education) belonged to the children absolutely. The purpose of educating the children was merely the motive for the gift; it was not a pre-condition to distribution to the children; the donations themselves were intended as absolute gifts, with the donors retaining no beneficial interest in the monies. Under this latter construction (which would not be possible if the trust were treated as a pure purpose trust), if X chooses not to pursue an education at all, X can still take the property.[261]

---

[255] Charitable Collections Act 1946, s 16(1).

[256] E Cairns, 'Appeals and Fund Raising' (1994) 2 *PCB* 126, 128.

[257] [1900] 2 Ch 326.

[258] JE Martin, *Hanbury and Martin Modern Equity* (17th edn, Sweet & Maxwell, London, 2005) 246.

[259] British Columbia LRC, *Report on Informal Public Appeal Funds* (1993) 16.

[260] [1905] 2 Ch 48. See also: *In re Osoba (decd); Osoba v Osoba* [1979] 1 WLR 247 (CA); *Barlow v Grant* (1684) 1 Vern 255.

[261] See p 184.

The British Columbia Law Reform Commission proposed[262] a third outcome for a surplus raised by public appeal for X, via legislation: a *cy-près* application of the surplus, which it envisaged would usually be at the application of the trustee or donor, but with a right reserved to X to appear and make submissions with respect to the use of the surplus. Notably, the types of Australian provisions considered in the previous section, which allowed for *cy-près* application of public appeal monies, could not apply to a public appeal for the benefit of X, given that the statutes required that the appeals be for the public or a section of it, or be of a public character. No such limitation was included by the British Columbia Commission, for it expressly recommended that public appeals for *specified individuals* ought to be covered by its proposals. The key provisions of the draft legislation provided:

> X.5.(2) Subject to subsection (8) and section X.6, the court may approve a scheme to distribute money or other property remaining in a public appeal fund if it is no longer needed or cannot be used for the purpose described in the appeal.
>
> (6) A scheme for distribution of money or other property remaining in a non-charitable public appeal fund may allow the money or other property to be used for either:
>
> (a) a charitable object, or
> (b) a non-charitable object consistent with the spirit of the appeal.
>
> . . .

If the *Andrew's* approach was held to apply, such that the surplus belonged beneficially to X for whose benefit the fund was raised, then the Commission recommended that the court should lack the power to approve a *cy-près* scheme to re-allocate the surplus without X's consent:

> (9) Subsections (2) to (8) do not apply if a person has a beneficial interest in the money or other property remaining in a public appeal fund that would entitle the person, if that person were under no legal disability, to demand the transfer to that person of the money or other property absolutely, unless that person consents to their application.

This draft legislation, however, has not been enacted to date.

A further non-charitable public appeal that has occurred from time to time is an appeal for the victims of a disaster, regardless of need. In such a case, none of the heads of *Pemsel's* case will be satisfied, even if the appeal arises out of a disastrous event, as Cairns explains:

> A gift for the benefit of . . . the victims of the disaster without reference to their needs will not be charitable since it will be for the benefit of individuals rather than for a public purpose. If, therefore, the intention is to make benefits available to the victims or relatives of those affected by the disaster in order to compensate them for their involvement regardless of need, which was apparently the case with the fund raised

---

[262] British Columbia LRC, *Report on Informal Public Appeal Funds* (1993) 24.

after the Penlee Lifeboat disaster, the fund should be established on a non-charitable basis. . . . The relief of those involved in the disaster or their relatives and dependants who are in financial need, the relief of those who are sick or injured as a result of the incident or the relief of hardship or suffering caused by or resulting from the disaster will be good charitable purposes.[263]

Failure to draft the appeal by reference to need on the part of the victims will render it non-charitable, and will preclude the *cy-près* doctrine from applying to any surplus.

---

[263] E Cairns, 'Appeals and Fund Raising' (1994) 2 *PCB* 126, 128.

Part II

The *Cy-près* Doctrine in the Context of Litigious Remedies

Part II discusses the application of the *cy-près* doctrine to the remedies granted in court actions—where the remedy sought by the plaintiffs is not possible or feasible, and the 'next best justice' is permitted. A *cy-près* solution has been variously allowed in class actions litigation (where damages are sought for and on behalf of a class of plaintiffs), and in contractual disputes (where the remedy of specific performance is sought). The *cy-près* doctrine, in this context, may entail some 'approximation' to justice in two respects—the persons who ultimately receive the damages or other property may vary from those recipients who were originally intended, or the property to be conveyed may vary somewhat from that which was originally stipulated. Whatever the context, not all jurisdictions have uniformly embraced these concepts. The *cy-près* doctrine, in respect of litigious remedies, remains controversial, inconsistent, and at times, ill-defined.

7

Class Actions Cy-près: An Introduction

A INTRODUCTION

THE NOTION UNDERPINNING class actions *cy-près* is that where a judgment or settlement has been achieved against a defendant, and where distribution to the class of plaintiffs who should strictly receive the sum is 'impracticable' or 'inappropriate', then (subject always to court approval) the damages should be distributed in the 'next best' fashion in order, as nearly as possible, to approximate the purpose for which they were awarded.[1] In other words, where a *cy-près* trigger manifests, the court orders that the damages, whose original purpose was to compensate those victims harmed by the defendant's unlawful conduct, be distributed 'for the indirect prospective benefit of the class.'[2] This phrase is something of a misnomer, for even non-class members—those who suffered no loss or damage whatsoever—may benefit under *cy-près* orders within the class actions context.

It has frequently been judicially acknowledged by American courts, in particular, that the *cy-près* doctrine applicable in class actions jurisprudence is derived from, and intended to be analogous to, the doctrine's application to charitable trusts.[3] For example, the charitable trust doctrine (it has been stated):

---

[1] *In re Folding Carton Antitrust Litig*, 557 F Supp 1091, 1108 (ND Ill 1983). Another good definition is drawn from the South African Law Comm, *The Recognition of a Class Action in South African Law* (Working Paper 57, 1995) [5.38] ('application of [an aggregate] award in a way which compensates or benefits the class members, where actual division and distribution of the award among the class members is impossible or impracticable').

[2] *Powell v Georgia-Pacific Corp*, 119 F 3d 703, 706 (8th Cir 1997), citing: HB Newberg and A Conte, *Newberg on Class Actions* (3rd edn, Shepard McGraw-Hill Inc, Colorado Springs, 1992) § 10.17. See also, for early American academic endorsement: Deems, 'The *Cy-près* Solution to the Damage Distribution Problems of Mass Class Actions' (1975) 9 *Georgia L Rev* 893, 904, and SR Shepherd, 'Damage Distribution in Class Actions: The *Cy-près* Remedy' (1972) 39 *U Chicago L Rev* 448, 452, both cited and explained further in: OLRC, *Report on Class Actions* (1982) 573.

[3] Eg: *In re Holocaust Victim Assets Litig*, 311 F Supp 2d 407, 415–16 (EDNY 2004) ('[t]he *cy-près* doctrine developed in the context of testamentary charitable trusts. Where a trust would otherwise fail, a court would attempt to fulfill the testator's charitable intent "as near as possible". . . . The same basic notion is now employed in class action settlements such as this one'). Also, the analogy is noted in, eg: *In re Compact Disc Minimum Advertised Price Antitrust Litig*, 2005 US Dist LEXIS 11332, at 7 (D Maine 2005); *Van Gemert v Boeing Co*, 573 F 2d 733, fn 7 (2nd Cir 1978); *Schwartz v Dallas Cowboys Football Club Ltd*, 362 F Supp 2d 574, 576 (ED Pa 2005); *In re 'Agent Orange' Prod Liab Litig*, 611 F Supp 1396, 1403 (EDNY 1985); *In re Department of Energy Stripper Well Exemption Litig*, 578 F Supp 586, 594 (D Kans 1983); *In re Matzo Food Prods Litig*, 156 FRD 600, 605 (DNJ 1994); *Brewer v Southern Union Co*, 1987 US Dist LEXIS 15940, at 7 (D Colo 1987); *In re Folding Carton Antitrust Litig*, 557 F Supp 1091, 1108–9 (ND Ill 1983); *Pray v Lockheed Aircraft Corp*,

originated to save testamentary charitable gifts that would otherwise fail. Under *cy-près*, if the testator had a general charitable intent, the court will look for an alternate recipient that will best serve the gift's original purpose. In the class action context, it may be appropriate for a court to use *cy-près* principles to distribute unclaimed funds. In such a case, the unclaimed funds should be distributed for a purpose as near as possible to the legitimate objectives underlying the lawsuit, the interests of class members, and the interests of those similarly situated.[4]

Essentially, the doctrine allows the damages award or settlement sum to be distributed to the 'next best' class whenever the class members (or some of them—*cy-près* funds often deal with residual parts of class actions judgments or settlements) are unable to be compensated individually.[5] The *cy-près* fund varies inversely with the number of claims made by individual class members,[6] and can also result from a 'trickle-on' effect where damages funds set aside for designated categories of plaintiffs have not been fully dispersed.[7]

This chapter will deal with some introductory matters concerning class actions *cy-près*. Section B discusses the various terminology, and the two main strands of application, associated with the doctrine. The manifestation of class actions *cy-près* in the leading jurisdictions which have implemented opt-out class action regimes is outlined in Section C, whilst the principal alternatives to *cy-près* orders in this context—from reversionary orders in favour of the defendant to the damages simply falling into governmental coffers—are explored in Section D.

B THE WIDE AND NARROW MEANINGS OF 'CY-PRÈS'

This field of jurisprudence is, unfortunately, rife with terminological obfuscation. The descriptors, '*cy-près*' and 'fluid recovery' appear, on occasion, to be

---

644 F Supp 1289, 1303 (DDC 1986); *In re Wells Fargo Securities Litig*, 991 F Supp 1193, 1194 (ND Cal 1998); *Six (6) Mexican Workers v Arizona Citrus Growers*, 641 F Supp 259, 265 (D Ariz 1986).

[4] *Airline Ticket Commission Antitrust Litig Travel Network Ltd v United Air Lines Inc*, 307 F 3d 679, 682 (8th Cir 2002), citing: *In re Airline Ticket Commission Antitrust Litig*, 268 F 3d 619, 625–26 (D Minn 2001); *Democratic Central Committee of District of Columbia v Washington Metro Area Transit Comm*, 84 F 3d 451, 455 fn 1 (DC Cir 1996).

[5] *Weber v Goodman*, 1998 US Dist LEXIS 22832, at 16 (EDNY 1998); *Democratic Central Committee of District of Columbia v Washington Metro Area Transit Comm*, 84 F 3d 451, 455 (DC Cir 1996).

[6] Note the discussion and cases cited in: RA Higgins, 'The Equitable Doctrine of Cy-près and Consumer Protection' (Annex 1, ACA Submission, Trade Practices Act Review, 15 Jul 2002) 4 and fn 13.

[7] As occurred in, eg: *Ford v F Hoffmann-La Roche Ltd* (SCJ, 23 Mar 2005) [65] ('no unclaimed money will be repaid to the Settling Defendants. Any monies not paid out of the Direct Purchaser Fund will trickle down to the Consumer Fund. The Intermediate Purchaser Fund and Consumer Fund will be fully distributed *cy-près*'). For lawyers' representatives' comments on this settlement outcome, see: J Jaffey, 'Settlement Reached on Vitamin Price-Fixing' (2005) *Lawyers' Weekly* Vol 24 No 6. Incidentally, termed a 'pour-over provision' by Higgins, *ibid*.

used interchangeably in American case law.[8] This tendency has met with critical comment. Leading American commentators Conte and Newberg note that 'fluid recovery' is an 'imprecise and misleading phrase,[9] whilst the OLRC declared that it would avoid use of the term altogether, explaining that it was a case whereby 'terminological confusion in the United States reache[d] its height', and that 'fluid class recovery' was used in many different ways by various commentators.[10]

The first coinage of the phrase, 'fluid class recovery'/'fluid recovery', appears to have occurred in *Eisen v Carlisle & Jacquelin*.[11] In circumstances where Judge Tyler was concerned with the potentiality of administering a fund against which many millions of class members could make claims,[12] he described 'fluid class recovery', somewhat obscurely, as 'distribution of damages to the class as a whole rather than to adopt, at this initial, planning stage, an inflexible mold of recovery running to specific class members.'[13] On another note, 'fluid recovery' has also been considered[14] to represent only one strand of *cy-près* distribution, namely, price-rollbacks (considered later in the chapter[15]). To avoid confusion, the term '*cy-près*' will be adopted exclusively throughout this Part.

1. The *Cy-près* Doctrine in its 'Narrow Sense'

In its strictest sense, the class actions *cy-près* doctrine encompasses two branches, as described in *Simer v Rios*: 'the money is either distributed through a market system in the way of reduced charges or is used to fund a project which

---

[8] Eg, as evidenced in: *Six (6) Mexican Workers v Arizona Citrus Growers*, 904 F 2d 1301, 1307 (9th Cir 1990); *In re Phenylpropanolamine (PPA) Products Liability Litig*, 214 FRD 614, 620 (WD Wash 2003); *Friedman v Lansdale Parking Authority*, Fed Sec L Rep (CCH) P98,676 (ED Pa 1995); *Weber v Goodman*, 1999 US Dist Lexis 22832, at 16 (EDNY 1998). Also noted by Deems, 'The *Cy-près* Solution to the Damage Distribution Problems of Mass Class Actions' (1975) 9 *Georgia L Rev* 893, 894–95, as cited in: *In re Folding Carton Antitrust Litig*, 557 F Supp 1091, 1108 (ND Ill 1983).

[9] A Conte and HB Newberg, *Newberg on Class Actions* (4th edn, Thomson West, St Paul Minn, 2002) vol 3, § 10.17 p 519.

[10] OLRC, *Report on Class Actions* (1982) 537.

[11] 52 FRD 253 (SDNY 1971), 'fluid class recovery'. A database search confirms that the first use of the term 'fluid recovery' occurred in: *In re Memorex Securities Cases*, 61 FRD 88, 102 (ND Cal 1973), which attributed that phrase to *Eisen*. Also, *Eisen* noted to be the first occurrence of the phrase in: RA Higgins, 'The Equitable Doctrine of *Cy-près* and Consumer Protection' (Annex 1, ACA Submission, Trade Practices Act Review, 15 Jul 2002) fn 12.

[12] The class action the subject of the litigation in *Eisen* involved approximately 6 million class members, who had engaged in odd-lot transactions (transfers involving less than 100 shares) during the period from May, 1962 to June, 1966, and who had been wrongfully charged an odd-lot differential per transaction.

[13] *Eisen, ibid*, 261. The phrase was quickly endorsed, although distinguished on the facts of the case, in: *City of Philadelphia v American Oil Co*, 53 FRD 45, 72 (DNJ 1971).

[14] Judicially indicated in: *In re 'Agent Orange' Products Liability Litig*, 597 F Supp 740, 840 (EDNY 1984); and academically indicated in: NA DeJarlais, 'The Consumer Trust Fund: A *Cy-près* Solution to Undistributed Funds in Consumer Class Actions' (1987) 38 *Hastings LJ* 729, fn 3.

[15] See pp 218–22.

will likely benefit the members of the class.'[16] In other words, and acknowledging differences in terminology to describe them,[17] a *cy-près* distribution in its narrow meaning embraces either, respectively, price-rollback distributions or organisational-benefit distributions.

The South African Law Commission provided illustrative examples of these two different methods of application:

> where an award assessed in respect of damages suffered as a result of pollution of the environment is used to clean up the environment for the benefit of those affected, or to provide a health service to remedy the ills caused by the pollution [organisational-benefit distribution *cy-près*] . . . . [or] where the individual claimants are regular users of a service in respect of which there has been an overcharge and the court orders compensation by way of a reduction in the charges for the service for a certain period of time [price-rollback *cy-près*].[18]

These two methods warrant some further inspection.

(a) *Price-rollback* cy-près

The price-rollback method requires that the unclaimed part of the damages fund is 'distributed'[19] by way of lowering the purchase price of the defendant's product (goods or services) for a set time period.[20] It particularly applies to those scenarios where defendants have sold a product to a large number of customers, and have illegally overcharged a great majority, if not all, of them—while each class member's damages are often too small to warrant a claim, the defendant

---

[16]   661 F 2d 655, 675 (7th Cir 1981) (footnotes omitted), cited, eg, in: *In re Motorsports Merchandise Antitrust Litig*, 160 F Supp 2d 1392, 1394 (ND Ga 2001); *Weber v Goodman*, 1998 US Dist LEXIS 22832, at 16 (EDNY 1998); *Democratic Central Comm*, 84 F 3d 451, 455 (DC Cir 1996). Also, see these two options as expressed in *Jones v National Distillers*, 56 F Supp 2d 355, 357 (SDNY 1999) : 'the funds are usually paid to a third party . . . for designated purposes. Alternatively, . . . undistributed class funds may be used for the prospective benefit of individual class members and others similarly situated, e.g., future class members who engage in future transactions of the type involved in the class litigation (price reduction or market distribution).' Also: *Mace v Van Ru Credit Corp*, 109 F 3d 338, 345 (7th Cir 1997) (it is a 'procedural device that distributes money damages either through a market system (eg, by reducing charges that were previously excessive), or through project funding (the project being designed to benefit the members of the class)').

[17]   Eg, the OLRC describes these as, respectively, price reduction and benefit distributions: *Report on Class Actions* (1982) 574–76. Also called 'lump sum distributions' and 'price mitigation distributions'.

[18]   South African Law Comm, *The Recognition of a Class Action in South African Law* (Working Paper 57, 1995) [5.38].

[19]   Although, strictly speaking, it is not—rather, the damages fund is never created: *State of California v Levi Strauss and Co*, 41 Cal 3d 460, 488, 224 Cal Rptr 605 (1986) ('I suggest that the "price rollback" remedy is not a method of distributing "residue" . . . but an alternative to the creation of residue': per Grodin J). However, as DeJarlais notes, notwithstanding, price-rollback *cy-près* is commonly regarded as under the umbrella of *cy-près* distributions: NA DeJarlais, 'The Consumer Trust Fund: A *Cy-près* Solution to Undistributed Funds in Consumer Class Actions' (1987) 38 *Hastings LJ* 729, fn 138.

[20]   As explained and applied in, eg: *Bebchick v Public Utilities Comm*, 318 F 2d 187, 203–4 (DC Cir 1963) (note that this was a non-class action brought for overcharging); *Colson v Hilton Hotels Corp*, 59 FRD 324, 326 (ND Ill 1972).

has reaped a substantial wrongful enrichment that the class action will seek to disgorge.[21]

Price-rollback *cy-près* has a number of key features. It is a distribution of damages to individuals, rather than an aggregate distribution to a deserving third party organisation which the alternative method of *cy-près* represents. It is directed to those who are engaged in future transactions, and invariably seeks to make the product the focus of the class action less expensive in the future.[22] Those who benefit from the price reduction may feasibly comprise all, most, some or none of the original class members for whom the class action was instituted. Judicially, price reduction has been noted[23] to be especially appropriate for 'remedying overcharges on items which are repeatedly purchased by the same individuals'; and academically, it has been said[24] to have the advantages of a low cost remedial method, whereby class members are not required to prove their claims, and the court only bears the cost of enforcing the price reductions.

The price-rollback *cy-près* alternative has been used in the following instances:[25]

- transit riders were overcharged by the defendant transit system owners—20% of the damages were distributed by reducing future fares;[26]
- defendant brokerage firms were accused of monopolising odd-lot trading on the New York Stock Exchange and of charging excessively high brokerage commissions—one proposal for distributing any unclaimed damages was to reduce the odd-lot differential until the unclaimed monies were depleted[27] (the proposal was not approved on appeal, however[28]);

[21] *In re 'Agent Orange' Products Liability Litig*, 597 F Supp 740, 840 (EDNY 1984).

[22] The distinctions are drawn out by, eg, A Conte and H Newberg, *Newberg on Class Actions* (4th edn, Thomson West, St Paul Minn, 2002) § 10.17 p 519, § 10.18 p 521.

[23] Eg: *Democratic Central Committee of District of Columbia v Washington Metropolitan Area Transit Comm*, 84 F 3d 451, 455 (DC Cir 1996), citing: *Bebchick v Public Utilities Comm*, 318 F 2d 187, 204 (DC Cir 1963). Overcharging is an oft-cited example of *cy-près* distribution, eg: GD Watson, 'Ontario's New Class Action Legislation' [1992] *Butterworths J of Intl Banking and Financial Law* 365, 366; M McGowan, 'Certification of Class Actions in Ontario' (1993), 16 CPC (3d) 172, 175.

[24] AL Durand, 'An Economic Analysis of Fluid Class Recovery Mechanisms' (1981) 34 *Stanford L Rev* 173, 181ff, and cited in: RA Higgins, 'The Equitable Doctrine of *Cy-près* and Consumer Protection' (Annex 1, ACA Submission, Trade Practices Act Review, 15 Jul 2002) fn 23.

[25] See, for discussion of some of these and other examples: *Brewer v Southern Union Co*, 1987 US Dist LEXIS 15940, at 14 (D Colo 1987), and in *In re 'Agent Orange' Products Liability Litig*, 597 F Supp 740, 841 (EDNY 1984).

[26] *Bebchick v Public Utilities Comm*, 318 F 2d 187, 203–4 (DC Cir 1963).

[27] *Eisen v Carlisle & Jacquelin*, 52 FRD 253, 265 (SDNY 1971).

[28] *Eisen v Carlisle & Jacquelin*, 479 F 2d 1005, 1010–12, 1017–18 (2d Cir 1973), where the District Court's use of a *cy-près* scheme was rejected on the basis that it avoided constitutionally required notice to each class member, dispensed with individual calculation of damages, and distributed the damages to future traders who were not necessarily members of the class. As Conte and Newberg note, this case is notable for the fact that the US Supreme Court vacated the decision (reported at 417 US 156, 94 S Ct 2140), and expressly left the question about the validity of the *cy-près* scheme open: *Newberg on Class Actions* (4th edn, Thomson West, St Paul Minn, 2002) § 10.18 p 522, § 10.20 p 527.

- taxi customers were overcharged because the defendant unlawfully altered the meters of its cabs—settlement funds were applied to reduce the fares below the authorised maximum fares;[29]
- the daily room rate at Hilton Hotels had been overcharged because of an improper charge on incoming phone calls—the room rate was reduced by $0.50 per night under the terms of the settlement;[30] and
- food was falsely labelled—and settlement funds were used to reduce beef prices.[31]

Despite the number of instances in which this *cy-près* method has been employed, some frequent criticisms of the method have emerged.[32] For example, price-rollbacks have been alleged to provide a competitive advantage to defendant manufacturers, compared to lawfully operating manufacturers in the same market. Essentially, the damages fund is being used to subsidise lower prices, which paradoxically may increase the defendant's business.[33] It also consolidates the defendant's market share, if the class members are forced to buy the defendant's product in order to recoup the losses that they sustained. The District Court of Colorado noted that the price-rollback method—

> is particularly appropriate in a monopolistic service industry . . . because the reduction of . . . prices would neither affect competitors nor a company's production decisions, but would provide a direct benefit to consumers, most of whom would be members of the litigating class.[34]

Given the abovementioned problems, Karas observes that, '[i]n competitive markets, therefore, price rollbacks must be minimal.'[35]

---

[29] *Daar v Yellow Cab Co*, 67 Cal 2d 695, 433, 63 Cal Rptr 724 (1967).

[30] *Colson v Hilton Hotels Corp*, 59 FRD 324 (ND Ill 1972).

[31] *Reich v Dominick's Finer Foods Inc*, No 78CH5667 (Ill Cir Ct Cook Co, 11 Jul 1980).

[32] For observations and criticisms listed in the text, see, academically: OLRC, *Report on Class Actions* (1982) 576–79; DA Crerar, 'The Restitutionary Class Action' (1998) 56 *U of Toronto Faculty of L Rev* 47, fn 223; A Conte and HB Newberg, *Newberg on Class Actions* (4th edn, Thomson West, St Paul Minn, 2002) § 10.18 p 523–24; S Karas, 'The Role of Fluid Recovery in Consumer Protection Litigation' (2002) 90 *Californian L Rev* 959, fn 71; A Borrell and W Branch, 'Power in Numbers: BC's Proposed Class Proceedings Act' (1995) 53 *Advocate* 515, 524–25; RA Higgins, 'The Equitable Doctrine of *Cy-près* and Consumer Protection' (Annex 1, ACA Submission, Trade Practices Review, 15 Jul 2002) 8; S Borenstein, 'Settling for Coupons: Discount Contracts as Compensation and Punishment in Antitrust Lawsuits' (1996) 39 *Journal of Law and Economics* 379; SB Farmer, 'More Lessons from the Laboratories: *Cy-près* Distributions in *Parens Patriae* Antitrust Actions Brought by State Attorneys General' (1999) 68 *Fordham L Rev* 361, 393; K Barnett, 'Equitable Trusts: An Effective Remedy in Consumer Class Actions' (1987) 96 *Yale LJ* 1591, 1598–99; NA DeJarlais, 'The Consumer Trust Fund: A *Cy-près* Solution to Undistributed Funds in Consumer Class Actions' (1987) 38 *Hastings LJ* 729, 754–55.

[33] *State of California v Levi Strauss and Co*, 41 Cal 3d 460, 473–74, 224 Cal Rptr 605 (1986) ('[t]his method is not appropriate in nonmonopoly markets like the jeans market since it compels consumers to collect their refunds by making further purchases of the defendant's products, to the detriment of the defendant's competitors').

[34] *Brewer v Southern Union Co*, 1987 US Dist LEXIS 15940, at 14 (D Colo 1987). Also noted in: *Democratic Central Committee of District of Columbia v Washington Metropolitan Area Transit Comm*, 84 F 3d 451, 456 (DC Cir 1996)

[35] S Karas, 'The Role of Fluid Recovery in Consumer Protection Litigation' (2002) 90 *Californian L Rev* 959, fn 71.

Secondly, and as intimated previously, matching victims to *cy-près* beneficiaries can be very difficult under price-rollback. The distribution method has been said[36] to have considerably less value when the nature of the product dictates that consumers are unlikely to repeatedly purchase the product or service, where the consumers alter their purchasing behaviour individually or *en masse* because of external factors (say, transport or access problems), or where the product or service falls in demand because it is replaced by something more attractive in the market place. Even where 'repeat business' does occur, if the price of the goods or services is fixed by independent retailers or other entities rather than by the defendant wrongdoer, then ensuring that price-rollbacks are indeed passed on to the consumer may be extremely difficult to verify.[37] Moreover, the defendant's customers may change, pre- to post-unlawful behaviour. Users of public transport, brokerage firms, hotel rooms, and food outlets fluctuate. A lack of cross-over between original class members and would-be *cy-près* beneficiaries has denied a price-rollback, for judicial fear that the order would thereby provide a windfall benefit to complete strangers to the litigation.[38]

Thirdly, if a price-rollback would adversely affect the consuming public, it is unlikely to be ordered. Such adversity can arise in a myriad of ways. For example, if one of the plaintiff class members would be disadvantaged (because reduced costs would impact upon one of those plaintiff's businesses too[39]), or if it would 'cost' the consumer in terms of time, effort or inconvenience to purchase at the lower price,[40] then the method will prove unsuitable. Alternatively, a defendant may try to 'counter' a price-rollback order at the consumers' expense—by compromising the quality of its product via cheaper manufacturing processes for the duration that the price is ordered to be reduced, or by simply producing less of it.[41] A court order that seeks to employ a *cy-près* distribution

---

[36] *State of California v Levi Strauss and Co*, 41 Cal 3d 460, 474, 224 Cal Rptr 605 (1986). See also: *In re Mexico Money Transfer Litig*, 164 F Supp 2d 1002, 1018 (ND Ill 2000) ('[t]he court recognizes the concern that a [*cy-près*] settlement benefits class members only to the extent they are willing to do repeat business with the alleged wrongdoers. Here that concern is ameliorated in part by the evidence that most class members engage in money transfer transactions relatively frequently and that these Defendants account for the vast majority of the market').

[37] *Levi Strauss, ibid* ('the price of jeans to the consumer is fixed not by the defendant, but by independent retailers. Hence, a price rollback would pose difficult if not insuperable management problems').

[38] Eg: *City of Philadelphia v American Oil Co*, 53 FRD 45, 72 (DNJ 1971), and cited with approval on this point in: *Six (6) Mexican Workers v Arizona Citrus Growers*, 904 F 2d 1301, 1308 (9th Cir 1990).

[39] *Brewer v Southern Union Co*, 1987 US Dist LEXIS 15940, at 14 (D Colo 1987) ('in this case, a price reduction distribution would result in a very small dividend to gas consumers, at a very large cost to the distributor, plaintiff Public Service Company of New Mexico. The Court rejects the price reduction distribution as a means to allocate the Surplus Funds').

[40] Noted, eg, in: NA DeJarlais, 'The Consumer Trust Fund: A *Cy-près* Solution to Undistributed Funds in Consumer Class Actions' (1987) 38 *Hastings LJ* 729, 755, citing the theories put forward in: 'An Economic Analysis of Fluid Class Recovery Mechanisms' (1980) 34 *Stanford L Rev* 173, 187.

[41] See DeJarlais, *ibid*, 755; RA Higgins, 'The Equitable Doctrine of *Cy-près* and Consumer Protection' (Annex 1, ACA Submission, Trade Practices Act Review, 15 Jul 2002) 8.

by dictating the price at which to sell does not fetter the defendant's discretion as to the quality or quantity of units sold. On a similar note, it has been judicially acknowledged that a price-rollback scheme will not be ordered if the cost to the defendant of implementing it would produce only 'nominal benefits' to the consumers of the product.[42]

A final criticism is that price-rollback schemes do have potential for permitting double recovery by class members who participate in individual recoveries and then also avail themselves of price reductions when the surplus of the judgment or settlement is applied via price-rollback.[43] Given that damages are finite, this double recovery must be at the expense of non-claiming class members.

(b) Organisational-distribution cy-près

Under this *cy-près* distribution method (also called 'earmarked escheat' or a 'consumer trust fund'), unclaimed class action fund monies are given to a designated entity, and used to fund a project, institution or study, which will be likely to indirectly assist the class members as a group. As the District Court of New York described in *Jones v National Distillers*:

> [a] frequent use of class funds not accruing to the class members is a donation to a public or otherwise non-profit entity combating harms similar to those that injured the class members. Such a donation may serve the *cy-près* principle of indirectly benefitting all class members.[44]

Industry representative bodies and foundations, consumer organisations, universities, research institutes, entities from each of the manufacturing, wholesaling and retailing sectors (say, farmers, distributors and pharmacies, respectively), consumer advocacy groups, an institution that can research or monitor the substantive law on which the litigation is based, law schools—all have directly benefited from the *cy-près* doctrine in this context, for the indirect benefit of those whom they serve or service. The recipient may be either newly established or long-existing.[45]

---

[42] As decided in: *Brewer v Southern Union Co*, 1987 US Dist LEXIS 15940, at 18 (D Colo 1987).

[43] A concern expressed in: *Eisen v Carlisle & Jacquelin*, 479 F 2d 1005, 1017 (2d Cir 1973), and subsequently reiterated in, eg: OLRC, *Report on Class Actions* (1982) 577; A Conte and HB Newberg, *Newberg on Class Actions* (4th edn, Thomson West, St Paul Minn, 2002) § 10.20 p 527.

[44] 56 F Supp 2d 355, 358 (SDNY 1999).

[45] JR McCall *et al*, 'Greater Representation for California Consumers—Fluid Recovery, Consumer Trust Funds and Representative Actions' (1995) 46 *Hastings LJ* 797, 850. For an interesting discussion of the establishment of the Institute for Consumer Antitrust Studies, a US non-partisan, independent academic centre designed to explore the impact of antitrust law enforcement on the individual consumer and to shape public policy, from *cy-près* distributions from antitrust class actions, see: SW Waller, 'The Future of Private Rights of Action in Antitrust' (2004) 16 *Loyola Consumer L Rev* 295.

North American examples of this application of *cy-près* include the following:[46]

- in a class action brought for damages for misrepresentation concerning a drug used to treat hypothyroidism, the parties agreed to distribute the aggregate amount of the settlement by way of a *cy-près* distribution to selected organisations, hospitals and universities (University Health Network, Hospital for Sick Children, Dalhousie University, University of Alberta, Centre for Research into Women's Health, and Thyroid Foundation of Canada), all of which were conducting research into thyroid disease, and providing education and outreach services, which would be likely to serve the interests of the class members;[47]
- in a class action for vitamin price-fixing, and because of significant problems in identifying possible class member plaintiffs below the manufacturer level, the monies allocated by settlement to intermediaries such as wholesalers and consumers were agreed to be paid by a *cy-près* distribution to specified not-for-profit entities;[48]
- in a class action for economic losses consequential upon a 1979 nuclear reactor accident, which achieved a settlement of $25 million, one-fifth of that sum was set aside 'for a Public Health Fund . . . to finance studies of the long term health effects of the . . . incident and to further evacuation planning for the future';[49] and
- in a class action for antitrust violations concerning the purchase by almost 2 million people of a satellite television package of National Football League (NFL) football games, approximately $436,000 in unclaimed funds remained, where cheques issued to class members were not cashed—the excess monies were paid to NFL Youth Education Town Centres.[50]

This method of damages distribution has received much favourable support.[51] It offers a cost-effective and judicially efficient *cy-près* distribution method; achieves the tripartite goals of disgorgement, deterrence and compensation; and

---

[46] For additional examples, see, in the US: *West Virginia v Chas Pfizer & Co*, 314 F Supp 710, 734 (SDNY 1970); *In re 'Agent Orange' Product Liability Litig*, 611 F Supp 1396, 1410 (EDNY 1985); *State of Calfornia v Levi Strauss & Co*, 224 Cal Rptr 605, 614, 617 (1986). In Canada: *Ford v F Hoffmann-La Roche Ltd* (SCJ, 23 Mar 2005) [92] (settlement monies 'distributed to consumer organizations for activities related to Vitamin Products, such as food and nutritional research, education and food programs, consumer services, or consumer protection activities for the indirect benefit of Consumers of all ages'). For a very recent example, involving a class suit against DuPont, the inventors of Teflon, in respect of its non-stick pan coating, in respect of which the set-up of a medical research facility was mooted, see: J Doran, 'DuPont sued for $5bn over Teflon cancer claims', The Times (Business), 20 Jul 2005, 41.

[47] *Tesluk v Boots Pharmaceutical plc* (2002), 21 CPC (5th) 196 (SCJ) [9] (520,000 class members).

[48] *Alfresh Beverages Canada Corp v Hoechst AG* (2002), 16 CPC (5th) 301 (SCJ) [15]. For a first-hand practitioner perspective of this important decision, see: CM Wright and MD Baer, 'The Growth of Private Rights of Action Outside the US: Price-fixing Class Actions—A Canadian Perspective' (2004) 16 *Loyola Consumer L Rev* 463.

[49] *In re Three Mile Island Litig*, 557 F Supp 96, 97 (MD Pa 1982).

[50] *Schwartz v Dallas Cowboys Football Club Ltd*, 362 F Supp 2d 574, 577 (ED Pa 2005).

[51] See, eg, the various arguments discussed in: RA Higgins, 'The Equitable Doctrine of *Cy-près* and Consumer Protection' (Annex 1, ACA Submission, Trade Practices Review, 15 Jul 2002) 10; NA DeJarlais, 'The Consumer Trust Fund: A *Cy-près* Solution to Undistributed Funds in Consumer Class Actions' (1987) 38 *Hastings LJ* 729, 763 ('it is the most effective way to benefit all injured consumers, regardless of their socio-economic status').

is more likely to reach lower socio-economic classes of plaintiffs. Not all proposals of this type will be successful, however. For example, where the plan is to designate funds to establish an institution that is regarded by the court as unnecessary and which would provide no benefit to the class members whatsoever, the proposal will be rejected.[52]

2. The *Cy-près* Doctrine in its 'Wider Sense'

(a) A *wider connotation of damages* distribution

In contrast to the two methods of *cy-près* outlined above, the doctrine within the class actions context has sometimes been judicially described in far wider terms in the United States. Where a settlement or judgment has been reached, and the time has arrived for distribution of the fund to the class members, the District Court of Colorado, in *Brewer v Southern Union Co*,[53] offered five options for such distribution. These do not entirely coalesce with the aforementioned categories: (1) plaintiff fund-sharing; (2) reversion; (3) general or specified escheat to a governmental body; (4) lump sum distribution; and (5) price reduction distribution. Only the fourth and fifth of these match the sense in which the South African Law Commission, for example, illustrated the *cy-près* doctrine. In this chapter, the other three categories will be considered as alternatives to the strict use of *cy-près*, and will be considered shortly.[54]

It should be noted at this juncture that, when considering the question of damages distribution, courts in the United States have been driven by four goals, all of which will become significant when considering the triggers for, and the recipients of, a *cy-près* distribution: 'direct compensation, disgorgement, deterrence, and equity for absentee class members.'[55]

(b) A *wider connotation of damages* computation

The *cy-près* doctrine and terminology, in its wider sense, extends to the very *calculation* of the damages to which the class is entitled. As the court explained in *Six (6) Mexican Workers v Arizona Citrus Growers*,[56] the terms '*cy-près*' or 'fluid recovery' have both been defined more widely by some courts to encompass the *whole* procedure of calculating damages on a classwide, aggregate basis, without reference to the individual losses sustained by the class

---

[52] *In re Folding Carton Antitrust Litig*, 744 F 2d 1252, 1254–55 (7th Cir 1984) (funds applied to establish an 'unneeded Foundation' that would provide no benefit to class members).

[53] 1987 US Dist LEXIS 15940, at 7 (D Colo 1987). Similar options were also described, for example, in: *Six (6) Mexican Workers v Arizona Citrus Growers*, 904 F 2d 1301, 1307 (9th Cir 1990).

[54] See pp 244 ff.

[55] K Barnett, 'Equitable Trusts: An Effective Remedy in Consumer Class Actions' (1987) 96 *Yale LJ* 1591, 1594.

[56] 641 F Supp 259, 265 (D Ariz 1986), citing: HB Newberg, *Newberg on Class Actions* (2nd edn, Shepard McGraw-Hill Inc, Colorado Springs, 1985) § 10.17 p 374 fn 127.

members, followed by distribution of the unclaimed fund in the 'next best' manner.

This much wider application of *cy-près*, for the purposes of damages *computation*, has been highly controversial in the United States. It has been held that the difficulties in proving individual damages, as required under antitrust statutes, for example, cannot be avoided by using some variation of the *cy-près* doctrine.[57] The Ninth Circuit noted,[58] in an early decision under the modern US class action regime that is contained in Rule 23 of the Federal Rules of Civil Procedure (FRCP),[59] that *cy-près* recovery significantly altered substantive rights under antitrust statutes, wrongfully dispensed with individualised proof of damages, and was 'clearly prohibited' by the Rules Enabling Act promulgating the FRCP. Over two decades later, the District Court of Pennsylvania was equally as troubled by yet another attempt to circumvent substantive legal requirements:

> Assuming that Losch, as class representative, establishes that PP&L violated the antitrust laws, such a finding amounts at most to the equivalent of a declaratory judgment on the issue of violation. To establish PP&L's liability for treble damages, individual plaintiffs must subsequently come forward armed with individualized proof of fact of damage and amount of damages ... Losch's 'aggregation' theory closely resembles 'fluid recovery,' a procedural vehicle used to avoid problems associated with determining individual damages issues by allowing gross damages on behalf of 'the class as a whole.' ... Once the factfinder determines cumulative classwide damages, the defendant pays that sum into court, and then each class member must individually prove fact of damage and amount of damages to claim her share of the aggregate fund. ... By certifying the Limited Class, I would effectively empower Losch, which only represents itself for individual damages, to impose upon PP&L at a settlement table the yet unsubstantiated claims of several hundred individual potential claimants who remain unrepresented for damages purposes. No tortured interpretation of Rule 23 supports such an untoward result, which in my judgment would impede rather than advance an orderly and amicable resolution of all the claims in this litigation.[60]

The most notable—and unsuccessful—attempt to alter substantive law in this manner occurred in *Eisen v Carlisle and Jacquelin*',[61] a statutory anti-trust class action suit involving some 6 million class members which was filed against two large odd-lot brokerage firms. The average recovery of each class member (even after trebling of damages as the statute permitted) was estimated to be about $3.90. As the cost of obtaining and processing proofs of claim by 6 million individual class members would render the recoveries negligible, the trial court

---

[57] In *Six (6) Mexican Workers v Arizona Citrus Growers*, 904 F 2d 1301, 1305 (9th Cir 1990), citing, eg: *Windham v American Brands Inc*, 565 F 2d 59, 72 (4th Cir 1977).
[58] *In re Hotel Telephone Charges*, 500 F 2d 86, 90 (9th Cir 1974) (antitrust allegations based on a surcharge for telephone services imposed at a number of different hotels nationwide).
[59] Dealing specifically with the damages class action contained in: FRCP 23(b)(3).
[60] *Yeager's Fuel Inc v Pennsylvania Power & Light Co*, 162 FRD 482, 486–87 (ED Pa 1995).
[61] 479 F 2d 1005, 1018 (2d Cir 1973).

determined that aggregate damages for the class as a whole could be substituted for individual proof of damages.[62] However, as it was envisaged that few claims would be filed, the trial court simultaneously determined to permit the residue to be used to benefit all the odd-lot traders by reducing the surcharge fees imposed on odd-lot investors until the fund was depleted. Judge Tyler also anticipated that there was an adequate pattern of repeat transactions by share purchasers that would benefit those who engaged in future transactions at the reduced price. This approach was rejected by the Second Circuit Court of Appeals as an illegal alteration of the substantive requirement that damages must be individually proved.[63] The court was also concerned that, if such a settlement were agreed to, there were two potentials for windfalls—to the class members who had already claimed their odd-lot differential, and to those who would purchase shares in the future and who had not been overcharged in the past, and were hence not class members. At Supreme Court level,[64] the case was rejected upon other grounds, and the issue of fluid class recovery was not resolved. In *Six (6) Mexican Workers*,[65] the Ninth Circuit explained *Eisen* on the basis that a *cy-près* recovery in that case was entirely improper where it 'avoided constitutionally required notice to each class member, *dispensed with individual calculation of damages*, and distributed the damages to future traders who were not necessarily members of the class'.

Note, however, that where the class has sought to use the *cy-près* doctrine for the much more limited purpose of *distributing* any remaining unclaimed damage funds after judgment or settlement, and after the defendant's liability to each individual plaintiff has been established according to permissible principles of legal accuracy, the *cy-près* doctrine *has* been more readily permitted. In other words, where the *cy-près* distribution is being proposed only as a device for distributing damages, where the basis of those damages has either been individually calculated per class member, or can be lawfully calculated on an aggregate basis, the doctrine has received a warmer judicial acceptance. Certainly, the plaintiff class members in *In re Phenylpropanolamine (PPA) Products Liability Litigation*[66] sought to distinguish *Eisen* on this basis. They asserted that *cy-près* in their case 'would be used only for the purpose of distributing unclaimed, rather than unproven, damages', and noted that the Ninth Circuit in *Six (6) Mexican Workers* was prepared to *prima facie* allow a *cy-près* distribution 'for the limited purpose of distributing unclaimed funds',[67] in circumstances where

[62] *Eisen*, 52 FRD 253 (SDNY 1971).

[63] *Eisen*, 479 F 2d 1005, 1010, 1017–18 (2d Cir 1973).

[64] *Eisen*, 417 US 156, 172, 94 S Ct 2140 (1974), but the Supreme Court did vacate the entire judgment of the Second Circuit Court of Appeals.

[65] 904 F 2d 1301, 1305 (9th Cir 1990) (emphasis added).

[66] 214 FRD 614, 620 (WD Wash 2003).

[67] *Six (6) Mexican Workers v Arizona Citrus Growers*, 904 F 2d 1301, 1309 (9th Cir 1990), although, ultimately, the Ninth Circuit rejected the distribution plan as an abuse of the trial court's discretion because it 'does not adequately target the plaintiff class and fails to provide adequate supervision over distribution'.

the class members in that case sought damages under a statute which allowed damages not dependent upon proof of actual injury.[68] Whilst that proposition was accepted to be correct, a *cy-près* distribution was ultimately disallowed in the *Phenylpropanolamine* case because '[h]ere, the court's concerns lie in more than simply how to distribute unclaimed damages.'[69]

(c) Coupon recovery

In the class actions context, individual class members may recover (notably so, in the United States' class actions settlements) property in lieu of monetary damages, such as discount coupon awards. Whilst this type of 'in-kind' compensation also represents an approximation to that which was originally intended, it is the 'next best class' to which settlement or judgment sums are distributed which has generally attracted the '*cy-près*' tag, *per se*, in class actions litigation.

Coupon recovery on the part of class members has been heavily (although not necessarily uniformly[70]) criticised.[71] The following comment from Jones typifies the negative sentiment that tends to accompany this manoeuvre:

> Sometimes, settlements can be reached that are of deceptively little utility to the class members. One method which is gaining popularity is known as the 'in kind' or 'scrip' settlement, involving coupons or some other 'benefit' which will accrue to class members who continue to patronise the defendant. These kinds of settlements can be inherently problematic because they come at minimum cost to the defendant (which might even generate a profit from them), and are therefore inadequate or illusory as deterrent. In some cases, they provide class members with only chimeric compensation as well.[72]

In one of the more notable class action settlement proposals, that of *In re General Motors Corp Pick-up Truck Fuel Tank Products Liability Litigation*,[73] the substance of the claim was the alleged abnormally high occurrence of fuel-fed fires following side-impact collisions involving GM trucks. The class

---

[68] That is, class member plaintiffs sought statutory damages under the Farm Labor Contractor Registration Act.

[69] 214 FRD 614, 620 (WD Wash 2003).

[70] Note, eg, the comments by the Associate Director of the US Division of Enforcement in the Bureau of Consumer Protection in: Kolish, 'FTC Workshop—Protecting Consumer Interests in Class Actions' (2005) 18 *Georgetown J of Legal Ethics* 1161, 1183; and LM Mezzetti and WR Case, 'The Coupon Can be the Ticket: The Use of "Coupon" and Other Non-Monetary Redress in Class Action Settlements' (2005) 18 *Georgetown J of Legal Ethics* 1431, 1431 ('[r]ecognizing that some changes can be valuable or necessary is far different from demanding radical or overly complex reforms that will create undue burdens on parties' ability to settle class actions').

[71] Eg, for excellent discussion of the problems, see: GP Miller and LS Singer, 'Non-Pecuniary Class Action Settlements' (1997) 60 *Law and Contemporary Problems* 97; and CR Leslie, 'A Market-Based Approach to Coupon Settlements in Antitrust and Consumer Class Action Litigation' (2002) 49 *UCLA L Rev* 991.

[72] C Jones, *Theory of Class Actions* (Irwin Law Inc, Toronto, 2003) ch 5C(3)(a) [accessed online via Quicklaw database], citing, at fn 25, the *General Motors* case discussed in text above.

[73] 55 F 3d 768 (3d Cir 1995).

sought an order requiring GM to recall the trucks or pay for their repair. Under the settlement agreement, members of the settlement class were to receive $1,000 coupons redeemable toward the purchase of any new GM truck or Chevrolet light duty truck. This coupon recovery proposal drew the following objections:

- the coupons provided no cash value to the class members whatsoever;
- there was a limited redemption period of 15 months, which meant that if some car dealer class members could not replace their fleets (up to 1,000 vehicles each) within that time due to budgetary restrictions, they would lose the value of the coupons;
- fleet buyers' purchase patterns were dictated to some degree by statutory and regulatory constraints (described as 'competitive bidding procurement rules'), again rendering the coupons of questionable utility;
- the settlement made no provision for repairing the allegedly life-threatening defect in the vehicle's fuel tank; and
- only 14% of the class indicated that they would 'definitely' or 'probably' buy a new vehicle ($1,000 coupons went little way toward the list price of between $11,000 and $33,000 per vehicle), hence forecasting very low redemption rates.[74]

Judicial approval for the settlement proposal was ultimately denied.

As some memorably put it, if coupons are such an attractive method of compensation, why are the lawyers not paid in the same 'currency'![75] When in-kind coupon recovery is combined (as is usually the case) with a *cy-près* 'next best class' distribution of those coupons, the results have been academically viscerated, as the following comment in respect of the Californian antitrust class action against Microsoft Corporation illustrates:

Private attorneys general purporting to represent fourteen million California consumers settled these consumers' antitrust claims for $1.1 billion in, essentially, $20 vouchers; however, if the full amount of vouchers are not redeemed—and how could they be?—two-thirds of the residuary value will be distributed as vouchers to underprivileged schools throughout the state. This so-called '*cy-près*' voucher settlement triggers a central concern about class action attorneys, namely, that they serve their own interests and not those of their clients.[76]

[74] *Ibid*, 781–82.
[75] Especially: NC Scott, 'Don't Forget Me! The Client in a Class Action Lawsuit' (2002) 15 *Georgetown J of Legal Ethics* 561, 592, citing: Sen Grassley, Class Action Fairness Act of 1999: Hearings on s 353 Before the Senate Judiciary Comm Administrative Oversight and the Courts Subcomm, 106th Cong 77 (1999) 2; CR Leslie, 'A Market-Based Approach to Coupon Settlements in Antitrust and Consumer Class Action Litigation' (2002) 49 *UCLA L Rev* 991, Pt V, especially 1086–98.
[76] WB Rubenstein, 'On What a "Private Attorney General" Is—And Why it Matters' (2004) 57 *Vanderbilt U L Rev* 2129, 2132. Simple mathematics means that, under the settlement, 55 million vouchers would require redeeming in order for the fund to be completely exhausted. For another concise description of the conflicts inherent in, and difficulties with, in-kind settlements, see: LW Hensler, 'Class Counsel, Self-Interest and Other People's Money' (2004) 35 *U Memphis L Rev* 53, 72–80.

In fact, in one study, redemption rates for coupons in class action settlements have been put as low as 15%.[77] With that in mind, whether coupon recovery promotes any of the goals of class actions litigation—disgorgement of ill-gotten gains, compensation for injury and loss, or punishment for unlawful behaviour—has been stridently questioned in the United States. The practice has yet to see any equivalent under either Canadian or Australian class actions regimes.

C A SNAPSHOT OF LEADING CLASS ACTION JURISDICTIONS

The treatment of the *cy-près* doctrine in each of the leading class action jurisdictions of the United States, Canada and Australia, varies enormously. Differences extend to whether *cy-près* distribution is permitted at all, and (if it is), how it is implemented—by statute or by judicial precedent—and in what circumstances it is permitted. No two jurisdictions agree on these matters.

The jurisdiction of England, which has not implemented a generalist opt-out class action (instead, it adheres to an opt-in 'group litigation order' regime[78]) will not be considered in this section. Interestingly, quite apart from the persistent refusal to adopt the practice of jurisdictions elsewhere and implement an opt-out class action, various studies that have considered multi-party litigation reform in England have ignored the topic of *cy-près* recovery altogether.[79] Notably, however, some isolated calls for the introduction of a class action in England which have appeared in academic literature from time to time have also been accompanied, on occasion, by the suggestion that 'it should also be possible to make more creative awards, such as "fluid recovery" schemes which have been adopted in the United States'.[80]

---

[77] Noted by: BA Vauter, 'The Next Best Thing: Unclaimed Funds From Class Action Settlements' (2001) 80 *Michigan Bar J* 68 (accessed online, no pp available). The problem of low redemption coupon rates is also referred to frequently in the collection of conference papers based upon the FTC Workshop, 'Protecting Consumer Interests in Class Actions', 13–14 Sept 2004, reproduced in: (2005) 18 *Georgetown J of Legal Ethics*.

[78] Contained in Civil Procedure Rules 1998, Pt 19.III. For further discussion, see, eg, RP Mulheron, *The Class Action in Common Law Legal Systems: A Comparative Perspective* (Hart Publishing, Oxford, 2004) ch 4.

[79] The doctrine makes no appearance in, eg: Law Society Civil Litigation Committee, *Group Actions Made Easier* (1995); Lord Woolf, *Access to Justice Inquiry: Issue Paper* (1996); Lord Chancellor's Department, *Multi-Party Situations: Consultation Paper (including Draft Rules and Practice Direction)* (1999); Lord Chancellor's Department, *Representative Claims: Proposed New Procedures*, Consultation Response (2002); Lord Woolf, *Access to Justice: Final Report to the Lord Chancellor on the Civil Justice System in England and Wales* (1996).

[80] WCH Ervine, 'Multi-Party Actions' (1995) 23 *Scots Law Times* 207, 209. For further positive comment about the *cy-près* doctrine in the context of group litigation, see: GG Howells, 'Mass Tort Litigation in the English Legal System: Have the Lessons from Opren Been Learned?' in J Bridge *et al* (eds), *United Kingdom Law in the 1990s* (UK National Committee of Comparative Law, London, 1994) 609, 616–17; and by the same author: 'Litigation in the Consumer Interest' (2002) 9 *J Intl and Comparative Law* 1, 40.

1. Australia

Of the leading class actions jurisdictions, Australia is the odd one out—the Australian federal class action regime, contained within Pt IVA of the Federal Court of Australia Act 1976,[81] does not statutorily reference a *cy-près* distribution of all or any part of the judgment that a class may obtain against a defendant. Nor has a *cy-près* distribution yet been judicially endorsed under Pt IVA as part of a settlement against the defendant. Instead, s 33ZA(1) and (5) provide that, where a court establishes a fund consisting of money to be distributed to class members, and where the date by which class members were to have established their entitlement to be paid out of the fund has passed, the court may order the payment of any unclaimed sum to the defendant. Thus, whilst an award of damages in an aggregate amount, without specifying amounts to be awarded to individual class members, is permitted under the regime,[82] no *cy-près* distribution of any or all of that aggregate amount is allowed. Reversion to the defendant of any unclaimed amount is preferred to a *cy-près* distribution.

This is no doubt principally attributable to the fact that the 1988 law reform report[83] which preceded enactment of the federal regime was strongly critical of *cy-près* distributions. A much earlier ALRC discussion paper[84] had appeared to leave the *cy-près* option open, in addition to canvassing the alternative of paying any unclaimed residue into a class actions fund for the funding of future actions.[85] Ultimately, neither of these was embraced by the legislature. In 1988, the ALRC's rejection of *cy-près* distributions was comprehensive and four-fold.[86] First (it was said), a class action procedure was intended to *compensate* class members. It was not intended to penalise defendants or to deter behaviour to any greater extent than provided for under existing law, and a *cy-près* award was inconsistent with that primary compensatory function. Secondly, any damages award payable by the defendant ought to be matched as closely as possible to the class members' entitlement (thus, only victims who came forward with valid claims should represent the defendant's liability to that class). That precluded organisational-distribution payments to some third party entity, or price-rollback reductions for future purchasers who were not repeat purchasers, and who were not plaintiffs themselves. Thirdly, and mirroring the concerns expressed previously in *Eisen*,[87] a *cy-près* distribution could result in a windfall gain to non-class members, obtaining damages in return for no loss or injury caused by the defendant—and it could also result in a windfall to class members,

---

[81]   Pt IVA was inserted in the Federal Court of Australia Act 1976 (FCA) by s 3 of the Federal Court of Australia Amendment Act 1991, and commenced operation on 4 Mar 1992.

[82]   FCA, s 33Z(1)(f).

[83]   ALRC, *Grouped Proceedings in the Federal Report* (Rep No 46, 1988).

[84]   ALRC, *Access to the Courts—II: Class Actions* (DP No 11, 1979).

[85]   *Ibid*, [52], and see also the preceding discussion at [47]–[51].

[86]   *Grouped Proceedings in the Federal Court* (1988) [237]–[239].

[87]   See fn 28 above.

if the same persons were the recipients of a direct distribution of damages *and* a *cy-près* distribution of any unclaimed funds. Fourthly, it was said, the mechanism of damages distribution had nothing to do with enhancing access to the courts, the primary goal of a class actions regime.

On a further dismissive note, somewhat earlier in 1978, the Law Reform Committee of South Australia had proposed a class action for that State,[88] in which it was provided that the balance of any unclaimed funds should be paid into consolidated revenue.[89] The Chairman of the ALRC at the time, Justice Kirby, appeared also to approve of this view, noting that the South Australian rules had avoided '[t]he more disquieting features of "fluid recovery" by which courts [had] disbursed large class action funds in the United States'.[90]

Interestingly, Australia's law reform position appears somewhat isolated. Other class actions law reform bodies around the world, from Ireland,[91] Manitoba,[92] Alberta,[93] Ontario,[94] federal Canada,[95] Victoria,[96] and South Africa,[97] have expressly approved of *cy-près* recoveries (Scottish law reform has exhibited some diverse views over time, with some favouring *cy-près*[98] and some against[99]). Some significant Australian academic commentary[100] has

---

[88] Law Reform Committee of South Australia, *Relating to Class Actions* (1978).

[89] *Ibid*, 10.

[90] MD Kirby (the Hon), 'Class Actions: A Panacea or Disaster?' [1978] *Aust Director* 25, 31. See also the comments by the same author in: 'Procedural Reform and Class Actions' in MD Kirby (the Hon), *Reform the Law* (OUP, Melbourne, 1983) 156, 159–60.

[91] Ireland LRC, *Consultation Paper on Multi-Party Litigation* (CP No 25, 2003) [4.96], although the *cy-près* recommendation is one of several notable omissions in the Commission's Final Report, *Multi-Party Litigation* (Rep 76, 2005), undoubtedly a casualty of the Commission's notable turnaround of opinion from an opt-out regime in the Consultation Paper to an opt-in arrangement recommended in the Final Report.

[92] Manitoba LRC, *Class Proceedings* (1992) 103.

[93] Alberta Law Reform Institute, *Class Actions* (Rep No 85, 2000) [349] and recommendation No 18.

[94] OLRC, *Report on Class Actions* (1982) 581–82.

[95] Federal Court of Canada Rules Committee, *Class Proceedings in the Federal Court of Canada* (DP, 2000) 80–85.

[96] Victorian A-G's Law Reform Advisory Council, *Class Actions in Victoria—Time for a New Approach* (1997) [6.43].

[97] South African Law Comm, *The Recognition of Class Actions and Public Interest Actions in South African Law* (1998), recommendation No 18 and Draft Bill s 9.

[98] Scottish Consumer Council, *Class Actions in the Scottish Courts: A New Way for Consumers to obtain Redress?* (1982) [7.6.2] ('fluid recovery and *cy-près* schemes may only be devised in exceptional cases but the idea of permitting such flexibility in the giving of an appropriate remedy seems to deserve serious consideration').

[99] Scottish Law Comm, *Multi-Party Actions: Court Proceedings and Funding* (DP No 98, 1994) [7.73] ('We think that the fairest arrangement would be that any residue should simply be repaid to the defenders', citing the Australian legislation). The SLC did not endorse *cy-près* distributions in its final report: *Multi-Party Actions* (1996) [4.102].

[100] RA Higgins, 'The Equitable Doctrine of *Cy-près* and Consumer Protection' (Annex 1, ACA Submission, Trade Practices Act Review, 15 Jul 2002) 19–22; L Sylvan, 'The Next Best Thing' (2003) 95 *Consuming Interest* 19, 19; D Nelthorpe, 'Consumer Trust Funds' (1988) 13 *Legal Services Bulletin* 26, 26. Cf the opinion of one New Zealand commentator about fluid recovery as 'quite exceptional . . . and has met with little judicial acceptance': J Scott Emerson, 'Class Actions' (1989)

also vouched for the flexibility and deterrent effect that a *cy-près* distribution mechanism would offer under that jurisdiction's class actions regime, with one commentator pointing out the 'creative settlements' in the consumer credit area which have utilised the doctrine in the context of regulatory proceedings.[101]

To date, however, no case has implemented such a scheme, and its introduction appears to be unlikely, given the strong ALRC opinion which preceded it. Opportunities to revisit the topic have been infrequent at best. A subsequent pass-through of the provisions of the class action regime by the ALRC in 1999[102] was notable for the fact that *cy-près* distributions did not merit a mention, and the ALRC's recommendation therein[103] that a full review of the operation of Pt IVA should be commissioned has not occurred to date.

However, given the moderation with which the doctrine has been treated in Canada (the jurisdiction of interest in the following section), and the several advantages afforded by such schemes that have been evident in American jurisprudence, it is this author's contention that the Australian legislature would do well to consider amending the class action regime in Pt IVA to expressly permit, but not mandate, *cy-près* distributions for that jurisdiction. In doing so, and in learning from the experiences of jurisdictions elsewhere, statutory restrictions of the type described below could be usefully imposed upon the use of the doctrine, and the worst excesses of coupon recovery could be either statutorily or judicially disallowed.

2. Canada

(a) Statutory invocations

In contrast to the position under the Australian federal regime, the Canadian provincial jurisdictions have been more receptive to *cy-près* distributions as part of their class actions jurisprudence.

For example, *cy-près* recoveries against the defendant are statutorily

---

19 *Victoria Uni of Wellington L Rev* 183, 197. Also cf: BM Debelle, 'Class Actions for Australia? Do They Already Exist?' (1980) 54 *ALJ* 508, 515 (although note that this author discusses *cy-près* in its widest sense, *viz*, as an assessment of damages on a classwide basis). As Morabito notes, one of the aspects of the goal of behaviour modification in class actions is to make available to class members 'legal remedies which would otherwise not be available to them': V Morabito, 'Taxpayers and Class Actions' (1997) 20 *U New South Wales LJ* 372, 381, and that the failure to bestow sufficient emphasis upon that particular goal has had other unfortunate consequences in Australian class actions jurisprudence: V Morabito, 'The Federal Court of Australia's Power to Terminate Properly Instituted Class Actions' (2004) 42 *Osgoode Hall LJ* 473, 490.

[101] A Cornwall, 'Class Actions Get Go Ahead' (1995) 20 *Alternative LJ* 138, 139, referring to the action by Consumer Credit Legal Service against HFC Financial Services in 1987; HFC agreed, by way of settlement, to pay $2.25 million to a consumer fund; most of this was used to found and fund the Consumer Law Centre Victoria. This and further examples also cited in: Nelthorpe, *ibid*.

[102] ALRC, *Managing Justice* (Rep No 89, 1999).

[103] See Recommendation # 81, and *ibid*, [7.128].

permitted in Ontario[104] by a provision within the Class Proceedings Act 1992[105] which has been judicially described as 'novel',[106] and which was the subject of a split in the OLRC which recommended it:[107]

Section 26 (1) The court may direct any means of distribution of amounts awarded under section 24 [damages in favour of the class] or 25 [individual damages in favour of individual class members] that it considers appropriate.

. . .

(4) The court may order that all or a part of an award under section 24 that has not been distributed within a time set by the court be applied in any manner that may reasonably be expected to benefit class members, even though the order does not provide for monetary relief to individual class members, if the court is satisfied that a reasonable number of class members who would not otherwise receive monetary relief would benefit from the order.

(5) The court may make an order under subsection (4) whether or not all class members can be identified or all of their shares can be exactly determined.

(6) The court may make an order under subsection (4) even if the order would benefit,

    (a) persons who are not class members; or
    (b) persons who may otherwise receive monetary relief as a result of the class proceeding.

Other Canadian common law provinces have enacted similar provisions within their class actions statutes[108] (and Quebec's civil law-based system also permits *cy-près* distributions[109]). The Ontario statute further

---

[104] CPA (Ont), s 26(4), (6).
[105] SO 1992, c 6, which commenced operation on 1 Jan 1993.
[106] *Smith v Canadian Tire Acceptance Ltd* (1995), 22 OR (3d) 433 (Gen Div) [41].
[107] See OLRC, *Report on Class Actions* (1982), 'Chairman's Reservations', 852.
[108] Class Proceedings Act 2002, CCSM 2002, c C 130, s 34 (Manitoba); Class Actions Act 2001, SS 2001, c C–12.01, s 37 (Saskatchewan); Class Actions Act 2001, SNL 2001, c C–18.1, s 34 (Newfoundland and Labrador); Class Proceedings Act 2003, SA 2003, c C–16.5, s 34 (Alberta); Class Proceedings Act 1996, RSBC 1996, c 50, s 34 (British Columbia).
[109] Code of Civil Procedure, RSQ c C–25 (Book IX) arts 1034, 1036, the latter providing, 'The court disposes of the balance in the manner it determines, taking particular account of the interest of the members, after giving the parties and any other person it designates an opportunity to be heard.' The OLRC noted that the Quebec regime, as drafted, was 'somewhat obscure on this point, [but] appears to authorize *cy-près* distributions': OLRC, *Report on Class Actions* (1982) 580, but since then, academic opinion has more robustly declared the availability of *cy-près* distributions: WA Bogart, 'Questioning Litigation's Role—Courts and Class Actions in Canada' (1987) 62 *Indiana LJ* 665, 686.

provides[110] that, as a last resort, any part of an award that remains undistributed after the time period set by the court should be returned to the defendant. On the other hand, the British Columbia statute prefers the view that a *cy-près* distribution should be ordered, even in those circumstances, such that *no* part of the judgment sum should be returned to the defendant.[111] Whether the defendant should ever receive back part of the judgment levied against it is a philosophical question upon which the Canadian provincial legislatures have plainly disagreed. The question of reversion to the defendant is considered later in the chapter.[112]

It has been judicially acknowledged in Canadian courts that *cy-près* provisions in class action regimes serve the important policy objectives of general and specific deterrence of wrongful conduct, and that 'the private class action litigation bar functions as a regulator in the public interest for public policy objectives.'[113] The statutory incorporation of the *cy-près* doctrine is further evidence that class suits in this jurisdiction do not serve a solely compensatory function (a view entirely at odds with Australian law reform, legislative and judicial opinion[114]). Moreover, would the Canadian courts be prepared to be so innovative with remedial options, were it not for the explicit statutory authorisation of the *cy-près* doctrine? Some doubt this.[115]

(b) Divided views

Academically, the *cy-près* solution in the Canadian class actions setting has been supported on the various bases: that it does not ultimately matter who the *cy-près* recipients are, provided that complete disgorgement of ill-gotten gains occurs;[116] that the *cy-près* mechanism for dealing with the unclaimed money 'represents not a substantive abandonment of private law principles, but rather a procedural lapse, analogous to the expiry of a limitation period';[117] that it is particularly useful for 'small but widespread consumer economic losses';[118] that

---

[110]   CPA (Ont), s 26(1).

[111]   CPA (BC), s 34(1). In this respect, the BC legislature chose to follow the OLRC's recommendations, whereas the Ontario legislature did not, as noted in: AL Close, 'British Columbia's New Class Action Legislation' (1997) 28 *Canadian Business LJ* 271, 274–75.

[112]   See pp 250–2.

[113]   *Alfresh Beverages Canada Corp v Hoechst AG* (2002), 16 CPC (5th) 301 (SCJ) [15]–[16]; *Tesluk v Boots Pharmaceutical plc* (2002), 21 CPC (5th) 196 (SCJ) [16], cited in: *Ford v F Hoffmann-La Roche Ltd* (SCJ, 23 Mar 2005) [133].

[114]   See pp 230–2.

[115]   BS Du Val, 'Book Review' (1983) 3 *Windsor Ybk of Access to Justice* 411, 436, cited with approval in:WA Bogart, 'Questioning Litigation's Role—Courts and Class Actions in Canada' (1987) 62 *Indiana LJ* 665, 695.

[116]   C Jones, *Theory of Class Actions* (Irwin Law Inc, Toronto, 2003) ch 5C(3)(a) [accessed via Quicklaw database].

[117]   DA Crerar, 'The Restitutionary Class Action: Canadian Class Proceedings Legislation as a Vehicle for the Restitution of Unlawfully Demanded Payments, *Ultra Vires* Taxes, and Other Unjust Enrichments' (1998) 56 *U Toronto Faculty of Law Rev* 47, [89].

[118]   I Ramsay, 'Class Action: Class Proceedings Act 1992' [1993] *Consumer LJ* CS39, CS39.

cy-près distributions achieve, by one stroke, compensation, deterrence and the prevention of unjust enrichment, to a greater extent than, say, forfeiting the unclaimed monies to consolidated revenue;[119] and that *cy-près* distributions offer an important alternative to the average or proportionate distribution of aggregate damages among known class members.[120]

Not all reception to the *cy-près* doctrine in class actions jurisprudence in this jurisdiction has been positive, however. For example, Macdonald and Rowley expressed the concern,[121] in the early days of the Ontario law reform proposal, that this was a substantive amendment to 'long-recognized fundamentals' that would not be permitted if the case were instituted by a unitary plaintiff, and which introduced distortions into Canadian civil procedure. Lindblom and Watson noted that *cy-près* recoveries tend to demonstrate 'the need to sacrifice the uncompensated individual on the altar of prevention'.[122] It was also suggested by Du Val that it did not follow that behaviour modification, deterrence and prevention of unjust enrichment were goals that all civil damages actions were intended to serve, and that *cy-près* distributions sat uncomfortably with the notion that the purpose of the suit was to compensate those injured by illegal conduct.[123]

Interestingly, the Ontario provision does not stipulate a trigger for the invoking of a *cy-près* distribution—other than that the court considers that distribution 'appropriate',[124] and that an aggregate award has not been distributed within time.[125] This omission is somewhat surprising. It has since been judicially clarified that the provision will operate when the amount recovered via the class action 'cannot be economically distributed to individual class members'.[126] In the absence of any really useful statutory guidance, the judicially-endorsed triggers for a *cy-près* distribution in the class actions context are discussed more fulsomely in the next chapter.

Although Ontario's provisions appear to be worded on the basis that any *undistributed residue* of an aggregate award can be distributed *cy-près* (and

---

[119]   BS Du Val, 'Book Review' (1983) 3 *Windsor Ybk of Access to Justice* 411, 432.

[120]   GD Watson, 'Ontario's New Class Action Legislation' [1992] *Butterworths J of Intl Banking and Financial Law* 365, 366. Also see support for the concept in: M McGowan, 'Certification of Class Actions in Ontario' (1993), 16 CPC (3d) 172, 175.

[121]   WA Macdonald and JW Rowley, 'Ontario Class Action Reform: Business and Justice System Impacts—A Comment' (1984) 9 *Canadian Business LJ* 351, 354, 356.

[122]   PH Lindblom and GD Watson, 'Complex Litigation—A Comparative Perspective' (1993) 12 *CJQ* 33, 74.

[123]   BS Du Val, 'Book Review' (1983) 3 *Windsor Ybk of Access to Justice* 411, 433. For a similar sentiment, within the English context, see: C Harlow and R Rawlings, *Pressure Through Law* (Routledge, London, 1992) 125 ('the deterrent function of civil liability . . . is taken far more seriously in the United States than in England where the general principle is that the purpose of an award of damages is to compensate the plaintiff, not to punish the defendant').

[124]   CPA (Ont), s 26(1).

[125]   CPA (Ont), s 26(4).

[126]   *Tesluk v Boots Pharmaceutical plc* (2002), 21 CPC (5th) 196 (SCJ) [16].

some academic opinion has seemingly preferred that view[127]), the provision has clearly been applied to entire judgments or settlements,[128] apparently on the basis that it would be impracticable to provide a more direct benefit by distributing any part of the monetary award to individual class members.

3. United States

(a) Creative judicial decision-making

In contrast to the Canadian position, there is no reference in the United States' class action regime[129] to a *cy-près* distribution of damages. Interestingly enough, that has occasionally prompted later law reform commissions to consider that, given this lead, no provision for dealing with an undistributed residue was required as part of class action reform.[130] That, however, is now the minority view. In the absence of any statutory course, it is by virtue of judicial innovation that the United States possesses the most developed *cy-près* jurisprudence relevant to class actions—although it is fair to say that the application of *cy-près* in this context has received a quite mixed reception among American courts.

On the one hand, it has been judicially acknowledged[131] that *cy-près* distributions are a 'pragmatic judicial solution', framed with the motivation of 'choos[ing] between compensating large numbers of demonstrably injured people in an imperfect manner or not compensating them at all'. They have served a useful purpose in consumer class action cases, especially.[132] The approval of this method of damages distribution has a long pedigree. Early

---

[127] See, eg, the example of 20 direct plaintiffs out of a class of 2,000 customers, and the residue left over, provided in: SJ Simpson, 'Class Action Reform: A New Accountability' (1991) 10 *Advocates' Society J* 19, 22. Also: JS Ziegel, 'Criminal Usury, Class Actions and Unjust Enrichment in Canada' (2002) 18 *Journal of Contract Law* 121, fn 50 ('The Quebec provisions make it clear that a *cy-près* award may apply to the whole award, not just to unclaimed amounts. Section 26(4) of the Ontario Act leaves this in doubt').

[128] Eg, in Canada, the entire settlement sum was distributed in: *Tesluk v Boots Pharmaceutical plc* (2002), 21 CPC (5th) 196 (SCJ) (class action for misrepresentation as a result of marketing and sale of pharmaceutical drug Synthroid, prescribed in the treatment of thyroid condition hypothyroidism; claim settled; defendants required to pay entire settlement of $2.25M as *cy-près* distribution).

[129] Contained within rule 23 of the Federal Rules of Civil Procedure, and commenced operation in 1966. For commentary by a contemporary Reporter for the Advisory Committee on Civil Rules, see: B Kaplan, 'Continuing Work of the Civil Committee: 1966 Amendments of the Federal Rules of Civil Procedure (Part I)' (1967) 81 *Harvard L Rev* 356.

[130] Scottish Law Comm, *Multi-Party Actions* (1996) [4.102]. This was also stated within the context of an opt-in, not an opt-out, regime.

[131] *In re 'Agent Orange' Products Liability Litig*, 597 F Supp 740, 841 (EDNY 1984). On this point about the role of the individual, and perfect outcomes being a 'legal fiction', see: S Karas, 'The Role of Fluid Recovery in Consumer Protection Litigation' (2002) 90 *California L Rev* 959, 989–90, and the references cited therein.

[132] *Ibid, Agent Orange*, citing: *In re Folding Carton Antitrust Litig*, 557 F Supp 1091 (ND Ill 1983); *West Virginia v Chas Pfizer & Co*, 314 F Supp 710 (SDNY 1970). For academic notation that *cy-près* is ultimately one facet of a complex cost-benefit analysis of all enforcement of substantive legal principles, see: EH Cooper, 'Rule 23: Challenges to the Rulemaking Process' (1996) 71 *NYU L Rev* 13, 18–19.

judicial authority in the 1940s certainly supported the concept of a *cy-près* recovery as a creative and flexible device,[133] as did some significant academic commentary.[134] Several federal appellate[135] and district[136] courts have approved of the use of *cy-près* distributions to the 'next best class'; State courts have also permitted or approved such distributions;[137] and certain State legislatures have expressly authorised employment of a *cy-près* remedy in class actions.[138]

[133] *Market Street Railway Co v Railroad Comm of California*, 28 Cal 2d 363, 171 P 2d 875 (1946) (refunds were ordered to identified passengers who had purchased fares in excess of approved rates; defendant streetcar company also ordered to use unclaimed funds for 'the rehabilitation of the physical [railway] properties ... and for the improvement of the service afforded thereby'; note that this was not a class action), and some significant decisions of the 1970s, cited in: *In re Folding Carton Antitrust Litig*, 557 F Supp 1091, fn 10 (ND Ill 1983), eg: *Lindy Bros Builders v American Radiator & Standard Sanitary Corp* (ED Pa, 28 Feb 1978) ($25,000 given to two law schools to establish student loan funds for poor and deserving students); *State of Illinois v J W Petersen Coal & Oil Co* (ND Ill 1976) (distribution of one-half of the unclaimed residue to the Chicago Bar Foundation and one-half to the Chicago Lawyers Committee for Civil Rights); *West Virginia v Chas Pfizer & Co*, 314 F Supp 710 (SDNY 1970).

[134] For some literature of the 1970s: Note, 'Developments in the Law—Class Actions' (1976) 89 *Harvard L Rev* 1318, 1522 ('Where funds cannot be delivered precisely to those with primary legal claims, the money should if possible be put to the "next best" use'); S Gordon, 'Manageability Under the Proposed Uniform Class Actions Act' (1977) 31 *Southwestern LJ* 715, 725; M Malina, 'Fluid Class Recovery as a Consumer Remedy in Antitrust Cases' (1972) 47 *NYU L Rev* 477; Deems, 'The *Cy-près* Solution to the Damage Distribution Problems of Mass Class Actions' (1975) 9 *Georgia L Rev* 893, 894; SR Shepherd, 'Damage Distribution in Class Actions: The *Cy-près* Remedy' (1972) 39 *U Chicago L Rev* 448; K Dam, 'Class Actions: Efficiency, Compensation, Deterrence, and Conflict of Interest' (1975) 4 *J of Legal Studies* 47.

[135] Eg: *Powell v Georgia-Pacific Corp*, 119 F 3d 703 (8th Cir 1997) (allowed *cy-près* distribution for scholarship programme); *Simer v Rios*, 661 F 2d 655 (7th Cir 1981) (rejected *Eisen* and permitted *cy-près* recovery); *In re Mexico Money Transfer Litig*, 267 F 3d 743 (7th Cir 2001); *Six (6) Mexican Workers v Arizona Citrus Growers*, 904 F 2d 1301 (9th Cir 1990).

[136] Eg: *Jones v National Distillers*, 56 F Supp 2d 355 (SDNY 1999) (*cy-près* distribution to Legal Aid Society Civil Division); *In re Wells Fargo Securities Litig*, 991 F Supp 1193 (ND Cal 1998) (*cy-près* distribution to law school programme); *Drennan v Van Ru Credit Corp*, 1997 US Dist Lexis 7776 (ND Ill 1997) (*cy-près* distribution to a legal aid foundation). Also: *Democratic Central Committee of District of Columbia v Washington Metropolitan Area Transit Comm*, 84 F 3d 451 (DC Cir 1996); *In re Holocaust Victim Assets Litig*, 302 F Supp 2d 89 (EDNY 2004).

[137] Eg, in California: *In re Vitamin Cases*, 107 Cal App 4th 820 (Ct App 2003); *People v Thomas Shelton Powers MD Inc*, 3 Cal Rptr 2d 34 (Ct App 1992); in District of Columbia: *Boyle v Giral*, 820 A 2d 561 (Ct App 2003); in Louisiana: *Cavalier v Mobil Oil Corp and Chelmette Refining LLC*, 898 So 2d 584 (La App 4 Cir 2005); in Missouri: *Buchholz Mortuaries Inc v Director of Revenue*, 113 SW 3d 192 (S Ct Mo 2003); in New Jersey: *Mui v GPU Inc*, 851 A 2d 799 (Sup Ct 2004); and note the comments about state courts' receptiveness in: *Superior Beverage Co v Owens-Illinois Inc*, 827 F Supp 477, 478–79 (ND Ill 1993). Also note the positive comment of DeJarlais that '*cy-près* remains a useful tool for consumer class actions in the generally more hospitable environment of state courts': NA DeJarlais, 'The Consumer Trust Fund: A *Cy-près* Solution to Undistributed Funds in Consumer Class Actions' (1987) 38 *Hastings LJ* 729, 740.

[138] Eg: Californian Code of Civil Procedure, s 384(b), which provides in part, '... the court shall ... direct the defendant to pay the sum of the unpaid residue ... to nonprofit organizations or foundations to support projects that will benefit the class or similarly situated persons, or that promote the law consistent with the objectives and purposes of the underlying cause of action, to child advocacy programs or to nonprofit organizations providing civil legal services to the indigent'. Also see the comment in A Conte and HB Newberg, *Newberg on Class Actions* (4th edn, Thomson West, St Paul Minn, 2002) § 10.25, p 540 ('*Cy-près* and other fluid recovery distributions of

On the other hand, the notion of class actions *cy-près* distributions has met with a 'good deal of resistance' from appellate courts.[139] There are numerous indicators of the controversy which accompanies the doctrine in the class actions context. A number of cases have featured a *cy-près* award which has been vacated by an appellate court.[140] The Supreme Court has declined to address the issue in two cases where the lower courts had opined on its validity.[141] Courts in some cases have refused to discuss other decisions of significance that were decided the other way.[142] To top off this, in *Van Gemert v Boeing Co*,[143] the Second Circuit called the *cy-près* remedy an 'extraordinary remedy' which it was not prepared to countenance on the facts of that case; in *Mace v Van Ru Credit Corp*,[144] the Seventh Circuit stated that 'it is important to stress that *cy-près* recovery should be reserved for unusual circumstances'; and in *Allapattah Services v Exxon Corp*,[145] it was noted that such distributions 'remain controversial'.

Some academic commentary has maintained a purposive campaign against the *cy-près* doctrine on various ethical fronts. Most notably, Coffee has remarked[146] that 'small recovery' class actions are not deemed by trial judges to be of particular importance, hence leading to a less-than-fulsome court scrutiny of the frequent *cy-près* settlements of these types of class actions; that *cy-près* settlements represent one arm of 'collusive settlements' between the plaintiff class lawyers and the defendants; and noting of a proposal to distribute matzo

unclaimed class funds have found growing acceptance among the law, procedural rules, and precedents of various states, as well as express authorization in federal statutes', citing New Jersey's Rules of Civil Procedure 4-32-2(c)).

[139] Noted in: *In re 'Agent Orange' Products Liability Litig*, 597 F Supp 740, 841 (EDNY 1984), citing: *Eisen v Carlisle & Jacquelin*, 479 F 2d 1005, 1010–12, 1018 (2d Cir 1973); *In re Hotel Telephone Charges*, 500 F 2d 86, 89–90 (9th Cir 1974). Both cases concerned claims under an anti-trust statute which limited damages to actual damages proven. Also: *Windham v American Brands Inc*, 565 F 2d 59, 72 (4th Cir 1977).

[140] A few instances of this are: *In re Folding Carton Antitrust Litig*, 744 F 2d 1252 (7th Cir 1984); *Airline Ticket Commission Antitrust Litig Travel Network Ltd v United Air Lines Inc*, 307 F 3d 679 (8th Cir 2002); *Wilson v Southwest Airlines Inc*, 880 F 2d 807 (5th Cir 1989); *Fogie v Thorn Americas Inc*, 190 F 3d 889 (8th Cir 1999).

[141] The Supreme Court did not take the opportunity to definitively decide the issue in: *Eisen v Carlisle and Jacquelin*, 417 US 156, 94 S Ct 2140 (1974); or in *Boeing Co v Van Gemert*, 444 US 472, 100 S Ct 745 (1980).

[142] Eg, in *In re Hotel Telephone Charges*, 500 F 2d 86 (9th Cir 1974), the Ninth Circuit omitted to refer to the identical fact scenario, decided a couple of years earlier, in: *Colson v Hilton Hotels Corp*, 59 FRD 324 (ND Ill 1972). Noted also in: OLRC, *Report on Class Actions* (1982) 577, fn 272.

[143] 553 F 2d 812, 816 (2d Cir 1977).

[144] 109 F 3d 338, 345 (7th Cir 1997).

[145] 157 F Supp 2d 1291, fn 11 (SD Fla 2001). Also: *Friedman v Lansdale Parking Authority*, Fed Sec L Rep (CCH) P98,676 (ED Pa 1995) ('this controversial theory'); *Powell v Georgia-Pacific Corp*, 119 F 3d 703, 706 (8th Cir 1997) ('controversial in the courts of appeals').

[146] JC Coffee, 'Class Wars: The Dilemma of the Mass Tort Class Action' (1995) 95 *Columbia L Rev* 1343, 1368–69, and also cited by Canadian commentator C Jones in: *Theory of Class Actions* (Irwin Law Inc, Toronto, 2003) ch 5C(3)(a) [accessed via Quicklaw database]. For similar concerns expressed from a practitioner viewpoint, see, eg: KA Lambert, 'Class Action Settlements in Louisiana' (2000) 61 *Louisiana L Rev* 89.

products to various charities over a four-year period in settlement of a price-fixing claim: '[t]he cynically disposed might see this settlement as an excellent way of simultaneously disposing of both stale matzos and a difficult litigation.'[147]

Some of the most strident criticism of *cy-près* (and in-kind coupon) recoveries has been reserved for the fee awards which lawyers have garnered, with little benefit realised by the class members themselves—thereby bringing the legal profession into disrepute. In its seminal report of damages class actions cases studies, the RAND Institute stated: 'The single most important action that judges can take to support the public goals of class action litigation is to reward class action attorneys only for lawsuits that actually accomplish something of value to class members and society.'[148] The lead author of the report subsequently reiterated this to be the Institute's 'strongest recommendation',[149] and legislature has certainly taken correlative steps to address this issue.[150] Recently, it has been provided that, in the case of coupon rather than cash settlements, fee awards are to be based upon the monetary value of coupons redeemed, not upon the overall value of the coupon settlement.[151] As Andreeva notes:

> Hence, class counsel will no longer be able to base their attorney's fees on a settlement value that assumes a hundred percent redemption rate. These new requirements may effectively eliminate coupon settlements as an option because plaintiffs' lawyers will be reluctant to agree to postpone the determination of the fees until the coupons are redeemed.[152]

The unfortunate mixture of extremely small recoveries per class member, coupon instead of cash settlements, and large fee awards for lawyers,[153] inevitably raises the conundrum of whether a preliminary merits threshold—that is, a minimum financial recovery per class member, a cost–benefit analysis, a probability of success of the class action, or a combination of any or all of these

---

[147] The case in issue was: *In re Matzo Food Products Litig*, 156 FRD 600 (DNJ 1994).

[148] DR Hensler *et al, Class Action Dilemmas: Pursuing Public Goals for Private Gain* (RAND Institute for Civil Justice, Santa Monica, 2000) 490.

[149] DR Hensler and TD Rowe, 'Complex Litigation at the Millennium: Beyond "It Just Ain't Worth It": Alternative Strategies for Damage Class Action Reform' (2001) 64 *Law and Contemporary Problems* 137, 151.

[150] Eg: the Private Securities Litigation Reform Act of 1995 provides, 'Total attorneys' fees and expenses awarded by the court to counsel for the plaintiff class shall not exceed a reasonable percentage of the amount of any damages and prejudgment interest actually paid to the class': s 78u-4(a)(6). Note the recent academic observation that 'the strong incentives to settle securities suits remain in spite of [this provision]': D Moos, 'Pleading Around the Private Securities Litigation Reform Act' (2005) 78 *U Southern California L Rev* 763, 772.

[151] Class Action Fairness Act of 2005, 28 USC § 1712(a) (2005).

[152] A Andreeva, 'Class Action Fairness Act of 2005: The Eight-Year Saga is Finally Over' (2005) 59 *U Miami L Rev* 385, 410–11.

[153] Witness, eg, one report of English shareholders of Cable & Wireless and Shell receiving documents that informed them of a settlement of a false disclosure suit, whereby 'the loss [is] estimated at $0.6487 per share. If everyone takes part in the claim, each stands to receive 0.61 per cent of the estimated damages owed to them. Not even a peppercorn': C Mortished, 'Lawyers cash in on wrong arm of the law', *The Times (Business)*, 20 Jul 2005, 45.

options—should be pursued in the class actions context.[154] Within the general damages class action of FRCP 23, none of these thresholds is explicitly provided on the face of the rule, although a cost–benefit analysis has been mooted in the recent past.[155]

Yet another criticism of *cy-près* distributions in the US is that some have arguably centred too much upon the individuals of the class, without due regard to funding projects that would benefit future groups of people (who were not class members at all). This has particularly arisen in the context of suits by Holocaust survivors against Swiss banks[156] for looting assets of Jewish depositors and for preventing heirs from claiming the assets of family members who had died. Dubinsky, for example, has commented that, in granting almost $600 million of unclaimed settlement funds *cy-près* to elderly Holocaust survivors who were living in the former Soviet Union in poverty and degradation, the court failed to take into account—

> forward-looking measures, such as Holocaust education, Holocaust scholarship, or rebuilding the properties and communal infrastructure of the Eastern European past. . . . In this respect our current jurisprudence under Rule 23, while perhaps adequate for much tort and commercial class action litigation, falls short of the pursuit of full and useful reparations in human rights class actions, where the effects of widespread and severe oppression go beyond individual injury.[157]

Fuelling the fire of controversy, it has also been suggested that *cy-près* distribution is unlawful. These allegations have been made on at least four separate fronts.

First, and on occasion, the ruling has been judicially made in circumstances where the *cy-près* remedy was to be potentially used to avoid the individual calculation of class members' damages in circumstances where that individual computation was compulsory. As noted above,[158] strident judicial criticisms have been made of those occasions on which *cy-près* has been used in its *wide* sense as a device for damages computation.

Secondly, FRCP 23 does not expressly authorise *cy-près* distributions—it was a theory driven by scholars and commentators in the rule's early jurisprudence,[159] and the controversy with which it has since been judicially considered motivated the OLRC, for example, to insist that the matter be expressly

---

[154] For further discussion of these options, see, eg: RP Mulheron, *The Class Action in Common Law Legal Systems: A Comparative Perspective* (Hart Publishing, Oxford, 2004) 130–43.

[155] See 'Proposed Amendments to the Federal Rules of Civil Procedure' (1996) 167 FRD 559, proposing, *inter alia*, the insertion of a new rule 23(c)(F) in respect of class actions suits for damages: 'whether the probable relief to individual class members justifies the costs and burdens of class litigation'. The rule was never implemented, for reasons discussed in: DR Hensler and TD Rowe, 'Complex Litigation at the Millennium: Beyond "It Just Ain't Worth It": Alternative Strategies for Damage Class Action Reform' (2001) 64 *Law and Contemporary Problems* 137.

[156] *In re Holocaust Victim Assets Litig*, 2000 US Dist LEXIS 20817 (EDNY 22 Nov 2000).

[157] PR Dubinsky, 'Book Reviews' (2004) 102 *Mich L Rev* 1152, 1179.

[158] See pp 224–7.

[159] Noted in: *In re Folding Carton Antitrust Litig*, 557 F Supp 1091, 1108 (ND Ill 1983).

dealt with in any legislation proposed for Ontario.[160] Given this lacuna in FRCP 23, some US federal courts have expressly derived their jurisdiction to award *cy-près* orders or approve *cy-près* settlements on the basis that, as courts of equitable jurisdiction, they 'should exercise . . . equitable control over these [residual] funds for the benefit of all consumers'.[161] Leading academic commentary concurs with this view.[162]

Thirdly, some have also queried whether the *cy-près* doctrine represents a modification of the substantive law that is beyond the scope of rules of court (given that such rules are specified not to abridge, enlarge or modify any substantive right[163]). The substantive law may be amended, as Cooper explains, in the following respect:

> Rule 23 does not authorize actions to enforce the public interest on behalf of the public and perhaps cannot do so. . . . Courts that experiment with such remedies must find implied authority from the statute being enforced or the development of common law principles. Even with such substantive roots, the result is at least slightly removed from the traditional view that courts in the United States act at the behest of private litigants to resolve private disputes. And justification must be found for the awkward complication that the fluid remedy either cuts off individual enforcement by class members—as a class action should—or leaves the defendant subject to double liability.[164]

Other commentary disagrees,[165] noting that the *cy-près* approach seeks to leave the policy of compensation undisturbed, is simply directed toward the fairness and efficiency of the litigious process, and is a tool for enforcing the substantive rights of victims, not to amend them. Interestingly, a similar point about whether the *cy-près* approach changes the substantive law of damages has been made by Canadian commentators.[166] Plainly the difficulties that can accompany any rule changes—which are intended to merely deal with matters of practice

[160] OLRC, *Report on Class Actions* (1982) 581.

[161] *West Virginia v Chas Pfizer & Co*, 314 F Supp 710, 728 (SDNY 1970), aff'd: 440 F 2d 1079 (2d Cir), cert denied: 404 US 871 (1971). The equitable powers of the court to make such distributions also referenced, eg, in: *Superior Beverage Co v Owens-Illinois Inc*, 827 F Supp 477, 479 (ND Ill 1993); *In re Folding Carton Antitrust Litig*, 557 F Supp 1091, 1104–6 (ND Ill 1983).

[162] A Conte and HB Newberg, *Newberg on Class Actions* (4th edn, Thomson West, St Paul Minn, 2002) § 10.22 p 532, citing: EL Fisch, *The Cy-près Doctrine in the United States* (Matthew Bender & Co, Albany NY, 1950), and § 11.20 p 28; OLRC, *Report on Class Actions* (1982) 573.

[163] Rules Enabling Act, 28 USC § 2072(b) (1982) ('Such rules shall not abridge, enlarge or modify any substantive right').

[164] EH Cooper, 'Class Action Advice in the Form of Questions' (2001) *Duke J of Comparative and Intl Law* 215, 244–45. See also, for similar comments by the same author: EH Cooper, 'The (Cloudy) Future of Class Actions' (1998) 40 *Arizona L Rev* 923, 931 ('Rule 23 does not explicitly authorize substituted relief that flows to the public at large . . . Adoption of a provision for "fluid" or "cy-près" class recovery would severely test the limits of the Rules Enabling Act'); and see too: W Simon, 'Class Actions—Useful Tool or Engine of Destruction' (1973) 55 FRD 375, 385–86.

[165] NA DeJarlais, 'The Consumer Trust Fund: A *Cy-près* Solution to Undistributed Funds in Consumer Class Actions' (1987) 38 *Hastings LJ* 729, 745;.

[166] A Borrell and WK Branch, 'Power in Numbers: BC's Proposed Class Proceedings Act' (1995) 53 *Advocate* 515, 524.

and procedure—simply do not exist when the class actions regime is introduced by way of statute instead.[167]

Lastly, *cy-près* distributions within the province of class actions further distances the device from the traditional unitary litigious model.[168] That, however, is surely no reason, of itself, to banish the former. Absolute precision in individual compensation is not always present in unitary litigation, and in any event, were the class to seek injunctive relief, Conte and Newberg make the point that such judgments 'benefit future parties who were not necessarily present members of an existing class.'[169] These authors also point out that, for the opponents of *cy-près* distributions, '[w]indfall recoveries sound like something never permitted, but they are well known and accepted in the law.'[170] For these reasons, it is not hard to agree with the American academic contention that the *cy-près* approach is a 'modest extension of those principles to class action [damages] relief.'[171]

(b) The practicalities

Cy-près distributions are more common in American jurisprudence for class actions *settlement* sums[172] rather than for judgment sums. There has been some dispute as to whether the latter are precluded from the *cy-près* doctrine altogether. Some authorities think not,[173] while others believe that settlement sums are the doctrine's *only* province of operation:

> the Second Circuit has not allowed for fluid recovery, see, eg, *Van Gemert v Boeing Co*, 553 F 2d 812, 815 (2d Cir 1977), except where made pursuant to a settlement agreement. See *Beecher v Able*, 575 F 2d 1010, 1015 (2d Cir 1978). Thus, application of the *cy-près* distribution may not ever occur in this case, and any eventual recovery [per judgment] may be distributed on a standard *pro-rata* basis.[174]

---

[167] Discussed further in: RP Mulheron, *The Class Action in Common Law Legal Systems: A Comparative Perspective* (Hart Publishing, Oxford, 2004) 38–42.

[168] JE Fisch, 'Class Action Reform, Qui Tam and the Role of the Plaintiff' (1997) 60 *Law and Contemporary Problems* 167.

[169] A Conte and HB Newberg, *Newberg on Class Actions* (4th edn, Thomson West, St Paul Minn, 2002) § 10.17 p 518.

[170] *Ibid*, § 10.22 p 531, citing, eg, punitive and liquidated damages.

[171] MC Weber, 'Managing Complex Litigation in the Illinois Courts' (1996) 27 *Loyola U Chicago LJ* 959, 982.

[172] Eg: *Powell v Georgia-Pacific Corp*, 119 F 3d 703 (8th Cir 1997); *In re Motorsports Merchandise Antitrust Litig*, 160 F Supp 2d 1392 (ND Ga 2001); *Jones v National Distillers*, 56 F Supp 2d 355 (SDNY 1999), and see also the comments in: A Conte and HB Newberg, *Newberg on Class Actions* (4th edn, Thomson West, St Paul Minn, 2002) § 10.17 p 522.

[173] Eg, in *Powell*, *ibid*, 497, the Eighth Circuit appeared to contemplate both scenarios in the following statement about the *cy-près* method: '[it] is most often used in the cases involving settlements of class actions rather than adjudicated class actions'. Similarly, the comment in *In re Matzo Food Products Litig*, 156 FRD 600, 605 (DNJ 1994) ('courts have employed *cy-près* principles to distribute class damages or settlement funds'). See also: *In re Toys 'R' Us Antitrust Litig*, 191 FRD 347 (EDNY 2000); *State of New York v Reebok Intl Ltd*, 903 F Supp 532 (SDNY 1995), aff'd, 96 F 3d 44 (2d Cir 1996).

[174] *Weber v Goodman*, 1998 US Dist LEXIS 22832, at 17 (EDNY 1998).

Certainly, greater flexibility is permitted when fashioning *cy-près* distributions of settlement, rather than judgment, sums.[175] According to leading class actions commentators in the United States, although the use of a *cy-près* distribution remains 'controversial and unsettled in an adjudicated class action context, courts are not in disagreement that *cy-près* distributions are proper in connection with a class settlement, subject to court approval of the particular application of the funds.'[176]

It is often the *unclaimed* (or *residual*) amount of a class actions judgment or settlement that is applied *cy-près* under the American federal class action regime,[177] with some judicial indications that the court is more prepared to order that these residual monies be distributed outside the strict category of class members.[178] This point was made in the case of *In re 'Agent Orange' Product Liability Litigation*,[179] where a *cy-près* distribution was permitted in circumstances where the class members had already benefited from direct distribution, so that 'non-class distribution is not an initial purpose of the fund, but only an eventual way to dispose of the unclaimed portion'. The unclaimed fund, of course, can amount to a significant amount of money —$125 million, in one case,[180] $600 million in another.[181]

---

[175]   Eg: *In re 'Agent Orange' Product Liability Litig*, 818 F 2d 179, 185 (2d Cir 1987) ('a district court may "provide broader relief [in a settlement context] than the court could have awarded after a trial." Indeed, we have previously recognized that some "fluidity" is permissible in the distribution of settlement proceeds', citing: *Local Number 93, Intl Assn of Firefighters v City of Cleveland*, 478 US 501, 106 S Ct 3063, 3077 (1986)).

[176]   See: A Conte and HB Newberg, *Newberg on Class Actions* (4th edn, Thomson West, St Paul Minn, 2002) § 11.20 p 28, and the cases cited fnn 7–15. According to one author, the most prominent example was the multi-billion dollar US tobacco settlement, which earmarked a large portion of the settlement for smoking prevention and other non-compensatory programmes: S Karas, 'The Role of Fluid Recovery in Consumer Protection Litigation' (2002) 90 *Californian L Rev 959*, fn 69.

[177]   Eg: *Nelson v Greater Gadsden Housing Authority*, 802 F 2d 405 (11th Cir 1986) (tenant class action; unclaimed part of settlement fund used to improve/repair building and defendant-supplied appliances); *Powell Georgia-Pacific Corp*, 119 F 3d 703 (8th Cir 1997) (race discrimination action; residual settlement funds distributed to nonprofit foundation to administer scholarship programme for African-Americans); *State of West Virginia v Chas Pfizer & Co*, 314 F Supp 710 (SDNY 1970), aff'd, 440 F 2d 1079 (2d Cir 1970) (antitrust class action against pharmaceutical companies re antibiotic sales; unclaimed part of settlement fund of up to $20M could be used for public health purposes, via *pro bono* projects that would benefit consumers who might have been injured by the defendants' illegal activities; such projects ultimately included drug abuse programmes, lead poisoning and sickle cell anaemia research, and community health clinics: discussed in OLRC, *Report on Class Actions* (1982) 575, fn 261); *Six (6) Mexican Workers v Arizona Citrus Growers*, 904 F 2d 1301, 1306–9 (9th Cir 1990).

[178]   *Jones v Distillers*, 56 F Supp 2d 355, 357 (SDNY 1999) ('the distribution is only of the residue of a fund that was used primarily for a *pro rata* distribution to all qualified claimants. Distribution of that fund residue outside the class thus is entirely proper, so long as the choice of recipient is appropriate under the circumstances'); *In re Matzo Food Products Litig*, 156 FRD 600, 605 (DNJ 1994) ('Cy-près principles have most commonly been used where unclaimed funds remain following distribution of the class fund to individual class members').

[179]   818 F 2d 179, 185 (2d Cir 1987).

[180]   As in: *Allapattah Services v Exxon Corp*, 157 F Supp 2d 1291 (SD Fla 2001).

[181]   *In re Holocaust Victim Assets Litig*, 2000 US Dist LEXIS 20817 (EDNY 22 Nov 2000).

A distribution of the entire settlement or judgment sum is not precluded in practice, however.[182] Veering away from direct distribution altogether has been supported[183] on the basis that it avoids the expense of notifying individual class members of their right to claim, plus the potential for fraud in claim procedures. The inevitable criticism of the practice is that it provides absolutely no opportunity for class members to claim their compensation directly, thus undermining the purpose of taking remedial action at all.[184] This concern has been downplayed on occasion. For example, in *In re Microsoft Corp Antitrust Litigation*, the District Court justified a total non-direct, *cy-près*, distribution, on this basis:

> Although the *cy-près* approach is most frequently used for the purpose of distributing the residue of a class settlement fund, it has also been utilized as a means for distributing the entirety of a class fund where the proceeds cannot be economically distributed to the class members. . . . As Professor Miller succinctly stated during the course of his presentation at the preliminary approval hearing, 'Courts are saying, the game isn't worth the candle.'[185]

Given the very many divided academic and judicial opinions that have been discussed in this section, the US legal position is far from clear. Notwithstanding, one of the leading class action commentaries proffers the hopeful view that—

> [t]he future of *cy-près* distributions of class recovery balances remains uncertain [in the United States but] . . . [t]hese issues may ultimately be decided on policy grounds because there appear to be no underlying substantive or procedural obstacles to the flexible distribution of unclaimed class funds under the particular circumstances involved.[186]

D THE ALTERNATIVES TO A *CY-PRÈS* DISTRIBUTION

In common with the charitable doctrine of *cy-près*, the court must eliminate the possibility of reversion of the property back to the payer (the defendant, in this case; the settlor/testator, in the context of charitable trusts), and satisfy itself

---

[182] Eg: *In re Mexico Money Transfer Litig*, 164 F Supp 2d 1002, 1031 (ND Ill 2000) ('Contrary to the California Objectors' contentions, approval of such a fund does not depend on its being composed of unclaimed or residual funds). Also: *Keele v Wexler*, 149 F 3d 589, 592 (7th Cir 1998); *Drennan v Van Ru Credit Corp*, 1997 US Dist LEXIS 7776, at 1 (ND Ill 1997); *In re Three Mile Island Litig*, 557 F Supp 96, 97 (MD Pa 1982).

[183] Postulated in: *State of California v Levi Strauss & Co*, 715 P 2d 564, 570 (Cal 1986), as noted also in: S Karas, 'The Role of Fluid Recovery in Consumer Protection Litigation' (2002) 90 *California L Rev* 959, 973. Also received strong academic support in, eg: SB Farmer, 'More Lessons from the Laboratories: *Cy-près* Distributions in Parens Patriae' (1999) 68 *Fordham L Rev* 361, 399.

[184] Eg: WB Rubenstein, 'On What a "Private Attorney General" Is—And Why it Matters' (2004) 57 *Vanderbilt U L Rev* 2129, fn 128. This article critiques, especially, the *Microsoft* decision, noted in text and in fn below.

[185] 185 F Supp 2d 519, 523 (MD 2002), with supporting authorities omitted from quote.

[186] A Conte and HB Newberg, *Newberg on Class Actions* (4th edn, Thomson West, St Paul Minn, 2002) § 10.25 pp 542–43.

that the distribution to the beneficiaries (the class members in this case; the beneficiaries of the trust in the context of charitable trusts) would be impossible, impracticable or infeasible. Thus, in *In re Wells Fargo Securities Litigation*,[187] the District Court ordered the enquiries as follows:

> before a court invokes its *cy-près* power to distribute the residue of a class settlement fund to an alternate recipient, it must ask three questions:
>
> (1) to whom does the residue belong,
> (2) would it be practicable to distribute the residue to its owners, and
> (3) if not, who is an appropriate alternate recipient?

Thus, there is a notable symmetry of analysis between the class actions and charitable trusts *cy-près* doctrines.

American courts commonly cite three alternative methods for disposing of any residual amount in the context of a class actions judgment or settlement, apart from *cy-près* distributions: plaintiff fund-sharing; reversion to the defendant; and escheat to the government.[188] Various of these have also been statutorily enacted in Canadian class actions provincial statutes, although with the admonishment that the legislature often does not provide any guidance as to how the court should choose between these alternatives,[189] and it (the legislature) should ideally do so.[190] Each of these options will be considered in turn.

1. Plaintiff Fund-sharing

Plaintiff fund-sharing means that the unclaimed pool is distributed *pro rata* to those class members who have been located, have filed valid claims, and have received earlier distributions.

The philosophy underpinning this type of distribution of the unclaimed funds is that the members of the class are the equitable owners of the damages recovered.[191] The approach also serves the tripartite goals of compensation, disgorgement and deterrence, given that no part of the fund is returned to the

---

[187] 991 F Supp 1193, 1195 (ND Cal 1998).

[188] Eg: *Powell v Georgia-Pacific Corp*, 119 F 3d 703, 705 (8th Cir 1997), and earlier: 843 F Supp 491, 495–97 (WD Ark 1994); *In re Motorsports Merchandise Antitrust Litig*, 160 F Supp 2d 1392, 1394 (ND Ga 2001); *Six (6) Mexican Workers v Arizona Citrus Growers*, 904 F 2d 1301, 1307–9 (9th Cir 1990); *Hayes v Arthur Young & Co*, 1994 US App LEXIS 23608, at 55 (9th Cir 1994); *Pruitt Cloud Land Trust v Powell Mountain Coal Co Inc*, 1996 US Dist LEXIS 5499, at 6 (WD Va 1996); *Nabal v BJ's Wholesale Club Inc*, 2002 US Dist LEXIS 15106, at 14 (ED Pa 2002); *In re Matzo Food Products Litig*, 156 FRD 600, fn 5 (DNJ 1994).

[189] See, eg, this point made in Alberta Law Reform Institute, *Class Actions* (2000) [348].

[190] *Ibid*, [354]. However, the legislation ultimately enacted in Alberta does not provide such guidance, allowing for *cy-près* distributions, and then providing for the court to 'make any order that the Court considers appropriate with respect to the distribution . . . of the unclaimed or undistributed portion of the award': Class Proceedings Act 2003, SA 2003, c C–16.5, s 34(5).

[191] *Boeing Co v Van Gemert*, 444 US 472, 481–82, and fn 7, 100 S Ct 745 (1980).

defendant, and all is applied toward the plaintiff class.[192] Coffee has further suggested[193] that, because class members rarely receive complete compensation via settlement agreements in any event, then sharing the residual amount amongst the claiming class members serves to better ensure their fullest compensation.

However, in *Hayes v Arthur Young & Co*,[194] the United States Court of Appeals for the Ninth Circuit expressed its disquiet about the procedure:

> In this particular case, we reject [plaintiff fund-sharing] because individual plaintiffs' recoveries on the § 10(b), § 11, and common law claims must be limited to their actual damages. . . . Distributing the unclaimed funds *pro rata* would thus give the claiming class members a windfall; it might also encourage the bringing of class actions likely to result in large uncollected damage pools and create conflicts of interest between named plaintiffs and other class members. . . . Thus, any excess unclaimed damages should not be distributed among the claiming plaintiffs.[195]

The Ninth Circuit also approved earlier authority which considered that any residual funds could *not* be used to defray the legal expenses of the claiming members of the class, because 'what [plaintiffs] may not gain directly, . . . they may not gain indirectly.'[196]

Quite apart from the problems of windfall gains and possible improper motives for bringing the action in the first place (both referred to in the passage above), the propriety of the distribution method has been seriously called into question by the judiciary for other reasons too. It means that silent (non-claiming) class members will not receive any compensation whatsoever; and it raises 'serious questions' as to the adequacy of representation where the interests of the claiming plaintiffs lay in keeping the other class members uninformed.[197] It may be that it would be impracticable (eg, too costly) to distribute the surplus to the claiming plaintiffs, and would consume in administrative costs the great majority of the damages left over.[198] Alternatively, it has been suggested that the

---

[192] RA Higgins, 'The Equitable Doctrine of *Cy-près* and Consumer Protection' (Annex 1, ACA Submission, Trade Practices Review, 15 Jul 2002) 9; A Conte and HB Newberg, *Newberg on Class Actions* (4th edn, Thomson West, St Paul Minn, 2002) § 10.15 p 513.

[193] JC Coffee, 'Class Wars: The Dilemma of the Mass Tort Class Action' (1995) 95 *Columbia L Rev* 1343, 1369, fn 96.

[194] 1994 US App LEXIS 23608 (9th Cir 1992).

[195] *Ibid*, 55, citing also: *Van Gemert v Boeing Co*, 553 F 2d 812, 815–16 (2d Cir 1977). See also: *Allapattah Services Inc v Exxon Corp*, 157 F Supp 2d 1291, 1306 (SD Fla 2001) ('Thus, under UCC principles, once all class members who assert valid claims are made whole, the compensatory purpose of any damage award has been completely satisfied').

[196] *Ibid*, 57, citing: *Van Gemert v Boeing Co*, 553 F 2d 812, 816 (2d Cir 1977). In addition, on this point: *In re Folding Carton Antitrust Litig*, 557 F Supp 1091, 1107 (ND Ill 1983), and later, aff'd: 744 F 2d 1252, 1254, 1257 (7th Cir 1984).

[197] *Van Gemert v Boeing Co*, 553 F 2d 812, 815 (2d Cir 1977), citing: Note, 'Damage Distribution in Class Actions: The *Cy-près* Remedy' (1972) 39 *U Chicago L Rev* 448, 453.

[198] *Brewer v Southern Union Co*, US Dist LEXIS 15940, at 18 (D Colo 1987). Also noted in, eg: *Schwartz v Dallas Cowboys Football Club Ltd*, 362 F Supp 2d 574, 577 (ED Pa 2005) ('payment of the excess funds to the members of the class is impractical (ie, after administrative costs, each member would receive approximately $3.50)').

benefits of plaintiff fund-sharing could only be realised in the (unusual) scenario where 'a large proportion of class members participated and submitted accurate claims'[199]—which tends to favour the better socio-economically placed plaintiffs, who (some evidence suggests[200]) are more likely to submit claims.

Apart from distribution to the class members, or a *cy-près* distribution, there remain two other options for distribution of a class actions judgment or settlement: escheat to the government, and reversion to the defendant.

2. Escheat to the Government

Invariably, money with no owner, including unclaimed damages sums, may find their way to governmental coffers. All States of Australia have legislation which provides that unclaimed funds will revert to State governments as consolidated revenue—for example, New South Wales, via its Unclaimed Money Act 1995, provides that unclaimed monies must be paid, under s 10 of that Act, into the Consolidated Fund, from whence it will be distributed for various purposes.[201] One Australian commentator has described escheat of monies to the Crown as a 'lengthy and tortuous process', and highly inappropriate where the money is rightfully the property of consumers.[202]

In Canada too, various statutes provide, in the general context rather than in the class actions-specific scenario, that unclaimed funds should escheat to the government. Manitoba's legislature, for example, has enacted that 'when property of any kind has become forfeited for any cause to the Crown, the Minister of Justice may cause possession thereof to be taken in the name of the Crown'.[203] Interestingly, the OLRC recommended, in its *Report on Class Actions*,[204] that an express statutory provision about escheat (or other destination of unclaimed funds) be included in the class actions statute, to avoid the inflexibility that had been evident in American case law if the matter was left to escheat statutes of general application.[205] This was provided for in the draft Bill prepared by the Commission,[206] but interestingly, no escheat provision in

---

[199] See: *State of California v Levi Strauss & Co*, 715 P 2d 564, 573.

[200] NA DeJarlais, 'The Consumer Trust Fund: A *Cy-près* Solution to Undistributed Funds in Consumer Class Actions' (1987) 38 *Hastings LJ* 729, 765, citing: T Bartsh *et al*, *A Class Action Suit that Worked: The Consumer Refund in the Anti-biotic Antitrust Litigation* (Lexington Books, Lexington Mass, 1978).

[201] The Unclaimed Money Act 1995 (NSW) applies to 'enterprises' that hold unclaimed money, which term is defined widely, and could include a court; furthermore, s 6 provides that the Act binds the Crown in all of its capacities. Other States have broadly similar legislation.

[202] D Nelthorpe, 'Consumer Trusts Funds' (1988) 13 *Legal Services Bulletin* 26, 26.

[203] Escheats Act, CCSM, c E140, s 1. Other provinces have broadly similar legislation.

[204] OLRC, *Report on Class Actions* (1982) 595.

[205] The OLRC cited Escheats Act, RSO 1980, c 142, in that regard. Now see: Escheats Act, RSO 1990, c E20.

[206] Cl 28 provided: 'The court may order that any money that has not been distributed ... be forfeited to the Crown or returned unconditionally to the defendant as the court considers proper.'

favour of the Crown was ultimately enacted in Ontario's Class Proceedings Act 1992. In fact, in that jurisdiction, any unclaimed amount from an aggregate award must be returned to the defendant,[207] and no option for escheat to consolidated revenue exists in the class actions legislation.[208] Other legislatures, however, have precisely followed the OLRC's advice. Manitoba, for example, expressly permits any part of an unclaimed damages award to be 'forfeited to the government', if the court considers that to be the most appropriate course.[209]

In the United States, and as noted previously, FRCP 23 contains no specific provisions governing the distribution of unclaimed amounts of class actions judgments or settlements. However, unclaimed funds in a judgment or settlement may escheat to the government under 28 USC §§ 2041, 2042, which provide, respectively, in part:

[a]ll moneys paid into any court of the United States . . . in any case pending or adjudicated in such court, shall be forthwith deposited with the Treasurer of the United States or a designated depositary, in the name and to the credit of such court

and:

[n]o money deposited under section 2041 of this title shall be withdrawn except by order of court. In every case in which the right to withdraw money deposited in court under section 2041 has been adjudicated or is not in dispute and such money has remained so deposited for at least five years unclaimed by the person entitled thereto, such court shall cause such money to be deposited in the Treasury in the name and to the credit of the United States.

Although these provisions appear to mandate that funds paid into United States courts and remaining unclaimed for five years will revert to the US Treasury, the provisions are truly permissive, as *Jones v National Distillers*[210] explained: '[t]he option may be appropriate in the absence of guidance either from *cy-près* principles or from the preferences of parties with equitable interests in the funds, but it remains a context-specific, discretionary determination.' From this, it would appear that greater flexibility is, at least, countenanced in recent case law from that jurisdiction, which is consistent with the OLRC's proposition several years earlier.

---

[207] See: Class Proceedings Act, SO 1992, c 6, s 26(10).

[208] This was actually the recommendation of the minority of the Commission, who proposed that any residue should be returned to the defendant, and never forfeited to the Crown: see OLRC, *Report on Class Actions* (1982) 596, fn 364, and 'Chairman's Reservations', 852, para (e) ('where a residue of an aggregate award remains after all feasible efforts at distribution to individual class members have been made, the Report recommends a discretionary *cy-près* distribution of the residue, or the forfeiture of the residue to the Crown. I share the view of my colleague, Barry A Percival, Esq, QC, that the undistributed residue of an aggregate award should be returned to the defendant, and I join in his dissent').

[209] Class Proceedings Act 2002, CCSM c C130, s 34(5)(b). Also see, in Saskatchewan: Class Actions Act, SS 2001, c C–12.01, s 37(5)(b); in St John's and Newfoundland: Class Actions Act 2001, SNL 2001, c C–18.1, s 34(5)(b); and in BC: CPA (BC), s 34(5)(b).

[210] 56 F Supp 2d 355, 358 (SDNY 1999), citing also: *Van Gemert v Boeing Co*, 739 F 2d 730, 735 (2d Cir 1984).

The court may prefer to directly order that any unclaimed funds be transferred to governmental coffers. The principle supporting a reversion to the government of unclaimed monies is that, as explained in *Folding Carton*:

> nonclaiming class members will benefit indirectly to the extent that the state uses the fund to benefit all of its citizens. Obviously, this results in an imperfect fit between the class harmed—the nonclaiming class members—and the class benefitted—all citizens. However, awarding the fund to either the defendants or the claiming class members results in an even less perfect fit because it ensures that nonclaiming members will receive no benefit.[211]

Transfer to the government is particularly apposite when a statute under which the class is claiming promotes the goals of deterrence, disgorgement and enforcement of the substantive law;[212] where the government is uniquely positioned to apply the unclaimed monies for the benefit of class members indirectly (eg, where an antitrust class action against drug companies accused of price-fixing was brought on behalf of consumers, and where the unclaimed balance of the settlement fund was distributed to State governments for application to and use in public health programmes[213]); where a transfer to the government 'would involve virtually no administrative expense, and would benefit the public at large by increasing federal revenues';[214] or where there is a clear cross-over between the public at large, and the injured class members (eg, where those injured were users of public transport), so that it could be said with reasonable confidence that a distribution to the government would probably serve the purpose of aiding the injured parties.[215] This distribution method also has the advantage of accruing only very minimal administrative costs.[216]

Transference to consolidated revenue of any damages sum has had its judicial critics, however. In *State of California v Levi Strauss & Co*,[217] the Californian

[211] *In re Folding Carton Antitrust Litig*, 744 F 2d 1252, 1258 (7th Cir 1984) (antitrust class action; settlement fund established to repay injured class members; *cy-près* distribution to charity rejected; unclaimed fund disposed of to US Treasury).
[212] *Six (6) Mexican Workers v Arizona Citrus Growers*, 904 F 2d 1301, 1307–8 (9th Cir 1990), citing, as examples of escheat: *Hodgson v YB Quezada*, 498 F 2d 5, 6 (9th Cir 1974); *Hodgson v Wheaton Glass Co*, 446 F 2d 527 (3d Cir 1971); *In re Folding Carton Antitrust Litig*, 744 F 2d 1252, 1254 (7th Cir 1984).
[213] *State of West Virginia v Chas Pfizer & Co*, 314 F Supp 710 (SDNY 1970).
[214] *In re Department of Energy Stripper Well Exemption Litig*, 578 F Supp 586, 595 (D Kans 1983).
[215] *Ibid*. Also: *United States v Exxon Corp*, 561 F Supp 816 (DDC 1983) (Dept of Energy sued for violation of oil price regulations by overcharging; impossible to trace all class members injured by conduct; monies ordered to be given to US Treasury, and divided among the States to be applied toward federal energy conservation programmes).
[216] K Barnett, 'Equitable Trusts: An Effective Remedy in Consumer Class Actions' (1987) 96 *Yale LJ* 1591, 1599; NA DeJarlais, 'The Consumer Trust Fund: A *Cy-près* Solution to Undistributed Funds in Consumer Class Actions' (1987) 38 *Hastings LJ* 729, 754.
[217] 41 Cal 3d 460, 475, 224 Cal Rptr 613 (1986), cited on this point in, eg: RA Higgins, 'The Equitable Doctrine of *Cy-près* and Consumer Protection' (Annex 1, ACA Submission, Trade Practices Review, 15 Jul 2002) fn 27; S Karas, 'The Role of Fluid Recovery in Consumer Protection Litigation' (2002) 90 *Californian L Rev* 959, fn 72; DeJarlais, *ibid*, 753.

Supreme Court noted that general escheat was 'the least focused compensation' and should be only used as a last resort, where other *cy-près* options are not workable. Furthermore, Higgins summarises its disadvantages thus:

> there is no real focus on future deterrence of the offence, benefits are thinly spread throughout the general public, and compensation may poorly map on to actual individual losses: there is likely to be some under- or over-inclusion of parties. Escheat introduces discretion as to the appropriate purpose to which to put the funds and creates a danger of funds being absorbed into Government allocations.[218]

Related concerns[219] that damages, in this context, are simply equated to civil fines that are paid into the government coffers, with no impetus to trace those funds to ensure that they are applied toward aligned projects, and with no brake to prevent the government from reducing its own funds in light of the influx of monies, may be difficult to refute—although the next alternative has its fair share of critics too.

3. Reversion to the Defendant

A return of any unclaimed damages award to the wrongdoing defendant has been embraced statutorily by some Canadian legislatures,[220] and by judicial approval in the United States.

In *Van Gemert v Boeing Co*,[221] the Court of Appeals for the Second Circuit upheld a decision reverting unclaimed funds to the defendant, having particular regard to the nature of the wrong committed: 'during each step of the process Boeing had acted without malice, without bad faith and relied on the advice of others before taking each step. . . . Boeing complied with the letter of the then existing law'. Earlier, in a separate hearing pertaining to that same case, the Supreme Court had mooted[222] that a defendant retains an interest in the unexpended funds of a class action suit; that the class members are the equitable owners of the unclaimed fund (whether they come forward or not); that any right that a defendant may establish is contingent on the failure of the absentee

---

[218] Higgins, *ibid*, 9.

[219] Noted by: WB Rubenstein, 'On What a "Private Attorney General" Is—And Why it Matters' (2004) 57 *Vanderbilt L Rev* 2129, fn 112, citing, eg: BH Thompson, 'The Continuing Innovation of Citizen Enforcement' (2000) *U Illinois L Rev* 185, 207–9; K Barnett, 'Equitable Trusts: An Effective Remedy in Consumer Class Actions' (1987) 96 *Yale LJ* 1591, 1599. Also see: NA DeJarlais, 'The Consumer Trust Fund: A *Cy-près* Solution to Undistributed Funds in Consumer Class Actions' (1987) 38 *Hastings LJ* 729, 753, citing also, on these points: 'Collecting Overcharges from the Oil Companies: The Department of Energy's Restitutionary Obligation' (1980) 32 *Stanford L Rev* 1039, 1052–53; 'An Economic Analysis of Fluid Class Recovery Mechanisms' (1980) 34 *Stanford L Rev* 173, 180.

[220] Eg, in Manitoba: Class Proceedings Act 2002, CCSM c C130, s 34(5)(c); in Saskatchewan: Class Actions Act, SS 2001, c C–12.01, s 37(5)(c); in Newfoundland and Labrador: Class Actions Act 2001, SNL 2001, c C–18.1, s 34(5)(c); in BC: CPA (BC), s 34(5)(c); in Ontario: CPA (Ont), s 26(10).

[221] 739 F 2d 730, 736–37 (2d Cir 1984).

[222] *Boeing Co v Van Gemert*, 444 US 472, 477–82, 100 S Ct 745 (1980).

class members to exercise their rights of possession; and that a defendant has 'a colorable claim' in the fund when it claims for return of the excess.

Furthermore, reversion to the defendant may be appropriate when compensation, not punishment, is the aim of the statute underlying the cause of action.[223] In the latter case, the defendant may cogently argue that once the claims of the members of the class are fulfilled, then it has an equitable claim to the money, given that 'it had been turned over for the specific and limited purpose of compensating the class.'[224]

In some cases, where the court decides that a *cy-près* distribution is inappropriate, the dispute will reduce to which of the defendant, or the class plaintiffs, has a better claim to the unused class action settlement or judgment—that is, should the court return the surplus to the defendant or disburse the entire fund to the claiming class members on a *pro rata* basis? It has been judicially said that neither has a legal right to the excess fund.[225] By way of illustration, in *Friedman v Lansdale Parking Authority*,[226] the competing arguments in this tug-of-war were summarised by the court in the following manner (where D = defendant, and C = class):

Arguments by C for plaintiff fund-sharing:	Arguments by D for return of the unused monies to it:
✓ the settlement made no provision for the return of excess money to D; ✓ C, unlike the defendant, has 'clean hands'; ✓ D had no legal right to the fund	✓ the non-claiming C members, despite ample time given to file a claim, had effectively waived their interest in the fund by their inaction; ✓ disbursing the surplus to C bestowed an undeserved windfall upon those claiming class members; ✓ since D did not admit wrongdoing in the settlement agreement, D also had, to some extent, 'clean hands' ✓ since both parties expected the fund to be exhausted, it is equitable to return the unused portion to D; ✓ to allow the claiming class members to retain the surplus may provide an incentive for future class action representatives to keep potential class members uninformed so large uncollected damage pools will be distributed to a few class members, and may deter Ds from pursuing settlements for fear of a punitive effect; ✓ where the excess is due to the mutually held erroneous assumption that the class would be approximately 200, it would be unfair to distribute the excess to C; ✓ since public funds paid for the settlement, it is only just that the excess be returned to D for the benefit of the entire community rather than disbursed to a few already fully compensated class members at taxpayers expense.

[223] *Six (6) Mexican Workers v Arizona Citrus Growers*, 904 F 2d 1301, 1306 (9th Cir 1990).
[224] Successfully claimed in, eg: *Wilson v Southwest Airlines Inc*, 880 F 2d 807, 812 (5th Cir 1989).
[225] Eg: *Wilson, ibid; Powell v Georgia-Pacific Corp*, 843 F Supp 491, 495 (WD Ark 1994); *In re Folding Carton Antitrust Litig*, 744 F 2d 1252, 1254 (7th Cir 1984).
[226] Fed Sec L Rep (CCH) P98,676 (ED Pa 1995).

The unclaimed settlement fund reverted to the defendant in this case, an approach which has been endorsed elsewhere.[227]

Where the court is asked to balance reversion with a *cy-près* distribution during the process of settlement approval, two experienced practitioners had this to say about which is appropriate:

> During the processes of negotiating a class action settlement, the subject of *cy-près* is often discussed. Experience dictates that stronger cases of liability and damages typically result in concessions made by one or more defendants that *cy-près* funding to certain groups or projects be part of the settlement makeup. Likewise, weaker cases of liability or damages typically result in a reversion of any unclaimed or undistributed funds to the defendant.[228]

Conversely, of course, it makes no sense to permit class action judgment or settlement monies to revert to the defendant, where deterrence is the primary goal of the action. Thus, drawing upon judicial examples under FRCP 23: where 'disgorgement and deterrence are concomitant policies' underlying the litigation;[229] where a defendant is directed to pay restitution by disgorging all of its profits made from its wrongdoing;[230] where to order reversion would simply reward the defendant for its poor record-keeping that rendered the class members unidentifiable;[231] or where damages are awarded with the express purpose of punishing the defendant and vindicating a public interest,[232] then any reversion to the defendant should, in the circumstances, be refuted.

---

[227] See, eg: *Kestenbaum v Emerson*, 1981 US Dist LEXIS 14794, at 5 (SDNY 1981) (any balance in the settlement fund to be repaid to the defendant Land Trust).

[228] JG Casurella and JR Bevis, 'Class Action Law in Georgia: Emerging Trends in Litigation, Certification and Settlement' (1997) 49 *Mercer L Rev* 39, 67.

[229] *Brewer v Southern Union Co*, 83 F 1173, 1987 US Dist LEXIS 15940, at 9 (D Colo 1987); *Six (6) Mexican Workers v Arizona Citrus Growers*, 904 F 2d 1301, 1306–8 (9th Cir 1990), citing: *Simer v Rios*, 661 F 2d 655, 676; *In re Compact Disc Minimum Advertised Price Antitrust Litig*, 2005 US Dist LEXIS 11332, at 9 (D Maine 2005).

[230] Noted in: *Nabal v BJ's Wholesale Club Inc*, 2002 US Dist LEXIS 15106, at 16 (ED Pa 2002) ('[i]nstead, a court could order escheat to the government or a *cy-près* distribution that provides the class members with an indirect benefit').

[231] *Six (6) Mexican Workers v Arizona Citrus Growers*, 641 F Supp 259, 268–69 (D Ariz 1986) (the defendants' 'violations of the housing and record-keeping requirements of FLCRA were intentional within the meaning of the Act. In contrast to having the undistributed damages revert back to the defendants, which would in effect reward the defendants for their inadequate record keeping, fluid recovery distribution would serve to compel observance of the statute').

[232] As occurred in: *Pray v Lockheed Aircraft Corp*, 644 F Supp 1289, 1304 (DDC 1986).

8

Class Actions Cy-près: *Principles*

A INTRODUCTION

A s WITH ANY OTHER application of the *cy-près* doctrine to the transfers of property, applying class action judgment or settlement sums *cy-près* represents an imperfect solution to a difficult problem. In seeking to set the parameters of the class actions *cy-près* doctrine, the American courts (and, to a lesser extent, the Canadian legislature and judiciary) have sought to establish a framework for its application.

This requires the existence of definable triggers, or tests, for its implementation, the analysis of which is contained in Section C. The framework also requires that appropriate guidelines for choosing the *cy-près* recipient (in the more frequent cases of organisational distribution *cy-près*) are delineated. These latter are discussed in Section D. Unfortunately, a considerable divide has emerged in American case law in answering the question—'how close must the purposes of the *cy-près* recipient be to the original purpose of the lawsuit'? However, before embarking upon our discussion of that framework, the interesting relationship—both analogies and contrasts—between the charitable trusts *cy-près* doctrine and the class actions doctrine, deserves some consideration in Section B next.

B RELATIONSHIP BETWEEN CLASS ACTIONS *CY-PRÈS* AND CHARITABLE TRUSTS *CY-PRÈS*

1. The Analogies

The doctrine has been said[1] to have a particularly analogous relationship to the trusts doctrine from whence it came, where the court holds a fund of unclaimed monies resulting from a class action judgment or settlement.

In both scenarios, the doctrine (note, the *one* doctrine) applies where distribution of the monies to the intended recipients is impossible, impracticable or infeasible; in both, the triggers for the operation of the doctrine have been gradually widened over time, either via judicial precedent or by statute; in both,

---

[1] *In re Folding Carton Antitrust Litig*, 557 F Supp 1091, 1109 (ND Ill 1983) ('We note that, because this fund already exists, the analogy between this case and the trust law origins of the *cy-près* doctrine is a particularly close one').

the property is to be applied 'as near as possible' to the original intention, although again, the degree of closeness between the *cy-près* application and that which was originally contemplated has been the subject of debate in both the charitable trusts and class actions contexts; and, in both scenarios, application of the doctrine can be ruled out where the document evidencing the disposition (trust instrument or judicially-approved class action settlement agreement, for example) indicates that, in the event of failure of the disposition, the property is to revert to the donor/defendant or pass to a nominated party.

It could be fairly said that the doctrine has been subject to discerning scrutiny in both applications to avoid any substantive change to the law being effected by the doctrine's use. For example, in charitable trusts *cy-près*, the doctrine cannot be used to convert a trust that was laudable and benevolent, but non-charitable at law, into a charitable trust. In the context of class actions *cy-près*, the doctrine cannot be used to circumvent individualised proof of damage, if that is expressly required by the relevant statute.[2]

An analogy may be drawn between a testator who gives funds for a specific charitable purpose that has been accomplished, and where a defendant pays monies over as a settlement but a portion of unclaimed funds remains at the end of the settlement. Just as the testator commits himself to disposing of his property to a charitable purpose, class members who participate in a settlement agreement similarly commit themselves to that specified manner of damages distribution—and in both cases, it is up to the court to divine what *cy-près* use of the property should be adopted when the property transfer is no longer possible or practicable in full or in part. Certainly, whether applied in the context of charitable trusts or class actions, the doctrine has a manifestly benevolent purpose, whereby the *cy-près* property distribution is intended to either directly or indirectly benefit the original beneficiaries or class members.

2. Defining the Purpose of the Class Actions *Cy-près* Doctrine

Some US authority, such as *Mirfasihi v Fleet Mortgage Corp*,[3] has sought to distance the charitable trusts *cy-près* principle from its application to class actions jurisprudence by pointing to two significant differences between the scenarios, which are addressed below. These perceived dual distinctions between

---

[2] *Molski v Gleich*, 318 F 3d 937, 954 (9th Cir 2003), citing also: *In re Hotel Telephone Charges*, 500 F 2d 86, 89–90 (9th Cir 1974) (*cy-près* disallowed because 'allowing gross damages by treating unsubstantiated claims of class members collectively significantly alters substantive rights under the antitrust statutes'); *Al Barnett & Son Inc v Outboard Marine Corp*, 64 FRD 43, 55 (D Del 1974) (*cy-près* distribution rejected; would alter the substantive law of antitrust by essentially eliminating plaintiffs' proof of injury and damage). Cf: *Six (6) Mexican Workers v Arizona Citrus Growers*, 904 F 2d 1301, 1306 (9th Cir 1990) (noting that concerns raised in *In re Hotel*, for example, did not apply 'where the underlying statute permits awards without a showing of actual damage').
[3] 356 F 3d 781 (7th Cir 2004).

the two applications of the *cy-près* doctrine prompted the Seventh Circuit to assert that the *cy-près* doctrine, 'or rather something parading under its name, has been applied in class action cases', and that the remedy was 'badly misnamed'.[4] Issue may be taken, however, with both perceived points of distinction.

(a) Focusing upon the 'donor' of the monies

In the class actions context, the Seventh Circuit remarked in *Mirfasihi* that the *cy-près* doctrine is used as a 'purely punitive' measure against the donor of the monies, the defendant, 'to prevent the defendant from walking away from the litigation scot-free because of the infeasibility of distributing the proceeds of the settlement [or] judgment'.[5] This, it was implied, was quite disparate from the benevolent function of *cy-près* in charitable trusts. At first glance, this may appear to be true. In the latter context, the doctrine seeks to adhere to the donor's wishes for the disposition of his property as near as possible to the original charitable purpose, rather than have that property revert to next-of-kin for which the donor may already have made adequate, or deliberately no, provision. Thus, it could certainly be reasoned that, when having regard to the parties from whence the monies came—settlor/testator, and defendant—in the former case, the doctrine acts benevolently, and in the latter case, punitively.

However, certain other US authority indicates that it would be a distinct mistake to overstate the punitive function of class actions *cy-près*. It would seem that to distinguish the charitable *cy-près* doctrine from the class actions *cy-près* doctrine by having regard to the effect upon the *donor* is not entirely valid, because the class actions *cy-près* doctrine is *not* primarily punitive. This is demonstrated via three propositions of note.

First, if the intended beneficiaries of the class action judgment or settlement—the class members—do not wish to benefit (as peculiar as it sounds), the argument that a *cy-près* distribution of the judgment or settlement sum should be ordered anyway, because it would punish or deter the defendant, will not stand. The leading example of this view is to be found in *In re Matzo Food Products Litigation*.[6] The class (a known class of 112 distributors), or more accurately, their lawyers, asked for a *cy-près* settlement because the class members themselves did not wish to participate in any recovery or judgment against the defendants. As the District Court put it:

> Indeed, class counsel go so far as to represent that were the case to proceed to trial, the class members would choose not to pursue the litigation and would opt out of the action. In other words, class counsel have pursued this litigation, and have created

---

[4] *Ibid*, 784.

[5] *Ibid*, 784. Also: *Van Gemert v Boeing Co*, 573 F 2d 733, fn 7 (2nd Cir 1978) (*cy-près* distribution 'primarily a deterrent against wrongful conduct'); *Simer v Rios*, 661 F 2d 655, 675–77 (7th Cir 1981) (*cy-près* distribution proper only where class sues under a statute that embraces all three policies of deterrence, disgorgement and compensation).

[6] 156 FRD 600 (DNJ 1994).

this settlement, on behalf of class members who apparently do not wish to have any-thing to do with the litigation. In short, class counsel are litigating this case without any clients. Counsel have not cited, and this court has not uncovered, any case which would support use of *cy-près* principles under such circumstances. . . . If it is true that the class members do not want to participate in any recovery, then this is a case where the fund never should have been created in the first place. Indeed, it appears that the proposed settlement is simply a thinly disguised ploy for the recovery of nearly $500,000 in attorneys' fees. Under these circumstances, I simply cannot conclude that the [*cy-près*] settlement, under which the class members recover nothing, is fair, adequate and reasonable.[7]

The class lawyers sought to argue that a *cy-près* settlement would nevertheless be appropriate because of its deterrent effect on the defendant, but the court disagreed. It noted that a *cy-près* distribution would achieve no further impact than a $1 million fine already imposed upon the defendants, and that the court's primary consideration in class litigation had to be the interests of the class members, and the compensation awarded to them. The court also noted that, under the proposed settlement, no class member distributors would receive either direct or indirect compensation. Thus, the *cy-près* settlement was rejected. Interestingly, it has been suggested[8] since, the deterrent effect of fines in this and similar cases may tend to be overstated, in comparison with the deterrent effects of class actions, given that the amount of compensation awarded against price-fixing defendants in class suits has far exceeded the amount of their criminal fines to date. In any event, the District Court in *Matzo* indicated that the deterrent rationale of the *cy-près* doctrine in the class litigation context is less than overriding.

Secondly, (and again, as peculiar as it may sound), a *cy-près* distribution may actually *benefit* the wrongdoing defendant—yet that will not affect the validity of the *cy-près* scheme in any way. That benefit may take the form of tax breaks. It has been judicially confirmed[9] in *obiter* that '[a]lthough it seems somewhat distasteful to allow a corporation to fulfil its legal and equitable obligations through tax-deductible donations to third parties' (via a *cy-près* distribution to organisations rather than to class members), that practice is permissible. A further illustration of benefit to the defendant occurred in the case of *Nelson v Greater Gadsden Housing Authority*,[10] which a later case has termed a 'very unusual use of the *cy-près* doctrine.'[11] In an action by a tenant class against the landlord Authority, unclaimed funds were applied *cy-près* to improve the building, and to repair and replace defendant-supplied appliances and equip-ment in the flats—in other words, the money was to be spent by the defendant

[7] *Ibid*, 606.
[8] S Calkins, 'An Enforcement Official's Reflections on Antitrust Class Actions' (1997) 39 *Arizona L Rev* 413, fn 155.
[9] *Molski v Gleich*, 318 F 3d 937, 954 (9th Cir 2003).
[10] 802 F 2d 405, 409 (11th Cir 1986).
[11] *Six (6) Mexican Workers v Arizona Citrus Growers*, 904 F 2d 1301, 1312 (9th Cir 1990).

on the defendant's *own property*. The *cy-près* aspect of the judgment was bolstered, however, by the fact that the defendant Authority appeared to be a public entity whose function it was to provide affordable housing, so that its funds may have already been committed to a public use, and only the nature of that use changed, and very slightly.

Thirdly, in *Six (6) Mexican Workers v Arizona Citrus Growers*, the court downplayed the punitive aspect of *cy-près*, by noting that it should never be used as a vehicle for 'social engineering', merely to benefit those who have no claim to the monies:

> in this case it is proposed that the doctrine be used in the absence of any expression of purpose or intent by any of those who have any right to the funds. Its use may well amount to little more than an exercise in social engineering by a judge, who finds it offensive that defendants have profited by some wrongdoing, but who has no legitimate plaintiff to give the money to. It is a very troublesome doctrine, which runs the risk of being a vehicle to punish defendants in the name of social policy, without conferring any particular benefit upon any particular wronged person. . . . [it is argued that] if the judge cannot find plaintiffs to give it to, he can do good by distributing that money to someone who has no claim whatever upon it. In my opinion, that is fundamentally wrong.[12]

In similar tone, where the defendants do not 'deserve' to be punished, then American courts, at least, have declined to award a *cy-près* distribution against them. For example, in *Simer v Rios*,[13] the court determined that a *cy-près* recovery was not needed to deter the defendant because: the defendant (CSA) was charged with administering a large and complex programme 'and it is inevitable that problems arise'; there was no sign that CSA's activities were carried out with *male fides* or with the specific intent of disobeying its statutory obligations; it was not a case of CSA having intentionally breached legislation which was intended to regulate 'socially opprobrious conduct' of the types regulated by antitrust or securities laws; CSA was, to some extent, uncertain of its obligations in light of some legislative changes; nor was it a case of a corporate defendant engaging in unlawful conduct for illegal profit, for neither CSA (nor its shareholders) benefitted financially from its allegedly unlawful behaviour. For all of these reasons, the court was satisfied that this was not an appropriate occasion for a *cy-près* distribution.

Thus, it is plain from the three propositions above that there is no particularly forceful punitive element in class actions *cy-près* that governs all else. Certainly, there is seemingly no 'bright-line' distinction between class actions and charitable *cy-près* on the basis that one is aimed solely toward the purpose of punishment and deterrence of the defendant, and the other toward the benevolent achievement of the donor's frustrated purpose. *Cy-près* distributions in the

---

[12] *Six (6) Mexican Workers, ibid.*
[13] 661 F 2d 655, 676–77 (7th Cir 1981).

class actions context serve the concomitant aims of compensation, deterrence, education and disgorgement. It is the benevolent effect of the *cy-près* distribution upon the intended recipients that is arguably the more crucial parallel between charitable *cy-près* and class actions *cy-près*.

(b) Focusing upon the intended recipient of the monies

The other alleged distinction between charitable and class actions *cy-près*, drawn by the Seventh Circuit in *Mirfasihi v Fleet Mortgage Corp*,[14] concerned those very recipients. The court declared that, unlike the position of beneficiaries under a trust who stood to gain from the application of the trust property toward an analogous charitable purpose to that selected by the donor, '[t]here is no indirect benefit to the class from the defendant's giving the money to someone else'.[15]

Against this, however, two assertions may be made. First, the importance of achieving a cross-over of benefit between the original class members and those who stand to gain from the *cy-près* application of class action judgment or settlement sums has been increasingly emphasised, in both American judicial statements,[16] and in Canadian statutory[17] and judicial[18] jurisprudence. The extent of this cross-over will be discussed later.[19] Secondly, and quite apart from the extent of any overlap between the original class members and the substituted beneficiaries under the *cy-près* scheme, the class members (say, consumers of vitamins) represent a 'proxy' for the 'larger amorphous class' (consumers generally) who stand to gain some advantage from the punitive and deterrent effect which the litigation will have upon the defendant's practices[20]—another 'indirect benefit' attainable from *cy-près* distributions.

[14] 356 F 3d 781 (7th Cir 2004).

[15] *Mirfasihi v Fleet Mortgage Corp*, 356 F 3d 781, 784 (7th Cir 2004).

[16] Note this typical statement: 'Such a doctrine has been extended to the distribution of funds in class action and overcharge cases and, where it is impossible to specifically identify the proper claimants, allows the funds to be used in a manner designed to benefit the claimants as a class': *In re Department of Energy Stripper Well Exemption Litig*, 578 F Supp 586, 594 (D Kans 1983). Also: *Jones v National Distillers*, 56 F Supp 2d 355, 357 (SDNY 1999) ('The *cy-près* approach ... puts the unclaimed fund to its next best compensation use, eg, for the ... indirect, prospective benefit of the class', citing HB Newberg and A Conte, *Newberg on Class Actions* (3rd edn, Shepard McGraw-Hill Inc, Colorado Springs, 1992) § 10.17); *Weber v Goodman*, 1998 US Dist LEXIS 22832, at 17 (EDNY 1998) (*cy-près* recovery 'does not necessarily mean that the class members will get "nothing" as defendants contend').

[17] Note the precise wording in CPA (Ont), s 26(4) (proviso: 'if the court is satisfied that a reasonable number of class members who would not otherwise receive monetary relief would benefit from the [*cy-près*] order').

[18] Note, eg, the statement in *Tesluk v Boots Pharmaceutical plc* (2002), 21 CPC (5th) 196 (SCJ) [16] that, where the settlement sum 'cannot be economically distributed to individual class members the court will approve a *cy-près* distribution to recognized organizations or institutions which will benefit class members').

[19] See pp 264 ff.

[20] See, on this point, eg: WB Rubenstein, 'On What a "Private Attorney General" Is—And Why it Matters' (2004) 57 *Vanderbilt L Rev* 2129, 2169.

C TRIGGERS FOR CY-PRÈS IN CLASS LITIGATION

In the class actions context, courts have utilised the *cy-près* doctrine to distribute class damages or settlement funds for the indirect benefit of the class where actual distribution to class members has been judicially stated to be 'impossible',[21] 'difficult' or 'inappropriate',[22] or 'not feasible'.[23]

It is worth noting that, in the view of some courts, at least, *cy-près* recovery will be considered to be premature until damages funds have been distributed to victims to the fullest extent that is feasible—if the victims can be identified, then even small entitlements to damages should be distributed, before any *cy-près* order is even contemplated.[24] To put the argument in another form, it is only justifiable to give the class members' money to others if those class members had the opportunity to actually claim their compensatory entitlements.[25] As discussed previously,[26] however, *cy-près* distributions of the *entirety* of a judgment or settlement sum have occurred in both Canada and the United States, rather negating the aforementioned emphasis upon the individuals' claims.

The 'unusual situations' (so-called,[27] although the volume of *cy-près* distributions evident from the case reports suggest otherwise) that may trigger the employment of *cy-près* principles in class actions litigation can be summarised in the following section. Not all factors require to be present in any one scenario, although their effect would appear to be cumulative:

Where recovery per class member would be extremely low. In *Jones v National Distillers*,[28] there were 17,198 class members, and the damages sum was $18,400.80. Given the postage and administrative costs of distributing that damages award to all eligible class members, the court concluded it would be prohibitive and the recovery negligible. Whilst not impossible, distribution of class funds to class members was 'infeasible', and a *cy-près* distribution followed.

---

[21] The term used in, eg: *In re Department of Energy Stripper Well Exemption Litig*, 578 F Supp 586, 591 (D Kans 1983), when describing the ultimate consumers of petroleum products who suffered from overcharging; also: *In re Matzo Food Products Litig*, 156 FRD 600, 605 (DNJ 1994) (*cy-près* allowed where 'distribution economically impossible'); *Mace v Van Ru Credit Corp*, 109 F 3d 338, 345 (7th Cir 1997).

[22] The terms used in, eg: *Mace v Van Ru Credit Corp*, 109 F 3d 338, 347 (7th Cir 1997), although no *cy-près* distribution was ordered in this case. Also: *In re Microsoft Corp Antitrust Litig*, 185 F Supp 2d 519, 523 (MD 2002) ('if . . . the proceeds of any class recovery could not be economically distributed to class members').

[23] The term used in, eg: *In re Matzo Food Products Litig*, 156 FRD 600, 605 (DNJ 1994); *Jones v National Distillers*, 56 F Supp 2d 355, 357 (SDNY 1999).

[24] *Weber v Goodman*, 1999 US Dist Lexis 22832, at 16 (EDNY 1998); *Mace v Van Ru Credit Corp*, 109 F 3d 338, 345 (7th Cir 1997).

[25] *In re Matzo Food Products Litig*, 156 FRD 600, 605–6 (DNJ 1994).

[26] See pp 235–6, 244.

[27] Noted in: *Mace v Van Ru Credit Corp*, 109 F 3d 338, 347 (7th Cir 1997).

[28] 56 F Supp 2d 355, 357 (SDNY 1999) (class action re securities fraud; *cy-près* settlement).

Where the recovery per class member is tiny, two problems can manifest: either the cost of *proving* the individual claim would be greater than the claim itself, or the cost of *distributing* the damages may exceed the value of the claim— in either event, a *cy-près* distribution may be triggered.[29] Essentially, the court employs a cost–benefit analysis: what is the amount of compensation per class member, compared with the costs of administering that recovery?[30] Unsurprisingly, a poor cost–benefit outcome has been the catalyst for judicial approval of substitute *cy-près* applications in both Canada[31] and in the United States.[32] In particular, recoveries of $1.00 per class member (or less) have invoked a *cy-près* distribution for the 'next best' application in more than one American[33] and Canadian[34] case.

Of course, the court may well have to assess conflicting evidence between the plaintiff class and the defendant as to the processing costs of individual claims, when determining whether or not individual distribution of the judgment or settlement sum is economically infeasible.[35]

Where the identities of the class members are not, and cannot be, known for purposes of distribution. Where class members are unidentifiable, *cy-près* distributions are appropriate. This may particularly occur in a distribution chain of plaintiff class members. For example, in *Alfresh Beverages Canada Corp v*

---

[29] *Six (6) Mexican Workers v Arizona Citrus Growers*, 904 F 2d 1301, 1305 (9th Cir 1990) ('When a class action involves a large number of class members but only a small individual recovery, the cost of separately proving and distributing each class member's damages may so outweigh the potential recovery that the class action becomes unfeasible'). Also, see eg: *In re Airline Ticket Commission Antitrust Litig*, 268 F 3d 619, 625 (8th Cir 2001); *Powell v Georgia-Pacific Corp*, 119 F 3d 703, 706 (8th Cir 1997); *Democratic Central Comm of District of Columbia v Washington Metro Area Transit Comm*, 84 F 3d 451, 455 fn 1 (DC Cir 1996).

[30] *State of California v Levi Strauss & Co*, 715 P 2d 564, 576 (Cal 1986).

[31] *Ford v F Hoffmann-La Roche Ltd* (SCJ, 23 Mar 2005) [80] ('the complexity and administrative costs associated with any direct distribution to each Intermediate Purchaser and Consumer would be prohibitive. Thus, the settlements contemplate *cy-près* distributions to these two groups of class members'); *Tesluk v Boots Pharmaceutical plc* (2002), 21 CPC (5th) (SCJ) [9] ('because of the large size of the class, some 520,000 members, the small dollar per claim damages [of between $30 and $70], and the costs associated with distribution the proper approach was to distribute the aggregate amount of the settlement by way of a *cy-près* distribution to selected recipient organizations, hospitals and universities conducting research into hypothyroidism which will likely serve the interests of the class members').

[32] Eg: *State of New York v Salton Inc*, 265 F Supp 2d 310, 314 (SDNY 2003), citing also: *State of New York v Keds Corp*, 1994 US Dist LEXIS 3362, at 3 (SDNY 1994); *In re Matzo Food Products Litig*, 156 FRD 600, 605 (DNJ 1994) ('[t]ypically, the court employs *cy-près* where class members cannot be located or where individual recoveries would be so small as to make distribution economically impossible').

[33] Eg: *State of California v Levi Strauss & Co*, 41 Cal 3d 460, 461, 715 P 2d 564, 565, 224 Cal Rptr 605 (1986) (antitrust class action; estimated claim per pair of jeans purchased only 35–40 cents); *State of New York v Keds Corp*, 1994 US Dist LEXIS 3362 (SDNY 1994) (antitrust class action; *cy-près* distribution of $5.7 million to charities where alleged overcharges were in the range of $1.00– $1.25 per pair of shoes purchased).

[34] Eg: *Gilbert v Canadian Imperial Bank of Commerce* (2004), 3 CPC (6th) 35 (SCJ) [15] (noting some class members' claims as low as $0.72).

[35] As occurred in: *In re Microsoft Corp Antitrust Litig*, 185 F Supp 2d 519, fn 2 (MD 2002).

Hoechst AG,[36] which was a price-fixing case involving food additives, the Ontario Superior Court of Justice favoured a *cy-près* distribution on the basis that there were 'significant problems' in identifying possible plaintiffs below the manufacturer level (that is, the wholesalers and consumers), and that a *cy-près* distribution to specified not-for-profit entities, 'in effect as surrogates for these categories of claimants, for the general, indirect benefit of such class members', was the best solution.

Alternatively, where the defendant and the class itself have not maintained purchase records, for example, a *cy-près* distribution may be called for.[37] Much Canadian[38] and American[39] authority has permitted *cy-près* distribution where this trigger has been met.

Where it is confidently predicted that some or all class members will not come forward. A *cy-près* distribution will be ordered where is it confidently forecast that there will be an unclaimed sum because either all or a portion of the class members will remain unidentifiable or will not come forward.[40] In such circumstances, a *cy-près* order renders the benefit of the judgment or settlement available to those silent, as well as claiming, class members.[41]

Reasons for class members' reluctance or inability to claim their loss could include any of the following: the class members cannot be given notice of the action;[42] they are possibly in breach of immigration requirements and 'may be reluctant to seek settlement benefits regardless of how simple the claims procedures are';[43] their migratory lifestyles make claims unlikely or practically

[36] (2002), 16 CPC (5th) 301 (SCJ) [15]–[16].

[37] SB Farmer, 'More Lessons From the Laboratories: *Cy-près* Distributions in Parens Patriae Antitrust Actions Brought by State Attorneys General' (1999) 68 *Fordham L Rev* 361, 405.

[38] Eg: *Gilbert v Canadian Imperial Bank of Commerce* (2004), 3 CPC (6th) 35 (SCJ) [16] (CIBC, chartered bank, issued credit cards, applied undisclosed and unauthorised percentage mark-up fees on transactions in foreign currency; past cardholders were omitted from distribution of damages; *cy-près* payment to organisation 'acceptable given the peregrinations involved in pursuing those claims. This approach is acceptable in the present circumstances given the impossibility of identifying such class members'); *Tesluk v Boots Pharmaceutical plc* (2002), 21 CPC (5th) (SCJ).

[39] Eg: *New York v Salton Inc*, 265 F Supp 2d 310, 314 (SDNY 2003) ('Because of the difficulty in identifying and locating individual purchasers of the Grills, and the minimal amount of recovery an individual consumer would be entitled to compared to the cost of administering individual relief, the Court finds that the *cy-près* method of distribution proposed in the Settlement Agreement is reasonable and adequate'), citing also: *New York v Reebok Intl Ltd*, 903 F Supp 532, 537 (SDNY 1995). Also: *State of New York v Keds Corp*, 1994 US Dist LEXIS 3362 (SDNY 1994) (more than five million pairs of shoes sold + almost impossible to locate individual consumers + cost of locating consumers would eliminate any economic benefit of settlement); *Mace v Van Ru Credit Corp*, 109 F 3d 338, 345 (7th Cir 1997); *In re Mexico Money Transfer Litig*, 164 F Supp 2d 1002 (ND Ill 2000).

[40] Flagged, and followed, in, eg: *In re Folding Carton Antitrust Litig*, 744 F 2d 1252, 1258 (7th Cir 1984) ('Because some nonclaiming class members will never come forward ... the task becomes to compensate them as nearly as possible'). Flagged, but not followed, in: *Mace v Van Ru Credit Corp*, 109 F 3d 338, 345 (7th Cir 1997).

[41] S Karas, 'The Role of Fluid Recovery in Consumer Protection Litigation' (2002) 90 *Californian L Rev* 959, 973, 991, citing: *State of California v Levi Strauss & Co*, 715 P 2d 564, 576 (Cal 1986).

[42] Noted in: *Mace v Van Ru Credit Corp*, 109 F 3d 338, 345 (7th Cir 1997); *Simer v Rios*, 661 F 2d 655, 675 (7th Cir 1981).

[43] *In re Mexico Money Transfer Litig*, 164 F Supp 2d 1002, 1031 (ND Ill 2000).

difficult;[44] there is a continuing lack of interest on the part of some class members about the action;[45] a great number of purchasers are unlikely to have retained proof of purchase dockets or receipts with which to claim;[46] or socio-economic factors, such as lack of education or affluence, reduce the likelihood that class members will come forward.[47]

For example, where a number of these factors were present in *In re Mexico Money Transfer Litigation*,[48] the defendants entered a settlement agreement in which they agreed to provide class members with coupons entitling them to a deduction off the price of one future wire transfer for every transfer made since November 1993, and that, in addition, they would pay $4.6 million to organisations that helped the Mexican-American community. This was judicially stated to be 'in recognition of the fact that many class members will prove to be unidentifiable, will not claim their coupons, or will not use all coupons they receive'.[49] As Draba pragmatically notes, it was also a common sense solution: '[a] *pro rata* distribution of $4.6 million in cash entitled each of the 13.5 million class members to 34 cents—less than the price of a first-class stamp.'[50]

Where the identity of the class members changes constantly. In *Powell v Georgia-Pacific Corp*,[51] the Court of Appeals for the Eighth Circuit noted that *cy-près* application of class action funds has traditionally been used in cases in which class members change constantly—where, for example, a service provider (eg, of public transport, electricity, or hotel rooms) is found liable for over-charging its customers. Large scale product purchases (eg, milk, petrol, vitamins) by a 'transient population' is also a scenario where a *cy-près* distribution is likely.

Where the sheer number of class members makes individual distribution of damages difficult. In a recent class action brought against Microsoft Corp in respect of case of computer software pricing, the District Court observed that, *inter alia*:

---

[44] *Six (6) Mexican Workers v Arizona Citrus Growers*, 641 F Supp 259, 265 (D Ariz 1986). Also mentioned as a relevant factor in: *Rodriguez v Berrybrook Farms Inc*, 1990 US Dist LEXIS 14646, at 6 (MD 1990).

[45] Suggested in: *Hayes v Arthur Young & Co*, 1994 US App LEXIS 23608, at 55 (9th Cir 1992).

[46] Eg: the many millions of purchasers of software in: *In re Microsoft Corp Antitrust Litig*, 185 F Supp 2d 519, fn 2 (MD 2002); the millions of purchasers of shoes in: *State of New York v Keds Corp*, 1994 US Dist LEXIS 3362 (SDNY 1994).

[47] Eg, Higgins cites the study by T Bartsh *et al*, *A Class Action Suit that Worked: The Consumer Refund in the Antibiotic Antitrust Litigation* (Lexington Books, Lexington Mass, 1978) as an example of a class in which the plaintiffs who came forward were better educated and higher earning than those that did not: RA Higgins, 'The Equitable Doctrine of *Cy-près* and Consumer Protection' (Annex 1, ACA Submission, Trade Practices Review, 15 Jul 2002) 5 and fn 17.

[48] 267 F 3d 743 (7th Cir 2001).

[49] *Ibid*, 745.

[50] RE Draba, 'Motorsports Merchandise: A *Cy-près* Distribution Not Quite "As Near as Possible" '(2004) 16 *Loyola Consumer L Rev* 121, 130–31.

[51] 119 F 3d 703, 706 (8th Cir 1997), also citing, by way of example: *Market Street Railway Co v Railroad Comm of California*, 28 Cal 2d 363, 171 P 2d 875, 881 (Cal 1946).

[t]he sheer number of potential class members (it has been estimated that there are as many as 100 million possible claimants), the transient nature of the US population, [and] the high rate of software piracy ... all point to the unfeasibility of economic distribution of class proceeds.[52]

A large class size has similarly influenced Canadian courts to confirm the wisdom of a *cy-près* distribution, with the Ontario Superior Court of Justice noting in *Tesluk v Boots Pharmaceutical plc* that the bigger the class size (in this case, 520,000), the larger the administration costs of the individual distributions, which would, in turn, significantly dissipate the settlement fund.[53]

Thus, in the absence of any statutory guidance in either Canadian statutes or American rules of court, it is possible to distill from relevant case law the following triggers for the propriety of a class actions *cy-près* distribution:

- ❏ a low damages recovery per class member;
- ❏ a poor cost–benefit analysis for individual damages distribution;
- ❏ class members cannot be identified;
- ❏ class members will not come forward to claim their damages, being unable or unwilling to do so;
- ❏ a constantly fluctuating class membership;
- ❏ a huge class, rendering individual damages distribution an 'impossible' task.

The triggers are, as with all instances of *cy-près*, only part of the equation— applying the damages to a like purpose is beset with the same sorts of difficulties that have been evident in charitable trusts *cy-près*. However, prior to any consideration of that third stage of the *cy-près* analysis, it is important to have regard to further objective factors that impact upon the availability of a *cy-près* distribution in the class actions context. In the case of charitable trusts *cy-près*, this second step of the analysis required our examination of any general charitable intent on the part of the donor; in the context of class actions *cy-près*, an acceptable degree of overlap must be established.

D A SUFFICIENT DEGREE OF OVERLAP

The purpose of a *cy-près* distribution, where a litigated or settled class action recovery (or part thereof) cannot be distributed to individual class members, is to apply those undistributed funds prospectively to the indirect benefit of the class—and for the *direct* benefit of a *substituted* class—such that '[t]he *cy-près*

---

[52] *In re Microsoft Corp Antitrust Litig*, 185 F Supp 2d 519, fn 2 (MD 2002). Also see: *Powell v Georgia-Pacific Corp*, 119 F 3d 703, 706 (8th Cir 1997); *Democratic Central Committee v Washington Metropolitan Area Transit Comm*, 84 F 3d 451, 455 (DC Cir 1996).

[53] *Tesluk v Boots Pharmaceutical plc* (2002), 21 CPC (5th) (SCJ) [14].

approach ... puts the unclaimed fund to its next best compensation use.'[54] Several objective factors have been developed by the US courts[55] and by the Canadian legislatures, in addition to the triggers outlined above, by which to determine whether the degree of overlap between the original and the substituted classes lends itself to a *cy-près* distribution. These factors are discussed in this section.

Essentially, wherever proposed damages or settlement monies are not being provided exclusively to the class members, there is a potential for those class members to decry the distribution as 'theft' of a sort—that 'their property' is being given to another.[56] There is also the potential for litigation not to be brought, if those who are injured by the defendant's practices believe that they will ultimately be denied reimbursement.[57] The authorities have sought to invoke a framework of principles for dealing with these types of criticism.

1. To What Extent will the *Cy-près* Distribution Benefit Original Class Members?

Whether achieved by a price-rollback or by an organisational lump sum distribution,[58] the extent to which class members receive their damages per a *cy-près* distribution is significant. It is undeniably a disadvantage of *cy-près* applications that original victims who comprised the class are not necessarily compensated under the *cy-près* scheme.[59] The permissibility of any *cy-près* proposal depends upon as great an overlap as reasonably possible between the original class members and potential *cy-près* recipients.

In *Six (6) Mexican Workers v Arizona Citrus Growers*,[60] the Ninth Circuit rejected the district court's *cy-près* application because it 'benefit[ed] a group far too remote from the plaintiff class. . . . [*cy-près*] will be rejected when the proposed distribution fails to provide the "next best" distribution. . . . The

---

[54] *In re Holocaust Victim Assets Litig*, 311 F Supp 2d 407, 416 (EDNY 2004), citing: A Conte and HB Newberg, *Newberg on Class Actions* (4th edn, Thomson West, St Paul Minn, 2002) § 10.17.

[55] See, eg, the lists of relevant factors in: *In re Compact Disc Minimum Advertised Price Antitrust Litig*, 2005 US Dist LEXIS 11332, at 7 (D Maine 2005), and refer to other cases/lists cited in fn 3 thereof. Another recent example is: *Schwartz v Dallas Cowboys Football Club Ltd*, 362 F Supp 2d 574, 576 (ED Pa 2005). Sets of differently-argued criteria are also outlined and discussed in: K Barnett, 'Equitable Trusts: An Effective Remedy in Consumer Class Actions' (1987) 96 *Yale LJ* 1591, Pt II; and SB Farmer, 'More Lessons from the Laboratories: *Cy-près* Distributions in Parens Patriae Antitrust Actions Brought By State Attorneys General' (1999) 68 *Fordham L Rev* 361, 405.

[56] As did some objectors to the settlement achieved in the antitrust class action in: *In re Microsoft Corp Antitrust Litig*, 185 F Supp 2d 519 (MD 2002), and noted in: WB Rubenstein, 'On What a "Private Attorney General" Is—And Why it Matters' (2004) 57 *Vanderbilt U L Rev* 2129, 2161.

[57] S Karas, 'The Role of Fluid Recovery in Consumer Protection Litigation' (2002) 90 *California L Rev* 959, 987; DW Welles, 'Charitable Punishment: A Proposal to Award Punitive Damages to Nonprofit Organizations' (1998) 9 *Stanford L and Policy Rev* 203, 211–12.

[58] See pp 218–24.

[59] As noted in, eg: *Gilbert v Canadian Imperial Bank of Commerce* (2004), 3 CPC (6th) 35 (SCJ) [15]; BS Du Val, 'Book Review' (1983) 3 *Windsor Ybk of Access to Justice* 411, 432.

[60] 904 F 2d 1301 (9th Cir 1990).

district court's plan permits distribution to areas where the class members may live, but there is no reasonable certainty that any [class] member will be benefited.'[61] Similarly, in *In re Airline Ticket Commission Antitrust Litigation*,[62] a *cy-près* distribution was rejected on the basis that the distribution of unclaimed funds to Minnesota law schools and charities, which were too remotely related to the subject matter of the litigation (caps on commissions paid to travel agencies), was an abuse of discretion.

As noted previously, the Ontario legislature sought to reiterate the importance of overlapping original and *cy-près* beneficiaries by statutorily requiring that 'the court is satisfied that a reasonable number of class members who would not otherwise receive monetary relief would benefit from the order.'[63] Alberta followed suit,[64] although some other provincial legislatures (such as British Columbia[65]) surprisingly omitted this proviso (presumably, the overlap would be required judicially in any event).

In fact, some significant US jurisprudence has demonstrated that the 'benefit' to original class members may be achieved by some tangential link that falls well short of conveying compensation to the precise class members injured, as the following types of association demonstrate:

Related interests and hobbies.   In *In re Compact Disc Minimum Advertised Price Antitrust Litigation*,[66] the court noted that the class members (members of a music club), by purchasing music CDs, showed a keen interest in music; and that, 'by definition, music club members are vitally interested in the availability of recorded music and in the performance of music and of musicians'.[67] A *cy-près* distribution along those lines, to a radio station and a community arts centre, was recently implemented by the District Court.[68]

Rectification of the injury of which the class members complained.   In *Tesluk v Boots Pharmaceutical plc*,[69] the class claimed damages for misrepresentation as a result of the marketing and sale of the pharmaceutical drug, Synthroid, which was prescribed for hypothyroidism. A *cy-près* distribution of the settlement sum to specified organisations, hospitals and universities researching into

---

[61] *Ibid*, 1308.

[62] 268 F 3d 619, 625–26 (8th Cir 2001).

[63] CPA (Ont), s 26(4).

[64] See, eg: Alberta's Class Proceedings Act 2003, SA 2003, c C–16.5, s 34(1), requiring the *cy-près* distribution to 'reasonably be expected to benefit class members or subclass members'.

[65] See CPA (BC), s 34(1). The legislative regimes in Newfoundland and Labrador, in Saskatchewan, and in Manitoba, are framed in the same manner as British Columbia's in this respect.

[66] 2005 US Dist LEXIS 11332 (D Maine 2005).

[67] *Ibid*, 8.

[68] *In re Compact Disc Minimum Advertised Price Antitrust Litig*, 2005 US Dist LEXIS 16468 (D Maine 9 Aug 2005), noting (at 6) that '[t]he funds will be used for purposes benefiting the class because the class interest is in having easy access to recorded music.'

[69] (2002), 21 CPC (5th) 196 (SCJ).

hypothyroidism was ordered, on the basis that it 'will likely serve the interests of the class members'.[70]

Assisting persons who are linked with the class members, but are economically worse off. Where class members were overcharged for a basic utility such as gas, where the small amounts of overcharge could not be distributed to energy consumers, and where price-rollback was not a feasible option, then in *Brewer v Southern Union Co*,[71] the court considered that the 'next best' class were those who were gas consumers and who were economically poorly off. The unclaimed funds were applied, via lump sum distributions, to two energy assistance programmes administered by the State of New Mexico's Energy and Minerals Department. Such a distribution 'will provide direct benefits to subeconomic class members still residing in New Mexico, and to other low income gas consumers who were not original members of the class.'[72]

The same principle was applied in *In re Holocaust Victim Assets Litigation*,[73] in which it was decided that a *cy-près* distribution in favour of the neediest survivors of Nazi persecution would be the 'next best' distribution solution for the Looted Assets Class in that litigation: '[w]hile the strategy I employed will by no means provide restitution to every member of the plaintiff class, it provides meaningful restitution to those "most in need of assistance".'[74]

2. Geographical Scope of the Original Class

Matching the *cy-près* recipients to the geographical scope of the original class suit has proven to be vital, and a failure to do so has lead to the unravelling of some *cy-près* proposals—note that a similar bias towards beneficiaries of comparable geographic area has also been espoused in the context of charitable trust dispositions.[75]

In *Powell v Georgia-Pacific Corp*,[76] the Eighth Circuit approved the *cy-près* distribution of unclaimed settlement funds, for use as a scholarship fund for black high school students in the geographic area around the factory at which alleged racial discrimination had occurred. The class of over 2,000 African American workers claimed that the Georgia-Pacific Corporation had violated their equal opportunity rights. After class members were compensated under the settlement package, nearly $1 million remained. The District Court ordered the parties to design a scholarship programme, to be administered by the

---

[70] *Ibid*, [9].
[71] US Dist LEXIS 15940 (D Colo 1987).
[72] *Ibid*, 18.
[73] 311 F Supp 2d 407 (EDNY 2004).
[74] *Ibid*, 416.
[75] See p 105.
[76] 119 F 3d 703 (8th Cir 1997).

Georgia-Pacific Foundation, under which scholarships were to be awarded over a decade to 112 African American high school students in the three counties in Arkansas and three parishes in Louisiana where most of the class members lived, with the remaining proceeds going to the United Negro College Fund. The scholarship programme had two perceived advantages. First, it addressed the subject matter of the class action—the employment opportunities available to African Americans living near the defendant's facilities, and secondly, it was likely that the 'scholarships [would] benefit the class members' younger relatives'.[77] Similarly, in *Nelson v Greater Gadsen Housing Authority*,[78] in a class action dispute involving an overcharge for tenants' utility allowances, the court affirmed a *cy-près* distribution that unclaimed funds be used to increase the energy efficiency of the very apartment block in which the tenant class members lived.

Where the class members are distributed widely, say, on a nationwide basis, then other factors demonstrating linkage and overlap will need to be relied upon to permit a *cy-près* distribution to occur,[79] or, given that selection of regional or provincial organisations would make equal treatment across the country difficult, the distribution will most feasibly be made to entities and organisations that have a national presence.[80] Thus, in *Airline Ticket Commission Antitrust Litigation Travel Network Ltd v United Air Lines Inc*,[81] the Eighth Circuit reversed the District Court's order for a *cy-près* distribution to local charities, indicating that the court had failed to consider the full geographic scope of the case:

> The district court did not fully carry out our mandate. Considering the evidence and the options before the district court, travel agencies in Puerto Rico and the US Virgin Islands were clearly the next best recipients of the funds. The lawsuit challenged the caps on ticket commissions for flights 'within and between the continental US, Alaska, Hawaii, Puerto Rico, and the US Virgin Islands.' Travel agencies in Puerto Rico and the US Virgin Islands, although not members of the class, were subject to the same allegedly unlawful caps. A *cy-près* distribution to these agencies would relate directly to the antitrust injury alleged in this lawsuit.[82]

Similarly, in *Houck v Folding Carton Administration Commission*,[83] the Seventh Circuit remanded for the District Court to 'consider to some degree a

---

[77] *Ibid*, 707.

[78] 802 F 2d 405 (11th Cir 1986).

[79] As in: *In re Compact Disc Minimum Advertised Price Antitrust Litig*, 2005 US Dist LEXIS 11332 (D Maine 2005), and see also the cases discussed in sub-sections 1, 3 and 4 of this chapter section.

[80] In Canada, see, eg: *Ford v F Hoffmann-La Roche Ltd* (SCJ, 23 Mar 2005) [158], [161]. In United States, see, eg: *Schwartz v Dallas Cowboys Football Club Ltd*, 362 F Supp 2d 574, 577 (ED Pa 2005).

[81] 268 F 3d 619 (8th Cir 2001), and discussed further in: LM Germano, 'Interpretation of "United States" '(2004) 69 *J of Air Law and Commerce* 195.

[82] *Ibid, Airline Ticket*, 623.

[83] 881 F 2d 494, 502 (7th Cir 1989).

broader nationwide use of its *cy-près* discretion' because the class suit involved a nationwide harm.

3. Will Non-class Members Receive a Windfall from the *Cy-près* Distribution?

It will be recalled[84] that one of the principal arguments raised by the Australian Law Reform Commission (ALRC) against the availability of a *cy-près* distribution under that jurisdiction's class action regime was that a windfall could accrue to persons who had suffered no loss or damage and were not members of the class. The problem is a common one: the mere fact that there may be a spillover benefit to non-class-members naturally follows from the inability to distribute the funds directly to class members.[85]

Whilst the same arguments as the ALRC raised against a *cy-près* distribution have been noted in US jurisprudence, they have been responded to in a manner which provides a reasonable basis for appropriate use of the method. For example, it has been academically[86] and judicially[87] recognised under FRCP 23 that, by operation of *cy-près* schemes, a windfall will probably accrue to persons who are not members of the class and to class members who have already recovered upon individual claims, but that the potential for those windfalls should not prompt an outright ban on the device. Instead, if there is a reasonable overlap between the injured class members and those who will likely benefit from the *cy-près* distribution, windfalls are less likely. In order to reiterate this objective criterion for *cy-près* distribution, the requirement of overlap was expressly inserted by the Ontario legislature[88] as a proviso to be satisfied before any *cy-près* order is made in that province. This was done on the

---

[84] See pp 230–1.

[85] *In re Compact Disc Minimum Advertised Price Antitrust Litig*, 2005 US Dist LEXIS 11332, at 7, 8 (D Maine 2005).

[86] Eg: A Conte and HB Newberg, *Newberg on Class Actions* (4th edn, Thomson West, St Paul Minn, 2002) § 10.22 pp 530–31; B Du Val, 'Book Review' (1983) 3 *Windsor Ybk of Access to Justice* 411, 431–35.

[87] *Brewer v Southern Union Co*, 1987 US Dist LEXIS 15940, at 19 (D Colo 1987) ('Any method of distribution would have a spillover effect on nonclass members; a spillover to nonclass members requiring energy assistance is beyond rebuke, and equitable under the circumstances presented'); *City of Philadelphia v American Oil Co*, 53 FRD 45, 72 (DNJ 1971) ('The motorist who purchased gasoline from a retail station during the relevant period [1955–65] is still likely, if he has not moved out of the trading area, to continue his purchases of gasoline. However, he will be joined by many persons who were either not old enough to have had a driver's licence or were not residing in the trading area [then]'; class action not certified). Also: *Airline Ticket Commission Antitrust Litig Travel Network Ltd v United Air Lines Inc*, 307 F 3d 679, fn 2 (8th Cir 2002) ('Our ruling that those travel agencies were not specific members of the class does not foreclose such a distribution. This much should be clear from *Powell*, where we approved a distribution of scholarship funds for the benefit of the younger relatives of class members. See *Powell*, 119 F 3d at 707'); *In re Mexico Money Transfer Litig*, 164 F Supp 2d 1002, 1032 (ND Ill 2000) ('The fact that non-class members may also benefit from the *cy-près* contribution does not support the conclusion that the court should disapprove this negotiated aspect of the parties' proposed deal').

[88] CPA (Ont), s 26(4).

recommendation of the OLRC[89]—precisely to handle the 'windfall' conundrum. There has been no ascertainable case law to date which has turned upon this Ontario proviso. As further reinforcement, the legislature also referred explicitly to the fact that windfalls to non-class members or to already-compensated class members does not bar a *cy-près* distribution.[90]

The incorporation of these express provisions, and the workability of such schemes under FRCP 23 in an appropriate case of overlap, give weight to the argument that the Australian legislature could reconsider in due course the express recognition of *cy-près* distributions under that jurisdiction's federal regime.

4. Will the *Cy-près* Distribution Promote the Purposes of the Underlying Cause/s of Action?

This question, oft-cited in US case law,[91] is another test of relatedness between the original class action and the *cy-près* distribution. The approach is intended to secure the goal of ensuring that unclaimed class action settlement or judgment funds will unreservedly be put to their 'next best use', and has been relied upon to both found and refute a *cy-près* order.

In the 2005 case of *Schwartz v Dallas Cowboys Football Club Ltd*,[92] the class consisted of approximately 1.8 million purchasers of a satellite television package of National Football League (NFL) football games, who claimed that the defendants' sale of a single package of bundled NFL programming violated the Sherman Act and the Clayton Act. Of the settlement sum of $7.5 million, about $436,000 remained unclaimed, as a result of a number of cheques that were issued to class members never being presented. A proposed *cy-près* distribution of these excess settlement funds to a student legal clinic was refused. The court was satisfied that the policies which those Acts strive to uphold—the prevention of monopolistic and collusive behaviour on the part of economic

---

[89] See OLRC, *Report on Class Actions* (1982) 581–82.

[90] CPA (Ont), s 26(6).

[91] Eg: *Six (6) Mexican Workers v Arizona Citrus Growers*, 904 F 2d 1301, 1309 (9th Cir 1990) ('After the claims period has expired and the amount of the unclaimed fund is known, the district court will be in a better position to determine what remedy will best effectuate the goals of FLCRA'); *Friedman v Lansdale Parking Authority*, Fed Sec L Rep (CCH) P98,676, at 7 (ED Pa 1995) ('When considering *cy-près* distribution, the court should take into consideration the substantive policies underlying the statute upon which the case was brought').

[92] 362 F Supp 2d 574 (ED Pa 2005). See also: *Friedman v Lansdale Parking Authority*, Fed Sec L Rep (CCH) P98,676 (ED Pa 1995) (underlying statute Securities Exchange Act of 1934, r 10(b); its purpose: to prevent deceptive and unfair practices and to protect the public from the dissemination of inaccurate, incomplete and misleading information; punitive damages not recoverable under this section (so disbursement of the unclaimed fund to a third party would not further any punitive goals of the underlying claim); small class (so no disciplinary goals would be achieved by awarding the fund to a third party); alleged injury stemmed from a discrete incident rather than from ongoing illegal conduct; no *cy-près* distribution appropriate).

entities which harms consumers and distorts the operation of a free market—
were adequately protected by a sophisticated plaintiff bar, with no suggestion
that any 'meritorious antitrust cases lie dormant for lack of adequate legal representation or that an appreciable increase in enforcement of the antitrust laws is
likely to result from bestowing upon a student legal clinic the benefits of the
excess funds.' Furthermore, the proposed distribution to either a law school's
legal clinic or a charter school for gifted underprivileged students did not touch
upon the subject matter of the action (which was the mode of access to football
or sports-related activities).[93]

On the other hand, in *Fears v Wilhelmina Model Agency Inc*,[94] a *cy-près*
distribution was ordered in favour of charities providing services to 'the
uninsured and women' in a case involving antitrust claims by models against
New York modeling agencies. There was a happy coincidence of the lawsuit's
purposes and the substituted beneficiaries of the damages award.

E CHOOSING THE CY-PRÈS RECIPIENTS IN CLASS ACTION LITIGATION

The third and final part of the *cy-près* analysis requires us to consider the
substituted beneficiaries of the property/settlement funds/damages. *Cy-près*
solutions in the class actions context are notable for their inventiveness;[95]
albeit that they inherently involve some subjective choice of a 'deserving'
recipient.

1. How Close must the Relationship between *Cy-près* and Original Purpose Be?

There is, as in other applications of *cy-près* considered in this book, a very real
tension about how close the *cy-près* distribution must be to the original purpose
of the class action. The degree of difficulty in identifying the 'next best use' of the
funds—the 'related purpose requirement', as one case puts it[96]—impacts upon
the utility of the *cy-près* doctrine.[97]

On the strict view, as expressed in *Airline Ticket Airline Ticket Commission
Antitrust Litigation Travel Network Ltd v United Air Lines Inc*,[98] '[a *cy-près*]
recipient must relate, as nearly as possible, to the original purposes of the class
action and its settlement.' The Ninth Circuit was even more emphatic: '[e]ven
where *cy-près* is considered, it will be rejected when the proposed distribution

[93] *Ibid, Schwartz,* 577.
[94] 2005 US Dist LEXIS 7961 (SDNY 2005).
[95] Noted, eg, in: P Rheingold, 'Settlement of Class Actions—American Style' (1997) 8 *Aust Product Liability Reporter* 91, 94.
[96] *In re Wells Fargo Securities Litig,* 991 F Supp 1193, 1194 (ND Cal 1998).
[97] *Fears v Wilhelmina Model Agency Inc,* 2005 US Dist LEXIS 7961, at 34 (SDNY 2005).
[98] 307 F 3d 679, 684 (8th Cir 2002).

fails to provide the "next best" distribution'.[99] Several cases have applied this strict view to reject a *cy-près* distribution as being too remote from the purpose or the class for which the litigation was instituted.[100]

In adopting this strict approach of relatedness, the District Court in *In re Wells Fargo Securities Litigation*[101] reasoned that, just as the charitable *cy-près* doctrine 'does not … enable courts to redirect this money to any alternate source that may represent a worthwhile endeavor, [but rather], courts must redirect the funds in a manner that best serves the original intent of the settlor or testator', then similarly, in the class actions context, a court must be careful to give the unclaimed funds to an organisation that will indirectly serve the interests of class members or other similarly positioned. In a rare tipping of the hat toward the French origin of the phrase, the District Court noted that 'the very term *cy-près* suggests this limitation on the principle; *cy-près* is Norman French for "as near" and signifies that the donor's intent must be followed "as nearly as possible".'[102]

However, there is no doubt that other judicial opinion has adopted a distinctly broader view—allowing that the link between the original class action and the *cy-près* recipient may be slight and tenuous, yet a *cy-près* distribution will still be permitted. In 1993, the District Court of Illinois stated:

> A threshold question is necessarily the scope of and the limits imposed by the *cy-près* doctrine. Historically, the *cy-près* concept was fairly limited and restricted to the closest comparable alternative to the original purpose for which the funds in question had been designated. … [for example] where the testator's dominant intent was that a separate building be built, using the funds to construct an addition to an existing building would not be allowable under *cy-près*, at least not where construction of a separate building was not actually impossible. … In recent years, the doctrine appears to have become more flexible. Funds remaining in antitrust cases have been awarded to law schools to support programs having little or no relationship to antitrust law, competition, or the operation of our economy. … While use of funds for purposes closely related to their origin is still the best *cy-près* application, the doctrine of *cy-près* and courts' broad equitable powers now permit use of funds for other public interest purposes by educational, charitable, and other public service organizations.[103]

---

[99] *Six (6) Mexican Workers v Arizona Citrus Growers*, 904 F 2d 1301, 1308 (9th Cir 1990) (action brought under the Farm Labor Contractor Registration Act on behalf of a class consisting of undocumented Mexican workers employed by defendant during the 1976–77 picking season; *cy-près* distribution ordered in favour of the Inter-American Fund for indirect distribution in Mexico; proposal permitted distribution to areas where the class members might live, but with no certainty that any member would be benefited).

[100] Eg: *In re Matzo Food Products Litig*, 156 FRD 600 (DNJ 1994); *In re Holocaust Victim Assets Litig*, 311 F Supp 2d 407 (EDNY 2004); *Shults v Champion Intl Corp*, 821 F Supp 520 (ED Tenn 1993); *City of Philadelphia v American Oil Co*, 53 FRD 45 (DNJ 1971).

[101] 991 F Supp 1193, 1195 (ND Cal 1998).

[102] *Ibid.*

[103] *Superior Beverage Co v Owens-Illinois Inc*, 827 F Supp 477, 478–79 (ND Ill 1993), cited with approval in: *Powell v Georgia-Pacific Corp*, 843 F Supp 491 (WD Kans). In the former case, 15 entities—legal service programmes, a museum, the National Association for Public Interest Law, and the AIDS Legal Council of Chicago—received *cy-près* distributions after presenting their case in a judicial hearing, together with supporting materials.

In 2001, the District Court of Georgia also opined[104] that, in its view, the doctrine had been so expanded by judicial precedent as to allow distributions to charitable organisations which were not directly associated with the original claims.

Thus, it would seem that, in the view of some US courts at least, the 'next best' class has been watered down to an 'unrelated' class, if the circumstances mean that there is no obvious application of the funds that would serve to bolster redressing the claims that the class brought, or the interests of the members that the class action was designed to protect. Perhaps the leading example of this occurred in *Jones v National Distillers*,[105] in which the District Court of New York admitted the traditional *cy-près* principles offered only 'limited guidance'. Unclaimed funds remained in a class action which had been instituted for misrepresentation. The court despaired that, owing to the passage of time, no clear 'next best' class manifested:

> there is no obvious use for the money that provides a particular benefit to class members. The alleged fraud in this action occurred more than twenty years ago—an eternity in the fast-changing world of securities markets. Twenty-two years after their ill-fated investment in Almaden Vineyards stock, it is unclear how many of the claimants remain active stock market investors. Any claimants who have continued to brave the markets after their Almaden Vineyards stock losses have weathered two recessions, the sky-rocketing interest rates of the early 1980s, the 1987 stock market crash, and markets injured by countless other frauds. While support for securities fraud research or prevention might benefit all participants in the global economy, the passage of time has eroded any assumption that it would benefit class members in any meaningfully additional way.[106]

The monies were eventually distributed to a legal aid society, on the basis that a disposition to a charity was a proper use of the funds where there was no obvious cause associated with the class, and that it was a more meaningful tie than giving the monies, say, to 'a dance performance or a zoo'.[107]

Significantly, over the past decade or so, American courts have shown a remarkable tendency to 'socially engineer' the application of monies for what are perceived to be worthwhile, charitable/benevolent purposes, even if they are completely unrelated to the class members or cause of action. (Note that this sentiment has not escaped judicial criticism.[108]) Examples abound of courts making *cy-près* distributions in favour of a wide range of charitable and

---

[104] *In re Motorsports Merchandise Antitrust Litig*, 160 F Supp 2d 1392, 1394 (ND Ga 2001), and the subject of an excellent discussion in: RE Draba, 'Motorsports Merchandise: A *Cy-près* Distribution Not Quite "As Near as Possible" ' (2004) 16 *Loyola Consumer L Rev* 121.

[105] 56 F Supp 2d 355 (SDNY 1999).

[106] *Ibid*, 358–59.

[107] *Ibid*, 359.

[108] See fnn 98–102, and the sources cited therein.

other 'worthy' public service institutions.[109] In favour of this approach is the contention that, if such recipients are efficient users of resources, the award is a 'socially beneficial transfer' and to be condoned on that basis.[110] Of course, it also upholds the disgorgement, punishment and deterrent functions of a *cy-près* remedy.

The disadvantage of this approach, however, is that the framework for determining between competing plaintiffs for the fund disappears—hunting for the 'next best' application of the monies becomes a highly subjective and discretionary exercise, akin, perhaps, to a lottery or prize for the most inventiveness. It rather calls to mind the cautionary note sounded in *Allapattah Services Inc v Exxon Corp*[111] that, when seeking to ensure that the defendant pays for the wrong that he has committed, 'the court only is to do so by applying settled or clearly stated principles of law, rather than by some process of divination.' Furthermore, Draba argues[112] that the judicial contention in *In re Motorsports Merchandise Antitrust Litigation*[113] that a broad-brush approach to selecting random charitable entities as objects of charitable munificence was supportable from earlier authorities, was patently not true—the cases to which the District Court of Georgia referred therein did not provide such unequivocal support for that position.

It is notable that the ability to choose a quite unrelated recipient for a *cy-près* distribution has clearly been counselled *against* by some Canadian class actions legislatures, where a closer adherence to the 'next best' class is envisaged on the face of the relevant statutes. The potential difference between an 'as near as possible'/related application of the residue and a 'next best'/unrelated

[109] Eg: *In re Motorsports Merchandise Antitrust Litig*, 160 F Supp 2d 1392 (ND Ga 2001) (*cy-près* distribution of residue to 10 different charities, including the Make-A-Wish Foundation, the American Red Cross, Children's Healthcare of Atlanta, the Atlanta Legal Aid Society, and the Lawyers Foundation of Georgia, all of which were unrelated to the class action; with the following court-ordered caveat: 'In general, the Court has attempted to identify charitable organizations that may at least indirectly benefit the members of the class of NASCAR racing fans'); *Superior Beverage Co v Owens-Illinois Inc*, 827 F Supp 477 (ND Ill 1993) (*cy-près* distribution to legal aid bureau, various law school programmes, a museum, a public television station, and other charities); *In re Folding Carton Antitrust Litig*, 934 F 2d 323 (7th Cir 1991) (anti-trust class action; *cy-près* distribution of surplus of $2.3M to National Assn for Public Interest Law (NAPIL) fellowships unrelated to antitrust law; under the fellowships, recent law school graduates selected for assignment to public interest organisations; fellowship paid part or all of their salaries for two years plus giving loan payment assistance to fellows with student loan obligations); and see further cases collected in: *Jones v National Distillers*, 56 F Supp 2d 355, 359 (SDNY 1999), which itself stated, '[t]he absence of an obvious cause to support with the funds does not bar a charitable donation'.

[110] RA Higgins, 'The Equitable Doctrine of *Cy-près* and Consumer Protection' (Annex 1, ACA Submission, Trade Practices Act Review, 15 Jul 2002) 15, and fn 44, citing: G Miller and L Singer, 'Nonpecuniary Class Action Settlements' (1997) 60(4) *Law and Contemporary Problems* (Feb 11, 1998).

[111] 157 F Supp 2d 1291, fn 11 (SD Fla 2001).

[112] RE Draba, 'Motorsports Merchandise: A *Cy-près* Distribution Not Quite "As Near as Possible" ' (2004) 16 *Loyola Consumer L Rev* 121, 149–52, arguing that the cases referred to in fn 109 above were only equivocally supportive of a wider 'next best' application.

[113] 160 F Supp 2d 1392, 1394 (ND Ga 2001).

application perhaps calls for some expression of preference. Which solution manifests the 'best practice' scenario? This author would suggest the latter. For one thing, it is undoubtedly true that flexibility 'constitutes much of the appeal of *cy-près* solutions',[114] which the 'next best' application offers. Furthermore, whilst the triggers and the further objective criteria for the application of *cy-près* should be stringently adhered to in order to ensure that the doctrine is not abused or fractured, once those 'narrow gates' have been safely negotiated, the court should arguably be permitted to apply the damages to the 'next best' use that it perceives. Sometimes this will entail a distribution for a purpose 'as near as possible' to the purpose for which the action was brought; and sometimes, the 'next best' use will benefit the class members in other ways, somewhat distinct from the class suit itself. A 'wide gate' at the stage at which the damages are applied for *cy-près* purposes ensures the optimal use of scarce resources, and allows for a greater degree of pragmatism and flexibility.

2. Focusing upon the *Cy-près* Recipient

Scrutiny of the proposed *cy-près* recipient represents the final aspect of the framework's analysis.

Is the cy-près recipient accountable and responsible? Is there appropriate supervision? In both Canada[115] and the United States,[116] the courts have demonstrated caution to ensure that the *cy-près* distribution will be properly administered. These authorities indicate that, with respect to an organisational recipient, approval is more likely if, for example: the organisation is well-respected and reputable, with an established and transparent record of providing public, charitable or non-profit services; that the administrators of the

---

[114] RA Higgins, 'The Equitable Doctrine of *Cy-près* and Consumer Protection' (Annex 1, ACA Submission, Trade Practices Act Review, 15 Jul 2002) fn 48. Also note: S Issacharoff, 'Group Litigation of Consumer Claims: Lessons from the US Experience' (1999) 34 *Texas Intl LJ* 135, fn 50 ('There are numerous examples of consumer class actions in which the difficulty of finding the actual victims of fraud has led courts to use *cy-près* remedies . . . in which the proceeds of the litigation are applied to help persons similarly situated to the victim class, *if not identical to it*. . . . Some courts have also applied *cy-près* remedies outside the context of the consumer class action', citing *Six (6) Mexican Workers v Arizona Citrus Growers*, 904 F 2d 1301 (9th Cir 1990)') (emphasis added).

[115] As outlined in: *Alfresh Beverages Canada Corp v Hoechst AG* (2002), 16 CPC (5th) 301 (SCJ) [18]; *Ford v F Hoffmann-La Roche Ltd* (SCJ, 23 Mar 2005) [158].

[116] For recent emphasis upon 'thoroughly vetting' the *cy-près* recipients, see: *Fears v Wilhelmina Model Agency Inc*, US Dist LEXIS 10764, at 17 (SDNY 6 Jun 2005); for emphasis upon the need for the recipient to demonstrate 'independent, disinterested judgment required to allocate limited funds to benefit the class as a whole', see: *In re 'Agent Orange' Product Liability Litig*, 818 F 2d 179, 185 (2d Cir 1987); and for reiteration that the *cy-près* fund would be administered by a board composed of leading Latino charitable groups with substantial records of service, and with a clear directive that the funds be used to benefit entities whose primary purposes include service to Mexican Americans or Mexican-American causes, see: *In re Mexico Money Transfer Litig*, 164 F Supp 2d 1002 (ND Ill 2000).

organisation have experience in implementing complex class action recoveries; that the costs of administration will be borne by the settlement fund and minimised; and that any disputes with respect to the distribution are to be determined by the court or other appropriate dispute resolution forum. The court may require a formal agreement to that effect before the *cy-près* scheme is approved.[117]

In *Six (6) Mexican Workers v Arizona Citrus Growers*,[118] a *cy-près* distribution in favour of the 'Inter-American Foundation' for distribution in Mexico was set aside as an abuse of discretion, given that, *inter alia*, the charity did not have a substantial record of service; the funds' application was not limited to specific projects conducted by the charity; and there was no procedure to ensure proper distribution of the funds. (The court was also concerned that the *cy-près* distribution benefited a group 'far too remote from the plaintiff class'.) In a very recent American federal decision, the *cy-près* distribution depended upon satisfactory answers being forthcoming from the proposed *cy-près* recipient to the following questions:

  (1) how the organisation will use the funds in a way that is related to the interests of music club members, including specification of what portion will go to administrative costs;
  (2) how that proposal, if funded, will result in additional benefit to those interests, and not just replace other monies;
  (3) a commitment to implement the proposal if awarded the funds;
  (4) a description of how and when the organisation will report on use of the funds; and
  (5) a commitment to report to the Court.[119]

In Canada, the would-be recipient of a *cy-près* distribution has been evaluated against the following set of judicially-set criteria:

  (1) the organisation's ability to deliver benefits in each province and territory;
  (2) the organisation's ability to reach one or more of the target age groups, being children, youth, adults, or the elderly;
  (3) whether the organisation was non-denominational;
  (4) whether the organisation had a charitable or non-profit designation;
  (5) the organisation's financial stability and budget; and

---

[117] Note the agreements and undertakings referred to in the recent settlement in: *In re Compact Disc Minimum Advertised Price Antitrust Litig*, 2005 US Dist LEXIS 16468 (D Maine 9 Aug 2005), and in later proceedings: *In re Compact Disc Minimum Advertised Price Antitrust Litig*, 2005 US Dist LEXIS 22273 (D Maine 30 Sep 2005). Also of relevance: *Valquez v Avco Financial Services*, No NCC-11933-B (LA Superior Ct 24 Apr 1984).

[118] 904 F 2d 1301, 1308–9 (9th Cir 1990) ('The tool for distribution, the IAF, is not an organization with a substantial record of service nor is it limited in its choice of projects. Under such circumstances, any distribution plan should be supervised by the court or a court appointed master to ensure that the funds are distributed in accordance with the goals of the remedy.... The plan ... fails to provide adequate supervision over distribution'), citing also: *In re 'Agent Orange' Product Liability Litig*, 818 F 2d 179, 185 (2d Cir 1987).

[119] *In re Compact Disc Minimum Advertised Price Antitrust Litig*, 2005 US Dist LEXIS 11332, at 9 (D Maine 2005).

(6) the organisation's history of advocacy, service delivery, research, or education relevant to Vitamin Products.[120]

The principal purpose of such evaluative lists, of course, is to provide the highest levels of confidence and reassurance to the public that the monies available for distribution will be responsibly used, while upholding respect for the judiciary as a fundamental institution of public safeguard.

The financial costs of finding a cy-près recipient. In *Airline Ticket Commission Antitrust Litigation Travel Network Ltd v United Air Lines Inc,*[121] the Eight Circuit stated that '[w]e recognize that the court's discretion in this regard must be guided, in part, by the amount of the remaining unclaimed funds and the costs of searching for another qualified recipient.' It was noted in earlier academic commentary that the costs of the *cy-près* scheme inevitably impact upon whether it is feasible:

> The acceptability of any *cy-près* damage distribution mechanism can be best measured by balancing (1) the extent to which the injured class receives the damages, (2) the cost of applying the remedy, and (3) the equitability of the distribution with respect to the potential of windfalls for nonclass members.[122]

F   *CY-PRÈS* IN UNITARY LITIGATION

On a final note, it should be observed that the use of the *cy-près* doctrine is not limited to the distribution of class action damages. There is some evidence in the United States that it has also been applied in regulatory litigation, where fines are cast against the defendant. Rather than pay a fine to the Treasury, an alternative recipient may be preferable, so as to devote the funds to a charitable or public service purpose. Again, it would follow in this context that the fine may be paid for the benefit of those who were not parties to the original unitary litigation, nor were injured by the defendant's illegal conduct. On this basis, in *Local 28 of the Sheet Metal Workers v EEOC,*[123] the Supreme Court approved of a remedy devised by the trial judge, whereby the proceeds of a contempt fine levied against a union defendant in a Title VII case was used to create a fund to aid minority prospective union members. The application of *cy-près* within the environmental context has also been noted.[124]

Other jurisdictions have also been prepared to utilise a *cy-près* distribution

---

[120] *Ford v F Hoffmann-La Roche Ltd* (SCJ, 23 Mar 2005) [96].

[121] 307 F 3d 679, 684 (8th Cir 2002).

[122] Note, 'Damage Distribution in Class Actions' (1972) 39 *U of Chicago L Rev* 448, 464, cited in: *Six (6) Mexican Workers v Arizona Citrus Growers,* 641 F Supp 259, 269 (D Ariz 1986).

[123] 478 US 421, 106 S Ct 3019 (1986).

[124] JA Rabkin, 'The Secret Life of the Private Attorney General' (1998) 61 *Law and Contemporary Problems* 179, 191, and cited in: WB Rubenstein, 'On What a "Private Attorney General" Is—And Why it Matters' (2004) 57 *Vanderbilt L Rev* 2129, fn 112.

(especially an organisational distribution scheme) in the regulatory context. Even in England, where the *cy-près* distribution of damages in the class actions context is unknown, actions launched on behalf of consumers in a regulatory context have netted *cy-près* awards. One example, cited by Howells, entailed Rover Car Company paying £1 million for car research to the Consumers' Association to compensate for breach of competition laws. As that author noted: '[o]nce again consumer disputes require reconsideration of existing principles.'[125]

In Australia too—a jurisdiction stridently against the use of the *cy-près* doctrine in class litigation—there is some precedent for *cy-près* orders in the consumer, non-class action, context, although the concept is controversial. In 2002, in a representative action brought against tobacco wholesalers and retailers, the New South Wales Supreme Court noted the different path which the United States had chosen to tread in this regard:

> Whatever may be the position in the United States of America there is no power in this court to make orders for disposition of a fund other than to persons who establish an entitlement to compensation out of such fund. Notions based on *cy-près* analogies, escheat, fluid recovery and deterrent distribution are just that. On no basis are they within the remedies available under s 87 of the Trade Practice Act.[126]

However, the fact remains that some Australian consumer organisations have been funded out of *cy-près* distributions, for example, where defendant lenders have failed to disclose as required by law, and have paid monies into a financial counselling trust fund.[127] Very recently, a trust fund was successfully established for the victims of unregistered finance brokers, where the action was commenced by the Director of Fair Trading on behalf of aggrieved consumers, and where the court accepted that such an order was within the broad discretion vested in the court to 'do justice'.[128]

These sorts of *cy-près* distributions within the context of consumer litigation have been praised on the basis that they 'provide an incentive for consumer organizations to bring actions to protect the consumer interest and then use the profits to bring further actions and thereby effectively police the market at the expense of the market.'[129] It is to be hoped that, given these non-class action examples of *cy-près* orders, the use of the doctrine will gain a greater acceptance within Australian litigious remedies than has hitherto been the case.

---

[125] GG Howells, 'Litigation in the Consumer Interest' (2002) *J Intl and Comparative Law* 1, 40, citing: D Nicholson-Lord, 'Rover "Pays" 1M Pounds Compensation', *The Independent (London)*, 17 Nov 1993, 2.
[126] *Cauvin v Phillip Morris Ltd* [2002] NSWSC 736.
[127] Discussed, eg, in: A Cornwall, 'Class Actions Get Go Ahead' (1995) 20 *Alternative LJ* 138, 139.
[128] *Commissioner for Fair Trading v Thomas* (NSWSC, 3 Jun 2004) [27]–[28].
[129] GG Howells, 'Litigation in the Consumer Interest' (2002) *J Intl and Comparative Law* 1, 41.

9

Cy-près *Specific Performance*

A INTRODUCTION

IN MOST CIRCUMSTANCES, the description of 'specific performance' is a misnomer. Definitions tend to construe this contractual remedy as if the breached contract were a collapsed house of cards that could, by judicial order, be reassembled into its original position again. The following sample statements[1] about specific performance—that it is an order directed to a defendant 'to perform the contract, and in accordance with its terms',[2] or 'to perform a promise that he has made'[3]—are, practically speaking, hardly ever precisely true of the remedy. In reality, some variation of the original contractual stipulations usually occurs by virtue of the order.

Specific performance then becomes a remedy of 'substituted', rather than 'specific', performance. Where ordered, the parties will perform 'as near as possible' to the original contractual specifications. Where property is to be transferred under the contract, and where that property transfer is subject to some form of substituted performance, this introduces the *cy-près* doctrine to this contractual remedy. McKendrick explains the inconsistency between the legal name and the legal reality in these terms:

> it can be argued that specific performance is not 'specific' at all in that, in the vast majority of cases, the defendant is not ordered 'specifically' to perform a contractual obligation. The obligation that the defendant is ordered to perform generally differs in some way from the initial obligation that was undertaken in the contract. Most claimants do not seek specific performance until the defendant has already broken the contract ... In such a case, the defendant obviously cannot perform exactly in accordance with the original contractual obligation in that, at the least, performance will take place at a different time from that originally agreed. On this basis it can be argued that specific performance is a *substitutionary* and not a specific remedy.[4]

Other leading commentary has similarly noted this terminological confusion.[5]

---

[1] For others, see, eg: GH Treitel, *The Law of Contract* (11th edn, Sweet & Maxwell, London, 2003) 1019; J Poole, *Contract Law* (7th edn, OUP, Oxford, 2004) 464; JC Smith, *The Law of Contract* (4th edn, Sweet & Maxwell, London, 2002) 234.

[2] J Beatson, *Anson's Law of Contract* (28th edn, OUP, Oxford, 2002) 632.

[3] R Upex and G Bennett, *Davies on Contract* (9th edn, Sweet & Maxwell, London, 2004) 288.

[4] E McKendrick, *Contract Law: Text, Cases and Materials* (2nd edn, OUP, Oxford, 2005) 1138.

[5] E Fry (the Hon), *A Treatise on the Specific Performance of Contracts* (6th edn, Stevens, London, 1921) 467, [1001] (noting that a mere incapacity to satisfy contractual obligations 'literally and exactly' is not a justification for declining to perform it 'in substance').

Quite apart from any requisite alterations in date, time or place of contractual performance that specific performance may necessitate (which are *not* the subject of this chapter), more radical variations may also ensue. Suppose that the contract requires the transfer of some stipulated property ('the Contractually Described Property'). It is, or becomes, impossible or impracticable for the Contractually Described Property to be transferred—because, say, in breach of contract, the vendor's title, or the quality or quantity of the property, have been wrongly described. Nevertheless, one party (the plaintiff) strongly desires the contract to proceed. That plaintiff would be willing for the contract to be performed on the basis of a different (even lesser) property transfer, rather than for the contract to end with no property being transferred at all and with each party left to his remedy in damages.

The question, then, is under what circumstances can the court award specific performance of the contract, and permit some substitution for the Contractually Described Property. This scenario hence falls squarely within the definition of the *cy-près* doctrine adopted earlier in this book:

> Where property is (or is to be) given by A to B for a designated purpose, under a legally enforceable obligation (by reason of a contractual obligation to do so); and it is, or becomes, impossible, impracticable, illegal or infeasible for the designated purpose to be effected (because the Contractually Described Property is deficient in some respect); and in accordance with relevant objective factors, it is legally appropriate that the original (contractual) transfer be carried out by approximation: then by court or other superior order, the original transfer can legally be altered in a material respect—namely, the nature of the property transferred is altered—to approximate 'as near as possible' the original contractual transfer[6]

By drawing upon a variety of English case law (with some supporting illustrations from other jurisdictions where helpful), this chapter considers the circumstances in which the court may exercise its discretion to award substituted specific performance where a party cannot transfer the Contractually Described Property. Following a brief description of the context in which substituted (*cy-près*) specific performance can be invoked to rescue a contract for property transfer (Section B), the circumstances in which either innocent party or contract-breaker may seek an appropriate order are examined (Section C). The chapter will conclude with a discussion of the principles governing an award of *cy-près* specific performance (Section D).

Finally, a note on terminology: the various scenarios of substituted specific performance discussed in this chapter have been disparately described, depending upon the jurisdiction and the context. For example, one of the scenarios where the vendor's estate in the land has been misdescribed has been labelled by English courts, 'the doctrine of partial performance'.[7] In another context where

---

[6] See ch 1, p 3.

[7] *Bankers Trust Co v Namdar* [1995] NPC 139 (Ch); *Thames Guaranty Ltd v Campbell* [1985] 1 QB 210 (CA) 235, cited in: *United Bank of Kuwait plc v Sahib* [1997] Ch 107 (CA) 121.

the subject matter of the contract was misdescribed in *Thomas v Dering*,[8] Longdale MR observed that the court was effectively executing the contract '*cy-près* ... [which is] in fact the execution of a new contract which the parties did not enter into'. In Canadian jurisprudence, reference has repeatedly been made to 'specific enforcement of the contract *cy-près*'.[9] Throughout this chapter, and for the sake of clarity and consistency, the terminology of '*cy-près* specific performance' will be adopted to refer to *any* instance of substituted specific performance discussed hereafter.

B SETTING THE CONTEXT

1. Finding a 'Middle Ground' in Contractual Remedies

Where a decree of substituted specific performance is made, the court must, in the first instance, adhere to those principles which govern *any* specific performance award, and hence, a brief revision of the overarching relevant principles may be helpful.

The remedy is notionally discretionary. It is oft-said, however, that the exercise of the court's discretion when awarding or refusing such a decree is now bound by a body of definable precedent and rules.[10] An award of specific performance involves a two-part analysis: whether it is available, and if so, its appropriate terms.[11] According to the longstanding and traditional view, specific performance is not to be ordered where (as of right) damages would be an adequate remedy. Historically then, specific performance occupied a supplementary, indeed exceptional, role to that of damages.[12] However, there are certain well-established circumstances in which an award of damages will *not* adequately compensate the innocent contracting party; for example, property which is unique, rare, special or difficult to substitute—such as land,[13] beautiful

[8] (1837) 1 Keen 729; [1835–42] All ER Rep 711, 717.

[9] Eg: *Webb and Reeves v Dipenta*, [1925] SCR 565, [1925] 1 DLR 216, 222, citing: Williams, *Vendor and Purchaser* (3rd edn) vol 1, 536; *Raaber v Coll-in-Wood Farms Ltd* (1971), 14 DLR (3d) 234 (Alta SC App Div) [58], [61]; *Wilson v Patterson* (1918), 39 DLR 642 (Alta SC) [6]. Note also the terminology, 'specific performance *cy-près*' used to describe this sort of case in, eg: SM Waddams, 'Profits Derived from Breach of Contract: Damages or Restitution' (1997) 11 *J of Contract Law* 115, 121, fn 27 ('the courts will be anxious to compel the execution of such a contract *cy-près* if it is otherwise unobjectionable', and also citing: Webb); and in: RJ Sharpe (the Hon), *Injunctions and Specific Performance* (3rd edn, Canada Law Book, Aurora, 2000) [11.320].

[10] J Beatson, *Anson's Law of Contract* (28th edn, OUP, Oxford, 2002) 633; GH Treitel, *The Law of Contract* (11th edn, Sweet & Maxwell, London, 2003) 1019; G Jones, *Jones and Goodhart's Specific performance* (2nd edn, Butterworths, London, 1996) 1, 5, 9; R Megarry R and W Wade, *Law of Real Property* (6th edn, Sweet & Maxwell, London, 2000) 721.

[11] Noted, eg, in: *Beaufort Western Ltd v Fellows* (CA, 26 May 2000).

[12] *Co-operative Ins Society Ltd v Argyll Stores (Holdings) Ltd* [1998] AC 1 (HL) 11 (Lord Hoffmann), explaining the 'exceptional' nature of the remedy and its historical development.

[13] *Adderley v Dixon* (1824) 1 Sims & St 607; 57 ER 239; *Sudbrook Trading Estate Ltd v Eggleton* [1983] 1 AC 444 (HL) 478 (Lord Diplock).

objects,[14] or petroleum products which are difficult to source alternatively[15]—will be the proper subject matter for a suit for specific performance. By contrast, where substitute goods can be readily acquired in the market place from an award of common law damages, specific performance will not be appropriate.[16] Further, if damages would be difficult to quantify,[17] would be nominal only,[18] or may never be paid because of the financial impecuniosity of the defendant,[19] they may be considered also to be inadequate.

Additionally, several factors, for and against, have been used to guide the exercise of the court's discretion when considering the suitability of this remedy.[20] Some factors weighing *against* the award of specific performance include: the ongoing execution of the contract will require the court's constant supervision; there is a lack of mutuality; some unfair conduct on the part of the plaintiff is evident; such an order would be futile, or against public policy; or he who is seeking the order has exhibited undue delay. Factors *favouring* such award include: the order would impose on neither party, nor any third party, great hardship or serious prejudice; and the contractual obligations to be performed are clearly defined and unambiguous. All of these factors potentially apply, whether specific performance is being sought in its usual or in its *cy-près* form.

Notwithstanding this definable body of precedent, there have been competing tensions evident in certain English decisions about the scope of the specific performance remedy. On the one hand, some cases have countenanced a wider availability of specific performance than hitherto envisaged. This is borne out from judicial statements, for example, that 'a court is not in modern times perhaps so constrained as once it was by black letter rules as to the availability of this discretionary remedy';[21] and that the outcome in each case will depend upon the 'cumulative effect' of the discretionary factors[22] and whether it is the

---

[14] *Falcke v Gray* (1859) 4 Drew 651; 62 ER 250.

[15] *Sky Petroleum Ltd v VIP Petroleum Ltd* [1974] 1 WLR 576 (Ch) 579.

[16] *Re Schwabacher* (1907) 98 LT 127 (securities); *Societe des Industries Metallurgiques SA v The Bronx Engineering Co Ltd* [1975] 1 Lloyd's Rep 465 (CA).

[17] Noted to be the case in *Co-operative Ins Society Ltd v Argyll Stores (Holdings) Ltd* [1998] AC 1 (HL) 11, although specific performance was ultimately refused because to so order would have compelled the defendant to carry on business, raising the spectre that constant supervision might be required by the court.

[18] *Beswick v Beswick* [1968] AC 58 (HL) 73 (Lord Reid) 88 (Lord Pearce).

[19] *Evans Marshall & Co Ltd v Bertola SA* [1973] 1 WLR 349 (CA) 382 ('Bertola being a wholly owned subsidiary of unknown financial status in Spain, and ISI a company with a £5,000 share capital, the chances of a judgment . . . being satisfied by them cannot be rated as other than questionable. So on that ground too, damages would *prima facie* in this case not be an adequate remedy').

[20] For a comprehensive elucidation of these factors, see, eg: GH Treitel, *The Law of Contract* (11th edn, Sweet & Maxwell, London, 2003) 1020–38; J Beatson, *Anson's Law of Contract* (28th edn, OUP, Oxford, 2002) 632–37; JE Martin, *Hanbury and Martin Modern Equity* (17th edn, Sweet & Maxwell, London, 2005) 735–55; R Megarry and W Wade, *Law of Real Property* (6th edn, Sweet & Maxwell, London, 2000) [12–116].

[21] *Internet Trading Clubs Ltd v Freeserve (Investments) Ltd plc* (QB, 19 Jun 2001) [30], citing: *Rainbow Estates Ltd v Tokenhold Ltd* [1999] Ch 64.

[22] *Co-operative Ins Society Ltd v Argyll Stores (Holdings) Ltd* [1998] AC 1 (HL) 16.

'more appropriate remedy'.[23] It is also evident that the bar of 'constant super-intendence by the court' is not the obstacle it once was,[24] and that seeking specific performance of only a part of the contract is not an insuperable hurdle,[25] as was previously held to be the case.[26] Widely stated, it is necessary to 'consider all the circumstances and assess whether or not it is just to confine the party seeking the injunction to damages, or rather, to grant specific relief by way of injunction or specific performance'[27], and indeed, to grant the latter 'if it can be done without injustice or unfairness to the defendant'.[28] In the light of this softened approach, some commentators[29] have viewed specific performance as having acquired a greater utility as a *frontline* remedy, to be accorded a more expansive role than its historically supplementary position.

On the other hand, there are distinct limits. In particular, as one court has recently reiterated, '[i]t is not the function of the court to impose upon the parties a contract which they did not make in circumstances where the contract which they did make has broken down and cannot be specifically enforced in its entirety'.[30] Indeed, some commentators adhere to the view (particularly since the decision of the House of Lords to refuse an order for specific performance in *Co-operative Insurance Society Ltd v Argyll Stores (Holdings) Ltd*[31]) that the remedy is (and should be) nothing more than secondary to that ultimate of substitutionary remedies, damages.[32]

In circumstances where some sort of *substituted* specific performance order has been sought, disquiet about widely construing the remedy has been particu-larly evident from time to time. In *Cato v Thompson*,[33] Jessel MR cautioned that

[23] *Beswick v Beswick* [1968] AC 58 (HL) 88 (Lord Pearce).

[24] GH Treitel, *The Law of Contract* (11th edn, Sweet & Maxwell, London, 2003) 1034, discussing *Co-operative Ins Society Ltd v Argyll Stores (Holdings) Ltd* [1998] AC 1 (HL).

[25] *Internet Trading Clubs Ltd v Freeserve (Investments) Ltd plc* (QB, 19 Jun 2001) [30].

[26] *Ryan v Mutual Tontine Westminster Chambers Assn* [1893] 1 Ch 116 (CA) 123 (Lord Esher), Kay and Lopes LLJ concurring.

[27] *Re SSSL Realisations (2002) Ltd (t/a Save Service Stations Ltd) (in liq)* [2004] EWHC 1760 (Ch) [76], citing, in this regard: *Rainbow Estates Ltd v Tokenhold Ltd* [1999] Ch 64, 72–73.

[28] *Price v Strange* [1978] Ch 337 (CA) 357, and adopted in: *Re SSSL Realisations, ibid.* Also: *Tito v Waddell (No 2)* [1977] Ch 106, 322 (specific performance awarded if it would 'do more perfect and complete justice' than damages). Also: *Rainbow Estates Ltd v Tokenhold Ltd* [1999] Ch 64, 72.

[29] E McKendrick, *Contract Law* (6th edn, Palgrave Macmillan, London, 2005) 450 ('the HL [in *Beswick*] envisaged a wider role for specific performance . . . rather than as a supplementary remedy in a hierarchical system of remedies'); GH Treitel, *The Law of Contract* (11th edn, Sweet & Maxwell, London, 2003) 1026 (citing certain of the authorities noted *ibid*).

[30] *Internet Trading Clubs Ltd v Freeserve (Investments) Ltd plc* (QB, 19 Jun 2001) [30].

[31] [1998] AC 1 (HL).

[32] R Upex and G Bennett, *Davies on Contract* (9th edn, Sweet & Maxwell, London, 2004) 288 ('any movement towards a more generous approach to the granting of specific performance has been checked by [*Co-operative*]'); J Beatson, *Anson's Law of Contract* (28th edn, OUP, Oxford, 2002) 633 (specific performance 'should remain a secondary remedy to damages'); J Poole, *Contract Law* (7th edn, OUP, Oxford, 2004) 464 ('The Chancery Court made specific performance available, by way of exception. It remains an exceptional remedy'). Cf: E McKendrick, *Contract Law* (6th edn, Palgrave Macmillan, London, 2005) 453 ('[*Co-operative*] may turn out to be no more than a temporary halt' in the more expansive approach toward specific performance).

[33] (1882) 9 QBD 616 (CA) 618.

'the cases of specific performance with compensation ought not to be extended. In many of them a bargain substantially different from that which the parties entered into has been substituted for it and enforced, which is not right.' In another leading substituted performance case, that of *Rudd v Lascelles*,[34] Farwell J noted that 'if I grant specific performance I shall decree specific performance not of the contract made by the parties, but of a new contract made for them by the Court.' In this latter decision—where a purchaser sued for specific performance of a contract for sale of four houses, a workshop, garden, and land, with compensation, on the ground of undisclosed restrictive covenants—specific performance was denied. Significantly, the parties had not contractually provided for compensation where the property was misdescribed: 'if I enforce the contract with compensation I am compelling the vendor to perform a contract into which she did not enter.'[35]

In light of these two disparate schools of thought, a closer analysis of *cy-près* specific performance is instructive because of the compromise that the remedy represents. If the Contractually Described Property cannot, for reasons of deficiency in title, quality, or quantity, be transferred as promised, then *cy-près* performance of a contract, in the various guises described in the next section, and as a substitute for intended contractual performance, provides contracting parties with a greater scope for achieving 'as near as possible' performance than the traditional subservience of this so-called ancillary remedy would perhaps indicate. On the spectrum between the readily available and substitutionary nature of damages at the one end, and the rarity of performance-oriented relief which specific performance affords at the other, *cy-près* specific performance occupies an important and useful middle ground.[36]

2. The Triggers for *Cy-près* Property Transfer

Given the propensity with which land contracts attract the remedy of specific performance because of the uniqueness of that species of property, most (but not all) *cy-près* specific performance cases arise in circumstances where the Contractually Described Property (a piece of land, or an estate or interest in land) cannot be transferred, but a substituted order can be made. In *cy-près* terms, the triggers for an order for substituted specific performance reflect the fact that it is impossible or impracticable to transfer the property as contractually intended. The following scenarios are indicative:[37]

---

[34] [1900] 1 Ch 815, 818.

[35] *Ibid.*

[36] RJ Sharpe (the Hon), *Injunctions and Specific Performance* (3rd edn, Canada Law Book, Aurora, 2000) [11.20].

[37] For further discussion of the matters considered hereafter, see: G Jones, *Jones and Goodhart's Specific performance* (2nd edn, Butterworths, London 1996) 289–99; Sharpe, *ibid*, ch 11; E Fry, *A Treatise on the Specific Performance of Contracts* (6th edn, Stevens, London, 1921) ch 11.

- ❏ the Contractually Described Property is burdened by encumbrances (eg, mortgage or restrictive covenant) that cannot be removed by the vendor, and the contract stipulates that the property is to be free from such encumbrances upon transfer—by court order, the property may be transferred with the encumbrance;[38]
- ❏ the vendor or mortgagor of the Contractually Described Property lacks the title to the entire estate or interest in that land which is purported to be sold or charged—by court order, the vendor or mortgagor may be required to sell or charge whatever interest he possesses;[39]
- ❏ the quantity of land actually available for transfer is less than that which was promised as the Contractually Described Property—the property may be ordered to be transferred in any event;[40]
- ❏ the quality of the land available for transfer is of lesser quality than that which the Contractually Described Property promised—again, even that lesser property may be ordered to be transferred;[41]
- ❏ the Contractually Described Property cannot be furnished, and may be replaced by another form of property altogether.[42]

In any of these circumstances, one contracting party may be prepared to accept specific performance of the 'lesser' property, with or without an 'abatement' (a reduction in the purchase price to take account of the difference, deficiency or defect[43]). It has been judicially stated that 'the power to make an order with abatement of the price [is] an example of the court's power to adapt

---

[38] As in, eg: *Rudd v Lascelles* [1900] 1 Ch 815 (sale of land, with house and other accoutrements; property subject to undisclosed restrictive covenants relating to building and user; purchaser sued for sp; sp refused, due to hardship considerations). For a Canadian example: *Wallace v Nichol* [1951], 1 DLR 449 (Ont CA) 454 (vendors of land undertook to obtain partial discharge of mortgage; mortgagee refused to grant discharge; specific performance refused; an essential condition of sale beyond the capacity of vendors to perform).

[39] As in, eg: *Cedar Holdings Ltd v Green* [1981] 1 Ch 129 (CA) (contract of charge to secure an overdraft; chargor held only a one-half share of the title over the security, the matrimonial home, instead of the entire interest as the charge stipulated; sp refused, although this case has been overruled on one crucial point, in *Williams and Glyn's Bank Ltd v Boland* [1981] AC 487 (HL) 507).

[40] *Aspinalls v Powell and Scholefield* (1889) 60 LT 595(sale of land; 'about 1200 square yards'; actually 935 square yards; vendor sued for sp, which was granted). Also: *Watson v Burton* [1957] 1 WLR 19 (Ch) (sp refused).

[41] *Shepherd v Croft* [1911] 1 Ch 521 (sale of land; a natural underground watercourse ran through it, undisclosed to the purchaser; vendor sued for sp, which was granted). Also, for a misdescription of the income generated by a property: *Gilchester Properties Ltd v Gomm* [1948] 1 All ER 493 (Ch).

[42] *Raaber v Coll-in-Wood Farms Ltd* (1971), 14 DLR (3d) 234 (Alta SC App Div) (sale of land; purchaser obliged to provide conditional sales agreement and guarantee, but unable to do so; vendor sued for sp, which was granted; provision of these security documents non-essential; cash sum (equal to face value of the conditional sales agreement) substituted). Also: *Waller v Roach* (BC SC, 14 Jul 1982) (contract for sale of land; sub-agreement for sale not furnished; sale could be completed *cy-près* by substituting a cash payment for the sub-agreement).

[43] C Harpum, 'Specific Performance with Compensation as a Purchaser's Remedy—A Study in Contract and Equity' (1981) 40 *CLJ* 47, 53. English courts tend to treat the terms of 'abatement' and 'compensation' synonymously, eg: *P & O Overseas Holdings Ltd v Rhys Braintree Ltd* (Ch, 5 Jul 2001) [52].

its orders to meet the justice of the case.'[44] The principle of 'specific performance + abatement' is longstanding, and founded in equitable doctrine.[45] As one of the few instances of an early equitable compensatory remedy,[46] it pre-dated,[47] and continues to stand apart from, specific performance with damages under Lord Cairns' Act.[48] In *Rudd v Lascelles*, the historical origins were described thus:

> [The jurisdiction] probably first arose in cases of small deficiency in the quantity, eg, if a vendor contracted to sell 100 acres, and it eventually turned out that he only had ninety-five. In such cases specific performance with compensation for the deficiency was only a *cy-près* execution of the contract, and the doctrine upon which the Court acted in granting such a remedy was clearly an equitable one.[49]

The abovementioned passage suggests that it is the purchaser as innocent party who will bring the suit. However, as discussed in the following section, both contract-breakers (such as the defaulting vendor above) and innocent parties may consider that 'near enough is good enough' and seek transfer of the deficient property via a decree of *cy-près* specific performance. Interestingly, under both categories of plaintiff, points of legal uncertainty have arisen.

C WHO MAY APPLY FOR A *CY-PRÈS* SPECIFIC PERFORMANCE ORDER?

1. Applications for *Cy-près* Specific Performance by the Innocent Party

When confronted with a vendor who can only transfer a deficient title, or a property which differs in quality or quantity from the Contractually Described Property, the innocent purchaser has an election under English law: 'the purchaser can either insist upon performance to the extent of the vendor's ability with an appropriate abatement in the purchase price, or be relegated to his remedy in damages'.[50] In other words, the innocent party should not be denied specific performance if he is willing to accept a lesser standard of performance than that contractually stipulated—but he should be entitled to claim some measure of compensation for that shortfall.[51]

---

[44] *Seven Seas Properties Ltd v Al-Essa* [1988] 1 WLR 1272 (Ch) 1274.

[45] JD Heydon and PL Loughlan, *Cases and Materials on Equity and Trusts* (5th edn, Butterworths, Sydney, 1997) 991.

[46] Another was the indemnity for misrepresentation, noted by Heydon and Loughlan, *ibid*.

[47] See, eg: *Mortlock v Buller* (1804) 10 Ves 292 (HL) 315 ('If the vendee chooses to take as much as he can have, he has a right to that, and to an abatement'); *Flight v Booth* (1834) 1 Bing NC 370. See also the very early case law on abatement referred to in: E Fry, *A Treatise on the Specific Performance of Contracts* (6th edn, Stevens, London, 1921) [1225]–[1259].

[48] Chancery Amendment Act 1858, c 27, s 2. On this point, see also; R Megarry and W Wade, *Law of Real Property* (6th edn, Sweet & Maxwell, London, 2000) 722.

[49] [1900] 1 Ch 815, 818.

[50] *Price v Strange* [1978] Ch 337 (CA) 364. Also see, for similar comment: *Grant v Dawkins* [1973] 1 WLR 1406 (Ch) 1412.

[51] J Berryman, *The Law of Equitable Remedies* (Irwin Law, Toronto, 2000) 190.

With reference to this election, some Commonwealth authorities have sought to emphasise that specific performance with abatement is in lieu of damages;[52] and that an abatement is not a remedial measure by which to recoup *all* the loss and damage accruing from the vendor's default.[53] As Megarry and Wade note, the precise relationship between abatement and damages is 'obscure'.[54]

Whatever the historical origins may have been, the innocent party's right to insist upon *cy-près* specific performance plus compensation, amounting to a transfer of the substituted property with abatement, has been afflicted by some confusion. Some relevant case law suggests that there are three possible approaches concerning the scope of the innocent party's right to this remedy.

A substantial discrepancy does not *lose the purchaser the remedy.* The first (and most significantly supported) of these approaches is that some trivial disparity between the available and the Contractually Described Property (such as the 100 versus 95 acres adverted to in *Rudd v Lascelles*) does not set the boundaries of recovery. Instead, the discrepancy can be much wider than that, and still the remedy will be awarded. In *Rutherford v Acton-Adams*,[55] the Privy Council noted that:

> [i]f it is the [innocent] purchaser who is suing, the Court holds him to have an *even larger right* [than the defaulting vendor]. Subject to considerations of hardship he may elect to take *all he can get*, and to have a proportionate abatement from the purchase money.

That is, when making his election between termination + damages, or specific performance + abatement, that innocent purchaser may elect to sue for the latter, whether the property being conveyed is *substantially* or trivially different from the Contractually Described Property. There is a significant body of judicial[56]

---

[52] *Ontario Asphalt Block Co v Montreuil* (1913), 15 DLR 703 (Ont CA) 710 ('the purchaser can elect to take what the [contract-breaker] can convey . . . with an abatement . . . [but] is not entitled to anything beyond that . . . what he in effect does when he makes his election is to agree to take the partial performance, with the abatement, in lieu of the rights he might otherwise have arising out of the contract or the breach of it'). See also: *Wallace v Nichol* [1951], 1 DLR 449 (Ont CA) [18].

[53] *King v Poggioli* (1923) 32 CLR 222 (HCA) 248 ('[Compensation by way of an] abatement in purchase-money is intelligible if the property is diminished or deteriorated in value by reason of a breach of contract; but it is not intelligible, to my mind, if the abatement claim is made, not in respect of a diminution or deterioration in value of the property, but in respect of loss or damage, however sustained, arising from the breach of contract. In the latter case the party is left to his remedy [in damages]': Starke J).

[54] R Megarry and W Wade, *Law of Real Property* (6th edn, Sweet & Maxwell, London, 2000) 722.

[55] [1915] AC 866 (PC) 870.

[56] The *Rutherford* proposition has been supported, both in England, eg: *Lipmans Wallpaper Ltd v Mason & Hodghton Ltd* [1968] 2 WLR 881 (Ch) 891; and in Canada, eg: *Wilson v Patterson* (1918), 39 DLR 642 (Alta SC) [6], [7]. In *Thames Guaranty Ltd v Campbell* [1985] 1 QB 210 (CA) 235, Slade LJ stated: '[i]t is a well-established principle of equity that where, in the course of concluding a contract, a person has represented that he can grant a certain property, or is entitled to a certain interest in that property and it later appears that there is a deficiency in his title or interest, the other party can obtain an Order compelling him to grant what he has got and, in an appropriate case, to submit to a reduction of the consideration for the grant.'

and academic[57] support for this evaluation of the innocent purchaser's position.

In respect of the *defaulting vendor's* right to insist on *cy-près* specific performance, he never possesses that option of suing for specific performance where the defect in the available property is substantial.[58] Succinctly put, 'if you get to a point . . . that the purchaser cannot get what he contracted to buy, the vendor cannot enforce specific performance.'[59] Hence, a defaulting vendor's action for specific performance with abatement can only succeed if the defect between what is being conveyed and the Contractually Described Property is small and immaterial.

The purported distinction between the wider rights of the innocent purchaser and the more restricted rights of the defaulting vendor, has been academically[60] and judicially[61] justified on the basis that, were a purchaser to be deprived of specific performance, even where the deficiency was substantial, the defaulting vendor could effectively take advantage of his own wrong. Moreover, if innocent parties are prepared to take what they can get, then performance of contracts should be encouraged.

The decision in *Topfell Ltd v Galley Properties Ltd*[62] provides a convenient illustration of this lastmentioned point. The defendant vendors advertised their house for sale, subject to an existing tenancy of the first floor, and with vacant possession of the ground floor. The plaintiff purchaser contracted to buy the house for £3,850. His intentions were to let the ground floor either on a long lease or alternatively, on a short-term furnished tenancy. Before settlement, however, he discovered a notice inside the front door, stipulating that the house was to be occupied by only one household. Consequently, the first floor tenancy precluded the leased occupation of the ground floor which the purchaser

---

[57] Eg: PV Baker and P St JLangan, *Snell's Principles of Equity* (28th edn, Sweet & Maxwell, London, 1982) 659 ('Although a substantial misdescription entitles the purchaser to refuse to be bound by the contract, in many cases he may nevertheless insist on the vendor conveying what he has with an abatement of the purchase-money as compensation'); *Emmet's Notes on Perusing Titles* (14th edn, 1955) 85, both of which are cited (Snell's 26th edn) with approval in: *Lipmans Wallpaper, ibid*; JE Martin, *Hanbury and Martin Modern Equity* (17th edn, Sweet & Maxwell, London, 2005) 743 ('the purchaser has a choice: he may elect to take the property, notwithstanding that it may be substantially different from the contract description'). This position is also approved in: R Megarry and W Wade, *Law of Real Property* (6th edn, Sweet & Maxwell, London, 2000) 686, 722; E Fry, *A Treatise on the Specific Performance of Contracts* (6th edn, Stevens, London, 1921) [1209]; RJ Sharpe (the Hon), *Injunctions and Specific Performance* (Canada Law Book, Aurora, 1983) [11.20], [11.90].

[58] Illustrated, eg, in: *Riverpath Properties Ltd v Brammall* (Ch, 31 Jan 2000); *King Bros (Finance) Ltd v North Western British Road Services Ltd* [1986] 2 EGLR 253 (Ch).

[59] *Jacobs v Revell* [1900] 2 Ch 858, 865 (Buckley J), and cited in: *Watson v Burton* [1957] 1 WLR 19 (Ch) 26.

[60] JE Martin, *Hanbury and Martin Modern Equity* (17th edn, Sweet & Maxwell, London, 2005) 753; R Megarry and W Wade, *Law of Real Property* (6th edn, Sweet & Maxwell, London, 2000) [12–118], [12–119].

[61] *Price v Strange* [1978] Ch 337 (CA) 364 ('A vendor who cannot convey what he has contracted to sell cannot, of course, rely upon the fact as a defence to a claim by the purchaser for specific performance. This would be to allow him to rely on his own fault.')

[62] [1979] 1 WLR 446 (1977 T No 734) (Ch) 452.

had envisaged. The purchaser sought an order for specific performance with abatement on the ground that the vendors were not able to give 'vacant possession' of the ground floor in accordance with the contract. The order was granted (on the basis that the ground floor was not in a state which would enable the purchasers to occupy it), together with an abatement of £1,000. Notably, the fairly substantial deviation from that which was contractually stipulated did not preclude this order for *cy-près* specific performance.

A substantial discrepancy does *lose the purchaser the remedy.*   The second school of thought, much-criticised as being a 'wrong-turn' in the law,[63] suggests that an innocent purchaser will lose his right to insist upon specific performance altogether where the deficiency in (especially) title is substantial in nature. Under this view, an innocent party is never able to demand a grant of some quite different subject matter in lieu of the Contractually Described Property.

The English Court of Appeal put the position thus in *Cedar Holdings Ltd v Green*:

> The doctrine [of partial performance] . . . is, in my opinion, directed to ensuring that the [innocent] grantee shall obtain, if he so elects, as much of the subject matter contracted to be granted as the [defaulting] grantor can convey, whether the deficiency be in respect of the physical extent of the subject matter or of the estate or interest of the grantor in the subject matter. It does not enable the grantee to demand a grant of some different subject matter in lieu of that contracted for.[64]

In this case, Mr and Mrs Green jointly owned their former home. Following their divorce, Mr Green and an imposter granted a mortgage over this home in favour of the lender. After the deception was discovered, the innocent lender sought a declaration (having the effect of *cy-près*, or partial, specific performance) that Mr Green should be compelled, at the lender's election, to charge his beneficial interest of one-half of the proceeds of sale and of any rents and profits until sale of the home in its favour. This was rejected on the basis that the Contractually Described Property was a legal estate or interest in the house; and a charge of the beneficial interest held by Mr Green was a different subject matter—it 'might be different' (said the court) if Mr Green had contracted to charge his share, but his only contract was to charge the entirety. Any order that a charge of *his share* be executed in favour of the lender would necessitate carrying into execution a new contract.[65]

This represents quite a different point of view from that expressed under

---

[63] R Megarry and W Wade, *Law of Real Property* (6th edn, Sweet & Maxwell, London, 2000) 722, fn 59; G Jones, *Jones and Goodhart's Specific Performance* (2nd edn, Butterworths, London, 1996) 294.

[64] [1981] 1 Ch 129 (CA) 142 (Buckley LJ), 146–47 (Goff LJ agreeing).

[65] *Ibid*, 147 (Buckley LJ). See also: *Watts v Spence* [1976] Ch 165, 173 (the only beneficial interest the grantor could convey was in the proceeds of sale of the matrimonial home under a trust for sale; '[t]he conveyance of such a beneficial interest could not be said to be a conveyance of a part of the fee simple in the land').

the first school of thought. To reiterate, under the *Topfell/Rutherford* principle, no matter how significant the difference between the Contractually Described Property and the available property, an innocent purchaser can insist upon *cy-près* specific performance. The *Cedar Holdings* view provides far narrower scope for the innocent purchaser to have (a version of) the contract performed. In actual fact, the opinion of Buckley LJ in *Cedar Holdings* that an interest in the proceeds of sale is substantially different from an interest in land, is probably overruled now, in the light of *Williams and Glyn's Bank Ltd v Boland*,[66] in which the House of Lords considered this particular aspect of *Cedar Holdings* to have been incorrectly decided. With sharp criticism, Lord Wilberforce remarked, 'to describe the interests of spouses in a house jointly bought to be lived in as a matrimonial home as merely an interest in proceeds of sale, or rents and profits until sale, is just a little unreal . . . contrast *Cedar Holdings Ltd v Green* (which I consider to have been wrongly decided).'[67]

In any event, and whilst not unanimously held,[68] significant academic opinion considers that the approach outlined in this section is wrong, on the basis that the vendor's narrower right to *cy-près* specific performance has been confused with the purchaser's remedy, to bring about this second (*Cedar Holdings*) school of thought. For example, Jones notes:

> There is some authority that specific performance [at the suit of the purchaser] will only be granted if the subject-matter to be conveyed is substantially the same as that described in the contract. This limitation is a misconceived importation from those decisions which have formulated the conditions governing a vendor's claim for specific performance. In our view it is wrong in principle and should be rejected.[69]

The more restricted right of the defaulting vendor to insist upon specific performance will be considered shortly.

A substantial discrepancy allows the purchaser specific performance, but with no abatement. The third approach, which has received the influential support of Treitel,[70] based upon an early decision of *Durham v Legard*,[71] is that where

---

[66] [1981] AC 487 (HL).

[67] *Ibid*, 507.

[68] See, eg: EH Burn, *Cheshire and Burn's Modern Law of Real Property* (16th edn, Butterworths, London, 2000) 837, who states, 'specific performance will not be decreed at the suit of the purchaser if the property which the vendor is in a position to convey is entirely different from that which he agreed to sell').

[69] G Jones, *Jones and Goodhart's Specific Performance* (2nd edn, Butterworths, London, 1996) 294. Jones cites *Rudd v Lascelles* [1900] 1 Ch 815, 819, where Farwell J noted: 'In my opinion the Court should confine this relief to cases where the actual subject-matter is substantially the same as that stated in the contract, and should not extend it to cases where the subject-matter is substantially different'. As Jones observes (at fn 9), Farwell J relied upon a statement by Jessel MR in *Cato v Thompson* (1882) 9 QBD 616 (CA) 618 to like effect, but failed to note that *Cato* involved a vendor's suit for specific performance.

[70] GH Treitel, *The Law of Contract* (11th edn, Sweet & Maxwell, London, 2003) 772, fn 64.

[71] (1865) 34 Beav 611; 55 ER 771.

the deficiency is substantial, the innocent purchaser may, instead of rescinding the contract, claim specific performance, but only *without* compensation. This view, if accepted, certainly counters the argument[72] that a wider scope of 'specific performance + abatement' recovery on the part of the innocent purchaser can potentially be the subject of abuse. If the purchaser realises that he has made an imprudent contract, and if abatement *is* permitted, he may feasibly seek to take advantage of a defaulting vendor by claiming that the vendor promised more under the contract than that which has been tendered, thereby entitling the purchaser to both the property and to a measure of compensation to cover that improvidence. This third solution, under which he is denied the right to an abatement, would prevent that particular scenario from occurring.

As noted previously, though, it is the first approach (per *Rutherford/Topfell*) which has received most judicial and academic support. The generally-accepted view is that some substantial discrepancy between the Contractually Described Property and the property actually available for transfer does not preclude the innocent purchaser from seeking and obtaining an award of *cy-près* specific performance with abatement.

2. Applications for *Cy-près* Specific Performance by the Contract-breaker

As controversial as it may appear, a defaulting party may also sue for specific performance plus abatement of a contract which he has broken. As the Privy Council made clear in *Rutherford v Acton-Adams*:

> [i]f a vendor sues and is in a position to convey substantially what the purchaser has contracted to get the court will decree specific performance with compensation for any small and immaterial deficiency, provided that the vendor has not, by misrepresentation or otherwise, disentitled himself to his remedy. Another possible case arises where a vendor claims specific performance and where the Court refuses it unless the purchaser is willing to consent to a decree on terms that the vendor will make compensation to the purchaser who agrees to such a decree on condition that he is compensated.[73]

This passage suggests that it is perfectly appropriate for the defaulting vendor to seek specific performance, and that the court can *impose* substituted specific performance in any case in which the discrepancy is not substantial; and that where it is substantial, the purchaser can choose to take the property in any event with an appropriate compensation. The former is the more legally interesting scenario, of course—for when will the purchaser be compelled to take property that he did not contract for?

---

[72] Postulated in: J Berryman, *The Law of Equitable Remedies* (Irwin Law, Toronto, 2000) 239.
[73] [1915] AC 866 (PC) 870 (Viscount Haldane).

A couple of points are significant about the above passage. The first is that it appears a somewhat unusual proposition to seek judicial help to maintain a contract on foot as against the innocent party, given that the party seeking the order for specific performance is not, in this instance, 'coming to equity with clean hands', but rather, as a party unable to convey the Contractually Described Property which he has promised. Immediately preceding the above passage, however, the Privy Council sought to justify this principle by stating that '[i]n exercising its jurisdiction over specific performance, courts of equity look at the substance and not merely at the letter of the contract'. In other words, to deprive the defaulting vendor of the benefit of the contract would introduce an inflexible rule capable of rendering injustice—an insistence upon literal performance or else—which equity will not countenance.[74] Jones justifies the defaulting vendor's right to sue for specific performance on an additional footing, that it is 'no more than the application to equitable relief of the common law principle that an innocent party may terminate a contract only if the other party's breach is fundamental.'[75] This proposition, that a defaulting vendor can claim 'specific performance + abatement' in the case of an insubstantial defect in that which he is in a position to convey, is now firmly entrenched in English law.[76]

As a second point of interest, must the innocent purchaser consent to the abatement before the court will grant the defaulting vendor's suit for *cy-près* specific performance? Opinion, both judicial and academic, suggests that where the discrepancy is *insubstantial*, the purchaser's consent is *not* required; he will be compelled to take the property if the court so orders. In *Watson v Burton*,[77] where the suit for *cy-près* specific performance was brought by the defaulting vendor, Wynn-Parry J noted: '[a]s I read that passage [in *Rutherford*], it is essential . . . that the purchaser should be agreeable to accept some compensation'. This particular comment, however, appears to relate to where the discrepancy in that case was, in any language, substantial. There, the purchaser was unwilling to accept any compensation for a considerably incorrect description of the size of the property, and the specific performance decree was refused. The Canadian commentator Di Castri also observes that 'the facts of a particular case may justify the court in refusing the decree unless the purchaser [innocent

---

[74] JE Martin, *Hanbury and Martin Modern Equity* (17th edn, Sweet & Maxwell, London, 2005) 752. See also: RJ Sharpe (the Hon), *Injunctions and Specific Performance* (3rd edn, Canada Law Book, Aurora, 2000) [11.90] ('the courts should not insist unduly upon literal performance').

[75] G Jones, *Jones and Goodhart's Specific Performance* (2nd edn, Butterworths, London, 1996) 290.

[76] See recently, eg: *Gill v Tsang* [2003] All ER (Ch) 175, [36] (vendor contracted to sell property, but was in default; 'a vendor can generally seek specific performance subject to an abatement, if he can comply substantially with the agreement. This illustrates the flexibility of the remedy', citing: R Megarry and W Wade, *The Law of Real Property* (6th edn, Sweet & Maxwell, London, 2000) [12–115]–[12–120]). Also: *Raineri v Miles* [1981] AC 1050, 1063 ('Equity does not need to expunge a breach of contract in order to award specific performance').

[77] [1957] 1 WLR 19 (Ch) 31. Given the substantial discrepancy between the area of the available property, and that of the Contractually Described Property—some 40%—it may be argued that no other result was feasibly open to the court.

party] consents thereto subject to being compensated by the vendor',[78] but again, this has been borne out in the case of substantial defects. Some earlier English authority certainly refers to the possibility of specific performance with compensation being 'enforced' upon the purchaser.[79] Consistent with this, and upon a review of Canadian authorities, Berryman comments: '[t]here are even instances where a vendor will be granted specific performance, imposing a property onto a purchaser and requiring the purchaser to accept compensation for the deficiency where the deficiency is not essential'.[80] Presumably, this point about consent will not often arise, for if the defaulting party is in a position to convey substantially that which he contractually promised, then the purchaser will usually accept such a transfer with an appropriate compensation for the deficiency.

Thirdly, if the consent of the innocent purchaser is not actually a pre-requisite to a decree of *cy-près* specific performance where the vendor seeks it, a further conundrum arises. Plainly this decree, in the absence of any consent, is only to be available at the suit of a defaulting vendor where there is a 'small and immaterial'/non-essential/insubstantial discrepancy between the available property and the Contractually Described Property. How, then, is that deficiency to be assessed: objectively or subjectively? Where the innocent purchaser is the plaintiff seeking the decree of specific performance, the court can readily assume that purchaser is willing to accept whatever degree of lesser performance the vendor is able to convey (with abatement)—otherwise, he would have presumably preferred his remedy in damages. Where it is the vendor who is the party seeking to impose *cy-près* specific performance, however, the degree of deficiency might be assessed by the court quite differently from how the purchaser would assess it.

English cases have clearly construed this assessment of deficiency as an objective test. For example, in *Watson v Burton*,[81] an innocent mistake on the vendor's part resulted in an overstatement of the area of the Contractually Described Property by almost 40%. In response to the vendor's suit for specific performance with compensation, the court remarked that 'the question whether or not the difference is substantial is a matter which is left to the court to decide in each case' (and, in this case, it was held to be substantial). The various factors to which courts have had regard when making this assessment will be considered more fulsomely in the next section. Interestingly, some Canadian case law[82] has

---

[78] JV Di Castri, *Canadian Law of Vendor and Purchaser* (Carswell, Toronto, 1968) 216; Also see JE Côté, *Introduction to the Law of Contract* (Juriliber, Edmonton, 1974) 252, citing the *Rutherford* proposition with the caveat 'if the plaintiff [purchaser] is willing'.

[79] See, eg: *Rudd v Lascelles* [1900] 1 Ch 815, 819 ('In the present case specific performance with compensation could not be enforced on the purchaser, as there was no provision that he should accept compensation, and the defect by his own shewing is substantial': Farwell J). Also: *Cato v Thompson* (1882) 9 QBD 616 (CA) 618.

[80] J Berryman, *The Law of Equitable Remedies* (Irwin Law, Toronto, 2000) 190.

[81] [1957] 1 WLR 19 (Ch) 27.

[82] *LeMesurier v Andrus* (1986), 54 OR (2d) 1, 25 DLR (4th) 424 (Ont CA) [17].

also supported a purely objective test on the basis that, were the materiality of any deficiency to be subjectively determined, 'no purchaser could ever be subject to specific performance and the test in *Rutherford v Acton-Adams* would be meaningless.' Subsequently, another Canadian court has been a little more qualified in its formulation of the relevant test:

> The materiality of the deficiency is to be determined essentially on an objective basis. However, this is not to say that the subjective views of the purchaser are to be ignored. Far from it. . . . the court, in carrying out its objective assessment, will give less weight to the subjective views of the purchaser if the needs alleged are more or less commonplace, not out of the ordinary and of little or no consequential effect to the use or enjoyment of the property as a whole. At the other extreme, the court will give no weight to the subjective views of the purchaser if it is felt that the so-called needs are capricious or arbitrary and contrived to avoid contractual obligations.[83]

This 'balanced' objective/subjective test has garnered both academic[84] and judicial[85] support, and is to be countenanced, in this author's view.

Thus, in summary, either an innocent purchaser or a defaulting vendor may apply for *cy-près* specific performance in circumstances where there is a discrepancy between the Contractually Described Property and the property actually available for transfer, although the pre-requisites for their doing so differ significantly.

D FURTHER CONDITIONS FOR CY-*PRÈS* SPECIFIC PERFORMANCE

Of course, the same previously-canvassed factors,[86] which are pertinent to the court's discretion when exercising its judgment about an award of specific performance, apply equally to decrees of *cy-près* specific performance. A study of the case law, however, reveals that there is one general overall pre-condition, and a number of particular indicators, which must additionally be found to exist, before *cy-près* orders will be made. In *cy-près* terms, this is the second stage of the doctrinal analysis—whether there are any further conditions that restrict or 'ring-fence' the capacity to award a substituted property transfer.

---

[83] In Ontario, eg: *Aquila v Hamilton General Homes (1971) Ltd* (SCJ, 24 Jun 2004) [14]. In BC, eg: *Bryson v Egerton* (1999), 25 RPR (3d) 113 (BC SC) [68], both of which cited: *Stefanovska v Kok* (1990), 73 OR (2d) 368 (HC) [30].

[84] J Berryman, *The Law of Equitable Remedies* (Irwin Law, Toronto, 2000) 242 (the degree of compliance/discrepancy 'is a matter of objective assessment, although it cannot be divorced from the legitimate subjective requirements of the purchaser'), citing *Stefanovska, ibid*.

[85] *Landucon-Yonge Ltd v Safeguard Real Estate Ltd* (1992), 30 RPR (2d) 87 (Ont Gen Div) (an easement covering 2.4% of the land was not a substantial discrepancy; specific performance at the suit of the defaulting vendor allowed).

[86] See p 282.

1. The *Cy-près* Order must fit the 'Spirit of the Contract'

It has been judicially reiterated in England[87] that where an order for *cy-près* specific performance is made, the courts have, in effect, made and enforced a different contract from that which the parties agreed. Any discretion to so order will hence be exercised most carefully. Further, as the Alberta Supreme Court has noted, the discrepancy between the available and contractually stipulated property must not be 'so great that . . . it removes the case altogether from the possibility of applying the *cy-près* doctrine to it.'[88] Another judicial formulation of this general precondition, reminiscent of the terminology used in the charitable trusts application of the doctrine, is that a *cy-près* order for substituted performance 'can be fashioned which will result in substantial compliance with the spirit of the agreement.'[89] Two indicators serve to assist the question as to whether that test has been met.

(a) Degree of difference between Contractually Described Property and available property

As explained previously, according to the *Rutherford/Topfell* school of thought, an innocent purchaser may bring a suit for specific performance plus abatement, whether the deviation between the available property and the Contractually Described Property is trivial or substantial. The purchaser's very decision to elect to sue for specific performance against the defaulting party imports that the 'spirit of the contract' will be met by granting to that disappointed party whatever the vendor can deliver, with an appropriate abatement.

However, in the case where the defaulting vendor is the plaintiff seeking the order, then relief will always be restricted to 'cases where the actual subject matter is substantially the same as that stated in the contract, and should not extend it to cases where the subject matter is substantially different.'[90] Under this category, the spectrum between the extremely trivial and the very substantial deficiencies which may afflict the Contractually Described Property involves much room for argument—for which reason it is said that these tests are readily

---

[87] *Rudd v Lascelles* [1900] 1 Ch 815, 818 ('But in this case, if I grant specific performance I shall decree specific performance not of the contract made by the parties, but of a new contract made for them by the Court'), citing: *Thomas v Dering* (1837) 1 Keen 729, 746–48. Also: *Bankers Trust Co v Namdar* [1995] NPC 139 (Ch); *Halsey v Grant* (1806) 13 Ves Jun 73, 76, 33 ER 222.

[88] *Boudreau v Reneault* (1911), 123 Alta LR 333 (SC) [9]. See also: *Webb v Dipenta* [1925] SCR 565, [1925] 1 DLR 216; *Punch v Chisholm* (1874), 9 NSR 469 (CA) 473; *Raaber v Coll-in-Wood Farms Ltd* (1971), 14 DLR (3d) 234 (Alta SC App Div) [56]; *Wilson v Patterson* (1918), 39 DLR 642 (Alta SC) [8]; *Nicola Valley Lumber Co v Meeker* (1917), 31 DLR 607 (BC CA) [47], [50].

[89] RJ Sharpe (the Hon), *Injunctions and Specific Performance* (Canada Law Book, Aurora, 1983) 420–21, cited with approval in: *Skariah v Praxl* (1990), 73 OR (2d) 1, 70 DLR (4th) 27 (HC) [70]. Now, see, by the same author (3rd edn, Canada Law Book, Aurora, 2000) [11.10], [11.30].

[90] *Rudd v Lascelles* [1900] 1 Ch 815, 819; *Flight v Booth* (1834) 1 Bing NC 370.

understood but difficult to apply.[91] A few examples of vendors' suits for *cy-près* specific performance will illustrate:

- in circumstances where the Contractually Described Property was residential land, and undisclosed to the purchaser, it had a natural underground watercourse running through it, specific performance was ordered on the basis that the purchaser had obtained substantially what she had contracted for.[92] In contrast, where the Contractually Described Property was land intended for house construction, but there was an undisclosed underground culvert that would have to be diverted to allow for construction, specific performance with abatement was refused;[93]
- in circumstances where the Contractually Described Property for sale consisted of a house, builder's yard, stables and 1,372 square yards, but it actually consisted of a smaller plot of 1,033 square yards with a substantially smaller builder's yard, specific performance with abatement was ordered because the misdescription did not go to the essence of the contract.[94] In contrast, where the Contractually Described Property was an industrial site of 3,290 square yards, and in reality, it was almost 40% less at 2,360 square yards, specific performance was refused.[95]

Other examples of insubstantial deviations from the Contractually Described Property have been gathered together elsewhere.[96] Given the inconsistencies among some of the authorities, as Sharpe reiterates, it would be improper and unhelpful to seek to explain some of these cases purely in terms of raw numbers or percentages.[97]

In summary, the objective factors which have determined whether the discrepancy between the Contractually Described Property and the available property is substantial or trivial have included: the percentage difference in land area; the purpose for which the purchaser sought to acquire the property; whether that purpose was known to the vendor; whether the property carried with it a restriction that, in the court's view, the purchaser would never have agreed to at any price; or whether the now-complained-of feature of the

---

[91] *In re Contract between Fawcett and Holmes* (1889) LR 42 Ch D 150 (CA) 156. See also: E Fry, *A Treatise on the Specific Performance of Contracts* (6th edn, Stevens, London, 1921) [1216]ff; JE Martin, *Hanbury and Martin Modern Equity* (17th edn, Sweet & Maxwell, London, 2005) 753.

[92] *Shepherd v Croft* [1911] 1 Ch 521.

[93] *In re Puckett and Smith's Contract* [1902] 2 Ch 258 (CA).

[94] *In re Contract between Fawcett and Holmes* (1889) LR 42 Ch D 150 (CA).

[95] *Watson v Burton* [1957] 1 WLR 19 (Ch).

[96] See, eg, the informative list compiled in: G Jones, *Jones and Goodhart's Specific Performance* (2nd edn, Butterworths, London, 1996) 291.

[97] RJ Sharpe (the Hon), *Injunctions and Specific Performance* (3rd edn, Canada Law Book, Aurora, 2000) [11.20].

property was one that the purchaser would not have minded, had it been known about before contracting.[98]

(b) No contradiction with the terms of the contract

Further qualifications upon a party's right to seek specific performance with abatement may be found within the contract itself. Whilst a fuller discussion of the myriad types of clauses that may oust *cy-près* specific performance is to be found elsewhere,[99] a couple of illustrations will suffice for present purposes.

Suppose that there is already a clause in the contract providing for compensation in the event of any shortcoming in the property:

> if through any mistake the estate should be improperly described, or any error or misstatement be inserted in that particular, such error or misstatement should not vitiate the sale thereof; but the vendor or purchaser, as the case might happen, should pay or allow a proportionate value according to the average of the whole purchase money as a compensation.[100]

In the light of such a clause, an order for *cy-près* specific performance with abatement, at either the request of the vendor or the purchaser, would appear likely—as Farwell J indicated, these sorts of clauses make the task easier, because 'compensation is part of the bargain.'[101] However, in practice, Sharpe notes[102] that such clauses actually seem to make little difference. If the clause is present, it simply confirms the court's jurisdiction to order specific performance with abatement; yet if there is no such clause, the parties are able to obtain specific performance with abatement in any event.[103]

Suppose that the vendor is contractually able to rescind the contract for any title defect that he is unable or unwilling to fix, and to return the deposit. In that event, can he be sued successfully for specific performance with abatement? A typical clause may read as follows:

> If the vendor is unable, or on some reasonable ground unwilling, to satisfy any requisition or objection made by the purchaser, the vendor may give the purchaser notice (specifying the reason for his inability or the ground of his unwillingness) to

---

[98] This list of factors is derived from the various judgments in *Jones v Edney* (1812) 3 Camp 285; *Jacobs v Revell* [1900] 2 Ch 858; *Flight v Booth* (1834) 1 Bing NC 370; *Shepherd v Croft* [1911] 1 Ch 521; *In re Puckett and Smith's Contract* [1902] 2 Ch 258 (CA), all of which are conveniently collected in *Watson v Burton* [1957] 1 WLR 19 (Ch). See also support for the objective test expressed in JE Martin, *Hanbury and Martin Modern Equity* (17th edn, Sweet & Maxwell, London, 2005) 752–53; and RJ Sharpe (the Hon), *Injunctions and Specific Performance* (3rd edn, Canada Law Book, Aurora, 2000) [11.110].

[99] Sharpe, *ibid*, [11.160]–[11.190]; E Fry, *A Treatise on the Specific Performance of Contracts* (6th edn, Stevens, London, 1921) [1239]–[1256], [1287]–[1296].

[100] The clause considered in: *Flight v Booth* (1834) 1 Bing NC 370; [1824–34] All ER Rep 43 (Ct of Com Pleas).

[101] *Rudd v Lascelles* [1900] 1 Ch 815, 818.

[102] RJ Sharpe (the Hon), *Injunctions and Specific Performance* (3rd edn, Canada Law Book, Aurora, 2000) [11.170].

[103] As in: *Shepherd v Croft* [1911] 1 Ch 521, cited *ibid*.

withdraw the same. If the purchaser does not withdraw the same within seven working days of service, either party may thereafter, notwithstanding any intermediate negotiation or litigation, rescind the contract by notice to the other.[104]

Presumably the effect of such a clause is that the vendor can never be forced to perform the contract with abatement. Berryman states the effect of these clauses succinctly: '[they prevent] the plaintiff [purchaser] imposing a judicially-determined abatement of purchase price on the vendor'.[105] They are not absolutely strict, however. In particular, they will not be permitted to be the subject of abuse. As the Court of Appeal noted in *Owen v Williams*,[106] a contractual 'escape hatch' of this sort, probably available earlier than the 19th century, must not be exercised by the vendor 'arbitrarily, or capriciously, or unreasonably . . . to get out of a sale . . . since by so doing he makes a nullity of the whole elaborate and protracted transaction.'

Suppose that a condition of the contract of sale expressly excludes the right of abatement, in the event of a discovery of a misstatement of title, quality or quantity:

> the property or (as the case may be) each lot is believed to be and shall be taken as correctly described as to quantity and otherwise, and any error, omission, or misstatement found in the contract (whether or not it materially affects the description of the property) shall not annul the sale, nor entitle a purchaser to be discharged from his purchase, nor shall the vendor, nor any purchaser, claim or be allowed any compensation in respect thereof: Provided that nothing in this condition shall entitle the vendor to compel the purchaser to accept, or the purchaser to compel the vendor to convey, property which differs substantially from the property agreed to be sold and purchased, whether in quantity, quality, tenure or otherwise, if the purchaser or the vendor respectively would be prejudiced by reason of such difference.[107]

In this event, could the vendor, having misdescribed the property available for conveyance, ever obtain an order for 'specific performance + abatement'? Presumably not—he is giving over deficient property, the clause precludes any compensation payable to the purchaser,[108] and case law confirms that the vendor cannot waive the clause, insist on transferring what he has, and pay compensation in spite of the clause.[109] Perhaps if the purchaser was prepared to

---

[104] Condition 16(1) of the Law Society's General Conditions of sale, 1980 Edn, considered in: *Owen v Williams* (CA, 21 Nov 1985). For another example: Condition 14 of the common form conditions of sale of the Birmingham Law Society, considered in: *In re Jackson and Haden's Contract* [1906] 1 Ch 412 (CA).

[105] J Berryman, *The Law of Equitable Remedies* (Irwin Law, Toronto, 2000) 241. Also: RJ Sharpe (the Hon), *Injunctions and Specific Performance* (3rd edn, Canada Law Book, Aurora, 2000) [11.190].

[106] (CA, 21 Nov 1985), also citing: *Selkirk v Romar Investments Ltd* [1963] 1 WLR 1415 (PC) 1422. For further discussion of attempts to abuse such a clause by the vendor, see: RJ Sharpe (the Hon), *Injunctions and Specific Performance* (3rd edn, Canada Law Book, Aurora, 2000) [11.190].

[107] Eg: Condition 35 of the England and Wales Law Society's Conditions of Sale (1953).

[108] *Jacobs v Revell* [1900] 2 Ch 858, 868–69.

[109] *Watson v Burton* [1957] 1 WLR 19 (Ch) 31, dealing with an offer to waive cl 35 of the Standard Conditions of Sale (1953).

take the property in its deficient condition without compensation, notwith-standing that clause, that would be permitted as a type of *cy-près* specific performance—certainly, Sharpe leaves open that possibility.[110]

2. Other Specific Indicators of *Cy-près* Specific Performance Suitability

The hardship exception. Any application for *cy-près* specific performance will be subject to the so-called 'hardship exception',[111] which has two limbs.

It has been clarified academically,[112] by early English authority,[113] as well as by more recent decisions,[114] that where the vendor has some estate or interest in the land, albeit less than he contracted to give, specific performance to the extent of his true estate or interest will not be ordered where the transfer or charge of the partial interest of the vendor might prejudice the rights of *third parties* interested in the estate. The proposition was well illustrated in *Thames Guaranty Ltd v Campbell*.[115] Unknown to his wife, Mr Campbell granted a mortgage over the matrimonial home, in favour of the lender, which was used to secure several overdraft facilities. The lender eventually claimed against Mr Campbell for the principal and interest due under those facilities, which it argued was secured by an equitable charge of Mr Campbell's interest in the home. Although the court accepted that Mr Campbell could have been ordered to grant a charge on whatever interest he had in the property as an application of the doctrine of partial performance, such an order would expose the wife, an innocent third party, to the risk of proceedings that would result in the sale of the property, depriving her of her home and the only asset she had. As the hardship that the wife would suffer on the making of the order far outweighed the hardship that the lender would suffer on a refusal to make it, *cy-près*, or partial, performance was not ordered.

Consistently with the general factors governing hardship and specific performance, *cy-près* specific performance also will not be granted if the order

[110] RJ Sharpe (the Hon), *Injunctions and Specific Performance* (3rd edn, Canada Law Book, Aurora, 2000) [11.180].

[111] *Thames Guaranty Ltd v Campbell* [1985] 1 QB 210 (CA).

[112] Eg: E Fry, *A Treatise on the Specific Performance of Contracts* (6th edn, Stevens, London, 1921) 588, [1270]; *Dart on Vendors and Purchasers* (6th edn) 1193; cited in *Rudd v Lascelles* [1900] 1 Ch 815, 816 (Farwell LJ); RJ Sharpe (the Hon), *Injunctions and Specific Performance* (3rd edn, Canada Law Book, Aurora, 2000) [11.40] fn 14.

[113] *Thomas v Dering* (1837) 1 Keen 729; [1835–42] All ER Rep 711.

[114] *Cedar Holdings Ltd v Green* [1981] 1 Ch 129 (CA) 147 (*cy-près* specific performance with abatement not applied; '[s]uch specific performance would, as it seems to me, prejudice the other co-owner, the second defendant, in two ways [under other potential proceedings]': Goff LJ). Also see: *Bankers Trust Co v Namdar* [1995] NPC 139 (Ch) (*cy-près* specific performance was applied; no prejudice to third party held), discussed further in: A Dunn, 'Subrogation, Partial Performance and Section 30 Orders for Sale' [1996] *Conv* 371; and also: *Thames Guaranty Ltd v Campbell* [1985] 1 QB 210 (CA) 239.

[115] *Ibid*.

would cause great hardship to the *other contracting party*. For example, in *Rudd v Lascelles*,[116] the vendor agreed to sell certain houses and land (formerly part of a building estate) to the purchaser for £3,500. It was then discovered, prior to settlement, that the property was encumbered with restrictive covenants relating to building and user. The innocent purchaser sought specific performance with abatement, the latter estimated (by the purchaser) to amount to some £1,000. The court refused to award specific performance, declaring that 'it would be a great hardship upon [the vendor] if specific performance were decreed, for, instead of obtaining £ 3,500 as she expected, she would receive almost one-third less—a serious matter for a woman with a limited income.'[117]

Abatement capable of quantification. The feasibility of calculating the amount of abatement has proven to be a crucial pre-condition for *cy-près* specific performance in the past, in that any inability to do so resulted in the order being refused. In the early authority of *Thomas v Dering*, Lord Langdale MR cautioned:

> It is impossible not to see that the *cy-près* execution of the contract which is given in these cases is in fact the execution of a new contract . . . in which there are no adequate means of ascertaining the just price. It is more easy to compute a just compensation when it is to be given for the defect in the quantity or the quality of the land sold than when it is to be given for the deficiency of the vendor's interest.[118]

There were other early authorities to like effect. Where a court formed the view that it was 'almost impossible' to assess what compensation should be granted to the innocent party for restrictive covenants existing over the property;[119] or where it was not a simple matter of taking the difference between what the property would have been worth with, and without, the encumbrance because it could not be assumed what price the parties would have contracted on, absent the encumbrances,[120] then no order for specific performance with abatement would be ordered. On the other hand, the threshold was not calculable perfection. Where expert evidence provided a spectrum of the minimum and maximum figures for the abatement, one court was willing to grant *cy-près* specific performance at the purchaser's request and assess the relevant abatement figure, albeit 'with very little assistance'.[121]

In fact, Sharpe notes that it is rare for this particular ground to be used to refuse an award of *cy-près* specific performance, and that courts will struggle manfully to value the defect or deficiency.[122] Jones further discredits this so-

---

[116] [1900] 1 Ch 815. Also: *Earl of Durham v Legard* (1865) 34 Beav 611; 55 ER 771.
[117] *Ibid*, but with this quote appearing in the version of the case reported at: [1900–3] All ER Rep Ext 1701.
[118] (1837) 1 Keen 729; [1835–42] All ER Rep 711, 717.
[119] *Cato v Thompson* (1882) 47 LT 491 (CA) 492.
[120] *Rudd v Lascelles* [1900] 1 Ch 815.
[121] *Topfell Ltd v Galley Properties Ltd* [1979] 1 WLR 446 (Ch) 451.
[122] RJ Sharpe (the Hon), *Injunctions and Specific Performance* (3rd edn, Canada Law Book, Aurora, 2000) [11.40] fn 3, citing: *Barnes v Wood* (1869), LR 8 Eq 424.

called bar to substituted specific performance, declaring that, given the age of the authorities which have held this particular factor to be important, and given also the robustness of the modern courts in tackling difficult assessments of compensation of all sorts, this principle has been, in effect, 'abandoned'.[123]

Misdescription a term of the contract.   Where there is a pre-contractual statement (inaccurate, but innocent) by a vendor inducing a contract, then the common law view is that the innocent purchaser is unable to obtain a decree for specific performance with an abatement of the purchase price. According to *Rutherford v Acton-Adams*,[124] *cy-près* specific performance applies only to a deficiency in the subject-matter as described in the contract, and does not apply to remedy a representation about that subject-matter made, not in the contract, but collaterally to it.

The reason for this position, as explained by Romer J in *Gilchester Properties Ltd v Gomm*,[125] was that, under common law principles,[126] no damages could be given for innocent misrepresentation, and to enforce a contract on the defaulting vendor with a compulsory deduction of part of the purchase money by way of abatement would be equivalent to awarding against the vendor damages for an innocent misrepresentation. In this case, innocent misrepresentations about the rents to be derived from four tenanted flats were made to the purchasers. Given that the statements complained of were inducements to the contract and did not constitute contractual terms, the purchaser's claim for specific performance of the contract of sale of the flats, with an abatement of the purchase price, failed.

Nowadays, however, a purchaser who wished to enforce the contract, in circumstances where the vendor made some misrepresentation as to the subject matter, could seek specific performance, plus damages, pursuant to s 2(1) of the Misrepresentation Act 1967, unless the vendor proved that he had reasonable grounds to believe, and did believe, that the representation was true.

E SOME CONCLUDING COMMENTS

Contractual transfers of property may potentially fall within the scope of the *cy-près* doctrine as defined for the purposes of this book. Under the first stage of the analysis that is adopted with respect to any *cy-près* application, the triggers must be delineated. In this scenario, it is, or becomes, impossible for the transfer to be effected, because the Contractually Described Property is deficient in some respect. In accordance with relevant objective factors, *viz*, the 'spirit of the contract', the extent of discrepancy, and which party is claiming the relief, it may be legally appropriate that the original (contractual) transfer be carried out by

---

[123] G Jones, *Specific performance* (2nd edn, Butterworths, London 1996) 290.
[124] [1915] AC 866 (PC) 870.
[125] [1948] 1 All ER 493 (Ch) 497.
[126] *Heilbut Symons & Co v Buckleton* [1913] AC 30 (HL) 47.

approximation. Then, by an order of substituted specific performance, the original transfer can legally be altered in a material respect—namely, the nature of the property transferred is altered—to approximate 'as near as possible' the original contractual transfer.

Clearly, contracting parties are not necessarily left to resort to their primary remedy of termination and damages if the Contractually Described Property cannot, for reasons of deficiency in title, quality, or quantity, be transferred as promised. The divide between substitutionary damages on the one hand, and specific performance of the promised contractual obligations on the other, is softened somewhat by the middle ground occupied by *cy-près* specific perform-ance. An even more expansive future treatment of *cy-près* specific performance is particularly justifiable, given the English Court of Appeal's statement of the 'struggle to grant specific performance if the justice of the case so demands, even if this involves *some tailoring of the unperformed contractual obligations* or the imposition of conditions or the grant of ancillary remedies.'[127]

In addition, it may be argued that contracts are often voluntarily performed after their breach, by an election of affirmation by the innocent party—*cy-près* performance (in this instance, by judicial order) is yet another instance of a contract going forth, despite non-adherence to its original terms. The doctrine partly underpins that school of thought which considers that contractual performance, rather than termination and damages, should be encouraged. It also has a close analogy to the *cy-près* doctrine in the context of charitable trusts, in which charitable giving is to be fostered by saving a bequest for charity wherever possible. Such doctrinal consistency across entirely different subject areas of property transfer is a hallmark of the wider definition of *cy-près* adopted in this book.

---

[127] *Progress Aviation SA v Americom Leasing Group Inc* (CA, 15 Mar 1988) (emphasis added).

10

Cy-près—*More than a Doctrine?*

BY VIRTUE OF LEGAL innovation, frequently born of law reform or judicial dissatisfaction, the modern *cy-près* doctrine is far more than a 'one-horse doctrine'—the 'law of *cy-près*' (cf the 'law of torts' or the 'law of restitution') has become a discrete and far-reaching discipline of law, whereby the principle that permits property transfers to be effected 'as near as possible' brings together various transfer scenarios under one overarching *cy-près* definition. Whilst many jurisdictions are at odds, or at least demonstrate some lack of uniformity, in their allowance of *cy-près* in its various manifestations, the number of jurisdictions which have adopted the doctrine beyond its traditional general law genesis in charitable trusts law, whether by statute or by judicial precedent, is significant. Notwithstanding adjustments for local political, cultural and societal circumstances, this willingness to embrace the doctrine demonstrably evidences its intrinsic worth and utility.

It is fascinating to reflect on how the old doctrine, with its seemingly Roman law parentage, has been reformed by generational succession to find acceptance and modernisation in a variety of legal areas—from charitable to non-charitable trusts, from class to unitary litigation, from charitable to non-charitable appeals, from contractual transfers to corporate dissolution. The doctrine has proven to be robust. Far from itself disappearing through obsolescence or under-use, it has flourished across a range of subject matter, with an ethos of pragmatism and flexibility. The modern *cy-près* doctrine is also notable for its local and *international* significance. Charitable giving occupies an important 'third sector' of any domestic economy, and takes in international events and global donors wishing to gift sums to causes from natural disaster relief to environmental redress. Statutory offshore developments in non-charitable purpose trusts for principally commercial transactions, and the international development of class actions jurisprudence, have flourished, and show no signs of abating, in extent or innovation. The *cy-près* doctrine has accompanied these cross-jurisdictional developments; and has done so in a manner which indicates that jurisdictions are continually seeking to learn lessons from others' experiences, whilst seeking to adapt their use of the doctrine to local conditions.

In light of the analysis that has been undertaken in previous chapters, it is convenient to revisit, and make some general observations upon, the revised definition of the *cy-près* doctrine that was adopted for the purposes of this book:

Where property is (or is to be) given by A to B for a designated purpose, under a legally enforceable obligation (the 'original transfer')

Transfers of property that may invoke the *cy-près* doctrine include: those given upon charitable or non-charitable trusts; those donated for public appeals whereby the appeal collector holds the donations on trust for the deserving cause; the court-ordered or sanctioned transfer of money by virtue of an award of damages or settlement sum in favour of a class of potential plaintiffs (or more rarely, in the context of unitary litigation, where a regulatory fine is imposed); and a transfer of property under a contract. In each instance, the property is to be transferred to the ultimate beneficiary under a legally enforceable obligation. As illustrated in preceding chapters, all of these scenarios of property being transferred for a specific purpose have been subject to some *cy-près* analysis.

AND it is or becomes impossible, impracticable, illegal or infeasible for the designated purpose to be effected

---

Careful delineation of the triggers of the *cy-près* doctrine (whether by statute or by judicial precedent) is absolutely vital for the efficacy and consistency of the doctrine.

Traditionally, the triggers were high: 'impossibility' or 'impracticability'. Consequential upon statutory enactment, the *charitable trusts cy-près* doctrine is now permitted in several jurisdictions where its application would make more 'suitable or effective' use of the property than the purpose intended by the donor. Lower threshold triggers of this sort inevitably require a considerable value judgment on the part of the court (or tribunal) when deciding whether deviation from the original charitable bequest is warranted. In the context of *non-charitable purpose trusts* also, the triggers are defined widely by those statutes which have validated them. Circumstances in which the non-charitable purpose has become 'obsolete' or 'by reason of changed circumstances, fails to achieve the general intent of the trust', are broadly phrased. In the case of damages distribution within the context of *class actions*, clearly individual distributions of

$3.00 per class member are entirely *possible*; but a *cy-près* distribution is likely in that scenario so as to achieve a more practicable application of the damages. The very notion of a cost–benefit analysis that is performed in class actions *cy-près* distributions admits, by corollary, that the distribution *is* possible. An analogously wide philosophy of contractual performance—whereby *cy-près specific performance* is recognised as a feasible alternative to the readily available and substitutionary remedy of damages—provides useful symmetry of law and consistency between this and other applications of the doctrine. In the context of non-charitable *public appeals*, the fund is frequently defined to 'fail' in circumstances which traverse much wider territory than the traditional *cy-près* doctrine (such as where the purpose was 'unlikely to be achieved within a reasonable time').

Occasionally, concerns and criticisms have been levelled at some applications of the doctrine—where the donor gives property on trust or for a public appeal—in that the original purpose should be adhered to, so that donors are not discouraged from conveying their property for good causes. The same sentiments conceivably arise where contracting parties intend to effect a property transfer for their mutual gain, but the proposed transfer is impossible. The objective of not discouraging such transfers is met, in this author's view, by viewing the triggers for the *cy-près* doctrine as a 'narrow gate', requiring a reasonably high threshold of difficulty to be met before the property transfer can be amended. The standard in trusts law (whether it concerns charitable or non-charitable bequests, or public appeal donations) is no longer impossibility, but neither is it mere inconvenience. Bolstering this approach, and in the context of class actions, the courts have emphasised the need to be vigilant in seeking to distribute the damages payable by the defendant to those *who are strictly entitled to them* (ie, the original class members), only resorting to a *cy-près* activation when the logistics of locating class members, and/or making distributions to them, renders this impossible or highly impracticable. Similarly, *cy-près* specific performance may only be sought by the parties in limited scenarios, as a secondary remedy to the more readily available remedy of damages. The triggers under each *cy-près* scenario indicate that the substituted property conveyance or distribution should not be effected frivolously or, for that matter, with unbridled frequency.

Adoption of a 'narrow gate' view of these triggers is the surest way of encouraging charitable and worthy giving; of retaining confidence of consumers and defendants alike in the litigious process; and of honouring the original purpose of a contractual transfer. It would surely be a mistake for the *cy-près* doctrine to march away from its genesis of impossibility or impracticability, and apply property differently, for other purposes or to other recipients, merely for the sake of convenience. This theme has been reiterated across all applications of the doctrine considered in this book.

> AND in accordance with relevant objective factors, it is legally appropriate that the original transfer be carried out by approximation

This second stage of the *cy-près* analysis requires that the court consider whether there are any other factors—apart from the triggers themselves—which 'ring-fence' the ability of the court (or tribunal) to apply the property for other purposes or to other recipients. Again, the strength of doctrinal consistency across various manifestations of *cy-près* is notable.

The application of the *cy-près* doctrine in the context of **charitable trusts** depends upon an objective test of appropriateness—'did the settlor have a general charitable intent when making his charitable bequest?' If so, then it is legally appropriate that the particular intent with which the original transfer was to be made be subordinated to that general intent, in order to effect the transfer. Equally, the case law on *cy-près* **specific performance** throws up several objective indicators to inform on which *cy-près* contractual performance determinations would comply with the 'spirit of the agreement', and which would fall outside the boundaries of the doctrine. Factors such as whether the Contractually Described Property has a 'substantial' defect, how third parties would be affected, and whether an appropriate measure of abatement is calculable, must all be assessed objectively. Similarly, in addition to the judicially-articulated triggers for *cy-près* damages distribution, the **class actions** *cy-près* doctrine requires proof of a sufficient degree of overlap between the original and the substituted classes before a *cy-près* distribution will be permitted. This typically requires, in US class actions jurisprudence, matching the geographical scope of the original and substituted beneficiaries, the injuries sustained by the class members and the means to redress that loss and damage, honouring the underlying purpose of the class action, and preventing undue windfalls to (undeserving) non-class members. As if to emphasise the 'narrow gate' application of the doctrine, certain Canadian legislatures have seen fit to enshrine the 'overlap requirement' in statute. As an objective 'ring-fence' around the *cy-près* power in the context of **non-charitable trusts**, several statutory enactments in offshore jurisdictions manifestly require that the settlor's general intent in conveying the property on trust be ascertained, and then be matched, should the non-charitable purpose fail.

These objectively-established factors, cumulative upon proof of suitable *cy-près* trigger/s, ensure that a careful brake is put upon the wrongful use or abuse of the doctrine across its various manifestations. They promote the reality that the original transfer will be honoured and adhered to in the vast majority of cases.

> THEN, by court or other superior order, the original transfer can legally be altered in a material respect—namely, the designated purpose for which the

property is given, or the nature of the property transferred for the designated purpose, or the recipients of the property, are altered—to approximate 'as near as possible' the original transfer

The third stage of the *cy-près* analysis, across all manifestations, considers how the property should be applied by approximation. Perhaps the most challenging issue with respect to the *cy-près* doctrine is precisely how '*cy-près*' must the substituted application of the property be—for instance, how 'near' must contractual performance be to what was promised; how 'near' must the donor's intent to benefit a charity be carried into effect; or how 'near' must the eventual recipients of an award of damages be?

On the one hand, the *cy-près* doctrine has been viewed, across all applications, on the basis that the substituted scheme ought to be 'as near as possible' to the original purpose of the transfer. Within the context of *charitable trusts cy-près* statutory incarnations, reference has been made in previous chapters to the judicial insistence that the substituted purpose closely resemble the charitable purpose which the donor originally designated. Even in circumstances where the New Zealand and Western Australian legislatures have statutorily permitted a *cy-près* application of property to 'another charitable purpose', this has been judicially read down, so that only purposes similar to the charitable purpose which failed have been judicially sanctioned. Similarly, a close correspondence of original and substituted schemes has been witnessed in the context of *non-charitable statutory trusts*—where legislatures have favoured terminology such as a *cy-près* purpose that 'is reasonably similar to the original purpose' or 'is consistent with the general intent of the trust'. Some legislatures (such as that of Queensland) which have permitted *cy-près* distributions in the case of *non-charitable public appeals* provide for application of the unused public donations, but only for analogous purposes to those for which the monies were donated. It may be recalled that the British Columbia Law Reform Commission strongly endorsed this view on the basis that donors' intentions must be, and be seen to be, respected in all cases of public appeals. Moreover, in the *class actions* context, certain courts have held that the *cy-près* recipient must relate, as nearly as possible, to the original purposes of the class action, and that it is not legally correct for the courts to redirect damages sums to alternative beneficiaries that may merely represent a worthwhile endeavour. Overriding all of these rather strict views of the *cy-près* power is that the courts must redirect the property in a manner that best serves the *original purpose* of the transfer.

On the other hand, it is equally apparent that the *cy-près* doctrine has been interpreted in some instances to equate to the 'next best' use of the property, rather than the 'as near as possible' use. These expressions, of course, may yield entirely different *cy-près* beneficiaries. The property or money may be put to very worthwhile use by a charitable or benevolent organisation that urgently requires such funds, and which will incidentally benefit the original beneficiaries—but that organisation's application of the money may bear little resemblance to the original charitable bequest, or the purpose underlying a class actions law suit. The very fact that the New Zealand and Western Australian legislatures saw fit to enact a liberal *cy-près* power with respect to *charitable trusts*, with strong approval by an eminent entity such as the OLRC, indicates that the concept of *cy-près* is continuing to evolve in some quarters in response to changing legal and social norms. In the context of *non-charitable trusts* too, some legislative provisions explicitly recognise that, where a reasonably similar purpose cannot be found, then some purpose should be chosen that is 'not against' the spirit of the trust. In the case of *non-charitable public appeals*, reference was made earlier to the provisions enacted in New South Wales, which expressly permit the application of dormant funds for other purposes, and in circumstances in which the legislature has specifically stated that the principles of *cy-près* do not apply to this re-allocation. By way of correlation, in the *class actions* context—and in the view of some US courts at least—the 'next best' class to whom the damages ought to be distributed has been watered down to an 'unrelated' class, if the circumstances mean that there is no obvious application of the funds that would serve to compensate the claims that the class brought, or the interests of the class members that the class action was designed to protect.

In rebuttal of the argument that such a 'wide gate' philosophy would serve to discourage donors of property, if they could not be assured that their property would be applied for like purposes in the event of failure of the original purpose, it may be contended that the donor should be ultimately protected by the establishment of carefully defined and clearly delineated *cy-près* triggers. A donor's property cannot be applied to some other purpose, merely because it would be convenient to do so. Once, however, the high threshold of difficulty in applying the property per the donor's wishes is reached, a fairly consistent liberal view has emerged across the manifestations of *cy-près* jurisprudence— that it is for the court to consider the next most useful application of the property.

Of course, such a 'wide gate' view involves contentious policy questions. The case in support of the wider application of property for its 'next best' use rests upon several bases, all of which have been adverted to in previous chapters, and which can be summarised as follows:

❑ strict compliance in distributing property may not be as essential as other social goals of the law—rather, a permissible degree of approximation should be accepted on the face of the facts in order to afford justice;

❑ the scarcity of resources means that property should be allocated where it is of most benefit to the community at large, or some section thereof, rather than closely analogous to where the donor may have wished (or where the class action's purpose may have dictated);

❑ it always remains within the court's discretion to order the substituted property transfer for a purpose 'as near as possible', but that this standard can be relaxed if the circumstances mean that there is no obvious application of the funds that would match the purpose which the donor favoured (or which would redress the claims that the class brought);

❏ to be permitted to alter a trust's objects, in particular, to achieve a more socially useful ('next best') outcome than the present impracticable object is the benefit that acts as the *quid pro quo* for the social cost of (favourable) tax treatment and perpetual withdrawal of assets from the economy which trusts facilitate; and

❏ flexibility and pragmatism constitute the essential appeal of *cy-près* inventiveness across all of its manifestations, and in that regard, the standing of the court, when exercising its discretion in favour of the 'next best' application, should be preserved as of paramount importance.

Notwithstanding the above, it is plain that there exists a considerable dichotomy of views between some legislatures and judiciaries as to whether the *cy-près* doctrine should optimally embrace 'as near as possible' or 'next best' use as the appropriate yardstick.

It is clear from the foregoing extrapolation of the *cy-près* definition that, in order for the doctrine to be applied consistently across a range of subject areas, it is important that it be examined in a strict tripartite analysis:

1. Appropriately-defined triggers are an essential pre-requisite, to the extent that they can be gleaned from case law, supplemented at times by legislation, and to the extent that they can be formulated objectively;

2. The further objective conditions necessary to permit a *cy-près* distribution of the property, howsoever arrived at, must be reasonably satisfied, having regard to the factual circumstances;

3. If the above two pre-requisites can be settled in broad terms, the third step of how the property ought to be applied should be settled in fairly non-contentious circumstances, and serve the overriding objective of access to justice.

Regardless of whether one is discussing *cy-près* specific performance or non-charitable purpose trusts, any possibility of *cy-près* application of the property should adhere to this analysis in order to achieve the symmetry of discussion that the doctrine now demands.

B SOME FURTHER COMMON THEMES

Some further common themes that arise from a consideration of the doctrine across a range of subject areas and jurisdictions are briefly outlined below:

An administrative function in 'uncharted waters'. Regardless of the particular subject area in which the courts are called upon to exercise a *cy-près* power in the case of property transfers, the fact is that, in order to decide who is the 'most deserving beneficiary', the court is exercising administrative functions. The value of precedent may be substantially discounted in this regard; *cy-près* distributions performed in other cases are not often referred to as illustrative or helpful.

The importance of this administrative function, when taken on a case-by-case basis, is not be understated. For one thing, the litigants in particular, and the public in general, rely upon judicial wisdom where the ultimate destination of large sums of money or very valuable property frequently is at stake. The importance of exercising this wisdom carefully, and with evenhandedness, is especially true where a 'next best' use of the property, rather than an 'as near as possible' use, is countenanced. There is also a question of the discretion which must be applied at the property distribution stage—appeals against *cy-près* orders are extremely rare (whether one or more of the *triggers* have been met has prompted appeals throughout the jurisdictions, but there is a scarcity of appeals based upon the argument that the 'wrong *cy-près* beneficiary was chosen').

A benevolent and 'outcome-oriented' doctrine.   The doctrine is intended as a 'salvage' tool, to retrieve a property transfer that has proven impossible or impracticable to effect, and to benefit (albeit indirectly) the originally-targeted recipients. In the case of charitable trusts *cy-près*, the beneficiaries under the trust stand to gain from the application of the trust property toward an analogous charitable purpose to that selected by the donor. Similarly, in the context of class actions, it has proven crucial to achieve an overlap between the original class members and those who stand to gain from the *cy-près* application of class action damages or settlement proceeds. It is also true that class members, particularly in damages actions, represent a 'proxy' for the 'larger amorphous class' (general society) who stand to benefit from the punitive and deterrent effect which the litigation will have upon either that defendant's practices or those of others in the industry—another 'indirect benefit' attainable from *cy-près* distributions.

Further, the *cy-près* doctrine prefers success to failure. Just as the courts have long been inclined to favour the continuation of a charitable trust, and to use the *cy-près* doctrine to effect that aim, *cy-près* specific performance promotes contractual performance rather than termination, and class actions *cy-près* promotes the goals of compensation, disgorgement and deterrence rather than unredressed wrongs. Certainly, the application of property to the 'next best' or 'as near as possible' use is preferred to (depending upon the context): *bona vacantia* dispositions; damages paid into Consolidated Revenue; or property wending its way to residuary beneficiaries.

It will be recalled that *cy-près* specific performance may be ordered at the behest of the contract-breaker—with the result that substituted property may be forced upon an innocent party who expected a different quantity, quality or subject-matter to be conveyed. What begins as a voluntary undertaking to the other party under a contract becomes, during the course of *cy-près* specific performance, a modified contractual obligation foisted upon the parties by court order. This mirrors the criticism, judicially cited, that *cy-près* specific performance involves the court in making a new contract for the parties. In contrast, the *cy-près* doctrine derived from charitable trusts law has sought to ensure consistency between the *cy-près* bequest and the supposed intentions of the settlor or testator. Is *cy-près* specific performance, then, an 'odd one out', a *cy-près* application which is not benevolent? Although it has been questioned whether the *cy-près* doctrine should ever be applied to property transfer and contractual remedies so as to achieve an outcome that is *contrary* to the expectations of the innocent contracting party, it has been noted in the previous chapter that this view is somewhat unrealistic. At common law, an innocent party cannot generally escape from a contract unless the breach is fundamental; and by corollary, an innocent purchaser must accept that *cy-près* specific performance with an abatement will be granted if the discrepancy is trivial.

Even in the class actions context, the *cy-près* doctrine has a certain benevolent overtone. In addition to seeking to match the damages awarded via judgment or settlement to as many of the original class of plaintiffs as possible, the doctrine is not *especially* punitive *vis à vis* the culpable defendant. A *cy-près* distribution of damages has been variously precluded: where it has been merely a tool of 'social engineering' that provided a benefit to persons who were not entitled to the damages fund whatsoever; or where the defendant did not 'deserve' punishment; or where the class members did not desire to bring any action against the defendant and would not claim their damages, even if such action were instituted. Moreover, the doctrine will be permitted, notwithstanding that the culpable defendant may actually *benefit* from the *cy-près* distribution of the monies.

Competing destinations for the property. First and foremost, a *cy-près* distribution will not be possible, in any context, where the court believes that the donor himself has the best claim upon the monies following failure of the original purpose. Considerable law has been generated in the context of charitable public appeals, whereby a resulting trust in favour of the donor may displace a *cy-près* distribution. In the context of non-charitable public appeals also, the tension between a resulting trust in favour of the donor, or the passing of the donation to the Crown as *bona vacantia*, should the public appeal fail, has been evident in English law, without a defined resolution. The terms of a charitable trust deed must be closely scrutinised to rule out the bequest resulting back to the settlor. Statutes validating non-charitable trusts frequently provide that a *cy-près* distribution is only permitted where the trust deed does not contain provisions for reform, on its own terms, in the face of a failed purpose. Finally, where legislation or judicial precedent permits *cy-près* within the class actions context, the courts must assess the equities in favour of the defendant when assessing whether that wrongdoer does, in fact, have a better claim upon the monies than any *cy-près* distribution.

Moreover, even where the property ought not to revert to the donor, *cy-près* distributions are generally a question of balancing the merits of various plaintiffs who could well lay valid claim to the money. In cases of charitable trusts *cy-près*, a variety of like-minded charities may seek to persuade the court that their purposes closely match those of the original beneficiary; and other organisations having similar purposes to the non-charitable trust or dissolved company may also seek to prove their worthiness as *cy-près* recipients. In the case of class actions *cy-près*, the court is similarly confronted with a variety of entities whose services could have benefited that particular group of plaintiffs who suffered loss as a result of the defendant's wrongdoing. Favour can potentially smile upon any one of a number of beneficiaries in these contexts.

Inter-relationship between statute and general law. This area of law has markedly demonstrated that the judiciary has been a herald for Parliamentary law-making. For example, the statutory *cy-près* doctrine was introduced in England in circumstances where Lord Nathan despaired of the lack of clarity and utility which plagued the general law doctrine prior to 1960. The failure to recognise the validity of non-charitable purpose trusts under English general law, and to judicially enunciate how the *cy-près* doctrine would apply to such trusts, saw the introduction, per the draftsman's pen, of offshore statutory regimes (and law reform proposals) that provided a framework and principled basis for *cy-près* applications of property devoted to non-charitable purposes.

The inability to apply non-charitable public appeal donations *cy-près* lead to the introduction of numerous statutes permitting that very application—various State enactments from Australia were analysed earlier in the book, with notations of how these enactments differed markedly in their *cy-près* triggers and powers of distribution. The enactment of class action regimes also introduced, by-the-by, *cy-près* powers with respect to damages distribution—a development which, it has been suggested, the Australian legislature would do well to embrace. Although the ALRC set its face against *cy-près* distributions, the care with which the triggers have been judicially framed elsewhere, the overlap requirement which cautious Canadian legislatures have enacted, and the success with which such distributions have assisted original class members who would otherwise have missed out on compensation entirely, have since demonstrated that a *cy-près* power within a class actions regime is surely warranted.

One of the dilemmas of the *cy-près* doctrine is the extent to which it should be codified, or left to the case-by-case development of the general law. Although legislatures have generally sought to articulate the various *triggers* for *cy-près* distributions in the charitable trust, non-charitable trust, public appeals, and class actions scenarios, the manner in which the property should be *applied* has been frequently left unaddressed (a 'gap' all the more unfortunate, given the potential dichotomy between the 'as near as possible' and 'next best' applications, adverted to previously). Notably, some non-charitable statutory trust regimes do cover the point (although most do not); and the perplexing refusal of the judiciaries to literally follow that which the New Zealand and Western

Australian legislatures have pronounced in respect of how charitable property should be applied *cy-près* has already been noted.

Avoiding use of the doctrine to effect improper legal change. Courts and academic commentary have constantly cautioned against using the *cy-près* doctrine in order to effect substantive changes to the law. For example, in charitable trusts *cy-près*, the doctrine cannot be used to convert a trust that is laudable and benevolent, but non-charitable at law, into a charitable trust. In the context of class actions *cy-près*, the doctrine cannot be used to circumvent individualised proof of damage, where that is expressly required by the relevant statute. In the context of non-charitable purpose trusts (and absent statutory validation), an invalid trust cannot be rendered enforceable because its designated purposes, whilst impossible to carry out, could be performed in favour of a charitable and closely-related purpose. In the context of *cy-près* specific performance, the same discretionary factors that govern any award of this remedy apply, such that if *cy-près* specific performance would cause hardship to a third party, it will not be granted.

Thus, across all of its manifestations, any tendency to use the *cy-près* doctrine as a vehicle to effect a substantive change to the law has been strenuously resisted.

C CONCLUDING OBSERVATIONS

The purposes of this book have been threefold. First, preceding chapters have examined, in common law jurisdictions, the modern scenarios in which the *cy-près* doctrine has been applied or contended for, whether judicially, legislatively or by law reform. Secondly, the marked differentiation that exists between common law countries' reception to *cy-près* in its various forms has been critiqued. Clearly, there are important lessons for the judiciary and for legislatures when considering the tripartite analysis in any application of *cy-près*: have the triggers been carefully delineated and satisfied; are the further objective requirements met; and how is the property to be applied to substitute purposes? These issues are not without difficulty within the province of charitable trusts. The encroachment of the doctrine into previously unfamiliar fields of class actions, non-charitable trusts, non-charitable public appeals, unitary litigation, and contractual (non)performance, has generated remarkably similar types of controversies and conundrums. The third objective of this book has been to emphasise that, whilst the doctrine is traditionally discussed in the context of trusts, succession and charity law, it occupies a far greater omnipresence in modern legal jurisprudence.

It is a remarkable doctrine, with both longevity and creativity as its hallmarks. The challenge ahead, for statutory and judicial law-makers, is to ensure that the *cy-près* doctrine serves to uphold property transfers where appropriate, reacts to societal demands for a diminution of complete accuracy and adherence to the 'strict letter of the law' where required, but does not over-reach its wish for success, and yet more success, at the expense of those who give of their property for a specified purpose. Above all, the modern doctrine, in all of its manifestations, and when reduced to its fundamentals, has been shown to provide both access to justice through disciplined application of principle, and a measured response to contested property transfers.

Bibliography

[The bibliography contains a record of materials cited in the book. Whilst every effort has been made to attribute and trace authorships correctly, where it has not been possible to do so, the author has indicated this with ——. The author apologises in the event of any errors contained in the bibliography of materials cited.]

TEXTS

Baker PV and P StJ Langan, *Snell's Principles of Equity* (28th edn, Sweet & Maxwell, London, 1982)

Bartsh T *et al*, *A Class Action Suit that Worked: The Consumer Refund in the Antibiotic Antitrust Litigation* (Lexington Books, Lexington Mass, 1978)

Baxendale-Walker P, *Purpose Trusts* (Butterworths, London, 1999)

Beatson J, *Anson's Law of Contract* (28th edn, OUP, Oxford, 2002)

Berryman J, *The Law of Equitable Remedies* (Irwin Law, Toronto, 2000)

Birks P (ed), *English Private Law* (OUP, Oxford, 2001)

Blake LL, *The Royal Law* (Shepheard Walwyn, London, 2000)

Brazier R, *Ministers of the Crown* (Clarendon Press, Oxford, 1997)

Bristowe LS and WI Cook, *The Law of Charities and Mortmain* (Reeves and Turner, London, 1889)

Brown A, *Snell's Principles of Equity* (16th edn, Stevens and Haynes, London, 1912)

Buckland WW, *Equity in Roman Law* (University of London Press, London, 1911)

Burn EH, *Cheshire and Burn's Modern Law of Real Property* (16th edn, Butterworths, London, 2000)

Cairns E, *Charities: Law and Practice* (3rd edn, Sweet & Maxwell, London, 1997)

Carter HG and MF Crawshaw, *Tudor on Charities* (5th edn, Sweet & Maxwell, London, 1929)

Chesterman M, *Charities, Trusts and Social Welfare* (Weidenfeld and Nicolson, London, 1979)

Conte A and HB Newberg, *Newberg on Class Actions* (4th edn, Thomson West, St Paul Minn, 2002)

Côté JE, *Introduction to the Law of Contract* (Juriliber, Edmonton, 1974)

Cracknell DG (ed), *Charities: The Law and Practice* (Thomson Sweet & Maxwell, London, 1994–) [looseleaf]

Dal Pont GE and DRC Chalmers, *Equity and Trusts in Australia and New Zealand* (LBC Information Services, Sydney, 1996)

Dal Pont G, *Charity Law in Australia and New Zealand* (OUP, Oxford, 2000)

Di Castri JV, *Canadian Law of Vendor and Purchaser* (Carswell, Toronto, 1968)

Duckworth A, *STAR Trusts* (Gostick Hall Publications, 1998)

Eskridge WN, *Dynamic Statutory Interpretation* (Harvard Uni Press, Camb Mass, 1994)

Evans M, *Outline of Equity and Trusts* (3rd edn, Butterworths, Sydney, 1996)

Fisch EL, *The Cy-près Doctrine in the United States* (Matthew Bender & Co, Albany NY, 1950)

Ford HAJ and IJ Hardingham, *Trusts Commentary and Materials* (6th edn, Law Book Co, Sydney, 1990)

Ford HAJ and WA Lee, *Principles of the Law of Trusts* (2nd edn, Law Book Co, Sydney, 1990)

Fry E, *A Treatise on the Specific Performance of Contracts* (6th edn, Stevens, London, 1921)

Gardner S, *An Introduction to the Law of Trusts* (2nd edn, OUP, Oxford, 2003)

Gladstone F, *Charity, Law and Social Justice* (Bedford Square Press, London, 1982)

Glasson J (ed), *International Trust Laws* (Jordan Publishing Ltd, Bristol, 1992–) [loose-leaf] vol 2, 'Source Material' tab

Grigsby WE, *Commentaries on Equity Jurisprudence* (first English edn, Stevens and Haynes, London, 1884)

Hackney J, *Understanding Equity and Trusts* (Fontana Press, London, 1987)

Harlow C and R Rawlings, *Pressure Through Law* (Routledge, London, 1992)

Hayton DJ (ed), *Modern International Developments in Trust Law* (Kluwer Law International, London, 1999)

Hayton DJ, *The Law of Trusts* (4th edn, Sweet & Maxwell, London, 2003)

Hayton DJ, *Underhill and Hayton Law Relating to Trusts and Trustees* (16th edn, Butterworths, London, 2003)

Hayton DJ and C Mitchell, *Hayton and Marshall Commentary and Cases on the Law of Trusts and Equitable Remedies* (12th edn, Sweet & Maxwell, London, 2005)

Hepburn S, *Principles of Equity and Trusts* (Cavendish Publishing, Sydney, 1997)

Hensler DR *et al*, *Class Action Dilemmas: Pursuing Public Goals for Private Gain* (RAND Institute for Civil Justice, Santa Monica, 2000)

Heydon JD and PL Loughlan, *Cases and Materials on Equity and Trusts* (5th edn, Butterworths, Sydney, 1997)

Hudson A, *Equity and Trusts* (4th edn, Cavendish Publishing, London, 2005)

Jolowicz HF, *Roman Foundations of Modern Law* (Clarendon Press, Oxford, 1957)

Jones C, *Theory of Class Actions* (Irwin Law Inc, Toronto, 2003) [online version, available via the Quicklaw database]

Jones G, *Jones and Goodhart's Specific Performance* (2nd edn, Butterworths, London, 1996)

Jones G, *History of the Law of Charity 1532–1827* (Cambridge Uni Press, Cambridge, 1969)

Keeton GW, *Modern Developments in the Law of Trusts* (Faculty of Law, Queen's University, Belfast, 1971)

Luxton P, *The Law of Charities* (OUP, Oxford, 2001)

McKendrick E, *Contract Law: Text, Cases and Materials* (2nd edn, OUP, Oxford, 2005)

McKendrick E, *Contract Law* (6th edn, Palgrave Macmillan, London, 2005)

McLoughlin P and C Rendell, *Law of Trusts* (MacMillan Publishers, London, 1992)

McMullen DH *et al*, *Tudor on Charities* (6th edn, Sweet & Maxwell, London, 1967)

Martin JE, *Hanbury and Martin Modern Equity* (17th edn, Sweet & Maxwell, London, 2005)

Maurice SG and DB Parker (eds), *Tudor on Charities* (7th edn, Sweet & Maxwell, London, 1984)

Maudsley RH, *The Modern Law of Perpetuities* (Butterworths, London, 1979)

Meagher RP and WMC Gummow (eds), *Jacobs' Law of Trusts in Australia* (6th edn, Butterworths, Sydney, 1997)

Megarry R and W Wade, *Law of Real Property* (6th edn, Sweet & Maxwell, London, 2000)

Moffat G, *Trusts Law Text and Materials* (4th edn, CUP, Cambridge, 2005)

Morris JHC and WB Leach, *The Rule Against Perpetuities* (2nd edn, Stevens, London, 1962)

Mowbray J *et al*, *Lewin on Trusts* (17th edn, Sweet & Maxwell, London, 2000)

Mowbray J *et al*, *Lewin on Trusts: First Supplement to the Seventeenth Edition* (Sweet & Maxwell, London, 2003)

Mulheron RP, *The Class Action in Common Law Legal Systems: A Comparative Perspective* (Hart Publishing, Oxford, 2004)

Nathan HL *et al*, *The Charities Act 1960* (Butterworths, London, 1962)

Newberg HB, *Newberg on Class Actions* (2nd edn, Shepard McGraw-Hill Inc, Colorado Springs, 1985)

Newberg HB and A Conte, *Newberg on Class Actions* (3rd edn, Shepard McGraw-Hill Inc, Colorado Springs, 1992)

Oakley AJ, *Parker and Mellows Modern Law of Trusts* (8th edn, Sweet & Maxwell, London, 2003)

Ong D, *Trusts Law in Australia* (Federation Press, Sydney, 1999)

Parker DB and AR Mellows, *The Modern Law of Trusts* (Sweet & Maxwell, London, 1983)

Pearce RA and J Stevens, *The Law of Trusts and Equitable Obligations* (3rd edn, Butterworths, London, 2002)

Pettit PH, *Equity and the Law of Trusts* (9th edn, Butterworths, London, 2001)

Picarda HAP, *The Law and Practice Relating to Charities* (3rd edn, Butterworths, London, 1999)

Poole J, *Contract Law* (7th edn, OUP, Oxford, 2004)

Randall AE, *Leading Cases in Equity* (Stevens and Sons, London, 1912)

Riddall JG, *The Law of Trusts* (6th edn, Butterworths, London, 2002)

Rivington HG and AC Fountaine, *Snell's Principles of Equity* (17th edn, Stevens and Haynes, London, 1915)

Roberts TA, *The Principles of the High Court of Chancery* (Wildy and Sons, London, 1852)

Scott AW and WF Fratcher, *The Law of Trusts* (4th edn, Little, Brown and Co, Boston, 1989), vol IVA

Sharpe RJ (the Hon), *Injunctions and Specific Performance* (3rd edn, Canada Law Book, Aurora, 2000)

Shebbeare GE and CP Sanger, *The Law of Charitable Bequests* (2nd edn, Sweet & Maxwell, London, 1921)

Sheridan LA, *Keeton and Sheridan's The Modern Law of Charities* (4th edn, Barry Rose Law Publishers, Chichester, 1992)

Sheridan LA and VTH Delany, *The Cy-près Doctrine* (Sweet & Maxwell, London, 1959)

Sheridan LA and VTH Delany, *The Cy-près Doctrine: First Supplement* (Sweet & Maxwell, London, 1961)

Sheridan LA, *The Barry Rose Charity Statutes* (Barry Rose Law Publishers, Chichester, 1998)

Smith HA, *The Principles of Equity* (Stevens and Sons, London, 1882)

Smith JC, *The Law of Contract* (4th edn, Sweet & Maxwell, London, 2002)

Snell EHT, *The Principles of Equity* (Stevens and Haynes, London, 1868)

Spence G, *Equitable Jurisdiction of the Court of Chancery* (Stevens and Norton, London, 1846)

Suddards RW, *Bradford Disaster Appeal: The Administration of an Appeal Fund* (Sweet & Maxwell, London, 1986)

Thomas G, *Thomas on Powers* (Sweet & Maxwell, London, 1998)

Thomas G and A Hudson, *The Law of Trusts* (OUP, Oxford, 2004)

Todd P and G Watt, *Cases and Materials on Equity and Trusts* (5th edn, OUP, Oxford, 2005)

Treitel GH, *The Law of Contract* (11th edn, Sweet & Maxwell, London, 2003)

Tyssen AD, *The Law of Charitable Bequests* (William Clowes and Sons, London, 1888)

Upex R and G Bennett, *Davies on Contract* (9th edn, Sweet & Maxwell, London, 2004)

Warburton J, *Annotated Charities Act 1993* (Sweet & Maxwell, London, 1993)

Warburton J (and assisted by D Morris and NF Riddle), *Tudor on Charities* (9th edn, Sweet & Maxwell, London, 2003)

Waters DWM, *Law of Trusts in Canada* (2nd edn, Carswell, Toronto, 1984)

Watt G, *Trusts and Equity* (OUP, Oxford, 2003)

Watt G, *Law of Trusts* (3rd edn, Blackstone Press, London, 2001)

Watt G, *Trusts* (OUP, Oxford, 2004)

Wilson S, *Todd and Wilson' Textbook on Trusts* (7th edn, OUP, Oxford, 2005)

GENERAL LAW SERIES

Canadian Encylopaedic Digest (Carswell Thomson, Toronto) [online version]

Halsbury's Laws of Australia (Butterworths, Sydney, 1991–) [looseleaf] [online version]

Halsbury's Laws of England (4th edn reissue, Butterworths, London, 1996) vols 5(2), 8(2), 35, 36

REPORTS and DISCUSSION PAPERS (in chronological order per jurisdiction)

Australia

Law Reform Committee of South Australia, *Relating to Class Actions* (Report No 36, 1978)

Australian Law Reform Commission, *Access to the Courts—II: Class Actions* (DP No 11, 1979)

Australian Law Reform Commission, *Grouped Proceedings in the Federal Court* (Report No 46, 1988)

Victorian Attorney-General's Law Reform Advisory Council (authored by V Morabito and J Epstein), *Class Actions in Victoria—Time for a New Approach* (1997)

Australian Law Reform Commission, *Managing Justice* (Report No 89, 1999)

Canada

Ontario Law Reform Commission, *Report on Class Actions* (1982)

Manitoba Law Reform Commission, *Non-Charitable Purpose Trusts* (Report No 77, 1982)

Law Reform Commission of British Columbia, *Non-Charitable Purpose Trusts* (Working Paper, 1991)

Manitoba Law Reform Commission, *Class Proceedings* (1992)

Law Reform Commission of British Columbia, *Report on Non-Charitable Purpose Trusts* (Report No 128, 1992)

Law Reform Commission of British Columbia, *Report on Informal Public Appeal Funds* (Report No 129, 1993)

Ontario Law Reform Commission, *Report on the Law of Charities* (1996)

Ontario Law Reform Commission, *Report on the Law of Trusts* (1996)

Alberta Law Reform Institute, *Class Actions* (Report No 85, 2000)

Federal Court of Canada Rules Committee, *Class Proceedings in the Federal Court of Canada* (Discussion Paper, 2000)

England and Wales

Report of the Committee on the Law and Practice relating to Charitable Trusts (Nathan Committee Report, Cmd 8710) (HMSO, London, 1952)

Report of the Charity Commissioners for England and Wales (1968)

Report of the Charity Commissioners for England and Wales (1970)

Report of the Charity Commissioners for England and Wales (1971)

Report of the Charity Commissioners for England and Wales (1972)

National Council of Social Services, *Charity Law and Voluntary Organisations* (Lord Goodman Report) (1976)

Report of the Charity Commissioners for England and Wales (1980)

Attorney-General, *Guidelines for Public Appeals* (1981)

Report of the Charity Commissioners for England and Wales (1982)

Report of the Charity Commissioners for England and Wales (1983)

Report of the Charity Commissioners for England and Wales (1984)

Report of the Charity Commissioners for England and Wales (1985)

Report of the Charity Commissioners for England and Wales (1986)

Report of the Charity Commissioners for England and Wales (1987)

Report of the Charity Commissioners for England and Wales (1988)

Report of the Charity Commissioners for England and Wales (1989)

Report of Sir Philip Woodfield *et al*, *Efficiency Scrutiny of the Supervision of Charities* (1987) (Woodfield Report)

Secretary of State for the Home Department, *Charities: A Framework for the Future* (1989) Cm 694 *Report of the Charity Commissioners for England and Wales* (1990)

Charity Commissioners for England and Wales, *Annual Report* (1992)

Charity Commissioners for England and Wales, *Charity Commission: Origin and Functions* (CC1, 1992)

Charity Commissioners for England and Wales, *Making a Scheme* (CC36, 1992)

Charity Commissioners for England and Wales, *Disaster Appeals, Attorney General's Guidelines* (CC40, 1992)

Charity Commissioners for England and Wales, *Responsibilities of Charity Trustees* (1992)

Law Society Civil Litigation Committee, *Group Actions Made Easier* (1995)

Lord Woolf, *Access to Justice Inquiry: Issues Paper* (1996)

Lord Woolf, *Access to Justice: Final Report to the Lord Chancellor on the Civil Justice System in England and Wales* (1996)

Charity Commissioners for England and Wales, *Annual Report* (1998)

Charity Commissioners for England and Wales, *Fundraising and Charities* (CC20)

Lord Chancellor's Department, *Multi-Party Situations: Consultation Paper (including Draft Rules and Practice Direction)* (1999)

Charity Commission for England and Wales, *Annual Report* (2000–01)

Lord Chancellor's Department, *Representative Claims: Proposed New Procedures, Consultation Response* (2002)

Cabinet Office Strategy Unit, *Private Action, Public Benefit: Review of Charities and the Wider Not-For-Profit Sector* (2002)

Cabinet Office Strategy Unit, *Providing Flexibility for Charities to Evolve and Merge* (2002)

Charity Commission for England and Wales, *Annual Report—Making a Difference* (2002–03)

Charity Commission for England and Wales, *Milestones: Managing Key Events in the Life of a Charity* (2003)

Charity Commission for England and Wales, *Small Charities* (2004)

Memorandum by the Home Office, *Charities Bill [HL]* (2005)

Ireland

Law Reform Commission of Ireland, *Consultation Paper on Multi-Party Litigation (Class Actions)* (CP No 25, 2003)

Law Reform Commission of Ireland, *Multi-Party Litigation: Final Report* (Report No 76, 2005)

Scotland

Scottish Consumer Council, *Class Actions in the Scottish Courts: A New Way for Consumers to obtain Redress?* (1982)

Scottish Law Commission, *Multi-Party Actions: Court Proceedings and Funding* (DP No 98, 1994)

Scottish Law Commission, *Multi-Party Actions* (1996)

South Africa

South African Law Commission, *The Recognition of a Class Action in South African Law* (Working Paper 57, 1995)

South African Law Commission, *The Recognition of Class Actions and Public Interest Actions in South African Law* (1998)

United States

American Law Institute, *American Restatement of the Law (Second), Trusts 2d* (ALI Publishers, St Paul Minn, 1959), vol II

American Law Institute, *Restatement of the Law (Third), Trusts (Tentative Draft No 3)* (ALI Publishers, St Paul Minn, 5 Mar 2001)

CONTRIBUTIONS TO EDITED TEXTS / CHAPTERS

Anderson AR, 'The Statutory Non-Charitable Purpose Trust: Estate Planning in the Tax Havens' in DWM Waters (ed), *Equity, Fiduciaries and Trusts* (Carswell, Toronto, 1993) 99

Beauchamp KA, 'Law Reform in Canada: The Proposed Introduction of the Non-Charitable Purpose Trust into Canada' in DWM Waters (ed), *Equity, Fiduciaries and Trusts* (Carswell, Toronto, 1993) 111

Cotterrell RBM, 'Some Sociological Aspects of the Controversy Around the Legal Validity of Private Purpose Trusts' in S Goldstein (ed), *Equity and Contemporary Legal Developments* (Hebrew University, Jerusalem, 1992) 302

Cotterrell RBM, 'Trusting in Law: Legal and Moral Concepts of Trust' in MDA Freeman and BA Hepple (eds), *Current Legal Problems, Collected Papers (Vol 46, Pt 2)* (OUP, Oxford, 1993) 75

Ford HAJ, 'Dispositions for Purposes' in PD Finn (ed), *Essays in Equity* (Law Book Co, Sydney, 1985) 159

Hayton DJ, 'Preface' in A Duckworth, *STAR Trusts* (Gostick Hall Publications, 1998) i

Hayton DJ, 'Anglo-Trusts, Euro-Trusts and Caribbo-Trusts: Whither Trusts?' in DJ Hayton (ed), *Modern International Developments in Trust Law* (Kluwer Law International, The Hague, 1999) 1

Hayton DJ, 'Modernising the Trustee Act 1925' in DJ Hayton (ed), *Modern International Developments in Trust Law* (Kluwer Law International, The Hague, 1999) 273

Hayton DJ, 'Modern Trust Law Reform in the United Kingdom' in DJ Hayton (ed), *Modern International Developments in Trust Law* (Kluwer Law International, The Hague, 1999) 299

Hayton DJ, 'Exploiting the Inherent Flexibility of Trusts' in DJ Hayton (ed), *Modern International Developments in Trust Law* (Kluwer Law International, The Hague, 1999) 319

Hayton DJ, 'Developing the Obligation Characteristic of the Trust' in DJ Hayton (ed), *Extending the Boundaries of Trusts and Similar Ring-Fenced Funds* (Kluwer Law International, The Hague, 2002) 189

Howells GG, 'Mass Tort Litigation in the English Legal System: Have the Lessons from *Opren* Been Learned?' in J Bridge *et al* (eds), *United Kingdom Law in the 1990s* (UK National Committee of Comparative Law, London, 1994) 609

Huxley A, 'Rhodes, Arakan, Grand Cayman: Three Versions of Offshore' in I Edge (ed), *Comparative Law in Global Perspective* (Transnational Publishers, London, 2001) 145

Kirby MD (the Hon), 'Procedural Reform and Class Actions' in MD Kirby (the Hon), *Reform the Law* (OUP, Melbourne, 1983) 156

Matthews P, 'From Obligation to Property, and Back Again? The Future of the Non-Charitable Purpose Trust' in DJ Hayton (ed), *Extending the Boundaries of Trusts and Similar Ring-Fenced Funds* (Kluwer Law International, The Hague, 2002) 203

Matthews P, 'The New Trust: Obligations without Rights?' in AJ Oakley (ed), *Trends in Contemporary Trust Law* (Clarendon Press, Oxford, 1996) 1

Petrow S, 'The History of Charity Law' in G Dal Pont, *Charity Law in Australia and New Zealand* (OUP, Oxford, 2000) 44

Swadling W, 'Orthodoxy' in W Swadling (ed), *The Quistclose Trust: Critical Essays* (Hart Publishing, Oxford, 2004) 9

Thomas G, 'Purpose Trusts' in J Glasson (ed), *International Trust Laws* (Jordan Publishing Ltd, Bristol, 1992) vol 1, ch 4

Warburton J, 'Trusts: Still Going Strong 400 Years after the Statute of Charitable Uses' in DJ Hayton (ed), *Extending the Boundaries of Trusts and Similar Ring-Fenced Funds* (Kluwer Law International, The Hague, 2002) 163

Waters DWM, 'The Protector: New Wine in Old Bottles' in AJ Oakley (ed), *Trends in Contemporary Trust Law* (Clarendon Press, Oxford, 1996) 63

PERIODICAL ARTICLES

——, 'Cy-près' [1998] *All ER Annual Review* 277

——, 'Civil Proceedings: Oldham Borough Council v A-G' (1992) 5(4) *Land Management and Environment Law Reporter* 166

——, 'Casenote' (1994) *ILT Digest* 201

——, 'The IHT Exemption for Charities' [1991] June *Trusts and Estates* 66

——, 'An Economic Analysis of Fluid Class Recovery Mechanisms' (1980) 34 *Stanford L Rev* 173

——, 'Collecting Overcharges from the Oil Companies: The Department of Energy's Restitutionary Obligation' (1980) 32 *Stanford L Rev* 1039

——, 'Damage Distribution in Class Actions: The *Cy-près* Remedy' (1972) 39 *U Chicago L Rev* 448

——, 'Developments in the Law—Class Actions' (1976) 89 *Harvard L Rev* 1318

——, 'Proposed Amendments to the Federal Rules of Civil Procedure' (1996) 167 FRD 559

——, 'Purpose Trusts introduced in The Bahamas' (2004) 11(1) *Trusts and Trustees* 20

Andreeva A, 'Class Action Fairness Act of 2005: The Eight-Year Saga is Finally Over' (2005) 59 *U Miami L Rev* 385

Atkinson R, 'Reforming *Cy-près* Reform' (1993) 44 *Hastings LJ* 1111

Barnett K, 'Equitable Trusts: An Effective Remedy in Consumer Class Actions' (1987) 96 *Yale LJ* 1591

Baxendale-Walker P, 'Purpose Trusts' (1999) 5 *Trusts and Trustees* 5

Baxter C, 'Trustees' Personal Liability and the Role of Liability Insurance' [1996] *Conv* 12

Bogart WA, 'Questioning Litigation's Role—Courts and Class Actions in Canada' (1987) 62 *Indiana LJ* 665

Borenstein S, 'Settling for Coupons: Discount Contracts as Compensation and Punishment in Antitrust Lawsuits' (1996) 39 *Journal of Law and Economics* 379

Borrell A and W Branch, 'Power in Numbers: BC's Proposed Class Proceedings Act' (1995) 53 *Advocate* 515

Bove AA, 'The Use of Purpose Trusts in the United States' (2004) 10(8) *Trusts and Trustees* 6

Bradford W, 'With a Very Great Blame on Our Hearts: Reparations, Reconciliation, and an American Indian Plea for Peace with Justice' (2002) 27 *American Indian L Rev* 1

Bright S, 'Charity and Trusts for the Public Benefit—Time for a Re-think?' [1989] *Conv* 28

Burchfield J, 'The Draft Charities Bill' [2004] 5 *Private Client Business* 310

Burchfield J, 'Private Action, Public Benefit' [2003] 2 *Private Client Business* 110

Cairns E, 'Appeals and Fund Raising' [1994] 2 *Private Client Business* 126

Calkins S, 'An Enforcement Official's Reflections on Antitrust Class Actions' (1997) 39 *Arizona L Rev* 413

Casurella JG and JR Bevis, 'Class Action Law in Georgia: Emerging Trends in Litigation, Certification and Settlement' (1997) 49 *Mercer L Rev* 39

Close AL, 'British Columbia's New Class Action Legislation' (1997) 28 *Canadian Business LJ* 271

Coffee JC, 'Class Wars: The Dilemma of the Mass Tort Class Action' (1995) 95 *Columbia L Rev* 1343

Coffee JC, 'The Mandatory/Enabling Balance in Corporate Law: An Essay on the Judicial Role' (1989) 89 *Columbia L Rev* 1618

Cooper EH, 'Rule 23: Challenges to the Rulemaking Process' (1996) 71 *NYU L Rev* 13

Cooper EH, 'The (Cloudy) Future of Class Actions' (1998) 40 *Arizona L Rev* 923

Cooper EH, 'Class Action Advice in the Form of Questions' (2001) *Duke J of Comparative and International Law* 215

Cornwall A, 'Class Actions Get Go Ahead' (1995) 20 *Alternative LJ* 138

Cotterrell RBM, 'Gifts to Charitable Institutions: A Note on Recent Developments' (1972) 36 *Conv* 198

Crerar DA, 'The Restitutionary Class Action: Canadian Class Proceedings Legislation as a Vehicle for the Restitution of Unlawfully Demanded Payments, Ultra Vires Taxes, and Other Unjust Enrichments' (1998) 56 *U Toronto Faculty of Law Rev* 47

Dam K, 'Class Actions: Efficiency, Compensation, Deterrence, and Conflict of Interest' (1975) 4 *J of Legal Studies* 47

Dash JA, 'Purpose Trusts: The Nevis Perspective' (2003) 9(8) *Trusts and Trustees* 8

Davies JD, 'Trusts' [1969] *Annual Survey of Commonwealth Law* 393

Davies JD, 'Trusts' [1972] *Annual Survey of Commonwealth Law* 261

Dawson N, 'Old Presbyterian Persons—A Sufficient Section of the Public?' [1987] *Conv* 114

Dawson N, '*Cy-près*: Means, Motive and Opportunity—and Other Matters' (1988) 39 *Northern Ireland Legal Quarterly* 177

Debelle DM, 'Class Actions for Australia? Do They Already Exist?' (1980) 54 *Australian LJ* 508

Deems, 'The *Cy-près* Solution to the Damage Distribution Problems of Mass Class Actions' (1975) 9 *Georgia L Rev* 893

DeJarlais NA, 'The Consumer Trust Fund: A *Cy-près* Solution to Undistributed Funds in Consumer Class Actions' (1987) 38 *Hastings LJ* 729

Delaney HA, 'Charitable Status and *Cy-près* Jurisdiction: An Examination of Some of the Issues Raised in *In Re The Worth Library*' (1994) 45 *Northern Ireland Legal Quarterly* 364

Delany VTH, '*Cy-près* Application of Gifts to Fictitious Institutions' (1957) 73 *Law Quarterly Review* 166

de Pourtales P, 'Purpose Trusts in the Bahamas' (2001 Oct) *Trusts and Trustees* 17

Draba RE, 'Motorsports Merchandise: A *Cy-près* Distribution Not Quite "As Near as Possible" ' (2004) 16 *Loyola Consumer L Rev* 121

Dubinksy PR, 'Book Reviews' (2004) 102 *Michigan L Rev* 1152

Duckworth A, 'STAR Wars: The Colony Strikes Back' (1998) 12 *Trust Law International* 16

Duckworth A, 'STAR Wars: Smiting the Bull' (1999) 13 *Trust Law International* 158

Duckworth A, 'Trust Law in the New Millennium: Part I—Retrospective' (Nov 2000) *Trusts and Trustees* 12

Dunn A, 'Subrogation, Partial Performance and Section 30 Orders for Sale' [1996] *Conv* 371

Durand AL, 'An Economic Analysis of Fluid Class Recovery Mechanisms' (1981) 34 *Stanford L Rev* 173

Du Val BS, 'Book Review' (1983) 3 *Windsor Yearbook of Access to Justice* 411

Emerson JS, 'Class Actions' (1989) 19 *Victoria University of Wellington L Rev* 183

Ervine WCH, 'Multi-Party Actions' (1995) 23 *Scots Law Times* 207

Evans D, 'Reverter of Sites Act 1987' [1987] *Conv* 408

Farmer SB, 'More Lessons from the Laboratories: *Cy-près* Distributions in *Parens Patriae* Antitrust Actions Brought by State Attorneys General' (1999) 68 *Fordham L Rev* 361

Flannery MFL, 'The Variation of the Charitable Trust' [1977] *New Zealand LJ* 368

Gardner S, 'New Angles on Unincorporated Associations' [1992] *Conv* 41

Germano LM, 'Interpretation of "United States" ' (2004) 69 *J of Air Law and Commerce* 195

Gordon S, 'Manageability Under the Proposed Uniform Class Actions Act' (1977) 31 *Southwestern LJ* 715

Gray H, 'The History and Development in England of the *Cy-près* Principle in Charities' (1953) 33 *Boston Uni L Rev* 30

Hackney J, 'Trusts' [1973] *Annual Survey of Commonwealth Law* 472

Hackney J, 'Trusts' [1974] *Annual Survey of Commonwealth Law* 514

Hackney J, 'Trusts' [1975] *Annual Survey of Commonwealth Law* 455

Hackney J, 'Trusts' [1976] *Annual Survey of Commonwealth Law* 412

Hargreaves P, 'Charitable, Purpose and Hybrid Trusts: A Jersey Perspective' [2002] 1 *Private Client Business* 30

Harpum C, 'Specific Performance with Compensation as a Purchaser's Remedy—A Study in Contract and Equity' (1981) 40 *Cambridge LJ* 47

Harris JW, 'Trust, Power and Duty' (1971) 87 *Law Quarterly Review* 31

Hayton DJ, 'Developing the Obligation Characteristic of the Trust' (2001) 117 *Law Quarterly Review* 96

Hayton DJ, 'STAR Trusts' (1998) 4 *Amicus Curiae* 13

Hensler DR and TD Rowe, 'Complex Litigation at the Millennium: Beyond "It Just Ain't Worth It": Alternative Strategies for Damage Class Action Reform' (2001) 64 *Law and Contemporary Problems* 137

Hensler LW, 'Class Counsel, Self-Interest and Other People's Money' (2004) 35 *U Memphis L Rev* 53

Hickling MA, 'The Destination of the Funds of Defunct Voluntary Associations' (1966) 30 *Conv* (NS) 117

Hill J, 'The Role of the Donee's Consent in the Law of Gift' (2001) 117 *Law Quarterly Review* 127

Histed EB, 'Finally Barring the Entail' (2000) 116 *Law Quarterly Review* 445

Howells GG, 'Litigation in the Consumer Interest' (2002) 9 *J International and Comparative Law* 1

Husbands J, 'Charity Trust Reform' (2004) 10(4) *Trusts and Trustees* 26

Issacharoff S, 'Group Litigation of Consumer Claims: Lessons from the US Experience' (1999) 34 *Texas International LJ* 135

Jaconelli J, 'Independent Schools, Purpose Trusts and Human Rights' [1996] *Conv* 24

Jaffey J, 'Settlement Reached on Vitamin Price-Fixing' (2005) *Lawyers' Weekly* Vol 24 No 6

Kaplan B, 'Continuing Work of the Civil Committee: 1966 Amendments of the Federal Rules of Civil Procedure (Part I)' (1967) 81 *Harvard L Rev* 356

Karas S, 'The Role of Fluid Recovery in Consumer Protection Litigation' (2002) 90 *Californian L Rev* 959

Kelledy M, 'Trusts, Charities and "Parklands"—The Olympic Sports Field Case' (1995) 1 *Local Government LJ* 65

Kirby MD (the Hon), 'Class Actions: A Panacea or Disaster?' [1978] *Australian Director* 25

Kolish, 'FTC Workshop—Protecting Consumer Interests in Class Actions' (2005) 18 *Georgetown J of Legal Ethics* 1161

Lambert KA, 'Class Action Settlements in Louisiana' (2000) 61 *Louisiana L Rev* 89

Leslie CR, 'A Market-Based Approach to Coupon Settlements in Antitrust and Consumer Class Action Litigation' (2002) 49 *UCLA L Rev* 991

Lindblom PH and GD Watson, 'Complex Litigation—A Comparative Perspective' (1993) 12 *Civil Justice Quarterly* 33

Lovell PA, 'Non-charitable Purpose Trusts—Further Reflections' (1970) 34 *Conv* 77

Luxton P, 'In Pursuit of "Purpose" Through Section 13 of the Charities Act 1960' [1985] *Conv* 313

Luxton P, 'Whither *Cy-près*? An Anglo-American Analysis of Practical Problems' [1987] *New Law Journal Annual Charities Review* 34

McCall JR *et al*, 'Greater Representation for California Consumers—Fluid Recovery, Consumer Trust Funds and Representative Actions' (1995) 46 *Hastings LJ* 797

McCormack G, 'The Eye of Equity: Identification Principles and Equitable Tracing' [1996] *J of Business Law* 225

Macdonald WA and JW Rowley, 'Ontario Class Action Reform: Business and Justice System Impacts—A Comment' (1984) 9 *Canadian Business LJ* 351

McGowan M, 'Certification of Class Actions in Ontario' (1993), 16 CPC (3d) 172

McKay L, 'Trusts for Purposes—Another View' (1973) 37 *Conv* 420

Malina M, 'Fluid Class Recovery as a Consumer Remedy in Antitrust Cases' (1972) 47 *NYU L Rev* 477

Martin J, 'The Construction of Charitable Gifts' (1974) 38 *Conv* 187

Matthews P, 'Trusts to Maintain Animals' (1983) 80 *Law Society Gazette* 2451

Matthews P, 'Shooting STAR: The New Special Trusts Regime from the Cayman Islands' (1997) 11 *Trust Law International* 67

Matthews P, 'STAR: Big Bang or Red Dwarf' (1998) 12 *Trust Law International* 98

McKay L, 'Trusts for Purposes—Another View' (1973) 37 *Conv* 420

Megarry RE, 'Perpetuities and the *Cy-près* Doctrine' (1939) 54 *Law Quarterly Review* 422

Mezzetti LM and WR Case, 'The Coupon Can be the Ticket: The Use of "Coupon" and Other Non-Monetary Redress in Class Action Settlements' (2005) 18 *Georgetown J of Legal Ethics* 1431

Miller GP and LS Singer, 'Non-Pecuniary Class Action Settlements' (1997) 60 *Law and Contemporary Problems* 97

Mitchell P, 'Just Do It! Eskridge's Critical Pragmatic Theory of Statutory Interpretation (Book Review)' (1996) 41 *McGill LJ* 713

Moerman S, 'Non-Charitable Purpose Trusts' (2000) 6(1) *Trusts and Trustees* 7

Moerman S, 'The Mauritius Purpose Trust' (2003) 9(4) *Trusts and Trustees* 21

Moerman S, 'BVI Purpose Trusts' (2004) 10(3) *Trusts and Trustees* 18

Moos D, 'Pleading Around the Private Securities Litigation Reform Act' (2005) 78 *U Southern California L Rev* 763

Morabito V, 'Taxpayers and Class Actions' (1997) 20 *U New South Wales LJ* 372

Morabito V, 'The Federal Court of Australia's Power to Terminate Properly Instituted Class Actions' (2004) 42 *Osgoode Hall LJ* 473

Morris D, 'Oldham Borough Council v A-G (Casenote)' (1992/93) 1 *Charity Law and Practice Review* 157

Morris D, 'Casenote' (2004) 18 *Trust Law International* 155

Nelthorpe D, 'Consumer Trust Funds' (1988) 13 *Legal Services Bulletin* 26

O'Malley R, 'Charitable Status and Fiscal Privileges: Two Separate Issues?' (2003) 4 *Hibernian LJ* 177

Paines AJS, 'Charity and the NHS—Use or Abuse' [1994] 5 *Private Client Business* 338

Parkinson P, 'Review Essay: *Trends in Contemporary Trust Law* by A Oakley' (1998) 20 *Sydney L Rev* 348

Partington D, 'Sharp Practice and the Law of Charities' [1988] *Conv* 288

Pascoe S, 'Solicitors: Be Bold—Create Entailed Interests [2001] *Conv* 396

Pawlowski M, 'Purpose Trusts: Obligations without Beneficiaries?' (2002) 9(1) *Trusts and Trustees* 10

Picarda HA, 'Charity in Roman Law: Roots and Parallels' (1992/93) *Charity Law and Practice Rev* 9

Rabkin JA, 'The Secret Life of the Private Attorney General' (1998) 61 *Law and Contemporary Problems* 179

Ramsay I, 'Class Action: Class Proceedings Act 1992' [1993] *Consumer LJ* CS39

Rheingold P, 'Settlement of Class Actions—American Style' (1997) 8 *Australian Product Liability Reporter* 91

Richardson N, 'Modern Problems for Ancient Charities' (2001) 15 *Trust Law International* 159

Rickett CEF, 'The Dead Hand's Grip' [1988] *New Zealand LJ* 335

Rickett CEF, 'Charitable Attitudes to Charity' [1989] *New Zealand LJ* 431

Rickett CEF, 'Politics and *Cy-près*' [1998] *New Zealand LJ* 55

Rickett CEF, 'Failure of Charities and the Conundrum of s 32' [2003] *New Zealand LJ* 59

Ridout P, 'From 1601 to 2004 and Onwards' (2004 Jul/Aug) *Trusts and Estates Law and Tax Journal* 16

Rubenstein WB, 'On What a "Private Attorney General" Is—And Why it Matters' (2004) 57 *Vanderbilt U L Rev* 2129

Santow GFK, 'Charity in its Political Voice—A Tinkling Cymbal or a Sounding Brass?' (1999) 18 *Australian Bar Rev* 225

Scott NC, 'Don't Forget Me! The Client in a Class Action Lawsuit' (2002) 15 *Georgetown J of Legal Ethics* 561

Shepherd SR, 'Damage Distribution in Class Actions: The *Cy-près* Remedy' (1972) 39 *U Chicago L Rev* 448

Sheridan LA, 'The *Cy-près* Doctrine' (1954) 32 *Canadian Bar Rev* 599

Sheridan LA, '*Cy-près* Application of Three Holloway Pictures' (1993/94) 2 *Charity Law and Practice Rev* 181

Sievers S, 'Incorporation and Regulation of Non-Profit Associations in Australia and Other Common Law Jurisdictions' (2001) 13 *Australian Journal of Corporate Law* 124

Simon D, 'Shopping for the Best Charitable Structure—Some Thoughts for Would-be Settlors and Trustees' (2000) 6(8) *Trusts and Trustees* 16

Simon W, 'Class Actions—Useful Tool or Engine of Destruction?' (1973) 55 FRD 375

Simpson SJ, 'Class Action Reform: A New Accountability' (1991) 10 *Advocates' Society J* 19

Sisson RG, 'Relaxing the Dead Hand's Grip: Charitable Efficiency and the Doctrine of Cy-près' (1988) 74 *Virginia L Rev* 635

Sladen M, 'The Charities Act 1985' [1986] *Conv* 78

Smith RJ, 'Trusts' [1977] *Annual Survey of Commonwealth Law* 298

Srivastava S, 'Administrative Efficiency in Charitable Trusts' (1994) *Law Society Journal* 31

Stein GJR, 'Cayman STAR Trusts: Three Years On' (2000 Nov) *Trusts and Trustees* 28

Swadling W, 'Quistclose Trusts and Orthodoxy' (2004) 11 *Journal of International Trust and Corporate Planning* 121

Sylvan L, 'The Next Best Thing' (2003) 95 *Consuming Interest* 19

Thompson BH, 'The Continuing Innovation of Citizen Enforcement' (2000) *U Illinois L Rev* 185

Thompson R, ' "Public" Charitable Trusts Which Fail: An Appeal for Judicial Consistency' (1971) 36 *Saskatchewan L Rev* 110

Todd ECE, 'The *Cy-près* Doctrine: A Canadian Approach' (1954) 32 *Canadian Bar Rev* 1100

Turnbull LA, 'Case Comment' (1991) 38 *Estates and Trusts Reports* 47

Vauter BA, 'The Next Best Thing: Unclaimed Funds From Class Action Settlements' (2001) 80 *Michigan Bar J* 68

Venables R, '*Cy-près* and Yet So Far Away' [May, 2002] *Legal Executive Journal* 54

Waddams SM, 'Profits Derived from Breach of Contract: Damages or Restitution' (1997) 11 *J of Contract Law* 115

Waller SW, 'The Future of Private Rights of Action in Antitrust' (2004) 16 *Loyola Consumer L Rev* 295

Warburton J, 'Charitable Companies and the *Cy-près* Rule' [1988] *Conv* 275

Warburton J, 'Charitable Trusts—Unique' [1999] *Conv* 20

Warburton J, 'The Spirit of the Gift' (1995/96) 3 *Charity Law and Practice Review* 1

Warburton J and W Barr, 'Charity Mergers—Property Problems' [2002] *Conv* 531

Waters DWM, 'Comment on *Re Hunter*' (1974) 52 *Canadian Bar Rev* 598

Watson GD, 'Ontario's New Class Action Legislation' [1992] *Butterworths J of Intl Banking and Financial Law* 365

Weber MC, 'Managing Complex Litigation in the Illinois Courts' (1996) 27 *Loyola U Chicago LJ* 959

Welles DW, 'Charitable Punishment: A Proposal to Award Punitive Damages to Nonprofit Organizations' (1998) 9 *Stanford L and Policy Rev* 203

Willard J, 'Illustrations of the Origin of *Cy-près*' (1894) 8 *Harvard L Rev* 69

Wilson D, 'Section 14 of the Charities Act 1960: A Dead Letter?' [1983] *Conv* 40

Winder WHD, '*Cy-près* Application of Surplus Funds' (1941) 5 *Conv* 198

Wright CM and MD Baer, 'The Growth of Private Rights of Action Outside the US: Price-fixing Class Actions—A Canadian Perspective' (2004) 16 *Loyola Consumer L Rev* 463

Young PW (the Hon), 'Charity and Politics' (1997) 71 *Australian Law Journal* 839

Ziegel JS, 'Criminal Usury, Class Actions and Unjust Enrichment in Canada' (2002) 18 *J of Contract Law* 121

UNPUBLISHED PAPER

Higgins RA, 'The Equitable Doctrine of *Cy-près* and Consumer Protection' (Annex 1, ACA Submission, Trade Practices Act Review, 15 July 2002)

DRAFT LEGISLATION

Charities Bill 2004 (December 2004)

Charities Bill [HL] (as amended on report) (HL Bill 27, 54/1, ordered to be printed 18 October 2005)

MODEL DOCUMENTS

Quint F, *Charity Law Association Model Documents—Memorandum and Articles of Association for a Charitable Company Limited by Guarantee* (NGO Finance, London, 1997)

Quint F, *Charity Law Association Model Documents—Trust Deed for a Charitable Trust* (NGO Finance, London, 1997)

Quint F, *Charity Law Association Model Documents—Constitution for a Charitable Unincorporated Association* (NGO Finance, London, 1997)

NEWSPAPER ARTICLES

Doran J, 'DuPont sued for $5bn over Teflon cancer claims', *The Times (Business)*, 20 July 2005, 41

Mortished C, 'Lawyers cash in on wrong arm of the law', *The Times (Business)*, 20 July 2005, 45

Nicholson-Lord D, 'Rover "pays" 1M pounds compensation', *The Independent* (London), 17 Nov 1993, 2

DICTIONARIES AND SIMILAR REFERENCES

——, *Words and Phrases* (Permanent edn, West Publishing Co, St Paul Minn, 1968–) vol 10A

Bone S (ed), *Osborn's Concise Law Dictionary* (9th edn, Sweet & Maxwell, London, 2001)

Burchfield RW, *The New Fowler's Modern English Usage* (Clarendon Press, Oxford, 1998)

Burke J, *Jowitt's Dictionary of English Law* (2nd edn, Sweet & Maxwell, London, 1977) vol 2

Cardiff Law School, *Cardiff Index to Legal Abbreviations* [accessed online at <www.legalabbrevs.cardiff.ac.uk>]

Garner BA, *A Dictionary of Modern Legal Usage* (OUP, New York, 1987)

Garner BA (ed), *Black's Law Dictionary* (8th edn, West Group, St Paul Minn, 2004)

Greenberg D and A Millbrook (eds), *Stroud's Judicial Dictionary of Words and Phrases* (6th edn, Sweet & Maxwell, London, 2000)

Nygh PE and P Butt (eds), *Butterworths Australian Legal Dictionary* (Butterworths, Sydney, 1997)

Rapalje S and RL Lawrence, *A Dictionary of American and English Law* (Lawbook Exchange Ltd, Union NJ, 1997)

Saunders JB (ed), *Words and Phrases Legally Defined* (Butterworths, London, 1988) vol 1

Walker DM, *The Oxford Companion to Law* (Clarendon Press, Oxford, 1980)

LEGISLATIVE AND CASE LAW DATABASE SOURCES

The case law and legislation cited in this book were obtained from the following database sources: (with pinpoints verified via hard copy where necessary):

Maintained by ILS Corporate Downloads, encompassing most non-charitable purpose trusts legislation: <www.ils-world.com/library/index.shtml>

Maintained by Lexis Nexis Butterworths Australia: <www.butterworthsonline.com>

Maintained by Lexis Nexis Professional UK (including full database access to Canadian, US and other international materials): <http://web.lexis-nexis.com>

Maintained by Lexis Nexis Butterworths UK: <www.butterworths.co.uk>
Maintained by Lexis Nexis Quicklaw Canada: <www.quicklaw.com>
Maintained by Justis Publishing Ltd: <www.justis.com>
Maintained by the joint law faculties of UTS and UNSW: <www.austlii.edu.au>
Maintained by the Canadian Legal Information Institute: <www.canlii.org>
Maintained by Sweet & Maxwell Westlaw (including full database access to Canadian, US and other international materials): <http://uk.westlaw.com>
Maintained by British and Irish Legal Information Institute: <http://bailii.org>
Maintained by Smith Bernal International: <www.casetrack.com>

Index

Abatement
  definition of 285
  scenarios giving rise to 286–7
Administrative function
  drafting *cy-près* schemes 309–10
Administrative schemes
  cy-près schemes
    comparison with 27–8, 95–6
    confusion with 28–30
  examples of 28, 30, 95–6
  inherent power to make 28, 96
Aggregate damages in class actions
  cy-près doctrine applied to 224–7
  individual damages, substituted for
    225–6
Amalgamation of charities
  cy-près scenario, whether a true 30–2
  cy-près trigger, as a 103–4
  rule of construction—*see Faraker* principle
Animal welfare, charitable trusts for 55,
  176–8
Anomalous cases
  cy-près doctrine, and 177–8, 186
  examples of 176
  non-charitable trusts, as 169, 175
  reasons for recognition 176–7
Anonymous donors
  charitable public appeals, in 158–63
  non-charitable public appeals, in 202–10
  statutory treatment of 163–6
Applying property *cy-près*
  administrative function 129
  charitable trusts, in class actions
    narrow approach 87
    wide approach 87–8
  criticisms of Charity Commissioners 130,
    132, 135–6
  discouraging donors, problem of 92, 125,
    129, 133, 305–8
  reference point for
    instrument, according to the 125
    testator's intent, according to the 126
  spectrum of closeness in charitable trusts
    'as near as possible' 86, 129–34
    'best practice' scenario 138
    within the same head of charity
      134–5
    to some other charitable purpose
      135–7
    maximising public benefit 137–8
Australia, class actions *cy-près* doctrine in
  class action regime 230–2
  resistance to *cy-près* doctrine

governmental review 232
  law reform opinion 230–1
  unitary litigation, in 277
Beneficiary principle
  definition of 171
  overcoming the 172–3
  non-charitable purpose trusts, and
    189–90
'Blue pencil' statutes
  effect of 54–5
  exclusively charitable purposes, compared
    with 54
Bona vacantia
  charitable public appeals, in 144,
    157–8, 161, 165
  competing destinations for property
    311
  Denley trusts, and 184
  non-charitable public appeals, and
    202–10
  non-charitable purpose trusts, and 192,
    194
  prerogative *cy-près*, and 23, 25
Breach of contract
  damages for 281–2
  specific performance, and 279–80
  rights to specific performance of
    contract-breaker 291–4
    innocent party 286–91
Breach of trust
  failure to apply for *cy-près* scheme 47

Canada, class actions *cy-près* doctrine in
  class action regime 232–6
  cy-près provisions in
    criticisms of 235
    drafting difficulties 235–6
    statutory enactments 232–4
    support for 234–5
    triggers for 235
Capricious and frivolous objects
  examples of 175
  non-charitable trusts generally 172–3,
    175–6
  non-charitable purpose trusts 200–1
Cayman Islands, non-charitable STAR trusts
  in 188, 195
Certainty
  object, of
    anomalous cases 177
    charitable trusts, for 27
    Denley trusts, for 185

Certainty (*cont*):
    non-charitable trusts, for 173,
      175–6, 178
    three types of 27
Charitable public appeals
    alternate scenarios 144
    destinations for monies given to 144–5
    over-subscribed public appeals
      Charities Act 1993, s 14, effect of
        148–9
      cy-près application 144, 147
      general charitable intent 147–8
      initial or subsequent failure 145–6
      resulting trust, not arising 146–7
      scenarios giving rise to 145–6
    under-subscribed public appeals
      anonymous donors
        collecting boxes, etc 150
        cross-infection of named donations
          160–1
        cy-près application, how arising
          158–9, 162
        general charitable intent 161
        resulting trust, how arising 158–60
      bona vacantia 157–8
      Charities Act 1993, s 14
        criticisms of 164–6
        effect of 163–4
        other jurisdictions 166–7
        judicial consideration 166
      conditional gift 151–2
      disclaiming donors in charitable
        appeals 165–6
      general charitable intent
        cross-infection problems 161–2
        identifiable donations 155–6
      identifiable and traceable donors—
        see named donors, below
      initial or subsequent failure 149–50
      named donors
        cy-près application 152–7
        out-and-out gift rationale 156–7
        resulting trust, when arising
          presumption of 151–2
          rebutting the presumption
          152–7
      rules governing public appeal 144
      scenarios giving rise to 149–50
    trust relationships in 143
Charitable status
    independent schools 107–8
    losing
      examples of 108
      trigger for *cy-près* application 107
Charitable trusts
    beneficial to the community, other
      purposes 54
    beneficiary principle 171–3

'blue pencil' statutes 54–5
Charity Commissioners, role of 92
definition
    according to *Pemsel* 54
    proposed new definition 189–90
education, advancement of 54
enforcement of 22–3
exclusively charitable purposes 54–8
general charitable intent—*see* General
    charitable intent
mixed charitable and non-charitable
    purposes 54–6
Pemsel's heads of charity 54, 56,
    135–6, 143
new definition of 189–90
perpetual 57–8
poverty, relief of 54
public benefit, requirement of 54, 56,
    87–8,
pre-requisite for statutory *cy-près* schemes
    98–9
rule against perpetuities 49–50
Charities Bill 2005
    effect upon *cy-près* doctrine 133–4,
      138
    obligation upon transferee charities under
      141
Charity Commissioners
    criticisms of 141
    role of 92
Class actions, application of property *cy-près*
    divergent views about closeness
      narrow approach—'as near as possible'
        270–1
      wide approach—'next best' 271–4
    suitability of recipient 274–6
    costs of locating recipients 276
Class actions *cy-près* doctrine
    Australia, in 230–2
    Canada, in—*see* Canada, class actions
      cy-près doctrine in
    charitable trusts *cy-près*,
      derivation from 215–6
      analogies to and distinctions from
        253–8
    coupon recovery 227–9
    damages assessment/computation,
      comparison with 224–7
    damages distribution, comparison with
      224
    England, reception in 229
    fluid recovery, comparison with 216–17,
      224–5
    goals of 216, 254
    indirect benefit, measures of 222, 258,
      260–1
    meaning of 215–216
    not necessarily punitive 255–8

overlap required for *cy-près* schemes—
see Overlap
terminology difficulties 216–17
triggers for *cy-près* schemes
huge classes 262–3
identities of class members changeable
262
low individual recoveries 259–60
non-claiming class members 262
unknown identities 260–1
types of—*see* Price-rollback and
Organisational Distribution
United States, in—*see* United States, class
actions *cy-près* doctrine in
Common *cy-près* themes
administrative function 309–10
benevolence 310–11
competing destinations 311–12
statutory enactments and general law
312–13
substantively changing the law 313
Conditional gifts—*see* Ouster of *cy-près*
schemes
Conditions precedent
doctrine applied to 14–15
Confusion between administrative and
cy-près schemes 28–30
Corporations
comparison with other entities 16
cy-près clauses applicable to
charitable corporations 15
corporations limited by guarantee
15
Coupon recovery
class actions, in 227
criticisms of 227–9, 232, 239
Cy-près schemes
administrative schemes, comparison with
27–8, 95–6
applying for *cy-près* schemes 139–40
definition of—*see* Definition of *cy-près*
derivation of term 1, 5
early judicial examples of 8–9
exclusively charitable purposes,
relationship to 54–8, 98–9
general charitable intent—*see* General
charitable intent
general law, under
continuing influence 93–5
relationship with statutory *cy-près*
powers 83
triggers for jurisdiction 59–62
initial failure, in cases of—*see* Initial failure
international recognition of 1–2, 91
period of immunity from *cy-près* 141
power of sale distinguished from 97–8
prerogative schemes—*see* Prerogative
cy-près

pronunciation of 5
reference point for developing 125–6
statutory authorisation
implementation in other jurisdictions
91, 118–24
relationship with
administrative schemes 95–6
ECHR articles of relevance 96
general law *cy-près* doctrine 92,
94–5
triggers—*see* Triggers for *cy-près*
schemes
subsequent failure, in cases of—
see Subsequent failure
surplus property, and 103
types of—*see* Judicial *cy-près* and
Prerogative *cy-près*

Damages for breach of contract
specific performance, election between
279–82
Definition of *cy-près*
American Restatement (2d) 2
class actions, and 215–16
'doctrine of approximation' 4
redefinition of the doctrine 2–5, 304–9
traditional charitable trustsdefinition 1–2,
53, 128
Denley trusts
cy-près schemes, likelihood of 185–6
examples of 180–1
leading authority 179–80
purposes impossible or impracticable,
alternatives
gift-over provisions, effect of 182–3
Saunders v Vautier, effect of rule in
183–4
private trust, construing as a 184
winding up, effect of 183
Disclaimers
beneficiary, by 61
donors to public appeals, by 165–6
trustees, by 60
Disasters, and *cy-près* schemes
non-charitable 143, 211–12
Discretionary factors governing specific
performance 282
Discrimination, and *cy-près* schemes 96–7,
116
'Doctrine of approximation' 4

Ecclesiastical courts
after-life, conferring rewards for 7
charitable gifts, special treatment of
6–7
exercise of *cy-près* schemes by 8–9
secular benefits 8
Education, trusts for 8, 50, 54, 57, 105

England, group litigation in
consumer protection litigation, contrast
unitary 277
group litigation orders 229
Escheat to the government
alternative to class actions *cy-près*
245
criticisms of 249–50
relevant statutes authorising 247
scenario giving rise to 249
European Convention on Human Rights
discriminatory trusts, and 96–7
relationship with *cy-près* doctrine 96–7
Exclusively charitable purposes
meaning of 54
non-charitable purposes 55–6
examples of difficulties 56–7
effect of gift-over provision 57–8
Extrinsic evidence, use of 126–8

***Faraker* principle**
charitable corporations, application to
38–9
Charities Act 1993, overlap with 35
examples of application 34
leading case explained 33–4
meaning of 33
pre-requisites
continued existence 36–9
overlap of purposes 35–6
'Fluid recovery'
meaning of 217, 224–5
origins of expression 216–17
Fulfilment of charitable purpose
cy-près trigger, as a 100
examples of 101

General charitable intent
abolishing the requirement
drafting difficulties 119–21
absence of 75–6
artificial applications 71, 77
drafting importance 76
guidelines for determining
connection between testator and
charity 85–6
difficulty in creating 76–7
limitations in expression 78–9
nestled among other charitable
dispositions 79–80
next-of-kin, provision for elsewhere
84–5
non-existent bodies, gifts to—
see Non-existent entities
precatory words, existence of 80–1
residue, charitable gifts of 84
specificity of detail of testator's
intention 79

trustee, who is nominated as 81
ultimate residuary a charity 85
initial failure, in cases of
date for determining whether 72–5
historical requirement 65
meaning and example 63
status of general charitable intent 64
whether presumption should operate
65–6
judicial expressions defining 76–7
modern requirement for, and realities 64
out-and-out gift rationale
displacement by 67–9
reasons against rationale 69–70
presuming the requirement
drafting difficulties 121–2
reasons for 65
statutory amendment of 118–22
statutory preservation of 99
subsequent failure, in cases of
date for determining whether 72–5
confusion in case law 66–7
meaning and example 63
presumption of 64
surplus, relevance to
arguments for 70–1
arguments against 71–2
Charities Act 1993, s 14, effect of
148–9
Gift-over provisions—*see* Ouster of *cy-près*

Hardship of specific performance order
contracting parties, on 282, 285, 299–300
third parties, on 299, 313

Illegality of
charitable trusts
trigger for *cy-près* doctrine 2, 3, 61,
123
non-charitable trusts 208
Immunity, period of for *cy-près* 141
Impossibility or impracticability
examples of 59–61
general law, under 58
cy-près trigger, as a 101–2
Incorporated association
cy-près doctrine applied to 16
Initial failure of charitable trust—*see* General
charitable intent
International/pure purpose trusts
cy-près doctrine under
clearest provisions 195–7
incomplete provisions 197–8
provisions entirely lacking in clarity
198–9
omission of *cy-près* provisions 199
jurisdictions enacting 194–9
protector, role of 194

Judicial *cy-près*
  meaning of 22, 24

Lease covenants
  doctrine applied to 4
  width of 4–5
Lose charitable status, trusts which
  cy-près application of property 107–9
  examples 108–9

Misdescription of charity name 83
Monuments, trusts for 169, 175–7
Mutuality, lack of, in specific performance
  282

Named institutions
  never existing 82
  no longer existing 82
  misdescription, compared with 83
Nathan Committee report 7, 91, 106, 113,
  141
Non-charitable public appeals
  bona vacantia 202–3, 205
  charitable public appeals, comparison
    with 202
  cy-près application
    scenarios for 206–7
    statutory authorisation for 207–10
  leading example 202–3
  private persons, for—*see* Private persons,
    public appeals for
  resulting trust
    criticisms of 204–5
    precedential support 202–4
Non-charitable purpose trusts
  alternatives to *cy-près* schemes 191–2
  benevolent purposes, and 174
  capricious purposes 174–5
  case for their recognition 186–9
  cy-près schemes relating to 173,
    190–4
  distinctions from other categories 170
  enforcement of
    difficulties with 170–1
    contrary views 171–3
  English reception to 173, 189–90
  examples of 169–70, 175
  lack of certainty in purposes, effect of
    191–2
  law reform proposals for 189–90,
    199–201
  mixed persons/non-charitable purpose
    trusts—*see Denley* trusts
  powers, treatment as a 201
  rule against perpetuities, effect of 174
  statutory recognition of 194–5
    cy-près schemes under 195–9
  whimsical settlors, problem of 174–5

Non-existent entities, gifts to
  differing legal positions among
    jurisdictions 83
  misdescription, compared to 83
  never existing versus once existing
    82

Object, certainty of
  charitable trusts, for 27
  purpose trusts, for 173, 175–6,
    178
Organisational distribution *cy-près*
  advantages of 223–4
  definition of 222
  recipients of 222
  scenarios giving rise to 223
Origins of *cy-près* schemes—*see* Roman law
  and Ecclesiastical courts
Ouster of *cy-près* schemes
  conditional gifts 51
  exclusively charitable intention,
    relationship to 57–8
  gift-over provisions
    meaning of 48
    valid provisions 49
    invalid provisions 49–50
  no subsisting trust, effect of 51
  private *cy-près* power
    meaning of 46
    advantages of 47
    sample clauses 47
  statutory fetters 51–2
Out-and-out gift rationale—*see* General
  charitable intent
Overlap, degree required for class actions
  cy-près
  judicial precedent for 264–5
  legislative requirement for 265
  guidelines for,
    assisting worse-off persons 266
    geographic overlap 266–8
    potential for windfall 268–9
    promotion of underlying cause of
      action 269–70
    related interest and hobbies 265
    similar injuries 265–6

Parks and recreational grounds, *cy-près*
  schemes relating to 97–8
Perpetuities, rule against
  charitable trusts, exempt from 88
  cy-près schemes, and 14
  gift-over provisions which are invalid
    49–50, 70
  meaning of 14
  non-charitable trusts, and 176, 188
  statutory non-charitable purpose trusts
    194

Plaintiff fund-sharing
    alternative to class actions *cy-près* 245
    criticisms of 246–7
    reasons supporting 245–6
Poverty, relief against 28, 35, 54, 56, 135
Powers of appointment
    cy-près doctrine applied to 16
Power of sale
    cy-près powers, and 97–8
Precatory words, and *cy-près* schemes 80–1
Prerogative *cy-près*
    delegation to Attorney-General 26
    judicial *cy-près*
        separation from 23–4
        divergent views 24–5
    modern practical application 26
    meaning of 23
Price-rollback *cy-près*
    criticisms of 220–2
    definition of 218
    features of 219
    scenarios giving rise to 219–20
Private persons, public appeals for
    cy-près, proposals for 211
    divergent traditional views 210–11
    examples of 210
Public appeals—*see* Charitable public appeals
            and Non-charitable public
            appeals
Purposes taken over
    cy-près trigger, as a 106
Purposes no longer charitable
    cy-près trigger, as a 107–9
Purpose trusts—*see* Statutory purpose trusts
            and Unincorporated charities

Recreation, trusts for 62, 131, 179–81,
            186
Religion, trusts for advancement of 8, 54,
            138
Resulting trusts
    anonymous donors, and 158–62
    gift-over provisions 48, 58
    initial versus subsequent failure 63–5
    public appeals
        over-subscribed 146–9
        under-subscribed 151–7
    private persons, public appeals for 210
Reversion to the defendant
    alternative to class actions *cy-près* 245
    criticisms of 252
    reasoning supporting 250–2
Roman law, origins in
    case law attributing links to 8–10
    ecclesiastical corporations 5–6
    illegal public games 6

Saunders v Vautier, rule in 183–4

Specific performance
    cy-près implications 280
    damages inadequate 279–80
    definition of 279
    discretionary factors governing exercise
            281–2
    frontline remedy, as a 283
    limitations upon 283–4
    terminology 280–1
Specific performance, *cy-près* orders in
    abatement, relationship with 285–6
    application by contract-breaker
        consent by innocent party 292–3
        requirements for 291–2
    application by innocent party for
        divergent views 287–91
        election 286–7
    bars to the remedy of 282
    'constant supervision' as bar 282
    definition of 280
    discretionary factors governing 281–2
    'inadequacy of damages' criterion
            281–2
    scenarios for 282
    spirit of the contract
        contradiction with the terms of the
            contract 297–9
        degree of discrepancy 295–7
        hardship factors 299–300
        misdescription a term of the contract
            301
        quantification of abatement 300–1
    triggers for 284–5
'Spirit of the contract'
    specific performance orders, in 295–9
'Spirit of the gift'
    derivation of 112
    guidelines for
        avoiding continuing disputes 114
        financial health of alternative charities
            116–17
        legal changes 116
        social, historical, economic and political
            changes 114–15
        spreading the fund too thinly 115–16
        whole charitable trust, taking account
            of 117
    judicial definitions of 112–13
STAR trusts in the Cayman Islands 188, 195
Statutory interpretation
    doctrine applied to 4
Statutory purpose trusts
    Canadian law reform proposals 199–200
    cy-près schemes within
        clearest provisions 195–7
        less explicit provisions 197–8
        omission of *cy-près* provisions 199
        unsatisfactory provisions 198–9

features of 194
relevant jurisdictions 194
Subsequent failure of charitable trust—
    see General charitable intent

Time limits for applying for *cy-près* scheme
    141
Tombs and monuments, trusts for 169,
    175–7
Triggers for *cy-près* schemes
    class actions, for—*see* Class actions
        cy-près
    general law, under charitable trusts
        traditional triggers 59–62
        wider interpretation 62
    specific performance
        generally 284–5
        'spirit of the contract' 295–9
    statutory triggers for charitable trusts
        cy-près
        amalgamation 103–4
        fulfilment of purpose 100–1
        impossibility or impracticability
            101–2
        ineffective purposes 109–12
        purposes no longer charitable
            107–9
        purposes taken over 106
        surplus property 103
        unsuitable class or area 104–6
    statutory triggers
        independence from each other 100
        law reform proposals 124
        other jurisdictions 122–4
Trustees' duties to apply for *cy-près* schemes
    breach of trust, doubts concerning
        140
    private *cy-près* power, under 47

statutory requirement
    arguments against 140
    international enactments 140–1
    relevant enactments 139–40

Unitary litigation, *cy-près* in 276–7
United States, class actions *cy-près* doctrine
    in
    class action regime 236–44
    cy-près recognition
        advantages of 236, 241, 244
        criticisms of 238
        ethical difficulties 238–40
        scenarios for 242–3
        substantive changes to the law alleged
            241–2
        support for 236–7
    non-charitable purpose trusts, recognition
        of 195
    unitary litigation, in 276
Unsuitable and ineffective purposes
    cy-près triggers, as 104–6, 109–12

Vernon presumption
    application of 40
    charitable corporations, application to
        status of presumption 44–5
        views in other jurisdictions 45–6
    comparison with *cy-près* schemes 41
    leading case 43–4
    meaning of 40
    pre-requisites
        continuing purposes 41–2
        not a gift for *that* institution 42–4

Whitby and Mitchell, rule in 13–14
Winding up of corporations
    cy-près doctrine applied to 15